STATISTICAL INFORMATION

RELATING TO CERTAIN

BRANCHES OF INDUSTRY

IN

MASSACHUSETTS,

For the Year ending June 1, 1855.

PREPARED FROM OFFICIAL RETURNS,

BY FRANCIS DEWITT,

SECRETARY OF THE COMMONWEALTH.

BOSTON:

WILLIAM WHITE, PRINTER TO THE STATE.

1856.

AN ACT

TO OBTAIN STATISTICAL INFORMATION RELATING TO CERTAIN BRANCHES OF INDUSTRY.

Be it enacted, &c., as follows:

SECT. 1. The assessors of each city or town in the Commonwealth shall, between the first day of June and the first day of October next, make return to the secretary of the Commonwealth, of the facts as they exist in each city or town on the first day of June next, in relation to the following matter, to wit:—

The number of cotton mills in the town; the whole number of cotton spindles; the quantity of cotton consumed during the year ending on the first day of June, one thousand eight hundred and fifty-five. The number of yards of cotton cloth manufactured during said year, with a description of the same. Gross value of the same. The number of pounds of cotton yarn manufactured and not made into cloth. Gross value of same. Quantity of cotton thread manufactured; value of cotton thread. Quantity of cotton batting manufactured; value of cotton batting. Quantity of pelisse wadding manufactured; value of pelisse wadding. Number of yards of cotton flannel manufactured; value of cotton flannel. The amount of capital invested in the manufacture of cotton. The number of males employed in said business. Number of females employed in same. The number of calico manufactories. Number of yards of calico printed during the year as aforesaid; gross value of calico printed. Number of yards of goods bleached and colored in said calico factories and not printed; value of the goods bleached and colored. The amount of capital invested in calico establishments. Number of males employed in said business. Number of females employed in same. The number of establishments for bleaching or coloring cotton goods and not connected with calico establishments; number of yards of goods bleached or colored in said establishments during said year; value of goods bleached or colored; amount of capital invested in said bleaching and coloring establishments. Number of hands employed in same.

The number of woollen mills; number of sets of woollen machinery; number of pounds of wool consumed during said year. Number of yards of broadcloth manufactured; value of the broadcloth manufactured.

Number of yards of cassimere manufactured; value of cassimere. Number of yards of satinet; value of satinet. Number of yards of Kentucky jeans; value of Kentucky jeans. Number of yards of flannel or blanketing; value of flannel or blanketing; number of pounds of woollen yarn manufactured and not made into cloth; value of woollen yarn; the amount of capital invested in said business. Number of males employed in the manufacture of wool; number of females in same.

The number of mills for the manufacture of carpeting; number of pounds of wool consumed in the manufacture of carpeting; number of yards of carpeting manufactured; value of carpeting manufactured; amount of capital invested in said business. Number of males employed in the manufacture of carpeting; number of females employed in same.

The number of establishments for the manufacture of worsted goods, or goods of which worsted is a component part; number of yards of such goods manufactured during said year; value of the same; number of pounds of worsted yarn manufactured and not made into cloth; value of worsted yarn; amount of capital invested in the manufacture of worsted. Number of males employed in said business; number of females employed in same.

The number of establishments for the manufacture of hosiery; quantity and description of hosiery manufactured; value of hosiery manufactured; number of pounds of yarn manufactured and not made into hosiery; value of yarn manufactured; amount of capital invested in said business. Number of males employed in same; number of females.

The number of establishments for the manufacture of linen; number of yards of linen manufactured; value of same; quantity of linen thread manufactured; value of linen thread; amount of capital invested in said business. Number of males employed in same; number of females in same.

The number of silk manufactories; number of yards of silk manufactured during said year; value of same; number of pounds of sewing silk manufactured; value of sewing silk; amount of capital invested in said business. Number of males employed in same; number of females employed in same.

The number of rolling, slitting and nail mills; quantity of iron manufactured by said rolling mills and not made into nails; value of iron thus manufactured; number of machines for manufacture of nails; quantity of nails manufactured during said year; value of nails manufactured; amount of capital invested in rolling, slitting and nail mills; number of hands employed in said business.

The number of forges; number of tons of bar iron, anchors, chain cables and other articles of wrought iron manufactured by said forges during said year; value of said bar iron, chain cables, anchors and other articles; amount of capital invested; number of hands employed; the number of furnaces for the manufacture of pig iron; number of tons of pig iron manufactured; value of the pig iron; amount of capital invested in said business; number of hands employed in same.

The number of furnaces for the manufacture of hollow ware and castings other than pig iron; number of tons of hollow ware and other castings manufactured; value of hollow ware and castings; amount of capital invested in said business; number of hands employed in same.

The number of establishments for the manufacture of cotton, woollen, and other machinery; gross value of machinery manufactured during said year; amount invested in said business; number of hands employed in same.

The number of establishments for the manufacture of steam engines and boilers; value of steam engines and boilers manufactured during said year; amount of capital invested in said business; number of hands employed in same.

The number of shops for the manufacture of fire engines; number of fire engines manufactured during said year; value of fire engines manufactured; number of hands employed in said business.

The number of scythe manufactories; number of scythes manufactured during said year; value of scythes manufactured; amount invested in said business; number of hands employed in same.

The number of axe manufactories; the number of axes, hatchets and other edge tools manufactured during said year; value of the same manufactured; amount of capital invested in said business; number of hands employed in same.

The number of establishments for the manufacture of cutlery; value of cutlery manufactured; amount of capital invested in said business; number of hands employed in same.

The number of screw manufactories; number of gross of screws manufactured during said year; value of screws manufactured; amount of capital invested in said business; number of hands employed in same.

The number of establishments for the manufacture of butts or hinges; number of dozen of iron butts or hinges manufactured; number of dozen of brass or composition butts or hinges manufactured; value of brass or composition butts or hinges; amount of capital invested in said business; number of hands employed in same.

The number of establishments for the manufacture of latches and door handles number of dozen of door handles and latches manufactured during said year; value of door handles and latches; amount of capital invested in said business; number of hands employed in same.

The number of lock manufactories; number of locks manufactured during said year; value of locks manufactured; amount of capital invested in said business; number of hands employed in same.

The number of tack and brad manufactories; quantity of tacks and brads manufactured; value of tacks and brads; amount of capital invested in said business; number of hands employed in same.

The number of manufactories of shovels, spades, forks and hoes; value of spades, shovels, forks and hoes manufactured; amount of capital invested in said business; number of hands employed in same.

The number of plough manufactories; number of ploughs and other agricultural tools manufactured during said year; value of the same; amount of capital invested in said business; number of hands employed in same.

The number of shops for the manufacture of iron railing, iron fences and iron safes; value of iron railing, iron fences and iron safes manufactured during said year; amount of capital invested in said business; number of hands employed in same.

The number of copper manufactories; quantity of copper manufactured during said year; value of the same; amount of capital invested in said business; number of hands employed in same.

The number of brass founderies; value of articles manufactured in said founderies during said year; amount of capital invested in said business; number of hands employed in same.

The number of establishments for the manufacture of britannia ware; value of britannia ware manufactured during said year; amount of capital invested in said business; number of hands employed in same.

The number of metal button manufactories; number of gross of metal buttons manufactured during said year; value of metal buttons manufactured; amount of capital invested in said business; number of hands employed in same.

The number of glass manufactories; quantity of window glass manufactured during said year; value of window glass; value of other glass manufactured; amount of capital invested in said business; number of hands employed in same.

The number of starch manufactories; quantity of starch manufactured from wheat or flour during said year; quantity of starch manufactured from potatoes; value of all starch manufactured; amount of capital invested in said business; number of hands employed in same.

The number of establishments for the manufacture of chemical preparations; value of chemical preparations manufactured during said year; amount of capital invested during said year; number of hands employed in same.

The number of paper manufactories; quantity of stock made use of during said year; quantity of paper manufactured; value of paper manufactured; amount of capital invested in said business; number of hands employed in same.

The number of piano-forte manufactories; number of piano-fortes manufactured during said year; amount of capital invested in said business; the number of all other musical instrument manufactories; value of musical instruments manufactured during said year; amount of capital invested in said business; number of hands employed in same.

The number of clock manufactories; number of clocks manufactured during said year; amount of capital invested in said business; number of hands employed in same.

The number of sewing machine manufactories; the number of sewing machines manufactured during said year; amount of capital invested in said business; number of hands employed in same.

The number of daguerreotype artists; number of daguerreotypes taken during said year; amount of capital invested in said business; number of hands employed in same.

The number of pin manufactories; quantity of pins manufactured; amount of capital invested in said business; number of hands employed in same.

The number of establishments for the manufacture of chronometers, watches, gold and silver ware and jewelry; value of the manufactures of said establishments; amount of capital invested in said business; number of hands employed in same.

The number of brush manufactories; value of brushes manufactured during said year; amount of capital invested in said business; number of hands employed in same.

The number of saddle, harness and trunk manufactories; value of saddles, harnesses and trunks manufactured during said year; amount of capital invested in said business; number of hands employed in same.

The number of upholstery manufactories; value of upholstery manufactured during said year; amount of capital invested in said business; number of hands employed in same.

The number of hat and cap manufactories; number of hats and caps manufactured during said year; amount of capital invested in said business; number of hands employed in same.

The number of cordage manufactories; quantity of cordage manufactured during said year; amount of capital invested in said business; number of hands employed in same.

The number of vessels launched during said year; amount of tonnage of said vessels; amount of capital invested in said business; number of hands employed in same.

The number of establishments for the manufacture of boats; number of boats built during said year; amount of capital invested in said business; number of hands employed in same.

The number of mast and spar sheds; number of masts and spars manufactured during said year; amount of capital invested in said business; number of hands employed in same.

The number of sail lofts; the number of sails made during said year, of American fabric; number of foreign fabric; value of sails manufactured of American fabric; value of sails manufactured of foreign fabric; amount of capital invested in said business; number of hands employed in same.

The number of card manufactories; value of cards of all kinds manufactured during said year; capital invested in said business; number of hands employed in same.

The number of establishments for the manufacture of salt; number of bushels of salt manufactured during said year; value of salt manufactured; amount of capital invested in said business; number of hands employed in same.

The number of establishments for the manufacture of railroad cars, coaches, chaises, wagons, sleighs and other vehicles; value of railroad cars, coaches, chaises, wagons, sleighs, and other vehicles manufactured during said year; amount of capital invested in said business; number of hands employed in same.

The number of lead manufactories; value of all manufactures of lead during said year; amount of capital invested in said business; number of hands employed in same.

The number of sugar refineries; quantity of sugar refined during said year; value of sugar refined; number of hands employed in same.

The number of establishments for the manufacture of oil and sperm candles; number of gallons of oil; value of oil manufactured; number of pounds of sperm candles manufactured during said year; value of sperm candles manufactured; amount of capital invested in said business; number of hands employed in same.

The number of establishments for the manufacture of soap, and tallow candles; quantity of soap manufactured during said year; value of soap manufactured; number of pounds of tallow candles manufactured during said year; value of tallow candles manufactured; amount of capital invested in said business; number of hands employed.

The number of powder mills; quantity of powder manufactured during said year; value of powder manufactured; amount of capital invested in said business; number of hands employed in same.

The number of establishments for the manufacture of fire-arms; number and description of fire-arms manufactured; value of fire-arms manufactured; amount of capital invested in said business; number of hands employed in same.

The number of establishments for the manufacture of cannon; number and description of cannon manufactured; value of cannon; amount of capital invested in said business; number of hands employed in same.

The number of chocolate mills; quantity of chocolate manufactured during said year; amount of capital invested in said business; number of hands employed in same.

The number of chair and cabinet ware manufactories; value of chairs and cabinet ware manufactured during said year; amount of capital invested in said business; number of hands employed in same.

The number of tin ware manufactories; value of tin ware manufactured during said year; amount of capital invested in said business; number of hands employed in same.

The number of comb manufactories; value of combs manufactured during said year; amount of capital invested in said business; number of hands employed in same.

The number of establishments for the manufacture of white lead and other paints; quantity of white lead manufactured; value of white lead manufactured; quantity and description of other paints manufactured; value of other paints; amount of capital invested in said business; number of hands employed in same.

The number of mills for the manufacture of linseed oil; quantity of oil manufactured; value of oil manufactured; amount of capital invested in said business; number of hands employed in same.

The number of establishments for the manufacture of camphene or burning fluid; number of gallons of camphene manufactured during said year; amount of capital invested in said business; number of hands employed in same.

The number of glue manufactories, and manufactories for the preparation of gums; value of glue and gums manufactured during said year; amount of capital invested in said business; number of hands employed in same.

The number of establishments for the manufacture of cotton gins; value of cotton gins manufactured during said year; amount of capital invested in said business; number of hands employed in same.

The number of flour mills; number of barrels of flour manufactured during said year; value of flour manufactured; amount of capital invested in said business; number of hands employed in same.

The number of tanneries; number of hides of all kinds tanned during said year; value of leather tanned and curried; amount of capital invested in said business; number of hands employed in same.

The number of manufactories of patent and enamelled leather; value of leather manufactured; amount of capital invested in said business; number of hands employed in same.

The number of pairs of boots of all kinds manufactured during said year; number of pairs of shoes of all kinds manufactured; value of boots and shoes manufactured; number of males employed in the manufacture of boots and shoes; number of females.

The number of establishments for the manufacture of straw bonnets and hats; number of straw bonnets manufactured during said year; number of straw hats; value of straw braid manufactured and not made into bonnets and hats; value of palm leaf hats; number of males employed in said business; number of females.

The number of bricks manufactured during said year; value of bricks manufactured; number of hands employed in the manufacture of bricks.

Value of mathematical instruments manufactured during said year; number of hands employed in the manufacture of mathematical instruments.

The value of snuff, tobacco and cigars manufactured during said year; number of males employed in said business; number of females.

The gross value of building stone quarried and prepared for building; number of hands employed in quarrying and preparing building stone.

The gross value of marble quarried and prepared for market during said year; number of hands employed in quarrying and preparing marble.

Number of casks of lime manufactured during said year; number of hands empnoyed in the manufacture of lime; value of lime manufactured.

The gross value of mineral coal and iron ore mined during said year; number of hands emplcyed in mining coal and iron ore.

The gross value of whips manufactured during said year; number of hands employed in the manufacture of whips.

Gross value of blacking manufactured during said year; number of hands employed in the manufacture of the same.

Gross value of blocks and pumps manufactured during said year; number of hands employed in the manufacture of blocks and pumps.

Gross value of mechanics' tools manufactured during said year; number of hands employed in the manufacture of mechanics' tools.

Gross value of all wooden ware not otherwise enumerated in this act, including farming utensils, manufactured during said year; number of hands employed in the manufacture of said wooden ware.

The number of corn and other brooms manufactured during said year; value of brooms manufactured; number of hands employed in the making of brooms.

The number of gold and steel pen manufactories; number of gold pens manufactured during said year; amount of capital invested in the manufacture of gold pens; number of hands employed in same; number of steel pens manufactured during said year; amount of capital invested in said business; number of males employed in same; number of females.

The quantity of lumber prepared for market; value of lumber thus prepared; number of hands employed in said business.

The number of cords of firewood prepared for market; value of firewood so prepared; number of hands employed in said business.

The gross value of all other articles manufactured in the town or city during said year, with a description of the same; amount of capital invested in the business; number of hands employed in the same.

The number of vessels employed in the whale fishery; amount of tonnage of vessels employed in the whale fishery; number of gallons of sperm oil imported during the year ending on the first day of January preceding; value of sperm oil imported; number of gallons of whale oil imported during said year; value of whale oil imported; number of pounds of whalebone imported during said year; value of whalebone imported; amount of capital invested in the whale fishery; number of hands employed in the same.

The number of vessels employed in the mackerel and cod fisheries; tonnage of vessels employed in said fisheries; number of barrels of mackerel taken during the year ending on said first day of January preceding; number of quintals of cod fish taken; value of mackerel taken; value of cod fish taken; also the value of cod liver sold for medicinal purposes; number of bushels of salt consumed in the mackerel and cod fisheries; amount of capital invested in said business; number of hands employed in same.

The number of Saxony sheep, of different grades; number of Merino sheep, of different grades; number of all other kinds of sheep; gross value of all the sheep; the number of pounds of wool produced from Saxony sheep; number of pounds from Merino sheep; number of pounds of all other wool produced; gross value of all wool produced in the town during the year.

The number of asses and mules; value of asses and mules; number of horses; value of the horses; number of neat cattle; value of neat cattle; number of swine; value of swine.

The number of bushels of Indian corn or maize raised during the year ending as aforesaid: value of the Indian corn or maize: number of bushels of whaat value of same; number of bushels of rye; value of same; number of bushels of barley; value of same; number of bushels of oats; value of same; number of bushels of potatoes; value of same; quantity of other esculent vegetables; value of same; quantity of millet raised; value of millet; number of tons of hay; value of hay; quantity of hemp raised; value of hemp; number of pounds of flax raised; value of flax.

Number of bushels of fruit of various kinds; value of fruit; number of pounds of hops raised; value of hops; number of pounds of tobacco; value of same. quantity of raw silk raised; value of same; quantity of teazles; value of teazles.

Number of pounds of butter produced during said year; value of butter; number of pounds of cheese; value of cheese; number of pounds of honey; value of honey.

Number of pounds of beeswax; value of beeswax; quantity of shoe pegs manufactured; value of same; number of bushels of charcoal manufactured during the year; value of same.

SECT. 2. The secretary of the Commonwealth shall cause to be printed, blank tables conveniently arranged for the return of the facts aforesaid, with blank columns for the return of facts such as are not enumerated in this act, and shall furnish three copies of the same, together with one copy of this act, to the assessors of each town or city, on or before the first day of June next.

SECT. 3. The secretary of the Commonwealth, after he shall have received the returns aforesaid, from the assessors of the several towns, shall cause to be prepared and printed a true abstract of the same, with each column of figures of such abstract added up for the use of the next legislature, at the next session thereof.

SECT. 4. Each assessor shall receive from the treasury of the Commonwealth, two dollars a day for every day that he shall be employed in making the return aforesaid, and the accounts of assessors for these services shall be audited by a committee of the legislature.

SECT. 5. The assessors of any town may authorize either of their number, or some other suitable person, to collect the information required by this act, to whom the same allowance per day shall be made from the treasury of the Commonwealth, as is provided for the services of the assessors.

SECT. 6. If the assessors of any town shall wilfully neglect to make the return aforesaid, in the manner aforesaid, such assessors shall forfeit to the Commonwealth a sum not exceeding one hundred dollars.

SECT. 7. This act shall take effect from and after its passage.

[Approved, May 21,1855.]

Commonwealth of Massachusetts.

SECRETARY'S OFFICE, May 16, 1856.

To the Honorable the Senate and House of Representatives:

In pursuance of a law passed by the Legislature of 1855, a copy of which accompanies this communication, I have the honor to submit an abstract report of the statistical information collected by the Assessors of the several cities and towns in the Commonwealth, touching the various branches of industrial pursuit in their respective precincts.

While this report fails to do full justice to the productive industry of the State, it is believed to be more comprehensive and complete than either of its predecessors, for an obvious reason that will be likely to make the next superior to this. That entire accuracy, which is so desirable, and which certainly lies within the scope of systematic and persistent effort, has not, I regret to say, been attained in the present instance. This may be, and is, I apprehend, in some measure, owing to the evident haste with which the law of 1855 was prepared. Many important interests, such as printing and publishing, in all their various departments, engraving, building, coasting, the manufacture of clothing, and various other pursuits which contribute largely to the wealth and prosperity of the State, were entirely overlooked, while there was a want of uniformity and completeness in the questions contemplated and proposed with reference to several other branches. For instance, no inquiry was made as to the value of clocks, sewing-machines, daguerreotypes, hats and caps, cordage, vessels and boats, masts and spars, chocolate, camphene, straw bonnets and hats, and gold pens. Neither was there any inquiry as to the amount of capital invested in sugar refineries, in the manufacture of fire engines, boots and shoes, mathematical instruments, straw bonnets and hats, whips, and twelve other articles which figure somewhat largely in the tables.

For the first and most important omission specified, a general inquiry as to all other branches than those specifically enumerated in the law, and in the blanks prepared in conformity with it, has been found to afford but an inadequate remedy. With regard to printing, publishing and book-binding, a remedy was sought in circulars addressed directly to the proprietors of the different printing and book-binding establishments in the State, so far as they could be ascertained. But these proved scarcely more effective than the general inquiry. The whole amount returned was less than one and a half million of dollars, while the book-publishing business, in the city of Boston alone, is estimated at over four millions. Out of eighty-nine printing establishments in Boston, answers were received from only twenty-six. From but one establishment in the county of Norfolk was there any response, and the proprietor of a newspaper establishment in Hampden County refused to answer. Full returns were received from three counties only—Barnstable, Dukes and Worcester. These returns, desultory and unsatisfactory as they were, are embodied in the appropriate tables, of which they constitute the principal basis. The number of newspapers and periodicals, however, has been made up from other sources.

In the instances specified, where the value was omitted, the omission has been supplied by estimates obtained from persons whose familiarity with the particular branches forming the subject of inquiry, qualified them to judge in the matter. The omission of capital was one for which no remedy suggested itself.

Another impediment to entire accuracy has been found in an apparent inability to comprehend the nature and scope of the questions proposed, or a culpable disregard of them, on the part of some of the Assessors. In numerous instances, these officers, instead of obtaining answers to such questions as were presented in the printed blanks prepared in conformity with the law, obtained answers to other and very different ones; which answers, for that reason, were of little or no consequence. In some few cases it would almost seem that special pains were taken to evade the real questions, and procure answers to others that had not been proposed. On the whole, however, the Assessors acquitted themselves of their duties with intelligence, precision and fidelity.

When the industrial statistics of the State were first collected, in 1837, they exhibited an annual production amounting to $86,282,616. In 1845, the amount was $124,749,457. It has now swelled to $295,820,681,— an increase of one hundred and thirty-eight per cent. since 1845, and of two hundred and forty-two, since 1837; and this, while the increase of population has been only thirty-four per cent. since 1845, and sixty-two in the longer period named. And this result, so surprising in itself, falls, manifestly, below the reality. Leaving out of the account those branches which were unfortunately omitted in the specific inquiries, and making all possible allowance for the greater accuracy attained in the collection of the information embodied in the accompanying pages, it is still apparent that the truth has not been reached. It is next to impossible for the tax-payer, when called upon by the Assessor to answer such questions as were propounded under the law, to divest his mind of the impression of an intimate connection between his answers and the assessment of his taxes. Hence, the general tendency to understate results, and an absolute refusal, in numerous instances, to answer at all. Had those branches which were overlooked been included in the returns, and honest and truthful answers obtained in all cases to the questions proposed, I am fully persuaded that instead of two hundred and ninety-five millions, we should have had an aggregate of at least three hundred and fifty millions, or considerable over one million of dollars per day for every working day in the year. As it is, the result exhibits a rapid and substantial growth in our industrial resources which is believed to be without a parallel in the history of the world.

Respectfully submitted,

FRANCIS DeWITT,
Secretary of the Commonwealth.

STATISTICAL RETURNS

Of the Assessors of the several Cities and Towns in the Commonwealth of Massachusetts, as to facts existing on June 1, 1855, *in relation to certain Branches of Industry.*

val. denotes	value.	f. emp. denotes	females employed.
cap. "	capital invested.	m. "	manufacture.
emp. "	persons employed.	m's. "	manufactures.
m. emp. "	males employed.	m'd. "	manufactured.

BARNSTABLE COUNTY.

BARNSTABLE.

Saddle, Harness and Trunk Manufactories, 2 ; val. of saddles, &c., $1,280 ; cap., $675; emp., 3.

Hat and Cap Manufactories, 1 ; Hats and Caps m'd., $675 ; cap., $200 ; emp., 1.

Establishments for m. of boats, 1; Boats built, 15; cap., $1,000 ; emp., 2.

Sail Lofts, 2 ; Sails made of Am. fabric, 225; val. of sails m'd. of Am. fabric, $9,000 ; cap., $1,800 ; emp., 8.

Establishments for m. of salt, 11 ; Salt m'd., 10,550 bush. ; val. of salt, $3,500 ; cap., $16,000 ; emp., 18.

Establishments for m. of railroad cars, coaches, chaises, wagons, sleighs, and other vehicles, 3 ; val. of railroad cars, &c., m'd., $2,200 ; cap., $1,350 ; emp., 5.

Tin Ware Manufactories, 3 ; val. of tin ware, $1,050 ; cap., $1,200 ; emp., 5.

Boots and shoes of all kinds m'd., 1,270 pairs; val. of boots and shoes, $3,000; m. emp., 15; f. emp., –.

Bricks m'd., 300,000; val. of bricks, $2,300; emp., 8.

Val. of blocks and pumps m'd., $500; emp., 1.

Firewood prepared for market, 3,000 cords; val. of firewood, $15,700; emp., 90.

Vessels employed in the mackerel and cod fisheries, 17; Tonnage, 1,300 tons; Mackerel taken, 465 bbls.; Codfish taken, 8,225 quintals; val. of mackerel taken, $4,400; val. of codfish taken, $29,000; Salt consumed, 9,000 bush.; cap., $38,500; emp., 160.

Saxony Sheep, of different grades, –; Merino Sheep, of different grades, –; all other kinds of sheep, 434; val. of all sheep, $1,050; Wool produced from Saxony sheep, – lbs.; Merino Wool produced, – lbs.; all other wool produced, 966 lbs.

Horses, 383; val. of horses, $41,750; Oxen over three years old, and Steers under three years old, 162; val. of oxen and steers, $6,700; Milch Cows, 640; Heifers, 198; val. of cows and heifers $24,688.

Butter 25,684 lbs.; val. of butter, $6,503; Cheese, 325 lbs.; val. of cheese, $32.50.

Indian Corn, 460 acres; Indian Corn, per acre, 25 bush.; val., $11,500.

Rye, 185 acres; Rye, per acre, 10 bush.; val., $2,312.

Barley, 1¾ acres; Barley, per acre, 15 bush.; val. $29.

Oats, 63 acres; Oats, per acre, 25 bush.; val., $950.

Potatoes, 113 acres; Potatoes, per acre, 50 bush.; val., $6,631.

Onions, 15 acres; Onions, per acre, 200 bush.; val., $1,600.

Turnips cultivated as a field crop, 16 acres; Turnips, per acre, 130 bush.; val., $625.

Carrots, 8 acres; Carrots, per acre, 200 bush.; val., $500.

Beets and other esculent vegetables, 17 acres; val., $1,150.

English Mowing, 890 acres; English Hay, 1,200 tons; val., $18,000.

Salt Hay, 1,466 tons; val., $8,154.

Apple Trees cultivated for their fruit, 3,384; val., $2,400.

Pear Trees cultivated for their fruit, 145; val., $89.
Cranberries, 33 acres; val., $1,532.
Cod Liver Oil, 100 bbls; val., $2,000.
Tallow Candles m'd., 4,000 lbs.; val., $600.
Swine, 631; val., $7,000.

BREWSTER.

Harness Manufactories, 1; val. of harnesses, &c., $500; cap., $200; emp., 1.

Establishments for m. of salt, 17; Salt m'd., 5,000 bush.; val. of salt, $1,500; cap., $4,200; emp., 10.

Establishments for m. of wagons, sleighs, and other vehicles, 2; val. of wagons, sleighs, &c., m'd., $500; cap., $200; emp., 2.

Tin Ware Manufactories, 2; val. of tin ware, $1,000; cap., $500; emp., 2.

Tanneries, 1; Hides of all kinds tanned, 1,500; val. of leather tanned, $4,500; cap., $2,000; emp., 2.

Currying Establishments, 2; val. of leather curried, $5,000; cap., $2,500; emp., 3.

Boots of all kinds m'd., 500 pairs; Shoes of all kinds m'd., 2,000 pairs; val. of boots and shoes, $3,000; m. emp., 10; f. emp., 3.

Firewood prepared for market, 220 cords; val. of firewood, $1,700; emp., 3.

Vessels employed in the mackerel and cod fisheries, 3; Tonnage, 210 tons; Mackerel taken, 1,500 bbls.; Codfish taken, – quintals; val. of mackerel taken, $10,000; val. of codfish taken, –; val. of cod liver oil sold for medicinal purposes, $50; Salt consumed, 1,500 bush.; cap., $4,000; emp., 30.

Alewives taken, 300 bbls.; val. of same, $300; emp., 2.

Saxony Sheep, of different grades, –; Merino Sheep, of different grades, –; all other kinds of sheep, 50; val. of all sheep,

$150; Wool produced from Saxony sheep, – lbs.; Merino Wool produced, – lbs.; all other wool produced, 150 lbs.

Horses, 150; val. of horses, $10,500; Oxen over three years old, 28; Steers under three years old, 30; val. of oxen and Steers, $2,250; Milch Cows, 300; Heifers 300; val. of cows and heifers, $1,350.

Butter, 30,000 lbs.; val. of butter, $6,000.

Indian Corn, 300 acres; Indian Corn, per acre, 15 bush.; val., $4,500.

Rye, 150 acres; Rye, per acre, 7 bush.; val., $1,050.

Barley, 20 acres; Barley, per acre, 10 bush.; val., $150.

Oats, 100 acres; Oats, per acre, 15 bush.; val., $750.

Potatoes, 100 acres; Potatoes, per acre, 50 bush.; val., $2,500.

Carrots, 5 acres; Carrots, per acre, 150 bush.; val., $225.

English Mowing, 450 acres; English Hay, 675 tons; val., $10,125.

Wet Meadow or Swale Hay, 200 tons; val., $1,600.

Salt Hay, 300 tons; val., $3,000.

Apple Trees cultivated for their fruit, 2,979; val., $516.

Pear Trees cultivated for their fruit, 359; val., $111.

Cranberries, 21 acres; val., $359.

Establishments for m. of sashes and door blinds, 1; cap., $200; val. m'd., $652; emp., 1.

Establishments for m. of fishing swivels, 1; cap., $100; val., $500; emp., 1.

Establishments for m. of grave stones, 1; cap., $200; val., $1,050; emp., 2.

Establishments for m. of Epsom salts, 1; cap., $100; val., $300; emp., 1.

Establishments for m. of fish weirs, 4; cap., $600; val., $2,200; emp., 6.

Freighting and Coasting vessels, 5,261 tons; cap., $211,332.

Swine, 300; val. $1,500.

CHATHAM.

Establishments for m. of boats, 2; Boats built, 15; cap., $2,000; emp., 3.

Establishments for m. of salt, 14; Salt m'd., 3,300 bush.; val. of salt, $1,320; cap., $4,500; emp., 14.

Tin Ware Manufactories, 2; val. of tin ware, $1,200; cap., $1,500; emp., 2.

Bricks m'd., 250,000; val. of bricks, $1,250; emp., 4.

Val. of blocks and pumps m'd., $3,000; emp., 4.

Vessels employed in the mackerel and cod fisheries, 27; Tonnage, 1,880 tons; Mackerel taken, 3,000 bbls.; Codfish taken, 15,000 quintals; val. of mackerel taken, $24,000; val. of codfish taken, $45,000; Salt consumed, 25,000 bush.; cap., $30,000; emp., 230.

Saxony Sheep, of different grades, –; Merino Sheep, of different grades, –; all other kinds of sheep, 60; val. of all sheep, $120; Wool produced from Saxony sheep, – lbs.; Merino Wool produced, – lbs.; all other wool produced, 150 lbs.

Horses, 138; val. of horses, $10,490; Oxen over three years old, 10; Steers under three years old, –; val. of oxen and steers, $375; Milch Cows, 244; Heifers, 69; val. of cows and heifers, $6,770.

Butter, 12,200 lbs.; val. of butter, $2,800.

Indian Corn, 226 acres; Indian Corn, per acre, 20 bush.; val., $4,200.

Rye, 150 acres; Rye, per acre, 7 bush.; val., $1,200.

Barley, 10 acres; Barley, per acre, 20 bush.; val., $200.

Oats, 50 acres; Oats, per acre, 20 bush.; val., $500.

Potatoes, 50 acres; Potatoes, per acre, 75 bush.; val., $2,812.

Onions, 2 acres; Onions, per acre, 125 bush.; val., $175.

Turnips cultivated as a field crop, 10 acres; Turnips, per acre, 200 bush.; val., $1,000.

English Mowing, 300 acres; English Hay, 400 tons; val., $7,760.

Salt Hay, 240 tons; val., $1,920.

DENNIS.

Vessels launched during said year, 2; Tonnage, 1,260 tons; cap., $78,000; emp., 50.

Sail Lofts, 1; Sails made of Am. fabric, –; val. of sails m'd. of Am. fabric, $5,000; cap., $1,200; emp., 2.

Establishments for m. of salt, 1; Salt m'd., 19,800 bush; val. of salt, $7,920; cap., $16,480; emp., 40.

Establishments for m. of railroad cars, coaches, chaises, wagons, sleighs, and other vehicles, 1; val. of railroad cars, &c. m'd., $1,500; cap., $700; emp., 2.

Tin Ware Manufactories, 2; val. of tin ware, $1,000; cap., $400; emp., 2.

Val. of blocks and pumps m'd., $150; emp., 1.

Firewood prepared for market, 450 cords; val. of firewood, $3,150; emp., 42.

Vessels employed in the mackerel and cod fisheries, 48; Tonnage, 2,130 tons; Mackerel taken, 11,036 bbls.; Codfish taken, 1,200 quintals; val. of mackerel taken, $77,252; val. of codfish taken, $42,000; Salt consumed, 30,500 bush.; cap., $96,000; emp., 500.

Bluefish taken, 450 bbls.; val., $2,400.

Alewives, Shad and Salmon taken, 2,125; val. of same, $6,375; emp., 35.

Horses, 195; val. of horses, $19,000; Oxen over three years old, 48; Steers under three years old, 14; val. of oxen and steers, $2,340; Milch Cows, 259; Heifers, 42; val. of cows and heifers, $9,010.

Butter, 9,840 lbs.; val. of butter, $1,568.

Indian Corn, 264 acres; Indian Corn, per acre, 20 bush.; val., $5,280.

Rye, 122 acres; Rye, per acre, 7 bush.; val. $1,020.

Oats, 20 acres; Oats, per acre, 23 bush.; val., $230.

Potatoes, 136 acres; Potatoes, per acre, 40 bush.; val., $4,300.

Onions, 2 acres; Onions, per acre, 200 bush.; val., $100.

Carrots, 6 acres; Carrots, per acre, 250 bush.; val., $375.

English Mowing, 276 acres; English Hay, 391 tons; val., $6,256.

Wet Meadow or Swale Hay, 75 tons; val., $450.

Salt Hay, 629 tons; val., $5,032.

Apple Trees cultivated for their fruit, 1,446; val., $300.

Pear Trees cultivated for their fruit, 290; val., $100.

Cranberries, 50 acres; val., $3,600.

EASTHAM.

Forges, 3; Bar Iron, Anchors, Chain Cables, and other articles of wrought iron, m'd., 10 tons; val. of bar iron, &c., $1,200; cap., $600; emp., 4.

Establishments for m. of salt, 28; Salt m'd., 13,722 bush.; val. of salt, $3,837; cap., $9,282; emp., 31.

Currying Establishments, 1; val. of leather curried, $2,000; cap., $1,200; emp., 3.

Val. of building stone quarried and prepared for building, $500; emp., 2.

Firewood prepared for market, 25 cords; val. of firewood, $200; emp., 1.

Vessels employed in the mackerel and cod fisheries, 3; Tonnage, 168 tons; Mackerel taken, 750 bbls.; Codfish taken, 300 quintals; val. of mackerel taken, $7,500; val. of codfish taken, $800; Salt consumed, 1,200 bush.; cap., $6,000; emp., 30.

Horses, 114; val. of horses, $5,000; Steers under three years old, 45; val. of steers, $500; Milch Cows, 202; Heifers, 137; val. of cows and heifers, $6,532.

Butter, 20,000 lbs.; val. of butter, $5,000.

Indian Corn, 401 acres; Indian Corn, per acre, 15 bush.; val., $6,015.

Wheat, 2 acres; Wheat, per acre, 12 bush.; val., $50.

Rye, 400 acres; Rye, per acre, 8 bush.; val., $4,000.

Barley, 5 acres; Barley, per acre, 12 bush.; val., $75.

Oats, 5 acres ; Oats, per acre, 20 bush. ; val., $180.

Potatoes, 40 acres ; Potatoes, per acre, 150 bush. ; val., $450.

Turnips cultivated as a field crop, 5 acres ; Turnips, per acre, 160 bush. ; val., $400.

English Mowing, 95 acres ; English Hay, 100 tons ; val., $1,200.

Wet Meadow or Swale Hay, 90 tons ; val., $800.

Salt Hay, 566 tons ; val., $3,400.

Apple Trees cultivated for their fruit, 1,804 ; val., $800.

Pear Trees cultivated for their fruit, 150 ; val., $75.

Cranberries, 5 acres ; val., $250.

Poultry, 5,520 ; val., $1,380.

Eggs, 50,600 doz. ; val., $8,096.

FALMOUTH.

Woollen Mills, 2 ; Sets of Machinery, 3 ; Wool consumed, 36,000 lbs. ; Flannel or Blanketing, 25,000 yds. ; val. of flannel or blanketing, $7,000 ; Yarn m'd. and not made into cloth, 22,400,000 yds. ; val. of yarn, $16,000 ; cap., $22,000 ; m. emp., 13 ; f. emp., 8.

Saddle, Harness and Trunk Manufactories, 1 ; val. of saddles, &c., $800 ; cap., $300 ; emp., 2.

Vessels launched during said year, 1 ; Tonnage, 260 tons ; cap., $12,000 ; emp., 18.

Establishments for m. of salt, 15 ; Salt m'd., 9,000 bush. ; val. of salt, $3,600 ; cap., $10,900 ; emp., 15.

Tin Ware Manufactories, 1 ; val. of tin ware, $600 ; cap., $200 ; emp., 1.

Boots of all kinds m'd., 179 pairs ; Shoes of all kinds m'd., 1,873 pairs ; val. of boots and shoes, $2,850 ; m. emp., 6.

Firewood prepared for market, 5,053 cords ; val. of firewood, $25,265 ; emp., 65.

Vessels employed in the whale fishery, 3 ; Tonnage, 1,096 tons ; Sperm Oil imported, 16,173½ galls. ; val. of sperm oil imported, $24,260.25; Whale Oil imported, 51,266 galls.; val. of whale oil imported, $30,760; Whalebone imported, 12,000 lbs.; val. of whalebone imported, $4,800; cap. in the whale fishery, $128,654; emp., 100.

Vessels employed in the mackerel and cod fisheries, 1; Tonnage, 51 tons; Codfish taken, 250 quintals; val. of codfish taken, $1,000; val. of cod liver oil sold for medicinal purposes, $83; Salt consumed, 300 bush.; cap., $600; emp., 8.

Alewives, Shad and Salmon taken, 500 bbls.; val. of same, $500; emp., –.

Saxony Sheep, of different grades, –; Merino Sheep, of different grades, –; all other kinds of sheep, 511; val. of all sheep, $1,022; Wool produced from Saxony sheep, – lbs.; Merino Wool produced, – lbs.; all other wool produced, 1,022 lbs.

Horses, 197; val. of horses, $9,850; Oxen over three years old, 78; Steers under three years old, 72; val. of oxen and steers, $4,560; Milch Cows, 421; Heifers, 159; val. of cows and heifers, $12,008.

Butter, 21,050 lbs.; val. of butter, $5,262; Cheese, 500 lbs.; val. of cheese, $50.

Indian Corn, 339 acres; Indian Corn, per acre, 25 bush.; val., $8,475.

Wheat, 25½ acres; Wheat, per acre, 15 bush.; val., $750.

Rye, 53 acres; Rye, per acre, 10 bush.; val., $795.

Barley, 74 acres; Barley, per acre, 20 bush.; val., $1,480.

Oats, 61 acres; Oats, per acre, 30 bush.; val., $915.

Potatoes, 115 acres; Potatoes, per acre, 80 bush.; val., $6,900.

Onions, 23 acres; Onions, per acre, 200 bush.; val., $1,840.

Turnips cultivated as a field crop, 10 acres; Turnips, per acre, 200 bush.; val., $500.

Carrots, 10 acres; Carrots, per acre, 200 bush.; val., $600.

English Mowing, 1,011 acres; English Hay, 898 tons; val., $13,470.

Salt Hay, 431 tons; val., $3,017.

Apple Trees cultivated for their fruit, 1,560 ; val., $780.

Cranberries, 26 acres ; val., $1,150.

Establishments for m. of casks, 1 ; cap., $3,000 ; Casks m'd., 2,600 ; val., $3,458 ; emp., 3.

Establishments for m. of gas, 1 ; cap., $800 ; val. m'd., $– ; emp., –.

Lard Oil Factory, 1 ; yearly m., 1,200 gall. ; val., $9,600 ; cap., $6,000.

HARWICH.

Establishments for m. of boats, 2 ; Boats built, 40 ; cap., $2,000 ; emp., 4.

Sail Lofts, 4 ; Sails made of Am. fabric, 207 ; val. of sails m'd. of Am. fabric, $8,280 ; cap., $4,000 ; emp., 10.

Establishments for m. of salt, 1 ; Salt m'd., 140 bush. ; val. of salt, $42 ; cap., $300 ; emp., 1.

Tin Ware Manufactories, 2 ; val. of tin ware, $1,000 ; cap., $400 ; emp., 3.

Boots of all kinds m'd., 200 pairs ; Shoes of all kinds m'd., 800 pairs ; val. of boots and shoes, $1,500 ; m. emp., 5 ; f. emp., 5.

Val. of blacking, $4,000 ; emp., 10.

Firewood prepared for market, 800 cords ; val. of firewood, $4,400 ; emp., 30.

Vessels employed in the mackerel and cod fisheries, 28 ; Tonnage, 2,040 tons ; Mackerel taken, 5,700 bbls. ; Codfish taken, 6,300 quintals ; val. of mackerel taken, $45,600 ; val. of codfish taken, $17,400 ; Salt consumed, 15,000 bush. ; cap., $84,000 ; emp., 280.

Alewives, Shad and Salmon taken, 500 bbls. ; val. of same, $500 ; emp., 4.

Saxony Sheep, of different grades, – ; Merino Sheep, of different grades, – ; all other kinds of sheep, 33 ; val. of all sheep,

$66; Wool produced from Saxony sheep, – lbs.; Merino Wool produced, – lbs.; all other wool produced 66 lbs.

Horses, 137; val. of horses, $10,200; Oxen over three years old, 12; steers under three years old, 30; val. of oxen and steers, $1,650; Milch Cows, 140; Heifers, 39; val. of cows and heifers, $4,085.

Butter, 9,012 lbs.; val. of butter, $2,253.

Indian Corn, 319 acres; Indian Corn, per acre, 20 bush.; val., $69,157.

Rye, 274 acres; Rye, per acre, 5 bush.; val., $1,995.

Barley, ½ acre; Barley, per acre, 8 bush.; val., $5.

Oats, 3 acres; Oats, per acre, 10 bush.; val., $18.

Potatoes, 90 acres; Potatoes, per acre, 30 bush.; val., $2,683.

Onions, 1½ acres; Onions, per acre, 186 bush.; val., $210.

Turnips cultivated as a field crop, 5 acres; Turnips, per acre, 106 bush.; val., $265.

Carrots, 1 acre; Carrots, per acre, 400 bush.; val., $100.

Beets and other esculent vegetables, ½ acre; val., $40; all other Grain or Root Crops, 1 acre; val., $200.

English Mowing, 60 acres; English Hay, 60 tons; val., $960.

Wet Meadow or Swale Hay, 136 tons; val., $1,360.

Salt Hay, 188 tons; val., $1,692.

Apple Trees cultivated for their fruit, 899; val., $125.

Pear Trees cultivated for their fruit, 65; val., $10.

Cranberries, 17 acres; val., $8,000.

Establishments for m. of sashes and door blinds, 1; cap., $2,000; val. m'd., $4,000; emp., 6.

Eggs, 36,000 doz.; value, $5,400.

ORLEANS.

Yarn m'd., 76 lbs.; val. of yarn, $76.

Establishments for m. of salt, 19; Salt m'd., 10,125 bush.; val. of salt, $3,037; cap., $10,000; emp., 19.

Establishments for m. of railroad cars, coaches, chaises, wagons, sleighs, and other vehicles, 2; val. of railroad cars, &c., m'd., $1,620; cap., $800; emp., 2.

Tin Ware Manufactories, 1; val. of tin ware, $1,500; cap., $500; emp., 2.

Boots of all kinds m'd., 250 pairs; Shoes, 1,000 pairs; val. of boots and shoes, $1,150; m. emp., 2.

Firewood prepared for market, 258 cords; val. of firewood, $1,806; emp., 10.

Vessels employed in the whale fishery, 4; Tonnage 620 tons; Sperm Oil imported, 4,000 galls.; val. of Sperm Oil imported, $7,000; Whale Oil imported, 15,000 galls.; val., of whale oil imported, $11,250; cap. in whale fishery, $40,000; emp., 125.

Vessels employed in the mackerel and cod fisheries, 8; Tonnage 670 tons; Mackerel taken, 800 bbls.; Codfish taken, 4,265 quintals; val. of mackerel taken, $6,000; val. of codfish taken, $11,728; Salt consumed, 6,160 bush.; cap., $21,000; emp., 72.

Saxony Sheep, of different grades, –; Merino Sheep, of different grades, –; all other kinds of sheep, 91; val. of all sheep, $273; Wool produced from Saxony sheep, – lbs.; Merino Wool produced, – lbs.; all other wool produced, 200 lbs.

Horses, 192; val. of horses, $12,350; Oxen over three years old, 36; Steers under three years old, 51; val. of oxen and steers, $3,330; Milch Cows, 295; Heifers, 96; val. of cows and heifers, $10,000.

Butter, 21,985 lbs.; val. of butter, $4,500; Cheese, 50 lbs.; val. of cheese, $5.

Indian Corn, 338 acres; Indian Corn, per acre, 20 bush.; val., $6,760.

Wheat, 13 acres; Wheat, per acre, 12 bush.; val., $234.

Rye, 237 acres; Rye, per acre, 10 bush.; val., $3,000.

Barley, 10 acres; Barley, per acre, 20 bush.; val., $200.

Oats, 46 acres; Oats, per acre, 20 bush.; val., $552.

Potatoes, 32 acres; Potatoes, per acre, 100 bush.; val., $2,400.

Onions, 140 bush.; val., $75.

Turnips cultivated as a field crop, 5 acres; Turnips, per acre, 200 bush.; val., $500.

Carrots, 2 acres; Carrots, per acre, 175 bush.; val., $100.50.

Beets and other esculent vegetables, 2 acres; val., $500.

English Mowing, 215 acres; English Hay, 300 tons; val., $3,600.

Wet Meadow or Swale Hay, 32 tons; val., $250.

Salt Hay, 610 tons; val., $3,660.

Apple Trees cultivated for their fruit, 4,000; val., $1,075.

Pear Trees cultivated for their fruit, 456; val., $125.

Cranberries, 8 acres; val., $375.

Swine, 194; val., $4,850.

Poultry, 4,888; val., $1,230.

Eggs, 40,000 doz.; val., $6,000.

Peat, 13,150 bbls.; val., $1,644.

Shellfish, 5,000 bush,; val., $2,000.

Bass and Bluefish, 150 bbls.; val., $900; emp., 6.

PROVINCETOWN.

Forges, 8; Bar Iron, Anchors, Chain Cables, and other articles of wrought iron, m'd., 40 tons; val. of bar iron, &c., $8,500; cap., $3,500; emp., 8.

Daguerreotype Artists, 1; Daguerreotypes taken, 300; cap., $100; emp., 1.

Establishments for m. of boats, 3; Boats built, 70; cap., $2,200; emp., 7.

Masts and Spar Sheds, 3; Masts and Spars m'd., 300; cap., $2,600; emp., 4.

Sail Lofts, 7; Sails made of Am. fabric, 473; val. of sails m'd. of Am. fabric, $33,700; cap., $22,000; emp., 20.

Establishments for m. of salt, 5; Salt m'd., 2,304 bush.; val. of salt, $702; cap., $200; emp., 2.

Boots of all kinds m'd., 2,200 pairs; Shoes of all kinds m'd.,

3,800 pairs; val. of boots and shoes, $5,600; m. emp., 10; f. emp., 8.

Val. of blocks and pumps m'd., $2,000; emp., 3.

Vessels employed in the whale fishery, 17; Tonnage, 1,885 tons; Sperm Oil imported, 61,582 galls.; val. of sperm oil imported, $92,373; Whale Oil imported, 44,100 galls.; val. of whale oil imported, $26,460; cap. in the whale fishery, $112,000; emp., 310.

Vessels employed in the mackerel and cod fisheries, 97; Tonnage, 8,495 tons; Mackerel taken, 6,000 bbls.; Codfish taken, 79,000 quintals; val. of mackerel taken, $60,000; val. of codfish taken, $246,875; val. of cod liver oil sold for medicinal purposes, $400; Salt consumed, 13,282 bush.; cap., $388,000; emp., 873.

Horses, 80; val. of horses, $6,000.

Salt Hay, 150 tons; val., $1,200.

Cranberries, 25 acres; val., $1,200.

Establishments for m. of casks, 1; cap., $2,000; Casks m'd., 2,000; val., $3,000; emp., 2.

Bakeries, 1; cap., $2,000; Flour consumed, 400 bbls.; val. of bread m'd., $5,600; emp., 3.

SANDWICH.

Nail Mills, 2; Machines for m. of nails, 15; Nails m'd., 200 tons; val. of nails, $15,000; cap., $12,000; emp., 10.

Furnaces for m. of hollow ware and castings other than pig iron, 1; Hollow Ware and other Castings m'd., 350 tons; val. of hollow ware and castings, $30,000; cap. $20,000; emp., 35.

Axe Manufactories, 1; Axes, Hatchets, and other Edge Tools m'd., 3,000; val., $2,500; cap., $1,800; emp., 6.

Tack and Brad Manufactories, 1; Tacks and Brads m'd., 100 tons; val. of tacks and brads, $20,000; cap., $15,000; emp., 25.

Glass Manufactories, 1; Window Glass m'd., –; val. of window glass, –; val. of other glass m'd., $600,000; cap., $400,000; emp., 500 men and boys.

Establishments for m. of railroad cars, coaches, chaises, wagons, sleighs, and other vehicles, 1; val. of railroad cars, &c., m'd., $6,000; cap., $4,000; emp., 10.

Firewood prepared for market, 2,443 cords; val. of firewood, $11,697; emp., 25.

Alewives, Shad and Salmon taken, 700 bbls.; val. of same, $1,400; emp., 6.

Saxony Sheep, of different grades, –; Merino Sheep, of different grades, –; all other kinds of sheep, 288; val. of all sheep, $576; Wool produced from Saxony sheep, –; Merino Wool produced, –; all other wool produced, 999 lbs.

Horses, 257; val. of horses, $20,478; Oxen over three years old, 192; Steers under three years old, 174; val. of oxen and steers, $12,385; Milch Cows, 593; Heifers, 149; val. of cows and heifers, $16,634.

Butter, 18,800; val. of butter, $4,700.

Indian Corn, 401 acres; Indian Corn, per acre, 25 bush.; val. $9,425.

Rye, 166 acres; Rye, per acre, 8 and 10 bush.; val. $1,987.

Barley, 17 acres; Barley, per acre, 15 bush.; val., $300.

Oats, 57 acres; Oats, per acre, 15 and 20 bush.; val., $609.

Potatoes, 109 acres; Potatoes, per acre, 125 bush.; val. $14,450.

English Mowing, 854 acres; English Hay, 1,031 tons; val., $18,605.

Wet Meadow or Swale Hay, 239 tons; val., $1,730.

Salt Hay, 999 tons; val., $5,994.

Apple Trees cultivated for their fruit, 5,959; val., $2,204.

Pear Trees cultivated for their fruit, 375; val., $193.

Cranberries, 5 acres; val., $250.

Establishments for m. of iron and steel axletrees, 1; val. of same, $6,000; cap., $4,000; emp., 10.

Establishments for m. of machinery, 1; Pig and other iron used, 250 tons; val. of machinery m'd., $10,000; emp., 25.

TRURO.

Sail Lofts, 2; Sails made of Am. fabric, 63; val. of sails m'd. of Am. fabric, $3,150; cap., $800; emp., 2.

Establishments for m. of salt, 15; Salt m'd., 5,078 bush.; val. of salt, $1,904.25; cap., $3,500; emp., 13.

Vessels employed in the mackerel and cod fisheries, 49; Tonnage, 2,843 tons; cap., $73,500; emp., 442.

Saxony Sheep, of different grades, –; Merino Sheep, of different grades, –; all other kinds of sheep, 10; val. of all sheep, $30; Wool produced from Saxony sheep, – lbs.; Merino Wool produced, – lbs.; all other wool produced, 25 lbs.

Horses, 112; val. of horses, $8,400; Oxen over three years old, 24; Steers under three years old, 2; val. of oxen and steers, $1,200; Milch Cows, 248; Heifers, 59; val. of cows and heifers, $6,790.

Butter, 9,176 lbs.; val. of butter, $2,294.

Indian Corn, 175 acres; Indian Corn, per acre, 15 bush.; val., $2,625.

Rye, 125 acres; Rye, per acre, 5 bush.; val., $812.50.

Potatoes, 40 acres; Potatoes, per acre, 50 bush.; val., $2,000.

Turnips, cultivated as a field crop, 20 acres; Turnips, per acre, 100 bush.; val., $1,000.

Carrots, 3 acres; Carrots per acre, 150 bush.; val., $150.

Beets and other esculent vegetables, 3 acres; val., $150.

English Mowing, 34 acres; English Hay, 69 tons; val., $1,035.

Wet Meadow or Swale Hay, 50 tons; val., $200.

Salt Hay, 657 tons; val., $5,256.

Apple Trees cultivated for their fruit, 1,200; val., $1,200.

Pear Trees cultivated for their fruit, 75; val., $75.

WELLFLEET.

Forges, 3.

Sail Lofts, 2; Sails made of Am. fabric, 100; val. of sails m'd. of Am. fabric, $4,000; cap., $500; emp., 4.

Establishments for m. of salt, 13; Salt m'd., 40,000 bush.; val. of salt, $12,000; cap., $4,600; emp., 10.

Tin Ware Manufactories, 2; val. of tin ware, $400.

Tanneries, 1; Hides of all kinds tanned, 200; val. of leather tanned, $400; cap., $100; emp., 1.

Boots of all kinds m'd., 100 pairs; Shoes of all kinds m'd., 200 pairs; val. of boots and shoes, $500; m. emp., 3.

Val. of blocks and pumps m'd., $200; emp., 1.

Vessels employed in the mackerel and cod fisheries, 80; Tonnage, 5,935 tons; Mackerel taken, 12,600 bbls.; Codfish taken, 8,528 quintals; val. of mackerel taken, $129,150; val. of codfish taken, $27,716; Salt consumed, 34,733 bush.; cap., $220,175; emp., 824.

Alewives, Shad and Salmon taken, 312,000; val. of same, $156; emp., 4.

Horses, 124; val. of horses, $8,680; Oxen over three years old, 8; Steers under three years old, 20; val. of oxen and steers, $440; Milch Cows, 196; Heifers, 61; val. of cows and heifers, $5,810.

Butter, 9,800 lbs.; val. of butter, $19,600.

Indian Corn, 131 acres; Indian Corn, per acre, 12 bush.; val., $1,729.20.

Rye, 83 acres; Rye, per acre, 8 bush.; val., $996.

Potatoes, 40 acres; Potatoes, per acre, 75 bush.; val., $3,000.

Turnips cultivated as a field crop, 10 acres; Turnips, per acre, 100 bush.; val., $500.

English Mowing, 46 acres; English Hay, 69 tons; val., $1,380.

Salt Hay, 734 tons; val., $5,872.

Apple Trees cultivated for their fruit, 2,425; val., $480.

Pear Trees cultivated for their fruit, 209; val., $25.

Cranberries, 2 acres; val., $100.

Bakeries, 1; cap., $700; Flour consumed, 400 bbls.; val. of bread m'd., $5,500; emp., 2.

YARMOUTH.

Establishments for m. of chemical preparations, 4; val. of chemical preparations, $3,165; cap., $6,600; emp., 5.

Harness Manufactories, 4; val. of harnesses, &c., $2,375; cap., $2,750; emp., 6.

Sail Lofts, 1; Sails made of Am. fabric, 20; val. of sails m'd. of Am. fabric, $700; cap., $200; emp., 1.

Establishments for m. of salt, 42; Salt m'd., 27,650 bush.; val. of salt, $8,295; cap., $21,350; emp., 34.

Chair and Cabinet Manufactories, 1; val. of chairs and cabinet ware, $100; cap., $200; emp., 1.

Tin Ware Manufactories, 3; val. of tin ware, $2,550; cap., $2,300; emp., 5.

Boots of all kinds m'd., 217 pairs; Shoes of all kinds m'd., 855 pairs; val. of boots and shoes, $1,640; m. emp., 5; f. emp., 2.

Firewood prepared for market, 385 cords; val. of firewood, $2,695; emp., 53.

Vessels employed in the mackerel and cod fisheries, 15; Tonnage, 1,035 tons; Mackerel taken, 1,217 bbls.; Codfish taken, 4,400 quintals; val. of mackerel taken, $9,082; val. of codfish taken, $9,350; Salt consumed, 6,881 bush.; cap., $33,481; emp., 170.

Alewives taken, 831 bbls.; val. of same, $2,027; emp., 26.

Horses, 156; val. of horses, $11,700; Oxen over three years old, 37; Steers under three years old, 27; val. of oxen and steers, $2,160; Milch Cows, 226; Heifers, 48; val. of cows and heifers, $7,500.

Butter, 6,780 lbs.; val. of butter, $1,356.

Indian Corn, 170 acres; Indian Corn, per acre, 25 bush.; val., $4,250.

Rye, 98 acres; Rye, per acre, 6 bush.; val., $882.

Oats, 5 acres; Oats, per acre, 16 bush.; val., $40.

Potatoes, 50 acres; Potatoes, per acre, 40 bush.; val., $2,000.

Carrots, 1 acre; Carrots, per acre, 240 bush.; val., $60.

Beets and other esculent vegetables, 40 acres; val., $1,000; all other Grain or Root Crops, 20 acres; val., $500.

English Mowing, 160 acres; English Hay, 325 tons; val., $4,875.

Wet Meadow or Swale Hay, 95 tons; val., $475.

Salt Hay, 400 tons; val., $2,800.

Apple Trees cultivated for their fruit, 283; val., $200.

Cranberries, 5 acres; val., $100.

Establishments for m. of casks, 1; cap., $300; Casks m'd., 1,000; val., $700; emp., 2.

Establishments for m. of sashes and door blinds, 1; cap., $300; val. m'd., $1,000; emp., 1.

Swine, 253; val. of same, $3,036.

Establishments for working marble, 1; cap., $500; val. m'd., $1,200; emp., 2.

Steam planing and sawing mills, 1; cap., $5,000; val. of products, $1,200; emp., 4.

BERKSHIRE COUNTY.

ADAMS.

Cotton Mills, 15; Spindles, 30,306; Cotton consumed, 1,983,395 lbs; Cloth m'd., 7,806,000 yds., (print cloths and sheetings,); val. of cloth, $373,985; Yarn m'd., 415,476 lbs.; val. of yarn, $160,000; cap., $661,000; m. emp., 318; f. emp., 387.

Calico Manufactories, 1; Calico printed, 3,640,000 yards;

val. of calico, $273,000; cap., $50,000; m. emp., 55; f. emp., 5.

Woollen Mills, 5; Sets of Machinery, 20; Wool consumed, 875,000 lbs.; Cassimere m'd., 850,000 yds.; val. of cassimere, $490,000; Satinet m'd., 575,000 yds.; val. of satinet, $287,500; cap., $405,000; m. emp., 208; f. emp., 136.

Furnaces for m. of pig iron, 1; Pig Iron m'd., 1,800 tons; val. of pig iron, $63,000; cap., $100,000; emp., 150.

Furnaces for m. of hollow ware and castings other than pig iron, 3; Hollow Ware and other Castings m'd., 150 tons; val. of hollow ware and castings, $12,000; cap., $9,000; emp., 8.

Establishments for m. of cotton, woollen and other machinery, 2; val. of machinery m'd., $20,000; cap., $9,000; emp. 17.

Paper Manufactories, 1; Stock made use of, 750,000 lbs.; Paper m'd., 563,000 lbs.; val. of paper, $90,000; cap., $90,000; emp., 76.

Piano-Forte Manufactories, 1; Piano-Fortes m'd., –; cap., $–; all musical instruments manufactured, 70; val. of musical instruments m'd., $7,000; cap., $2,500; emp., 7.

Daguerreotype Artists, 2; Daguerreotypes taken, 750; cap., $400; emp., 2.

Saddle, Harness and Trunk Manufactories, 3; val. of saddles, &c., $3,550; cap., $3,550; emp., 7.

Establishments for m. of railroad cars, coaches, chaises, wagons, sleighs, and other vehicles, 4; val. of railroad cars, &c., m'd., $11,175; cap., $7,000; emp., 19.

Establishments for m. of soap and tallow candles, 1; Soap m'd., 50 lbs.; val. of soap, $200; Tallow Candles m'd., 42,000 lbs.; val. of tallow candles, $6,300; cap., $3,000; emp., 3.

Establishments for m. of fire arms, 2; Fire Arms m'd., 60 rifles; val. of fire arms, $1,900; cap., $600; emp., 2.

Chair and Cabinet Manufactories, 3; val. of chairs and cabinet ware, $4,600; cap., $6,300; emp., 9.

Tin Ware Manufactories, 2; val. of tin ware, $11,000; cap., $7,500; emp., 9.

Tanneries, 2; Hides of all kinds tanned, 17,300; val. of leather tanned, $49,500; cap., $20,000; emp., 17.

Boots of all kinds m'd., 17,250 pairs; Shoes of all kinds m'd., 15,650 pairs; val. of boots and shoes, $47,500; m. emp., 51; f. emp., 22.

Bricks m'd., 300,000; val. of bricks, $2,000; emp., 6.

Val. of marble quarried and prepared for market, $23,200; emp., 11.

Casks of Lime m'd., 10,000; val. of lime, $15,000; emp., 15.

Val. of mineral coal and iron ore mined, $7,500; emp., 14.

Charcoal m'd., 200 bush.; val. of same, $20.

Val. of blocks and pumps m'd., $1,500; emp., 3.

Val. of mechanics' tools m'd., $2,500; emp., 4.

Val. of wooden ware not otherwise enumerated, including farming utensils m'd., $1,500; emp., 6.

Lumber prepared for market, 887,406 ft.; val. of lumber, $11,500; emp., 20.

Firewood prepared for market, 9,895 cords; val. of firewood, $29,553; emp., 40.

Saxony Sheep, of different grades, 10; Merino Sheep, of different grades, 2,263; all other kinds of sheep, 169; val. of all sheep, $3,747; Wool produced from Saxony sheep, 40 lbs.; Merino Wool produced, 6,429 lbs.; all other wool produced, 657 lbs.; gross val. of all wool produced, $2,851.

Horses, 475; val. of horses, $50,925; Oxen over three years old, 109; Steers under three years old, 77; val. of oxen and steers, $7,751; Milch Cows, 1,409; Heifers, 274; val. of cows and heifers, $48,379.

Butter, 81,956 lbs.; val. of butter, $18,031; Cheese, 300,347 lbs.; val. of cheese, $27,912; Honey, 400 lbs.; val. of honey, $64.

Indian Corn, 422 acres; Indian Corn, per acre, 33½ bush.; val., $15,946.

Wheat, 9 acres; Wheat, per acre, 15 bush.; val., $278.

Rye, 54 acres; Rye, per acre, 13½ bush.; val., $908.

Barley, 54 acres; Barley, per acre, 26½ bush.; val., $1,608.

Oats, 356 acres; Oats, per acre, 32⅓ bush.; val., $7,217.

Potatoes, 198 acres; Potatoes, per acre, 101 bush.; val., $10,000.

Carrots, $1\frac{1}{2}$ acre ; Carrots, per acre, 804 bush. ; val. $362.

English Mowing, 4,820 acres ; English Hay, 4,151 tons ; val., $62,265.

Apple Trees cultivated for their fruit, 12,818 ; val., $4,756.

Pear Trees cultivated for their fruit, 310 ; val., $120.

Beeswax, 15 lbs. ; val., $4.

Establishments for m. of casks, 2 ; cap., $3,000 ; Casks m'd., 48,240 ; val., $8,500 ; emp., 17.

Establishments for m. of sashes and door blinds, 1 ; cap., $1,400 ; val. m'd., $4,500 ; emp., 3.

Bakeries, 1 ; cap., $3,000 ; Flour consumed, 350 bbls. ; val. of bread m'd., $5,460 ; emp., 4.

Establishments for m. of boxes, for transportation, 2 ; cap., $2,300 ; val. of boxes m'd., $2,450 ; emp., 3.

Barrel and Keg staves manufactured, 2,640,600 ; val., $15,712 ; cap., $900 ; emp., 17.

Poultry, 12,633 lbs.

Eggs, 8,165 doz. ; val., $2,611.

Bark, 274 cords ; val., $1,141.

Number of Swine, 646 ; val., $5,775.

Buckwheat, 25 acres ; 20 bush. per acre ; val., $495.

ALFORD.

Chair and Cabinet Manufactories, 1 ; val. of chairs and cabinet ware, $642 ; cap., $100 ; emp., 1.

Val. of building stone quarried, $3,500 ; emp., 5.

Charcoal m'd., 57,500 bush. ; val. of same, $4,450 ; emp., 12.

Lumber prepared for market, 26,700 ft. ; val. of lumber, $326 ; emp., 3.

Saxony Sheep, of different grades, – ; Merino Sheep, of different grades, 309 ; all other kinds of Sheep, 174 ; val. of all sheep, $850 ; Wool produced from Saxony sheep, – ; Merino Wool produced, 1,053 lbs. ; all other Wool produced, 535 lbs.

Horses, 100; val. of horses, $6,531; Oxen over three years old, 48; Steers under three years old, 14; val. of oxen and steers, $3,273; Milch Cows, 239; Heifers, 52; val. of cows and heifers, $7,665.

Butter, 26,470 lbs.; val. of butter, $4,764.60; Cheese, 2,965 lbs.; val. of cheese, $296.50; Honey, 185 lbs.; val. of honey, $23.

Indian Corn, 344 acres; Indian Corn, per acre, 28 bush.; val., $9,633.

Wheat, 14½ acres; Wheat, per acre, 11 bush.; val., $319.

Rye, 117 acres; Rye, per acre, 14 bush.; val., $1,842.

Oats, 406 acres; Oats, per acre, 22 bush.; val., $4,912.60.

Potatoes, 33 acres; Potatoes, per acre, 100 bush.; val., $1,650.

Beets and other esculent vegetables, – acres; val., $–; all other Grain or Root Crops, 60 acres; val., $1,200.

English Mowing, 870 acres; English Hay, 832 tons; val., $7,488.

Wet Meadow or Swale Hay, 25 tons; val., $150.

Apple Trees cultivated for their fruit, 2,227; val., $689.50.

Pear Trees cultivated for their fruit, 104; val., $53.

Number of Swine, 186; val., $469.25.

BECKET.

Tanneries, 2; Hides of all kinds tanned, 30,000; val. of leather tanned, $75,000; cap., $10,000; emp., 20.

Currying Establishments, 1; val. of leather curried, $120,-000; cap., $5,000; emp., 25.

Boots of all kinds m'd., – pairs; Shoes of all kinds m'd., unknown pairs; val. of boots and shoes, $4,000; m. emp., 6; f. emp., –.

Charcoal m'd., 109,500 bush.; val. of same, $10,950; emp., 10.

Lumber prepared for market, 3,114,000 ft.; val. of lumber, $381,200; emp., 50.

Firewood prepared for market, 7,619 cords; val. of firewood, $11,500; emp., 25.

Saxony Sheep, of different grades, –; Merino Sheep, of different grades, 895; all other kinds of Sheep, 636; val. of all sheep, $2,300; Wool produced from Saxony sheep, – lbs.; Merino Wool produced, 3,132 lbs.; all other Wool produced, 2,544 lbs.

Horses, 192; val. of horses, $11,750; Oxen over three years old, 217; Steers under three years old, 138; val. of oxen and steers, $355; Milch Cows, 503; Heifers, 158; val. of cows and heifers, $14,552.

Butter, 35,000 lbs.; val. of butter, $5,950; Cheese, 20,600 lbs.; val. of cheese, $1,442.

Indian Corn, 110 acres; Indian Corn, per acre, 30 bush.; val., $3,367.

Wheat, ½ acre; Wheat, per acre, 7 bush.; val., $15.

Rye, 18 acres; total, 436 bush.; val., $436.

Barley, 4 acres; total, 20 bush.; val., $20.

Oats, 86 acres; Oats, per acre, 31 bush.; val. $1,332.

Potatoes, 104 acres; Potatoes, per acre, 126 bush.; val., $6,091.

Turnips, cultivated as a field crop, 5 acres; Turnips, per acre, 370 bush.

Carrots, ¾ acre; Carrots, per acre, 450 bush.; val., $150.

English Mowing, 3,613 acres; English Hay, 3,295 tons; val., $26,360.

Wet Meadow or Swale Hay, 240 tons; val., $1,000.

Apple Trees cultivated for their fruit, 2,847; val., $1,370.

CHESHIRE.

Cotton Mills, 1; Spindles, 1,500; Cotton consumed, 140,000 lbs.; Cloth, m'd., 663,848 yds. of Sheeting and Printing cloths; val. of cloth, $40,000; cap., $50,000; m. emp., 30; f. emp., 20.

Furnaces for m. of pig iron, 1; Pig Iron m'd., 1,500 tons; val. of pig iron, $50,000; cap., $40,000; emp., 15.

Glass Manufactories, 1; Window Glass m'd., –; val. of window glass, $–; val. of other (rough plate) glass m'd., $40,000; cap., $80,000; emp., 25.

Establishments for m. of railroad cars, coaches, chaises, wagons, sleighs, and other vehicles, 2; val. of railroad cars, &c., m'd., $7,500; cap., $3,600; emp., 12.

Chair and Cabinet Manufactories, 1; val. of chairs and cabinet ware, $800; cap., $600; emp., 1.

Tin Ware Manufactories, 1; val. of tin ware, $2,500; cap., $1,500; emp., 2.

Flour Mills, for manufacturing feed, 1; number of tons of feed, 144; val., $5,760; cap., $3,000; emp., 2.

Tanneries, 2; Hides of all kinds tanned, 12,200; val. of leather tanned, $44,000; cap., $37,000; emp., 18.

Boots of all kinds m'd., 1,050 pairs; Shoes of all kinds m'd., 500 pairs; val. of boots and shoes, $3,500; m. emp., 4; f. emp., –.

Bricks m'd., 225,000; val. of bricks, $900; emp., 3.

Casks of Lime m'd., 4,075; emp., 6; val. of lime, $5,000.

Iron ore mined during the year, 4,000 tons; emp., 12.

Charcoal m'd., 200,000 bush.; val. of same, $14,000; emp., 10.

Lumber prepared for market, 1,050,000 ft.; val. of lumber, $10,500; emp., 10.

Firewood prepared for market, 3,000 cords; val. of firewood, $8,000; emp., 12.

Saxony Sheep, of different grades, –; Merino Sheep, of different grades, –; all other kinds of Sheep, 579; val. of all sheep, $1,600; Wool produced from Saxony sheep, – lbs.; Merino Wool produced, – lbs.; all other Wool produced, 1,750 lbs.

Horses, 210; val. of horses, $16,000; Oxen over three years old, 98; Steers under three years old, 150; val. of oxen and steers, $8,000; Milch Cows, 1,153; Heifers, 150; val. of cows and heifers, $36,000.

Butter, 23,325 lbs.; val. of butter, $4,000; Cheese, 304,500 lbs.; val. of cheese, $24,360; Honey, 500 lbs.; val. of honey, $83.

Indian Corn, 292 acres; Indian Corn, per acre, 25 bush.; val. $1,655.

Buckwheat, 50 acres; Buckwheat, per acre, 20 bush.; val., $750.

Rye, 49 acres; Rye, per acre, 16 bush.; val., $980.

Barley, 50 acres; total, 1,000 bush.; val., $1,000.

Oats, 358 acres; Oats, per acre, 25 bush.; val., $5,375.

Potatoes, 140 acres; Potatoes, per acre, 100 bush.; val., $7,000.

Onions, 100 bush.; val., $50.

Turnips cultivated as a field crop, 200 bush.; val., $50.

Carrots, 1 acre; Carrots, per acre, 400 bush.; val., $100.

Beets and other esculent vegetables, 2 acres; val., $300.

English Mowing, 3,139 acres; English Hay, 3,139 tons; val., $31,390.

Wet Meadow or Swale Hay, 100 tons; val., $600.

Apple Trees cultivated for their fruit, 5,000; val., $3,000.

Pear Trees cultivated for their fruit, 100; val., $200.

Tobacco, 2 acres; val., $250.

Establishments for m. of casks, 1; cap., $2,000; Casks, m'd., 18,000; val., $5,500; emp., 3.

Establishments for m. of sashes and door blinds, 1; cap., $2,000; val. m'd., $500; emp., 2.

Establishments for m. of cheese boxes, 1; cap., $1,500; val. of boxes m'd., $1,950; emp., 2.

Mills for m. of staves and heading, and heading machines, 1; val., $6,500; cap., $3,000; emp., 8.

White Glass Sand dug, 4,000 tons; val. per ton, $5.50; gross val., $22,000; cap., $15,000; emp., 30.

Number of Swine, 245; val. of same, $2,000.

CLARKSBURG.

Powder Mills, 1; Powder m'd., 375,000 lbs.; val. of powder, $33,750; cap., $9,000; emp., 7.

Lumber prepared for market, 240,000 ft.; val. of lumber, $2,400; emp., 8.

Firewood prepared for market, 6,125 cords; val. of firewood $16,843.75; emp., 50.

Saxony Sheep, of different grades, –; Merino Sheep, of different grades, –; all other kinds of Sheep, 62; val. of all sheep, $248; Wool produced from Saxony sheep, – lbs.; Merino Wool produced, – lbs.; all other Wool produced, 217 lbs.

Horses, 83; val. of horses, $5,615; Oxen over three years old, 50; Steers under three years old, 28; val. of oxen and steers, $3,000; Milch Cows, 150; Heifers, 45; val. of cows and heifers, $4,425.

Butter, 22,500 lbs.; val. of butter, $4,500; Cheese, 3,000 lbs.; val. of cheese, $300; Honey, 300 lbs.; val. of honey, $50.

Indian Corn, 85 acres; Indian Corn, per acre, 40 bush.; val., $4,250.

Wheat, 1¾ acre; Wheat, per acre, 20 bush.; val., $87.50.

Rye, 30 acres; Rye, per acre, 15 bush.; val., $675.

Barley, 3 acres; Barley, per acre, 34 bush.; val., $102.

Oats, 78 acres; Oats, per acre, 40 bush.; val., $1,560.

Potatoes, 88 acres; Potatoes, per acre, 100 bush.; val., $4,400.

Onions, ½ acre; Onions, per acre, 400 bush.; val., $100.

Turnips cultivated as a field crop, 1 acre; Turnips, per acre, 400 bush.; val., $200.

Carrots, 1 acre; Carrots, per acre, 320 bush.; val., $160.

English Mowing, 580 acres; English Hay, 580 tons; val., $6,960.

Apple Trees cultivated for their fruit, 2,582; val., $1,032.80.

Establishments for m. of boot, shoe, and dry goods boxes, and cloth boards, 1; cap., $5,000; val. of boxes m'd., $2,691; emp., 4.

Number of Swine, 105; val., $525.

The Assessors append to their Report the following general statement, without details:—"There are in this town six saw mills, one grist mill, one carding machine for carding wool, and one establishment for dressing cloth. Thirty thousand staves for hogsheads have been prepared for market, valued at thirty dollars per thousand. There is one establishment for cutting barrel staves which has just commenced operations. There are quite a number of young orchards of choice fruit, that begin to bear some apples, pears, plums, and cherries."

DALTON.

Paper Manufactories, 5; Stock made use of, 725 tons; Paper m'd., 555 tons; val. of paper, $174,000; cap., $200,000; emp., 155.

Saddle, Harness and Trunk Manufactories, 1; val. of saddles, &c., $680; cap., $200; emp., 1.

Tanneries, 1; Hides of all kinds tanned, 3,000; val. of leather tanned, $8,000; cap., $11,000; emp., 6.

Currying Establishments, 1; val. of leather curried, $8,000; cap., $11,000; emp., 2.

Boots of all kinds m'd., 680 pairs; Shoes of all kinds m'd., 160 pairs; val. of boots and shoes, $2,360; m. emp., 4; f. emp., –.

Val. of palm leaf hats, $40; m. emp., –; f. emp., 1.

Casks of Lime m'd., 6,000; val. of lime, $6,000; emp., 12.

Lumber prepared for market, 1,983,000 ft.; val. of lumber, $17,847; emp., 48.

Firewood prepared for market, 4,620 cords; val. of firewood, $9,240; emp., 37.

Saxony Sheep, of different grades, –; Merino Sheep of different grades, –; all other kinds of Sheep, 1,199; val. of all sheep, $2,997.50; Wool produced from Saxony sheep, – lbs.; Merino Wool produced, – lbs.; all other Wool produced, 3,597 lbs.

Horses, 135; val. of horses, $12,350; Oxen over three years old, 71; Steers under three years old, 61; val. of oxen and steers, $5,415; Milch Cows, 216; Heifers, 45; val. of cows and heifers, $7,155.

Butter, 21,600 lbs.; val. of butter, $4,320; Cheese, 3,550 lbs.; val. of cheese, $284.

Indian Corn, 133 acres; Indian Corn, per acre, 30 bush.; val., $3,990.

Wheat, 2 acres; Wheat, per acre, 15 bush.; val., $60.

Rye, 24 acres; Rye, per acre, 12 bush.; val., $288.

Barley, 3½ acres; Barley, per acre, 20 bush.; val., $70.

Oats, 138 acres; Oats, per acre, 30 bush.; val., $2,070.

Potatoes, 86 acres; Potatoes, per acre, 100 bush.; val., $4,300.

Carrots, 1½ acre; Carrots, per acre, 400 bush.; val., $200.

English Mowing, 1,502 acres; English Hay, 1,502 tons; val., $15,020.

Wet Meadow or Swale Hay, 232 tons; val., $1,392.

Apple Trees cultivated for their fruit, 5,280; val., $1,191.

Pear Trees cultivated for their fruit, 100; val., $100.

Beeswax, 17 lbs.; val., $5.50.

Buckwheat, 50 acres; val., $450.

Bark for market, 400 cords; val., $1,200.

Number of Swine, 198; val., $990.

EGREMONT.

Saddle, Harness and Trunk Manufactories, 1; val. of harnesses, &c., $500; cap., $300; emp., 2.

Establishments for m. of railroad cars, coaches, chaises, wagons, sleighs, and other vehicles, 1; val. of railroad cars, &c., m'd., $25,000; cap., $10,000; emp., 20.

Chair and Cabinet Manufactories, 1; val. of chairs and cabinet ware, $3,000; cap., $500; emp., 3.

Flour Mills, 1; Flour m'd., 1,500 bbls.; val. of flour m'd., $15,000; cap., $12,000; emp., 2.

Boots of all kinds m'd., 425 pairs; Shoes of all kinds m'd., 500 pairs; val. of boots and shoes, $2,025; m. emp., 4; f. emp., –.

Charcoal m'd., 52,000 bush.; val., of same, $36,400; emp., 20.

Firewood prepared for market, 2,655 cords; val. of firewood, $7,965; emp., 10.

Saxony Sheep, of different grades, –; Merino Sheep, of different grades, 190; all other kinds of Sheep, 420; val. of all sheep, $1,748; Wool produced from Saxony sheep, – lbs.; Merino Wool produced, 669 lbs.; all other Wool produced, 953 lbs.

Horses, 225; val. of horses, $19,850; Oxen over three years old, 96; Steers under three years old, 12; val. of oxen and steers, $6,240; Milch Cows, 380; Heifers, 92; val. of cows and heifers, $10,565.

Butter, 29,180 lbs.; val. of butter, $5,836; Cheese, 4,600 lbs.; val. of cheese, $460.

Indian Corn, 630 acres; Indian Corn, per acre, 30 bush.; val., $14,175.

Wheat, 20 acres; Wheat, per acre, 20 bush.; val., $800.

Rye, 640 acres; Rye, per acre, 12 bush.; val., $7,680.

Oats, 684 acres; Oats, per acre, 40 bush.; val., $13,680.

Potatoes, 60 acres; Potatoes, per acre, 100 bush.; val., $1,500.

Beets and other esculent vegetables, – acres; val., $–; all other Grain or Root Crops, 3,000 acres; val., $2,880.

English Mowing, 1,223 acres; English Hay, 1,730 tons; val., $17,300.

Apple Trees cultivated for their fruit, 943; val., $347.

Pear Trees cultivated for their fruit, 28; val., $32.

FLORIDA.

Val. of Palm Leaf Hats, $250 ; f. emp., 3.

Lumber prepared for market, 311,000 ft. ; val. of lumber, $2,177 ; emp., 5.

Firewood prepared for market, 1,666 cords ; val. of firewood, $1,666 ; emp., 10.

Saxony Sheep, of different grades, – ; Merino Sheep, of different grades, – ; all other kinds of Sheep, 482 ; val. of all sheep, $1,205 ; Wool produced from Saxony sheep, – lbs. ; Merino Wool produced, – lbs. ; all other Wool produced, 1,566 lbs.

Horses, 112 ; val. of horses, $840 ; Oxen over three years old, 146 ; Steers under three years old, 138 ; val. of oxen and steers, $8,054 ; Milch Cows, 262 ; Heifers, 228 ; val. of cows and heifers, $8,760.

Butter, 22,180 lbs. ; val. of butter, $2,992 ; Cheese, 8,061 lbs. ; val. of cheese, $725.49 ; Honey, 670 lbs. ; val. of honey, $76,25.

Indian Corn, 51 acres ; Indian Corn, per acre, 32 bush. ; val., $1,632.

Wheat, 1½ acre ; Wheat, per acre, 18 bush. ; val., $54.

Rye, 2 acres ; Rye, per acre, 23 bush. ; val., $28.35.

Barley, 6½ acres ; Barley, per acre, 15$\frac{5}{13}$ bush. ; val., $15.45.

Oats, 80½ acres ; Oats, per acre, 36 bush. ; val., $1,800.

Potatoes, 138 acres ; Potatoes, per acre, 163 bush. ; val., $6,175.

Turnips cultivated as a field crop, 2½ acres ; Turnips, per acre, 112 bush. ; val., $18.00.

Carrots, ½ acre ; Carrots, per acre, 300 bush. ; val., $112.50.

Buckwheat and all other Grain or Root Crops, 45 acres ; val., $2,250.

English Mowing, 1,971 acres ; English Hay, 1,577 tons ; val., $12,616.

Apple Trees cultivated for their fruit, 1,326 ; val., $513.87.

Pear Trees cultivated for their fruit, 8 ; val., $17.

Beeswax, 64½ lbs. ; val., $25.80.

Val. of oak staves for molasses hogsheads, $3,270; cap., $1,500; emp., 10.

GREAT BARRINGTON.

Cotton Mills, 1; Spindles, 2,036; Cotton consumed, 80,000 lbs.; Sheeting Cloth, m'd., 350,000 yds.; val. of cloth, $14,000; cap., $30,000; m. emp., 35; f. emp., 43.

Woollen Mills, 1; Sets of Machinery, 8; Wool consumed, 300,000 lbs.; Cassimere m'd., 500,000 yds.; val. of cassimere, $250,000; cap., $85,000; m. emp., 95; f. emp., 50.

Furnaces for m. of Pig Iron, 1; Pig Iron m'd., 1,093 tons; val. of pig iron, $40,465; cap., $27,000; emp., 18.

Daguerreotype Artists, 1; Daguerreotypes taken, –; cap., $–; emp., 1.

Saddle, Harness and Trunk Manufactories, 2; val. of same, $4,000; cap., $2,000; emp., 6.

Cordage Manufactories, 1; Cordage m'd., 1,000 lbs.; cap., $300; emp., 2.

Chair and Cabinet Manufactories, 1; val. of chairs and cabinet ware, $1,000; cap., $200; emp., 2.

Tin Ware Manufactories, 1; val. of tin ware, $8,000; cap., $2,000; emp., 4.

Flour Mills, 2; Flour m'd., 12,000 bbls.; val. of flour m'd., $90,000; cap., $16,000; emp., 6.

Tanneries, 1; Hides of all kinds tanned, 1,250; val. of leather tanned, $1,500; cap., $500; emp., 2.

Boots of all kinds m'd., 700 pairs; Shoes of all kinds m'd., 800 pairs; val. of boots and shoes, $2,800; m. emp., 8.

Val. of building stone quarried and prepared for building, $1,500; emp., 6.

Charcoal m'd., 60,000 bush.; val. of same, $4,200; emp., 25.

Lasts manufactured, 44,000; val., $7,000.

Lumber prepared for market, 457,000 ft.; val. of lumber, $5,027; emp., 18.

Firewood prepared for market, 10,183 cords; val. of firewood, $20,360; emp., 25.

Saxony Sheep, of different grades, 224; Merino Sheep, of different grades, 800; all other kinds of Sheep, 345; val. of all sheep, $1,642.80; Wool produced from Saxony sheep, 672 lbs.; Merino Wool produced, 2,600 lbs.; all other Wool produced, 1,207 lbs.

Horses, 320; val. of horses, $28,800; Oxen over three years old, 208; Steers under three years old, 269; val. of oxen and steers, $15,526; Milch Cows, 662; Heifers, 408; val. of cows and heifers, $21,446.

Butter, 75,000 lbs.; val. of butter, $12,500; Cheese, 3,500 lbs.; val. of cheese, $280; Honey, 300 lbs.; val. of honey, $37.50.

Indian Corn, 802 acres; Indian Corn, per acre, 33 bush.; val., $26,466.

Wheat, 55 acres; Wheat, per acre, 12 bush.; val., $1,165.

Rye, 752 acres; Rye, per acre, 14 bush.; val., $12,107.

Oats, 830 acres; Oats, per acre, 34 bush.; val., $14,110.

Potatoes, 170 acres; Potatoes, per acre, 110 bush.; val., $9,350.

Turnips, cultivated as a field crop, 6 acres; Turnips, per acre, 300 bush.; val., $108.

Carrots, 2¼ acres; Carrots, per acre, 500 bush.; val., $250.

Beets and other esculent vegetables, – acres; val., $–; Buckwheat and all other Grain or Root Crop, 245 acres; val., $2,940.

English Mowing, 2,485 acres; English Hay, 3,546 tons; val., $28,368.

Wet Meadow or Swale Hay, 164 tons; val., $984.

Apple Trees cultivated for their fruit, 1,607; val., $1,607.

Pear Trees cultivated for their fruit, 156; val., $156.

Establishments for m. of casks, 4; cap., $300; Casks m'd., 1,450; val., $708; emp., 4.

Establishments for m. of gas, 1; cap., $2,000; val. m'd., $750; emp., 1.

Distilleries, 1; cap., $2,000; Alcohol distilled, 900 bbls.; all other Liquors distilled, (cider brandy,) 100 bbls.; val., $13,500; emp., 4.

Establishments for m. of India-rubber goods, 1; cap., –; val. of goods m'd., $40,000; m. emp., 14; f. emp., 6.

Bakeries, 1; cap., $1,250; Flour consumed, 1,200 bbls.; val. of bread m'd., $10,937.50; emp., 4.

Gross value of all other articles manufactured in the town, including the Warp Mill, $43,255; cap., $16,500; emp., 40.

Establishments for m. of wagons and sleighs, 5; cap., $700; val., $4,600.

Blacksmiths' Shops, 7; cap., $900; val. of m's., $1,455.

Shingle Mills, 1; gross val., $1,200; cap., $300.

Cotton Warp Mills, 1; cap., $15,000; yearly m., 1,004,000; Cotton consumed, 135,000 lbs.; val. of warp, $36,000; m. emp., 15; f. emp., 13.

HANCOCK.

Woollen Mills, 3; Sets of Machinery, 5; Wool consumed, 111,000 lbs.; Broadcloth m'd., 500 yds.; val. of broadcloth, $1,000; Satinet m'd., 101,200 yds.; val. of satinet, $50,600; Blanketing for horses, 3,000 yds.; val. of blanketing, $2,250; m. emp., 16; f. emp., 10.

Furnaces for m. of hollow ware and castings other than pig iron, 1; Hollow Ware and other Castings m'd., 10 tons; val. of hollow ware and castings, $800; cap., $600; emp., 1.

Saddle, Harness and Trunk Manufactories, 1; val. of saddles, &c., $200; emp., 1.

Chair and Cabinet Manufactories, 1; val. of chairs and cabinet ware, $200; emp., 1.

Tanneries, 2; Hides of all kinds tanned, 3,018; val. of leather tanned, $7,500; cap., $4,100; emp., 5.

Boots of all kinds, m'd., 400 pairs; Shoes of all kinds m'd., 250 pairs; val. of boots and shoes, $1,625; m. emp., 3; f. emp., 1.

Corn and other Brooms m'd., 4,400; val. of brooms, $1,100; emp., 2.

Firewood prepared for market, 688 cords; val. of firewood, $1,376.

Saxony Sheep, of different grades, –; Merino Sheep, of different grades, –; all other kinds of Sheep, 4,033; val. of all sheep, $8,066; Wool produced from Saxony sheep, – lbs.; Merino Wool produced, – lbs.; all other Wool produced, 12,070 lbs.

Horses, 153; val. of horses, $15,300; Oxen over three years old, 64; Steers under three years old, 40; val. of oxen and steers, $5,000; Milch Cows, 424; Heifers, 71; val. of cows and heifers, $7,425.

Butter, 16,535 lbs.; val. of butter, $3,307; Cheese, 773,000 lbs.; val. of cheese, $6,184; Honey, 1,774 lbs.; val. of honey, $211.

Indian Corn, 209 acres; Indian Corn, per acre, 35⅓ bush.; val., $7,315.

Wheat, 38 acres; Wheat, per acre, 13¾ bush.; val., $1,044.

Rye, 50 acres; Rye, per acre, 11⅖ bush.; val., $600.

Oats, 501 acres; Oats, per acre, 27 bush.; val., $6,888.

Potatoes, 83 acres; Potatoes, per acre, 89 bush.; val., $3,648.

Onions, ¼ acre; Onions, per acre, 400 bush.; val., $50.

Turnips, cultivated as a field crop, 1 acre; Turnips, per acre, 200 bush; val., $50.

Carrots, ¾ acre; Carrots, per acre, 300 bush.; val., $75.

English Mowing, 3,400 acres; English Hay, ¾ ton per acre; val., $25,500.

Apple trees cultivated for their fruit, 1,369; val., $272.

Pear trees cultivated for their fruit, 12.

Beeswax, 30 lbs.; val., $7.

Buckwheat, 12 acres; buckwheat, per acre, 15 bush.; val., $90.

HINSDALE.

Woollen Mills, 3; Sets of Machinery, 11; Wool consumed, 397,000 lbs.; Broadcloth m'd., 115,000 yds.; val. of broadcloth, $101,000; Satinet m'd., 185,000 yds.; val. of satinet, $90,000; cap., $87,000; m. emp., 105; f. emp., 69.

Manufactories of shovels, spades, forks and hoes, 2; val. of shovels, &c., $2,615; cap., $2,350; emp., 6.

Tin Ware Manufactories, 1; val. of tin ware, $3,000; cap., $1,400; emp., 4.

Flour Mills, 1; Flour m'd., 150 bbls.; val. of flour m'd., $1,500; emp., 1.

Tanneries, 1; Hides of all kinds tanned, 1,000; val. of leather tanned, $4,000; cap., $25,000; emp., 2.

Boots of all m'd., 300 pairs; val. of boots, $1,000; m. emp., 2.

Casks of Lime m'd., 2,087; val. of lime, $2,087; emp., 6.

Lumber prepared for market, 840,000 ft.; val. of lumber, $7,917; emp., 16.

Firewood prepared for market, 4,754 cords; val. of firewood, $13,156; emp., 20.

Saxony Sheep, of different grades, 655; Merino Sheep, of different grades, 5,370; all other kinds of Sheep, 708; val. of all sheep, $20,199; Wool produced from Saxony sheep, 2,485 lbs.; Merino Wool produced, 17,599 lbs.; all other Wool produced, 2,354 lbs.

Horses, 180; val. of horses, $15,740; Oxen over three years old, 95; Steers under three years old, 146; val. of oxen and steers, $8,943; Milch Cows, 371; Heifers, 162; val. of cows and heifers, $15,488.

Butter, 36,763 lbs.; val. of butter, $7,352.60; Cheese, 8,592 lbs.; val. of cheese, 768.60; Honey, 765 lbs.; val. of honey, $127.50.

Indian Corn, 140 acres; Indian Corn, per acre, 37$\frac{5}{7}$ bush.; val., $5,281.

Wheat, 32 acres; Wheat, per acre, 15$\frac{1}{2}$ bush.; val., $990.

Rye, 33 acres; Rye, per acre, 14$\frac{2}{3}$ bush.; val., $650.70.

Barley, 29 acres; Barley, per acre, 24$\frac{5}{7}$ bush.; val., $896.25.

Oats, 179 acres; Oats, per acre, 30$\frac{1}{3}$ bush.; val., $3,471.65.

Potatoes, 167 acres; Potatoes, per acre, 130 bush.; val., $14,091.

Turnips cultivated as a field crop, $\frac{3}{4}$ acre; Turnips, per acre, 400 bush.; val., $68.

Carrots, $\frac{5}{8}$ acre; Carrots, per acre, 800 bush.; val., $154.60.

Beets and other esculent vegetables, 1 acre; val., $30; all other Grain or Root Crops, 28$\frac{1}{2}$ acres; val., $603.

English Mowing, 2,257 acres; English Hay, 2,143 tons; val., $23,573.

Wet Meadow or Swale Hay, 998 tons; val., $7,984.

Apple Trees cultivated for their fruit, 4,000; val., $1,800.

Beeswax, 54 lbs.; val., $18.

Number of Shingles m'd., 44,000; val., $132.

Maple Sugar m'd., 5,625 lbs.; val., $562.50.

Plaster m'd., 200 tons; val., $1,600.

Meal m'd., 80,000 lbs.; val., $1,600.

LANESBOROUGH.

Furnaces for m. of Pig Iron, 1; Pig Iron m'd., 1,300 tons; val. of pig iron, $39,000; cap., $100,000; emp., 15.

Glass Manufactories, 1; Window Glass m'd., 14,069 boxes; val. of window glass, $35,000; val. of other glass m'd., $5,000; cap., $50,000; emp., 75.

Establishments for m. of wagons, sleighs, and other vehicles, 1; val. of same, $600; cap., $600; emp., 2.

Casks of Lime m'd., 6,000; emp., 10; val. of lime, $6,000.

Val. of mineral coal and iron ore mined, $6,000; emp., 15.

Charcoal m'd., 300,000 bush.; val. of same, $21,000; emp., 70.

Lumber prepared for market, 131,000 ft.; val. of lumber, $1,824; emp., 4.

Firewood prepared for market, 1,730 cords; val. of firewood, $2,595.

Merino Sheep, of different grades, 6,931; val. of all sheep, $13,862; Merino Wool produced, 21,690 lbs.

Horses, 199; val. of horses, $13,680; Oxen over three years old, 93; steers under three years old, 60; val. of oxen and steers, $6,599; Milch Cows, 504; Heifers, 120; val. of cows and heifers, $1,440.

Butter, 27,675 lbs.; val. of butter, $5,535; Cheese, 83,850 lbs.; val. of cheese, $6,708; Honey, 1,000 lbs.; val. of honey, $166.

Indian Corn, 289¼ acres; Indian Corn, per acre, 40 bush.; val., $9,256.

Wheat, 18¾ acres; Wheat, per acre, 15 bush.; val., $562.

Rye, 78 acres; Rye, per acre, 15 bush.; val., $1,170.

Barley, 32 acres; Barley, per acre, 25 bush.; val., $600.

Oats, 366½ acres; Oats, per acre, 35 bush.; val., $6,413.

Potatoes, 126 acres; Potatoes, per acre, 100 bush.; val., $4,200.

Turnips, cultivated as a field crop, 1 acre; Turnips, per acre, 500 bush.; val., $62.50.

Carrots, ¼ acre; Carrots, per acre, 1,000 bush.; val., $3,125.

Beets and other esculent vegetables, ⅛ acre; val., $18.75; all other Grain or Root Crops, 70½ acres; val., $528.50.

English Mowing, 3,067 acres; English Hay, 2,509 tons; val., $25,090.

Wet Meadow or Swale Hay, 419 tons; val., $2,095.

Apple Trees cultivated for their fruit, 1,000; val., $800.

Establishments for m. of glass boxes, 1; cap., $4,000; val. of boxes m'd., $2,000; emp., 3.

Establishments for m. of felloes, 1; number manufactured, 11,000 sets.

Auger and Chisel handles m'd., 400 gross.

Val. of articles m'd. in the two last named establishments, $12,500; cap., $7,000.

Ash and Oak lumber consumed in the town for manufacturing purposes, during the year, 290,000 ft.

LEE.

Cotton Mills, 1; Spindles, 756; Cotton consumed, 150,000 lbs.; Cloth, m'd., No. of yds. m'd. not returned; Grain Bags m'd. yearly, 150,000; val. of cloth, $30,000; Batting m'd., 3,900 lbs.; val. of batting, $350; cap., $12,000; m. emp., 14; f. emp., 19.

Woollen Mills, 3; Sets of Machinery, 13; Wool consumed, 345,000 lbs.; Cassimere m'd., 250,000 yds.; val. of cassimere, $240,000; Satinet m'd., 245,000 yds.; val. of satinet, $125,000; cap., $120,000; m. emp., 134; f. emp., 66.

Establishments for m. of cotton, woollen and other machinery, 2; val. of machinery m'd., $50,000; cap., $26,000; emp., 32.

Repair Machine Shop, 1; emp., 14.

Axe Manufactories, 1; Axes, Hatchets, and other Edge Tools m'd., 600; val., $5,750; cap., $4,000; emp., 4.

Paper Manufactories, 20; Stock made use of, 5,500 tons; Paper m'd., 3,172 tons; val. of paper, $1,010,000; cap., $550,000; m. emp., 228; f. emp., 505.

Daguerreotype Artists, 1; Daguerreotypes taken, 600; cap., $200; emp., 1.

Saddle, Harness and Trunk Manufactories, 2; val. of saddles, &c., $3,000; cap., $750; emp., 3.

Hat and Cap Manufactories, 1; Hats and Caps m'd., $1,300; cap., $500; emp., 4.

Establishments for m. of wagons, sleighs, and other vehicles, 1; val. of same, $5,000; cap., $1,000; emp., 5.

Powder Mills, 1; Powder m'd., 75,000 lbs.; val. of powder, $7,875; cap., $1,500; emp., 3.

Chair and Cabinet Manufactories, 2; val. of chairs and cabinet ware, $1,500; cap., $1,300; emp., 3.

Tin Ware Manufactories, 1; val. of tin ware, $3,000; cap., $1,000; emp., 3.

Flour Mills, 1; Flour m'd., 3,000 bbls.; val. of flour m'd., $30,000; cap., $15,000; emp., 3; val. of other productions of the flour mill, including Corn Meal, Feed, Rye Flour, &c., $20,000.

Tanneries, 1; Hides of all kinds tanned, 700; val. of leather tanned, $1,700; cap., $500; emp., 1.

Boots of all kinds m'd., 750 pairs; Shoes of all kinds m'd., 1,760 pairs; val. of boots and shoes, $5,361; m. emp., 12; f. emp., 4.

Bricks m'd., 200,000; val. of bricks, $11,000; emp., 5.

Val. of building stone quarried and prepared for building, $75,000; emp., 75.

Val. of marble quarried and prepared for market, $15,000; emp., 20.

Charcoal m'd., 160,704 bush.; val. of same, $16,000; emp., 40.

Lumber prepared for market, 1,468,500 ft.; val. of lumber, $18,399; emp., 14.

Firewood prepared for market, 7,141 cords; val. of firewood, $11,956; emp., 15.

Saxony Sheep, of different grades, –; Merino Sheep, of different grades, 910; all other kinds of Sheep, 115; val. of all sheep, $1,629; Wool produced from Saxony sheep, – lbs.; Merino Wool produced, 2,998 lbs.; all other Wool produced, 357 lbs.

Horses, 300; val. of horses, $29,486; Oxen over three years old, 150; Steers under three years old, 211; val. of oxen and steers, $14,897; Milch Cows, 681; Heifers, 266; val. of cows and heifers, $24,318.

Butter, 75,722 lbs.; val. of butter, $15,144.40; Cheese, 40,643 lbs.; val. of cheese, $2,457.87; Honey, 906 lbs.; val. of honey, $151.

Indian Corn, 323 acres; Indian Corn, per acre, 41 bush.; val., $13,243.

Wheat, 17 acres; Wheat, per acre, 15 bush.; val., $637.50.

Rye, 109 acres; Rye, per acre, 11 bush.; val., $1,798.50.

Barley, 16 acres; Barley, per acre, 17 bush.; val., $204.

Oats, 324 acres; Oats, per acre, 32 bush.; val., $6,480.

Potatoes, 149 acres; Potatoes, per acre, 105 bush.; val., $7,822.50.

Turnips cultivated as a field crop, 5½ acres; Turnips, per acre, 300 bush.; val., $495.

Carrots, 4½ acres; Carrots, per acre, 324 bush.; val., $437.40.

Beets and other esculent vegetables, (Cabbages,) 1 acre; val., $250.

English Mowing, 2,669 acres; English Hay, 3,480 tons; val., $34,800.

Wet Meadow or Swale Hay, 160 tons; val., $960.

Apple Trees cultivated for their fruit, 11,993; val., $4,285.

Pear Trees cultivated for their fruit, 813; val., $182.

Bakeries, 1; Flour consumed, 125 bbls.; val. of bread m'd., $2,125; cap., $500; emp., 2.

Establishments for m. of boxes for packing cloth and paper, 1; val. of boxes m'd., $1,300; cap., $800; emp., 1.

Establishments for m. of monuments and grave stones, 1; val. of monuments and grave stones, $3,000; cap., $1,000; emp., 2.

Buckwheat, 65 acres; val., $828.75.

Swine raised and slaughtered, 374; producing 129,358 lbs. of pork; val., $9,701.85.

Val. of milk sold, $1,215.

LENOX.

Furnaces for m. of Pig Iron, 1; Pig Iron m'd., 1,500 tons; val. of pig iron, $55,500; cap., $70,000; emp., 15.

Manufactories of shovels, spades, forks and hoes, 1; val. of shovels, &c., $50; cap., $25; emp., 1.

Glass Manufactories, 1; Window Glass m'd., 3,800 boxes; val. of window glass, $13,125; cap., $15,000; emp., 50.

Saddle, Harness and Trunk Manufactories, 2; val. of saddles, &c., $1,500; cap., $800; emp., 2.

Establishments for m. of railroad cars, coaches, chaises, wag-

6

ons, sleighs, and other vehicles, 2; val. of railroad cars, &c., m'd., $1,406; cap., $1,000; emp., 3.

Tanneries, 1; Hides of all kinds tanned, 400; val. of leather tanned, $800; cap., $500; emp., 1.

Currying Establishments, 1; val. of leather curried, $800; cap., $500; emp., 1.

Boots of all kinds m'd., 250 pairs; Shoes of all kinds m'd., 325 pairs; val. of boots and shoes, $1,362; m. emp., 3.

Bricks m'd., 50,000; val. of bricks, $200; emp., 2.

Val. of mathematical instruments, $50; emp., 1.

Val. of marble quarried and prepared for market, $600; emp., 2.

Casks of Lime m'd., 26,000; val. of lime, $26,000; emp., 27.

Val. of mineral coal and iron ore mined, $10,000; emp., 24.

Lumber prepared for market, 693,000 ft.; val. of lumber, $8,116; emp., 15.

Firewood prepared for market, 9,866 cords; val. of firewood, $26,625; emp., 30.

Saxony Sheep, of different grades, 232; Merino Sheep, of different grades, 965; all other kinds of Sheep, 863; val. of all sheep, $4,120; Wool produced from Saxony sheep, 696 lbs.; Merino Wool produced, 3,377 lbs.; all other Wool produced, 3,452 lbs.

Horses, 289; val. of horses, $17,264; Oxen over three years old, 102; Steers under three years old, 135; val. of oxen and steers, $9,165; Milch Cows, 429; Heifers, 210; val. of cows and heifers, $15,390.

Butter, 42,900 lbs.; val. of butter, $8,580; Cheese, 7,000 lbs.; val. of cheese, $700; Honey, 3,660 lbs.; val. of honey, $610.

Indian Corn, 311 acres; Indian Corn, per acre, 36 bush.; val., $11,196.

Wheat, 40 acres; Wheat, per acre, 13 bush.; val., $520.

Rye, 108 acres; Rye, per acre, 10 bush.; val., $1,350.

Barley, 3 acres; Barley, per acre, 14 bush.; val., $42.

Oats, 333 acres; Oats, per acre, 30 bush.; val., $3,240.

Potatoes, 108 acres; Potatoes, per acre, 140 bush.; val., $9,828.

Turnips cultivated as a field crop, 2 acres; Turnips, per acre, 494 bush.; val., $246.

English Mowing, 2,739 acres; English Hay, 2,739 tons; val., $27,390.

Wet Meadow or Swale Hay, 101 tons; val., $505.

Apple Trees cultivated for their fruit, 9,201; val., $5,266.

Pear trees cultivated for their fruit, 820; val., $155.

Beeswax, 20 lbs.; val., $6.67.

Establishments for m. of casks, 2; Casks m'd., 24,000; val., $5,000; emp., 10.

Establishments for m. of boxes for packing glass, 1; capital and value not given.

MONTEREY.

Cotton Mills, 1; Spindles, 332; Cotton consumed, 25,000 lbs.; Yarn m'd., 18,000 lbs.; val. of yarn, $2,800; cap., $3,000; m. emp., 5; f. emp., 9.

Paper Manufactories, 1; Stock made use of, 100 tons of straw; Paper m'd., 34,453 reams; val. of paper, $6,090.60; cap., $3,000; emp., 6.

Comb Manufactories, 2; val. of combs m'd., $1,000; cap., $160; emp., 7.

Lumber prepared for market, 200,000 ft. and 400,000 shingles; val. of lumber, $2,400; emp., 4.

Firewood prepared for market, 500 cords; val. of firewood, $750; emp., 4.

Saxony Sheep, of different grades, –; Merino Sheep, of different grades, –; all other kinds of Sheep, 844; val. of all sheep, $1,688; Wool produced from Saxony sheep, –; Merino Wool produced, –; all other Wool produced, 2,052 lbs.

Horses, 122; val. of horses, $8,970; Oxen over three years old, 144; Steers under three years old, 39; val. of oxen and steers, 8,331; Milch Cows, 645; Heifers, 115; val. of cows and heifers, $17,326.

Butter, 25,155; val. of butter, $4,527.90; Cheese, 76,000 lbs.; val. of cheese, $6,840; Honey, 275 lbs.; val. of honey, $45.83.

Indian Corn, 126 acres; Indian Corn, per acre, 33 bush.; val. $4,158.

Wheat, ½ acre; Wheat, per acre, 24 bush.; val., $24.

Rye, 68 acres; Rye, per acre, 16 bush.; val., $1,088.

Barley, 6 acres; Barley, per acre, 24 bush.; val., $144.

Oats, 172 acres; Oats, per acre, 32 bush.; val., $3,027.20.

Potatoes, 103 acres; Potatoes, per acre, 102 bush.; val., $6,303.60.

Turnips, cultivated as a field crop, 4 acres; Turnips, per acre, 202 bush.; val., $202.

Carrots, 2 acres; Carrots, per acre, 258 bush.; val., $170.28.

English Mowing, 750 acres; English Hay, 1,116 tons; val., $11,160.

Wet Meadow or Swale Hay, 478 tons; val., $2,868.

Apple Trees cultivated for their fruit, 829; val., $835.

Pear Trees cultivated for their fruit, 40; val., $70.

Establishments for m. of casks, 2; cap., $200; Casks m'd., 2,000; val., $600; emp., 2.

Establishments for m. of mouse traps, 1; number m. 180,000; val., $1,600.

Maple Sugar m'd., 8,000 lbs.; val., $640.

Buckwheat raised, 700 bush.; val., $525.

MOUNT WASHINGTON.

Charcoal m'd., 16,000 bush.; val. of same, $12,800; emp., 25.

Lumber prepared for market, 225,000 ft.; val. of lumber, $2,475; emp., 10.

Saxony Sheep, of different grades, –; Merino Sheep, of different grades, 60; all other kinds of Sheep, 105; val. of all sheep, $450; Wool produced from Saxony sheep, – lbs.; Merino Wool produced, 120 lbs.; all other Wool produced, 300 lbs.

Horses, 49; val. of horses, $3,500; Oxen over three years old, 45; Steers under three years old, 25; val. of oxen and steers, $2,600; Milch Cows, 116; Heifers, 50; val. of cows and heifers, $3,650.

Butter, 11,600 lbs.; val. of butter, $1,856.

Indian Corn, 37 acres; Indian Corn, per acre, 21 bush.; val., $777.

Rye, 150 acres; Rye, per acre, 6½ bush.; val., $1,218.

Oats, 107 acres; Oats, per acre, 19 bush.; val., $1,550.

Potatoes, 47 acres; Potatoes, per acre, 76 bush.; val., $1,800.

Beets and other esculent vegetables, – acres; val., $–; all other Grain or Root Crops, 64 acres; val., $850.

English Mowing, 574 acres; English Hay, 497 tons; val., $4,970.

Wet Meadow or Swale Hay, 45 tons; val., $225.

Apple Trees cultivated for their fruit, 100; val., $200.

NEW ASHFORD.

Establishments for m. of railroad cars, coaches, chaises, wagons, sleighs, and other vehicles, 1; val. of railroad cars, &c. m'd., $300; cap., $500; emp., 1.

Charcoal m'd., 20,000 bush.; val. of same, $1,200; emp., 4.

Lumber prepared for market, 5,500 ft.; val. of lumber, $138; emp., 1.

Firewood prepared for market, 100 cords; val. of firewood, $200; emp., 3.

Saxony Sheep, of different grades, 26; Merino Sheep, of different grades, 1,240; all other kinds of Sheep, 4; val. of all sheep, $2,540; Wool produced from Saxony sheep, 62 lbs.;

Merino Wool produced, 3,720 lbs.; all other Wool produced, 16 lbs.

Horses, 48; val. of horses, $5,000; Oxen over three years old, 16; Steers under three years old, 28; val. of oxen and steers, $3,500; Milch Cows, 133; Heifers, 47; val. of cows and heifers, $6,120.

Butter, 5,645 lbs.; val. of butter, $1,242; Cheese, 24,580 lbs.; val. of cheese, $1,966.40; Honey, 250 lbs.; val. of honey, $25.

Indian Corn, 71½ acres; Indian Corn, per acre, 30 bush.; val., $2,845.

Wheat, 1½ acre; Wheat, per acre, 30 bush.; val., $90.

Rye, 1 acre; Rye, per acre, 11 bush.; val., $13.75.

Oats, 109 acres; Oats, per acre, 30 bush.; val., $1,962.

Potatoes, 33½ acres; Potatoes, per acre, 100 bush.; val., $2,010.

Onions raised during the year, 4 bush.; val., $3.

Turnips cultivated as a field crop, ½ acre; Turnips, per acre, 250 bush.; val., $10.

English Mowing, 759 acres; English Hay, 759 tons; val., $6,072.

Wet Meadow or Swale Hay, 57 tons; val., $285.

Apple Trees cultivated for their fruit, 1,023; val., $304.

Pear Trees cultivated for their fruit, 20; val., $25.

Maple Sugar produced, 2,840 lbs.; val., $198.80.

Buckwheat raised, 550 bush.; val., $350.

NEW MARLBOROUGH.

Furnaces for m. of hollow ware and castings other than pig iron, 1; Hollow Ware and other Castings m'd., 150 tons; val. of hollow ware and castings, $12,000; cap., $7,000; emp., 12.

Axe Manufactories, 1; Axes, Hatchets and other Edge Tools m'd., 1,000; val., $1,000; cap., $2,000; emp., 2.

Paper Manufactories, 3; val. of stock consumed, $41,000;

Paper m'd., 85,000 reams; val. of paper, $66,000; cap., $40,000; emp., 47.

Tin Ware Manufactories, 1; val. of tin ware, $1,200; cap., $1,000; emp., 1.

Flour Mills, 3; Flour m'd., 59,000 bush.; val. of mills, $8,000; emp., 4.

The Assessors state, in a note, that "the Mills are for custom work. They grind 35,000 bushels of corn, 1,000 bushels of wheat, 14,000 bushels of rye, and 9,000 bushels of buckwheat." They return the value of the mills, but not the value of the flour manufactured nor the amount of capital invested in the business, as required by the Act of the Legislature.

Tanneries, 1; Hides of all kinds tanned, 1,700; val. of leather tanned, $4,500; cap., $3,000; emp., 3.

Boots of all kinds m'd., 900 pairs; Shoes of all kinds m'd., 1,500 pairs; val. of boots and shoes, $2,800; m. emp., 6.

Bricks m'd., 150,000; val. of bricks, $1,050; emp., 2.

Casks of Lime m'd., 15,000; val. of lime, $15,000; emp., 10.

Charcoal m'd., 85,000 bush.; val. of same, $4,500; emp., 20.

Val. of whip lashes m'd., $12,000; m. emp., 4; f. emp., 35.

Lumber prepared for market, 1,000 bundles of shingles and 420,000 feet of boards; val. of lumber, $6,700; emp., 10.

Firewood prepared for market, 3,000 cords; val. of firewood, $4,500.

Merino Sheep, of different grades, 3,895; val. of all sheep, $4,844; Merino Wool produced, 11,400 lbs.

Horses, 312; val. of horses, $18,720; Oxen over three years old, 203; Steers under three years old, 210; val. of oxen and steers, $23,450; Milch Cows, 1,069; Heifers, 276; val. of cows and heifers, $30,500.

Butter, 65,000 lbs.; val. of butter, $11,700; Cheese, 50,000 lbs.; val. of cheese, $5,000; Honey, 890 lbs.; val. of honey, $120.

Indian Corn, 688 acres; Indian Corn, per acre, 30 bush.; val., $20,640.

Wheat, 21 acres; Wheat, per acre, 14 bush.; val., $588.

Rye, 452 acres; Rye, per acre, 12 bush.; val., $1.20 per bush.

Oats, 604 acres; Oats, per acre, 30 bush.; val., 50 cts. per bush.

Potatoes, 222 acres; Potatoes, per acre, 100 bush.; val., 40 cts. per bush.

Turnips, cultivated as a field crop, 19 acres; Turnips, per acre, 200 bush.; val., 10 cts. per bush.

Carrots, 6 acres; Carrots per acre, 500 bush.; val., 25 cts. per bush.

English Mowing, 3,382 acres; English Hay, 3,382 tons; val., $8 per ton.

Buckwheat, 273 acres; per acre, 15 bush.; val., 60 cts. per bush.

Apple Trees cultivated for their fruit, 1,500; val., $1,385.

Beeswax, 53 lbs.; val., 30 cts. per lb.

Establishments for m. of casks, 6; cap., $3,000; Casks m'd., 13,000; val., $4,000; emp., 12.

OTIS.

Furnaces for m. of hollow ware and castings other than pig iron, reported "idle," 1.

Paper Manufactories, 1; reported "idle."

Saddle, Harness and Trunk Manufactories, 1; val. of saddles, &c., $500; cap., $500; emp., 1.

Establishments for m. of railroad cars, coaches, chaises, wagons, sleighs, and other vehicles, 1; val. of railroad cars, &c., m'd., $500; cap., $300; emp., 1.

Chair and Cabinet Manufactories, 1; val of chairs and cabinet ware, $2,000; cap., $1,000; emp., 3.

Tanneries, 2; Hides of all kinds tanned, 4,000; val. of leather tanned, $10,000; cap., $6,000; emp., 4.

Charcoal m'd., 55,000 bush.; val. of same, $2,750.

Val. of wooden ware not otherwise enumerated, including farming utensils m'd., $2,650 ; emp., 6.

Lumber prepared for market, 1,175,200 ft. ; val. of lumber, $8,226 ; emp., 12.

Firewood prepared for market, 469 cords ; val. of firewood, $703 ; emp., 2.

Saxony Sheep, of different grades, – ; Merino Sheep, of different grades, – ; all other kinds of Sheep, 697 ; val. of all sheep, $1,000 ; Wool produced from Saxony sheep, – lbs. ; Merino Wool produced, – lbs. ; all other Wool produced, 2,074 lbs.

Horses, 179 ; val. of horses, $10,740 ; Oxen over three years old, 178 ; Steers under three years old, 156 ; val. of oxen and Steers, $20,920 ; Milch Cows, 577 ; Heifers 215 ; val. of cows and heifers, $17,005.

Butter, 27,760 lbs. ; val. of butter, $4,996 ; Cheese, 42,825 lbs. ; val. of cheese, $3,854 ; Honey, 453 lbs. ; val. honey, $47.

Indian Corn, 112 acres ; Indian Corn, per acre, 30 bush. ; val., $3,360.

Rye, 1 acre ; Rye, per acre, 15 bush. ; val., $15.

Barley, 5 acres ; Barley, per acre, 23 bush. ; val., $71.

Oats, 83 acres ; Oats, per acre, 25 bush. ; val., $1,245.

Potatoes, 111 acres ; Potatoes, per acre, 89 bush. ; val., $4,945.

Onions, 6 acres ; Onions, per acre, 155 bush. ; val., $140.

English Mowing, 2,586 acres ; English Hay, 2,102 tons ; val., $16,816.

Wet Meadow or Swale Hay, 521 tons ; val., $2,605.

Apple Trees cultivated for their fruit, 3,343 ; val., $714.

Gross value of all other articles manufactured in the town, including the production of maple sugar, $1,290.

7

PERU.

Lumber prepared for market, 136,000 ft.; val. of lumber, $9,520; emp., 10.

Firewood prepared for market, 560 cords; val. of firewood, $840; emp., 17.

Saxony Sheep, of different grades, –; Merino Sheep, of different grades, 2,367; all other kinds of Sheep, 43; val. of all sheep, $2,958; Wool produced from Saxony sheep, – lbs.; Merino Wool produced, 8,284 lbs.; all other Wool produced, 125 lbs.

Horses, 105; val. of horses, $6,725; Oxen over three years old, 92; Steers under three years old, 59; val. of oxen and steers, $4,874; Milch Cows, 417; Heifers, 280; val. of cows and heifers, $9,629.

Butter, 24,675 lbs.; val. of butter, $4,935; Cheese, 27,226 lbs.; val. of cheese, $1,633.56; Honey, 75 lbs.; val. of honey, $12.

Indian Corn, 49 acres; whole number, 1,340 bush.; val., $1,340.

Rye, 1 acre; Rye, per acre, 4 bush.; val., $6.25.

Buckwheat, 53 acres; total, 846 bush.; val., $423.

Barley, 11 acres; Barley, per acre, 25 bush.; val., $229.

Oats, 52 acres; Oats, per acre, 25 bush.; val., $654.

Potatoes, 83 acres; Potatoes, per acre, 125 bush.; val., $5,206.

English Mowing, 1,976 acres; English Hay, 1,363 tons; val., $13,630.

Wet Meadow or Swale Hay, 359 tons; val., $1,795.

Apple Trees cultivated for their fruit, 2,695; val., $250.99.

Number of Swine raised, 113; val. $604.

PITTSFIELD.

Cotton Mills, 4; Spindles, 5,892; Cotton consumed, 691,000 lbs.; Cloth, m'd., 1,300,000 yds.; (manufacture Sheetings one yd. wide—four yds. to the pound—No. 18 yarn); val. of cloth, $78,000; Yarn m'd., 192,400 lbs.; val. of yarn, $42,640; Pelisse Wadding m'd., 5,000 bales; val. of wadding, $50,000; cap., $93,000; m. emp., 50; f. emp., 111.

Woollen Mills, 8; Sets of Machinery, 40; Wool consumed, 1,355,500 lbs.; Broadcloth m'd., 267,400 yds.; val. of broadcloth, $373,600; Satinet m'd., 860,000 yds.; val. of satinet, $350,000; cap., $475,000; m. emp., 340; f. emp., 178.

Furnaces for m. of hollow ware and castings other than pig iron, 2; Hollow Ware and other Castings m'd., 265 tons; val. of hollow ware and castings, $18,000; cap., $7,500; emp., 15.

Establishments for m. of cotton, woollen and other machinery, 2; val. of machinery m'd., $10,000; cap., $5,000; emp., 12.

Establishments for m. of steam-engines and boilers, 1; val. of steam-engines and boilers, $65,000; cap., $20,000; emp., 50.

Paper Manufactories, 1; Stock made use of, 150 tons; Paper m'd., 100 tons; val. of paper, $40,000; cap., $25,000; emp., 23.

Piano-Forte Manufactories, -; all other musical instrument manufactories, 1; val. of musical instruments m'd., $8,000; cap., $4,000; emp., 8.

Daguerreotype Artists, 2; Daguerreotypes taken, 2,700; cap., $1,000; emp., 2.

Establishments for m. of chronometers, watches, gold and silver ware and jewelry, 1; val. of m's., $16,000; cap., $2,500; emp., 8.

Saddle, Harness and Trunk Manufactories, 4; val. of saddles, &c., $15,000; cap., $4,300; emp., 17.

Hat and Cap Manufactories, 2; Hats and Caps m'd., $6,800; cap., $5,500; emp., 10.

Establishments for m. of railroad cars, coaches, chaises, wagons, sleighs, and other vehicles, 6; val. of railroad cars, &c., m'd., $44,000; cap., $30,000; emp., 60.

Establishments for m. of soap and tallow candles, 1; Soap m'd., 1,000 lbs.; val. of soap, $60; Tallow Candles m'd., 1,000 lbs.; val. of tallow candles, $140; cap., $100; emp., 1.

Chair and Cabinet Manufactories, 1; val. of chairs and cabinet ware, $5,000; cap., $3,000; emp., 6.

Tin Ware Manufactories, 3; val. of tin ware, $20,000; cap., $7,000; emp., 15.

Tanneries, 1; Hides of all kinds tanned, 3,000; val. of leather tanned, $18,000; cap., $5,000; emp., 5.

Currying Establishments, 1; val. of leather curried, $22,000; cap., $5,000; emp., 4.

Boots of all kinds m'd., 2,025 pairs; Shoes of all kinds m'd., 2,100 pairs; val. of boots and shoes, $12,375; m. emp., 21; f. emp., 5.

Bricks m'd., 610,000; val. of bricks, $3,050; emp., 10.

Val. of snuff, tobacco and cigars, $3,000; m. emp., 3.

Val. of building stone quarried and prepared for building, $1,500; emp., 2.

Val. of marble quarried and prepared for market, $15,000; emp., 18.

Casks of Lime m'd., 4,640; val. of lime, $4,640; emp., 7.

Val. of mineral coal and iron ore mined, $5,000; emp., 10.

Val. of mechanics' tools m'd., $1,000; emp., 2.

Gross val. of wooden ware m'd., $1,000; emp. 2.

Corn and other Brooms m'd, 3,600; val. of brooms, $600; emp., 2.

Lumber prepared for market, 300,000 ft.; val. of lumber, $3,000; emp., 3.

Firewood prepared for market, 2,100 cords; val. of firewood, $6,315; emp., 10.

Saxony Sheep, of different grades, –; Merino Sheep, of different grades, 3,500; all other kinds of Sheep, 190; val. of all sheep, $9,225; Wool produced from Saxony sheep, – lbs.;

Merino Wool produced, 10,500 lbs.; all other Wool produced, 605 lbs.

Horses, 550; val. of horses, $56,650; Oxen over three years old, 120; Steers under three years old, 150; val. of oxen and steers, $11,910; Milch Cows, 972; Heifers, 300; val. of cows and heifers, $35,304.

Butter, 95,000 lbs.; val. of butter, $19,000; Cheese, 28,000 lbs.; val. of cheese, $2,520; Honey, 1,315 lbs.; val. of honey, $220.

Indian Corn, 580 acres; Indian Corn, per acre, 37⅓ bush.; val., $21,653.

Wheat, 72 acres; Wheat, per acre, 17½ bush.; val., $2,520.

Rye, 495 acres; Rye, per acre, 16½ bush.; val., $10,210.

Barley, 20½ acres; Barley, per acre, 21½ bush.; val., $364.

Oats, 652 acres; Oats, per acre, 40 bush.; val., $13,040.

Potatoes, 287 acres; Potatoes, per acre, 113 bush.; val., $16,215.

Onions, 4 acres; Onions, per acre, 200 bush.; val., $400.

Turnips cultivated as a field crop, 10 acres; Turnips, per acre, 200 bush.; val., $500.

Carrots, 2½ acres; Carrots, per acre, 400 bush.; val., $250.

Beets and other esculent vegetables, 2 acres; val., $200; all other Grain or Root Crops, 4 acres; val., $400.

English Mowing, 4,062 acres; English Hay, 5,004 tons; val., $50,040.

Wet Meadow or Swale Hay, 190 tons; val., $1,140.

Apple Trees cultivated for their fruit, 5,140; val., $1,500.

Pear Trees cultivated for their fruit, 200; val., $160.

Establishments for m. of sashes and door blinds, 3; cap., $6,500; val. m'd., $14,000; emp., 12.

Establishments for m. of gas, 1; cap., $35,000; val. m'd., $14,600; emp., 3.

Bakeries, 1; cap., $5,000; Flour consumed, 1,500 bbls.; val. of bread m'd., $15,000; emp., 10.

Val. of soda m'd., $5,000; cap., $1,500; emp., 3.

RICHMOND.

Furnaces for m. of pig iron, 1; Pig Iron m'd., 1,600 tons; val. of pig iron, $48,000; cap., $5,400; emp., 20.

Saddle, Harness and Trunk Manufactories, 1; val. of saddles, &c., $1,000; cap., $400; emp., 2.

Tanneries, 1; Hides of all kinds tanned, 1,000; val. of leather tanned, $1,500; cap., $800; emp., 1.

Boots of all kinds m'd., 100 pairs; Shoes of all kinds m'd., 100 pairs; val. of boots and shoes, $450; m. emp., 1.

Casks of Lime m'd., 13,730; emp., 14; val. of lime, $14,030.

Val. of mineral coal and iron ore mined, $18,975; emp., 50.

Firewood prepared for market, 825 cords; val. of firewood, $2,475; emp., 5.

Saxony Sheep, of different grades, 268; Merino Sheep, of different grades, 2,688; val. of all sheep, $3,887; Wool produced from Saxony sheep, 755 lbs.; Merino Wool produced, 8,064 lbs.

Horses, 200; val. of horses, $15,252; Oxen over three years old, 62; Steers under three years old, 54; val. of oxen and steers, $5,011; Milch Cows, 285; Heifers, 120; val. of cows and heifers, $8,919.

Butter, 30,000 lbs.; val. of butter, $5,500; Cheese, 4,100 lbs.; val. of cheese, $3,690; Honey, 1,750 lbs.; val. of honey, $218.

Indian Corn, 235 acres; Indian Corn, per acre, 25 bush.; val., $5,475.

Wheat, 25 acres; Wheat, per acre, 15 bush.; val., $562.

Rye, 17 acres; Rye, per acre, 20 bush.; val., $340.

Buckwheat, 247 acres; Buckwheat, per acre, 17 bush.; val., $4,148.

Barley, 26 acres; Barley, per acre, 20 bush.; val., $520.

Oats, 396 acres; Oats, per acre, 30 bush.; val., $47,520.

Potatoes, 65 acres; Potatoes, per acre, 80 bush.; val., $1,560.

Turnips, cultivated as a field crop, 5 acres; Turnips, per acre, 200 bush.; val., $200.

English Mowing, 1,760 acres; English Hay, 1,760 tons; val., $15,840.

Wet Meadow or Swale Hay, 131 tons; val., $655.

Apple Trees cultivated for their fruit, 3,400; val., $1,428.

Pear Trees cultivated for their fruit, 25; val., $75.

Beeswax, 25 lbs.; val., $7.50.

The number of Swine raised during the year, 175; val., $1,110.

SANDISFIELD.

Plough Manufactories, –; Hay Rakes m'd., 40,000; val., $4,000; cap., $1,000; emp., 12.

Paper Manufactories, 1; Stock made use of, 220 tons; Paper m'd., 160 tons; val. of paper, $23,000; cap., $14,000; emp., 12.

Saddle, Harness and Trunk Manufactories, 1; val. of saddles, &c., $180; cap., $50; emp., 1.

Establishments for m. of railroad cars, coaches, chaises, wagons, sleighs, and other vehicles, 1; val. of railroad cars, &c., m'd., $1,800; cap., $1,200; emp., 5.

Chair and Cabinet Manufactories, 1; val. of chairs and cabinet ware, $1,200; cap., $500; emp., 2.

Tanneries, 2; Hides of all kinds tanned, 5,000; val. of leather tanned, $30,000; cap., $5,000; emp., 12.

Currying Establishments, 1; val. of leather curried, $1,000; cap., $500; emp., 1.

Boots of all kinds m'd., 5,700 pairs; Shoes of all kinds m'd., 1,100 pairs; val. of boots and shoes, $13,650; m. emp., 16; f. emp., 5.

Charcoal m'd., 188,000 bush.; val. of same, $9,400; emp., 50.

Val. of wooden ware not otherwise enumerated, including farming utensils m'd., $600 ; emp., 2.

Lumber prepared for market, 940,000 ft. ; val. of lumber, $6,200 ; emp., 18.

Firewood prepared for market, 300 cords ; val. of firewood, $600 ; emp., 4.

Saxony Sheep, of different grades, – ; Merino Sheep, of different grades, – ; all other kinds of Sheep, 466 ; val. of all sheep, $700 ; Wool produced from Saxony sheep, – lbs. ; Merino Wool produced, – lbs. ; all other Wool produced, 1,617 lbs.

Horses, 285 ; val. of horses, $20,057 ; Oxen over three years old, 300 ; Steers under three years old, 149 ; val. of oxen and steers, $18,487 ; Milch Cows, 1,273 ; Heifers, 373 ; val. of cows and heifers, $36,700.

Butter, 24,790 lbs. ; val. of butter, $4,131.66 ; Cheese, 175,700 lbs. ; val. of cheese, $17,570 ; Honey, 150 lbs. ; val. of honey, $25.

Indian Corn, 171 acres ; Indian Corn, per acre, 20 bush. ; val. $3,420.

Oats, 196 acres ; Oats, per acre, 25 bush. ; val., $2,450.

Potatoes, 150 acres ; Potatoes, per acre, 100 bush. ; val., $5,625.

Onions, ¼ acre ; Onions, per acre, 400 bush. ; val., $50.

Turnips, cultivated as a field crop, 9 acres ; Turnips, per acre, 250 bush. ; val., $375.

Carrots, 4 acres ; Carrots, per acre, 400 bush. ; val., $320.

English Mowing, 3,000 acres ; English Hay, 3,000 tons ; val., $27,000.

Wet Meadow or Swale Hay, 300 tons ; val., $1,300.

Establishments for m. of casks, 1 ; cap., $25 ; Casks m'd., 500 ; val., $150 ; emp., 1.

Establishments for m. of cheese boxes, 3 ; cap., $300 ; val. of boxes m'd., $1,100 ; emp., 6.

Maple Sugar m'd., 76,000 lbs. ; val., $6,080.

Hemlock Bark cut, 600 cords ; val., $1,800.

Swine, 304 ; val., $1,520.

SAVOY.

Sugar Refineries, –; Maple Sugar refined, 1,700 lbs.; val. of sugar, $180; emp., 5.

Tanneries, 1; Hides of all kinds tanned, 2,000; val. of leather tanned, $8,000; cap., $7,000; emp., 5.

Val. of palm leaf hats, $500; f. emp., 10.

Lumber prepared for market, 1,130,000 ft.; val. of lumber, $8,300; emp., 30.

Firewood prepared for market, 2,000 cords; val. of firewood, $2,500; emp., 10.

Saxony Sheep, of different grades, –; Merino Sheep, of different grades, –; all other kinds of Sheep, 371; val. of all sheep, $928; Wool produced from Saxony sheep, – lbs.; Merino Wool produced, – lbs.; all other Wool produced, 1,286 lbs.

Horses, 198; val. of horses, $13,487; Oxen over three years old, 78; Steers under three years old, 87; val. of oxen and steers, $5,672; Milch Cows, 568; Heifers, 155; val. of cows and heifers, $16,270.

Butter, 22,776 lbs.; val. of butter, $5,000; Cheese, 69,490 lbs.; val. of cheese, $5,559.20; Honey, 600 lbs.; val. of honey, $60.

Indian Corn, 67 acres; Indian Corn, per acre, 26½ bush.; val., $1,975.

Wheat, ½ acre; Wheat, per acre, 30 bush.; val., $37.50.

Rye, 3 acres; Rye, per acre, 10 bush.; val., $37.50.

Barley, 17 acres; Barley, per acre, 21 bush.; val., $359.

Oats, 100 acres; Oats, per acre, 35½ bush.; val., $1,773.50

Potatoes, 147 acres; Potatoes, per acre, 117 bush.; val., $8,615.

Turnips cultivated as a field crop, 2 acres; Turnips, per acre, 162 bush.; val., $81.

Carrots, ½ acre; Carrots, per acre, 1,000 bush.; val. $250.

Beets and other esculent vegetables, 2 acres; val., $200.

English Mowing, 2,642 acres; English Hay, 2,120 tons; val., $21,200.

Wet Meadow or Swale Hay, 180 tons; val., $1,080.

Apple Trees cultivated for their fruit, 1,640; val., $423.

Beeswax, 16 lbs.; val., $6.

Establishments for m. of casks, 1; cap., $100; Casks m'd., 3,000; val., $900.

Establishments for m. of cheese boxes, 1; cap., 100; val. of boxes m'd., $300; emp., 2.

Shingles m'd., 400,000; val., $800.

Number of Swine raised, 160; val., $1,000.

SHEFFIELD.

Daguerreotype Artists, 1; Daguerreotypes taken, 1,000; cap., $700; emp., 2.

Tanneries, 1; Hides of all kinds tanned, 1,400; val. of leather tanned, $4,800; cap., $2,000; emp., 4.

Bricks m'd., 600,000; val. of bricks, $3,000; emp., 14.

Lumber prepared for market, 250,000 ft.; val. of lumber, $4,100; emp., 4.

Firewood prepared for market, 1,575 cords; val. of firewood, $4,287; emp., 4.

Saxony Sheep, of different grades, 750; Merino Sheep, of different grades, 210; all other kinds of Sheep, 1,618; val. of all sheep, $7,509; Wool produced from Saxony sheep, 2,050 lbs.; Merino Wool produced, 776 lbs.; all other Wool produced, 4,313 lbs.

Horses, 522; val. of horses, $43,138; Oxen over three years old, 313; Steers under three years old, 264; val. of oxen and steers, $24,182; Milch Cows, 1,465; Heifers, 483; val. of cows and heifers, $45,977.

Butter, 165,225 lbs.; val. of butter, $33,045; Cheese, 179,890 lbs.; val. of cheese, $17,989; Honey, 2,700 lbs.; val. of honey, $337.

Indian Corn, 1,360 acres; Indian Corn, per acre, 29 bush.; val., $39,440.

Wheat, 50 acres; Wheat, per acre, 13 bush.; val., $1,300.

Rye, 1,270 acres; Rye, per acre, 15 bush.; val., $22,225.

Oats, 493 acres; Oats, per acre, 27 bush.; val., $8,856.

Potatoes, 286 acres; Potatoes, per acre, 86 bush.; val., $18,447.

Beets and other esculent vegetables, – acres; all other Grain or Root Crops, 319 acres; val., $3,190.

English Mowing, 4,047 acres; English Hay, 6,013 tons; val., $60,130.

Wet Meadow or Swale Hay, 207 tons; val., $1,035.

Apple Trees cultivated for their fruit, 11,718; val., $9,111.

Pear Trees cultivated for their fruit, 186; val., $285.

Hops, 3 acres; Hops, per acre, 600 lbs.; val., $324.

Number of Swine, 708; val., $5,518.

STOCKBRIDGE.

Woollen Mills, –; Wool and Cotton consumed, 275,000 lbs.; Satinet m'd., 520,000 yds.; val. of satinet, $208,000; cap., $125,000; m. emp., 70; f. emp., 35.

Furnaces for m. of pig iron, 1; Pig Iron m'd., 3,000 tons; val. of pig iron, $90,000; cap., $125,000; emp., 50.

Furnaces for m. of hollow ware and castings other than pig iron, 1; Hollow Ware and other Castings m'd., 15 tons; val. of hollow ware and castings, $1,000; cap., $2,500; emp., 2.

Tack and Brad Manufactories, 1; Tacks and Brads m'd., 2,000 lbs.; val. of tacks and brads, $350; cap., $450; emp., 1.

Paper Manufactories, 1; Stock made use of, 270 tons; Paper m'd., 180 tons; val. of paper, $45,000; cap., $30,000; emp., 20.

Saddle, Harness and Trunk Manufactories, 1; val. of saddles, &c., $1,500; cap., $400; emp., 1.

Establishments for m. of wagons, sleighs, and other vehicles, 4; val. of wagons, &c., m'd., $1,000; cap., $500; emp., 5.

Chair and Cabinet Manufactories, 4; val. of chairs and cabinet ware, $12,200; cap., $7,100; emp., 20.

Tin Ware Manufactories, 1; val. of tin ware, $6,000; cap., $2,800; emp., 4.

Boots of all kinds m'd., 800 pairs; Shoes of all kinds m'd., 1,350 pairs; val. of boots and shoes, $4,500; m. emp., 7; f. emp., 2.

Casks of Lime m'd., 400; emp., 1; val. of lime, $350.

Charcoal m'd., 90,000 bush.; val. of same, $6,300; emp., 12.

Lumber prepared for market, 80,000 ft.; val. of lumber, $1,000.

Firewood prepared for market, 2,217 cords; val. of firewood, $4,987; emp., 12.

Saxony Sheep, of different grades, –; Merino Sheep, of different grades, –; all other kinds of Sheep, 1,720; val. of all sheep, $4,529; Wool produced from Saxony sheep, – lbs.; Merino Wool produced, – lbs.; all other Wool produced, 5,000 lbs.

Horses, 261; val. of horses, $20,235; Oxen over three years old, 143; Steers under three years old, 204; val. of oxen and steers, $11,344; Milch Cows, 526; Heifers, 220; val. of cows and heifers, $19,200.

Butter, 83,475 lbs.; val. of butter, $16,695; Cheese, 12,035 lbs.; val. of cheese, $1,203.50; Honey, 3,625 lbs.; val. of honey, $453⅛.

Indian Corn, 365 acres; Indian Corn, per acre, 43⅕ bush.; val., $15,775.

Wheat, 25 acres; Wheat, per acre, 18½ bush.; val., $865.

Rye, 221½ acres; Rye, per acre, 11 bush.; val., $3,045.62½.

Barley, 20 acres; Barley, per acre, 20 bush.; val., $376.

Oats, 418½ acres; Oats, per acre, 34¼ bush.; val., $8,598.

Potatoes, 124 acres; Potatoes, per acre, 122 bush.; val., $7,545.50.

Onions, 1 acre; Onions, per acre, 550 bush.; val., $308.

Turnips, cultivated as a field crop, 6 acres; Turnips, per acre, 300 bush.; val., $360.

Carrots, 8 acres; Carrots, per acre, 528¼ bush.; val., $1,056.50.

English Mowing, 2,750 acres; English Hay, 3,370 tons; val., $33,700.

Wet Meadow or Swale Hay, 25 tons; val., $150.

Apple Trees cultivated for their fruit, 10,429; val., $6,446.

Pear Trees cultivated for their fruit, 1,222; val., $2,690.

Beeswax, 155 lbs.; val., $38.75.

Val. of birdseye maple and black walnut veneering m'd., $1,000; cap., 500; emp., 1.

Buckwheat, 45 acres; total number of bushels, 2,625; val., $2,625.

TYRINGHAM.

Val. of wooden ware not otherwise enumerated, including farming utensils, rakes, &c. m'd., $4,300; emp., 15.

Corn and other Brooms m'd., 1,081; val. of brooms, $200; emp., 2.

Lumber prepared for market, 250,000 ft. hemlock, 75,000 ft. chestnut and pine; val. of lumber, $2,875; emp., 25 to 30 men.

Firewood prepared for market, 3,130 cords; val. of firewood, $7,042.50.

Saxony Sheep, of different grades, –; Merino Sheep, of different grades, 350; all other kinds of Sheep, 75; val. of all sheep, $1,000; Wool produced from Saxony sheep, – lbs.; Merino Wool produced, 1,050 lbs.; all other Wool produced, 250 lbs.

Horses, 75; val. of horses, $90 each; Oxen over three years old, 118; val., $60 each; Steers three years old, 64; val., $50 each; two years old, 50; val., $25 each; yearlings, 90; val., $10 each; Milch Cows, 250; val., $25 each; Heifers, 69; val., $20 each.

Butter, 10,500 lbs.; val. of butter, 20 cts. per lb.; Cheese, 53,000 lbs.; val. of cheese, 8 cts. per lb.

Indian Corn, 90 acres; Indian Corn, per acre, 35 bush.; val., $1.25 per bush.

Wheat, 5 acres; Wheat, per acre, 15 bush.; val., $2.50 per bush.

Rye, 25 acres; Rye, per acre, 15 bush.; val., $1.25 per bush.

Oats, 90 acres; Oats, per acre, 30 bush.; val., 60 cts. per bush.

Potatoes, 80 acres; Potatoes, per acre, 125 bush.; val., 60 cts. per bush.

Beets and other esculent vegetables, 400 bush.; all other Grain or Root Crops, 33 acres of buckwheat; val., 75 cts. per bush.

English Mowing, 1,200 acres; English Hay, 1,500 tons; val., $12 per ton.

Apple Trees cultivated for their fruit, 200.

Pear Trees cultivated for their fruit, 25.

Saw Mills, 7; val., $3,500; running part of the time; emp. 10 or 14 men.

Letter and Note Paper Manufactories, 2. The "Turkey Mill" works 400,000 lbs. of rags, and 6,000 lbs. of chloride of lime, and consumes 2,000 cords of wood; paper m'd., 25,000 reams; val., $60,000; m. emp., 21; f. emp., 50; mill inventory, $1,200. The "Bay State" Mill works 100 tons of rags, worth $9,000, which produces 65 tons of paper, valued at $14,300; m. emp., 4; f. emp., 1; mill inventory, $3,000.

Maple Sugar produced, 10,000 lbs.; val., $1,000; emp., 30 or 40 hands from 4 to 6 weeks during the year.

Rake Manufactories, 4; val. of rakes m'd., $400.

Val. of pails and cheese tubs m'd., $300.

WASHINGTON.

Bricks m'd., 200,000; val. of bricks, $1,200; emp., 4.

Charcoal m'd., 140,000 bush.; val., of same, $9,800; emp., 36.

Lumber prepared for market, 1,528,000 ft.; val. of lumber, $152,800; emp., 30.

Firewood prepared for market, 9,753 cords; val. of firewood, $14,629.50; emp., 39.

Merino Sheep, of different grades, 1,256; val. of all Sheep, $3,581; Merino Wool produced, 3,768 lbs.

Horses, 129; val. of horses, $9,137; Oxen over three years old, 126; Steers under three years old, 195; val. of oxen and steers, $10,908; Milch Cows, 318; Heifers, 170; val. of cows and heifers, $11,169.

Butter, 23,118 lbs.; val. of butter, $4,623.60; Cheese, 14,238 lbs.; val. of cheese, $1,139.04; Honey, 340 lbs.; val. of honey, $56.66.

Indian Corn, 82 acres; Indian Corn, per acre, 28 bush.; val., $2,240.

Wheat, 2 acres; Wheat, per acre, 12½ bush.; val., $50.

Rye, 10 acres; Rye, per acre, 13$\frac{4}{10}$ bush.; val., $134.

Barley, 29 acres; Barley, per acre, 29 bush.; val., $669.60.

Oats, 100 acres; Oats, per acre, 33½ bush.; val., $1,678.50.

Potatoes, 126 acres; Potatoes, per acre, 114 bush.; val., $5,741.60.

English Mowing, 2,659 acres; English Hay, 2,224 tons; val., $17,794.

Apple Trees cultivated for their fruit, 362; val., $261.08.

Beeswax, 60 lbs.; val., $18.

Number of cords of hemlock bark, 425; val., $1,275.

Gross val. of wool raised, $1,431.84.

Number of swine raised, 110; val., 550.

WEST STOCKBRIDGE.

Furnaces for m. of pig iron, 1; Pig Iron m'd., 10,023 tons; val. of pig iron, $256,575; cap., $100,000; emp., 40.

Paper Manufactories, 1; Stock made use of, 3,955 tons; Paper m'd., 25,000 reams; val. of paper, $7,500; cap., $5,000; emp., 8.

Saddle, Harness and Trunk Manufactories, 2; val. of saddles, &c., $2,820; cap., $600; emp., 4.

Establishments for m. of railroad cars, coaches, chaises, wagons, sleighs, and other vehicles, 2; val. of railroad cars, &c., m'd., $10,000; cap., $5,000; emp., 12.

Tin Ware Manufactories, 1; val. of tin ware, $1,500; cap., $200; emp., 3.

Flour Mills, 3; Flour consumed, 11,650 bbls.; val. of flour, $109,580; cap., $52,000; emp., 12.

Boots of all kinds m'd., 100 pairs; Shoes of all kinds m'd., 100 pairs; val. of boots and shoes, $600; m. emp., 1.

Bricks m'd., 250,000; val. of bricks, $1,000; emp., 3.

Val. of marble quarried and prepared for market, $29,000; emp., 32.

Val. of mineral coal and iron ore mined, $64,000; emp., 100.

Lumber prepared for market, 250,000 ft.; val. of lumber, $2,950; emp., 6.

Firewood prepared for market, 4,755 cords; val. of firewood, $14,265; emp., 8.

Saxony Sheep, of different grades, –; Merino Sheep, of different grades, 1,205; all other kinds of Sheep, 168; val. of all sheep, $3,683; Wool produced from Saxony sheep, – lbs.; Merino Wool produced, 5,237 lbs.; all other Wool produced, 599 lbs.

Horses, 248; val. of horses, $24,795; Oxen over three years old, 60; Steers under three years old, 45; val. of oxen and steers, $4,500; Milch Cows, 222; Heifers, 75; val. of cows and heifers, $8,017.

Butter, 22,405 lbs.; val. of butter, $4,481; Cheese, 3,250 lbs.; val. of cheese, $325.

Indian Corn, 236 acres; Indian Corn, per acre, 35 bush.; val., $8,260.

Wheat, 14 acres; Wheat, per acre, 15 bush.; val., $420.

Rye, 168 acres; Rye, per acre, 15 bush.; val., $3,175.

Barley, 12 acres; Barley, per acre, 25 bush.; val., $300.

Oats, 324 acres; Oats, per acre, 30 bush.; val. $5,832.

Potatoes, 84 acres; Potatoes, per acre, 100 bush.; val., $60.

Turnips, cultivated as a field crop, 11 acres; Turnips, per acre, 200 bush; val., $550.

Carrots, 2 acres; Carrots, per acre, 300 bush.; val., $150.

English Mowing, 1,515 acres; English Hay, 1,515 tons; val., $15,150.

Wet Meadow or Swale Hay, 170 tons; val., $1,190.

Apple Trees, cultivated for their fruit, 5,000; val., $2,400.

Pear Trees, cultivated for their fruit, 54; val., $120.

Feed m'd. at flouring mills, 900 tons; val., $36,000; Grain used, 40,500 bush.; val., $34,000.

Cotton Spindles m'd., 3,000; val., $900; val. of stock used, $395; cap., $3,000; emp., 2.

WILLIAMSTOWN.

Cotton Mills, 1; Spindles, 2,114; Cotton consumed, 124,320 lbs.; Cloth m'd., 685,420 yds.; (Printing Cloth, 28 inch. wide, 52x56;) val. of cloth, $25,703; Batting m'd., 50,000 lbs.; val. of batting, $4,000; cap., $5,000; m. emp., 23; f. emp., 35.

Saddle, Harness and Trunk Manufactories, 2; val. of saddles, &c., $3,000; cap., $500; emp., 3.

Establishments for m. of railroad cars, coaches, chaises, wagons, sleighs, and other vehicles, 1; val. of railroad cars, &c., m'd., $4,000; cap., $2,000; emp., 12.

Chair and Cabinet Manufactories, 3; val. of chairs and cabinet ware, $1,700; cap., $1,000; emp., 3.

Tin Ware Manufactories, 1; val. of tin ware, $2,000; cap., $1,200; emp., 2.

Boots of all kinds m'd., 790 pairs; Shoes of all kinds m'd., 1,050 pairs; val. of boots and shoes, $4,980; m. emp., 9.

Bricks m'd., 250,000; val. of bricks, $1,200; emp., 4.

Charcoal m'd., 130,000 bush.; val. of same, $10,400; emp., 18.

Lumber prepared for market, 108,500 ft.; val. of lumber, $3,910; emp., 11.

Firewood prepared for market, 2,000 cords; val. of firewood, $7,000; emp., 50.

Saxony Sheep, of different grades, 520; Merino Sheep, of different grades, 4,000; all other kinds of Sheep, 310; val. of all sheep, $9,491; Wool produced from Saxony sheep, 1,483 lbs.; Merino Wool produced, 12,341 lbs.; all other Wool produced, 904 lbs.

Horses, 371; val. of horses, $31,415; Oxen over three years old, 102; Steers under three years old, 76; val. of oxen and steers, $7,121; Milch Cows, 1,052; Heifers, 166; val. of cows and heifers, $30,032.

Butter, 46,655 lbs.; val. of butter, $8,187; Cheese, 172,650 lbs.; val. of cheese, $13,379; Honey, 200 lbs.; val. of honey, $24.

Indian Corn, 648 acres; Indian Corn, per acre, $23\frac{151}{216}$ bush.; val., $15,357.

Wheat, 45 acre; Wheat, per acre, $36\frac{23}{45}$ bush.; val., $1,643.

Rye, 86 acres; Rye, per acre, $16\frac{12}{43}$ bush.; val., $1,400.

Barley, 53 acres; Barley, per acre, $23\frac{36}{53}$ bush.; val., $1,255.

Oats, 912 acres; Oats, per acre, $20\frac{109}{114}$ bush.; val., $9,556.

Potatoes, 205 acres; Potatoes, per acre, $97\frac{61}{205}$ bush.; val., $9,973.

Onions, 5 acres; Onions, per acre, 500 bush.; val., $250.

Turnips cultivated as a field crop, 5 acres; Turnips, per acre, 200 bush.; val., $50.

Carrots, 6 acre; Carrots, per acre, 800 bush.; val., $200.

Beets and other esculent vegetables, 10 acres; val., $200; all other Grain or Root Crops, 500 acres; val., $5,000.

English Mowing, 4,233 acres; English Hay, 3,660 tons; val., $36,802.

Apple Trees, cultivated for their fruit, 11,703; val., $3,930.

Pear Trees, cultivated for their fruit, 498; val., $69.

Establishments for m. of casks, 2; cap., $200; Casks m'd., 1,500; val., $600; emp., 3.

Establishments for m. of sashes and door blinds, 1; cap., $200; val. m'd., $1,000; emp., 2.

Distilleries, 1; cap., $100; Alcohol distilled, – bbls.; all other Liquors distilled, 2 bbls.; val., $100; emp., 1.

Plane Stock Manufactory, 1; Plane Stocks m'd., 15,000; cap., $5,000; gross val., $10,000; emp., 15.

Corn Baskets m'd., 2,000; val., $840; emp., 10.

WINDSOR.

Establishments for m. of cotton, woollen and other machinery, 1; val. of machinery m'd., $2,500; cap., $1,300; emp., 2.

Axe Manufactories, 1; Axes, Hatchets and other Edge Tools m'd., 1,700; val., $1,400; cap., $2,000; emp., 2.

Chair and Cabinet Manufactories, 1; val. of chairs and cabinet ware, $1,000; cap., $600; emp., 2.

Tanneries, 1; Hides of all kinds tanned, 800; val. of leather tanned, $1,200; cap., $2,000; emp., 1.

Lumber prepared for market, 351,000 ft.; val. of lumber, $2,104; emp., 5.

Firewood prepared for market, 1,000 cords; val. of firewood, $2,000; emp., 5.

Merino Sheep of different grades, 1,611; val. of all sheep, $3,718; Merino Wool produced, 4,833.

Horses, 168; val. of horses, $11,420; Oxen over three years old, 108; Steers under three years old, 152; val. of oxen and steers, $6,640; Milch Cows, 725; Heifers, 185; val. of cows and heifers, $23,070.

Butter, 53,860 lbs.; val. of butter, $10,772; Cheese, 161,000 lbs.; val. of cheese, $12,880.

Indian Corn, 100 acres; Indian Corn, per acre, 40 bush.; val., $4,000.

Wheat, 2 acres; Wheat, per acre, 24 bush.; val., $54.

Rye, 2 acres; Rye, per acre, 20 bush.; val., $25.

Barley, 42 acres; Barley, per acre, 40 bush.; val., $1,265.

Oats, 122 acres; Oats, per acre, 30 bush.; val., $1,830.

Potatoes, 155 acres; Potatoes, per acre, 200 bush.; val., $9,300.

English Mowing, 4,732 acres; English Hay, 2,790 tons; val., $33,480.

Wet Meadow or Swale Hay, 140 tons; val., $840.

Val. of carpenter's bench screws and scythe stones, $9,200; cap., $6,500; emp., 14.

Val. of wagon "hubs" and window shades, $1,100; cap., $225; emp., 4.

BRISTOL COUNTY.

ATTLEBOROUGH.

Cotton Mills, 7; Spindles, 16,300; Cotton consumed, 550,400 lbs.; Cloth m'd., 1,466,000 yds.; val. of cloth, $151,420; Yarn m'd., 60,000 lbs.; val. of yarn, $16,800; Thread m'd., 1,100,000 doz. of spool thread; val. of thread, $78,000; cap., $200,000; m. emp., 116; f. emp., 197.

Brass Founderies, 1; val. of articles m'd., $6,000; cap., $2,500; emp., 4.

Metal Button Manufactories, 2; Metal Buttons m'd., 1,538,000 gross; val. of metal buttons, $27,620; cap., $8,000; emp., 26.

Glass Manufactories, 2; Window Glass m'd., –; val. of window glass, –; val. of other glass m'd., $9,000; cap., $2,500; emp., 6.

Clock Manufactories, 1; Clocks m'd., 800; cap., $2,000; emp., 4.

Establishments for m. of chronometers, watches, gold and silver ware and jewelry, 24; val. of m's., $946,200; cap., $350,000; emp., 724.

Establishments for m. of boats – : Boats built, 10 ; val., $500 : cap., $200 ; emp., 1.

Establishments for m. of railroad cars, coaches, chaises, wagons, sleighs, and other vehicles, 2 : val. of railroad cars, &c., m'd., $1,400.

Gold Refineries, 1 : Gold refined, – lbs. : val. of gold refined, $50,000 ; emp., 2.

Tin Ware Manufactories, 2 : val. of tin ware, $4,000 ; cap., $2,000 ; emp., 4.

Comb Manufactories, 1 : val. of combs m'd., $8,300 : cap., $2,000 : emp., 5.

Tanneries, 1 ; Hides of all kinds tanned, 6,000 ; val. of leather tanned, $12,000 ; cap., $2,000 ; emp., 6.

Boots of all kinds m'd., 880 pairs ; Shoes of all kinds m'd., 125 pairs : val. of boots and shoes, $4,500 : m. emp., 10 : f. emp., 1.

Establishments for m. of straw bonnets and hats, 2 ; Straw Bonnets m'd., 2,000 ; val., $4,500 ; Straw Hats, m'd., – ; val. of straw braid m'd. and not made into bonnets and hats, $3,278 ; m. emp., 2 ; f. emp., 65.

Charcoal m'd., 3,200 bush. ; val. of same, $400.

Val. of mechanics' tools m'd., $57,000 ; emp., 31.

Val. of wooden ware not otherwise enumerated, including farming utensils m'd., $2,000 ; emp., 2.

Lumber prepared for market, 500,000 ft. ; val. of lumber, $10,000 ; emp., 7.

Firewood prepared for market, 5,337 cords : val. of firewood, $26,685 ; emp., 7.

Saxony Sheep, of different grades, – ; Merino Sheep, of different grades, – ; all other kinds of Sheep, 20 ; val. of all sheep, $40 ; Wool produced from Saxony sheep – lbs. ; Merino Wool produced, – lbs. ; all other Wool produced, 100 lbs.

Horses, 377 ; val. of horses, $29,861 ; Oxen over three years old, 222 ; Steers under three years old, 75 ; val. of oxen and steers, $13,856 ; Milch Cows, 750 ; Heifers, 123 ; val. of cows and heifers, $13,973.

Butter, 25,170 lbs. ; val. of butter, $5,034 ; Cheese, 3,250 lbs.; val. of cheese, $237.50; Honey, 500 lbs.; val. of honey, $238.54.

Indian Corn, 421 acres; Indian Corn, per acre, 28 bush.; val., $11,788.

Rye, 134 acres; Rye, per acre, 12 bush.; val., $2,213.

Barley, 2 acres; Barley, per acre, 10 bush.; val., $20.

Oats, 95 acres; Oats, per acre, 15 bush.; val., $720.

Potatoes, 187 acres; Potatoes, per acre, 88 bush.; val., $12,672.

Turnips, cultivated as a field crop, 6 acres; Turnips, per acre, 250 bush.; val., $557.62.

Carrots, 1 acre; Carrots, per acre, 80 bush.; val., $20.

Beets and other esculent vegetables, 116 acres; val., $6,387: all other Grain or Root Crops, 100 acres; val., $2,587.50.

Millet, 37 acres; val., $600.

English Mowing, 2,488 acres; English Hay, 2,170 tons; val., $43,400.

Wet Meadow or Swale Hay, 790 tons; val., $7,900.

Apple Trees, cultivated for their fruit, 17,032; val., $7,350.

Pear Trees, cultivated for their fruit, 100; val., $127.

Cranberries, 132 acres; val., $4,251.

Establishments for m. of boxes, 3; cap., $2,000; val. of jewellers' and fancy boxes m'd., $6,000; wooden do., $600; Total, $6,600; emp., 11.

Val. of shoe-lacings m'd., $5,000.

Val. of daguerreotype articles m'd., $40,000.

Cap. in the two last named branches, $12,000; m. emp., 25; f. emp., 12.

Gross val. of shuttles m'd., $7,250; emp., 8.

Spools for thread m'd., 31,300 gross; val., $3,700; emp., 6.

Val. of goggles m'd., $6,000; cap., $2,500; emp., 9.

Hooks and Eyes m'd., 300,000 gross; val., $25,000; cap., $10,000; emp., 80.

Plated Pencils m'd., 624 gross; val., $7,485; cap., $3,000; emp., 8.

Val. of poultry, $3,575.50.

BERKLEY.

Vessels launched during said year, 1; Tonnage, 112 tons; cap., $10,000; emp., 10.

Boots of all kinds m'd., 150 pairs; Shoes of all kinds m'd., 12,970 pairs; val. of boots and shoes, $13,320; m. emp., 7; f. emp., 2.

Lumber prepared for market, 8,000 ft.; val. of lumber, $144; emp., 2.

Firewood prepared for market, 680 cords; val. of firewood, $3,060; emp., 3.

Alewives, Shad and Salmon taken, 595,135; val. of same, $5,292.70; emp., 37.

Saxony Sheep, of different grades, 4; Merino Sheep, of different grades, 125; all other kinds of Sheep, 255; val. of all sheep, $877; Wool produced from Saxony sheep, 21 lbs.; Merino Wool produced, 301 lbs.; all other Wool produced, 716 lbs.

Horses, 94; val. of horses, $5,615; Oxen over three years old, 94; Steers under three years old, 42; val. of oxen and steers, $5,595; Milch Cows, 237; Heifers, 38; val. of cows and heifers, $6,593.

Butter, 11,532 lbs.; val. of butter, $2,883; Cheese, 3,000 lbs.; val. of cheese, $300; Honey, 55 lbs.; val. of honey, $7.

Indian Corn, 276 acres; Indian Corn, per acre, 20½ bush.; val., $5,662.

Rye, 100 acres; Rye, per acre, 8 bush.; val., $1,017.

Barley, 4 acres; Barley, per acre, 10 bush.; val., $41.

Oats, 16 acres; Oats, per acre, 12 bush.; val., $96.

Potatoes, 147 acres; Potatoes, per acre, 48 bush.; val., $4,917.

Onions, ⅛ acre; Onions, per acre, 320 bush.; val., $20.

Turnips, cultivated as a field crop, 2 acres; Turnips, per acre, 200 bush.; val., $66.

Millet, 4 acres; val., $60.

English Mowing, 834 acres; English Hay, 585 tons; val., $10,530.

Wet Meadow or Swale Hay, 202 tons: val., $2,020.

Salt Hay, 141 tons; val., $1,600.

Apple Trees cultivated for their fruit, 5,385; val., $5,150.

Pear Trees cultivated for their fruit, 87; val., $16.

Cranberries, 2 acres; val., $60.

Establishments for m. of stone and earthenware, 1; cap., $50; val. of stone and earthenware, $50; emp., 1.

Swine raised, 85; val., $700.

Straw Bonnets m'd. in private families, 3,255.

Straw Hats m'd. in private families, 4,340.

DARTMOUTH.

Cotton Mills, 1; Batting m'd., 200,000 lbs.; val. of batting, $18,000; cap., $8,000; m. emp., 6.

Vessels launched during said year, 2: Tonnage, 670 tons; cap., $92,000; emp., 30.

Establishments for m. of salt, 3; Salt m'd., 9,000 bush.; val. of salt, $4,500; cap., $12,562; emp., 6.

Establishments for m. of railroad cars, coaches, chaises, wagons, sleighs, and other vehicles, 5; val. of railroad cars, &c., m'd., $1,400; cap., $600; emp., 5.

Tanneries, 2; Hides of all kinds tanned, 150; val. of leather tanned, $900; cap., $2,200; emp., 2.

Boots of all kinds m'd., 355 pairs; Shoes of all kinds m'd., 1,370 pairs; val. of boots and shoes, $4,000; m. emp., 7.

Charcoal m'd., 12,200 bush.; val. of same, $1,708; emp., 8.

Lumber prepared for market, 276,000 ft.; val. of lumber, $5,520; emp., 12.

Firewood prepared for market, 5,427 cords; val. of firewood, $20,300; emp., 50.

Vessels employed in the whale fishery, 5; Tonnage, 1,584 tons; Sperm Oil imported, 28,382 galls.; val. of sperm oil imported, $51,087; cap. in the whale fishery, $197,000; emp., 155.

Saxony Sheep, of different grades, 35; Merino Sheep, of different grades, 48; all other kinds of Sheep, 1,045; val. of all sheep, $1,567; Wool produced from Saxony sheep, 146 lbs.; Merino Wool produced, 154 lbs.; all other Wool produced, 2,696 lbs.

Horses, 385; val. of horses, $33,295; Oxen over three years old, 428; Steers under three years old, 75; val. of oxen and steers, $24,450; Milch Cows, 1,018; Heifers, 169; val. of cows and heifers, $31,629.

Butter, 25,900 lbs.; val. of butter, $6,475; Cheese, 3,475 lbs.; val. of cheese, $417; Honey, 877 lbs.; val. of honey, $175.

Indian Corn, 712 acres; Indian Corn, per acre, 29 bush.; val., $20,648.

Wheat, 2 acres; Wheat, per acre, 26 bush.; val., $104.

Rye, 24 acres; Rye, per acre, 20 bush.; val., $720.

Barley, 31 acres; Barley, per acre, 23 bush.; val., $713.

Oats, 389 acres; Oats, per acre, 26 bush.; val., $6,574.10.

Potatoes, 151 acres; Potatoes, per acre, 87 bush.; val., $13,137.

Onions, 2 acres; Onions, per acre, 565 bush.; val., 282.50.

Turnips, cultivated as a field crop, 75 acres; Turnips, per acre, 200 bush.; val., $4,950.

Carrots, 1 acre; Carrots, per acre, 300 bush.; val., $75.

Beets and other esculent vegetables, – acres; val., $6,861; all other Grain or Root Crops, 50 acres; val., $5,300.

English Mowing, 4,102 acres; English Hay, 3,205 tons; val., $51,280.

Wet Meadow or Swale Hay, 192 tons; val., $1,920.

Salt Hay, 374 tons; val., $2,618.

Apple Trees, cultivated for their fruit, 14,835; val., $4,079.

Pear Trees, cultivated for their fruit, 689; val., $243.

Cranberries, 3 acres; val., $127.

Beeswax, 45 lbs.; val., $15.

Shingles Mills, 5; Shingles m'd., 1,200,000; val., $3,000; emp., 8.

Strawberries, 2 acres; val., $500.

Cabbages, 2 acres; val., $450.

Swine raised, 850; val., $5,000.
Milk, 423,534 quarts; val., $16,941.36.
Ship Timber, 462 tons; val., $3,696.

DIGHTON.

Cotton Mills, 1; Spindles, 3,000; Cotton consumed, 300 bales; Cloth m'd., 342,000 yds.; Print Cloth, 52x56; val. of cloth, $15,000; Thread m'd., 57,000 lbs.; val. of thread, $17,000; cap., $40,000; m. emp., 9; f. emp., 40.

Tack and Brad Manufactories, 2; Tacks and Brads m'd., 70 tons; val. of tacks and brads, $10,000; cap., $10,000; emp., 10.

Paper Manufactories, 1; Stock made use of, 800 tons; Paper m'd., 450 tons; val. of paper, $40,500; cap., $15,000; emp., 20.

Vessels launched during said year, 1; Tonnage, 42 tons; cap., $2,000; emp., 4, during 4 months.

Establishments for m. of railroad cars, coaches, chaises, wagons, sleighs, and other vehicles, 1; val. of railroad cars, &c., m'd., $500; cap., $100; emp., 1.

Boots of all kinds m'd., 110 pairs; Shoes of all kinds m'd., 1,190 pairs; val. of boots and shoes, $930; m. emp., 4.

Charcoal m'd., 4,950 bush.; val. of same, $594; emp., 4, during 4 months.

Lumber prepared for market, 400,000 shingles; val. of lumber, $1,200; emp., 2.

Firewood prepared for market, 1,084 cords; val. of firewood, $5,150; emp., 13.

Alewives, Shad and Salmon taken, 406,500; val. of same, $3,473; emp., 26, during 2 months.

Saxony Sheep, of different grades, –; Merino Sheep, of different grades, –; all other kinds of Sheep, 95; val. of all sheep, $251; Wool produced from Saxony sheep, – lbs.; Merino Wool produced, – lbs.; all other Wool produced, 270 lbs.

Horses, 156; val. of horses, $12,110; Oxen over three years old, 111; Steers under three years old, 39; val. of oxen and steers, $5,398; Milch Cows, 315; Heifers, 62; val. of cows and heifers, $9,272.

Butter, 12,285 lbs.; val. of butter, $2,991; Cheese, 3,435 lbs.; val. of cheese, $447; Honey, 293 lbs.; val. of honey, $45.

Indian Corn, 275 acres; Indian Corn, per acre, 25 bush.; val., $6,531.

Rye, 103 acres; Rye, per acre, 11 bush.; val., $1,473.

Oats, 91 acres; Oats, per acre, 25 bush.; val., $1,138.

Potatoes, 169 acres; Potatoes, per acre, 68 bush.; val., $7,619.

Onions, $\frac{3}{4}$ acre; Onions, per acre, 115 bush.; val., $69.

Turnips, cultivated as a field crop, $1\frac{1}{4}$ acre; Turnips, per acre, 40 bush.; val., $19.

English Mowing, 1,324 acres; English Hay, 963 tons; val., $17,334.

Wet Meadow or Swale Hay, 277 tons; val., $2,770.

Salt Hay, 122 tons; val., $1,220.

Apple Trees, cultivated for their fruit, 4,708; val., $1,286.

Pear Trees, cultivated for their fruit, 262; val., $42.

Cranberries, 1 acre; val., $100.

Establishments for m. of casks, 1; cap., $10,000; Casks m'd., 60,000; val., $8,700; emp., 11.

Establishments for m. of sashes and door blinds, 1; cap., $3,300; val. m'd., $4,000; emp., 4.

Bakeries, 1; cap., $2,500; Flour consumed, 325 bbls.; val. of bread m'd., $8,000; emp., 4.

Val. of other articles produced in the town during the year, $5,225, as follows: Nail Key Hoops, 577,000; Hogshead Hoops, 79,000; Ship Timber, 271 tons; cap., $1,000; emp., 20.

EASTON.

Cotton Mills, 6; Spindles, 2,390; Cotton consumed, 132,800 lbs.; Yarn m'd., 82,000 lbs.; val. of yarn, $16,500; Thread m'd., 36,700 lbs.; val. of thread, $27,600; Batting m'd.,

4,050 lbs.; val. of batting, $524; cap., $43,500; m. emp., 21; f. emp., 48.

Furnaces for m. of hollow ware and castings other than pig iron, 2; Hollow Ware and other Castings m'd., 554 tons; val. of hollow ware and castings, $44,500; cap., $11,000; emp., 50.

Establishments for m. of cotton, woollen and other machinery, 1; val. of machinery m'd., $2,000; cap., $2,500; emp., 4.

Manufactories of shovels, spades, forks and hoes, 1; val. of shovels, &c., $600,000; cap., $200,000; emp., 330.

Daguerreotype Artists, 1; Daguerreotypes taken, 500; cap., $600; emp., 1.

Establishments for m. of railroad cars, coaches, chaises, wagons, sleighs, and other vehicles, 4; val. of railroad cars, &c. m'd., $46,000; cap., $4,675; emp., 23.

Boots of all kinds m'd., 38,000 pairs; Shoes of all kinds m'd., 87,700 pairs; val. of boots and shoes, $153,200; m. emp., 215; f. emp., 92.

Charcoal m'd., 9,190 bush.; val. of same, $1,003; emp., 15.

Lumber prepared for market, 202,500 ft.; val. of lumber, $2,680; emp., 28.

Firewood prepared for market, 2,577 cords; val. of firewood, $9,807; emp., 115.

Saxony Sheep, of different grades, –; Merino Sheep, of different grades, –; all other kinds of Sheep, 51; val. of all sheep, $125; Wool produced from Saxony sheep, – lbs.; Merino Wool produced, – lbs.; all other Wool produced, 135 lbs.

Horses, 230; val. of horses, $20,252; Oxen over three years old, 157; Steers under three years old, 33; val. of oxen and steers, $9,176; Milch Cows, 451; Heifers, 59; val. of cows and heifers, $14,965.

Butter, 18,440 lbs.; val. of butter, $4,610; Cheese, 6,980 lbs.; val. of cheese, $837; Honey, 160 lbs.; val. of honey, $32.

Indian Corn, 252 acres; Indian Corn, per acre, 26 bush.; val., $6,552.

Wheat, 1½ acre; Wheat, per acre, 10 bush.; val., $30.

Rye, 44 acres; Rye, per acre, 9 bush.; val., $590.

Barley, 22½ acres; Barley, per acre, 12 bush.; val., $270.

Oats, 29 acres; Oats, per acre, 16½ bush.; val., $310.

Potatoes, 187⅓ acres; Potatoes, per acre, 84 bush.; val., $11,780.

Onions, 1 acre; Onions, per acre, 560 bush.; val., $336.

Turnips, cultivated as a field crop, 5 acres; Turnips, per acre, 350 bush.; val., $440.

Carrots, ¼ acre; Carrots, per acre, 200 bush.; val., $12.

Beets and other esculent vegetables, 1 acre; val., $100; all other Grain or Root Crops, 1 acre; val., $120.

Millet, 3 acres; val., $40.

English Mowing, 1,581 acres; English Hay, 1,144 tons; val., $22,880.

Wet Meadow or Swale Hay, 639 tons; val., $6,390.

Apple Trees, cultivated for their fruit, 11,044; val., $3,488.

Pear Trees, cultivated for their fruit, 619; val., $85.

Fruit of various kinds raised during the year, 1,750 bush.

Cranberries, 78 acres; val., $1,109.

Beeswax, 17 lbs.; val., $6.

Gross val. of all other articles m'd. in the town during the year, $24,152; cap., $9,600; emp., 51. Said articles are reported to be "Wooden Hoops, Philosophical Instruments, Mathematical Instruments, Shoemakers' Awls, Cord, Twine and Wicking Castors, Piano-Forte Tools, Spools, Deck Scrapers and Washers."

Swine raised, 352; val., $3,137.

FAIRHAVEN.

Cotton Mills, 2; Spindles, 4,980; Cotton consumed, 510,000 lbs.; Cloth m'd., 300,000 yds. of Sheeting; val. of cloth, $24,000; Yarn m'd., 375,000 lbs.; val. of yarn, $67,500; cap., $80,000; m. emp., 36; f. emp., 51.

Brass Founderies, 1; val. of articles m'd., $8,000; cap., $2,700; emp., 2.

Paper Manufactories, 1; Stock made use of, 160,000 lbs.; Paper m'd., 130,000 lbs.; val. of paper, $13,068; cap., $1,000; emp., 16.

Vessels launched during said year, 4; Tonnage, 2,434 tons; cap., $30,000; emp., 140.

Establishments for m. of boats, 5; Boats built, 105; cap., $3,900; emp., 8.

Masts and Spar Sheds, 2; Masts and Spars m'd. in one shed, 140; cap., $800; emp., 2. The Assessors report that "no information could be obtained of one."

Sail Lofts, 1; Sails made of Am. fabric, 240; of For. fabric, 80; val. of sails m'd. of Am. fabric, $18,000; val. of sails of For. fabric, $2,000; cap., $100; emp., 10.

Establishments for m. of salt, 1; Salt m'd., 811 bush.; val. of salt, $406; cap., $1,000; emp., 1.

Establishments for m. of oil and sperm candles, 1; Whale Oil m'd., 150,000 galls.; val. of oil m'd., $120,000; cap., $20,000; emp., 5.

Establishments for m. of soap and tallow candles, 1; Soap m'd., 10 tons; val. of soap, $600; emp., 1.

Chair and Cabinet Manufactories, 1; val. of chairs and cabinet ware, $1,380; cap., $400; emp., 2.

Tin Ware Manufactories, 1; val. of tin ware, $4,000; cap., $1,500; emp., 4.

Boots of all kinds m'd., 530 pairs; Shoes of all kinds m'd., 1,050 pairs; val. of boots and shoes, $3,517; m. emp., 9.

Val. of snuff, tobacco, and cigars, $800; m. emp., 1.

Charcoal m'd., 1,850 bush.; val. of same, $166; emp., 3.

Val. of blocks and pumps m'd., $2,190; emp., 6.

Lumber prepared for market, 139,000 ft.; val. of lumber, shingles and boards, $2,892; emp., 29, part of the time.

Firewood prepared for market, 1,374 cords; val. of firewood, $6,870.

Vessels employed in the whale fishery, 46; Tonnage, 15,532 tons; Sperm Oil imported, 95,628 galls.; val. of sperm oil imported, $150,829; Whale Oil imported, 662,622 galls.; val. of whale oil imported, $392,613; Whalebone imported, 243,448 lbs.; val. of whalebone imported, $94,917; cap. in the whale fishery, $1,620,394; emp., 1,324.

Saxony Sheep, of different grades, 4; Merino Sheep, of different grades, 86; all other kinds of Sheep, 187; val. of all sheep, $686; Wool produced from Saxony sheep, 25 lbs.; Merino Wool produced, 194 lbs.; all other Wool produced, 548 lbs.

Horses, 351; val. of horses, $34,321; Oxen over three years old, 143; Steers under three years old, 56; val. of oxen and steers, 8,071; Milch Cows, 531; Heifers, 116; val. of cows and heifers, $13,378.

Butter, 24,873 lbs.; val. of butter, $5,974.60; Cheese, 350 lbs.; val. of cheese, $35; Honey, 647 lbs.; val. of honey, $161.75.

Indian Corn, 304 acres; Indian Corn, per acre, 30 bush.; val., $9,120.

Wheat, 9½ acres; Wheat, per acre, 8 bush.; val., $152.

Rye, 40 acres; Rye, per acre, 11 bush.; val., $550.

Barley, 21 acres; Barley, per acre, 16½ bush.; val., $346.

Oats, 121 acres; Oats, per acre, 20 bush.; val., $830.

Potatoes, 82 acres; Potatoes, per acre, 74 bush.; val., $3,951.

Onions, 1 acre; Onions, per acre, 237 bush.; val., $118.

Turnips, cultivated as a field crop, 15 acres; Turnips, per acre, 200 bush.; val., $750.

Carrots, 4 acres; Carrots, per acre, 400 bush.; val., $320.

Beets and other esculent vegetables, 1⅘ acre; val., $87.

English Mowing, 2,144 acres; English Hay, 1,984 tons; val., $31,744.

Wet Meadow or Swale Hay, 194 tons; val., $1,552.

Salt Hay, 371 tons; val., $1,855.

Apple Trees, cultivated for their fruit, 10,737; val., $2,167.

Pear Trees, cultivated for their fruit, 6,365; val., $364.

Beeswax, 18 lbs.; val., $7.55.

Establishments for m. of casks, 15; cap., $19,797; Casks m'd., 4,965; val., $34,310; emp., 30.

Bakeries, 2; cap., $5,500; Flour consumed, 1,750 bbls.; val. of bread m'd., $18,845; emp., 7.

Establishments for m. of boxes, 2; cap., $125; val. of boxes, $3,600; emp., 7.

Swine raised, 605; val., $9,421.

Establishments for m. of "Whaling Craft," 4; cap., $4,000; Harpoons m'd., 1,700; Lances m'd., 550; Spades m'd., 350; emp., 9, in part; val. of "Whaling Craft" m'd., $3,495.

FALL RIVER.

Cotton Mills, 8; Spindles, 106,584; Cotton consumed, 4,286,-000 lbs.; Cloth m'd., 21,985,000 yds., of which 3,000,000 yds. are 39 inch. "Pocasset Sheeting"—18,985,000 yds. of printing cloths, from 64 to 74 picks to the inch; val. of cloth, $1,189,250; Yarn m'd. as knitting cotton, 150,000 lbs.; val. of yarn, $40,000; cap., $1,365,000; m. emp., 786; f. emp., 925.

Calico Manufactories, 2; Calico printed, 19,000,000 yards; val. of calico, $1,330,000; cap., $230,000; m. emp., 325; f. emp., 25.

Establishments for m. of linen, 1; Linen m'd., 1,600,000 yds.; val. of linen, $240,000; cap., $365,000; m. emp., 300; f. emp., 250.

Rolling Mills, 1; Nail Mills, 1; Iron m'd. and not made into nails, 1,800 tons; val. of iron, $135,000; number of Machines for m. of nails, 100; Nails m'd., 111,000 casks, of 100 lbs. each; val. of nails, $444,000; cap., $300,000; emp., 250.

Forges. "None, except for repairs and light work, usually done by common blacksmiths."

Furnaces for m. of hollow ware and castings other than pig iron, 2; Hollow Ware and other Castings m'd., 2,036 tons; val. of hollow ware and castings, $152,600; cap., $55,000; emp., 74.

Establishments for m. of cotton, woollen and other machinery, 3; val. of machinery m'd., $200,000; cap., $105,000; emp., 150.

Brass Founderies, 1; val. of articles m'd., $14,000; cap., $6,000; emp., 7.

Daguerreotype Artists, 2; Daguerreotypes taken, 3,500; cap., $2,000; emp., 4.

Establishments for repairing of chronometers, watches, gold and silver ware and jewelry, 4.

Saddle, Harness and Trunk Manufactories, 4; val. of saddles, &c., $54,500; cap., $5,550; m. emp., 32; f. emp., 6.

Upholstery Manufactories, 1; val. of upholstery, $12,000; cap., $3,000; m. emp., 12; f. emp., 3.

Hat and Cap Manufactories, 1; Hats and Caps m'd., $750; cap., $1,000; emp., 3.

Vessels launched during said year, 2; Tonnage, 515 tons; cap., $10,000; emp., 20.

Sail Lofts, 1; Sails made of Am. fabric, 150; val. of sails m'd. of Am. fabric, $12,000; cap., $2,200; emp., 6.

Establishments for m. of coaches, chaises, wagons, sleighs, and other vehicles, 3; val. of coaches, &c., m'd., $24,000; cap., $13,000; emp., 30.

Establishments for m. of soap, 2; Soap m'd., 750,000 lbs.; val. of soap, $50,000; cap., $7,500; emp., 10.

Cabinet Manufactories, 2; val. of cabinet ware, $10,500; cap., $8,700; emp., 12.

Tin Ware Manufactories, 5; val. of tin ware, $35,000; cap., $11,000; emp., 26.

Flour Mills, 2; Flour m'd., 60,000 bbls.; val. of flour m'd., $670,000; cap., $150,000; m. emp., 28; f. emp., 8.

Tanneries, 2; Hides of all kinds tanned, 4,550; val. of leather tanned, $13,200; cap., $7,500; emp., 10.

Boots of all kinds m'd., 1,100 pairs; Shoes of all kinds m'd., 3,100 pairs; val. of boots and shoes, $5,700; m. emp., 15.

Val. of cigars, $4,000; m. emp., 7; f. emp., 1.

Val. of building stone quarried and prepared for building, $7,500; emp., 20.

Charcoal m'd., 1,100 bush.; val. of same, $140; emp., 5.

Val. of stove blacking, $22,000; emp., 6.

Val. of blocks and pumps m'd., $350; emp., 1.

Lumber prepared for market, 150,000 ft.; val. of lumber, $4,500.

Vessels employed in the whale fishery, 4; Tonnage, 1,144 tons; cap. in the whale fishery, $101,000; emp., 105.

Vessels emplyed in the mackerel and cod fisheries, 2; Tonnage, 159 tons; cap., $7,500; emp., 20.

Saxony Sheep, of different grades, –; Merino Sheep, of different grades, –; all other kinds of Sheep, 316; val. of all sheep, $800; Wool produced from Saxony sheep, – lbs.; Merino Wool produced, – lbs.; all other Wool produced, 1,000 lbs.

Horses, 292; val. of horses, $30,000; Oxen over three years old, 92; Steers under three years old, 37; val. of oxen and steers, $7,650; Milch Cows, 411; Heifers, 44; val. of cows and heifers, $13,210.

Butter, 4,615 lbs.; val. of butter, $1,154; Honey, 410 lbs.; val. of honey, $75.

Indian Corn, 184 acres; Indian Corn, per acre, 30 bush.; val., $5,545.

Rye, 10 acres; Rye, per acre, 20 bush.; val., $327.

Barley, 2 acres; Barley, per acre, 43 bush.; val., $86.

Oats, 10 acres; Oats, per acre, 30 bush.; val., $150.

Potatoes, 62 acres; Potatoes, per acre, 75 bush.; val., $4,650.

Turnips, cultivated as a field crop, 8 acres; Turnips, per acre, 300 bush.; val., $800.

Beets and other esculent vegetables, 20 acres; val., $4,000.

English Mowing, 600 acres; English Hay, 25 tons; val., $16,500.

Salt Hay, 8 tons; val., $80.

Flax, 2 acres; Flax, per acre, 2,000 lbs.; val., $32.

Apple Trees, cultivated for their fruit, 5,215; val., $1,530.

Pear Trees, cultivated for their fruit, 740; val., $444.

Cranberries, 5 acres; val., $300.

Beeswax, 25 lbs.; val., $10.

Establishments for m. of gas, 1; cap., $40,000; val. m'd., $15,000; emp., 10.

Breweries, –; Small Beer m'd., 1,000 bbls.; val., $3,500; emp., 3.

Bakeries, 3; cap., $10,800; Flour consumed, 2,400 bbls.; val. of bread m'd., $49,000; emp., 20.

Establishments for m. of boxes for calico packing, 1; cap., $8,000; val. of boxes m'd., $18,000; emp., 4.

Val. of bookbinding done, $4,750.

Val. of water stops m'd., $15,000.

Val. of perfumery m'd. during the year, $18,000.

Cap. in the three branches of business last named, $9,800 m. emp., 19; f. emp., 10.

The Assessors state that they "have one Ice Company, with houses sufficiently large for storing 5,000 tons of ice, annually. The sales of the Company average some 3,000 tons annually. Capital, as near as can be ascertained, $10,000." They also present the following statistical view of the city:—

Stores.—Groceries, 47; Provisions, 7; Dry Goods, 15; Merchant Tailors, 6; Hat and Cap, 1; Apothecary, 11; Auction, 3; Millinery, 12; Coal Dealers, 7; Flour and Grain, 5; Stove Dealers, 4; Confectioners, 3; Ready Made Clothing, 7; Hardware, 3; Furniture, 5; Music, 1; Book and Stationery, 3; Boot and Shoe, 12; Restorators, 5.

Hotels.—1.

Professions.—Editors, 4; Doctors, 13; Lawyers, 13; Clergymen, 15; Male Teachers, 6; Female Teachers, 25 to 40; Civil Engineers, 4; Dentists, 2.

Vessels owned, including ships, barks, brigs, steamers and schooners, 60; Tonnage, 12,000. [Value not returned, nor capital invested in commerce.]

Mechanics, &c.—Master Mechanics, 12; Engineers, 12; Barbers, 5.

Churches.—Congregational, 2; Calvinistic Baptist, 2; Christian Baptist, 2; Methodist, 3; Unitarian, 1; Universalist, 1; Episcopal, 1; Associated Presbyterian, 1; New Jerusalem, 1; Friends, 2; Catholics, 1.

Banks.—3, Fall River, Massasoit, Metacomet, and Institution for Savings.

Livery Stables.—6.

FREETOWN.

Rolling, Slitting and Nail Mills, 2; Machines for m. of nails, 12; Nails m'd., 66 tons; val. of nails, $6,600; cap., $3,375; emp., 12.

Axe Manufactories, 1; Axes, Hatchets, and other Edge Tools m'd., 1,300; val., $1,015; cap., $1,000; emp., 2.

Establishments for m. of fire arms, 1; Fire Arms m'd., 350—250 rifles, 100 carbine guns; val. of fire arms, $2,500; cap., $300; emp., 7.

Tanneries, 1; Hides of all kinds tanned, 150; val. of leather tanned, $500; cap., $300; emp., 2.

Currying Establishments, 1; val. of leather curried, $1,000; cap., $500; emp., 1.

Boots of all kinds m'd., 150 pairs; Shoes of all kinds m'd., 6,000 pairs; val. of boots and shoes, $5,700; m. emp., 10; f. emp., 5.

Charcoal m'd., 18,750 bush.; val. of same, $2,344; emp., 56.

Lumber prepared for market, 746,500 ft.; val. of lumber, $6,520; emp., 13.

Firewood prepared for market, 4,657 cords; val. of firewood, $18,600; emp., 133.

Saxony Sheep, of different grades, –; Merino Sheep, of different grades, –; all other kinds of Sheep, 307; val. of all sheep, $651; Wool produced from Saxony sheep, – lbs.; Merino Wool produced, – lbs.; all other Wool produced, 765 lbs.

Horses, 117; val. of horses, $7,875; Oxen over three years old, 102; Steers under three years old, 45; val. of oxen and steers, $6,220; Milch Cows, 261; Heifers, 51; val. of cows and heifers, $9,045.

Butter, 13,729 lbs.; val. of butter, $3,432; Cheese, 1,145 lbs.; val. of cheese, $114; Honey, 160 lbs.; val. of honey, $32.

Indian Corn, 186 acres; Indian Corn, per acre, 21 bush.; val., $3,906.

Rye, 60 acres; Rye, per acre, 9½ bush.; val., $712.

Potatoes, 117 acres; Potatoes, per acre, 62 bush.; val., $6,528.

Onions, 733 bush.; val., $440.

Turnips, cultivated as a field crop, 781 bush.; val., $312.

Beets and other esculent vegetables, 1,315 bush.; val., $600.

Millet, 5 acres; val., $80.

English Mowing, 712 acres; English Hay, 610½ tons; val., $9,768.

Wet Meadow or Swale Hay, 58¼ tons; val., $348.

Salt Hay, 118½ tons; val., $948.

Apple Trees, cultivated for their fruit, 4,834; val., $2,175.

Pear Trees, cultivated for their fruit, 184; val., $295.

Cranberries, 42 acres; val., $1,600.

Establishments for m. of sashes, doors and blinds, 1; cap., $1,500; val. m'd., $4,000; emp., 4.

Establishments for m. of wrapping twine, 1; cap., $1,200; Twine m'd., 45,000 lbs.; val., $6,300; emp., 6.

Establishments for m. of window blind trimmings, &c., 1; cap., $2,000; Trimmings m'd., 3 tons; val., $780; Whale Blubber Spades, 600; val., $540.

Hoops prepared for market, 105,000; val., $2,100; emp., 21.

Boxboard Logs prepared for market, 117; val., $585.

Swine raised, 213; val., $2,076.

MANSFIELD.

Cotton Mills, 4; Spindles, 2,728; Cotton consumed, 115,000 lbs.; Thread m'd., 90,000 lbs.; val. of thread, $36,000; Batting m'd., 80,000 lbs.; val. of batting, $6,000; cap., $22,550; m. emp., 24; f. emp., 40.

Furnaces for m. of hollow ware and castings other than pig iron, 1; Hollow Ware and other Castings m'd., 30,000 tons; val. of hollow ware and castings, $25,000; cap., $5,000; emp., 24.

Establishments for m. of cotton, woollen and other machinery, 2; val. of machinery m'd., $58,500; cap., $38,000; emp., 43.

Tack and Brad Manufactories, 2; Tacks and Brads m'd., 150 tons; val. of tacks and brads, $21,000; cap., $4,700; emp., 8.

Saddle, Harness and Trunk Manufactories, 1; val. of saddles, &c., $600; cap., $100; emp., 1.

Establishments for m. of railroad cars, coaches, chaises, wagons, sleighs, and other vehicles, 3; val. of railroad cars, &c., m'd., $6,000; cap., $2,500; emp., 8.

Establishments for m. of soap and tallow candles, 2; soap m'd., 1,000 lbs.; val. of soap, $4,000; cap., $1,200; emp., 4.

Tin Ware Manufactories, 1; val. of tin ware, $1,000; cap., $400; emp., 2.

Boots of all kinds m'd., 5,000 pairs; Shoes of all kinds m'd., 3,000 pairs; val. of boots and shoes, $13,000; m. emp., 28; f. emp., 10.

Establishments for m. of straw bonnets and hats, 1; Straw Bonnets m'd., 150,000; Straw Hats, m'd., 27,500; val. of straw bonnets and hats, $110,000; m. emp., 20; f. emp., 275.

Val. of marble quarried and prepared for market, $3,000; emp., 5.

Charcoal m'd., 3,500 bush.; val. of same, $437.50; emp., 2.

Val. of mechanics' tools m'd., $15,000; emp., 31.

Lumber prepared for market, 75,000 ft.; val. of lumber, $1,125; emp., 8.

Firewood prepared for market, 625 cords; val. of firewood, $2,812.50; emp., 25.

Saxony Sheep, of different grades, –; Merino Sheep, of different grades, –; all other kinds of Sheep, 10; val. of all sheep, $30; Wool produced from Saxony sheep, – lbs.; Merino Wool produced, – lbs.; all other Wool produced, 40 lbs.

Horses, 199; val. of horses, $11,940; Oxen over three years old, 82; Steers under three years old, 25; val. of oxen and steers, $4,600; Milch Cows, 311; Heifers, 29; val. of cows and heifers, $9,910.

Butter, 12,595 lbs.; val. of butter, $3,148.75; Cheese, 4,675 lbs.; val. of cheese, $467.50; Honey, 385 lbs.; val. of honey, $61.60.

Indian Corn, 267 acres; Indian Corn, per acre, 22 bush.; val., $5,874.

Wheat, 5 acres; Wheat, per acre, 16 bush.; val., $140.

Rye, 50 acres; Rye, per acre, 8 bush.; val., $560.

Barley, 2 acres; Barley, per acre, 12 bush.; val., $24.

Oats, 130 acres; Oats, per acre, 25 bush.; val., $1,625.

Potatoes, 162 acres; Potatoes, per acre, 80 bush.; val., $6,480.

Turnips, cultivated as a field crop, 10 acres; Turnips, per acre, 100 bush.; val., $250.

Beets and other esculent vegetables, 50 acres; val., $500.

Millet, 30 acres; val., $300.

English Mowing, 1,200 acres; English Hay, 570 tons; val., $11,400.

Wet Meadow or Swale Hay, 450 tons; val., $3,600.

Apple Trees, cultivated for their fruit, 2,440; val., $1,215.

Pear Trees, cultivated for their fruit, 100; val., $50.

Cranberries, 17 acres; val., $330.

Beeswax, 25 lbs.; val., $10.

Bakeries, 1; cap., $500; Flour consumed, 400 bbls.; val. of bread m'd., $7,000; emp., 4.

Baskets m'd., 56,000; val., $13,650.

Boots and Shoes bottomed for manufacturers out of town, 12,000 pairs; val., $3,000.

Val. of sewing, fancy and florence braid, for manufacturers out of town, $11,500.

NEW BEDFORD.

Cotton Mills, 1; Spindles, 31,540; Cotton consumed, 1,200,000 lbs.; Cloth m'd., 2,500,000 yds.; val. of cloth, $350,000; cap., $600,000; m. emp., 300; f. emp., 200.

Furnaces for m. of hollow ware and castings other than pig iron, 1; Hollow Ware and other Castings m'd., 600 tons; val. of hollow ware and castings, $51,000; cap., $20,000; emp., 22.

Brass Founderies, 2; val. of articles m'd., $95,000; cap., $28,000; emp., 26.

Establishments for m. of chemical preparations, 1; val. of chemical preparations, $14,000; cap., $10,000; emp., 8.

Piano-Forte Manufactories, 1; Piano-Fortes m'd., 3; cap., $–; all other musical instrument manufactories, 1; val. of musical instruments m'd., $7,500; cap., $1,200; emp., 4.

Daguerreotype Artists, 6; Daguerreotypes taken, 11,150; cap., $2,800; emp., 12.

Establishments for m. of chronometers, watches, gold and silver ware and jewelry, 1.

Saddle, Harness and Trunk Manufactories, 5; val. of saddles, &c., $38,300; cap., $10,500; emp., 20.

Upholstery Manufactories, 6; val. of upholstery, $14,000; cap., $4,500; emp., 6.

Hat and Cap Manufactories, 1; Hats and Caps m'd., 15,600; cap., $1,500; emp., 6.

Cordage Manufactories, 1; Cordage m'd., 1,000 tons; cap., $75,000; emp., 60.

Vessels launched during said year, 1; Tonnage, 420 tons; emp., 15.

Establishments for m. of boats, 12; Boats built, 373; cap., $12,000; emp., 40.

Masts and Spar Sheds, 4; Masts and Spars m'd., 1,470; cap., $8,000; emp., 26.

Sail Lofts, 10; Sails made of Am. fabric, 2,311; of For. fabric, 408; val. of sails m'd. of Am. fabric, $175,231.84; val. of sails of For. fabric, $18,553.75; cap., 28,000; emp., 102.

Establishments for m. of salt, 1; Salt m'd., 5,000 bush.; val. of salt, $2,500; cap., $20,000; emp., 2.

Establishments for m. of railroad cars, coaches, chaises, wagons, sleighs, and other vehicles, 7; val. of railroad cars, &c., m'd., $41,270; cap., $11,000; emp., 47.

Establishments for m. of oil and sperm candles, 18; Oil m'd., $3,270,268 galls.; val. of oil m'd., $3,042,296.18; Sperm Candles m'd., 678,110 lbs.; val. of sperm candles, $189,970.80; cap., $1,390,000; emp., 123.

Establishments for m. of soap and tallow candles, 1; Soap m'd., 75,000 lbs.; val. of soap, $4,500; Tallow Candles m'd., 80,000 lbs.; val. of tallow candles, $10,800; cap., $7,000; emp., 5.

Tin Ware Manufactories, 12; val. of tin ware, $72,000; cap., $20,000; emp., 32.

Tanneries, 1; Hides of all kinds tanned, 500.

Boots of all kinds m'd., 1,425 pairs; Shoes of all kinds m'd., 9,300 pairs; val. of boots and shoes, $20,950; m. emp., 18.

Val. of mathematical instruments, $2,500; emp., 3.

Val. of snuff, tobacco and cigars, $1,400; m. emp., 1; f. emp., 4.

Val. of building stone quarried and prepared for building, $25,000; emp., 20.

Val. of blocks and pumps m'd., $26,000; emp., 20.

Val. of wooden ware not otherwise enumerated, including farming utensils m'd., $1,000; emp., 2.

Lumber prepared for market, 200,000 ft.; val. of lumber, $48,000; emp., 3.

Firewood prepared for market, 600 cords; val. of firewood, $2,100.

Vessels employed in the whale fishery, 311; Tonnage, 104,690 tons; Sperm Oil imported, 1,352,106 galls.; val. of sperm oil imported, $2,011,257.68; Whale Oil imported, 5,483,780 galls.; val. of whale oil imported, $3,214,866.02; Whalebone imported, 1,646,200 lbs.; val. of whalebone imported, $650,249; cap. in the whale fishery, $9,827,100; emp., 6,775.

Saxony Sheep of different grades, –; Merino Sheep, of different grades, –; all other kinds of Sheep, 7.

Horses, 699; val. of horses, $104,500; Oxen over three years old, 86; steers under three years old, 9; val. of oxen and steers, $6,450; Milch Cows, 366; Heifers, 8; val. of cows and heifers, $12,049.

Indian Corn, 794 acres; Indian Corn, per acre, 50 bush.; val., $3,973.

Rye, $5\frac{1}{2}$ acres; Rye, per acre, 15 to 18 bush.; val., $127.67.

Oats, $37\frac{1}{2}$ acres; Oats, per acre, 30 bush.; val., $677.60.

Potatoes, $15\frac{1}{3}$ acres; Potatoes, per acre, 175 bush.; val., $1,745.25.

Onions, 2 acres; Onions, per acre, 370 bush.; val., $310.

Turnips, cultivated as a field crop, $1\frac{3}{4}$ acre; Turnips, per acre, 400 bush.; val., $227.70.

Beets and other esculent vegetables, 7 acres; val., $1,250.

English Mowing, 1,190 acres; English Hay, 1,370 tons; val., $25,800.

Salt Hay, 25 tons; val., $160.

Apple Trees, cultivated for their fruit, 3,106; val., $740.

Pear Trees, cultivated for their fruit, 156; val., $325.

Establishments for m. of casks, 12; cap., $36,000; Casks m'd., 118,500; val., $154,125; emp., 115.

Establishments for m. of sashes and door blinds, 2; cap., $3,200; val. m'd., $17,450; emp., 18.

Establishments for m. of gas, 1; cap., $100,000; val. m'd., $26,059.95; emp., 6.

Bakeries, 7; cap., $38,300; Flour consumed, 14,912 bbls.; val. of bread m'd., $182,662; emp., 45.

Establishments for m. of boxes, 2; one for wooden candle boxes, 14,000 m'd.; one for paper boxes, 69,404 m'd.; cap., $3,200; val. of boxes m'd., $7,900; emp., 7.

Sperm Oil m'd., 1,094,474 galls.; val., $1,628,030.08.

Whale Oil m'd., 2,175,794 galls.; val., $1,414,266.10.

Steam Mills for grinding paints, 2; cap., $20,000; gross proceeds, $60,000; emp., 4.

Steam Mills for planing, 2; cap., $14,000; gross proceeds, $16,000; emp., 12.

Blacksmiths' Shops, 12; cap., $26,000; proceeds, $121,200; emp., 74.

Machine Shops, 4; cap., $10,000; proceeds, $25,000; emp., 18.

Book Binderies, 2; cap., $850; proceeds, $7,500; emp., 4.

Rivet Manufactory, 1; cap., $25,000; proceeds, $70,500; emp., 8.

Whale Oil Soap m'd., 1,238,076 lbs.; val., $34,047.09.

"Whale Foots" Soap m'd., 212,771 lbs.; val., $14,893.79.

Sperm Oil Soap m'd., 176,451 lbs.; val., $8,822.55.

Nurseries, 2; Trees, 48,000.

Corn Meal consumed in bakeries, 2,867 bush.; Rye consumed, 1,433 bush.; val. of bread m'd., $7,045.17.

Saleratus Manufactory, 1; cap., $5,000; proceeds, $6,000; emp., 5.

NORTON.

Cotton Mills, 3; Spindles, 3,656; Cotton consumed, 175,000 lbs.; Cloth m'd., 376,320 yds., from No. 35 to 40; val. of cloth, $42,336; Yarn m'd., 45,720 lbs.; Batting m'd., 25,836 lbs.; val. of batting, $2,325.24; Pelisse Wadding m'd., 3,000 doz.; val. of wadding, $225; cap., $85,000; m. emp., 53; f. emp., 33.

Furnaces for m. of hollow ware and castings other than pig iron, 1; Hollow Ware and other Castings m'd., 500 tons; val. of hollow ware and castings, $50,000; cap., $25,000; emp., 30.

Copper Manufactories, 1; cap., $60,000; emp., 60.

Establishments for m. of railroad cars, coaches, chaises, wagons, sleighs, and other vehicles, 2; val. of railroad cars, &c., m'd., $3,615; cap., $2,000; emp., 5.

Establishments for m. of straw bonnets and hats, 1; Straw Bonnets m'd., 35,000; Straw Hats m'd., 36,000; m. emp., 19; f. emp., 250.

Charcoal m'd., 20,000 bush.; val. of same, $2,000.

Lumber prepared for market, 1,205,000 ft.; val. of lumber, $11,715.

Firewood prepared for market, 2,588 cords; val. of firewood, $8,210.

Saxony Sheep, of different grades, –; Merino Sheep, of different grades, –; all other kinds of Sheep, 92; val. of all sheep, $210; Wool produced from Saxony sheep, – lbs.; Merino Wool produced, – lbs.; all other Wool produced, 287 lbs.

Horses, 211; val. of horses, $16,156; Oxen over three years old, 90; Steers under three years old, 47; val. of oxen and steers, $10,785; Milch Cows, 420; Heifers, 82; val. of cows and heifers, $12,161.

Butter, 12,358 lbs.; val. of butter, $2,471.60; Cheese, 8,538 lbs.; val. of cheese, $1,024.76.

Indian Corn, 275 acres; Indian Corn, per acre, 28½ bush.; val., $7,637.

Wheat, 2¼ acres; Wheat, per acre, 31¼ bush.; val., $170.

Rye, 92 acres; Rye, per acre, 10 bush.; val., $1,380.

Barley, 9 acres; Barley, per acre, 18 bush.; val., $165.

Oats, 97 acres; Oats, per acre, 14 bush.; val., $819.60.

Potatoes, 187 acres; Potatoes, per acre, 61 bush.; val., $6,844.20.

Turnips, cultivated as a field crop, 8 acres; Turnips, per acre, 81 bush.; val., $120.

English Mowing, 1,602 acres; English Hay, 871 tons; val., $17,420.

Wet Meadow or Swale Hay, 521 tons; val., $5,210.

Apple Trees, cultivated for their fruit, 3,428; val., $1,389.

Pear Trees, cultivated for their fruit, 150; val., $93.

Cranberries, 22 acres; val., $1,440.

Establishments for m. of boxes, 1; cap., $2,000; val. of boxes m'd., $6,000; emp., 3.

Round Timber sent to market, 500 tons; val., $3,000.

Swine, 367; val., $3,070.

PAWTUCKET.

Cotton Mills, 6; Spindles, 16,522; Cotton consumed, 794,000 lbs.; Cloth m'd., 3,498,900 yds., about one-half Print Cloth, ¾ y'd. wide; 1,592,000 yds. Shirting, ¾ and ⅛ y'd. wide; about 220,000 yds. for Sheeting, 1 y'd. wide; val. of cloth, $234,700;

Yarn m'd., 40,000 lbs.; val. of yarn, $12,800; Batting m'd., 104,000 lbs.; val. of batting, $7,800; cap., $283,000; m. emp., 102; f. emp., 226.

Calico Manufactories, 1; Calico printed, 16,500,000 yds.; val. of calico, $1,650,000; Goods bleached and colored and not printed, 1,000,000 yds.; val. of goods bleached, &c., $70,000; cap., $700,000; m. emp., 300; f. emp., 75.

Saddle, Harness and Trunk Manufactories, 1; val. of saddles, &c., $2,000; cap., $600; emp., 3.

Establishments for m. of railroad cars, coaches, chaises, wagons, sleighs, and other vehicles, 1; val. of railroad cars, &c., m'd., $3,100; cap., $2,000; emp., 2.

Establishments for m. of soap and tallow candles, 1; Soap m'd., 625 bbls.; val. of soap, $1,575; cap., $400; emp., 3.

Tin Ware Manufactories, 1; val. of tin ware, $10,000; cap., $5,000; emp., 5.

Lumber prepared for market, 44,000 ft.; val. of lumber, $759; emp., 4.

Firewood prepared for market, 950 cords; val. of firewood, $4,700; emp., 8.

Horses, 147; val. of horses, $14,000; Oxen over three years old, 8; Steers under three years old, –; val. of oxen and steers, $800; Milch Cows, 155; Heifers, 5; val. of cows and heifers, $4,500.

Indian Corn, 106 acres; Indian Corn, per acre, 25 bush.; val., $2,600.

Rye, 40 acres; Rye, per acre, 10 bush.; val., $600.

Oats, 10 acres; Oats, per acre, 10 bush.; val., $60.

Potatoes, 64 acres; Potatoes, per acre, 75 bush.; val., $2,400.

Millet, 4 acres; val., $120.

English Mowing, 114 acres; English Hay, 125 tons; val., $3,100.

Wet Meadow or Swale Hay, 25 tons; val., $375.

Bakeries, 1; cap., $3,000; Flour consumed, 1,600 bbls.; val. of bread m'd., $20,000; emp., 10.

Establishments for m. of boxes, 1; cap., $2,000; val. of boxes m'd., $10,000; emp., 5.

Swine, 200 ; val., $1,600.

White Beans, 1 acre ; White Beans, per acre, 6 bush. ; val., $15.

RAYNHAM.

Rolling, Slitting and Nail Mills, 3 ; Machines for m. of nails, 134 ; Nails m'd., 5,749 tons ; val. of nails, $493,814 ; cap., $57,700 ; emp., 125.

Forges, 1 ; Bar Iron, Anchors, Chain Cables, and other articles of wrought iron, m'd., 250 tons ; val. of bar iron, &c., $35,000 ; cap., $20,000 ; emp., 15.

Tack and Brad Manufactories, 3 ; Tacks and Brads m'd., 85 tons ; val. of tacks and brads, $18,260 ; cap., $1,300 ; emp., 8.

Manufactories of shovels, spades, forks and hoes, 2 ; val. of shovels, &c., $24,000 ; cap., $9,000 ; emp., 24.

Establishments for m. of railroad cars, coaches, chaises, wagons, sleighs, and other vehicles, 2 ; val. of railroad cars, &c., m'd., $500 ; cap., $250 ; emp., 3.

Boots of all kinds m'd., – pairs ; Shoes of all kinds m'd., 250,000 pairs ; val. of boots and shoes, $250,000 ; m. emp., 120 ; f. emp., 80.

Bricks m'd., 300,000 ; val. of bricks, $800 ; emp., 2.

Charcoal m'd., 1,000 bush. ; val. of same, $100.

Lumber prepared for market, 840,000 shingles, 312,500 ft. ; val. of lumber, $7,144 ; emp., 14.

Firewood prepared for market, 2,571 cords ; val. of firewood, $9,037 ; emp., 8.

Alewives, Shad and Salmon taken, 125,000 ; val. of same, $1,000 ; emp., 2.

Saxony Sheep, of different grades, – ; Merino Sheep, of different grades, 2 ; all other kinds of Sheep, 91 ; val. of all sheep, $265 ; Wool produced from Saxony sheep, – lbs. ; Merino Wool produced, 2 lbs. ; all other Wool produced, 207 lbs.

Horses, 194; val. of horses, $16,643; Oxen over three years old, 140; Steers under three years old, 20; val. of oxen and steers, $6,652; Milch Cows, 352; Heifers, 38; val. of cows and heifers, $10,247.

Butter, 8,110 lbs.; val. of butter, $2,027.50; Cheese, 5,329 lbs.; val. of cheese, $639.48; Honey, 780 lbs.; val. of honey, $156.

Indian Corn, 288 acres; Indian Corn, per acre, $2\frac{29}{144}$ bush.; val., $5,813.

Wheat, 1 acre; Wheat, per acre, 14 bush.; val., $25.

Rye, 40 acres; Rye, per acre, 52 bush.; val., $423.

Barley, $5\frac{1}{2}$ acres; Barley, per acre, 14 bush.; val., $78.

Oats, $117\frac{1}{2}$ acres; Oats, per acre, $12\frac{2}{2}\frac{1}{3}$ bush.; val., $1,060.

Potatoes, 162 acres; Potatoes, per acre, $49\frac{3}{4}$ bush.; val., $5,932.50.

Turnips, cultivated as a field crop, $9\frac{3}{4}$ acres; Turnips, per acre, $142\frac{1}{2}$ bush.; val., $560.

Carrots, $1\frac{1}{8}$ acre; Carrots, per acre, 392 bush.; val., $78.40.

Millet, $1\frac{3}{4}$ acre; val., $25.

English Mowing, 1,445 acres; English Hay, 883 tons; val., $17,660.

Wet Meadow or Swale Hay, 348 tons; val., $3,480.

Apple Trees, cultivated for their fruit, 8,470; val., $1,178.

Pear Trees, cultivated for their fruit, 524; val., $88.

Cranberries, 8 acres; val., $396.

Beeswax, 5 lbs.; val., $1.67.

Swine, 336; val., $2,654.

REHOBOTH.

Cotton Mills, 3; Spindles, 2,504; Cotton consumed, 185,000 lbs.; Cloth, m'd., 350,000 yds. Printing Cloths, 60 x 64; val. of cloth, $17,000; Batting m'd., 85,000 lbs.; val. of batting, $5,100; cap., $32,000; m. emp., 29; f. emp., 34.

Val. of snuff, tobacco and cigars, $450; m. emp., 1.

Charcoal m'd., 50,100 bush.; val. of same, $12,525; emp., 35.

Val. of wooden ware not otherwise enumerated, including farming utensils m'd., $1,200; emp., 3.

Lumber prepared for market, 311,000 ft.; val. of lumber, $1,075; emp., 3.

Firewood prepared for market, 2,717 cords; val. of firewood, $10,868; emp., 40.

Alewives, Shad and Salmon taken, 3,500; val. of same, $320; emp., 4.

Saxony Sheep, of different grades, –; Merino Sheep, of different grades, –; all other kinds of Sheep, 371; val. of all sheep, $985; Wool produced from Saxony sheep, – lbs.; Merino Wool produced, – lbs.; all other Wool produced, 1,030 lbs.

Horses, 324; val. of horses, $21,329; Oxen over three years old, 284; Steers under three years old, 69; val. of oxen and steers, $13,613; Milch Cows, 755; Heifers, 163; val. of cows and heifers, $25,648.

Butter, 43,837 lbs.; val. of butter, $8,767.40; Cheese, 16,861 lbs.; val. of cheese, $1,686.10; Honey, 180 lbs.; val. of honey, $36.

Indian Corn, 754 acres; Indian Corn, per acre, 25 bush.; val., $18,660.

Rye, 195 acres; Rye, per acre, 9 bush.; val., $1,785.

Oats, 279 acres; Oats, per acre, 16¾ bush.; val., $2,332.

Potatoes, 306 acres; Potatoes, per acre, 66 bush.; val., $15,135

Beets and other esculent vegetables, – acres; val., $–; all other Grain or Root Crops, 15 acres; val., $3,500.

English Mowing, 2,995 acres; English Hay, 1,946 tons; val., $36,028.

Wet Meadow or Swale Hay, 982 tons; val., $8,838.

Salt Hay, 34 tons; val., $340.

Apple Trees, cultivated for their fruit, 12,135; val., $3,850.

Pear Trees, cultivated for their fruit, 140; val., $75.

Cranberries, 10 acres; val., $891.

Twine m'd., 125,000 lbs.; val., $15,000.

Val. of ring travellers, for cotton manufacturers, baskets and wood turning, $1,500; cap., $3,000; emp., 2.

Swine, 694; val., $6,623.

Milk, 20,125 galls.; val., $2,415.

Hogshead Hoops, prepared for market, 333,800; val., $6,676.

Nail Keg Hoops, 597,000; val., $1,791; emp., 16.

SEEKONK.

Cotton Mills, 3; Spindles, 3,700; Cotton consumed, 30,000 lbs.; Cloth m'd., 85,000 yds. 52 x 56 Prints; val. of cloth, $4,500; cap., $5,000; m. emp., 27; f. emp., 27.

Saddle, Harness and Trunk Manufactories, 1; val. of saddles, &c., $200; cap., $50; emp., 1.

Establishments for m. of railroad cars, coaches, chaises, wagons, sleighs, and other vehicles, 2; val. of railroad cars, &c., m'd., $650; cap., $150; emp., 3.

Boots of all kinds m'd., 100 pairs; Shoes of all kinds m'd., 25 pairs; val. of boots and shoes, $450; m. emp., 1.

Bricks m'd., 400,000; val. of bricks, $2,500; emp., 10.

Val. of snuff, tobacco and cigars, $800; m. emp., 3.

Val. of building stone quarried and prepared for building, $1,500; emp., 3.

Lumber prepared for market, 365,000 ft.; val. of lumber, $4,500; emp., 3.

Firewood prepared for market, 2,396 cords; val. of firewood, $9,584; emp., 24.

Horses, 255; val. of horses, $20,455; Oxen over three years old, 194; Steers under three years old, 33; val. of oxen and steers, $11,410; Milch Cows, 683; Heifers, 99; val. of cows and heifers, $22,307.

Butter, 17,628 lbs.; val. of butter, $3,526; Cheese, 1,050 lbs.; val. of cheese, $105; Honey, 100 lbs.; val. of honey, $20.

Indian Corn, 667 acres; Indian Corn, per acre, 24⅔ bush.; val., $16,599.

Wheat, 3 acres; Wheat, per acre, 15 bush.; val., $90.

Rye, 262 acres; Rye, per acre, 9 bush.; val., $2,357.50.

Barley, 4 acres; Barley, per acre, 10 bush.; val., $40.

Oats, 147 acres; Oats, per acre, 18 bush.; val., $1,402.

Potatoes, 184 acres; Potatoes, per acre, 74 bush.; val., $16,240.

Onions, 4 acres; Onions, per acre, 280 bush.; val., $570.

Turnips, cultivated as a field crop, 4 acres; Turnips, per acre, 220 bush.; val., $170.

Carrots, 4 acres; Carrots, per acre, 300 bush.; val., $240.

Beets and other esculent vegetables, 10 acres; val., $500.

Millet, 21 acres; val., $450.

English Mowing, 2,564 acres; English Hay, 2,297 tons; val., $45,940.

Wet Meadow or Swale Hay, 576 tons; val., $5,760.

Salt Hay, 93 tons; val., $950.

Apple Trees, cultivated for their fruit, 10,886; val., $3,867.

Pear Trees, cultivated for their fruit, 1,315; val., $195.

Basket Willow cultivated, 3 acres; val., $15.

Cranberries, 19 acres; val., $560.

Establishments for m. of pails and tubs, 1; val. of pails and tubs m'd., $1,000.

SOMERSET.

Furnaces for m. of hollow ware and castings other than pig iron, 1; Hollow Ware and other Castings m'd., 9,300 tons; val. of hollow ware and castings, $32,000; cap., $25,000; emp., 25.

Vessels launched during said year, 6; Tonnage, 2,150 tons; cap., $168,000; emp., 115.

Chair and Cabinet Manufactories, 1; val. of chairs and cabinet ware, $150; cap., $200; emp., 1.

Tin Ware Manufactories, 1; val. of tin ware, $800; cap., $300; emp., 2.

Boots of all kinds m'd., 100 pairs; Shoes of all kinds m'd., 1,500 pairs; val. of boots and shoes, $2,050; m. emp., 4.

Bricks m'd., 240,000; val. of bricks, $7,200; emp., 10.

Firewood prepared for market, 136 cords; val. of firewood, $680; emp., 6.

Alewives, Shad and Salmon taken, 150,000; val. of same, $7,500; emp., 10.

Saxony Sheep, of different grades, –; Merino Sheep, of different grades, –; all other kinds of Sheep, 446; val. of all sheep, $1,374; Wool produced from Saxony sheep, – lbs.; Merino Wool produced, – lbs.; all other Wool produced, 1,488 lbs.

Horses, 117; val. of horses, $12,161; Oxen over three years old, 123; Steers under three years old, 99; val. of oxen and steers, $9,935; Milch Cows, 207; Heifers 27; val. of cows and heifers, $4,581.

Butter, 10,690 lbs.; val. of butter, $2,681; Cheese, 1,200 lbs.; val. of cheese, $149; Honey, 50 lbs.; val. of honey, $10.

Indian Corn, 299 acres; Indian Corn, per acre, 30 bush.; val., $8,970.

Rye, 58 acres; Rye, per acre, 20 bush.; val., $1,160.

Barley, 12 acres; Barley, per acre, 25 bush.; val., $300.

Oats, 168 acres; Oats, per acre, 35 bush.; val., $2,940.

Potatoes, 117 acres; Potatoes, per acre, 85 bush.; val., $7,020.

Onions, 7 acres; Onions, per acre, 400 bush.; val., $1,400.

Turnips, cultivated as a field crop, 5 acres; Turnips, per acre, 500 bush.; val., $625.

Carrots, 1 acre; Carrots, per acre, 800 bush.; val., $100.

Beets and other esculent vegetables, 2 acres; val., $200.

Millet, 2 acres; val., $24.

English Mowing, 1,265 acres; English Hay, 1,665 tons; val., $29,970.

Wet Meadow or Swale Hay, 9 tons; val., $100.

Salt Hay, 34 tons; val., 269.

Apple Trees, cultivated for their fruit, 3,338; val., $1,675.

Pear Trees, cultivated for their fruit, 414; val., $179.

Establishments for m. of stone and earthenware, 4; cap., $15,500; val. of stone and earthenware, $13,200; emp., 16.

Bakeries, 1; cap., $400; val. of bread m'd., $1,000; emp., 2.

Rolling, Slitting and Nail Mills, 1 erecting; cap., $60,000 assessed and paid in.

SWANZEY.

Vessels launched during said year, 2; Tonnage, 1,500 tons; cap., $50,000; emp., 20.

Establishments for m. of railroad cars, coaches, chaises, wagons, sleighs, and other vehicles, 3; val. of railroad cars, &c., m'd., $2,000; cap., $900; emp., 7.

Tanneries, 1; Hides of all kinds tanned, 725; val. of leather tanned, $2,200; cap., $2,000; emp., 1.

Boots of all kinds m'd., – pairs; Shoes of all kinds m'd., 10,000 pairs; val. of boots and shoes, $8,000; m. emp., 16; f. emp., 16.

Firewood prepared for market, 982 cords; val. of firewood, $3,437; emp., 4.

Alewives, Shad and Salmon taken, 5,537; val. of same, $430; emp., 4.

Saxony Sheep, of different grades, –; Merino Sheep, of different grades, 227; all other kinds of Sheep, 227; val. of all sheep, $1,021; Wool produced from Saxony sheep, – lbs.; Merino Wool produced, 675 lbs.; all other Wool produced, 605 lbs.

Horses, 187; val. of horses, $15,560; Oxen over three years old, 167; Steers under three years old, 119; val. of oxen and

steers, $10,977; Milch Cows, 405; Heifers, 83; val. of cows and heifers, $12,832.

Butter, 24,229 lbs.; val. of butter, $5,338; Cheese, 3,745 lbs.; val. of cheese, $374.

Indian Corn, 556 acres; Indian Corn, per acre, 25 bush.; val., $14,333.

Rye, 189 acres; Rye, per acre, 13 bush.; val., $2,261.

Barley, 14 acres; Barley, per acre, 22 bush.; val., $306.

Oats, 287 acres; Oats, per acre, 26 bush.; val., $3,691.

Potatoes, 246 acres; Potatoes, per acre, 64 bush.; val., $7,909.

Onions, 2 acres; Onions, per acre, 300 bush.; val., $300.

Turnips, cultivated as a field crop, 4 acres; Turnips, per acre, 400 bush.; val., $266.

English Mowing, 1,885 acres; English Hay, 1,737 tons; val., $27,792.

Wet Meadow or Swale Hay, 195 tons; val., $1,365.

Salt Hay, 125 tons; val., $1,000.

Apple Trees, cultivated for their fruit, 11,381; val., $2,000.

Pear Trees, cultivated for their fruit, 160; val., $50.

Cranberries, 2 acres; val., $210.

Hoops m'd., 15,200; val., $3,000.

Swine, 414; val., $3,257.

Timber, 50 tons; val., $300.

Quince Trees, 175.

TAUNTON.

Cotton Mills, 5; Spindles, 22,087; Cotton consumed, 1,426,355 lbs.; Cloth m'd., 4,331,504 yds., viz.: Printing Cloths, 1,853,000 yds., Jeans, 1,785,000 yds., Cotton Flannel, 693,504 yds.; val. of cloth, $354,415; cap., $302,000; m. emp., 187; f. emp., 349.

Woollen Mills, 1; Sets of Machinery, 5; Wool consumed,

90,000 lbs.; Cassimere m'd., 90,000 yds.; val. of cassimere, $95,000; cap., $30,000; m. emp., 50; f. emp., 18.

Rolling, Slitting and Nail Mills, 1; Iron m'd. and not made into nails, 1,565; val. of iron, $140,850; cap., $130,000; emp., 240.

Furnaces for m. of hollow ware and castings other than pig iron, 4; Hollow Ware and other Castings m'd., 1,410 tons; val. of hollow ware and castings, $122,000; cap., $66,000; emp., 119.

Establishments for m. of cotton, woollen and other machinery, 2; val. of machinery m'd., $340,000; cap., $250,000; emp., 480.

Establishments for m. of steam-engines and boilers, 2; val. of steam-engines and boilers, $325,000; cap., $275,000; emp., 400.

Screw Manufactories, 1; Screws m'd., 400,000 gross; val. of screws, $150,000; cap., $105,000; emp., 200.

Tack and Brad Manufactories, 4; Tacks and Brads m'd., 1,635 tons; val. of tacks and brads, $312,500; cap., $172,000; emp., 195.

Manufactories of shovels, spades, forks and hoes, 1; val. of shovels, &c., $35,000; cap., $20,000; emp., 40.

Copper Manufactories, 1; Copper m'd., 1,000 tons; val., $500,000; cap., $240,000; emp., 90.

Brass Founderies, 1; val. of articles m'd., $4,000; cap., $1,500; emp., 4.

Establishments for m. of britannia ware, 4; val. of britannia ware, $99,000; cap., $56,000; emp., 160.

Paper Manufactories, 1; Stock made use of, 300,000 lbs.; Paper m'd., 250,000 reams; val. of paper, $25,000; cap., $1,600; emp., 14.

Daguerreotype Artists, 2; Daguerreotypes taken, 2,715; cap., $1,200; emp., 2.

Saddle, Harness and Trunk Manufactories, 5; val. of saddles, &c., $4,373; cap., $2,550; emp., 14.

Upholstery Manufactories, 1; val. of upholstery, $3,000; cap., $1,200; emp., 2.

Vessels launched during said year, 1; Tonnage, 150 tons; cap., $2,000; emp., 10.

Establishments for m. of boats, 1; Boats built, 2; cap., $60; emp., 1.

Sail Lofts, 1; Sails made of Am. fabric, 30; of For. fabric, 10; val. of sails m'd. of Am. fabric, $1,500; val. of sails of For. fabric, $500; cap., $150; emp., 4.

Establishments for m. of railroad cars, coaches, chaises, wagons, sleighs, and other vehicles, 4; val. of railroad cars, &c., m'd., $2,290; cap., $1,420; emp., 9.

Establishments for m. of soap and tallow candles, 2; Soap m'd., 628 lbs.; val. of soap, $3,140; cap., $3,000; emp., 4.

Tin Ware Manufactories, 4; val. of tin ware, $6,500; cap., $4,800; emp., 10.

Tanneries, 1; Hides of all kinds tanned, 600; val. of leather tanned, $1,900; cap., $700; emp., 2.

Boots of all kinds m'd., 800 pairs; Shoes of all kinds m'd., 21,500 pairs; val. of boots and shoes, $21,366; m. emp., 26; f. emp., 6.

Bricks m'd., 4,980,000; val. of bricks, $32,690; emp., 62.

Val. of cigars m'd., $2,000; cap., $500; m. emp., 5.

Val. of building stone quarried and prepared for building, $5,000; emp., 21.

Charcoal m'd., 6,400 bush.; val. of same, $760; emp., 6.

Val. of mechanics' tools m'd., $50,000; emp., 66.

Lumber prepared for market, 183,000 ft.; val. of lumber, $3,176; emp., 7.

Firewood prepared for market, 5,300 cords; val. of firewood, $21,380; emp., 126.

Saxony Sheep, of different grades, 174; val. of all sheep, $585; Wool produced from Saxony sheep, - lbs.; all other Wool produced, 505 lbs.

Horses, 758; val. of horses, $70,532; Oxen over three years old, 203; Steers under three years old, 84; val. of oxen and steers, $11,813; Milch Cows, 823; Heifers, 113; val. of cows and heifers, $23,554.

Butter, 26,037 lbs.; val. of butter, $5,207; Cheese, 8,600

lbs.; val. of cheese, $860; Honey, 202 lbs.; val. of honey, $35.

Indian Corn, 474 acres; Indian Corn, per acre, 25 bush.; val., $11,850.

Wheat, 2 acres; Wheat, per acre, 19 bush.; val., $75.

Rye, 146 acres; Rye, per acre, 9 bush.; val., $1,971.

Barley, 11 acres; Barley, per acre, 12 bush.; val., $165.

Oats, 32 acres; Oats, per acre, 14 bush.; val., $223.

Potatoes, 298 acres; Potatoes, per acre, 65 bush.; val., $13,777.

Turnips, cultivated as a field crop, 12 acres; Turnips, per acre, 150 bush.; val., $450.

Carrots, 1 acre; Carrots, per acre, 300 bush.; val., $66.

English Mowing, 2,472 acres; English Hay, 2,361 tons; val., $47,220.

Wet Meadow or Swale Hay, 556 tons; val., $5,560.

Apple Trees, cultivated for their fruit, 12,024; val., $4,000.

Pear Trees, cultivated for their fruit, 10,000; val., $1,000.

Cranberries, 33 acres; val., $778.

Establishments for m. of casks, 2; cap., $16,000; Casks m'd., 270,000; val., $33,500; emp., 45.

Establishments for m. of stone and earthenware, 1; cap., $1,500; val. of stone and earthenware, $15,000; emp., 5.

Establishments for m. of sashes and door blinds, 2; cap., $9,000; val. m'd., $15,000; emp., 15.

Establishments for m. of gas, 1; cap., $60,000; val. m'd., $100,000; emp., 5.

Bakeries, 3; cap., $2,500; Flour consumed, 1,300 bbls.; val. of bread m'd., $24,000; emp., 10.

Establishments for m. of boxes, (candle and soap,) 2; cap., $9,500; val. of boxes m'd., $27,000; emp., 13.

Swine, 1,279; val., $17,419.

File Manufactories, 2; val., $6,400; cap., $1,300; emp., 13.

Ice Establishments, 2; cap., $6,000; val. of ice, $10,000; number of tons, 13,200; emp., 10.

Crucible Manufactory, 1; cap., $11,000; val., $36,000; emp., 25.

Establishments for m. of stove linings, 2 ; cap., $2,100 ; val., $7,500 ; emp., 7.

Oil Cloth Manufactories, 1 ; cap., $8,000 ; val., $37,000 ; emp., 18.

Car Lining Manufactories, 1 ; cap., $5,000 ; val., $10,000 ; emp., 14.

Marble Manufactories, 2 ; cap., $2,000 ; val., $9,000 ; emp., 15.

Shingle Mills, 1 ; cap., $200 ; val., $1,500.

Grist Mills, 5 ; cap., $7,000 ; grain ground, 8,000 bush. ; emp., 5.

Steam Grist Mills, 1 ; cap., $8,000 ; grain ground, 100,000 bush. ; emp., 3.

Copper and Brass Kettle Manufactories, 1 ; cap., $25,000 ; val. m'd., $109,000 ; number of kettles m'd., 300,000 ; emp., 10.

Knob Manufactories, 1 ; cap., $500 ; val., $1,000 ; emp., 2.

WESTPORT.

Cotton Mills, 1 ; Spindles, 808 ; Cotton consumed, 20,000 lbs. ; Carpet Warp m'd., 16,000 lbs. ; val. of carpet warp, $2,250.

Saddle, Harness, and Trunk Manufactories, 1 ; val. of saddles, &c., $500 ; cap., $200 ; emp., 2.

Vessels launched during said year, 1 ; Tonnage, 326 tons ; cap., $1,000 ; emp., 15.

Sail Lofts, 1 ; Sails made of Am. fabric, 52 ; of For. fabric, 9 ; val. of sails m'd. of Am. fabric, 2,550 ; val. of sails of For. fabric, $400 ; cap., $800 ; emp., 3.

Establishments for m. of railroad cars, coaches, chaises, wagons, sleighs, and other vehicles, 3 ; val. of railroad cars, &c., m'd., $6,000 ; cap., $3,000 ; emp., 10.

Tanneries, 1 ; Hides of all kinds tanned, 200 ; val. of leather tanned, $650 ; cap., $500 ; emp., 1.

Boots of all kinds m'd., 200 pairs ; Shoes of all kinds m'd., 500 pairs ; val. of boots and shoes, $1,400 ; m. emp., 4.

Charcoal m'd., 6,000 bush. ; val. of same, $1,000 ; emp., 1.

Val. of wooden ware not otherwise enumerated, including farming utensils m'd., $200.

Lumber prepared for market, 300,000 ft.; val. of lumber, $6,000; emp., 2.

Firewood prepared for market, 2,700 cords; val. of firewood, $8,100.

Vessels employed in the whale fishery, 22; Tonnage, 4,592 tons; Sperm Oil imported, 70,245 galls.; val. of sperm oil imported, $105,000; Whale Oil imported, 15,200 galls.; val. of whale oil imported, $9,120; Whalebone imported, 1,100 lbs.; val. of whalebone imported, $440; cap. in the whale fishery, $355,000; emp., 462.

Vessels employed in the tautog and lobster fisheries, 11; Tonnage, 185 tons; val. of fish taken, $11,000; cap., $7,500; emp., 31.

Alewives, Shad and Salmon taken, 50,000; val. of same, $250.

Saxony Sheep, of different grades, –; Merino Sheep, of different grades, –; all other kinds of Sheep, 2,019; val. of all sheep, $4,780; Wool produced from Saxony sheep, – lbs.; Merino Wool produced, – lbs.; all other Wool produced, 3,829 lbs.

Horses, 337; val. of horses, $26,293; Oxen over three years old, 392; Steers under three years old, 85; val. of oxen and steers, $23,691; Milch Cows, 855; Heifers, 146; val. of cows and heifers, $27,849.

Butter, 41,825 lbs.; val. of butter, $9,830; Cheese, 8,000 lbs.; val. of cheese, $800; Honey, 678 lbs.; val. of honey, $83.50.

Indian Corn, 696½ acres; Indian Corn, per acre, 28⅔ bush.; val., $19,971.

Wheat, ¾ acre; Wheat, per acre, 14 bush.; val., $20.

Rye, 20 acres; Rye, per acre, 12 bush.; val., $525.

Barley, 36 acres; Barley, per acre, 24 bush.; val., $965.

Oats, 270 acres; Oats, per acre, 27½ bush.; val., $4,000.

Potatoes, 112 acres; Potatoes, per acre, 86 bush.; val., $7,500.

Onions, 1¾ acre; Onions, per acre, 375 bush.; val., $325.

Turnips, cultivated as a field crop, 62 acres; Turnips, per acre, 216 bush.; val., $3,375.

Carrots, 1 acre; Carrots, per acre, 550 bush.; val., $110.

Beets and other esculent vegetables, ½ acre; val., $75; all other Grain or Root Crops, 75 acres; val., $3,000.

English Mowing, 4,086 acres; English Hay, 2,923 tons; val., $43,800.

Wet Meadow or Swale Hay, 10 tons; val., $50.

Salt Hay, 200 tons; val., $1,000.

Apple Trees, cultivated for their fruit, 16,163; val., $5,121.

Pear Trees, cultivated for their fruit, 163; val., $66.

Cranberries, 6 acres; val., $130.

Beeswax, 30 lbs.; val., $10.

Establishments for m. of casks, 3; cap., $1,500; Casks m'd., 560; val., $3,750; emp., 7.

Establishments for m. of rules, 1; cap., $4,000; val. of rules, $6,000; m. emp., 16; f. emp., 2.

Establishments for m. of candle, soap, and other kinds of boxes, 1; cap., $4,000; val. of boxes m'd., $1,200; emp., 4.

Val. of spokes, felloes and hubs m'd., $1,500; cap., $2,000; emp., 2.

Swine, 758; val., $5,468.

Val. of spool blocks m'd., $1,000.

Milk carried to market, 115,000 qts.; val., $5,000.

DUKES COUNTY.

CHILMARK.

Bricks m'd., 700,000; val. of bricks, $3,000; emp., 14.

Saxony Sheep, of different grades, –; Merino Sheep, of different grades, –; all other kinds of Sheep, 6,088; val. of all sheep, $13,720; Wool produced from Saxony sheep, – lbs.;

Merino Wool produced, – lbs.; all other Wool produced, 12,037 lbs.

Horses, 131; val. of horses, $8,245; Oxen over three years old, 165; Steers under three years old, 189; val. of oxen and steers, $14,129; Milch Cows, 289; Heifers, 158; val. of cows and heifers, $11,155.

Butter, 10,342 lbs.; val. of butter, $2,275; Cheese, 2,987 lbs.; val. of cheese, $373.

Indian Corn, 168 acres; Indian Corn, per acre, 27 bush.; val., $5,443.

Rye, 28 acres; Rye, per acre, 6 bush.; val., $252.

Oats, 93 acres; Oats, per acre, 18 bush.; val. $1,004.

Potatoes, 30 acres; Potatoes, per acre, 59 bush.; val., $1,170.

Turnips cultivated as a field crop, 6 acres; Turnips, per acre, 264 bush.; val., $713.

English Mowing, 629 acres; English Hay, 755 tons; val., $10,570.

Wet Meadow or Swale Hay, 293 tons; val., $2,051.

Salt Hay, 203 tons; val., $1,827.

Apple Trees, cultivated for their fruit, 1,521; val., $521.

Pear Trees, cultivated for their fruit, 118; val., $100.

Swine, 146; val., $1,460.

EDGARTOWN.

Establishments for m. of boats, 2; Boats built, 30; cap., $500; emp., 4.

Sail Lofts, 1; Sails made of Am. fabric, 100; val. of sails m'd. of Am. fabric, $2,200; cap., $200; emp., 2.

Establishments for m. of salt, 1; Salt m'd., 75 bush.; val. of salt, $37; cap., $100; emp., 1.

Establishments for m. of oil and sperm candles, 1; Whale Oil m'd., 449,000 galls.; Sperm, 10,380 galls.; val. of oil m'd., $448,215; Sperm Candles m'd., 68,800 lbs.; val. of sperm candles, $20,640; cap., $100,000; emp., 12.

Tin Ware Manufactories, 1; val. of tin ware, $200; cap., $500; emp., 1.

Boots of all kinds m'd., 50 pairs; Shoes of all kinds m'd., 300 pairs; val. of boots and shoes, $675; m. emp., 2.

Val. of blocks and pumps m'd., $300; emp., 2.

Firewood prepared for market, 100 cords; val. of firewood, $600; emp., 2.

Vessels employed in the whale fishery, 12; Tonnage, 3,863 tons; Sperm Oil imported, 3,150 galls.; val. of sperm oil imported, $5,550; Whale Oil imported, 63,000 galls., val. of whale oil imported, $37,800; Whalebone imported, 20,000 lbs.; val. of whalebone imported, $6,000; cap. in the whale fishery, $390,000; emp., 360.

Saxony Sheep, of different grades, –; Merino Sheep, of different grades, –; all other kinds of Sheep, 800; val. of all sheep, $1,700; Wool produced from Saxony sheep, – lbs.; Merino Wool produced, – lbs.; all other Wool produced, 2,000 lbs.

Horses, 112; val. of horses, $8,960; Oxen over three years old, 92; Steers under three years old, 55; val. of oxen and steers, $5,700; Milch Cows, 253; Heifers, 55; val. of cows and heifers, $8,690.

Butter, 6,950 lbs.; val. of butter, $1,732.

Indian Corn, 427 acres; Indian Corn, 5,027 bush.; val., $5,027.

Rye, 145 acres; Rye, 728 bush.; val., $910.

Oats, 36 acres; Oats, 365 bush.; val., $182.

Potatoes, 50 acres; Potatoes, per acre, 120 bush.; val., $6,000.

Turnips, cultivated as a field crop, 18 acres; Turnips per acre, 120 bush.; val., $900.

English Mowing, 500 acres; English Hay, 542 tons; val., $8,672.

Wet Meadow or Swale Hay, 189 tons; val., $1,700.

Salt Hay, 67 tons; val., $600.

Cranberries, 6 acres; val., $162.

Establishments for m. of casks, 1; cap., $500; Casks m'd., 1,000; val., $1,200; emp., 2.

Bakeries, 1; cap., $600; Flour consumed, 300 bbls; val. of bread m'd., $6,000; emp., 3.

TISBURY.

Woollen Mills, [number not given]; Satinet m'd., 3,000 yds.; val. of satinet, $1,500; Flannel or Blanketing, 5,000 yds.; val. of flannel or blanketing, $1,900; m. emp., 2; f. emp., 3.

Establishments for m. of hosiery, –; Yarn m'd. and not made into hosiery, 3,500 lbs.; val. of yarn, $3,040; m. emp., 2; f. emp., 3.

Vessels launched during said year, 1; Tonnage, 192 tons; cap. $11,000; emp. 7.

Tanneries, 1; Hides of all kinds tanned, 600; val. of leather tanned, $2,500; cap., $3,500; emp., 2.

Boots of all kinds m'd., 275 pairs; Shoes of all kinds m'd., 725 pairs; val. of boots and shoes, $2,393.75; m. emp., 5.

Firewood prepared for market, 470 cords; val. of firewood, $3,290.

Alewives, Shad and Salmon taken, 600,000; val. of same, $3,000; emp., 65.

Saxony Sheep, of different grades, –; Merino Sheep, of different grades, 1,351; all other kinds of Sheep, 899; val. of all sheep, $6,187.50; Wool produced from Saxony sheep, – lbs.; Merino Wool produced, 3,650 lbs.; all other Wool produced, 2,204 lbs.

Horses, 124; val. of horses, $11,090; Oxen over three years old, 90; Steers under three years old, 57; val. of oxen and steers, $6,090; Milch Cows, 222; Heifers, 65; val. of cows and heifers, $8,404.

Butter, 11,090 lbs.; val. of butter, $3,105.20; Cheese, 1,000 lbs.; val. of cheese, $120.

Indian Corn, 168 acres; Indian Corn, per acre, 25 bush.; val., $4,746.

Rye, 24 acres; Rye, per acre, 10 bush.; val., $360.

Barley, 2 acres; Barley, per acre, 17 bush.; val., $42.50.

Oats, 39 acres; Oats, per acre, 25 bush.; val., 604.50

Potatoes, 22 acres; Potatoes, per acre, 160 bush.; val., $2,992.

Onions, ¼ acre; Onions, per acre, 632 bush.; val., $106.

Turnips, cultivated as a field crop, 4½ acres; Turnips, per acre, 300 bush.; val. $540.

Carrots, 2 acre; Carrots, per acre, 350 bush.; val., $210.

English Mowing, 410 acres; English Hay, 513 tons; val., $7,715.

Wet Meadow or Swale Hay, 130 tons; val., $1,300.

Salt Hay, 129 tons; val., $1,032.

Apple Trees, cultivated for their fruit, 6,212; val., $1,000.

Pear Trees, cultivated for their fruit, 255; val., $50.

Cranberries, 8 acres; val., $1,135.

Establishments for m. of casks, 1; cap., $1,250; Casks m'd., 1,000; val., $1,250; emp., 1.

Codfish taken in boats, 600 quintals; val., $2,700.

Swordfish, 100 bbls.; val., $800.

Menhaden and Scuppog, 1,000 bbls.; val., $200.

ESSEX COUNTY.

AMESBURY.

Woollen Mills. [See "Salisbury" for details.]

Harness Manufactories, 4; val. of harnesses, &c., $6,210; cap., $500; emp., 6.

Hat Manufactories, 1; Hats m'd., 25,000; cap., $6,000; m. emp., 12; f. emp., 4.

Vessels launched during said year, 1; Tonnage, 500 tons.

Establishments for m. of chaises, carryalls, buggies, and other vehicles, 20; val. of chaises, carryalls, &c., m'd., $287,525; cap., $250,000; emp., 280.

Tanning and Currying establishments, 2; Hides of all kinds tanned, 4,000; val. of leather tanned and curried, $11,500; cap., $6,000; emp., 11.

Boots of all kinds m'd., 11,400 pairs; Shoes of all kinds m'd., 41,420 pairs; val. of boots and shoes, $29,136; m. emp., 54; f. emp., 40.

Bricks m'd., 300,000; val. of bricks, $1,200; emp., 3.

Lumber prepared for market, 250,000 ft.; val. of lumber, $3,000; emp., 3.

Firewood prepared for market, 100 cords; val. of firewood, $600; emp., 3.

Vessels employed in the mackerel fishery, 1; Tonnage, 45 tons; Mackerel taken, 210 bbls.; val. of mackerel taken, $1,600; Salt consumed, 200 bush.; cap., $1,000; emp., 8.

Merino Sheep, of different grades, 150; val. of all sheep, $350; Merino Wool produced, 450 lbs.

Horses, 215; val. of horses, $15,515; Oxen over three years old, 189; Steers under three years old, 49; val. of oxen and steers, $10,759; Milch Cows, 354; Heifers, 48; val. of cows and heifers, $10,585.

Butter, 18,670 lbs.; val. of butter, $4,667; Cheese, 7,764 lbs.; val. of cheese, $776.

Indian Corn, 208 acres; Indian Corn, per acre, 25 bush.; val., $5,200.

Wheat, 11 acres; Wheat, per acre, 10 bush.; val., $210.

Rye, 37 acres; Rye, per acre, 10 bush.; val., $400.

Barley, 30 acres; Barley, per acre, 18 bush.; val., $436.

Oats, 46 acres; Oats, per acre, 25 bush.; val., $500.

Potatoes, 111 acres; Potatoes, per acre, 75 bush.; val., $4,178.

Onions, 3 acres; Onions, per acre, 2 bush.; val., $300.

Carrots, 2 acres; Carrots, per acre, 350 bush.; val., $175.

Beets and other esculent vegetables, 2 acres; val. $100; all other Grain or Root Crops, 3 to 4 acres; val., $400.

English Mowing, 1,397 acres; English Hay, 1,118 tons; val., $16,770.

Wet Meadow or Swale Hay, 312 tons; val., $2,184.

Apple Trees, cultivated for their fruit, 6,984; val., $3,853.

Pear Trees, cultivated for their fruit, 300; val., $100.

Establishments for m. of stone and earthenware, 1; cap., $250; val. of stone and earthenware, $1,000.

Val. of 1,800 sets of carriage wheels m'd., $16,200; val. of "carriage stuff" sawed out, $3,500; cap., $30,000; emp., 19.

Establishments for m. of steel eliptic springs and axletrees, 1; number turned out during the year, 540 sets; val., $3,240; axletrees produced, 500 sets; val., $3,000.

Horse Collars m'd., 350; val., $525.

Swine raised, 225; val., $1,350.

ANDOVER.

Woollen Mills, 4; Sets of Machinery, 25; Wool consumed, 600,000 lbs.; Flannel or blanketing, 1,525,000 yds.; val. of flannel or blanketing, $500,000; cap., $230,000; m. emp., 171; f. emp., 160.

Establishments for m. of linen, 1; Linen Thread m'd., 1,150,000 lbs., val. of thread, $200,000; cap., $85,000; m. emp., 100; f. emp., 120.

Piano-Forte Manufactories, 1; Piano-Fortes m'd., 200; cap., $5,000; emp., 16.

Saddle, Harness and Trunk Manufactories, 1; val. of saddles, &c., $1,000; cap., $200; emp., 2.

Establishments for m. of railroad cars, coaches, chaises, wagons, sleighs, and other vehicles, 3; val. of railroad cars, &c., m'd., $3,750; cap., $3,400; emp., 8.

Establishments for m. of soap and tallow candles, 2; Soap m'd., 500,000 lbs.; val. of soap, $15,000; cap., $1,800; emp., 5.

Chair and Cabinet Manufactories, 4; val. of chairs and cabinet ware, $5,800; cap., $7,350; emp., 9.

Tin Ware Manufactories, 2; val. of tin ware, $1,500; cap., $1,000; emp., 8.

Boots of all kinds m'd., 600 pairs; Shoes of all kinds m'd., 80,134 pairs; val. of boots and shoes, $55,787; m. emp., 76; f. emp., 34.

Lumber prepared for market, 316,800 ft.; val. of lumber, $3,869; emp., 6.

Firewood prepared for market, 3,208 cords; val. of firewood, $16,040; emp., 11.

Saxony Sheep, of different grades, –; Merino Sheep, of different grades, –; all other kinds of Sheep, 19; val. of all sheep, $57; Wool produced from Saxony sheep, – lbs.; Merino Wool produced, – lbs.; all other Wool produced, 50 lbs.

Horses, 294; val. of horses, $21,855; Oxen over three years old, 222; Steers under three years old, 28; val. of oxen and steers, $15,200; Milch Cows, 619; Heifers, 92; val. of cows and heifers, $17,807.

Butter, 25,380 lbs.; val. of butter, $6,230; Cheese, 2,725 lbs.; val. of cheese, $218; Honey, 200 lbs.; val. of honey, $40.

Indian Corn, 291 acres; Indian Corn, per acre, 35 bush.; val., $10,185.

Wheat, 3¾ acres; Wheat, per acre, 23½ bush.; val., $176.

Rye, 164 acres; Rye, per acre, 13 bush.; val., $2,665.

Barley, 56½ acres; Barley, per acre, 20 bush.; val., $1,130.

Oats, 84 acres; Oats, per acre, 22 bush.; val., $1,082.40.

Potatoes, 220 acres; Potatoes, per acre, 100 bush.; val., $22,000.

Onions, 300 acres; Onions, per acre, 200 bush.; val., $150.

Turnips cultivated as a field crop, 8 acres; Turnips, per acre, 300 bush.; val., $800.

Carrots, 12 acres; Carrots, per acre, 450 bush.; val., $1,350.

Beets and other esculent vegetables, 8 acres; val., $1,280; Beans, 150 bush.; val., $300.

English Mowing, 1,541½ acres; English Hay, 1,632½ tons; val., $32,650.

Wet Meadow or Swale Hay, 759 tons; val., $7,590.

Apple Trees, cultivated for their fruit, 25,891; val., $8,581.

Pear Trees, cultivated for their fruit, 1,000; val., $500.

Cranberries, 14 acres; val., $1,400.

Establishments for m. of sashes and door blinds, 1; cap, $2,000; val. m'd., $200; emp., 3.

Bakeries, 1; cap., $200; Flour consumed, 300 bbls.; val. of bread m'd., $4,000; emp., 2.

Type and Stereotype Founderies, 1; cap., $2,000; val. of type, &c., m'd., $4,500; m. emp., 3.

Whole number of Inhabitants, 4,823; m., 2,289; f., 2,534; Houses, 689; Families, 921.

BEVERLY.

Forges, 7; Bar Iron, Anchors, Chain Cables, and other articles of wrought iron, m'd., 51; tons; val. of bar iron, &c., $9,100; cap., $7,000; Furnaces for m. of pig iron, 9.

Establishments for m. of britannia ware, 2; val. of britannia ware, $5,000; cap., $2,000; emp., 4.

Piano-Forte Manufactories, –; all other musical instrument manufactories, 1; val. of musical instruments m'd., $1,500; cap., $300; emp., 1.

Saddle, Harness and Trunk Manufactories, 1; val. of saddles, &c., $500; cap., $400; emp., 1.

Vessels launched during said year, 5; Tonnage, 579 tons; cap., $18,000; emp., 50.

Sail Lofts, 2; Sails made of Am. fabric, 82; val. of sails m'd. of Am. fabric, $5,600; cap., $2,500; emp., 6.

Establishments for m. of railroad cars, coaches, chaises, wagons, sleighs, and other vehicles, 5; val. of railroad cars, &c., m'd., $4,000; cap., $1,500; emp., 7.

Establishments for m. of soap and tallow candles, 1; Soap m'd., 100,000 lbs.; val. of soap, $5,000; Tallow Candles m'd., 25,000 lbs.; val. of tallow candles, $3,500; cap., $8,000; emp., 5.

Chair and Cabinet Manufactories, 5; val. of chairs and cabinet ware, $90,000; cap., $25,000; emp., 113.

Tin Ware Manufactories, 2; val. of tin ware, $3,000; cap., $1,500; emp., 4.

Boots of all kinds m'd., 2,600 pairs; Shoes of all kinds m'd., 285,000 pairs; val. of boots and shoes, $171,000; m. emp., 511; f. emp., 300.

Bricks m'd., 2,283,000; val. of bricks, $20,700; emp., 25.

Val. of blacking, $200; emp., 1.

Val. of blocks and pumps m'd., $1,500; emp. 2.

Corn and other brooms m'd., 250; val. of brooms, $30; emp., 2.

Firewood prepared for market, 500 cords; val. of firewood, $2,500; emp., 10.

Vessels employed in the whale fishery, 5; Tonnage, 987 tons, Sperm Oil imported, 26,845 galls; val. of sperm oil imported, $41,500; Whale Oil imported, 1,575 galls; val. of whale oil imported, $1,250; cap. in the whale fishery, $80,000; emp., 117.

Vessels employed in the mackerel and cod fisheries, 48; Tonnage, 3,680 tons; Mackerel taken, 200 bbls.; Codfish taken, 33,414 quintals; val. of mackerel taken, $1,500; val. of codfish taken, $108,600; val. of cod liver oil sold for medicinal purposes, $50; Salt consumed, 42,400 bush.; cap., $152,000; emp., 384.

Saxony Sheep, of different grades, –; Merino Sheep, of different grades, –; all other kinds of Sheep, 30; val. of all sheep, $90; Wool produced from Saxony sheep, – lbs.; Merino Wool produced, – lbs.; all other Wool produced, 120 lbs.

Horses, 334; val. of horses, $18,000; Oxen over three years old, 128; Steers under three years old, 20; val. of oxen and steers, $5,300; Milch Cows, 572; Heifers, 55; val. of cows and heifers, $14,500.

Butter, 15,000 lbs.; val. of butter, $3,750; Cheese, 1,500 lbs.; val. of cheese, $150; Honey, 500 lbs.; val. of honey, $100.

Indian Corn, 300 acres; Indian Corn per acre, 33 bush.; val., $9,900.

Wheat, 5 acres; Wheat, per acre, 20 bush.; val., $150.

Rye, 45 acres; Rye, per acre, 20 bush.; val., $1,200.

Barley, 55 acres; Barley, per acre, 18 bush.; val., $990.

Oats, 10 acres; Oats, per acre, 20 bush.; val., $100.

Potatoes, 175 acres; Potatoes, per acre, 70 bush.; val., $12,250.

Onions, 31 acres; Onions, per acre, 400 bush.; val., $6,200.

Turnips, cultivated as a field crop, 15 acres; Turnips, per acre, 400 bush; val., $1,200.

Carrots, 20 acres; Carrots, per acre, 400 bush.; val., $1,600.

Beets and other esculent vegetables, – acres; all other Grain or Root Crops, 23 acres; val., $5,100.

English Mowing, 2,590 acres; English Hay, 2,590 tons; val., $46,620.

Wet Meadow or Swale Hay, 205 tons; val., $1,640.

Salt Hay, 95 tons; val., $950.

Apple Trees, cultivated for their fruit, 6,450; val., $6,450.

Pear Trees, cultivated for their fruit, 200; val., $150.

Establishments for m. of casks, 1; cap., $200; Casks m'd., 400; val., $500; emp., 1.

Establishments for m. of India-rubber goods, 1; cap., $60,000; val. of goods m'd., 125,000; m. emp., 16; f. emp., 33.

Bakeries, 2; cap., $4,000; Flour consumed, 1,400 bbls.; val. of bread m'd., $19,000; emp., 9.

Grist Mills, 5; grinding 100,000 bushels per annum.

Turning Mills, 1; val. of labor, $250.

Mustard Factories, 1; val. of Mustard m'd., $4,000.

Ice, 400 tons; val., $1,200.

Curing fish for foreign vessels, $500.

Codfish Oil, 425 bbls.; val., $8,925.

Tongues and Sounds, 600 bbls.; val., $4,200.

Halibut salted, 2,500 quintals; val., $6,250.

Val. of curled hair m'd., $75,000; emp., 15.

BOXFORD.

Cotton Mills, 1; Spindles, 612.

Establishments for m. of railroad cars, coaches, chaises, wagons, sleighs, and other vehicles, 2; val. of railroad cars, &c., m'd., $500; cap., $1,200; emp., 4.

Boots of all kinds m'd., – pairs; Shoes of all kinds m'd., 61,550 pairs; val. of boots and shoes, $52,550; m. emp., 50; f. emp., 47.

Shoe Pegs m'd., 800 bush.; val., $800.

Lumber prepared for market, 189,000 ft.; val. of lumber, $4,507; emp., 10.

Firewood prepared for market, 1,570 cords; val. of firewood, $5,545; emp., 6.

Saxony Sheep of different grades, –; Merino Sheep, of different grades, –; all other kinds of Sheep, 333; val. of all sheep, $832; Wool produced from Saxony sheep, – lbs.; Merino Wool produced, – lbs.; all other Wool produced, 914 lbs.

Horses, 131; val. of horses, $10,535; Oxen over three years old, 117; Steers under three years old, 38; val. of oxen and steers, $12,196; Milch Cows, 412; Heifers, 64; val. of cows and heifers, $11,329.

Butter, 20,542 lbs.; val. of butter, $3,711; Cheese, 3,500 lbs.; val. of cheese, $350.

Indian Corn, 213 acres; Indian Corn, per acre, 21 bush.; val., $4,700.

Wheat, 4 acres; Wheat, per acre, 10 bush.; val., $90.

Rye, 16 acres; Rye, per acre, 12 bush.; val., $245.

Barley, 16½ acres; Barley, per acre, 17 bush.; val., $257.

Oats, 83 acres; Oats, per acre, 19 bush.; val., $1,010.

Potatoes, 79 acres; Potatoes, per acre, 66 bush.; val., $4,297.

Turnips, cultivated as a field crop, 7 acres; Turnips, per acre, 70 bush.; val., $150.

English Mowing, 1,496 acres; English Hay, 968 tons; val., $16,000.

Wet Meadow or Swale Hay, 686 tons ; val., $5,220.

Apple Trees, cultivated for their fruit, 6,180 ; val., $4,170.

Pear Trees, cultivated for their fruit, 80 ; val., $77.

Cranberries, 23 acres ; val., $288.

Establishments for m. of shoe boxes, 1 ; cap., $2,500 ; val. of boxes m'd., $3,000 ; emp., 5.

BRADFORD.

Saddle, Harness and Trunk Manufactories, 2 ; val. of saddles, &c., $1,500 ; cap., $400 ; emp., 2.

Boots of all kinds m'd., 75 pairs ; Shoes of all kinds m'd., 20,000 pairs ; val. of boots and shoes, $1,000 ; m. emp., 12 ; f. emp., 11.

Bricks m'd., 250,000 ; val. of bricks, $1,250 ; emp., 3.

Horses, 84 ; val. of horses, $9,160 ; Oxen over three years old, 94 ; Steers under three years old, 30 ; val. of oxen and steers, $6,235 ; Milch Cows, 258 ; Heifers, 30 ; val. of cows and heifers, $8,110.

Butter, 17,060 lbs. ; val. of butter, $4,265 ; Cheese, 3,825 lbs. ; val. of cheese, $382 ; Honey, 325 lbs. ; val. of honey, $60.

Indian Corn, 142 acres ; Indian Corn, per acre, 35 bush. ; val., $5,494.

Wheat, 4 acres ; Wheat, per acre, 18 bush. ; val., $144.

Rye, 17 acres ; Rye, per acre, 20 bush. ; val., $376.

Barley, 2 acres ; Barley, per acre, 25 bush. ; val., $50.

Oats, 98 acres ; Oats, per acre, 40 bush. ; val., $2,352.

Potatoes, 61 acres ; Potatoes, per acre, 100 bush. ; val., $5,490.

Onions, 1 acre ; Onions, per acre, 30 bush. ; val., $180.

Turnips, cultivated as a field crop, 4 acres ; Turnips, per acre, 150 bush. ; val., $150.

Carrots, 2 acres ; Carrots, per acre, 300 bush. ; val., $180.

English Mowing, 1,130 acres ; English Hay, 1,240 tons ; val., $18,600.

Wet Meadow or Swale Hay, 40 tons; val., $320.
Apple Trees, cultivated for their fruit, 6,850; val., $6,580.
Pear Trees, cultivated for their fruit, 420; val., $225.
Shoes made the past year, 102,700.
Jack Screws, 200; val., $1,000.

DANVERS.

Mills for m. of carpeting, 1; Wool consumed, 180,000 lbs.; Carpeting m'd., 100,000 yds.; val. of carpeting, $55,000; cap., $20,000; m. emp., 85; f. emp., 45.

Rolling, Slitting and Nail Mills, 1; Iron m'd. and not made into nails, 1,000 tons; Machines for m. of nails, 6; emp., 8.

Daguerreotype Artists, 1; emp., 1.

Saddle, Harness and Trunk Manufactories, 2; val. of saddles, &c., $5,000; cap., $3,000; emp., 3.

Vessels launched during said year, 1; Tonnage, 130 tons; cap., $5,000; emp., 11.

Establishments for m. of railroad cars, coaches, chaises, wagons, sleighs, and other vehicles, 3; val. of railroad cars, &c., m'd., $4,000; cap., $2,000; emp., 7.

Tin Ware Manufactories, 1; val. of tin ware, $5,000; cap., $2,500; emp., 2.

Tanneries, 3; Hides of all kinds tanned, 13,000; val. of leather tanned, $40,000; cap., $30,000; emp., 8.

Currying Establishments, 3; val. of leather curried, $60,000; cap., $25,000; emp., 25.

Manufactories of patent and enamelled leather, 1; val. of leather m'd., $25,000; cap., $8,000; emp., 6.

Boots of all kinds m'd., – pairs; Shoes of all kinds m'd., $1,330,000 pairs; val. of boots and shoes, $1,000,000; m. emp., 1,300; f. emp., 1,500.

Bricks m'd., 1,500,000; val. of bricks, $15,000; emp., 30.

Saxony Sheep of different grades, –; Merino Sheep of different grades, –; all other kinds of Sheep, 40; val. of all sheep,

$120 ; Wool produced from Saxony sheep, – lbs. ; Merino Wool produced, – lbs. ; all other Wool produced, 160 lbs.

Horses, 284 ; val. of horses, $28,400 ; Oxen over three years old, 84 ; Steers under three years old, – ; val. of oxen and steers, $5,040 ; Milch Cows, 314 ; Heifers, 24 ; val. of cows and heifers, $8,450.

Butter, 5 tons ; val. of butter, $2,500 ; Honey, 1,000 lbs. ; val. of honey, $180.

Indian Corn, 250 acres ; Indian Corn, per acre, 50 bush. ; val., $12,500.

Rye, 50 acres ; Rye, per acre, 20 bush. ; val., $1,000.

Barley, 20 acres ; Barley, per acre, 30 bush. ; val., $600.

Oats, 25 acres ; Oats, per acre, 40 bush. ; val., $700.

Potatoes, 116 acres ; Potatoes, per acre, 100 bush. ; val., $5,800.

Onions, 81 acres ; Onions, per acre, 300 bush. ; val., $13,365.

Turnips, cultivated as a field crop, 4 acres ; Turnips, per acre, 300 bush. ; val., $120.

Carrots, 20 acres ; Carrots, per acre, 320 bush. ; val., $64.

Beets and other esculent vegetables, 2 acres. [Neither the number of bushels per acre, nor value, are returned.]

English Mowing, 1,225 acres ; English Hay, 1,000 tons ; val., $22,000.

Wet Meadow or Swale Hay, 175 tons ; val., $1,750.

Salt Hay, 35 tons ; val., $350.

Apple Trees, cultivated for their fruit, 6,000 ; val., not given.

Pear Trees, cultivated for their fruit, 1,000 ; val., not given.

Cranberries, 58 bush. ; val., $174.

Establishments for m. of casks, 1 ; cap., $3,000 ; Casks m'd., 4,500 ; val., $4,500 ; emp., 3.

Establishments for m. of sashes, doors and blinds, 1 ; cap., $1,000 ; val. m'd., $6,000 ; emp., 4.

Bakeries, 1 ; cap., $8,000 ; Flour consumed, 1,000 bbls. ; val. of bread m'd., $20,000 ; emp., 8.

Establishments for m. of boxes, (shoe,) 1 ; cap., $7,000 ; val. of boxes m'd., $16,000 ; emp., 8.

Grain ground—74,000 bush. corn, 13,000 bush. rye, 10,000 bush. barley; 4 run of stones used for grinding the above.

Cabbages raised, 200 doz.

Cucumbers, for pickles, 700,000.

Squashes, 30 tons.

Fuel sold—Coal, 1,500 tons; Wood, 1,000 cords.

Morocco Manufactories, 1; Goat Skins tanned and dressed, 45,000; Sheep Skins tanned and dressed, 75,000.

In addition to the above, the Assessors report:—

Asses, 1; Grocery and Dry Goods Stores, 12; Millinery Establishments, 3; Toy and Fancy Goods Stores, 2; Apothecary Stores, 1; Tailoring Establishments, 2.

ESSEX.

Cotton Mills, 1; Spindles, 256. [Lately commenced operation.]

Daguerreotype Artists, 1; Daguerreotypes taken, 100; cap., $200; emp., 1.

Saddle, Harness and Trunk Manufactories, 1; val. of saddles, &c., $62; cap., $25; emp., 1.

Cordage (Line and Twine) Manufactories, 3; Cordage m'd., 4,230 doz. lines; cap., $11,700; emp., 10.

Vessels launched during said year, 23; Tonnage, 2,960 tons; cap., $27,000; emp., 120.

Establishments for m. of boats, 1; Boats built, 20; cap., $160; emp., 2.

Masts and Spar Sheds, 2; Masts and Spars m'd., 50 sets; cap., $1,700; emp., 5.

Establishments for m. of railroad cars, coaches, chaises, wagons, sleighs, and other vehicles, 1; val. of railroad cars, &c., m'd., $500; cap., $200; emp., 2.

Tanneries, 1; Hides of all kinds tanned, 1,100; val. of leather tanned, $3,000; cap., $2,000; emp., 2.

Currying Establishments, 1; val. of leather curried, $4,000; cap., $200; emp., 2.

Boots of all kinds m'd., 2,550 pairs; Shoes of all kinds m'd., 2,300 pairs; val. of boots and shoes, $7,470; m. emp., 15; f. emp., 7.

Bricks m'd., 125,000; val. of bricks, $750; emp., 3.

Val. of blocks and pumps m'd., $1,500; emp., 3.

Firewood prepared for market, 150 cords; val. of firewood, $750; emp., 2.

Saxony Sheep, of different grades, –; Merino Sheep, of different grades, 1; all other kinds of Sheep, 2; val. of all sheep, $13; Wool produced from Saxony sheep, – lbs.; Merino Wool produced, 3 lbs.; all other Wool produced, 7 lbs.

Horses, 96; val. of horses, $1,000; Oxen over three years old, 150; Steers under three years old, 9; val. of oxen and steers, $9,600; Milch Cows, 372; Heifers, 10; val. of cows and heifers, $9,390.

Butter, 15,000 lbs.; val. of butter, $3,750; Cheese, 2,600 lbs.; val. of cheese, $312; Honey, 100 lbs.; val. of honey, $20.

Indian Corn, 143 acres; Indian Corn, per acre, 30 bush.; val., $4,300.

Rye, 7 acres; Rye, per acre, 10 bush.; val., $100.

Barley, 60 acres; Barley, per acre, 17 bush.; val., $1,000.

Oats, 3 acres; Oats, per acre, 10 bush.; val., $15.

Potatoes, 50 acres; Potatoes, per acre, 70 bush.; val., $3,513.

Onions, 1 acre; Onions, per acre, 125 bush.; val., $62.50.

Turnips, cultivated as a field crop, 2 acres; Turnips, per acre, 125 bush.; val., $87.

Carrots, 3 acres; Carrots, per acre, 300 bush.; val., $150.

Beets and other esculent vegetables, 10 acres; val., $400.

English Mowing, 1,000 acres; English Hay, 810 tons; val., $14,580.

Wet Meadow or Swale Hay, 68 tons; val., $408.

Salt Hay, 1,151 tons; val., $10,350.

Apple Trees, cultivated for their fruit, 3,700; val., $3,722.

Pear Trees, cultivated for their fruit, 250; val., $150.

Clams taken, 865 bbls.; val., $3,027; emp., 30.

Mast Hoops m'd., 1,200; val., $250; emp., 1.

Jib Hanks, 75 doz.; val., $25.

Coopers, 1; Barrels m'd., 300; val., $250.

Oars m'd, 800; val., $500; emp., 1.

Net Buoys m'd., 150 doz.; val., $45.

GEORGETOWN.

Establishments for m. of railroad cars, coaches, chaises, wagons, sleighs, and other vehicles, 1; val. of railroad cars, &c., m'd., $2,000; cap., $300; emp., 2.

Tin Ware Manufactories, 1; val. of tin ware, $300; cap., $200; emp., 1.

Tanneries, 2; Hides of all kinds tanned, 300; val. of leather tanned, $600; cap., $300; emp., 2.

Currying Establishments, 5; val. of leather curried, $48,250; cap., $5,000; emp., 11.

Boots of all kinds m'd., 57,640 pairs; Shoes of all kinds m'd., 281,900 pairs; val. of boots and shoes, $336,320; m. emp., 356; f. emp., 239.

Lasts m'd., 4,000; val., $800.

Lumber prepared for market, 150,000 ft.; val. of lumber, $2,500; emp., 2.

Firewood prepared for market, 1,383 cords; val. of firewood, $6,770; emp., 6.

Saxony Sheep, of different grades, –; Merino Sheep, of different grades, –; all other kinds of Sheep, 63; val. of all sheep, $195; Wool produced from Saxony sheep, – lbs.; Merino Wool produced, – lbs.; all other Wool produced, 205 lbs.

Horses, 166; val. of horses, $13,060; Oxen over three years old, 98; Steers under three years old, 11; val. of oxen and steers, $5,682; Milch Cows, 336; Heifers, 54; val. of cows and heifers, $12,127.

Butter, 22,486 lbs.; val. of butter, $5,621; Cheese, 3,449 lbs.; val. of cheese, $344; Honey, 200 lbs.; val. of honey, $40.

Indian Corn, 158 acres; Indian Corn, per acre, 28 bush.; val., $5,482.

Wheat, 3½ acres; Wheat, per acre, 10 bush.; val., $87.50.

Rye, 16 acres; Rye, per acre, 8 bush.; val., $224.

Barley, 6½ acres; Barley, per acre, 20 bush.; val., $160.

Oats, 32 acres; Oats, per acre, 20 bush.; val., $382.

Potatoes, 90 acres; Potatoes, per acre, 91 bush.; val., $6,165.

Turnips, cultivated as a field crop, 1 acre; Turnips, per acre, 90 bush.; val., $30.

English Mowing, 808 acres; English Hay, 761 tons; val., $13,698.

Wet Meadow or Swale Hay, 481 tons; val., $3,848.

Salt Hay, 303 tons; val., $3,030.

Apple Trees, cultivated for their fruit, 10,366; val., $4,702.

Pear Trees, cultivated for their fruit, 313; val., $216.

Cranberries, 15 acres; val., $385.

Shoe String Manufactories, 2; Strings m'd., 1,400,000 pairs; val., $4,700; cap., $1,000; emp., 6.

Establishments for m. of medicines, essences and perfumeries, 1; val. of medicines, &c., m'd., $10,000; cap., $1,000; emp., 5.

Establishments for m. of shoe patterns, 1; val. of patterns m'd., $425; emp., 1.

GLOUCESTER.

Forges, 23; Bar Iron, Anchors, Chain Cables, and other articles of wrought iron m'd, 257 tons; val. of bar iron, &c., $50,800; cap., $15,500; emp., 33.

Daguerreotype Artists, 1; Daguerreotypes taken, 1,000; cap., $1,000; emp., 1.

Saddle, Harness and Trunk Manufactories, 1; val. of saddles, &c., $1,500; cap., $500; emp., 2.

Vessels launched during said year, 7; Tonnage, 605 tons; cap., $10,500; emp., 37.

Establishments for m. of boats, 2; Boats built, 102; cap., $1,400; emp., 4.

Masts and Spar Sheds, 2; Masts and Spars m'd., 500; cap., $5,000; emp., 7.

Sail Lofts, 6; Sails made of Am. fabric, 1,270; val. of sails m'd. of Am. fabric, $95,250; cap., $40,400; emp., 54.

No regular establishments for m. of oil and sperm candles. Oil m'd., 23,700 galls.; val. of oil m'd., $13,035.

Establishments for m. of soap and tallow candles, 1; Soap m'd., 150,000 lbs. hard, 200 bbls. soft; val. of soap, $9,800; Tallow Candles m'd., 12,000 lbs.; val. of tallow candles, $1,680; cap., $5,000; emp., 4.

Tin and Sheet Iron Ware Manufactories, 3; val. of tin and sheet iron ware, $13,000; cap., $7,500; emp., 14.

Boots of all kinds m'd., 2,950 pairs; Shoes of all kinds m'd., 21,150 pairs; val. of boots and shoes, $21,375; m. emp., 89; f. emp., 110.

Val. of snuff, tobacco, and cigars, $4,000; m. emp., 3; f. emp., 5.

Val. of building stone quarried and prepared for building, $75,000; emp., 178.

Val. of blacking, $800.

Val. of blocks and pumps m'd., $720; m'd. at mast and spar establishments.

Firewood prepared for market, 450 cords; val. of firewood, $2,250.

Vessels employed in the mackerel and cod fisheries, 282; Tonnage, 19,374 tons; Mackerel taken, 43,201 bbls.; Codfish taken, 97,950 quintals; val. of mackerel taken, $388,809; val. of codfish taken, $293,850; val. of cod liver oil sold for medicinal purposes, $1,020; Salt consumed, 16,000 bush.; cap., $989,250; emp., 2,820.

Horses, 268; val. of horses, $20,100; Oxen over three years old, 110; Steers under three years old, 30; val. of oxen and

steers, $7,000; Milch Cows, 212; Heifers, 35; val. of cows and heifers, $6,275.

Butter, 8,750 lbs.; val. of butter, $2,188.

Indian Corn, 107 acres; Indian Corn, per acre, 42 bush.; val., $4,454.

Beets and other esculent vegetables, – acres; val. $ –; al other Grain or Root Crops, 1,285 acres; val., $25,700.

English Mowing, 600 acres; English Hay, 847 tons; val., $16,940.

Salt Hay, 550 tons; val., $8,250.

Apple Trees, cultivated for their fruit, 8,000; val., $8,000.

Pear Trees, cultivated for their fruit, 525; val., $775.

Cranberries, – acres; val., $600.

Establishments for m. of casks, 3; cap., $800; Casks m'd., 800; val., $1,800; emp., 4.

Establishments for m. of gas, 1; cap., $40,000; val. m'd., $4,760; emp., 3.

Bakeries, 4—one steam; cap., $29,500; Flour consumed, 5,608 bbls.; val. of bread m'd., $69,500; emp., 20.

Newspaper establishments, 1; number of papers, 3; cap., $2,000; m. emp., 5; f. emp., 8.

Fish barrels m'd., 2,500; val., $1,700; Nets and Seines, 700; cap., $5,000; emp., 25.

Halibut smoked, 210 tons; val., $25,200; emp., 16.

Marine Railways, 3; cap., $37,000; emp., 8.

Breweries, 2; cap., $2,000; val. of beer m'd., $5,000; emp., 4.

Ice cut, 6,500 tons; val., 15,000; emp., 65.

Establishments for burning and grinding coffee, 1; Coffee burnt and ground, 150 tons; val., $30,000; cap., $9,000; emp., 3.

Grist mills, 2; grain ground, $50,000 bush.; emp., 6.

Livery Stables, 2; Horses, 23; Carriages, 35; Sleighs, 22; Hay consumed, 70 tons; Grain consumed, 2,700 bush.; cap., $15,000; emp., 5.

Imports of For. merchandise, $185,064; Exports, Foreign and Domestic, $112,133.

Tonnage of Am. vessels entered, 7,358; number of vessels, 60; emp., 339.

Tonnage of For. vessels entered, 9,517 ; number of vessels, 126 ; emp., 602.

Tonnage of Am. vessels cleared, 6,223 ; number of vessels, 60 ; emp., 302.

Tonnage of For. vessels cleared, 9,570 ; number of vessels, 127 ; emp., 604.

Vessels in coasting trade entered, 4,162 tons ; number of vessels, 46 ; emp., 177.

Vessels in coasting trade cleared, 10,280 tons ; number of vessels, 121 ; emp., 454.

GROVELAND.

Tanneries, 3 ; Hides of all kinds tanned, 700 ; val. of leather tanned, $2,625 ; cap., $500 ; emp., 2.

Currying Establishments, 1 ; val. of leather curried, $3,325 ; cap., $500 ; emp., 2.

Boots of all kinds m'd, 19,544 pairs ; Shoes of all kinds m'd., 141,870 pairs ; val. of boots and shoes, $152,039 ; m. emp., 261 ; f. emp., 193.

Lumber prepared for market, 100,000 ft. ; val. of lumber, $1,200 ; emp., 3.

Firewood prepared for market, 792 cords ; val. of firewood, $4,150 ; emp., 27.

Alewives, Shad and Salmon taken, 3,000 ; val. of same, $300 ; emp., 6.

Saxony Sheep, of different grades, – ; Merino Sheep, of different grades, – ; all other kinds of Sheep, 47 ; val. of all sheep, $153 ; Wool produced from Saxony sheep, – lbs. ; Merino Wool produced, – lbs. ; all other Wool produced, 79 lbs.

Horses, 119 ; val. of horses, $8,870 ; Oxen over three years old, 82 ; Steers under three years old, 11 ; val. of oxen and steers, $4,550 ; Milch Cows, 219 ; Heifers, 51 ; val. of cows and heifers, $8,030.

Butter, 15,416 lbs.; val. of butter, $3,834; Cheese, 6,020 lbs.; val. of cheese, $640; Honey, 62 lbs.; val. of honey, $8.

Indian Corn, 110 acres; Indian Corn, 3,467 bush.; val., $3,519.

Rye, 7½ acres; Rye, 97 bush.; val., $138.

Barley, 1¾ acre; Barley, 68 bush.; val., $68.

Oats, 36 acres; Oats, 1,057 bush.; val., $624.

Potatoes, 57½ acres; Potatoes, 4,093 bush.; val., $3,194.

Carrots, 1 acre; Carrots, per acre, 183 bush.; val., $48.

English Mowing, 671 acres; English Hay, 595 tons; val., $11,001.

Wet Meadow or Swale Hay, 299 tons; val., $2,703.

Salt Hay, 69 tons; val., $703.

Apple Trees, cultivated for their fruit, 3,830; val., $3,322.

Pear Trees, cultivated for their fruit, 126; val., $101.

Cranberries, 9 acres; val., $74.

Beeswax, 7 lbs.; val., $2.

Swine raised, 148; val., $1,117.

Groveland Mills Company. This Company consumed during the year, 240,000 lbs. cotton.

Seamless Meal Bags m'd., 210,000; val., $50,250; m. emp., 17; f. emp., 45.

HAMILTON.

Woollen Mills, 1; Wool consumed, 60,000 lbs.; Yarn m'd. and not made into cloth, – yds.; val. of yarn, $24,000; cap., $15,000; m. emp., 12; f. emp., 6.

Boots of all kinds m'd., 15,000 pairs; Shoes of all kinds m'd., 8,000 pairs; val. of boots and shoes, $8,200; m. emp., 93; f. emp., 56.

Firewood prepared for market, 50 cords; val. of firewood, $300.

Vessels employed in the mackerel and cod fisheries, 2; Tonnage, 200 tons; Codfish taken, 1,000 quintals; val. of codfish taken, $2,500; cap., $6,000; emp., 12.

Horses, 144; val. of horses, $10,800; Oxen over three years old, 162; Steers under three years old, 69; val. of oxen and steers, $10,660; Milch Cows, 376; Heifers, 72; val. of cows and heifers, $15,760.

Butter, 18,800 lbs.; val. of butter, $4,600; Cheese, 2,000 lbs.; val. of cheese, $200; Honey, 125 lbs.; val. of honey, $30.

Indian Corn, 252 acres; Indian Corn, per acre, 40 bush.; val., $10,584.

Rye, 40 acres; Rye, per acre, 15 bush.; val., $900.

Barley, 47 acres; Barley, per acre, 20 bush.; val., $750.

Oats, 33 acres; Oats, per acre, 20 bush.; val., $400.

Potatoes, 160 acres; Potatoes, per acre, 80 bush.; val., $7,680.

Onions, 5 acres; Onions, per acre, 300 bush.; val., $1,000.

Carrots, 3 acres; Carrots, per acre, 600 bush.; val., $525.

English Mowing, 1,082 acres; English Hay, 800 tons; val., $17,600.

Wet Meadow or Swale Hay, 582 tons; val., $3,488.

Salt Hay, 547 tons; val., $5,470.

Apple Trees, cultivated for their fruit, 5,900; val., $3,000.

Pear Trees, cultivated for their fruit, 255; val., $250.

Cranberries, 15 acres; val., $450.

HAVERHILL.

Woollen Mills, 1; Sets of Machinery, 4; Wool consumed, 100,000 lbs.; cap., $25,000; m. emp., 30; f. emp., 15.

Furnaces for m. of hollow ware and castings other than pig iron, 1; Hollow Ware and other Castings m'd., 60 tons; val. of hollow ware and castings, $4,200; cap., $3,000; emp., 4.

Tack and Awl Manufactories, 1; Tacks and Awls m'd., –; val. of tacks and awls, $1,400; cap., $200; emp., 2.

Shops for m. of iron railing, iron fences and iron safes, 1; val. of iron railing, &c., $3,000; cap., $1,000; emp., 3.

Piano-Forte Manufactories, –; Piano-Fortes m'd., –; cap., –; all other musical instrument manufactories, 1; val. of fifty-two musical instruments m'd., $3,000; cap., $500; emp., 5.

Daguerreotype Artists, 2; Daguerreotypes taken, 3,500; cap., $750; emp., 2.

Saddle, Harness and Trunk Manufactories, 1; val. of saddles, &c., $2,900; cap., $500; emp., 3.

Hat and Cap Manufactories, 7; Hats and Caps m'd., 200,100; cap., $23,500; emp., 90.

Establishments for m. of boats, 1; Boats built, 14; cap., $500; emp., 3.

Establishments for m. of railroad cars, coaches, chaises, wagons, sleighs, and other vehicles, 3; val. of railroad cars, &c., m'd., $31,000; cap., $11,000; emp., 32.

Establishments for m. of soap and tallow candles, 1; Soap m'd., 800 bbls.; val. of soap, $3,200; Tallow Candles m'd., 6,000 lbs.; val. of tallow candles, $900; cap., $3,000; emp., 4.

Tin Ware Manufactories, 3; val. of tin ware, $9,500; cap., $2,100; emp., 17.

Tanneries, 1; Hides of all kinds tanned, 7,750; val. of leather tanned, $50,000; cap., $10,000; emp., 15.

Currying Establishments, 5; val. of leather curried, $184,500; cap., $15,000; emp., 61.

Manufactories of patent and enamelled leather, 2; val. of leather m'd., $107,120; cap., $15,000; emp., 27.

Boots of all kinds m'd., 1,040,729 pairs; Shoes of all kinds m'd., 3,291,286 pairs; val. of boots and shoes, $2,782,930; m. emp., 4,087; f. emp., 2,257.

Bricks m'd., 1,450,000; val. of bricks, $8,050; emp., 19.

Val. of marble quarried and prepared for market, $4,200; emp., 4.

Val. of mechanics' tools m'd., $7,000; emp., 13.

Corn and other Brooms m'd., 3,000; val. of brooms, $600; emp., 1.

Lasts m'd., 58,000; val., $11,000.

Lumber prepared for market, 3,641,000 ft.; val. of lumber, $63,555; emp., 27.

Firewood prepared for market, 2,843 cords; val. of firewood, $14,909; emp., 38.

Alewives, Shad and Salmon taken, 30,000; val. of same, $3,000; emp., 30.

Saxony Sheep, of different grades, 9; Merino Sheep, of different grades, -; all other kinds of Sheep, 163; val. of all sheep, $498; Wool produced from Saxony sheep, 27 lbs.; Merino Wool produced, - lbs.; all other Wool produced, 382 lbs.

Horses, 518; val. of horses, $49,375; Oxen over three years old, (see end of the Return.)

Butter, 35,490 lbs.; val. of butter, $8,558.50; Cheese, 9,750 lbs.; val. of cheese, $1,085; Honey, 171 lbs.; val. of honey, $33.

Indian Corn, 37,854 bush.; val., $37,854.

Wheat, 12¾ acres; Wheat, per acre, 13⅓ bush.; val., $353.50.

Rye, 1,024 bush.; val., $1,406.

Barley, 588 bush.; val., $588.

Oats, 40 acres; Oats, per acre, 25 bush.; val., $750.

Potatoes, 17,266 bush.; val., $15,461.25.

Onions, ½ acre; Onions, 305 bush.; val., $203.

Carrots, 1 acre; Carrots, per acre, 279 bush.; val., $89.

Beets and other esculent vegetables, - acres; val., $11,337; all other Grain or Root Crops, 1,004 bush.; val., $566.

English Hay, 3,084¼ tons; val., $51,488.

Wet Meadow or Swale Hay, 827 tons; val., $7,513.

Val. of all kinds of fruit, $12,852.

Hops, 2 lbs.; val., 80 cts.

Cranberries, 8 acres; val., $306.

Establishments for m. of sashes and blinds, 3; cap., $1,300; val. m'd., $15,000; emp., 13.

Establishments for m. of gas, 1; cap., $45,000; val. m'd., $5,000; emp., 4.

Bakeries, 1; cap., $15,000; Flour consumed, 650 bbls.; val. of bread m'd., $14,300; emp., 6.

Establishments for m. of boxes, 3; cap., $2,000; val. of boxes m'd., $17,600; emp., 13.

Swine raised, 1,048; val., $18,223.
Val. of blacksmithing, $12,000.
Val. of silver ware m'd., $7,000.
Val. of millinery business, $17,000.
Val. of clothing m'd., $15,000.
Val. of confectionery m'd., $5,000.
Val. of bookbindery business, $1,500.
Val. of artificial teeth m'd., $1,500.
Sweet Potatoes, 10 bush.; val., $12.

Four separate returns were made from this town. Those relating to "neat cattle," are as follows:—

District No. 1.—Neat Cattle, 281; val., $10,564.

District No. 2.—Oxen over three years old, 132; Steers under three years old, 25; val. of oxen and steers, $6,957; Milch Cows, 228; Heifers, 40; val. of cows and heifers, $5,920.

District No. 3.—Neat Cattle, 377; val., $11,875.

District No. 4.—Neat Cattle, 193; val., $6,777.

IPSWICH.

Cotton Mills, 1; Spindles, 3,000; Cotton consumed, 150,000 lbs.; Cloth m'd., 900,000 yds., Printing Cloths; val. of cloth, $54,000; cap., $40,000; m. emp., 25; f. emp., 45.

Establishments for m. of hosiery, 5; Hosiery m'd., ribbed wool, 3,800 doz. pairs; val. of hosiery, $13,300; m. emp., 8; f. emp., 6.,

Establishments for m. of stocking frames, 1; val. of machinery m'd., $500; emp., 2.

Vessels launched during said year, 3; Tonnage, 254 tons; cap., $5,000; emp., 6.

Establishments for m. of wagons and sleighs, 5; val. of wagons and sleighs m'd., $2,000; emp., 3.

Establishments for m. of soap and tallow candles, 1; Soap m'd., 400 bbls., 500 boxes; val. of soap, $4,000; Tallow Candles m'd., –; val. of tallow, candles, &c., $1,000; cap., $1,500; emp., 2.

Tin Ware Manufactories, 1; val. of tin ware, $1,500; emp., 2.

Tanneries, 1; Hides of all kinds tanned, 3,000; val. of leather tanned and curried, $21,000; cap., $5,000; emp., 6.

Currying Establishments, 1.

Boots of all kinds m'd., 22,000 pairs; Shoes of all kinds m'd., 20,000 pairs; val. of boots and shoes, $69,000; m. emp., 78; f. emp., 60.

Bricks m'd., 100,000; val. of bricks, $600; emp., 2.

Val. of cigars, $500; emp., 1.

Val. of blacking, $500; emp., 2.

Firewood prepared for market, 1,000 cords; val. of firewood, $6,000.

Alewives taken, 300 bbls.; val. of same, $1,200; emp., 6.

Saxony Sheep, of different grades, –; Merino Sheep, of different grades, –; all other kinds of Sheep, 158; val. of all sheep, $632; Wool produced from Saxony sheep, – lbs.; Merino Wool produced, – lbs.; all other Wool produced, 600 lbs.

Horses, 291; val. of horses, $25,080; Oxen over three years old, 394; Steers under three years old, 150; val. of oxen and steers, $33,320; Milch Cows, 760; Heifers, 151; val. of cows and heifers, $21,251.

Butter, 42,445 lbs.; val. of butter, $1,064.25; Cheese, 6,000 lbs.; val. of cheese, $600; Honey, 500 lbs.; val. of honey, $125.

Indian Corn, 505 acres; Indian Corn, per acre, 35 bush.; val., $17,675.

Rye, 183 acres; Rye, per acre, 12 bush.; val., $2,296.

Barley, 182 acres; Barley, per acre, 10 bush.; val., $1,456.

Oats, 83 acres; Oats, per acre, 12 bush.; val., $996.

Potatoes, 226 acres; Potatoes, per acre, 100 bush.; val., $16,962.

Onions, 5 acres; Onions, per acre, 600 bush.; val., $1,500.

Turnips, cultivated as a field crop, 7 acres; Turnips, per acre, 600 bush.; val., $1,000.

Carrots, 8 acres; Carrots, per acre, $500 bush.; val., $1,200.

Beets and other esculent vegetables, 15 acres; val., $1,450.

English Mowing, 2,478 acres; English Hay, 2,930 tons; val., $37,170.

Wet Meadow or Swale Hay, 474 tons; val., $2,844.

Salt Hay, 2,294 tons; val., $16,058.

Apple Trees, cultivated for their fruit, 10,307; val., $7,630.

Pear Trees, cultivated for their fruit, 213; val., $346.

Cranberries, 250 bush.; val., $500.

Establishments for m. of casks, 2; cap., $300; Casks m'd., 882; val., $617.40; emp., 2.

Bakeries, 2; Flour consumed, 700 bbls.; emp., 3.

Shoe Boxes m'd., 1,000; cap., $400.

Guernsey Frocks m'd., 2,700 doz.; val., $29,200; m. emp., 10; f. emp., 20.

Shirts and Drawers m'd., 1,000 pieces; val., $1,600; m. emp., 1; f. emp., 2.

Clambait obtained, 3,125 bbls.; val., $17,020; m. emp., 106.

Milk, 20,000 galls.; val., $2,400.

Whortleberries, 800 bush.; val., $1,600.

Bayberry Tallow, 2,000 lbs.; val., $500.

LAWRENCE.

Cotton Mills, 6; Spindles, 127,644; Cotton consumed, 7,544,704 lbs.; Cloth m'd., 19,981,015 yds. of Sheeting, Shirting, Denims, Tickings, Striped Shirting, and Duck; val. of cloth, $1,888,015; Yarn m'd., 12,000 lbs.; val. of yarn, $2,100; Flannel m'd., 196,000 yds.; val. of flannel, $21,000; cap., $3,800,000; m. emp., 712; f. emp., 1,873.

Woollen Mills, 5; Sets of Machinery, 103; Wool consumed, 2,218,534 lbs.; Woven and Felt Beavers m'd., 132,227½ yds.; val. of beavers, $107,800.62; Cassimere m'd., 147,217 yds.; val. of cassimere, $87,321.65; Satinet m'd., 200,161 yds.; val.

of satinet, $80,064.40; Felting Cloth and Carpets, 110,050 yds.; val., $87,368.08; Fancy Plaids, 147,428 yds.; val., $73,714; Flannel, 2,073,115 yds.; val. of flannel, $696,950.47; cap., $1,800,000; m. emp., 1,300; f. emp., 1,000.

Shawls m'd., 161,934; val., $647,736.

Mills for m. of carpeting, 1; Wool consumed, 150,000 lbs.; Carpeting m'd., 75,000 yds.; val. of carpeting, $45,000; cap., $15,000; m. emp., 25; f. emp., 10.

Establishments for m. of de laines, 1. [The Assessors do not state whether this establishment is embraced in the five woollen mills returned.] De Laines m'd., 3,216,998 yds.; val. of goods, $536,000; Wool consumed, 475,000 lbs.; Cotton consumed, 200,000 lbs.; cap., about $700,000; m. emp., 109; f. emp., 192.

Print Works connected with the de laine establishment; Sets of Woollen Machinery, 13; m. emp., 273; f. emp., 25.

Furnaces for m. of hollow ware and castings other than pig iron, 3; Hollow Ware and other Castings m'd., 2,400 tons; val. of hollow ware and castings, $155,000; cap., $170,000; emp., 100.

Establishments for m. of cotton, woollen and other machinery, 2; val. of machinery m'd., $220,000; cap., $198,000; emp., 215.

Establishments for m. of steam-engines and boilers, 1; val. of steam-engines and boilers, $270,000; cap., $200,000; emp., 150.

Axe Manufactories, 1; Axes, Hatchets and other Edge Tools, m'd., 6,000; cap., $2,000; emp., 5.

Brass Founderies, 1; val. of articles m'd., $12,000; cap., $8,000; emp., 3.

Paper Manufactories, 3; Stock made use of, 2,150 tons; Paper m'd., 1,500 tons; val. of paper, $300,000; cap., $150,000; emp., 100.

Piano-Forte Manufactories, 1; val. of piano-fortes m'd., (only the wood-word,) $83,000; cap., $25,000; emp., 33.

Daguerreotype Artists, 3; Daguerreotypes taken, 7,100; cap., $3,000; emp., 7.

Saddle, Harness and Trunk Manufactories, 4; val. of saddles, &c., $7,350; cap., $1,000; emp., 7.

Upholstery Manufactories, 2; val. of upholstery, $4,000; cap., $500; emp., 2.

Hat and Cap Manufactories, 2; number of hats and caps m'd., 3,700; val. of hats and caps m'd., $3,225; cap., $1,500; emp., 13.

Card Manufactories, 1; val. of cards for mill machinery m'd., $20,000; cap., $10,000; emp., 6.

Establishments for m. of railroad cars, coaches, chaises, wagons, sleighs, and other vehicles, 2; val. of railroad cars, &c., m'd., $61,103; cap., $21,000; emp., 68.

Establishments for m. of soap and tallow candles, 3; Soft Soap m'd., 2,500 bbls.; Hard Soap m'd., 160,000 lbs.; val. of soap, $15,800; Tallow Candles m'd., 16,000 lbs.; val. of tallow candles, $2,240; cap., $14,500; emp., 16.

Chair and Cabinet Manufactories, 2; val. of chairs and cabinet ware, $6,250; cap., $2,500; emp., 14.

Tin Ware Manufactories, 6; val. of tin ware, $30,260; cap., $13,500; emp., 29.

Boots of all kinds m'd., 8,367 pairs; Shoes of all kinds m'd., 15,816 pairs; val. of boots and shoes, $24,925; m. emp., 31; f. emp., 30.

Val. of building stone quarried and prepared for building, $26,000; emp., 29.

Lumber prepared for market, 5,255,463 ft.; val. of lumber, $67,235.23; emp., 57.

Firewood prepared for market, 2,060 cords; val. of firewood, $10,300; emp., 23.

Horses, 196; val. of horses, $25,480; Oxen over three years old, 74; Steers under three years old, 4; val. of oxen and steers, $5,310; Milch Cows, 201; Heifers, 8; val. of cows and heifers, $6,270.

Butter, 3,650 lbs.; val. of butter, $949; Cheese, 200 lbs.; val. of cheese, $20.

Indian Corn, 25½ acres; Indian Corn, per acre, 40 bush.; val., $1,122.

Rye, $10\frac{3}{4}$ acres; Rye, per acre, 25 bush.; val., $322.50.

Barley, $\frac{3}{4}$ acre; Barley, per acre, 32 bush.; val. $30.

Oats, 12 acres; Oats, per acre, 25 bush.; val., $180.

Potatoes, $30\frac{1}{2}$ acres; Potatoes, per acre, 100 bush.; val., $2,745.

Onions, 10 bush.; val., $6.

Turnips, cultivated as a field crop, $3\frac{1}{2}$ acres; Turnips, per acre, 300 bush.; val., $346.50.

Carrots, $\frac{1}{4}$ acre; Carrots, per acre, 300 bush.; val., $24.75.

Beets and other esculent vegetables, 6 acres; val., $597.50.

English Mowing, 300 acres; English Hay, 226 tons; val., $3,842.

Wet Meadow or Swale Hay, 26 tons; val., $260.

Apple Trees, cultivated for their fruit, 2,500; 1,984 bush. apples raised; val., $596.40.

Pear Trees, cultivated for their fruit, 165; bush., 20; val., $50.

Establishments for m. of sashes, doors and blinds, 3; cap., $12,000; val. m'd., $37,219.46; emp., 25.

Establishments for m. of gas, 1; cap., $100,000; val. m'd., $28,000; emp., 6.

Bakeries, 2; cap., $4,000; Flour consumed, 1,300 bbls.; val. of bread m'd., $22,000; emp., 16.

Establishment for m. of boxes, (for boots, shoes, and woollen goods,) 1; cap., $10,000; val. of boxes m'd., $30,000; emp., 6.

Swine, 183; val., $3,205.

Establishments for m. of belting, banding and harness for mill machinery, 1; val. m'd., $65,000; cap., $27,500; m. emp., 19; f. emp., 20.

Blank Book Manufactories, 1; val. m'd., $1,200; cap., $300; emp., 2.

Establishments for m. of machinists' tools, 1; val. m'd., $50,000; cap., $80,000; emp., 80.

Establishments for m. of paper machinery, 1; val. m'd., $200,000; cap., $112,000; emp., 100.

Cotton Ducking Mills, 1; Spindles, 5,000; Cotton consumed,

$1,200,000 lbs.; Cotton Duck m'd., 1,100,000 yds.; val., $200,000; cap., $300,000; m. emp., 75; f. emp., $150.

File Manufactories, 2; val. m'd., $21,000; cap., $5,000; emp., 32.

LYNN.

Silk Manufactories, 1; Sewing Silk m'd., 8,000 lbs.; val. of sewing silk, $85,000; cap., $7,000; m. emp., 8; f. emp., 5.

Establishments for m. of cotton, woollen and other machinery, 3; val. of machinery m'd., $17,500; cap., $2,600; emp., 12.

Establishments for m. of steam-engines and boilers, 1; val. of steam-engines and boilers, $3,000; cap., $1,000; emp., 3.

Shops for m. of iron railing, iron fences and iron safes, 2; val. of iron railing, &c., $4,200; cap., $1,500; emp., 5.

Daguerreotype Artists, 3; Daguerreotypes taken, 17,800; cap., 3,100; emp., 5½.

Saddle, Harness and Trunk Manufactories, 3; val. of saddles, &c., $10,500; cap., $3,700; emp., 10.

Upholstery Manufactories, 2; val. of upholstery, $12,000; cap., $5,000; emp., 4.

Hat and Cap Manufactories, 1; Hats and Caps m'd., 2,000; cap., $400; emp., 2.

Cordage Manufactories, 1; Cordage m'd., 27,200 lbs.; cap., $1,000; emp., 3.

Sail Lofts, 1; Sails made of Am. fabric, 9; val. of sails m'd. of Am. fabric, $400; cap., $350; emp., 1.

Establishments for m. of railroad cars, coaches, chaises, wagons, sleighs, and other vehicles, 5; val. of railroad cars, &c., m'd., $6,200; cap., $2,350; emp., 11.

Establishments for m. of soap and tallow candles, 2; Hard Soap m'd., 362,000 lbs.; Soft Soap, 500 bbls.; val. of soap, $23,550; cap., $7,500; emp., 7.

Chocolate Mills, 1; Chocolate m'd., 80,000 lbs.; cap., $10,000; emp., 2.

Chair and Cabinet Manufactories, 2; val. of chairs and cabinet ware, $3,150; cap., $600; emp., 6.

Tin Ware Manufactories, 5; val. of tin ware, $12,500; cap., $7,150; emp., 10.

Glue Manufactories, and Manufactories for the preparation of Gums, 2; val. of glue and gums m'd., $20,000; cap., $10,000; emp., 9.

Tanneries, 11; Hides of all kinds tanned, 590,264; val. of leather tanned and finished, $407,485; cap., $74,160; emp., 196.

Boots of all kinds m'd., 3,274,893 pairs; Shoes of all kinds m'd., 6,000,700 pairs; val. of boots and shoes, $4,165,529; m. emp., 4,545; f. emp., 11,021.

Bricks m'd., 800,000; val. of bricks, $6,400; emp., 12.

Val. of snuff, tobacco and cigars, $5,000; m. emp., 14; f. emp., 1.

Val. of blacking, $3,500; emp., 5.

Val. of blocks and pumps m'd., $500; emp., 1.

Val. of mechanics' tools m'd., $77,300; emp., 52.

Val. of wooden ware not otherwise enumerated, including farming utensils m'd., $11,744; emp., 6.

Lasts m'd., 75,600; val., $15,320.

Firewood prepared for market, 2,947 cords; val. of firewood, $15,491; emp., 40.

Vessels employed in the whale fishery, 1; Tonnage, 323 tons; cap. in the whale fishery, $25,000; emp., 32.

Alewives, 250,000; val. of same, $500; emp., unknown.

Saxony Sheep, of different grades, –; Merino Sheep, of different grades, –; all other kinds of Sheep, 300; val. of all sheep, $900; Wool produced from Saxony sheep, – lbs.; Merino Wool produced, – lbs.; all other Wool produced, 900 lbs.

Horses, 684; val. of horses, $82,490; Oxen over three years old, 28; Steers under three years old, –; val. of oxen and steers, $1,200; Milch Cows, 274; Heifers, 13; val. of cows and heifers, $10,930.

Butter, 912 lbs.; val. of butter, $228.

Indian Corn, 42 acres; Indian Corn, per acre, 43 bush.; val., $1,806.

Rye, 15 acres; Rye, per acre, 9 bush.; val., $135.

Barley, 7 acres; Barley, per acre, 23 bush.; val., $161.

Potatoes, 67 acres; Potatoes, per acre, 80½ bush.; val., $5,164.

Onions, 17½ acres; Onions, per acre, 422 bush.; val., $4,431.

Turnips, cultivated as a field crop, 3 acres; Turnips, per acre, 279 bush.; val., $251.

Carrots, 8 acres; Carrots, per acre, 510 bush.; val., $1,020.

Beets and other esculent vegetables, 61 acres; val., $6,012; all other Grain or Root Crops, 6 acres; val., $874.75.

English Mowing, 643 acres; English Hay, 820 tons; val., $16,400.

Wet Meadow or Swale Hay, 22½ tons; val., $337.

Salt Hay, 465 tons; val., $5,580.

Apple Trees, cultivated for their fruit, 22,177; val., $5,428.25.

Pear Trees, cultivated for their fruit, 12,450; val., $2,799.45.

Establishments for m. of sashes, doors and blinds, 2; cap., $2,300; val. m'd., $5,500; emp., 5.

Establishments for m. of gas, 1; cap., $40,000; val. m'd., $9,895.26; emp., 4.

Breweries, 2; cap., $1,400; Beer m'd., 305 bbls.; val., $2,469.60; emp., 5.

Bakeries, 6; cap., $30,400; Flour consumed, 12,700 bbls.; val. of bread m'd., $191,000; emp., 42.

Establishments for m. of boxes, 4; number of boxes, 209,800, viz.: wooden, for spice and coffee, 23,400—wooden, for shoes, 61,400—paste-board, for shoes, 125,000; cap., 20,000; val. of boxes m'd., $32,890; emp., 25.

Val. of Milk produced, $18,139.93.

Spice and Coffee Mills, 4; Coffee ground, 1,268,000 lbs.; val., $126,800; Spices and Cream Tartar ground, 225,717 lbs.; val., $42,727.52; cap., $39,500; emp., 22.

Establishments for preparation of wool and hair for upholstery purposes, 1; Cape Good Hope Wool prepared, 4,000 lbs.;

val., $1,600; Hair prepared, 80,000 lbs.; val., $2,000; cap., $600; emp., 2.

Establishments for m. of needles for sewing-machines, 1; Needles m'd., 60,000; val., $6,000; cap., $1,000; emp., 3.

Establishments for m. of confectionery, 2; Confectionery m'd., 99,200 lbs.; val., $13,076; cap., $4,000; emp., 6.

Handkerchief Printing Establishments, 1; number printed, 33,600; val., $9,000; cap., $6,000; m. emp., 23; f. emp., 1.

Establishments for m. of paper hangings, 1; Paper m'd., 960,000 rolls; val., $192,000; cap., $50,000; m. emp., 44; f. emp., 6.

Establishments for m. of tin and zinc shoe patterns, (connected with last manufactories,) 5; Patterns m'd., 51,600; val., $4,448.

Establishments for m. of lightning rods, 1; val. of rods m'd., $5,000; cap., $600; emp., 4.

Quince Trees, 1,200; val. of quinces produced, $1,500.

Peat prepared for market, 53 cords; val., $265.

Ice cut, 7,000 tons; val., $20,000.

Swine, 830; val., $16,913.50.

Other articles m'd., Coffins, Fireworks, Shoe-cutting Boards, Essences, Horse Shoes, Iron for Carriages, Silk Bonnets, Copal Varnish, Signs, Bitters, Shoemakers' Wax; gross val., $29,010; cap., $11,000.

LYNNFIELD.

Woollen Mills, 1; Sets of Machinery, 1; Wool consumed, 15,000 lbs.; Flannel or Blanketing, 50,000 yds.; val. of flannel or blanketing, $8,500; cap., $7,000; m. emp., 8.

Establishments for m. of boats, 1; Boats built, 6; cap., $300; emp., 1.

Boots of all kinds m'd., – pairs; Shoes of all kinds m'd., 33,000 pairs; val. of boots and shoes, $31,200; m. emp., 41; f. emp., 39.

Val. of building stone quarried and prepared for building, $6,000; emp., 7.

Lumber prepared for market, 11,800 ft.; val. of lumber, $17,700; emp., "at odd jobs," 7.

Firewood prepared for market, 1,410 cords; val. of firewood, $4,230; emp., 10.

Horses, 58; val. of horses, $3,875; Oxen over three years old, 54; Steers under three years old, –; val. of oxen and steers, $3,085; Milch Cows, 169; Heifers, 16; val. of cows and heifers, $5,310.

Butter, 16,900 lbs.; val. of butter, $4,225.

Indian Corn, 85 acres; Indian Corn, per acre, 30 bush.; val., $2,550.

Rye, 26 acres; Rye, per acre, 12 bush.; val., $312.

Barley, 7 acres; Barley, per acre, 25 bush.; val., $157.50.

Oats, 17 acres; Oats, per acre, 30 bush.; val., $306.

Potatoes, 45 acres; Potatoes, per acre, 100 bush.; val., $3,375.

Onions, 5 acres; Onions, per acre, 300 bush.; val., $750.

Carrots, 3 acres; Carrots, per acre, 500 bush.; val., $296.

English Mowing, 368 acres; English Hay, 276 tons; val., $2,760.

Wet Meadow or Swale Hay, 289 tons; val., $2,890.

Apple Trees, cultivated for their fruit, 2,618; val., $1,309.

Pear Trees, cultivated for their fruit, 123; val., $100.

Cranberries, 100 acres; val., $200.

Establishments for m. of sashes, doors and blinds, 1; val. m'd., $8,000; cap., $7,000; emp., 10.

MANCHESTER.

Chair and Cabinet Manufactories, 20; val. of chairs and cabinet ware, $151,500; cap., $105,000; emp., 222.

Tanneries, 1; Hides of all kinds tanned, 7,000; val. of leather tanned, $40,000; cap., $25,000; emp., 20.

Currying Establishments, included above.

Boots of all kinds m'd., – pairs; Shoes of all kinds m'd., 2,500 pairs; val. of boots and shoes, $1,200; m. emp., 1; f. emp., 2.

Bricks m'd., 530,000; val. of bricks, $3,065; emp., 7.

Val. of building stone quarried and prepared for building, $2,000; emp., 2.

Lumber prepared for market, 60,000 ft.; val. of lumber, $825; emp., 2.

Firewood prepared for market, 570 cords; val. of firewood, $2,650; emp., 15.

Vessels employed in the cod fishery, 10; Tonnage, 549 tons; Codfish taken, 4,943 quintals; val. of codfish taken, $16,325; Salt consumed 5,368 bush.; cap., $16,400; emp., 71.

Horses, 60; val. of horses, $5,725; Oxen, over three years old, 40; Steers under three years old, 4; val. of oxen and steers, $2,720; Milch Cows, 85; Heifers, 2; val. of cows and heifers, $3,125.

Butter, 1,500 lbs.; val. of butter, $338.

Indian Corn, 45 acres; Indian Corn, per acre, 47½ bush.; val., $2,137.

Rye, 2 acres; Rye, per acre, 25 bush.; val., $75.

Barley, 10 acres; Barley, per acre, 28 bush.; val., $224.

Oats, 2 acres; Oats, per acre, 40 bush.; val., $48.

Potatoes, 44 acres; Potatoes, per acre, 70 bush.; val., $3,080.

Onions, 3½ acres; Onions, per acre, 432 bush.; val., $757.

Turnips, cultivated as a field crop, 2½ acres; Turnips, per acre, 260 bush.; val., $260.

Carrots, 2 acres; Carrots, per acre, 600 bush.; $300.

Beets and other esculent vegetables, 4 acres; val., $600; all other Grain or Root Crops, 5 acres; val., $375.

English Mowing, 430 acres; English Hay, 418 tons; val., $8,360.

Wet Meadow or Swale Hay, 22 tons; val., $154.

Salt Hay, 55 tons; val., $660.

Apple Trees, cultivated for their fruit, 522; val., $609; not of age to bear fruit, 980.

Pear Trees, cultivated for their fruit, 23; val., $50.

Bakeries, 1; cap., $2,000; Flour consumed, 458 bbls.; val. of bread m'd., $8,000; emp., 3.

Establishments for sawing of mahogany and black walnut plank boards and veneers, 1; val., $60,000; cap., $12,000; emp., 9.

MARBLEHEAD.

Cordage Manufactories, 1; Cordage m'd., 1,270,718 lbs.; emp., 50.

Vessels launched during said year, 2; Tonnage, 1,428 tons; cap., $85,680; emp., 20.

Sail Lofts, 3; Sails made of Am. fabric, 60; of For. fabric, 2; val. of sails m'd. of Am. fabric, $4,264; val. of sails of For. fabric, $241; cap., $1,000; emp., 6.

Tin Ware Manufactories, 2; val. of tin ware, $2,500; cap., $7,000; emp., 4.

Glue Manufactories, 1; val. of glue m'd., $20,000; cap., $22,000; emp., 10.

Boots of all kinds m'd., 9,500 pairs; Shoes of all kinds m'd., 2,826,224 pairs; val. of boots and shoes, $1,020,373.20; m. emp., 1,080; f. emp., 1,485.

Vessels employed in the cod fishery, 45; Tonnage, 3,805 tons; Codfish taken, 41,690 quintals; val. of codfish taken, $143,764; val. of cod liver oil sold for currying purposes, $7,217; Salt consumed, 62,832 bush.; cap., $138,050; emp., 280.

Horses, 209; val. of horses, $18,280; Oxen over three years old, 26; Steers under three years old, 2; val. of oxen and steers, $1,645; Milch Cows, 192; Heifers, 12; val. of cows and heifers, $7,695.

Butter, 2,350 lbs.; val. of butter, $542.

Indian Corn, 26 acres; Indian Corn, per acre, 46 bush.; val., $1,324.

Wheat, $1\frac{1}{4}$ acre; Wheat, per acre, 10 bush.; val., $26.

Rye, $15\frac{1}{4}$ acres; Rye, per acre, $30\frac{1}{2}$ bush.; val., $587.25.

Barley, $13\frac{1}{2}$ acres; Barley, per acre, $24\frac{1}{3}$ bush.; val., $315.75.

Oats, $2\frac{1}{2}$ acres; Oats, per acre, 30 bush.; val., $57.

Potatoes, $73\frac{1}{2}$ acres; Potatoes, per acre, $159\frac{1}{2}$ bush.; val., $6,581.

Onions, 69 acres; Onions, per acre, 377 bush.; val., $14,997.

Turnips, cultivated as a field crop, 12 acres; Turnips, per acre, 325 bush.; val., $1,346.50.

Carrots, 16 acres; Carrots, per acre, 750 bush.; val., $2,629.80.

Beets and other esculent vegetables, – acres; val., $9,487.

English Mowing, 690 acres; English Hay, 805 tons; val., $16,240.

Wet Meadow or Swale Hay, 8 tons; val. $104.

Salt Hay, 5 tons; val., $55.

Apple Trees, cultivated for their fruit, 4,248; val., $960.

Cranberries, 6 acres; val., $100.

Establishments for m. of gas, 1; cap., $37,100; val. m'd., $3,863.20; emp., 3.

Bakeries, 4; cap., $9,500; Flour consumed, 2,350 bbls.; val. of bread made, $35,850; emp., 15.

Establishments for m. of boxes, 1; cap., $5,000; val. of boxes m'd., $15,000; emp., 7.

Establishments for m. of machines for cutting sole leather, 1; number m'd., 75 to 100; cap., $9,000; val. of machines, $10,000; emp., 8.

Establishments for m. of oakum, 1; quantity m'd., 250,000 lbs.; cap., $3,000; val. of oakum, $17,600; emp., 7.

Cabbages, 30 acres; Heads per acre, 2,707; val., $4,120.

Squashes, 30 acres; Squashes, per acre, 6 tons; val., $4,175.

METHUEN.

Cotton Mills, 2; Spindles, 5,500; Cotton consumed, 442,356 lbs.; Cloth m'd., 1,200,000 yds. Tickings, Denims and Ducks; val. of cloth, $150,000; m. emp., 25; f. emp., 150.

Saddle, Harness and Trunk Manufactories, 1; val. of saddles, &c., $625; cap., $300; emp., 1.

Hat and Cap Manufactories, 6; Hats and Caps m'd., 321,400; cap., $105,000; emp., 178.

Establishments for m. of railroad cars, coaches, chaises, wagons, sleighs, and other vehicles, 2; val. of railroad cars, &c., m'd., $2,340; cap., $650; emp., 3.

Boots of all kinds m'd., – pairs; Shoes of all kinds m'd., 304,500 pairs; val. of boots and shoes, $300,500; m. emp., 280; f. emp., 210.

Bricks m'd., 1,500,000; val. of bricks, $7,500; emp., 16.

Lumber prepared for market, 150,000 ft.; val. of lumber, $1,500; emp., 5.

Firewood prepared for market, 2,500 cords; val. of firewood, $12,500; emp., 12.

Saxony Sheep, of different grades, –; Merino Sheep, of different grades, –; all other kinds of Sheep, 40; val. of all sheep, $133; Wool produced from Saxony sheep, – lbs.; Merino Wool produced, – lbs.; all other Wool produced, 141 lbs.

Horses, 213; val. of horses, $18,940; Oxen over three years old, 188; Steers under three years old, 40; val. of oxen and steers, $12,185; Milch Cows, 716; Heifers, 57; val. of cows and heifers, $20,129.

Butter, 30,070 lbs.; val. of butter, $7,516; Cheese, 500 lbs.; val. of cheese, $50.

Indian Corn, 240 acres; Indian Corn, per acre, 33 bush.; val., $8,000.

Wheat, 3 acres; Wheat, per acre, 11 bush.; val., $66.

Rye, 36 acres; Rye, per acre, 16 bush.; val., $750.

Barley, 7 acres; Barley, per acre, 19 bush.; val., $133.

Oats, 127 acres ; Oats, per acre, 32 bush. ; val., $2,032.

Potatoes, 185 acres ; Potatoes, per acre, 78 bush. ; val., $10,882.

Beets and other esculent vegetables, 2 acres ; val., $200 ; all other Grain or Root Crops, 6 acres ; val., $1,200.

English Mowing, 1,916 acres ; English Hay, 2,112 tons ; val., $37,836.

Wet Meadow or Swale Hay, 468 tons ; val., $3,744.

Apples raised, 14,740 bush. ; val., $7,370.

Cranberries, 10 acres ; val., $500.

Milk, 408,736 qts. ; val., $20,436.

MIDDLETON.

Paper Manufactories, 1 ; val. of stock made use of, $10,000 ; val. of paper m'd., $25,000 ; cap., $3,000 ; emp., 6.

Establishments for m. of soap and tallow candles, 1 ; Soap m'd., 1,200 bbls. of soft soap and 10 tons of hard soap ; val. of soap, $5,200 ; emp., 2.

Boots of all kinds m'd., – pairs ; Shoes of all kinds m'd., 180,000 pairs ; val. of boots and shoes, $117,000 ; m. emp., 165 ; f. emp., 140.

Lumber prepared for market, 70,000 ft. ; val. of lumber, $1,120.

Firewood prepared for market, 2,000 cords ; val. of firewood, $6,000 ; emp., 25 three months.

Saxony Sheep, of different grades, – ; Merino Sheep, of different grades, – ; all other kinds of Sheep, 23 ; val. of all sheep, $69 ; Wool produced from Saxony sheep, – lbs. ; Merino Wool produced, – lbs. ; all other Wool produced, 92 lbs.

Horses, 73 ; val. of horses, $5,490 ; Oxen over three years old, 43 yoke ; Steers under three years old, 2 yoke ; val. of oxen and steers, $4,360 ; Milch Cows, 132 ; Heifers, 22 ; val. of cows and heifers, $5,191.

Butter, 21,330 lbs. ; val. of butter, $5,332.50.

Indian Corn, 107 acres; Indian Corn, per acre, 35 bush.; val., $3,745.

Rye, 17 acres; Rye, per acre, 20 bush.; val., $340.

Barley, 24 acres; Barley, per acre, 20 bush.; val., $480.

Oats, 15 acres; Oats, per per acre, 20 bush.; val., $180.

Potatoes, 97 acres; Potatoes, per acre, 100 bush.; val., $7,275.

Onions, 4 acres; Onions, per acre, 200 bush.; val., $400.

Turnips, cultivated as a field crop, 2 acres; Turnips, per acre, 200 bush.; val., $100.

Carrots, 1 acre; Carrots, per acre, 500 bush.; val., $100.

English Mowing, 730 acres; English Hay, 550 tons; val., $11,000.

Wet Meadow or Swale Hay, 501 tons; val., $2,505.

Apple Trees, cultivated for their fruit, 3,000; val., $1,500.

Pear Trees, cultivated for their fruit, 100; val., $100.

Cranberries, 40 acres; val., $1,600.

NAHANT.

Forges, 3; emp., 4.

Val. of mathematical instruments, $300; emp., 2.

Firewood prepared for market, 8 cords; val. of firewood, $72; emp., 1.

Vessels employed in the mackerel and cod fisheries, 4; Tonnage, 150 tons; Mackerel taken, 530 bbls.; Codfish taken, 2,500 quintals; val. of mackerel taken, $4,000; val. of codfish taken, $6,000; val. of cod liver oil sold for medicinal purposes, $300; emp., 30.

Horses, 33; val. of horses, $2,850; Oxen over three years old, 4; Steers under three years old, 1; val. of oxen and steers, $415; Milch Cows, 33; Heifers, 1; val. of cows and heifers, $1,440.

Butter, 1,350 lbs.; val. of butter, $372.

Indian Corn, 17 acres; Indian Corn, per acre, 37 bush.; val., $691.90.

Wheat, 2½ acres; Wheat, per acre, 10 bush.; val., $35.

Rye, 1½ acres; Rye, per acre, 15 bush.; val., $22.

Potatoes, 17 acres; Potatoes, per acre, 150 bush.; val., $1,912.50.

Val. of onions, $2.50.

Turnips, cultivated as a field crop, ¼ acre; Turnips, per acre, 80 bush.; val., $25.

Carrots, 2 acres; Carrots, per acre, 300 bush.; val., $150.

Beets and other esculent vegetables, 1½ acre; val., $75.

English Mowing, 70 acres; English Hay, 105 tons; val., $2,625.

Wet Meadow or Swale Hay, 4 tons; val., $60.

Salt Hay, 6 tons; val., $90.

Apple Trees, cultivated for their fruit, 1,420; val., $250.

Pear Trees, cultivated for their fruit, 200; val., $500.

Val. of cranberries, $4.

Establishments for m. of gas, 1; val. m'd., $4,000; cap., $3,000.

NEWBURY.

Forges, 4; Bar Iron, Anchors, Chain Cables, and other articles of wrought iron, m'd., 10 tons; val. of bar iron, &c., $2,400.

Chair and Cabinet Manufactories, 1; val. of chairs and cabinet ware, $6,000; cap., $4,000; emp., 12.

Bricks m'd., 500,000; val. of bricks, $2,000; emp., 4.

Val. of snuff, tobacco and cigars, $6,000; m. emp., 4; f. emp., 5.

Lumber prepared for market, 2,500 ft. ship timber; val. of lumber, $37,500; emp., 25.

Firewood prepared for market, 500 cords; val. of firewood, $2,500; emp., 6.

Saxony Sheep, of different grades, –; Merino Sheep, of dif-

ferent grades, –; all other kinds of Sheep, 113; val. of all sheep, $300; Wool produced from Saxony sheep, – lbs.; Merino Wool produced, – lbs.; all other Wool produced, 350 lbs.

Horses, 166; val. of horses, $11,835; Oxen over three years old, 261; Steers under three years old, 143; val. of oxen and steers, $17,855; Milch Cows, 643; Heifers 138; val. of cows and heifers, $15,235.

Butter, 21,000 lbs.; val. of butter, $5,250; Cheese, 6,000 lbs.; val. of cheese, $360; Honey, 300 lbs.; val. of honey, $50.

Indian Corn, 352 acres; Indian Corn, per acre, 38 bush.; val., $11,000.

Wheat, 4 acres; Wheat, per acre, 15 bush.; val., $65.

Rye, 85 acres; Rye, per acre, 15 bush.; val., $2,000.

Barley, 50 acres; Barley, per acre, 25 bush.; val., $1,000.

Oats, 28 acres; Oats, per acre, 30 bush.; val., $500.

Potatoes, 80 acres; Potatoes, per acre, 125 bush.; val., $10,000.

Onions, 60 acres; Onions, per acre, 300 bush.; val., $9,000.

Carrots, 7 acres; Carrots, per acre, 500 bush.; val., $900.

Beets and other esculent vegetables, 2 acres; val., $300; all other Grain or Root Crops, 20 acres; val., $4,000.

English Mowing, 1,200 acres; English Hay, 1,300 tons; val., $23,400.

Wet Meadow or Swale Hay, 250 tons; val., $2,500.

Salt Hay, 1,200 tons; val., $10,000.

Apple Trees, cultivated for their fruit, 16,184; val., $16,000.

Pear Trees, cultivated for their fruit, 598; val., $620.

Milk, 110,800 galls.; val., $13,296.

Grist Mills, 3; Grain ground, 85,000 bush.

NEWBURYPORT.

Cotton Mills, 6; Spindles, 64,640; Cotton consumed, 1,890,600 lbs.; Cloth m'd., 10,501,835 yds, Sheets, Shirtings, Drillings and Printing Cloths; val. of cloth, $790,273; cap., $1,180,000; m. emp., 441; f. emp., 879.

Forges, 42; Bar Iron, Anchors, Chain Cables, and other articles of wrought iron m'd., 600 tons; val. of bar iron, &c., $84,000; cap., $14,000; emp., 84.

Furnaces for m. of hollow ware and castings other than pig iron, 1; Hollow Ware and other Castings m'd., 300 tons; val. of hollow ware and castings, $35,000; cap., $8,000; emp., 14.

Establishments for m. of cotton, woollen and other machinery, 1; val. of machinery m'd., $20,000; cap., $8,000; emp., 16.

Shops for m. of iron railing, iron fences and iron safes, 1; val. of iron railing, &c., $25,000; cap., $5,000; emp., 10.

Seraphine Manufactories, 1; Seraphines m'd., 12; val. of musical instruments m'd., $1,200; cap., $200; emp., 2.

Daguerreotype Artists, 2; Daguerreotypes taken, 20,000; cap., $3,000; emp., 5.

Establishments for repairing of chronometers, watches, gold and silver ware and jewelry, 2; val. of m's., $25,000; cap., $8,000; emp., 9.

Saddle, Harness and Trunk Manufactories, 2; val. of saddles, &c., $6,000; cap., $2,000; emp., 6.

Upholstery Manufactories, 2; val. of upholstery, $2,000; cap., $600; emp., 3.

Hat and Cap Manufactories, 2; Hats and Caps m'd., 2,000; cap., 1,000; emp., 9.

Line Manufactories, 5; val. of line m'd., $24,500; cap., $6,000; emp., 24.

Vessels launched during said year, 15; Tonnage, 12,794 tons; val., $650,000; cap., $100,000; emp., 540.

Establishments for m. of boats, 2; Boats built, 40; val., $3,000; cap., $1,000; emp., 4.

Masts and Spar Sheds, 2; val. of masts and spars m'd., $20,000; cap., $3,000; emp., 12.

Sail Lofts, 4; Sails made of Am. fabric, (ships' suits) 25; val. of sails m'd. of Am. fabric, $47,000; Am. Duck used, 150,000; Bolt-rope used, 18; cap., $10,000; emp., 23.

Establishments for m. of railroad cars, coaches, chaises,

wagons, sleighs, and other vehicles, 4; val. of railroad cars, &c., m'd., $6,000; cap., $1,000; emp., 8.

Establishments for m. of soap and tallow candles, 4; Soap m'd., 230,000 lbs.; val. of soap, $8,000; Soft Soap, 650 lbs.; val., $2,000; Tallow Candles m'd., 180,000 lbs; val. of tallow candles, $27,000; cap., $7,000; emp., 10.

Chair and Cabinet Manufactories, 4; val. of chairs and cabinet ware, $3,000; cap., $800; emp., 4.

Tin Ware Manufactories, 4; val. of tin ware, $6,000; cap., $1,000; emp., 6.

Comb Manufactories, 1; val. of combs m'd., $40,000; cap., $10,000; emp., 18.

Glue Manufactories, and Manufactories for the preparation of Gums, 1; val. of glue and gums m'd., $500; cap., $100; emp., 1.

Tanneries, 1; Hides of all kinds tanned, 200; val. of leather tanned, $500; cap., $100; emp., 1.

Boots of all kinds m'd., 4,400 pairs; Shoes of all kinds m'd., 424,000 pairs; val. of boots and shoes, $398,600; m. emp., 361; f. emp., 258.

Bricks m'd., 950,000; val. of bricks, $5,700; emp., 8.

Val. of snuff, tobacco and cigars, $70,000; m. emp., 12; f. emp., 72.

Val. of blocks and pumps m'd., $17,000; emp., 19.

Firewood prepared for market, 200 cords; val. of firewood, $1,200; emp., 2.

Vessels employed in the mackerel and cod fisheries, 56; Tonnage, 3,857 tons; Mackerel taken, 7,995 bbls.; Codfish taken, 15,000 quintals; val. of mackerel taken, $86,000; val. of codfish taken, $30,000; Cod Liver Oil m'd., 450 bbls.; val., $9,000; Salt consumed, 29,000 bush.; cap., $138,000; emp., 665.

Herring taken, 500 bbls.; val. of same, $2,500.

Saxony Sheep of different grades, –; Merino Sheep, of different grades, –; all other kinds of Sheep, 71; val. of all sheep, $200; Wool produced from Saxony sheep, – lbs.; Merino Wool produced, – lbs.; all other Wool produced, 200 lbs.

Horses, 465; val. of horses, $53,000; Oxen over three years old, 74; Steers under three years old, 20; val. of oxen and steers, $4,500; Milch Cows, 552; Heifers, 36; val. of cows and heifers, $17,280.

Butter, 2,850 lbs.; val. of butter, $700.

Indian Corn, 117 acres; Indian Corn, per acre, 40 bush.; val., $4,680.

Wheat, 5 acres; Wheat, per acre, 20 bush.; val., $300.

Rye, 13 acres; Rye, per acre, 20 bush.; val., $325.

Barley, 24 acres; Barley, per acre, 25 bush.; val., $750.

Oats, 35 acres; Oats, per acre, 25 bush.; val., $437.50.

Potatoes, 63 acres; Potatoes, per acre, 100 bush.; val., $6,300.

Onions, 13 acres; Onions, per acre, 400 bush.; val., $2,600.

Carrots, 14 acres; Carrots, per acre, 600 bush.; val., $1,680.

Beets and other esculent vegetables, 6 acres; val., $720.

Squashes, 100 tons; val. of same, $2,000.

Cabbages, 40,000 heads; val., $1,200.

English Mowing, 1,100 acres; English Hay, 1,250 tons; val., $22,500.

Wet Meadow or Swale Hay, 250 tons; val., $2,500.

Salt Hay, 260 tons; val., $3,120.

Apple Trees, cultivated for their fruit, 11,500; val., $8,100.

Pear Trees, cultivated for their fruit, 3,200; val., $800.

Val. of all other fruit, $1,000.

Establishments for m. of casks, 3; cap., $1,500; Casks m'd., 2,375; val., $4,750; emp., 8.

Establishments for m. of gas, 1; cap., $80,000; val. m'd., $9,200; emp., 3.

Distilleries, 1; cap., $5,000; Alcohol distilled, – bbls.; all other Liquors distilled, 1,600 bbls.; val., $17,500; emp., 4.

Bakeries, 4; cap., $12,000; Flour consumed, 4,200 bbls.; val. of bread m'd., $72,500; emp., 30.

Swine, 636; val., $12,720.

Milk produced, 220,000 galls.; val., $36,000.

NORTH ANDOVER.

Woollen Mills, 3; Sets of Machinery, 23; Wool conumed, 590,000 lbs.; Flannel or Blanketing, 1,800,000 yds.; val. of flannel or blanketing, $365,000; cap., $150,000; m. emp., 117; f. emp., 95.

Furnaces for m. of hollow ware and castings other than pig iron, 1; Hollow Ware and other Castings m'd., 350 tons; val. of hollow ware and castings, $18,000; cap., $3,000; emp., 20.

Establishments for m. of cotton, woollen and other machinery, 1; val. of machinery m'd., 80,000; cap., $25,000; emp., 65.

Saddle, Harness and Trunk Manufactories, 1; val. of saddles, &c., $6,000; cap., $1,000; emp., 3.

Establishments for m. of soap and tallow candles, 1; Soap m'd., 300 bbls.; val. of soap, $1,000.

Boots and Shoes of all kinds m'd., 50,000 pairs; val. of boots and shoes, $36,000; m. emp., 60; f. emp., 25.

Lumber prepared for market, 50,000 ft.; val. of lumber, $1,000; emp., 2.

Firewood prepared for market, 1,000 cords; val. of firewood, $4,000; emp., 3.

Alewives, Shad and Salmon taken, 12,000; val. of same, $1,500; emp., 8, during 2 months.

Saxony Sheep, of different grades, –; Merino Sheep, of different grades, –; all other kinds of Sheep, 83; val. of all sheep, $250; Wool produced from Saxony sheep, – lbs.; Merino Wool produced, – lbs.; all other Wool produced, 260 lbs.

Horses, 187; val. of horses, $16,000; Oxen over three years old, 232; Steers under three years old, 25; val. of oxen and steers, $13,000; Milch Cows, 534; Heifers, 96; val. of cows and heifers, $18,103.

Butter, 41,590 lbs.; val. of butter, $10,397.50.

Indian Corn, 249 acres; Indian Corn, per acre, 30 bush.; val., $7,490.

Wheat, 14 acres; Wheat, per acre, 12 bush.; val., $336.

Rye, 16 acres; Rye, per acre, 15 bush.; val., $288.

Barley, 25 acres; Barley, per acre, 25 bush.; val., $625.

Oats, 133 acres; Oats, per acre, 30 bush.; val., $2,394.

Potatoes, 107 acres; Potatoes, per acre, 100 bush.; val., $8,025.

Beets and other esculent vegetables, 4 acres; val., $640; all other Grain or Root Crops, 4 acres; val., $980.

English Mowing, 1,515 acres; English Hay, 1,370 tons; val., $27,400.

Wet Meadow or Swale Hay, 610 tons; val., $4,904.

Apple Trees, cultivated for their fruit, –; val., $10,000.

Establishments for m. of reed and loom harnesses, 1; number m'd., 600; val., $4,000; Reeds, 4,500; val., $12,000; cap., $3,000; emp., 16.

Cabbages, 4 acres; val. of total amount raised, $640.

ROCKPORT.

Cotton Mills, 1; Spindles, 3,888; Cotton consumed, 1,033,745 lbs.; Cloth m'd., 855,842 yds., Duck or Sail-cloth, 22 inches wide; val. of cloth, $196,843.66; Yarn m'd., 74,997 lbs.; val. of yarn, $15,749.37; cap., $200,000; m. emp., 48; f. emp., 135.

Sail Lofts, 1; Sails made of Am. fabric, 60; val. of sails m'd. of Am. fabric, $3,000; cap., $1,000; emp., 3.

Curriers' Oil m'd., 8,550 galls.; val. of same, $5,700.

Establishments for m. of soap and tallow candles, 1; Soap m'd., 200 bbls.; val. of soap, $800; cap., $500; emp., 1.

Chair and Cabinet Manufactories, 1; val. of chairs and cabinet ware, $10,000; cap., $8,000; emp., 12.

Tin Ware Manufactories, 2; val. of tin ware, $2,000; cap., $800; emp., 3.

Boots of all kinds m'd., 900 pairs; Shoes of all kinds m'd., 14,000 pairs; val. of boots and shoes, $8,000; m. emp., 17.

Val. of building stone quarried and prepared for building, $224,000; emp., 284; 20 sloops employed in transporting stone from the town; 6 men in each.

Vessels employed in the mackerel and cod fisheries, 65; Tonnage, 1,895 tons; Mackerel taken, 3,524 bbls.; Codfish taken, 17,700 quintals; val. of mackerel taken, $33,182; val. of codfish taken, $53,000; val. of cod liver oil sold for medicinal purposes, $7,392; Salt consumed, 43,774 bush.; cap., $46,250; emp., 357.

Fresh Fish sold, 1,050,000 lbs.; val. of same, $15,750.

Horses, 72; val. of horses, $5,775; Oxen over three years old, 130; Steers under three years old, 15; val. of oxen and steers, $10,150; Milch Cows, 127; Heifers, 10; val. of cows and heifers, $5,040.

Butter, 2,000 lbs.; val. of butter, $500.

Indian Corn, 39 acres; Indian Corn, per acre, 40 bush.; val., $1,560.

Barley, 25 acres; Barley, per acre, 40 bush.; val., $1,000.

Potatoes, 50 acres; Potatoes, per acre, 100 bush.; val., $5,000.

Turnips, cultivated as a field crop, 18 acres; Turnips, per acre, 200 bush.; val., $900.

Carrots, 5 acres; Carrots, per acre, 800 bush.; val., $1,000.

Beets and other esculent vegetables, 40 acres; val., $4,000; all other Grain or Root Crops, 20 acres; val., $2,000.

English Mowing, 625 acres; English Hay, 575 tons; val., $11,500.

Wet Meadow or Swale Hay, 75 tons; val., $750.

Apple Trees, cultivated for their fruit, 8,000; val., $4,000.

Pear Trees, cultivated for their fruit, 500; val., $250.

Cranberries, 3 acres; val., $375.

Bakeries, 1; cap., $500; Flour consumed, 350 bbls.; val. of bread m'd., $4,000; emp., 2.

Val. of fish glue or isinglass m'd., $6,000; cap., $4,000; emp., 12, during 3 months in winter.

ROWLEY.

Boots of all kinds m'd., 30,800 pairs; Shoes of all kinds m'd., 134,000 pairs; val. of boots and shoes, $195,600; m. emp., 209; f. emp., 114.

Firewood prepared for market, 771 cords; val. of firewood, $4,626; emp., 25.

Saxony Sheep, of different grades, –; Merino Sheep, of different grades, –; all other kinds of Sheep, 172; val. of all sheep, $ –; Wool produced from Saxony sheep, – lbs.; Merino Wool produced, – lbs.; all other Wool produced, 516 lbs.

Horses, 158; val. of horses, $11,060; Oxen over three years old, 126; steers under three years old, 28; val. of oxen and steers, $7,700; Milch Cows, 419; Heifers, 75; val. of cows and heifers, $9,880.

Butter, 25,140 lbs.; val. of butter, $6,285; Cheese, 5,825 lbs.; val. of cheese, $582; Honey, 150 lbs.; val. of honey, $37.

Indian Corn, 220 acres; Indian Corn, per acre, 30 bush.; val., $6,600.

Rye, 53 acres; Rye, per acre, 8 bush.; val., $530.

Barley, 21 acres; Barley, per acre, 12 bush.; val., $252.

Oats, 32 acres; Oats, per acre, 15 bush.; val., $288.

Potatoes, 151 acres; Potatoes, per acre, 50 bush.; val., $750.

Onions, 5 acres; Onions, per acre, 200 bush.; val., $500.

English Mowing, 618 acres; English Hay, 618 tons; val., $12,360.

Wet Meadow or Swale Hay, 190 tons; val., $1,520.

Salt Hay, 1,022 tons; val., $10,222.

Apple Trees, cultivated for their fruit, 8,463; val., $2,500.

Pear Trees, cultivated for their fruit, 253; val., $126.

SALEM.

Cotton Mills, 1; Spindles, 32,768; Cotton consumed, 1,810,000 lbs.; Cloth m'd., 5,300,000 yds., Brown Sheetings or Shirtings; val. of cloth, $500,000; Flannel m'd., 200,000 yds.; val. of flannel, $22,000; cap., $700,000; m. emp., 200; f. emp., 400.

Factories for m. of painted carpeting, 2; Carpeting m'd., 3,500 yds.; val. of carpeting, $3,100; cap., $1,500; m. emp., 3.

Establishments for m. of hosiery, 1; Hosiery (Hose and Vests), m'd., 1 pair; val. of hosiery, $400; emp., 1.

Forges, 20; Bar Iron, Anchors, Chain Cables, and other articles of wrought iron, m'd., 220 tons; val. of bar iron, &c., $58,000; cap., $20,000; emp., 38.

Furnaces for m. of hollow ware and castings other than pig iron, 1; Hollow Ware and other Castings m'd., 400 tons; val. of hollow ware and castings, $24,000; cap., $15,000; emp., 15.

Establishments for m. of steam-engines and boilers, 4; val. of steam-engines and boilers, $69,000; cap., $22,000; emp., 47.

Brass Founderies, 2; val. of articles m'd., $13,000; cap., $7,000; emp., 7.

Establishments for m. of chemical preparations, 1; val. of chemical preparations, $66,500; cap., $600,000; emp., 20.

Daguerreotype Artists, 3; Daguerreotypes taken, $4,500; cap., $1,100; emp., 6.

Establishments for m. of chronometers, watches, gold and silver ware and jewelry, 5; val. of m's., $6,000; cap., $3,500; emp., 6.

Saddle, Harness and Trunk Manufactories, 7; val. of saddles, &c., $12,600; cap., $7,000; emp., 15.

Upholstery Manufactories, 2; val. of upholstery, $4,300; cap., $2,000; emp., 6.

Cordage Manufactories, 3; Cordage m'd., 66 tons; cap., $12,600; emp., 21.

Vessels launched during said year, 2; Tonnage, 483 tons; cap., $19,320; emp., 18.

Masts and Spar Sheds, 2; Masts and Spars m'd., 253; cap., $1,700; emp., 3.

Sail Lofts, 5; Sails made of Am. fabric, 370; val. of sails m'd. of Am. fabric, $15,300; emp., 12.

Establishments for m. of railroad cars, coaches, chaises, wagons, sleighs, and other vehicles, 10; val. of railroad cars, &c., m'd., $21,000; cap., $10,500; emp., 16.

Lead Manufactories, also White Lead, 1; val. of sheet lead m'd., $15,000; cap., inclusive of white lead, $70,000; emp., 30.

Establishments for m. of oil and adamantine candles, 1; Oil m'd., (Extract from Palm Oil,) 25,000 galls.; val. of oil m'd., $20,000; Adamantine Candles m'd., 1,000,000 lbs.; val. of adamantine candles, $200,000; cap., $60,000; emp., 25.

Establishments for m. of soap and tallow candles, 1; Soap m'd., 292,500 lbs.; val. of soap, $17,000; Tallow Candles m'd., 25,000 lbs.; val. of tallow candles, $5,000; emp., 6.

Chair and Cabinet Manufactories, 6; val. of chairs and cabinet ware, $13,100; cap., $4,000; emp., 24.

Tin Ware Manufactories, 4; val. of tin ware, $3,200; cap., $1,500; emp., 4.

Establishments for m. of white lead and other paints, 1; White Lead m'd., 1,800,000 lbs.; val. of white lead m'd., $144,000.

Manufactories for the preparation of gum copal and gum arabic, 1; val. of gums m'd., $225,000; cap., $8,300; emp., 40.

Tanneries, 41; Hides of all kinds tanned, 328,000; val. of leather tanned, $1,127,000; cap., $563,000; emp., 218.

Currying Establishments, 52; val. of leather curried, $1,310,400; cap., $435,000; emp., 364.

Manufactories of patent and enamelled leather, 2; val. of leather m'd., $113,000; cap., $35,000; emp., 20.

Boots of all kinds m'd., 500 pairs; Shoes of all kinds m'd., 138,725 pairs; val. of boots and shoes, $96,000; m. emp., 128; f. emp., 148.

Stove Linings and Fire Bricks m'd., uncertain; val. of bricks, $7,000; emp., 6.

Val. of mathematical instruments, $100,000; emp., 1.

Val. of snuff, tobacco and cigars, $63,000; m. emp., 32; f. emp., 28.

Val. of building stone prepared for building, $25,000; emp., 21.

Val. of marble quarried for market, $4,200; emp., 3.

Val. of blocks and pumps m'd., $3,300; emp., 5.

Horses, 406; val. of horses, $45,000; Oxen over three years old, 55; Steers under three years old, –; val. of oxen and steers, $3,300; Milch Cows, 386; Heifers, – ; val. of cows and heifers, $15,440.

Indian Corn, 236 acres; Indian Corn, per acre, 40 bush.; val., $8,532.

Rye, 3 acres; Rye, per acre, 20 bush.; val., $66.

Barley, 16 acres; Barley, per acre, 20 bush.; val., $288.

Oats, 13 acres; Oats, per acre, 20 bush.; val., $148.

Potatoes, 168 acres; Potatoes, per acre, 45 bush.; val., $7,680.

Onions, 15 acres; Onions, per acre, 90 bush.; val., $8,100.

Turnips, cultivated as a field crop, 10 acres; Turnips, per acre, 70 bush.; val., $140.

Carrots, 12 acres; Carrots, per acre, 80 bush.; val., $250.

Beets and other esculent vegetables, 20 acres; val., $700; all other Grain or Root Crops, 43 acres; val., $1,290.

English Mowing, 730 acres; English Hay, 1,100 tons; val., $22,000.

Wet Meadow or Swale Hay, 15 tons; val., $150.

Salt Hay, 112 tons; val., $1,008.

Apple Trees, cultivated for their fruit, 6,500; val., $5,500.

Pear Trees, cultivated for their fruit, 570; val., $1,710.

Establishments for m. of casks, 10; cap., $34,000; Casks m'd., larger part kegs, 153,900; val., $60,500; emp., 79.

Establishments for m. of sashes, doors and blinds, 2; cap., $6,000; val. m'd., $12,000; emp., 12.

Establishments for m. of gas, 2; cap., $110,000; val. m'd., $28,000; emp., 11.

Distilleries, 2; cap., $18,000; Alcohol distilled, – bbls.; all other Liquors distilled, 3,237 bbls.; val., $39,704; emp., 5.

Bakeries, 16; cap., $41,000; Flour consumed, 8,900 bbls.; val. of bread m'd., $126,850; emp., 44.

Establishments for m. of confectioneries, 2; val. m'd., $28,000; cap., $2,000; emp., 14.

SALISBURY.

Cotton Mills, 1; Spindles, 765; Cotton consumed, 125,200 lbs.; Yarn m'd., 112,680 lbs.; val. of yarn, $20,282.40; cap., $12,000; m. emp., 6; f. emp., 9.

Woollen Mills. Under this head the Assessors return the following Report from the Agent of the Salisbury Manufacturing Company:—

"The Works of the Salisbury Manufacturing Company are located both in Salisbury and Amesbury, (the dividing line of the towns being only a small river,) and so arranged that the machinery in both towns is connected in the operation.

There are in both towns 6 mills, with 50 sets of machinery, 1 Printing Mill, together with Dye Houses, Dry Houses, Machine Shops, Sorting House, and other buildings.

Wool used, 502,306 lbs.; Flannel m'd., 476,768 yds.; val., $137,000; Tweeds, Cassimeres, &c., m'd., 395,360 yds.; val., $283,000; Satinet m'd., 71,468 yds.; val., $30,000; Table Covers embossed, 15,094; val., $25,000; Total val., $475,000; cap., $661,000; m. emp., 440; f. emp., 400.

Owing to the long continued drought, the stream upon which the S. M. Co's. works are situated gave out, and the Company were obliged to suspend operations for something over three months last year, by which means the product was materially smaller than it would otherwise have been. The Company have, therefore, only given their business for the six months ending June 1st, 1855. This should be divided about equally between the two towns."

Saddle, Harness and Trunk Manufactories, 3; val. of saddles, &c., $1,750; cap., $1,000; emp., 3.

Vessels launched during said year, 4; Tonnage, 274 tons; cap., $7,500; emp., 18.

Establishments for m. of boats, 8; Boats built, 589; cap., $4,150; emp., 18.

Establishments for m. of wagons, sleighs, and other vehicles, 4; val. of wagons, sleighs, &c., m'd., $7,940; cap., $4,000; emp., 9.

Establishments for m. of oil and sperm candles, 1; Lard Oil m'd., 5,000 galls.; val. of oil m'd., $5,000; cap., $4,000; emp., 2.

Establishments for m. of soap and tallow candles, 2; Soap m'd., 40,000 lbs.; val. of soap, $2,034; Tallow Candles m'd., 6,250 lbs.; val. of tallow candles, $937.50; cap., $2,500; emp., 4.

Tin Ware Manufactories, 2; val. of tin ware, $4,500; cap., $2,250; emp., 6.

Glue Manufactories, and Manufactories for the preparation of Gums, 1; val. of glue and gums m'd., $6,000; cap., $4,000; emp., 4.

Tanneries, 5; Hides of all kinds tanned, 7,250; val. of leather tanned, $22,925; cap., $21,500; emp., 15.

Currying Establishments, 4; val. of leather curried, $18,600; cap., $12,800; emp., 5.

Manufactories of patent and enamelled leather, 1; val. of leather m'd., $4,500; cap., $1,000; emp., 4.

Boots of all kinds m'd., 6,571 pairs; Shoes of all kinds m'd., 11,593 pairs; val. of boots and shoes, $15,019.75; m. emp., 33; f. emp., 48.

Lumber prepared for market, 35,700 ft.; val. of lumber, $404; emp., 2.

Firewood prepared for market, 1,808 cords; val. of firewood, $7,283; emp., 15.

Vessels employed in the mackerel and cod fisheries, 4; Tonnage, 248 tons; Mackerel taken, 990 bbls.; val. of mackerel taken, $7,020; Salt consumed, 1,260 bush.; cap., $9,600; emp., 40.

Saxony Sheep, of different grades, –; Merino Sheep, of different grades, –; all other kinds of Sheep, 125; val. of all sheep, $421; Wool produced from Saxony sheep, – lbs.; Merino Wool produced, – lbs.; all other Wool produced, 400 lbs.

Horses, 145; val. of horses, $11,635; Oxen over three years old, 302; Steers under three years old, 97; val. of oxen and steers, $17,035; Milch Cows, 393; Heifers, 50; val. of cows and heifers, $11,670.

Butter, 18,520 lbs.; val. of butter, $4,216; Cheese, 3,985 lbs.; val. of cheese, $326.

Indian Corn, 133 acres; Indian Corn, per acre, 40⅓ bush.; val., $5,333.

Wheat, 7 acres; Wheat, per acre, 12 bush.; val., $194.

Rye, 17 acres; Rye, per acre, 16 bush.; val., $456.

Barley, 12 acres; Barley, per acre, 15 bush.; val., $180.

Oats, 47 acres; Oats, per acre, 20 bush.; val., $571.

Potatoes, 135 acres; Potatoes, per acre, 100 bush.; val., $13,500.

English Mowing, 1,078 acres; English Hay, 1,078 tons; val., $15,765.

Wet Meadow or Swale Hay, 160 tons; val., $1,280.

Salt Hay, 1,338 tons; val., $10,644.

Apple Trees, cultivated for their fruit, 9,725; val., $8,402.

Pear Trees, cultivated for their fruit, 1,015; val., $325.

Establishments for m. of casks, 3; cap., $2,500; Casks m'd., 1,800; val., $3,600; emp., 8.

Establishments for m. of sashes, doors and blinds, 1; val. m'd., $15,000; cap., $9,000; emp., 15.

Val. of milk sold, $1,120.

Val. of garden productions, $3,971.

Grist Mills, 1; grain ground, 16,000 bush.

Saw Mills, 2; Lumber sawed, 400,000 ft.

Ship Plug Manufactories, 1; val. of plugs m'd., $600; emp., 1.

Barrels m'd., 600; val., $450.

SAUGUS.

Woollen Mills, 2; Sets of Machinery, 10; Wool consumed, 325,300 lbs.; Flannel or Blanketing, 825,000 yds.; val. of flannel or blanketing, $206,250; cap., $85,000; m. emp., 52; f. emp., 39.

Boots of all kinds m'd., 50,000 pairs; Shoes of all kinds m'd., 84,000 pairs; val. of boots and shoes, $96,000; m. emp., 152; f. emp., 120.

Bricks m'd., 470,000; val. of bricks, $28,900; emp., 12.

Val. of snuff, tobacco, and cigars, $63,025; m. emp., 25; f. emp., 45.

Firewood prepared for market, 1,050 cords; val. of firewood, $5,200; emp., 20.

Indian Corn, 104 acres; Indian Corn, per acre, 40 bush.; val., $4,160.

Rye, 8 acres; Rye, per acre, 17 bush.; val., $170.

Potatoes, 60 acres; Potatoes, per acre, 80 bush.; val., $4,800.

Onions, 6 acres; Onions, per acre, 225 bush.; val., $810.

Turnips, cultivated as a field crop, 7 acres; Turnips, per acre, 200 bush.; val., $630.

Beets and other esculent vegetables, 10 acres; val., $2,000.

English Mowing, 460 acres; English Hay, 450 tons; val., $9,000.

Wet Meadow or Swale Hay, 70 tons; val., $700.

Salt Hay, 450 tons; val., $6,750.

Apple Trees, cultivated for their fruit, 700; val., $650.

SOUTH DANVERS.

Establishments for bleaching or coloring cotton goods, not connected with calico establishments, –; Goods bleached or colored, 100 tons; cap., $150,000; emp., 60.

Establishments for m. of railroad cars, coaches, chaises, wagons, sleighs, and other vehicles, 3; val. of railroad cars, &c., m'd., $5,500; cap., $1,000; emp., 5.

Establishments for m. of soap and tallow candles, 2; Soap m'd., 230,000 lbs.; val. of soap, $17,500; Tallow Candles m'd., 5,000 lbs.; val. of tallow candles, $700; cap., $10,000; emp., 3.

Glue Manufactories, 3; val. of glue m'd., $120,000; cap., $40,000; emp., 21.

Tanneries, 27; Hides of all kinds tanned, 131,000; val. of leather tanned, $660,000; cap., $436,000; emp., 122.

Currying Establishments, 24; val. of leather curried, $805,-000; cap., $450,000; emp., 153.

Manufactories of patent and enamelled leather, 1; val. of leather m'd., $20,000; cap., $8,000; emp., 7.

Boots of all kinds m'd., – pairs; Shoes of all kinds m'd., 747,600 pairs; val. of boots and shoes, $597,259; m. emp., 562; f. emp., 481.

Val. of building stone quarried and prepared for building, $5,000; 10 pairs mill-stones, val., $1,250; emp., 7.

Lasts m'd., 60,000; val., $16,000.

Firewood prepared for market, 1,460 cords; val. of firewood, $9,500.

Saxony Sheep, of different grades, –; Merino Sheep, of different grades, –; all other kinds of Sheep, 36; val. of all sheep, $150; Wool produced from Saxony sheep, – lbs.; Merino Wool produced, – lbs.; all other Wool produced, 75 lbs.

Horses, 407; val. of horses, $46,700; Oxen over three years old, 98; Steers under three years old, –; val. of oxen and steers, $6,190; Milch Cows, 447; Heifers, 9; val. of cows and heifers, $13,575.

Butter, 7,650 lbs.; val. of butter, $1,912.50.

Indian Corn, 171 acres; Indian Corn, per acre, 42 bush.; val., $7,180.

Rye, 20 acres; Rye, per acre, 30 bush.; val., $900.

Potatoes, 102 acres; Potatoes, per acre, 120 bush.; val., $6,130.

Onions, 188 acres; Onions, per acre, 410 bush.; val., $77,080.

Carrots, 300 acres; Carrots, per acre, 600 bush.; val., $4,050.

Beets and other esculent vegetables, 82 acres; val., $3,280.

English Mowing, 1,200 acres; English Hay, 1,207 tons; val., $24,140.

Wet Meadow or Swale Hay, 363 tons; val., $3,267.

Apple Trees, cultivated for their fruit, 4,214.

Establishments for m. of earthenware, 2; val. of earthenware, $2,300; emp., 4.

Bakeries, 2; cap., $6,000; Flour consumed, 1,750 bbls.; val. of bread m'd., $35,000; emp., 15.

Establishments for m. of cloth and shoe boxes, 1; cap., $2,000; val. of boxes m'd., $2,800; emp., 3.

Establishments for m. of morocco, shoe-linings and binding skins, 13; Skins m'd., 82,900; val., $258,000; cap., $50,000; emp., 111.

SWAMPSCOTT.

Vessels launched during said year, 3; Tonnage, 57½ tons; cap., $2,500; emp., 6.

Establishments for m. of boats, –; Boats built, 250; cap., $5,000; emp., 7.

Tin Ware Manufactories, 1; val. of tin ware, $205.14; cap., $1,500; emp., 1.

Boots of all kinds m'd., 20,600 pairs; Shoes of all kinds m'd., – pairs; val. of boots and shoes, $49,300; m. emp., 76; f. emp., 141.

Vessels employed in the mackerel and cod fisheries, 39; Tonnage, 1,000 tons; Mackerel taken, 5,000 bbls.; Codfish taken, 56,160 quintals; val. of mackerel taken, $50,000; val. of codfish taken, $196,560; val. of cod liver oil sold for medicinal purposes, $5,300; Salt consumed, 19,040 bush.; cap., $689,150; emp., 226.

Horses, 94; val. of horses, $14,052; Oxen over three years

old, 15; Steers under three years old, –; val. of oxen and steers, $1,000; Milch Cows, 112; Heifers, –; val. of cows and heifers, $3,595.

Butter, 200 lbs.; val. of butter, $50.

Indian Corn, 375 bush.; val., $375.

Rye, 379 bush.; val., $379.

Barley, 42 bush.; val., $42.

Potatoes, 2,145 bush.; val., $2,145.

Onions, 5⅓ acres; Onions, per acre, 448⅕ bush.; val., $2,152.

Turnips, 1,200 bush.; val., $575.

Beets and other esculent vegetables, 100 acres; val., $2,100.

English Mowing, 382 acres; English Hay, 487 tons; val., $10,965.

Salt Hay, 62 tons; val., $773.

Apple Trees, cultivated for their fruit, 1,082; val., $1,100.

Pear Trees, cultivated for their fruit, 1,225; val., $455.

TOPSFIELD.

Daguerreotype Artists, 1; Daguerreotypes taken, 800; cap., $500; emp., 1.

Saddle, Harness and Trunk Manufactories, 1; val. of saddles, &c., $300; cap., $200; emp., 1, one-half the time.

Establishments for m. of railroad cars, coaches, chaises, wagons, sleighs, and other vehicles, 2; val. of railroad cars, &c., m'd., $1,800; cap., $400; emp., 3.

Boots of all kinds m'd., 700 pairs; Shoes of all kinds m'd., 97,650 pairs; val. of boots and shoes, $90,260; m. emp., 104; f. emp., 121.

Firewood prepared for market, 238 cords; val. of firewood, $1,077; emp., 1.

Saxony Sheep, of different grades, –; Merino Sheep, of different grades, –; all other kinds of Sheep, 45; val. of all sheep, $144; Wool produced from Saxony sheep, – lbs.; Merino Wool produced, – lbs.; all other Wool produced, 144 lbs.

Horses, 146 ; val. of horses, $11,385 ; Oxen over three years old, 146 ; Steers under three years old, 19 ; val. of oxen and steers, $9,053 ; Milch Cows, 410 ; Heifers, 58 ; val. of cows and heifers, $12,601.

Butter, 21,386 lbs. ; val. of butter, $5,278 ; Cheese, 2,000 lbs. ; val. of cheese, $198 ; Honey, 110 lbs. ; val. of honey, $25.

Indian Corn, 166 acres ; Indian Corn, per acre, 29½ bush. ; val., $4,892.

Wheat, 1¼ acre ; Wheat, per acre, 10 bush. ; val., $25.

Rye, 25 acres ; Rye, per acre, 11¼ bush. ; val., $314.

Barley, 29 acres ; Barley, per acre, 15½ bush. ; val., $476.

Oats, 22 acres ; Oats, per acre, 16 bush. ; val., $206.

Potatoes, 107 acres ; Potatoes, per acre, 83 bush. ; val., $6,733.

English Mowing, 1,166½ acres ; English Hay, 885 tons ; val., $15,912.

Wet Meadow or Swale Hay, 887 tons ; val., $7,103.

Salt Hay, 822 tons ; val., $7,810.

Apple Trees, cultivated for their fruit, 15,616 ; val., $3,221.

Pear Trees, cultivated for their fruit, 1,084 ; val., $227.

Cranberries, 34 acres ; val., $482.

Beeswax, 7 lbs. ; val., $2.62½.

Swine, 299 ; val., $2,681.

WENHAM.

Establishments for m. of railroad cars, coaches, chaises, wagons, sleighs, and other vehicles, 1 ; val. of railroad cars, &c., m'd., $4,250 ; cap., $1,000 ; emp., 4.

Boots of all kinds m'd., 4,200 pairs ; Shoes of all kinds m'd., 25,000 pairs ; val. of boots and shoes, $20,000 ; m. emp., 46 ; f. emp., 20.

Val. of blocks and pumps m'd., $175 ; emp., 2 one month.

Firewood prepared for market, 615 cords ; val. of firewood, $3,000 ; emp., 12 two months.

Merino Sheep, of different grades, 30; val. of all sheep, $100; Merino Wool produced, 75 lbs.

Horses, 115; val. of horses, $8,750; Oxen over three years old, 70; Steers under three years old, 6; val. of oxen and steers, $3,750; Milch Cows, 226; Heifers, 14; val. of cows and heifers, $7,500.

Butter, 14,655 lbs.; val. of butter, $3,663.75; Honey, 230 lbs.; val. of honey, $46.

Indian Corn, 120 acres; Indian Corn, per acre, 30 bush.; val., $3,600.

Rye, 33 acres; Rye, per acre, 15 bush.; val., $742.50.

Barley, 10 acres; Barley, per acre, 15 bush.; val., $150.

Oats, 12 acres; Oats, per acre, 22 bush.; val., $150

Potatoes, 56 acres; Potatoes, per acre, 106 bush.; val., $5,936.

English Mowing, 780 acres; English Hay, 555 tons; val., $10,530.

Wet Meadow or Swale Hay, 286 tons; val., $2,288.

Apple Trees, cultivated for their fruit, 5,300; val., $5,250.

Pear Trees, cultivated for their fruit, 500; val., $275.

Cranberries, 20 acres; val., $750.

There are 205,000 pairs of shoes made in this town for dealers in Danvers and Lynn; val., $36,560; m. emp., 160.

Val. of blacksmiths' work done, $2,500; emp., 3.

Establishment for cutting ice, 1; val. of iee sold, $40,000; cap., $25,000.

Stores, 2; val. of business done, $40,000.

House Carpenters, 8; products of their labor, $4,000.

WEST NEWBURY.

Establishments for m. of railroad cars, coaches, chaises, wagons, sleighs, and other vehicles, 2; val. of railroad cars, &c., m'd., $10,000; cap., $6,000; emp., 15.

Comb Manufactories, 15; val. of combs m'd., $186,500; cap., $134,900; emp., 212.

Boots of all kinds m'd., – pairs; Shoes of all kinds m'd., 275,200 pairs; val. of boots and shoes, $231,138; m. emp., 231; f. emp., 138.

Bricks m'd., 600,000; val. of bricks, $3,600; emp., 4.

Firewood prepared for market, 540 cords; val. of firewood, $3,780; emp., 10.

Saxony Sheep, of different grades, –; Merino Sheep, of different grades, –; all other kinds of Sheep, 164; val. of all sheep, $656; Wool produced from Saxony sheep, – lbs.; Merino Wool produced, – lbs.; all other Wool produced, 525 lbs.

Horses, 169; val. of horses, $12,565; Oxen over three years old, 282; Steers under three years old, 55; val. of oxen and steers, $18,872; Milch Cows, 520; Heifers, 102; val. of cows and heifers, $16,632.

Butter, 35,761 lbs.; val. of butter, $8,940; Cheese, 11,420 lbs.; val. of cheese, $1,142; Honey, 250 lbs.; val. of honey, $50.

Indian Corn, 298 acres; Indian Corn, 45 bush.; val., $13,410.

Wheat, 8 acres; Wheat, per acre, 13 bush.; val., $208.

Rye, 33 acres; Rye, per acre, 12 bush.; val., $594.

Barley, 66 acres; Barley, per acre, 24 bush.; val., $1,590.

Oats, 97 acres; Oats, per acre, 33 bush.; val., $2,081.

Potatoes, 125 acres; Potatoes, per acre, 96 bush.; val., $11,875.

Onions, 8 acres; Onions, per acre, 540 bush.; val., $2,590.

Turnips, cultivated as a field crop, 3 acres; Turnips per acre, 400 bush.; val., $360.

Carrots, 6 acres; Carrots, per acre, 650 bush.; val., $1,080.

Millet, 10 acres; val., $324.

English Mowing, 1,545 acres; English Hay, 1,831 tons; val., $34,780.

Wet Meadow or Swale Hay, 720 tons; val., $7,380.

Salt Hay, 581 tons; val., $5,810.

Apple Trees, cultivated for their fruit, 14,900; val., $24,150.

Pear Trees, cultivated for their fruit, 325 ; val., $950.
Cranberries, 15 acres ; val., $300.
Beeswax, 25 lbs. ; val., $10.
Val. of milk sold, $3,200.

FRANKLIN COUNTY.

ASHFIELD.

Saddle, Harness and Trunk Manufactories, 1 ; val. of saddles, &c., $600 ; cap., $100 ; emp., 1.

Tanneries, 2 ; Hides of all kinds tanned, 400 ; val. of leather tanned $1,500 ; cap., $1,800 ; emp., 2.

Currying Establishments, 1 ; val. of leather curried, $800 ; cap., $900 ; emp., 1.

Boots of all kinds m'd., 165 pairs ; Shoes of all kinds m'd., 215 pairs ; val. of boots and shoes, $695 ; m. emp., 1 ; f. emp., 1.

Val. of palm leaf hats m'd., $2,300 ; m. emp., 4 ; f. emp., 60.

Charcoal m'd., 400 bush. ; val. of same, $36 ; emp., 1.

Val. of mechanics' tools m'd., $4,500 ; emp., 8.

Val. of wooden ware not otherwise enumerated, including farming utensils m'd., $75 ; emp., 1.

Lumber prepared for market, 1,290,000 ft. ; val. of lumber, $11,610 ; emp., 18.

Firewood prepared for market, 992 cords ; val. of firewood, $2,480 ; emp., 8.

Saxony Sheep, of different grades, – ; Merino Sheep, of different grades, 2,624 ; all other kinds of Sheep, 520 ; val. of all sheep, $7,860 ; Wool produced from Saxony sheep, – lbs. ; Merino Wool produced, 10,062 lbs. ; all other Wool produced, 2,068 lbs.

Horses, 246 ; val. of horses, $23,210 ; Oxen over three years old, 200 ; Steers under three years old, 314 ; val. of oxen and steers, $1,726 ; Milch Cows, 625 ; Heifers, 240 ; val. of cows and heifers, $24,455.

Butter, 80,150 lbs. ; val. of butter, $17,633 ; Cheese, 15,900 lbs. ; val. of cheese, $1,590 ; Honey, 150 lbs. ; val. of honey, $30.

Indian Corn, 283 acres ; Indian Corn, per acre, 46 bush. ; val., $13,018.

Wheat, 40 acres ; Wheat, per acre, 20 bush. ; val., $1,800.

Rye, 40 acres ; Rye, per acre, 25 bush. ; val., $1,000.

Barley, 43 acres ; Barley, per acre, 27 bush. ; val., $870.75.

Oats, 90 acres ; Oats, per acre, 30 bush. ; val., $1,350.

Potatoes, 139 acres ; Potatoes, per acre, 114 bush. ; val., $7,923.

Onions, 2 acres ; Onions, per acre, 270 bush. ; val., $405.

Turnips, cultivated as a field crop, 4 acres ; Turnips, per acre, 300 bush. ; val., $300.

Carrots, 3 acres ; Carrots, per acre, 365 bush. ; val., $328.50.

English Mowing, 2,951 acres ; English Hay, 2,874 tons ; val., $34,488.

Wet Meadow or Swale Hay, 905 tons ; val., $6,335.

Apple Trees, cultivated for their fruit, 5,176 ; val., $3,334.

Pear Trees, cultivated for their fruit, 258 ; val., $320.

Establishments for m. of stone and earthenware, 1 ; cap., $1,500 ; val. of stone and earthenware, $4,950 ; emp., 4.

Val. of surgical splints m'd., $1,400 ; emp., 3.

Faucets m'd., 60,000 ; val., $1,600 ; cap., $1,000 ; emp., 3.

Canes m'd., 35,000 ; val., $1,500 ; cap., $400 ; emp., 3.

Washboards m'd., 1,000 ; val., $250.

Val. of shirts and collars m'd., $4,000 ; emp., 38.

Val. of mincing knives, $1,200.

Val. of rolling pins, pill boxes, &c., $500.

Shingles m'd., 410,000 ; val., $1,025.

Maple Sugar, 40,000 lbs. ; val. of maple sugar, $4,000.

Val. of quinces, $150.

Swine raised, 315 ; val., $4,200.

BERNARDSTON.

Manufactories of shovels, spades, forks and hoes, 1; val. of shovels, &c., $650; cap., $6,000; emp., 3.

Saddle, Harness, and Trunk Manufactories, 1; val. of saddles, &c., $300; cap., $200; emp., 1.

Firewood prepared for market, 1,500 cords; val. of firewood, $3,750; emp., 10.

Saxony Sheep, of different grades, –; Merino Sheep, of different grades, 777; all other kinds of Sheep, 259; val. of all sheep, $2,590; Wool produced from Saxony sheep, – lbs.; Merino Wool produced, 2,331 lbs.; all other Wool produced, 777 lbs.

Horses, 114; val. of horses, $9,280; Oxen over three years old, 136; Steers under three years old, 212; val. of oxen and steers, $12,599; Milch Cows, 300; Heifers, 160; val. of cows and heifers, $12,474.

Butter, 26,865 lbs.; val. of butter, $5,372; Cheese, 4,390 lbs.; val. of cheese, $439.

Indian Corn, 244 acres; Indian Corn per acre, 32 bush.; val., $7,808.

Wheat, 9 acres; Wheat, per acre, 13½ bush.; val., $243.

Rye, 186 acres; Rye, per acre, 10 bush.; val., $2,325.

Barley, 2 acres; Barley, per acre, 15 bush.; val., $30.

Oats, 90 acres; Oats, per acre, 30 bush.; val., $1,350.

Potatoes, 93 acres; Potatoes, per acre, 72 bush.; val., $3,348.

English Mowing, 1,333 acres; English Hay, 1,616 tons; val., $24,240.

Apple Trees, cultivated for their fruit, 3,000; val. of apples, 50 cts. per bush.

Pear Trees, cultivated for their fruit, 47; val. of pears, $1 per bush.

Hops, 16½ acres; Hops, per acre, 712 lbs.; val., $2,892.50.

BUCKLAND.

Establishments for m. of cutlery, 1; val. of cutlery, $175,000; cap., $150,000; emp., 250.

File Manufactories, 1; Files m'd., – gross; val. of files, $2,000; cap., $500; emp., 4.

Daguerreotype Artists, 1; Daguerreotypes taken, 500; cap., $300; emp., 1.

Tanneries, 1; Hides of all kinds tanned, 1,200; val. of leather tanned, $8,000; cap., $2,700; emp., 2.

Currying Establishments, 1; val. of leather curried, $4,000; cap., $1,300; emp., 3.

Val. of building stone quarried and prepared for building, $2,000; emp., 3.

Charcoal m'd., 6,000 bush.; val. of same, $480; emp., 1.

Lumber prepared for market, 350,000 ft.; val. of lumber, $2,800; emp., 6.

Firewood prepared for market, 3,000 cords; val. of firewood, $9,000; emp., 12.

Saxony Sheep, of different grades, –; Merino Sheep, of different grades, 731; all other kinds of Sheep, 170; val. of all sheep, $2,062; Wool produced from Saxony sheep, – lbs.; Merino Wool produced, 2,193 lbs.; all other Wool produced, 680 lbs.

Horses, 156; val. of horses, $11,145; Oxen over three years old, 114; Steers under three years old, 164; val. of oxen and steers, $8,457; Milch Cows, 389; Heifers, 141; val. of cows and heifers, $11,522.

Butter, 77,000 lbs.; val. of butter, $13,000; Cheese, 38,500 lbs.; val. of cheese, $3,080.

Indian Corn, 146 acres; Indian Corn, per acre, 40 bush.; val., $4,860.

Rye, 20 acres; Rye, per acre, 15 bush.; val., $300.

Barley, 6 acres; Barley, per acre, 20 bush.; val., $80.

Oats, 75 acres; Oats, per acre, 30 bush.; val., $1,125.

Potatoes, 75 acres; Potatoes, per acre, 100 bush.; val., $3,750.

English Mowing, 223 acres; English Hay, 260 tons; val., $2,600.

Wet Meadow or Swale Hay, 1,060 tons; val., $5,300.

Apple Trees, cultivated for their fruit, 1,500; val., $3,000.

Establishments for m. of knife, shaving, pen and pencil boxes, 3; cap., $1,200; val. of boxes m'd., $2,150; emp., 4.

Gross val. of all other articles m'd., $7,500; cap., $4,000; emp., 10. The articles are as follows:—Broom Handles, Pen Holders, Splints, Carpenters' Gauges, Twine Reels, Lemon Squeezers, Towel Rollers, Meat Mauls, Scythes, Sticks, and Brush Handles.

Swine raised, 143; val., $968.

CHARLEMONT.

Plough Manufactories, –; Ploughs and other Agricultural Tools m'd., (100 corn-planters, 30 cultivators,) 130; val., $330; cap., $100; emp., 1.

Establishments for m. of railroad cars, coaches, chaises, wagons, sleighs, and other vehicles, 1; val. of railroad cars, &c., m'd., $1,000; cap., $400; emp., 3.

Tanneries, 2; Hides of all kinds tanned, 3,800; val. of leather tanned, $7,900; cap., $1,500; emp., 4.

Boots of all kinds m'd., 280 pairs; Shoes of all kinds m'd., 195 pairs; val. of boots and shoes, $1,035; m. emp., 4.

Val. of palm leaf hats, $3,612; f. emp., 200.

Val. of marble prepared for market, $2,000; emp., 3.

Val. of wooden ware not otherwise enumerated, including farming utensils m'd., (20,000 hoe handles, 85,000 broom handles,) $1,490; emp., 3.

Lumber prepared for market, 625,000 ft.; val. of lumber, $4,375; emp., 9.

Firewood prepared for market, 525 cords; val. of firewood, $1,000; emp., 3.

Saxony Sheep of different grades, –; Merino Sheep, of different grades, – ; all other kinds of Sheep, 990 ; val. of all sheep, $1,980 ; Wool produced from Saxony sheep, – lbs. ; Merino Wool produced, – lbs. ; all other Wool produced, 2,970 lbs.

Horses, 150 ; val. of horses, $8,500 ; Oxen over three years old, 154 ; Steers under three years old, 184 ; val. of oxen and steers, $9,000 ; Milch Cows, 411 ; Heifers, 180 ; val. of cows and heifers, $12,700.

Butter, 34,900 lbs. ; val. of butter, $6,322 ; Cheese, 12,700 lbs. ; val. of cheese, $1,016 ; Honey, 200 lbs. ; val. of of honey, $30.

Indian Corn, 238 acres, Indian Corn, per acre, 40 bush. ; val., $9,520.

Wheat, 10 acres ; Wheat, per acre, 14½ bush. ; val., $292.

Rye, 125 acres ; Rye, per acre, 11 bush. ; val., $1,485.

Barley, 10 acres ; Barley, per acre, 17 bush. ; val., $127.50.

Oats, 90 acres ; Oats, per acre, 30 bush. ; val., $1,350.

Potatoes, 99 acres ; Potatoes, per acre, 80 bush. ; val., $3,960.

Turnips, cultivated as a field crop, 1⅝ acre ; Turnips, per acre, 400 bush ; val., $83.

English Mowing, 2,150 acres ; English Hay, 1,946 tons ; val., $23,352.

Apple Trees, cultivated for their fruit, 4,500 ; val., $2,500.

Swine, 225 ; val., $1,350.

Val. of all other articles produced, $20,304 ; cap. invested in the following branches of industry, $2,000 ; emp., 24, as follows :—

Buckwheat, 15 acres ; Buckwheat, per acre, 11$\frac{1}{15}$; val., $132.

Maple Sugar, 4,600 lbs. ; val., $4,060.

Val. of flagging stone quarried, $200.

Scythe Sticks m'd., 3,750 doz. ; val., $15,000.

Friction Matches, 4,000 gross ; val., $1,000 ; val. of match-boxes, $1,000.

Val. of silk and other bonnets m'd., $2,400.

Val. of axe handles and ox bows m'd., $112.

COLERAINE.

Cotton Mills, 2; Spindles, 7,500; Cotton consumed, 450,000 lbs.; Cloth m'd., 2,800,000 yds., Print Cloths; val. of cloth, $85,000; Batting m'd., 7,500 lbs.; val. of batting, $750; m. emp., 55; f. emp., 85.

Plough Manufactories, 1; Ploughs and other Agricultural Tools m'd., 55; val., $300; emp., 1.

Tanneries, 1; Hides of all kinds tanned, 1,500; val. of leather tanned, $4,200; cap., $2,500; emp., 2.

Boots of all kinds m'd., 1,500 pairs; Shoes of all kinds m'd., 30 pairs; val. of boots and shoes, $2,600; m. emp., 2.

Val. of palm leaf hats m'd., $267.

Val. of mechanics' tools m'd., $3,000; emp. 3.

Val. of wooden ware not otherwise enumerated, including farming utensils m'd, $5,340; emp., 13.

Lumber prepared for market, 176,000 ft.; val. of lumber, $10,081; emp., 12.

Firewood prepared for market, 1,632 cords; val. of firewood, $2,448; emp., 5.

Saxony Sheep, of different grades, –; Merino Sheep, of different grades, 1,293; all other kinds of Sheep, 1,177; val. of all sheep, $7,410; Wool produced from Saxony sheep, – lbs.; Merino Wool produced, 3,161 lbs.; all other Wool produced, 3,531 lbs.

Horses, 211; val. of horses, $18,155; Oxen over three years old, 267; Steers under three years old, 325; val. of oxen and steers, $24,834; Milch Cows, 578; Heifers, 209; val. of cows and heifers, $18,856.

Butter, 39,335 lbs.; val. of butter, $7,180.30; Cheese, 8,880 lbs.; val. of cheese, $710; Honey, 445 lbs.; val. of honey, $74.

Indian Corn, 401 acres; Indian Corn, per acre, 30 bush.; val., $12,030.

Wheat, 22 acres; Wheat, per acre, 15 bush.; val., $660.

Rye, 71 acres; Rye, per acre, 15 bush.; val., $1,329.

Barley, 17 acres; Barley, per acre, 20 bush.; val., $266.

Oats, 250 acres; Oats, per acre, 25 bush.; val., $3,125.

Potatoes, 152 acres; Potatoes, per acre, 125 bush.; val., $5,430.

English Mowing, 3,111 acres; English Hay, 2,536 tons; val., $25,360.

Wet Meadow or Swale Hay, 1,156 tons; val., $5,780.

Apple Trees, cultivated for their fruit, 4,437; val., $3,063.

Maple Sugar produced, 15,481 lbs.; val., $1,238.

CONWAY.

Cotton Mills, 3; Spindles, 1,854; Cotton consumed, 300,387 lbs.; Cloth m'd., 207,542 yds. of Grain Bags, and 59,080 yds. of Duck; val. of cloth, $41,867; cap., $34,200; m. emp., 27; f. emp., 53.

Woollen Mills, 1; Sets of Machinery, 4; Wool consumed, 200,000 lbs.; Satinet m'd., 300,000 yds.; val. of satinet, $150,000; cap., $65,000; m. emp., 46; f. emp., 26.

Establishments for m. of cutlery, 1; val. of cutlery, $40,000; cap., $30,000; emp., 50.

Saddle, Harness and Trunk Manufactories, 1; val. of saddles, &c., $1,000; cap., $150; emp., 1.

Establishments for m. of railroad cars, coaches, chaises, wagons, sleighs, and other vehicles, 1; val. of railroad cars, &c., m'd., $1,000; cap., $200; emp., 1.

Chair and Cabinet Manufactories, 1; val. of chairs and cabinet ware, $2,000; cap., $1,800; emp., 2.

Tin Ware Manufactories, 1; val. of tin ware, $1,800; cap., $1,000; emp., 1.

Tanneries, 1; Hides of all kinds tanned, 4,000; val. of leather tanned, $20,000; cap., $10,000; emp., 8.

Boots of all kinds m'd., 130 pairs; Shoes of all kinds m'd., 650 pairs; val. of boots and shoes, $1,315; m. emp., 4.

Charcoal m'd., 550 bush.; val. of same, $38.50; emp., 1.

Lumber prepared for market, 35,000 ft.; val. of lumber, $3,500; emp., 1.

Firewood prepared for market, 1,459 cords; val. of firewood, $2,918; emp., 5.

Saxony Sheep, of different grades, –; Merino Sheep, of different grades, 77; all other kinds of Sheep, 742; val. of all sheep, $1,787; Wool produced from Saxony sheep, – lbs.; Merino Wool produced, 283 lbs.; all other Wool produced, 2,148 lbs.

Horses, 224; val. of horses, $18,584; Oxen over three years old, 286; Steers under three years old, 191; val. of oxen and steers, $21,183; Milch Cows, 449; Heifers, 163; val. of cows and heifers, $18,059.

Butter, 35,975 lbs.; val. of butter, $6,475.50; Cheese, 17,105 lbs.; val. of cheese, $1,539.45; Honey, 166 lbs.; val. of honey, $26.56.

Indian Corn, 306 acres; Indian Corn, per acre, 44½ bush.; val., $13,617.

Wheat, 27 acres; Wheat, per acre, 16⅛ bush.; val., $870.75.

Rye, 76 acres; Rye, per acre, 13½ bush.; val., $1,026.

Barley, 12 acres; Barley, per acre, 29⅓ bush.; val., $352.

Oats, 124 acres; Oats, per acre, 27½ bush.; val., $1,688.88.

Potatoes, 115½ acres; Potatoes, per acre, 77 bush.; val. $2,964.50.

Onions, ¼ acre; Onions, per acre, 200 bush.; val., $18.75.

Turnips, cultivated as a field crop, 1 acre; Turnips, per acre, 300 bush.; val., $75.

Carrots, 1 acre; Carrots, per acre, 400 bush.; val., $100.

Beets and other esculent vegetables, – acres; all other Grain or Root Crops, 6 acres; val., $90.

English Mowing, 3,052 acres; English Hay, 3,229 tons; val., $32,290.

Wet Meadow or Swale Hay, 79 tons; val., $474.

Apple Trees, cultivated for their fruit, 1,563; val., $1,015.

Pear Trees, cultivated for their fruit, 56; val., $56.

Tobacco, 4 acres; val., $623.

Broom Handles m'd., 75,000; val., $750.

Brush Handles m'd., 37,000; val., $111.

Swine raised, 262; val., $2,620.

Maple Sugar, 18,270 lbs.; val., $1,827.

DEERFIELD.

Establishments for m. of cutlery, 1; val. of cutlery, $250,000; cap., $175,000; emp., 300.

Establishments for m. of railroad cars, coaches, chaises, wagons, sleighs, and other vehicles, 3; val. of railroad cars, &c., m'd., $5,200; emp., 8.

Tanneries, 1; Hides of all kinds tanned, 700; val. of leather tanned, $1,500; cap., $700; emp., 2.

Currying Establishments, 1; val. of leather curried, $1,000; emp., 1.

Boots of all kinds m'd., 68 pairs; Shoes of all kinds m'd., 1,250 pairs; val. of boots and shoes, $1,630; m. emp., 4; f. emp., 1.

Val. of palm leaf hats, $100; f. emp., 1.

Bricks m'd., 400,000; val. of bricks, $1,600; emp., 5.

Corn and other Brooms m'd., 36,000; val. of brooms, $6,100; emp., 7.

Lumber prepared for market, 180,000 ft.; val. of lumber, $2,000; emp., 6.

Firewood prepared for market, 1,485 cords; val. of firewood, $3,085; emp., 7.

Saxony Sheep, of different grades, –; Merino Sheep, of different grades, –; all other kinds of Sheep, 784; val. of all sheep, $1,694; Wool produced from Saxony sheep, – lbs.; Merino Wool produced, – lbs.; all other Wool produced, 2,400 lbs.; val. of wool, $690.

Horses, 337; val. of horses, $24,000; Oxen over three years old, 351; Steers under three years old, 284; val. of oxen and steers, $32,335; Milch Cows, 695; Heifers, 285; val. of cows and heifers, $28,670.

Butter, 66,630 lbs.; val. of butter, $11,105; Cheese, 5,650 lbs.; val. of cheese, $565; Honey, 100 lbs.; val. of honey, $16.

Indian Corn, 1,280 acres; Indian Corn, per acre, 35 bush.; val., $44,800; Broom Corn, 283 acres; Broom Bush, per acre,

550 lbs.; val., $12,400; Broom Seed, per acre, 39 bush.; val., $2,750.

Wheat, 71 acres; Wheat, per acre, 13 bush.; val., $1,425.

Rye, 744 acres; Rye, per acre, 10 bush.; val., $7,440.

Barley, 33 acres; Barley, per acre, 20 bush.; val., $585.

Oats, 492 acres; Oats, per acre, 28 bush.; val., $6,850.

Potatoes, 192 acres; Potatoes, per acre, 100 bush.; val., $5,000.

Onions, ½ acre; Onions, per acre, 150 bush.; val., $70.

Turnips, cultivated as a field crop, 1 acre; Turnips, per acre, 50 bush.; val., $15.

Carrots, 1¾ acre; Carrots, per acre, 200 bush.; val., $150.

Beets and other esculent vegetables, ¼ acre; val., $10.

Millet, ¾ acre; val., $20.

English Mowing, 3,173 acres; English Hay, 4,000 tons; val., $45,000.

Wet Meadow or Swale Hay, 98 tons; val., $700.

Apple Trees, cultivated for their fruit, 3,323; val., $2,430.

Pear Trees, cultivated for their fruit, 20; val., $20.

Hops, 1½ acre; Hops, per acre, 1,000 lbs.; val., $300.

Tobacco, 13½ acres; val., $1,850.

Cranberries, 2 acres; val., $180.

Establishments for m. of paper boxes, 2; cap., $800; val. of boxes m'd., $3,600; emp., 9.

Swine raised, 502; val., $3,924.

Deer, 1;—(the Assessors defiantly remark, "produce another if you can,")—val. of deer, $12.

Buckwheat, 18 acres; Buckwheat, per acre, 12 bush.; val. of buckwheat, $215.

Beans, 5 acres; Beans, per acre, 11 bush.; val., $80.

Beds m'd., 130; val. of beds, $850; emp., 2.

Maple Sugar m'd., 2,400 lbs.; val. of sugar, $300.

Corn Planters, 100; val., $1,500; cap., $300; emp., 2.

Porte-Monnaies m'd., 62,000 doz.; val., $180,000; cap., $20,000; m. emp., 35; f. emp., 120.

Pocket-Books and Wallets, 19,400 doz.; val., $27,300; cap., $3,000; m. emp., 14; f. emp., 57.

ERVING.

Chair and Cabinet Manufactories, 1 ; val. of chairs and cabinet ware, $25,000 ; cap., $8,000 ; emp., 12.

Val. of palm leaf hats, $574 ; f. emp., 26.

Charcoal m'd., 100,000 bush. ; val. of same, $8,000 ; emp., 3.

Lumber prepared for market, 1,155,000 ft. ; val. of lumber, $103,950 ; emp., 12.

Firewood prepared for market, 2,285 cords ; val. of firewood, $5,141.25 ; emp., 5.

Saxony Sheep, of different grades, – ; Merino Sheep, of different grades, – ; all other kinds of Sheep, 50 ; val. of all sheep, $75 ; Wool produced from Saxony sheep, – lbs. ; Merino Wool produced, – lbs. ; all other Wool produced, 150 lbs.

Horses, 34 ; val. of horses, $2,750 ; Oxen over three years old, 55 ; Steers under three years old, 33 ; val. of oxen and steers, $4,000 ; Milch Cows, 79 ; Heifers, 27 ; val. of cows and heifers, $2,875.

Butter, 4,525 lbs. ; val. of butter, $905 ; Cheese, 2,325 lbs. ; val. of cheese, $186.

Indian Corn, 90 acres ; Indian Corn, per acre, 20 bush. ; val., $1,800 ; Broom Corn, 8½ acres ; Broom Bush, per acre, 450 lbs. ; val., $372.50 ; Broom Seed, per acre, 45 bush. ; val., $133.87.

Rye, 118 acres ; Rye, per acre, 7 bush. ; val., $1,032.50.

Oats, 25 acres ; Oats, per acre, 20 bush. ; val., $250.

Potatoes, 31 acres ; Potatoes, per acre, 80 bush. ; val., $1,240.

English Mowing, 380 acres ; English Hay, 285 tons ; val., $4,275.

Wet Meadow or Swale Hay, 33 tons ; val., $231.

Apple Trees, cultivated for their fruit, 1,000 ; val., $500.

Establishments for m. of casks, 1 ; cap., $800 ; Casks m'd., 400 ; val., $500 ; emp., 1.

Establishments for m. of friction match wood, 1 ; cap., $1,900 ; Match woods m'd., 52,000 gross ; val., $5,200 ; emp., 8.

Establishments for m. of piano-forte cases and legs, 1; articles m'd., 40 cases and 1,200 sets of legs; val., $1,000; cap., $3,000.

Railroad Ties m'd., 5,745; val., $1,273.90.

Swine, 90; val., $720.

GILL.

Establishments for m. of railroad cars, coaches, chaises, wagons, sleighs, and other vehicles, –; val. of railroad cars, &c., m'd., $500; emp., 3.

Tanneries, 1; Hides of all kinds tanned, 400; val. of leather tanned, $1,500; cap., $1,000; emp., 2.

Val. of palm leaf hats m'd., $1,375.

Val. of wooden ware not otherwise enumerated, including farming utensils m'd., $2,500; emp., 3.

Corn and other Brooms m'd., 1,200; val. of brooms, $240; emp., 1, part of the year.

Lumber prepared for market, 50,000 ft.; val. of lumber, $600.

Firewood prepared for market, 500 cords; val. of firewood, $1,500.

Saxony Sheep, of different grades, –; Merino Sheep, of different grades, –; all other kinds of Sheep, 170; val. of all sheep, $510; Wool produced from Saxony sheep, – lbs.; Merino Wool produced, – lbs.; all other Wool produced, 510 lbs.

Horses, 123; val. of horses, $9,840; Oxen over three years old, 154; Steers under three years old, 140; val. of oxen and steers, $11,500; Milch Cows, 339; Heifers, 107; val. of cows and heifers, $11,150.

Butter, 48,000 lbs.; val. of butter, $10,560; Cheese, 5,500 lbs.; val. of cheese, $550; Honey, 400 lbs.; val. of honey, $66.

Indian Corn, 332 acres; Indian Corn, per acre, 35 bush.; val., $11,620; Broom Corn, 39 acres; Broom Bush, per acre, 700 lbs.; val., $2,454; Broom Seed, per acre, 40 bush.; val., $597.

Wheat, 20 acres; Wheat, per acre, 12 bush.; val., $480.
Rye, 245 acres; Rye, per acre, 10 bush.; val., $3,062.
Oats, 130 acres; Oats, per acre, 30 bush.; val., $1,950.
Potatoes, 80 acres; Potatoes, per acre, 100 bush.; val., $4,000.
Onions, 1 acre; Onions, per acre, 400 bush.; val., $300.
Carrots, 2 acres; Carrots, per acre, $600 bush.; val., $300.
English Mowing, 1,004 acres; English Hay, 1,255 tons; val., $12,550.
Wet Meadow or Swale Hay, 200 tons; val., $1,000.
Apple Trees, cultivated for their fruit, 3,000; val., $1,250.
Pear Trees, cultivated for their fruit, 40; val., $25.
Hops, 2 acres; Hops, per acre, 600 lbs.; val., $300.

GREENFIELD.

Woollen Mills, 1; Sets of Machinery, 5; Wool consumed, 150,000 lbs.; Cassimere m'd., 140,000 yds.; val. of cassimere, $150,000; cap., $80,000; m. emp., 70; f. emp., 50.

Furnaces for m. of hollow ware and castings other than pig iron, 1; Hollow Ware and other Castings m'd., 200 tons; val. of hollow ware and castings, $16,000; cap., $8,000; emp., 5.

Daguerreotype Artists, 2; Daguerreotypes taken, 2,100; cap., $1,400; emp., 2.

Saddle, Harness and Trunk Manufactories, 2; val. of saddles, &c., $3,000; cap., $2,000; emp., 7.

Establishments for m. of railroad cars, coaches, chaises, wagons, sleighs, and other vehicles, 2; val. of railroad cars, &c., m'd., $3,700; cap., $2,500; emp., 6.

Chair and Cabinet Manufactories, 1; val. of chairs and cabinet ware, $1,700; cap., $2,000; emp., 4.

Tin Ware Manufactories, 2; val. of tin ware, $1,700; cap., $1,400; emp., 6.

Tanneries, 1; Hides of all kinds tanned, 400; val. of leather tanned, $2,000; cap., $800; emp., 1.

Boots of all kinds m'd., 590 pairs; Shoes of all kinds m'd., 2,255 pairs; val. of boots and shoes, $4,640; m. emp., 7.

Bricks m'd., 500,000; val. of bricks, $2,500; emp., 6.

Val. of blacking, $800; emp., 2.

Val. of mechanics' tools m'd., $120,000; cap., $70,000; emp., 80.

Lumber prepared for market, 554,000 ft.; val. of lumber, $6,000; emp., 13.

Firewood prepared for market, 1,663 cords; val. of firewood, $5,848; emp., 6.

Saxony Sheep, of different grades, –; Merino Sheep, of different grades, –; all other kinds of Sheep, 399; val. of all sheep, $1,238; Wool produced from Saxony sheep, – lbs.; Merino Wool produced, – lbs.; all other Wool produced, 931 lbs.

Horses, 252; val. of horses, $23,659; Oxen over three years old, 209; Steers under three years old, 243; val. of oxen and steers, $24,415; Milch Cows, 583; Heifers, 127; val. of cows and heifers, $19,655.

Butter, 49,035 lbs.; val. of butter, $10,905; Cheese, 5,920 lbs.; val. of cheese, $545; Honey, 437 lbs.; val. of honey, $68.

Indian Corn, 404 acres; Indian Corn, per acre, 35 bush.; val., $15,801.

Wheat, 15 acres; Wheat, per acre, 18 bush.; val., $604.

Rye, 261 acres; Rye, per acre, 9 bush.; val., $2,952.

Oats, 121 acres; Oats, per acre, 30 bush.; val., $2,201.

Potatoes, 72 acres; Potatoes, per acre, 100 bush.; val., $3,923.

Onions, 1 acre; Onions, per acre, 38 bush.; val., $38.

Turnips, cultivated as a field crop, 2½ acres; Turnips, per acre, 411 bush.; val., $351.

Carrots, 2 acres; Carrots, per acre, 330 bush.; val., $220.

Beets and other esculent vegetables, – acres; all other Grain or Root Crops, 16 acres; val., $240.

English Mowing, 1,779 acres; English Hay, 2,637 tons; val., $31,644.

Wet Meadow or Swale Hay, 159 tons; val., $1,161.

Apple Trees, cultivated for their fruit, 480; val., $960.

Pear Trees, cultivated for their fruit, 50; val., $150.

Hops, 1 acre; Hops, per acre, 500 lbs.; val., $85.

Establishments for m. of sashes, doors and blinds, 1; cap., $5,000; val. m'd., $12,000; emp., 10.

Bakeries, 1; Flour consumed, 500 bbls.; val. of bread m'd., $6,000; cap., $2,000; emp., 5.

Establishments for m. of baby carriages, 3; carriages m'd., 1,700; val., $17,000; cap., $3,500; emp., 14.

White Beans, 10 acres; White Beans, per acre, 12 bush.; val., $180.

HAWLEY.

Tanneries, 1; Hides of all kinds tanned, 2,500; val. of leather tanned, $12,000; cap., $2,000; emp., 3.

Val. of palm leaf hats, $597; m. emp., 1; f. emp., 4.

Lumber prepared for market, 364,000 ft.; val. of lumber, $18,200; emp., 2.

Firewood prepared for market, 459 cords; val. of firewood, $650; emp., 2.

Saxony Sheep, of different grades, –; Merino Sheep, of different grades, –; all other kinds of Sheep, 1,286; val. of all sheep, $2,572; Wool produced from Saxony sheep, – lbs.; Merino Wool produced, – lbs.; all other Wool produced, 3,858 lbs.

Horses, 165; val. of horses, $11,338; Oxen over three years old, 129; Steers under three years old, 205; val. of oxen and steers, $11,585; Milch Cows, 300; Heifers, 180; val. of cows and heifers, $8,506.

Butter, 22,440 lbs.; val. of butter, $4,488; Cheese, 4,251 lbs.; val. of cheese, $425; Honey, 230 lbs.; val. of honey, $40.

Indian Corn, 137 acres; Indian Corn, per acre, 30 bush.; val., $4,110.

Wheat, 22 acres; Wheat, per acre, 20 bush.; val., $880.

Rye, 23 acres; Rye, per acre, 20 bush.; val., $460.

Barley, 34 acres; Barley, per acre, 20 bush.; val., $680.

Oats, 67 acres; Oats, per acre, 30 bush.; val., $1,005.

Potatoes, 126 acres; Potatoes, per acre, 100 bush.; val., $6,300.

Carrots, 3 acres; Carrots, per acre, 1,500 bush.; val., $500.

English Mowing, 1,616 acres; English Hay, 1,234 tons; val., $12,340.

Wet Meadow or Swale Hay, 205 tons; val., $1,025.

Apple Trees, cultivated for their fruit, 1,000; val., $1,000.

Pear Trees, cultivated for their fruit, 12; val., $20.

Establishments for m. of cheese and butter boxes, 2; val. of boxes m'd., $1,550; cap., $500.

Broom Handles m'd., 502,000; val., $5,020; emp., 10.

Shingles m'd., 227,000; val., $454.

Swine, 137; val., $685.

HEATH.

Tanneries, 1; Hides of all kinds tanned, 1,000; val. of leather tanned, $8,000; cap., $4,650; emp., 2.

Val. of palm leaf hats, $1,061; [not a regular business.]

Lumber prepared for market, 200,000 ft.; val. of lumber, $1,000; emp., 4.

Saxony Sheep, of different grades, –; Merino Sheep, of different grades, –; all other kinds of Sheep, 403; val. of all sheep, $1,294; Wool produced from Saxony sheep, – lbs.; Merino Wool produced, – lbs.; all other Wool produced, 1,612 lbs.

Horses, 175; val. of horses, $12,000; Oxen over three years old, 187; Steers under three years old, 177; val. of oxen and steers, $13,158; Milch Cows, 370; Heifers, 211; val. of cows and heifers, $13,500.

Butter, 24,757 lbs.; val. of butter, $4,952; Cheese, 15,479 lbs.; val. of cheese, $1,083.

Indian Corn, 182 acres; Indian Corn, per acre, 33 bush.; val., $6,726.72.

Wheat, 35 acres; Wheat, per acre, 15 bush.; val., $1,312.50.

Rye, 14 acres; Rye, per acre, 17 bush.; val., $296.75.

Barley, 56 acres; Barley, per acre, 18 bush.; val., $1,008.

Oats, 80 acres; Oats, per acre, 25 bush.; val., $1,200.

Potatoes, 130 acres; Potatoes, per acre, 110 bush.; val., $7,150.

Carrots, 4 acres; Carrots, per acre, 400 bush.; val., $533.

English Mowing, 2,800 acres; English Hay, 1,600 tons; val., $16,000.

Apple Trees, cultivated for their fruit, 3,900; val., $2,500.

All other articles produced are as follows:—

Chair-backs, val., $700; cap. $400; emp., 1.

Swine, 137; val., $1,030.

Maple Sugar, 6,000 lbs.; val., $480.

LEVERETT.

Woollen Mills, 1; Sets of Machinery, 1; Wool consumed, 4,000 lbs.; Satinet m'd., 1,000 yds.; val. of satinet, $600; Yarn m'd. and not made into cloth, 300 lbs.; val. of yarn, $250; cap., $2,500; m. emp., 3; f. emp., 2.

Scythe Manufactories, 2; Scythes m'd., 340; val. of scythes, $260; cap., $500; emp., 2.

Manufactories of Hoes, 2; val. of hoes, &c., $700; cap., $600; emp., 2.

Establishments for m. of railroad cars, coaches, chaises, wagons, sleighs, and other vehicles, 2; val. of railroad cars, &c., m'd., $1,675; cap., $1,000; emp., 4.

Tanneries, 2; Hides of all kinds tanned, 2,100; val. of leather tanned, $8,000; cap., $4,500; emp., 5.

Currying Establishments, 2; val. of leather curried, $4,000; cap., $300; emp., 3.

Boots of all kinds m'd., 125 pairs; Shoes of all kinds m'd., 125 pairs; val. of boots and shoes, $450; m. emp., 2.

Val. of palm leaf hats, $2,500; emp., 147.

Charcoal m'd., 60,300 bush., val. of same, $4,824; emp., 14.

Val. of whips m'd., $700; emp., 2.

Corn and other Brooms, 15,000; val. of brooms, $2,900; emp., 4.

Lumber prepared for market, 965,000 ft.; val. of lumber, $8,520; emp., 25.

Firewood prepared for market, 700 cords; val. of firewood, $1,275; emp., 8.

Saxony Sheep, of different grades, –; Merino Sheep, of different grades, –; all other kinds of Sheep, 413; val. of all sheep, $753; Wool produced from Saxony sheep, –; lbs.; Merino Wool produced, – lbs.; all other Wool produced, 997 lbs.

Horses, 130; val. of horses, $10,040; Oxen over three years old, 189; Steers under three years old, 128; val. of oxen and steers, $12,290; Milch Cows, 286; Heifers, 123; val. of cows and heifers, $90,400.

Butter, 23,510 lbs.; val. of butter, $4,231.80; Cheese, 10,225 lbs.; val. of cheese, $920.25.

Indian Corn, 342 acres; Indian Corn, per acre, 21 bush.; val., $7,182; Broom Corn, 4 acres; Broom Bush, per acre, 725 lbs.; val., $261; Broom Seed, per acre, 52½ bush.; val., $84.

Rye, 278 acres; Rye, per acre, 7½ bush.; val., $2,651.25.

Oats, 88 acres; Oats, per acre, 14 bush.; val., $625.

Carrots, ½ acre; Carrots, per acre, 300 bush.; val., $30.

English Mowing, 926 acres; English Hay, 839 tons; val., $10,068.

Wet Meadow or Swale Hay, 472 tons; val., $3,304.

Apple Trees, cultivated for their fruit, 6,070; val., $2,347.

Pear Trees, cultivated for their fruit, 72; val., $25.

Cranberries, 1 acre; val., $60.

Establishments for m. of sashes, doors and blinds, 1; cap., $300; val. m'd., $200; emp., 1.

Distilleries, 1; cap., $500; Alcohol distilled, 40 bbls.; val., $1,024; emp., 1.

Mills for grinding rye or corn, 2; Rye Flour, 266 bbls; val., $1,596; Corn, 462 bbls.; val., $1,386; emp., 2.

Plaster Mills, 1; Plaster ground, 70 tons; val., $490; emp., 1.

Establishments for m. of scythe snathe irons, 1; scythe snath irons m'd., 90,000; val., $9,000; emp., 5.

Machine Shops, 1; val. machinery m'd., $2,000; cap., $1,000; emp., 3.

LEYDEN.

Charcoal m'd., 4,000 bush.; val. of same, $320; emp., 1, during 60 days.

Lumber prepared for market, 30,000 ft.; val. of lumber, $240; emp., 1.

Firewood prepared for market, 563 cords; val. of firewood, $1,126; emp., 2.

Saxony Sheep, of different grades, –; Merino Sheep, of different grades, 1,340; all other kinds of Sheep, 456; val. of all sheep, $3,084; Wool produced from Saxony sheep, – lbs.; Merino Wool produced, 3,500 lbs.; all other Wool produced, 1,500 lbs.

Horses, 143; val. of horses, $10,500; Oxen over three years old, 154; Steers under three years old, 140; val. of oxen and steers, $11,810; Milch Cows, 260; Heifers, 109; val. of cows and heifers, $8,395.

Butter, 21,920 lbs.; val. of butter, $3,945.60; Cheese, 3,000 lbs.; val. of cheese, $240.

Indian Corn, 203 acres; Indian Corn, per acre, 30 bush.; val., $5,481.

Wheat, 23 acres; Wheat, per acre, 15 bush.; val., $603.75.

Rye, 32 acres; Rye, per acre, 12 bush.; val., $384.

Barley, 3 acres; Barley, per acre, 25 bush.; val., $50.

Oats, 128 acres; Oats, per acre, 25 bush.; val., $1,600.

Potatoes, 63 acres; Potatoes, per acre, 100 bush.; val., $2,100.

Carrots, 2 acres; Carrots, per acre, 500 bush.; val., $250.

English Mowing, 1,000 acres; English Hay, 1,000 tons; val., $6,500.

Wet Meadow or Swale Hay, 363 tons; val., $1,452.

Apple Trees, cultivated for their fruit, 200; val., $400.

Establishments for m. of broom handles, 1; Broom Handles m'd., 115,000; val., $1,150; cap., $400; emp., 2.

Maple Sugar m'd., 4,000 lbs.; val., $320.

Swine, 103; val., $618.

MONROE.

Boots of all kinds m'd., 22 pairs; Shoes of all kinds m'd., 13 pairs; val. of boots and shoes, $83; m. emp., 2.

Val. of palm leaf hats m'd., $429; m. emp., 4; f. emp., 15.

Lumber prepared for market, 249,000 ft.; val. of lumber, $1,495; emp., 7.

Saxony Sheep, of different grades, –; Merino Sheep, of different grades, –; all other kinds of Sheep, 140; val. of all sheep, $439; Wool produced from Saxony sheep, – lbs.; Merino Wool produced, – lbs.; all other Wool produced, 311 lbs.

Horses, 46; val. of horses, $2,755; Oxen, over three years old, 42; Steers under three years old, 51; val. of oxen and steers, $2,299; Milch cows, 141; Heifers, 78; val. of cows and heifers, $4,112.

Butter, 14,110 lbs.; val. of butter, $2,822; Cheese, 2,525 lbs.; val. of cheese, $202; Honey, 367 lbs.; val. of honey, $55.

Indian Corn, 25½ acres; Indian Corn, 32⅓ bush.; val., $825.

Wheat, 3½ acres; Wheat, per acre, 18 bush.; val., $130.

Barley, 1 acre; Barley, per acre, 32 bush.; val., $24.

Oats, 19½ acres; Oats, per acre, 31 bush.; val., $299.

Potatoes, 28¾ acres; Potatoes, per acre, 143¾ bush.; val., $1,736.70.

Onions, ¼ acre; Onions, per acre, 10 bush.; val., $7.50.

Carrots, ⅓ acre; Carrots, per acre, 90 bush.; val., $10.

Beets and other esculent vegetables, ¼ acre; val., $20.

English Mowing, 747 acres; English Hay, 713 tons; val., $5,704.

Apple Trees, cultivated for their fruit, 1,908; val., $202.90.

Pear Trees, cultivated for their fruit, 10; val., $5.

Beeswax, 21 lbs.; val., $7.87.

Swine raised, 37; val., $239.

MONTAGUE.

Scythe Snathe Manufactories, 1; Scythe Snathes m'd., 8,000; val. of scythe snathes, $3,500; cap., $3,000; emp., 3.

Piano-Forte Case Manufactories, 1; Piano-Forte Cases m'd., 300; cap., $4,500; emp., 16.

Establishments for m. of railroad cars, coaches, chaises, wagons, sleighs, and other vehicles, 2; val. of railroad cars, &c., m'd., $6,000; cap., $4,000; emp., 5.

Tin Ware Manufactories, 1; val. of tin ware, $700; cap., $1,400; emp., 2.

Tanneries, 1; Hides of all kinds tanned, 4,000; val. of leather tanned, $25,000; cap., $5,000; emp., 6.

Val. of palm leaf hats m'd., $11,225.

Bricks m'd., 200,000; val. of bricks, $800; emp., 2.

Val. of building stone quarried and prepared for building, $300; emp., 1.

Charcoal m'd., 17,600 bush.; val. of same, $895; emp., 2.

Corn and other Brooms m'd., 33,000; val. of brooms, $7,210; emp., 5.

Lumber prepared for market, 2,547,500 M.; val. of lumber, $34,259; emp., 39.

Firewood prepared for market, 3,732 cords; val. of firewood, $8,192; emp., 23.

Saxony Sheep, of different grades, 3; Merino Sheep, of different grades, –; all other kinds of Sheep, 197; val. of all sheep, $503; Wool produced from Saxony Sheep, 12 lbs.; Merino Wool produced, – lbs.; all other Wool produced, 549. lbs.

Horses, 183; val. of horses, $14,780; Oxen over three years old, 227; Steers under three years old, 209; val. of oxen and steers, $16,657; Milch Cows, 361; Heifers, 172; val. of cows and heifers, $12,695.

Butter, 40,780 lbs.; val. of butter, $6,796; Cheese, 6,310 lbs.; val. of cheese, $631; Honey, 183 lbs.; val. of honey, $30.

Indian Corn, 537 acres; Indian Corn, per acre, 27$\frac{1}{6}$ bush.; val., $14,816; Broom Corn, 36 acres; Broom Bush, per acre, 555 lbs.; val., $1,505; Broom Seed, per acre, 46 bush.; val., $835.

Wheat, 41 acres; Wheat, per acre, 11$\frac{1}{8}$ bush.; val., $810.

Rye, 641 acres; Rye, per acre, 7$\frac{1}{6}$ bush.; val., $6,492.

Oats, 122 acres; Oats, per acre, 21$\frac{1}{5}$ bush.; val., $1,311.50.

Potatoes, 116 acres; Potatoes, per acre, 103$\frac{1}{5}$ bush.; val., $6,003.

Onions, $\frac{1}{4}$ acre; Onions, per acre, 335 bush.; val., $73.

Turnips, cultivated as a field crop, 1$\frac{5}{8}$ acre; Turnips, per acre, 200 bush.; val., $78.

Carrots, 1$\frac{5}{16}$ acre; Carrots, per acre, 600 bush.; val., $259.

Millet, 4 acres; val., $72.

English Mowing, 1,216 acres; English Hay, 1,531 tons; val., $24,581.

Wet Meadow or Swale Hay, 348 tons; val., $3,041.

Apple Trees, cultivated for their fruit, 4,842; val., $2,250.

Pear Trees, cultivated for their fruit, 81; val., $44.

Hops, 1 acre; Hops, per acre, 600 lbs.; val., $100.

Cranberries, $\frac{1}{8}$ acre; val., $5.

Beeswax, 20 lbs.; val., $8.

Establishments for m. of sashes, doors and blinds, 1; cap., $200; val. m'd., $1,450; emp., 3.

Establishments for m. of cutlery boxes, 1; cap., $200; val. of boxes m'd., $400; emp., 1.

Quinces, 255 bush.; val., $223.

Maple Sugar, 8,220 lbs.; val., $822.

Swine raised, 376; val., $2,997.

Plough Handles m'd., 1,600; val., $800.

Huckleberries, 450 bush.; val., $900.

Rakes m'd., 6,000; val., $900; Fork Handles m'd., 1,200; val., $75; Hoe Handles m'd., 2,400; val., $100; cap., $500; emp., 2.

Establishments for m. of confectionery, 2; cap., $2,800; val. of confectionery m'd., $7,000; emp., 5½.

Railroad Ties m'd., 12,600; val., $2,900; emp., 6.

Buckwheat, 28 acres; Buckwheat, per acre, 10⁴⁄₇ bush.; val., $216.

Grist Mills, 1; 17,000 bush. rye meal, 24,000 bush. corn meal, 16,000 bush. provender, ground; cap., $2,000; emp., 2.

NEW SALEM.

Tanneries, 2; Hides of all kinds tanned, 3,300; val. of leather tanned, $16,000; cap., $5,333; emp., 3.

Currying Establishments, 2; val. of leather curried, $16,000; cap., $5,333; emp., 4.

Boots of all kinds m'd., 2,655 pairs; Shoes of all kinds m'd., 700 pairs; val. of boots and shoes, $6,052; m. emp., 9.

Val. of palm leaf hats, $7,115; m. emp., 11; f. emp., 187.

Bricks m'd., 70,000; val. of bricks, $350; emp., 2.

Charcoal m'd., 1,700 bush.; val. of same, $85; emp., 1.

Lumber prepared for market, 2,505,000 ft.; val. of lumber, $34,060; emp., 17.

Firewood prepared for market, 360 cords; val. of firewood, $515; emp., 2.

Saxony Sheep, of different grades, –; Merino Sheep, of

different grades, –; all other kinds of Sheep, 310; val. of all sheep, $845; Wool produced from Saxony sheep, – lbs.; Merino Wool produced, – lbs.; all other Wool produced, 958 lbs.

Horses, 182; val. of horses, $12,952; Oxen over three years old, 192; Steers under three years old, 118; val. of oxen and steers, $13,595; Milch Cows, 391; Heifers, 122; val. of cows and heifers, $11,773.

Butter, 23,840 lbs.; val. of butter, $4,768; Cheese, 15,600 lbs.; val. of cheese, $1,560; Honey, 30 lbs.; val. of honey, $5.

Indian Corn, 255 acres; Indian Corn, per acre, 28 bush.; val., $8,925.

Wheat, 2½ acres; Wheat, per acre, 22 bush.; val., $110.

Rye, 103 acres; Rye, per acre, 824 bush.; val., $1,060.

Barley, 28 acres; Barley, per acre, 16 bush.; val., $448.

Oats, 115 acres; Oats, per acre, 18 bush.; val., $1,138.50.

Potatoes, 155 acres; Potatoes, per acre, 68 bush.; val., $5,270.

Carrots, 1½ acre; Carrots, per acre, 515 bush.; val., $291.

English Mowing, 1,817 acres; English Hay, 1,350 tons; val., $16,200.

Wet Meadow or Swale Hay, 449 tons; val., $2,694.

Apple Trees, cultivated for their fruit, 3,408; val., $2,033.

Cranberries, 2 acres; val., $60.

Beeswax, 7 lbs.; val., $2.94.

Establishments for m. of match-boxes, 2; val. of boxes m'd., $5,480; cap., $2,500; emp., 8.

Swine, 126; val., $1,007.

NORTHFIELD.

Saddle, Harness and Trunk Manufactories, 1; val. of saddles, &c., $400; cap., $100; emp., 1.

Tanneries, 1; Hides of all kinds tanned, 1,700; val. of leather tanned, $10,000; cap., $3,000; emp., 2.

Boots of all kinds m'd., 200 pairs; Shoes of all kinds m'd., 100 pairs; val. of boots and shoes, $600.

Bricks m'd., 30,000; val. of bricks, $120; emp., 2.

Charcoal m'd., 50,000 bush.; val. of same, $4,000; emp., 2.

Val. of wooden ware not otherwise enumerated, including farming utensils m'd., $9,700.

Corn and other Brooms m'd., 155,000; val. of brooms, $27,000; emp., 18.

Lumber prepared for market, 1,579,000 ft.; val. of lumber, $17,750; emp., 25.

Firewood prepared for market, 350 cords; val. of firewood, $875; emp., 6.

Saxony Sheep, of different grades, 300; Merino Sheep, of different grades, 200; all other kinds of Sheep, 723; val. of all sheep, $1,528; Wool produced from Saxony sheep, 1,200 lbs.; Merino Wool produced, 600 lbs.; all other Wool produced, 2,169 lbs.

Horses, 324; val. of horses, $22,180; Oxen over three years old, 290; Steers under three years old, 201; val. of oxen and steers, $17,900; Milch Cows, 572; Heifers 230; val. of cows and heifers, $18,900.

Butter, 42,377 lbs.; val. of butter, $8,475.40; Cheese, 5,325 lbs.; val. of cheese, $426; Honey, 250 lbs.; val. of honey, $37.50.

Indian Corn, 700 acres; Indian Corn, per acre, 35 bush.; val., $26,250; Broom Corn, 275 acres; Broom Bush, per acre, 600 lbs.; val., $13,200; Broom Seed, per acre, 50 bush.; val., $2,750.

Wheat, 16 acres; Wheat, 141 bush.; val., $282.

Rye, 516 acres; Rye, per acre, 12 bush.; val., $7,740.

Barley, 11 acres; Barley, per acre, 16 bush.; val., $171.

Oats, 305 acres; Oats, per acre, 40 bush.; val., $6,100.

Potatoes, 188 acres; Potatoes, per acre, 80 bush.; val., $6,016.

Onions, ½ acre; Onions, per acre, 115 bush.; val., $78.

Turnips, cultivated as a field crop, ½ acre; Turnips, per acre, 150 bush.; val., $30.

English Mowing, 2,424 acres; English Hay, 2,961 tons; val., $29,610.

Apple Trees, cultivated for their fruit, 2,190; val., $2,190.

Hops, 30 acres; Hops, per acre, 830 lbs.; val., $6,225.

Beeswax, 40 lbs.; val., $12.

Establishments for m. of sashes, doors and blinds, 1; cap., $600; val. m'd., $1,000; emp., 2.

Gross val. of ploughs and carts m'd., $300.

Buckwheat, 320 bush.; val., $240.

Beans, 40 bush.; val., $100.

Shooks m'd., 1,000 bunches; val., $1,000.

Shingles m'd., 150,000; val., $375.

Val. of essence oils m'd., $300.

Grist Mills, 4; income, $1,600.

Ferries, 3; income, $900.

Toll Bridge income, $700.

ORANGE.

Furnaces for m. of hollow ware and castings other than pig iron, 1; Hollow Ware and other Castings m'd., 50 tons; val. of hollow ware and castings, $4,000; cap., $1,000; emp., 3.

Plough Manufactories, 1; Ploughs and other Agricultural Tools m'd., 100; val., $600; cap., $200; emp., 1.

Saddle, Harness and Trunk Manufactories, 3; val. of saddles, &c., $2,000; cap., $600; emp., 4.

Establishments for m. of railroad cars, coaches, chaises, wagons, sleighs, and other vehicles, 2; val. of railroad cars, &c., m'd., $6,700; cap., $3,300; emp., 8.

Chair and Cabinet Manufactories, 2; val. of chairs and cabinet ware, $18,000; cap., $8,000; m. emp., 22; f. emp., 25.

Tin Ware Manufactories, 1; val. of tin ware, $400; cap., $200; emp., 1.

Tanneries, 1; Hides of all kinds tanned, 2,500; val. of leather tanned, $15,000; cap., $2,500; emp., 3.

Boots of all kinds m'd., 13,000 pairs; Shoes of all kinds m'd., – pairs; val. of boots and shoes, $16,000; m. emp., 20.

Val. of palm leaf hats m'd., $2,686; f. emp., 27.

Val. of wooden ware not otherwise enumerated, including farming utensils or bows and axletrees m'd., $500; emp., 1.

Lumber prepared for market, 1,031,000 ft.; val. of lumber, $15,000; emp., 20.

Firewood prepared for market, 500 cords; val. of firewood, $750; emp., 1.

Saxony Sheep, of different grades, –; Merino Sheep, of different grades, –; all other kinds of Sheep, 266; val. of all sheep, $588; Wool produced from Saxony sheep, – lbs.; Merino Wool produced, – lbs.; all other Wool produced, 745 lbs.

Horses, 225; val. of horses, $18,345; Oxen, over three years old, 188; Steers under three years old, 159; val. of oxen and steers, $14,093; Milch Cows, 520; Heifers, 143; val. of cows and heifers, $15,405.

Butter, 20,305 lbs.; val. of butter, $4,061; Cheese, 8,885 lbs.; val. of cheese, $710.80.

Indian Corn, 223 acres; Indian Corn, per acre, $28\frac{1}{14}$ bush.; val., $6,170.

Rye, 94 acres; Rye, per acre, $15\frac{1}{7}$ bush.; val., $1,594.12.

Barley, 21 acres; Barley, per acre, $20\frac{3}{7}$ bush.; val., $357.50.

Oats, 116 acres; Oats, per acre, 25 bush.; val., $1,450.

Potatoes, 130 acres; Potatoes, per acre, 49 bush.; val., $3,185.

Turnips, cultivated as a field crop, $1\frac{1}{2}$ acre; Turnips, per acre, 100 bush.; val., $25.

Carrots, $\frac{1}{8}$ acre; Carrots, per acre, 240 bush.; $10.

English Mowing, 1,680 acres; English Hay, 1,153 tons; val., $17,295.

Wet Meadow or Swale Hay, 615 tons; val., $6,150.

Apple Trees, cultivated for their fruit, 2,384; val., $1,830.

Pear Trees, cultivated for their fruit, 44; val., $82.

Establishments for m. of sashes, doors and blinds, 3; cap., $6,000; val. m'd., $14,000; emp., 16.

Pail Manufactories, 3; Pails m'd., 200,000; val., $25,000; cap., $13,000; emp., 32.

Swine, 282; val., $8,231.

Val. of all other articles m'd., $14,000; cap., $8,000; emp., 11.

ROWE.

Woollen Mills, 1; Sets of Machinery, 1; Wool consumed, 4,000 lbs.; Satinet m'd., 12,000 yds.; val. of satinet, $6,000; cap., $4,000; m. emp., 2; f. emp., 2.

Chair and Cabinet Manufactories, 1; val. of chairs and cabinet ware, $600; cap., $600; emp., 2.

Tanneries, 1; Hides of all kinds tanned, 800; val. of leather tanned, $3,000; cap., $2,500; emp., 2.

Currying Establishments, 1; val. of leather curried, $3,500; cap., $2,500; emp., 2.

Val. of palm leaf hats m'd., $730; f. emp., 51.

Val. of mechanics' tools m'd., $300; emp., 1.

Val. of wooden ware not otherwise enumerated, including farming utensils m'd., $1,200; emp., 4.

Saxony Sheep, of different grades, –; Merino Sheep, of different grades, 354; all other kinds of Sheep, 395; val. of all sheep, $2,222; Wool produced from Saxony Sheep, lbs. –; Merino Wool produced, 1,486 lbs.; all other Wool produced, 1,188 lbs.

Horses, 117; val. of horses, $7,075; Oxen over three years old, 88; Steers under three years old, 193; val. of oxen and steers, $9,447; Milch Cows, 236; Heifers, 187; val. of cows and heifers, $8,012.

Butter, 22,596 lbs.; val. of butter, $3,766; Cheese, 5,215 lbs.; val. of cheese, $365.05; Honey, 485 lbs.; val. of honey, $80.83.

Indian Corn, 108 acres; Indian Corn, per acre, 34 bush.; val., $3,672.

Wheat, 51 acres; Wheat, per acre, 17 bush.; val., $1,734.

Rye, 12 acres; Rye, per acre, 13 bush.; val., $195.

Barley, 6 acres; Barley, per acre, 20 bush.; val., $96.

Oats, 50 acres; Oats, per acre, 28 bush.; val., $700.

Potatoes, 76 acres; Potatoes, per acre, 124 bush.; val., $3,141.33.

English Mowing, 2,400 acres; English Hay, 1,800 tons; val., $12,600.

Apple Trees, cultivated for their fruit, 1,334; val., $1,014.

Maple Sugar produced, 15,135 lbs.; val., $1,135.12.

SHELBURNE.

Establishments for m. of steam-engines and boilers, 1; val. of steam-engines and boilers, $10,000; cap., $5,000; emp., 2.

Axe Manufactories, 1; Axes m'd., 7,600; val., 7,000; cap., $5,000; emp., 6.

Daguerreotype Artists, 1; Daguerreotypes taken, 600; cap., $600; emp., 1.

Saddle, Harness and Trunk Manufactories, 1; val. of saddles, &c., $1,150; cap., $800; emp., 2.

Establishments for m. of railroad cars, coaches, chaises, wagons, sleighs, and other vehicles, 1; val. of railroad cars, &c., m'd., $3,000; cap., $1,000; emp., 3.

Chair and Cabinet Manufactories, 2; val. of chairs and cabinet ware, $5,070; cap., $2,400; emp., 6.

Tin Ware Manufactories, 2; val. of tin ware, $1,400; cap., $1,000; emp., 3.

Tanneries, 2; Hides of all kinds tanned, 670; val. of leather tanned, $2,700; cap., $1,500; emp., 2.

Boots of all kinds m'd., 900 pairs; Shoes of all kinds m'd., 1,500 pairs; val. of boots and shoes, $3,300; m. emp., 4.

Firewood prepared for market, 1,000 cords; val. of firewood, $2,000; emp., 3.

Saxony Sheep, of different grades, –; Merino Sheep, of dif-

ferent grades, –; all other kinds of Sheep, 685; val. of all sheep, $1,757; Wool produced from Saxony sheep, – lbs.; Merino Wool produced, – lbs.; all other Wool produced, 2,069 lbs.

Horses, 210; val. of horses, $19,210; Oxen over three years old, 184; Steers under three years old, 249; val. of oxen and steers, $19,075; Milch Cows, 380; Heifers, 171; val. of cows and heifers, $15,367.

Butter, 38,460 lbs.; val. of butter, $7,692; Cheese, 13,270 lbs.; val. of cheese, $1,327.

Indian Corn, 234 acres; Indian Corn, per acre, 40 bush.; val., $9,360.

Wheat, 39 acres; Wheat, per acre, 15 bush.; val., $1,200.

Rye, 40 acres; Rye, per acre, 14 bush.; val., $770.

Barley, 10 acres; Barley, per acre, 20 bush.; val., $150.

Oats, 100 acres; Oats, per acre, 24 bush.; val., $1,200.

Potatoes, 59 acres; Potatoes, per acre, 100 bush.; val., $2,940.

Turnips, cultivated as a field crop, 2 acres; Turnips, per acre, 400 bush.; val., $320.

Carrots, 1 acre; Carrots, per acre, 700 bush.; val., $280.

English Mowing, 1,597 acres; English Hay, 2,306 tons; val., $27,672.

Apple Trees, cultivated for their fruit, 2,837; val., $2,934.

Pear Trees, cultivated for their fruit, 25; val., $50.

Auger Bits, Car Bits and Augers m'd., 30,000; Automatic Apple Pealers m'd., 33,300; cap., invested in both of these branches of business, $30,000; emp., 47.

SHUTESBURY.

Chair and Cabinet Manufactories, 1; val. of chairs and cabinet ware, $800; cap., $500; emp., 2.

Boots of all kinds m'd., 8,238 pairs; Shoes of all kinds m'd., – pairs; val. of boots and shoes, $12,631; m. emp., 16.

Val. of palm leaf hats, $4,830 ; f. emp., 195.

Charcoal m'd., 6,200 bush. ; val. of same, $310 ; emp., 1.

Lumber prepared for market, 2,281,000 ft. ; val. of lumber, $18,248 ; emp., 66.

Firewood prepared for market, 800 cords ; val. of firewood, $800 ; emp., 3.

Saxony Sheep, of different grades, – ; Merino Sheep, of different grades, – ; all other kinds of Sheep, 100 ; val. of all sheep, $250 ; Wool produced from Saxony sheep, – lbs. ; Merino Wool produced, – lbs. ; all other Wool produced, 357 lbs.

Horses, 116 ; val., of horses, $7,780 ; number of neat cattle, 517 ; val. of neat cattle, $15,865.

Butter, 20,000 lbs. ; val. of butter, $5,000 ; Cheese, 5,000 lbs. ; val. of cheese, $400.

Indian Corn, 152 acres ; Indian Corn, per acre, 20 bush. ; val., $3,805.

Rye, 63 acres ; Rye, per acre, 10 bush. ; val., $840.

Barley, 8 acres ; Barley, per acre, 11 bush. ; val., $100.

Oats, 64 acres ; Oats, per acre, 15 bush. ; val., $481.

Potatoes, 188 acres ; Potatoes, per acre, 50 bush. ; val., $4,699.

English Mowing, 1,440 acres ; English Hay, 770 tons ; val., $9,240.

Wet Meadow or Swale Hay, 195 tons ; val., $1,170.

Val. of apples, $600.

Cranberries, 4 acres ; val., $200.

Val. of baskets m'd., $200.

Swine, 181 ; val., $1,810.

SUNDERLAND.

Cotton Mills, 1 ; Cotton m'd. into Wicking, 15,000 lbs. ; val. of wicking, $2,550 ; m. emp., 1 ; f. emp., 2.

Flour Mills, 1 ; Flour m'd., 500 bbls. ; val. of flour m'd., $4,000 ; cap., $4,000 ; emp., 1.

Boots of all kinds m'd., 135 pairs; Shoes of all kinds m'd., 340 pairs; val. of boots and shoes, $875; emp., 2.

Corn and other Brooms m'd., 31,400; val. of brooms, $5,055; emp., 4.

Lumber prepared for market, 234,000 ft.; val. of lumber, $2,300; emp., 4.

Firewood prepared for market, 391 cords; val. of firewood, $976; emp., 1.

Saxony Sheep, of different grades, –; Merino Sheep, of different grades, –; all other kinds of Sheep, 152; val. of all sheep, $190; Wool produced from Saxony Sheep, – lbs.; Merino Wool produced, – lbs.; all other Wool produced, 500 lbs.

Horses, 164; val. of horses, $13,760; Oxen over three years old, 65; Steers under three years old, 50; val. of oxen and steers, $5,257; Milch Cows, 274; Heifers, 100; val. of cows and heifers, $8,393.

Dry Cows, 63; val., $1,926.

Butter, 35,146 lbs.; val. of butter, $7,099.20; Cheese, 4,070 lbs.; val. of cheese, $447.70; Honey, 441 lbs.; val. of honey, $70.56.

Indian Corn, 397 acres; Indian Corn, per acre, 34 bush.; val., $13,382; Broom Corn, 248 acres; Broom Bush, per acre, 556 lbs. val., $12,416; Broom Seed, per acre, 49 bush.; val., $4,809.

Wheat, 46 acres; Wheat, per acre, 10⅓ bush.; val., $1,192.

Rye, 351 acres; Rye, per acre, 9½ bush.; val., $3,617.90.

Barley, 3 acres; Barley, per acre, 10⅔ bush.; val., $32.

Oats, 71 acres; Oats, per acre, 26½ bush.; val., $952.50.

Potatoes, 62 acres; Potatoes, per acre, 94½ bush.; val., $2,926.50.

Turnips, cultivated as a field crop, 2 acres; Turnips, per acre, 233½ bush.; val., $93.40.

Carrots, 2¼ acres; Carrots, per acre, 616 bush.; val., $346.50.

English Mowing, 775 acres; English Hay, 1,034 tons; val., $15,510.

Wet Meadow, or Swale Hay, 70 tons; val., $490.

Apple Trees, cultivated for their fruit, 4,659; val., $1,240.

Pear Trees, cultivated for their fruit, 187; val., $52.
Hops, 2 acres; Hops, per acre, 800 lbs.; val., $400.
Tobacco, 7 acres; val., $765.
Raw Silk raised, 2½ lbs.; val., $15.
Beeswax, 11½ lbs.; val., $4.68.
Feed, ground at flour mill, 15,000 bush.; val., $12,750.
Swine, 567; val., $6,955.
Val. of poultry, $837.
Eggs, 9,665 doz.; val., $1,739.70.
Maple Sugar m'd., 8,950 lbs.; val., $895.
Beans, 49 bush.; val., $73.50.
Quinces, 56 bush.; val., $28.

WARWICK.

Glue Manufactories, and Manufactories for the preparation of Gums, 1; val. of glue and gums m'd., $800; cap., $800; emp., 2.

Tanneries, 2; Hides of all kinds tanned, 2,750; val. of leather tanned, $5,000; cap. $4,500; emp., 4.

Currying Establishments, 2; val. of leather curried, $5,000; cap., $4,500; emp., 4.

Boots of all kinds m'd., 105 pairs; Shoes of all kinds m'd., 95 pairs; val. of shoes made, $350; emp., 1.

Val. of palm leaf hats, $3,465. "Some made in nearly every family."

Charcoal m'd., 1,900 bush.; val. of same, $195.

Lumber prepared for market, 1,098 ft.; val. of lumber, $11,390; emp., "Not able to ascertain."

Firewood prepared for market, 824 cords; val. of firewood, $1,644.

Saxony Sheep, of different grades, –; Merino Sheep, of different grades, –; all other kinds of Sheep, 305; val. of all sheep, $773; Wool produced from Saxony sheep, – lbs.; Merino Wool produced, – lbs.; all other Wool produced, 871 lbs.

Horses, 161; val. of horses, 11,798; Oxen over three years old, 161; Steers under three years old, 242; val. of oxen and steers, $12,753; Milch Cows, 388; Heifers, 177; val. of cows and heifers, $11,147.

Butter, 21,091 lbs.; val. of butter, $4,218; Cheese, 7,525 lbs.; val. of cheese, $602; Honey, 35 lbs.; val. of honey, $12.

Indian Corn, 147 acres; Indian Corn, per acre,. 31 bush.; val., $6,242.

Wheat, 6 acres; Wheat, per acre, 12 bush.; val., $180.

Rye, 63 acres; Rye, per acre, 11 bush.; val., $1,086.

Barley, 33 acres; Barley, per acre, 21 bush.; val., $526.

Oats, 86 acres; Oats, per acre, 26 bush.; val., $1,119.

Potatoes, 115 acres; Potatoes, per acre, 87 bush.; val., $5,033.

Carrots, $\frac{3}{4}$ acre; Carrots, per acre, 807 bush.; val., $160.

English Mowing, 1,793 acres; English Hay, 876 tons; val., $13,140.

Wet Meadow or Swale Hay, 483 tons; val., $4,064.

Apple Trees, cultivated for their fruit, 1,598; val., $1,337.

Pear Trees, cultivated for their fruit, 26; val., $26.

Val. of staves for pails, $2,575.

Val. of oak staves for hogsheads, $1,660.

Val. railroad ties, $2,180.

Val. hemlock bark, $900.

Swine, 170; val. $1,209.

Val. of chestnut shingles, (268,000) m'd., $599.

Val. of wooden ware m'd., $2,440; emp., not stated.

WENDELL.

Daguerreotype Artists, 1; Daguerreotypes taken, 125; cap., $75.

Boots of all kinds m'd., 3,100 pairs; Shoes of all kinds m'd., 1,700 pairs; val. of boots and shoes, $4,650; m. emp., 14; f. emp., 6.

Val. of palm leaf hats, $2,846 ; f. emp., 133.

Lumber prepared for market, 1,257,000 ft. ; val. of lumber, $8,600 ; emp., 19.

Firewood prepared for market, 1,673 cords; val. of firewood, $2,409 ; emp., 12.

Saxony Sheep, of different grades, – ; Merino Sheep, of different grades, – ; all other kinds of Sheep, 87 ; val. of all sheep, $151.

Horses, 93 ; val. of horses, $4,003 ; Oxen over three years old, 114 ; Steers under three years old, 96 ; val. of oxen and steers, $7,745 ; Milch Cows, 193 ; Heifers, 49 ; val. of cows and heifers, $4,406.

Butter, 8,120 lbs. ; val. of butter, $1,461.60 ; Cheese, 1,970 lbs. ; val. of cheese, $158.

Indian Corn, 110 acres ; Indian Corn, per acre, 21 bush. ; val., $2,693.80.

Rye, 38 acres ; Rye, per acre, 10 bush. ; val., $483.75.

Barley, 17 acres ; Barley, per acre, 15 bush. ; val., $252.

Oats, 34 acres ; Oats, per acre, 17 bush. ; val., $302.

Potatoes, 88 acres ; Potatoes, per acre, 79 bush. ; val., $3,509.

Carrots, $4\frac{1}{2}$ acres ; Carrots, per acre, 325 bush. ; val., $429.66.

English Mowing, 874 acres ; English Hay, 587 tons ; val., $7,044.

Wet Meadow or Swale Hay, 407 tons ; val., $2,442.

Swine, 97 ; val., $670.

Val. hemlock bark, $375.

WHATELY.

Woollen Mills, 1 ; Sets of Machinery, 1 ; Wool consumed, 35,000 lbs. ; Satinet m'd., 47,000 yds. ; val. of satinet, $18,800 ; cap., $10,000 ; m. emp., 8 ; f. emp., 4.

Tanneries, 2 ; Hides of all kinds tanned, 1,300 ; val. of leather tanned, $5,300 ; cap., $5,300 ; emp., 4.

Bricks m'd., 25,000; val. of bricks, $2,500; emp., 1.

Val. of blacking, $10,000; emp., 8.

Val. of wooden ware not otherwise enumerated, including farming utensils m'd., $1,582.

Corn and other Brooms m'd., 107,000; val. of brooms, $18,800; emp., 20.

Lumber prepared for market, 43,000 ft.; val. of lumber, $430.

Firewood prepared for market, 1,100 cords; val. of firewood, $2,830.

Saxony Sheep, of different grades, –; Merino Sheep, of different grades, –; all other kinds of Sheep, 229; val. of all sheep, $458; Wool produced from Saxony sheep, – lbs.; Merino Wool produced, – lbs.; all other Wool produced, 916 lbs.

Horses, 186; val. of horses, $14,780; Oxen over three years old, 159; Steers under three years old, 223; val. of oxen and steers, $13,090; Milch Cows, 381; Heifers, 137; val. of cows and heifers, $23,650.

Butter, 42,440 lbs.; val. of butter, $8,488; Cheese, 7,877 lbs.; val. of cheese, $787; Honey, 120 lbs.; val. of honey, $20.

Indian Corn, 449 acres; Indian Corn, per acre, 25 bush.; val., $11,225; Broom Corn, 111 acres; Broom Bush, per acre, 510 lbs.; val., $5,661; Broom Seed, per acre, 31 bush.; val., $1,147.

Wheat, 43 acres; Wheat, per acre, 7 bush.; val., $602.

Rye, 272 acres; Rye, per acre, 9 bush.; val., $3,060.

Oats, 127 acres; Oats, per acre, 18 bush.; val., $1,371.

Potatoes, 85 acres; Potatoes, per acre, 88 bush.; val., $4,000.

Carrots, 1 acre; Carrots, per acre, 800 bush.; val., $266.

English Mowing, 788 acres; English Hay, 1,000 tons; val., $16,000.

Wet Meadow or Swale Hay, 660 tons; val., $6,600.

Apple Trees, cultivated for their fruit, 1,700; val., $1,000.

Pear Trees, cultivated for their fruit, 25; val., $25.

Tobacco, 69 acres; val., $9,165.

Establishments for m. of stone and earthenware, 1; cap., $3,000; val. of stone and earthenware, $8,000; emp., 7.

Drain Tile Establishments, 1; val. of tiles m'd., $2,000; cap., $1,000; emp., 6.

Val. of broom corn and brushes m'd., $8,000; emp., 7.

Swine, 350; val., $2,000.

HAMPDEN COUNTY.

AGAWAM.

Woollen Mills, 1; Sets of Machinery, 1; Wool consumed, 10,500 lbs.; Satinet m'd., 8,000 yds.; val. of satinet, $3,200; Flannel or Blanketing, 1,800 yds.; val. of flannel or blanketing, $900; Yarn m'd., and not made into cloth, 800 lbs.; val. of yarn, $640; cap., $9,000; m. emp., 5; f. emp., 4.

Val. of snuff, tobacco, and cigars, $68,510; m. emp., 56; f. emp., 20.

Corn and other Brooms m'd., 6,000; val. of brooms, $1,500; emp., 2.

Firewood prepared for market, 361 cords; val. of firewood, $1,444; emp., 5.

Alewives, Shad and Salmon taken, 6,000; val. of same, $950; emp., 18, during 3 months.

Saxony Sheep, of different grades, –; Merino Sheep, of different grades, –; all other kinds of Sheep, 439; val. of all sheep, $1,317; Wool produced from Saxony Sheep, – lbs.; Merino Wool produced, – lbs.; all other Wool produced, 1,317 lbs.

Horses, 207; val. of horses, $18,015; Oxen over three years old, 179; Steers under three years old, 111; val. of oxen and steers $14,411; Milch Cows, 505; Heifers, 154; val. of cows and heifers, $1,684.50.

Butter, 48,743 lbs.; val. of butter, $9,748.60; Cheese, 2,298 lbs.; val. of cheese, $229.80.

Indian Corn, 458½ acres; Indian Corn, per acre, 30½ bush.; val., $14,023; Broom Corn, 5 acres; Broom Bush, per acre, 700 lbs.; val., $343; Broom Seed, per acre, 57 bush.; val., $71.25.

Wheat, 18¼ acres; Wheat, per acre, 8½ bush.; val., $232.69.

Rye, 639 acres; Rye, per acre, 10 bush.; val., $6,390.

Oats, 145 acres; Oats, per acre, 24 bush.; val., $1,740.

Potatoes, 201 acres; Potatoes, per acre, 97 bush.; val., $9,748.50.

Onions, 2¼ acres; Onions, per acre, 391 bush.; val., $659.

Turnips, cultivated as a field crop, 74 acres; Turnips, per acre, 100 bush.; val., $1,850.

Carrots, 1 acre; Carrots, per acre, 745 bush.; val., $248.33.

Beets and other esculent vegetables, 2 acres; val., $600; all other Grain or Root Crops, 122 acres; val., $1,403.

Millet, 1 acre; val., $25.

English Mowing, 1,553 acres; English Hay, 2,000 tons; val., $30,000.

Wet Meadow or Swale Hay, 300 tons; val., $2,100.

Apple Trees, cultivated for their fruit, 6,958; val., $2,293.

Tobacco, 26 acres; val., $2,161.74.

Distilleries, 1; cap., $15,000; Alcohol distilled, – bbls.; all other Liquors (gin) distilled, 800 bbls.; val., $12,500; emp., 5.

Grist Mills, 2; used as custom or toll mills for grinding wheat, rye, corn, &c.

Milk sold, 77,475 qts.

Swine raised, 458; val., $3,664.

White Beans, 31 acres; Beans, per acre, 14 bush.; val., $651.

Winter Squashes, 4 acres; tons, 17; val., $510.

Water Melons, 2 acres; tons, 8; val., $128.

Cabbages, 4 acres; val., $1,000.

BLANDFORD.

Val. of bedsteads m'd., $2,700 ; cap., $700 ; emp., 5.

Tanneries, 4; Hides of all kinds tanned, 7,600; val. of leather tanned, $49,000; cap., $25,000; emp., 24.

Currying Establishments, 4 ; val. of leather curried, $49,000; cap., $25,000 ; emp., 24.

Val. of wooden ware not otherwise enumerated, including farming ("dishes") utensils m'd., $1,800 ; emp., 4.

Lumber prepared for market, 1,045,000 ft.; val. of lumber, $58,600; emp., "prepared by farmers who do not make it a business."

Firewood prepared for market, 1,780 cords; val. of firewood, $2,870 ; emp., "prepared by farmers, not wholly as a business."

Saxony Sheep, of different grades, –; Merino Sheep, of different grades, –; all other kinds of Sheep, 976; val. of all sheep, $1,952; Wool produced from Saxony Sheep, – lbs.; Merino Wool produced, – lbs.; all other Wool produced, 2,153 lbs.

Horses, 223; val. of horses, $21,150; Oxen over three years old, 348; Steers under three years old, 221; val. of oxen and steers, $22,381; Milch Cows, 1,020; Heifers, 293; val. of cows and heifers, $28,973.

Butter, 60,250 lbs.; val. of butter, $10,845; Cheese, 121,250 lbs.; val. of cheese, $10,912.50; Honey, 400 lbs.; val. of honey, $6,800.

Indian Corn, 234 acres; Indian Corn, per acre, 30 bush.; val., $7,000.

Wheat, 4 acres; Wheat, per acre, 21 bush.; val., $168.

Rye, 50 acres; Rye, per acre, 21 bush.; val., $766.

Barley, 19 acres; Barley, per acre, 21 bush.; val., $390,

Oats, 127 acres; Oats, per acre, 31 bush.; val., $1,935.

Potatoes, 192 acres; Potatoes, per acre, 80 bush.; val., $6,144.

Turnips, cultivated as a field crop, 4 acres; Turnips, per acre, 250 bush.; val., $250.

Carrots, 6 acres; Carrots, per acre, 325 bush.; val., $646.

English Mowing, 4,876 acres; English Hay, 3,650 tons; val., $29,200.

Wet Meadow or Swale Hay, 224 tons; val., $896.

Apple Trees, cultivated for their fruit, 7,320; val., $1,440.

Cranberries, 2 acres; val., $75.

Beeswax, 25 lbs.; val., $7.50.

Distilleries, 2. [These, according to the report of the Assessors, are "out of employ and of no value."]

Swine raised, 325; val., $2,600.

BRIMFIELD.

Shoe Tack Manufactories, 1; Tacks m'd., 9 tons; val., $1,500; cap., $1,000; emp., 1.

Currying Establishments 1; val. of leather curried, $30,000; cap., $5,000; emp., 3.

Lumber prepared for market, 270,000 ft.; val. of lumber, $6,750; emp., 4.

Firewood prepared for market, 300 cords; val. of firewood, $800; emp., 2.

Saxony Sheep, of different grades, –; Merino Sheep, of different grades, –; all other kinds of Sheep, 711; val. of all sheep, $2,032; Wool produced from Saxony sheep, – lbs.; Merino Wool produced, – lbs.; all other Wool produced, 2,880 lbs.

Horses, 187; val. of horses, $13,970; Oxen over three years old, 361; Steers under three years old, 210; val. of oxen and steers, $21,821; Milch Cows, 785; Heifers, 210; val. of cows and heifers, $24,069.

Butter, 46,925 lbs.; val. of butter, $9,385; Cheese, 48,250 lbs.; val. of cheese, $3,377; Honey, 300 lbs.; val. of honey, $50.

Indian Corn, 429 acres; Indian Corn, per acre, 30 bush.; val., $12,870.

Rye, 170 acres; Rye, per acre, 12 bush.; val., $2,040.

Barley, 5 acres; Barley, per acre, 15 bush.; val., $52.

Oats, 416 acres; Oats, per acre, 26 bush.; val., $4,867.

Potatoes, 323 acres; Potatoes, per acre, 115 bush.; val., $14,818.

English Mowing, 2,464 acres; English Hay, 2,398 tons; val., $23,980.

Wet Meadow or Swale Hay, 1,544 tons; val., $9,264.

Apple Trees, cultivated for their fruit, 15,093; val., $5,450.

Pear Trees, cultivated for their fruit, 257; val., $150.

Beeswax, 50 lbs.; val., $20.

Milk, 32,940 galls.; val., $3,623.

Shoes Bottomed, 30,700; val., $4,298; emp., 30.

Railroad Sleepers m'd., 11,000; val., $3,300.

Buckwheat, 340 bush.; val., $338.

CHESTER.

Cotton Mills, 1; Spindles, 1,500; Cotton consumed, 33,000 lbs.; Cloth m'd., 156,000 yds. 4-4 yd. wide, $4\frac{41}{100}$ yds. to the pound, used for finishing into Silesia; val. of cloth, $9,000; cap., $5,000; m. emp., 18; f. emp., 18.

Tanneries, 3; Hides of all kinds tanned, 15,700; val. of leather tanned, $59,700; cap., $23,200; emp., 17.

Boots of all kinds m'd., 700 pairs; Shoes of all kinds m'd., 550 pairs; val. of boots and shoes, $2,677.50; m. emp., 5.

Val. of building stone quarried and prepared for building, $1,000; emp., 2.

Charcoal m'd., 50,000 bush.; val. of same, $5,000; emp., 4.

Shoe Pegs m'd., 800 bush.; val., $1,200.

Lumber prepared for market, 1,080,000 ft.; val. of lumber, $10,800; emp., 20.

Firewood prepared for market, 3,590 cords; val. of firewood, $7,180; emp., 12.

Saxony Sheep, of different grades, 539; Merino Sheep, of different grades, 661; all other kinds of Sheep, 268; val. of all sheep, $3,303; Wool produced from Saxony sheep, 1,617 lbs.; Merino Wool produced, 2,123 lbs.; all other Wool produced, 998 lbs.

Horses, 173; val. of horses, $13,557; Oxen over three years old, 268; Steers under three years old, 225; val. of oxen and steers, $17,255; Milch Cows, 441; Heifers, 244; val. of cows and heifers, $16,398.

Butter, 29,750 lbs.; val. of butter, $5,950; Cheese, 8,750 lbs.; val. of cheese, $875; Honey, 1,020 lbs.; val. of honey, $170.

Indian Corn, 117 acres; Indian Corn, per acre, 41¾ bush.; val., $5,858.40.

Wheat, 11 acres; Wheat, per acre, 19$\frac{1}{11}$ bush.; val., $420.

Rye, 47 acres; Rye, per acre, 11⅓ bush.; val., $666.25.

Barley, 8 acres; Barley, per acre, 31¼ bush.; val., $250.

Oats, 47 acres; Oats, per acre, 31⅔ bush.; val., $1,115.25.

Potatoes, 118 acres; Potatoes, per acre, 102¾ bush.; val., $6,063.

Turnips, cultivated as a field crop, 10 acres; Turnips, per acre, 103¼ bush.; val., $207.

Carrots, 2 acres; Carrots, per acre, 300 bush.; val., $198.

Beets and other esculent vegetables, – acres; all other Grain or Root Crops, 15 acres; val., $315.

English Mowing, 959 acres; English Hay, 974 tons; val., $9,740.

Wet Meadow or Swale Hay, 1,212 tons; val., $9,696.

Apple Trees, cultivated for their fruit, 6,949; val., $2,748.

Pear Trees, cultivated for their fruit, 75; val., $50.

Beeswax, 25 lbs.; val., $10.50.

Distilleries, 1; cap., $200; Alcohol distilled, 16½ bbls.; val., $500; emp., 1.

Swine, 143; val., $858.

Peaches, 586 bush.; val., $363.32.

Establishments for m. of bobbins, 1; cap., $1,000; val., $1,200; emp., 2.

Establishments for m. of bedsteads, 3; Bedsteads m'd., 8,900; val., $22,200; cap., $10,500; emp., 23.

Establishments for m. of cradles, 1; Cradles m'd., 700; val., $825.

CHICOPEE.

Cotton Mills, 11; Spindles, 81,958; Cotton consumed, 6,451,966 lbs.; Cloth m'd., 25,848,583 yds.; Sheetings, 5,437,066 yds.; Printing Cloths, 2,330,120 yds.; Shirtings, 9,398,450 yds.; Cotton Flannel, 1,231,576 yds.; val. of cloth, $1,508,564.89; cap., $2,400,000; m. emp., 688; f. emp., 1,653.

Woollen Mills, 1; Sets of Machinery, –; Wool consumed, 40,000 lbs.; Cassimere m'd., 45,000 yds.; val. of cassimere, $35,000; m. emp., 15; f. emp., 10.

Furnaces for m. of hollow ware and castings other than pig iron, 1; Hollow Ware and other Castings m'd., 200 tons; val. of hollow ware and castings, $16,000; cap., $3,000; emp., 10.

Establishments for m. of cotton, woollen and other machinery, 1; val. of machinery m'd., $35,000; cap., $30,000; emp., 35.

Establishments for m. of steam-engines and boilers, 1; val. m'd., $30,000; cap., $2,000; emp., 9.

Plough Manufactories, –; Ploughs and other Agricultural Tools m'd., 5,384; val., $18,412.86; cap., $8,000; emp., 30.

Brass Founderies, 1.

Paper Manufactories, 1; Stock made use of, 540,000 lbs.; Paper m'd., 420,000 lbs.; val. of paper, $44,100; cap., $33,000; emp., 25.

Daguerreotype Artists, 3; Daguerreotypes taken, 300; emp., 3.

Brush Manufactories, 1; val. of brushes, $3,500; cap., $800; emp., 4.

Saddle, Harness and Trunk Manufactories, 2; val. of saddles, &c., $1,500; cap., $2,000; emp., 3.

Establishments for m. of railroad cars, coaches, chaises, wagons, sleighs, and other vehicles, 2; val. of railroad cars, &c., m'd., $18,000; cap., $8,000; emp., 22.

Establishments for m. of fire arms, 1; Fire Arms m'd., 3,000 sporting guns, breech-loading carbines, revolvers and pistols; val. of fire arms, $36,000; cap., $40,000; emp., 40.

Tin Ware Manufactories, 3; val. of tin ware, $1,500; cap., $600; emp., 8.

Boots of all kinds m'd., 5,675 pairs; Shoes of all kinds m'd., 2,150 pairs; val. of boots and shoes, $16,950; m. emp., 30; f. emp., 8.

Bricks m'd., 2,500,000; val. of bricks, $125,000; emp., 35.

Corn and other Brooms m'd., 50,000; val. of brooms, $10,000; emp., 6.

Lumber prepared for market, 129,000 ft.; val. of lumber, $2,193.

Firewood prepared for market, 3,026 cords; val. of firewood, (pine and oak,) $12,104.

Saxony Sheep, of different grades, –; Merino Sheep, of different grades, –; all other kinds of Sheep, 29; val. of all sheep, $60; Wool produced from Saxony sheep, – lbs.; Merino Wool produced, – lbs.; all other Wool produced, 100 lbs.

Horses, 323; val. of horses, $28,632; Oxen over three years old, 91; Steers under three years old, 41; val. of oxen and steers, $7,117; Milch Cows, 391; Heifers, 71; val. of cows and heifers, $14,121.

Butter, 21,955 lbs.; val. of butter, $4,391; Cheese, 115 lbs.; val. of cheese, $14.50; Honey, 500 lbs.; val. of honey, $62.

Indian Corn, 540 acres; Indian Corn, per acre, 24 bush.; val., $13,080; Broom Corn, 7 acres; Broom Bush, per acre, 700 lbs.; val., $490; Broom Seed, per acre, 175 bush.; val., $87.

Wheat, 10 acres; Wheat, per acre, 15 bush.; val., $225.

Rye, 789 acres; Rye, per acre, $7\frac{5}{8}$ bush.; val., $7,641.

Oats, 138 acres; Oats, per acre, 23 bush.; val., $1,929.

Potatoes, 165 acres; Potatoes, per acre, 122 bush.; val., $13,425.

Onions, 2 acres; Onions, per acre, 300 bush.; val., $400.

Turnips, cultivated as a field crop, 19 acres; Turnips, per acre, 500 bush.; val., $1,187.

Carrots, 4 acres; Carrots, per acre, 650 bush.; val., $866.

English Mowing, 902 acres; English Hay, 1,345 tons; val., $22,865.

Wet Meadow or Swale Hay, 123 tons; val., $861.

Apple Trees, cultivated for their fruit, 7,088; val., $2,000.

Pear Trees, cultivated for their fruit, 100; val., $25.

Tobacco, 18 acres; val., $2,660.

Establishments for m. of gas, 1; cap., $30,000; val. m'd., -; emp., 3.

The Ames Manufacturing Company make Cotton and all other kinds of machinery, Machinists' Tools, Turbine Water Wheels, Iron Castings, of every description, Brass and Bronze Castings, Bronze Guns—Field and Navy, Statuary, Swords, Sword Belts and Trimmings, Plated Ware, all varieties, Belting and Engine Hose, Pump Augers and Reamers, Ring-Travellers, Shafting, Pullies, &c.; cap., $250,000; m. emp. on platina ware, 56; f. emp., 10; m. emp. in furnace, 50; in machinery, 184.

Establishments for m. of belting, 1; val. of belting m'd., $7,000; cap., $3,600; emp., 2.

GRANVILLE.

Tin Ware Manufactories, 1; val. of tin ware, $200; cap., $75; emp., 1.

Tanneries, 2; Hides of all kinds tanned, $1,500; val. of leather tanned, $4,000; cap., $3,000; emp., 4.

Bricks m'd., 100,000; val. of bricks, $500; emp., 2.

Val. of snuff, tobacco and cigars, $400; m. emp., 2; f. emp., 3.

Charcoal m'd., 2,000 bush.; val. of same, $120; emp., 2.

Val. of whips m'd., $1,400; emp., 5.

Lumber prepared for market, 581,000 ft.; val. of lumber $3,750; emp., 20.

Firewood prepared for market, 520 cords; val. of firewood, $1,050; emp., 20.

Saxony Sheep, of different grades, –; Merino Sheep, of different grades, –; all other kinds of Sheep, 179; val. of all sheep, $355; Wool produced from Saxony sheep, – lbs.; Merino Wool produced, – lbs.; all other Wool produced, 536 lbs.

Horses, 205; val. of horses, $14,585; Oxen over three years old, 310; Steers under three years old, 224; val. of oxen and steers, $22,413; Milch Cows, 688; Heifers, 249; val. of cows and heifers, $20,215.

Butter, 30,000 lbs.; val. of butter, $7,833; Cheese, 16,130 lbs.; val. of cheese, $1,513.

Indian Corn, 259 acres; Indian Corn, per acre, 24 bush.; val., $2,598.

Wheat, 9 acres; Wheat, per acre, 12 bush.; val., $242.

Rye, 175 acres; Rye, per acre, 9½ bush.; val., $1,672.

Oats, 111 acres; Oats, per acre, 27 bush.; val., $242.

Potatoes, 175 acres; Potatoes, per acre, 72 bush.; val., $4,272.

Turnips, cultivated as a field crop, 5 acres; Turnips, per acre, 140 bush.; val., $160.

English Mowing, 1,537 acres; English Hay, 1,456 tons; val. $14,560.

Wet Meadow or Swale Hay, 1,134 tons; val., $5,192.

Apple Trees, cultivated for their fruit, 3,198; val., $1,834.

Pear Trees, cultivated for their fruit, 20; val., $30. James P. Cooley has one tree that bears two crops in one year.

Powder Kegs m'd., 95,000; val. of kegs m'd., $5,300; cap., $1,775; emp., 28.

Val. of toy drums m'd., $1,000; emp., 2.

Val. of spectacles m'd., $1,000; cap., $600; emp., 3.

Val. of wagon hubs, $500; emp., 1.

HOLLAND.

Firewood prepared for market, 230 cords; val. of firewood, $460; emp., 1.

Saxony Sheep, of different grades, –; Merino Sheep, of different grades, –; all other kinds of Sheep, 581; val. of all sheep, $695; Wool produced from Saxony sheep, – lbs.; Merino Wool produced, – lbs.; all other Wool produced, 1,307 lbs.

Horses, 47; val. of horses, $2,493; Oxen over three years old, 92; Steers under three years old, 88; val. of oxen and steers, $5,135; Milch Cows, 172; Heifers, 54; val. of cows and heifers, $3,626.

Butter, 4,460 lbs.; val. of butter, $910; Cheese, 7,443 lbs.; val. of cheese, $657; Honey, 215 lbs.; val. of honey, $28.

Indian Corn, 102 acres; Indian Corn, per acre, 25 bush.; val., $2,550.

Rye, 56 acres; Rye, per acre, 8 bush.; val., $448.

Oats, 73 acres; Oats, per acre, 20 bush.; val., $730.

Potatoes, 87 acres; Potatoes, per acre, 85 bush.; val., $3,697.50.

Turnips, cultivated as a field crop, 1½ acre; Turnips, per acre, 125 bush.; val., $31.

Beets and other esculent vegetables, – acres; all other Grain or Root Crops, 20 acres; val., $100.

English Mowing, 583 acres; English Hay, 400 tons; val., $4,000.

Wet Meadow or Swale Hay, 360 tons; val., $1,963.

Apple Trees, cultivated for their fruit, 327; val., $228.

Cranberries, 7 acres; val., $165.

HOLYOKE.

Cotton Mills, 3; Spindles, 53,000; Cotton consumed, 4,267,985 lbs.; Cloth m'd., 12,517,119 yds.—970,000 yds. Cotton Cassimeres for "pantaloonery," 8,199,370 yds. No. 14 Sheeting and Shirting, 3,447,749 yds. No. 70 and 90 Lawns, Jaconets, Checks and Brilliants; val. of cloth, $1,161,178.36; Yarn m'd., 108,000 lbs.; val. of yarn, $20,000; cap., $1,600,000; m. emp., 458; f. emp., 1,035.

Establishments for m. of cotton, woollen and other machinery, 1; val. of machinery m'd., $325,000; cap., $305,000; emp., 300.

Paper Manufactories, 1; Stock made use of, 175 tons; Paper m'd., 125 tons; val. of paper, $50,000; cap., $60,000; emp., 100.

Daguerreotype Artists, 1; Daguerreotypes taken, 1,000; cap., $300; emp., 1.

Saddle, Harness and Trunk Manufactories, 1; val. of saddles, &c., $2,500; cap., $500; emp., 2.

Card Manufactories, 1; val. of cards of all kinds m'd., (Clothing for Cotton and Woollen Cards,) $30,240; cap., $10,000; emp., 11.

Establishments for m. of railroad cars, coaches, chaises, wagons, sleighs, and other vehicles, 2; val. of railroad cars, &c., m'd., $1,640; cap., $400; emp., 3.

Tin Ware Manufactories, 2; val. of tin ware, $9,000; cap., $3,000; emp., 8.

Flour Mills, 1. [This mill was not run last year, but is now in operation, and can turn out 3,500 bbls. flour, 25,000 bush. of other grain, and 18,000 bbls. of cement.]

Tanneries, 1; Hides of all kinds tanned, 1,800; val. of leather tanned, $10,125; cap., $5,000; emp., 11.

Boots of all kinds m'd., 600 pairs; Shoes of all kinds m'd., 1,275 pairs; val. of boots and shoes, $3,515; m. emp., 5; f. emp., 1.

Bricks m'd., 2,000,000; val. of bricks, $9,500; emp., 20, during 6 months.

Val. of building stone quarried and prepared for building, $15,000; emp., 25. This stone was quarried within the limits of Northampton, but owned and used in this town by the Hadley Falls Company.

Charcoal m'd., 3,000 bush.; val. of same, $300; emp., 4, during 2 months.

Lumber prepared for market, 436,000 ft.; val. of lumber, $5,668; emp., 7.

Firewood prepared for market, 4,336 cords; val. of firewood, $14,792; emp., 9.

Alewives, Shad and Salmon taken, 500; val. of same, $100.

Saxony Sheep, of different grades, –; Merino Sheep, of different grades, –; all other kinds of Sheep, 82; val. of all sheep, $205; Wool produced from Saxony sheep, – lbs.; Merino Wool produced, – lbs.; all other Wool produced, 369 lbs.

Horses, 213; val. of horses, $21,925; Oxen over three years old, 103; Steers under three years old, 39; val. of oxen and steers, $8,296; Milch Cows, 363; Heifers, 55; val. of cows and heifers, $13,286.

Butter, 25,074 lbs.; val. of butter, $5,014.75; Cheese, 550 lbs.; val. of cheese, $68.75; Honey, 278 lbs.; val. of honey, $49.33.

Indian Corn, 277 acres; Indian Corn, per acre, 31 bush.; val., $9,875.05; Broom Corn, 4 acres; Broom Bush, per acre, 825 lbs.; val., $330; Broom Seed, per acre, 34 bush.; val., $57.12.

Wheat, 6 acres; Wheat, per acre, 14½ bush.; val., $174.

Rye, 349 acres; Rye, per acre, 7½ bush.; val., $3,934.50.

Oats, 132 acres; Oats, per acre, 18¼ bush.; val., $1,445.40.

Potatoes, 143 acres; Potatoes, per acre, 105 bush.; val., $11,261.25.

Onions, 1½ acre; Onions, per acre, 474⅔ bush.; val., $498.40.

Turnips, cultivated as a field crop, 20 acres; Turnips, per acre, 410¾ bush.; val., $1,643.

Carrots, ½ acre; Carrots, per acre, 360 bush.; val., $90.

Beets and other esculent vegetables, 3½ acres; val., $695.

English Mowing, 946 acres; English Hay, 1,211 tons; val. $18,165.

Wet Meadow or Swale Hay, 146 tons; val., $1,168.

Apple Trees, cultivated for their fruit, 3,218; val., $2,784.

Pear Trees, cultivated for their fruit, 19; val., $17.

Tobacco, 3 acres; val., $264.

Beeswax, 17 lbs.; val., $5.67.

Establishments for m. of gas, 1; cap., $37,000; val. m'd., $9,074.26; val. of coke m'd., $107.88; emp., 2.

Breweries, 1; cap., $250; Small Beer m'd., 170 bbls.; val., $841.50; emp., 2.

Bulls, 3; val., $110.

Swine, 392; val., $8,527.97.

White Beans, 4 acres; Beans, per acre, 14 bush.; val., $112.

Buckwheat, 20 acres; Buckwheat, per acre, 12½ bush.; val., $250.

Hens, 2,035; val., $678.33.

Eggs, 7,902 doz.; val., $1,317.

Turkies, 127; val. of same, $159.

Milk produced, 46,012 galls.; val., $7,362.

Card and Piano-Forte Wire Manufactories, 1; cap., $1,600; val. of stock (coarse wire) used, $10,000; val. of card wire, $5,000; val. of piano-forte and broom wire, $9,000; emp., 4.

Power Loom Reed Manufactories, 1; cap., $1,000; val. of reeds m'd., $1,200; val. of stock consumed, $300; emp., 1.

Loom Harness Manufactories, 1; cap., $3,000; val. of harness m'd., $8,000; emp., 15.

LONGMEADOW.

Covered Button Manufactories, 1; Covered Buttons m'd., 90,000 gross; val. of covered buttons, $30,000; cap., $3,000; emp., 25.

Establishments for m. of soap, 1; Soap m'd., 100 bbls.; val. of soap, $225.

Val. of building stone quarried and prepared for building, $12,460; emp., 26.

Lumber prepared for market, 75,000 ft.; val. of lumber, $1,125; emp., 3.

Firewood prepared for market, 1,850 cords; val. of firewood, $6,650; emp., 4.

Saxony Sheep, of different grades, –; Merino Sheep, of different grades, –; all other kinds of Sheep, 180; val. of all sheep, $270; Wool produced from Saxony sheep, – lbs.; Merino Wool produced, – lbs.; all other Wool produced, 578 lbs.

Horses, 266; val. of horses, $19,957; Oxen over three years old, 167; steers under three years old, 150; val. of oxen and steers, $10,989; Milch Cows, 549; Heifers, 156; val. of cows and heifers, $18,350.

Butter, 50,020 lbs.; val. of butter, $8,503; Cheese, 3,280 lbs.; val. of cheese, $328; Honey, 104 lbs.; val. of honey, $12.

Indian Corn, 680 acres; Indian Corn, per acre, 25 bush.; val., $25 per acre; Broom Corn, 8 acres; Broom Bush, per acre, 625 lbs.; val., $50 per acre; Broom Seed, per acre, 45 bush.; val., $16 per acre.

Wheat, 2 acres; Wheat, per acre, 10 bush.; val., $15 per acre.

Rye, 507 acres; Rye, per acre, 10 bush.; val., $10 per acre.

Barley, 1 acre; Barley, per acre, 12 bush.; val., $8.

Oats, 285 acres; Oats, per acre, 25 bush.; val., $12 per acre.

Potatoes, 135 acres; Potatoes, per acre, 100 bush.; val., $50 per acre.

Onions, ½ acre; Onions, per acre, 520 bush.; val., $260 per acre.

Turnips, cultivated as a field crop, 3¼ acres; Turnips, per acre, 320 bush.; val., $54 per acre.

Carrots, 1 acre; Carrots, per acre, 284 bush.; val., $71 per acre.

Beets and other esculent vegetables, 4 acres; val., $240; all other Grain or Root Crops, 12 acres; val., $100.

Millet, 2 acres; val., $16.

English Mowing, 1,642 acres; English Hay, 2,024 tons; val., $20,240.

Wet Meadow or Swale Hay, 596 tons; val., $2,980.

Apple Trees, cultivated for their fruit, 3,509; val., $1,511.

Tobacco, 10 acres; val., $1,400.

Swine, 352; val., $2,100.

Establishments for m. of spectacles and thimbles, 4; cap., $5,500; Silver Spectacles m'd., 9,000; val., $6,300; Gold Spectacles m'd., 8,150; val., $28,525; Thimbles m'd., 3,000 doz.; val., $8,450; emp., 27.

Establishments for m. of shoulder braces, 1; Braces m'd., 700 doz.; val., $4,200; cap., $1,000; m. emp., 2; f. emp., 12.

Establishments for m. of husks, 1; cap., $500; val. of husks m'd., $2,000; emp., 1.

LUDLOW.

Cotton Mills, 1; Spindles, 3,520; Cotton consumed, 204,400 lbs.; Cloth, m'd., 649,573 yds., 36 inches wide; val. of cloth, $42,222.24; cap., $25,000; m. emp., 31; f. emp., 35.

Woollen Mills, 1; Sets of Machinery, 1; Wool consumed, 1,500 lbs.; Satinet m'd., 1,500 yds.; val. of satinet, $750; Yarn m'd. and not made into cloth, 600 lbs.; val. of yarn, $600; cap., $2,000; m. emp., 3; f. emp., 2.

Corn and other Brooms m'd., 1,500; val. of brooms, $250; emp., 1, during six months.

Lumber prepared for market, 100,000 ft.; val. of lumber, $1,200; emp., 2.

Firewood prepared for market, 5,210 cords; val. of firewood, $10,420; emp., 30, during six months.

Saxony Sheep, of different grades, –; Merino Sheep, of different grades, –; all other kinds of Sheep, 164; val. of all sheep, $410; Wool produced from Saxony sheep, – lbs.; Merino Wool produced, – lbs.; all other Wool produced, 492 lbs.

Horses, 211; val. of horses, $15,825; Oxen over three years

old, 204; Steers under three years old, 151; val. of oxen and steers, $12,918; Milch Cows, 467; Heifers, 161; val. of cows and heifers, $14,090.

Butter, 31,350 lbs.; val. of butter, $5,643; Cheese, 9,000 lbs.; val. of cheese, $810; Honey, 500 lbs.; val. of honey, $75.

Indian Corn, 632 acres; Indian Corn, per acre, 20 bush.; val., $12,640; Broom Corn, 2 acres; Broom Bush, per acre, 800 lbs.; val., $150; Broom Seed, per acre, 50 bush.; val., $40.

Rye, 1,147 acres; Rye, per acre, 7 bush.; val., $8,026.

Oats, 112 acres; Oats, per acre, 20 bush.; val., $1,120.

Potatoes, 150 acres; Potatoes, per acre, 100 bush.; val., $7,500.

Turnips, cultivated as a field crop, 5 acres; Turnips, per acre, 200 bush.; val., $200.

Beets and other esculent vegetables, 25 acres; val., $250; all other Grain or Root Crops, 50 acres; val., $300.

English Mowing, 1,193 acres; English Hay, 1,193 tons; val., $16,702.

Wet Meadow or Swale Hay, 509 tons; val., $2,545.

Apple Trees, cultivated for their fruit, 3,000; val., $1,250.

Establishments for m. of sashes, doors and blinds, 1; val. m'd., $2,500; cap., $1,500; emp., 2.

The income from labor in sewing shirts and drawers, sent from other places, amounts to $2,500, per annum.

Grist Mills, 2; affording an income of $1,500.

Saw Mills, 3; furnishing 200,000 ft. of lumber, one-half for home use.

Shingle Mills, 1; furnishing 200,000 ft. chestnut shingles; val. of shingles, $400.

Shops for m. of printers' composing sticks, 1; val. m'd., $500.

Shops for m. of carriages, 1; val. m'd., $500.

MONSON.

Cotton Mills, 1; Spindles, 3,200; Cotton consumed, 95,625 lbs.; Cloth m'd., 480,000 yds., 7-8 yds. wide, measuring 5 yds. to the pound; val. of cloth, $30,000; cap., $15,000; m. emp., 22; f. emp., 23.

Woollen Mills, 4; Sets of Machinery, 10; Wool conumed, 400,000 lbs.; Satinet m'd., 616,000 yds.; val. of satinet, $254,400; cap., $92,000; m. emp., 85; f. emp., 53.

Saddle, Harness and Trunk Manufactories, 1; val. of saddles, &c., $200; cap., $200; emp., 1.

Establishments for m. of soap and tallow candles, 1; Soap m'd., 125 bbls.; val. of soap, $500; Tallow Candles m'd., 4,300 lbs.; val. of tallow candles, $650; emp., 1.

Chair and Cabinet Manufactories, 1; val. of chairs and cabinet ware, $400; cap., $300; emp., 1.

Grain Mills, 5; Grain ground, 33,550 bush.; val. of grain, $31,450; cap., $6,000; emp., 6.

Tanneries and Currying Shops, 1; Hides of all kinds tanned, 488; val. of leather tanned and curried, $14,456; cap., $6,000; emp., 7.

Boots of all kinds m'd., 250 pairs; Shoes of all kinds m'd., 400 pairs; val. of boots and shoes, $2,075; m. emp., 3.

Establishments for m. of straw bonnets, 1; Straw Bonnets m'd., 150,000; val. of straw bonnets m'd., $120,000; cap., $16,000; m. emp., 14; f. emp., 200. Stock for the bonnets belongs to New York.

Val. of building stone quarried and prepared for building, $5,000; emp., 15.

Charcoal m'd., 34,300 bush.; val. of same, $2,434.

Establishments for m. of gold and silver spectacles, 1; Gold Spectacles m'd., 1,321; val. of gold spectacles m'd., $6,600; Silver Spectacles m'd., 2,890; val. of silver spectacles m'd., $2,475; emp., 5.

Lumber prepared for market, 1,055,000 feet; val. of lumber, $13,410; emp., 12.

Firewood prepared for market, 8,703 cords; val. of firewood, $24,768.

Saxony Sheep, of different grades, –; Merino Sheep, of different grades, –; all other kinds of Sheep, 825; val. of all sheep, $2,352; Wool produced from Saxony sheep, – lbs.; Merino Wool produced, – lbs.; all other Wool produced, 2,569 lbs.

Horses, 273; val. of horses, $19,090; Neat Cattle, 1,692; val. of neat cattle, $42,108.

Butter, 47,950 lbs.; val. of butter, $9,590; Cheese, 24,100 lbs.; val. of cheese, $2,410; Honey, 348 lbs.; val. of honey, $48.

Indian Corn, 9,662 bush.; val., $9,662.

Rye, 3,372 bush.; val., $3,372.

Oats, 6,876 bush.; val., $3,438.

Potatoes, 20,942 bush.; val., $10,471.

White Beans, 257 bush.; val., $514.

Turnips, 2,195 bush.; val., $219.

Buckwheat, 909 bush.; val., $674.

Hay of all kinds, 3,847 tons; val., 36,280.

Fruit, 4,530 bush; val., $1,274.

Shingle Mills, 5; Shingles m'd., 410,000; val., $914; emp., 5.

Swine, 255; val., $1,722.

Establishments for m. of collars and bosoms, 1; cap., $400; Collars and Bosoms m'd., 1,000 doz.; val., $1,600; m. emp., 1; f. emp., 1.

Establishments for m. of shirts, 1; cap., $600; val., $3,500; m. emp., 1; f. emp., 12.

Plough Handle Factories, 1; cap., $5,000; val. of plough handles m'd., $10,000; emp., 7.

Gross val. of wheel rims and ox bows m'd., $8,000; emp., 4.

Axe Handles m'd., 300 doz.; val., $600.

Hatchet Handles m'd., 200 doz.; val., $250.

Val. of machinery built for turning handles, $300; cap., $1,500; emp., 3.

MONTGOMERY.

Charcoal m'd., 4,448 bush.; val. of same, $266.88; emp., 4.

Lumber prepared for market, 70,000 ft.; val. of lumber, $700; emp., 3.

Firewood prepared for market, 1,826 cords; val. of firewood, $2,789; emp., 50, during a part of the year.

Saxony Sheep, of different grades, –; Merino Sheep, of different grades, –; all other kinds of Sheep, 268; val. of all sheep, $804; Wool produced from Saxony sheep, – lbs.; Merino Wool produced, – lbs.; all other Wool produced, 804 lbs.

Horses, 61; val. of horses, $3,050; Oxen over three years old, 86; Steers under three years old, 89; val. of oxen and steers, $5,635; Milch Cows, 171; Heifers, 70; val. of cows and heifers, $5,325.

Butter, 16,050 lbs.; val. of butter, $2,675; Cheese, 1,890 lbs.; val. of cheese, $189; Honey, 600 lbs.; val. of honey, $75.

Indian Corn, 125 bush.; Indian Corn, per acre, 2,500 bush.; val., $2,500.

Wheat, 1½ acre; Wheat, per acre, 6 bush.; val., $18.

Rye, 78 acres; Rye, per acre, 8 bush.; val., $624.

Oats, 79 acres; Oats, per acre, 30 bush.; val., $888.75.

Potatoes, 45 acres; Potatoes, per acre, 50 bush.; val., $562.

English Mowing, 583 acres; English Hay, 583 tons; val., $5,830.

Wet Meadow or Swale Hay, 150 tons; val., $750.

Apple Trees, cultivated for their fruit, 610; val., $610.

Pear Trees, cultivated for their fruit, 23; val., $40.

Distilleries, 2; Alcohol distilled, – bbls.; all other Liquors distilled, 30 bbls.; val., $750; cap., $150; emp., 2.

PALMER.

Cotton Mills, 4; Spindles, 48,580; Cotton consumed, 3,415,000 lbs.; Cloth, m'd., 7,577,000 yds.; 1,650,000 yds. for Printing, 1,710,000 yds. Duck Cloth, 1,217,000 yds. 34 inch Cloth, 3,000,000 yds. Stripe Tick and Denims; val. of cloth, $628,707; cap., $957,000; m. emp., 505; f. emp., 541.

Furnaces for m. of hollow ware and castings other than pig iron, 1; Hollow Ware and other Castings m'd., 50 tons; val. of hollow ware and castings, $4,000; cap., $1,000; emp., 4.

Scythe Manufactories, 1; Scythes m'd., 14,000; val. of scythes, $9,000; cap., $4,000; emp., 15.

Saddle, Harness and Trunk Manufactories, 2; val. of saddles, &c., $2,500; cap., $800; emp., 3.

Hat and Cap Manufactories, 1; Hats and Caps m'd., 300; cap., $300; emp., 1.

Establishments for m. of railroad cars, coaches, chaises, wagons, sleighs, and other vehicles, 1; val. of railroad cars, &c., m'd., $15,000; cap., $2,000; emp., 15.

Establishments for m. of soap and tallow candles, 1; Soap m'd., 936 bbls.; val. of soap, $2,808; Tallow Candles m'd., 6,000 lbs.; val. of tallow candles, $840; cap., $1,050; emp., 3.

Tin Ware Manufactories, 1; val. of tin ware, $1,000; cap., $1,800; emp., 2.

Currying Establishments, 1; val. of leather curried, $32,000; cap., $5,000; emp., 7.

Boots of all kinds m'd., 500 pairs; Shoes of all kinds m'd., 1,000 pairs; val. of boots and shoes, $3,000; m. emp., 7.

Establishments for m. of straw bonnets and hats, 1; Straw Bonnets and Straw Hats, m'd., 8,295 doz.; Bonnets and Hats, unfinished, 10,200; val. of straw hats and bonnets, $10,000; m. emp., 15; f. emp., 262.

Lumber prepared for market, 1,350,000 ft.; val. of lumber, $9,600; emp., 8.

Firewood prepared for market, 9,500 cords; val. of firewood, $23,750.

Saxony Sheep, of different grades, –; Merino Sheep, of different grades, –; all other kinds of Sheep, 441; val. of all sheep, $1,146; Wool produced from Saxony sheep, – lbs.; Merino Wool produced, – lbs.; all other Wool produced, 1,421 lbs.

Horses, 292; val. of horses, $21,905; Oxen over three years old, 205; Steers under three years old, 176; val. of oxen and steers, $15,010; Milch Cows, 483; Heifers, 226; val. of cows and heifers, $17,273.

Butter, 38,000 lbs.; val. of butter, $7,600; Cheese, 20,000 lbs.; val. of cheese, $2,000; Honey, 85 lbs.; val. of honey, $14.

Indian Corn, 550 acres; Indian Corn, per acre, 28 bush.; val., $15,400.

Wheat, 1 acre; Wheat, per acre, 10 bush.; val., $20.

Rye, 393 acres; Rye, per acre, 10 bush.; val., $4,912.

Oats, 335 acres; Oats, per acre, 25 bush.; val., $4,188.

Potatoes, 160 acres; Potatoes, per acre, 100 bush.; val., $8,000.

English Mowing, 1,596 acres; English Hay, 1,596 tons; val., $19,152.

Wet Meadow or Swale Hay, 618 tons; val., $4,226.

Apple Trees, cultivated for their fruit, 2,888; val., $2,350.

There is $1,000 invested in the m. of reeds; val. of reeds m'd., $1,400; emp., 2.

Swine, 268; val., $1,921.

Beans, 800 bush.; val. of beans, $2,000.

Buckwheat, 2,000 bush.; val. of buckwheat, $1,500.

The Assessors add to their "industrial statistics" the following facts:—Churches, 6; School-Houses, 13; Public Houses, 6; Grist Mills, 3; Saw Mills, 4; Blacksmiths' Shops, 6; Stores, 17.

RUSSELL.

Paper Manufactories, 1; Stock made use of, 400 tons; Paper m'd., 200 tons; val. of paper, $60,000; cap., $15,000; emp., 80.

Tanneries, 1; Hides of all kinds tanned, 2,000; val. of leather tanned, $12,000; cap., $6,000; emp., 6.

Lumber prepared for market, 233,000 ft.; val. of lumber, $20,970; emp., 8.

Firewood prepared for market, 2,500 cords; val. of firewood, $5,625; emp., 12.

Merino Sheep, of different grades, 205; val. of all sheep, $552; Merino Wool produced, 615 lbs.

Horses, 70; val. of horses, $5,600; Oxen over three years old, 104; Steers under three years old, 32; val. of oxen and steers, $5,776; Milch Cows, 152; Heifers, 66; val. of cows and heifers, $4,460.

Butter, 11,400 lbs.; val. of butter, $2,280; Cheese, 3,000 lbs.; val. of cheese, $270.

Indian Corn, 80 acres; Indian Corn, per acre, 20 bush.; val., $1,600.

Rye, 40 acres; Rye, per acre, 12 bush.; val., $480.

Oats, 40 acres; Oats, per acre, 25 bush.; val., $580.

Potatoes, 56 acres; Potatoes, per acre, 40 bush.; val., $840.

English Mowing, 544 acres; English Hay, 544 tons; val., $5,440.

Apple Trees, cultivated for their fruit, 851; val., $850.

Swine, 100; val., $800.

All other articles m'd. are as follows:—Val. of R. R. Blocking, $5,250; Fishing Rods, $3,000; Brake Blocks, $700; cap. invested in the above branches, $2,000; emp., 12.

SOUTHWICK.

Powder Mills, 1; Powder m'd., 200,000 lbs.; val. of powder, $20,000; cap., $8,000; emp., 3.

Tanneries, 2; Hides of all kinds tanned, 6,000; val. of leather tanned, $9,000; cap., $2,000; emp., 3.

Val. of cigars, $21,685; m. emp., 12; f. emp., 5.

Lumber prepared for market, 35,000 ft.; val. of lumber, $665; emp., 3.

Firewood prepared for market, 1,917 cords; val. of firewood, $4,792; emp., 25.

Saxony Sheep, of different grades, –; Merino Sheep, of different grades, –; all other kinds of Sheep, 729; val. of all sheep, $1,500; Wool produced from Saxony sheep, – lbs.; Merino Wool produced, – lbs.; all other Wool produced, 1,795 lbs; val. of wool, $628.

Horses, 224; val. of horses, $15,407; Oxen over three years old, 260; Steers under three years old, 191; val. of oxen and steers, $14,453; Milch Cows, 389; Heifers, 148; val. of cows and heifers, $12,904.

Butter, 38,681 lbs.; val. of butter, $7,736; Cheese, 4,565 lbs.; val. of cheese, $547; Honey, 1,000 lbs.; val. of honey, $125.

Indian Corn, 578 acres; Indian Corn, per acre, 30 bush.; val., $17,340.

Wheat, 2 acres; Wheat, per acre, 20 bush.; val., $55.

Rye, 975 acres; Rye, per acre, 10 bush.; val., $9,750.

Oats, 253 acres; Oats, per acre, 25 bush.; val., $3,162.

Potatoes, 221 acres; Potatoes, per acre, 75 bush.; val., $8,287.

Onions, 2 acres; Onions, per acre, 400 bush.; val., $200.

Turnips cultivated as a field crop, 10 acres; Turnips, per acre, 100 bush.; val., $250.

Millet, $\frac{3}{4}$ acre.

English Mowing, 1,085 acres; English Hay, 1,200 tons; val., $15,600.

Wet Meadow or Swale Hay, 725 tons; val., $5,075.

Apple Trees, cultivated for their fruit, 10,000; val., $2,500.

Pear Trees, cultivated for their fruit, 100; val., $50.

Tobacco, 11 acres; val., $1,100.

Cranberries, $1\frac{1}{2}$ acre; val., $30.

Distilleries, 3; cap., $1,000; Alcohol distilled, – bbls.; all other Liquors distilled, 30 bbls. (C. B.); val., $750; emp., 2.

Buckwheat, 211 acres; val., $1,055.

Val. of split baskets, $400.
Val. of philosophical instruments, $1,000.
Whip Lashes, 3,500 doz.; val., $3,500.
Swine raised, 200; val., $2,000.

SPRINGFIELD.

Cotton Mills, [commenced operating Jan. 1, 1855,] 1; Spindles, 13,656; Cotton consumed, 277,852 lbs.; Cloth, m'd., 633,057 yds. Fine 4-4 Sheeting; val. of cloth, $56,975.17; cap., $250,000; m. emp., 82; f. emp., 188.

Woollen Mills, 1; Sets of Machinery, 2; Wool consumed, 52,000 lbs.; Cassimere m'd., 62,000 yds.; val. of cassimere, $46,500; cap., $10,000; m. emp., 18; f. emp., 7.

Forges, 1; Bar Iron, Anchors, Chain Cables, and other articles of wrought iron m'd, 75 tons car axles; val. of bar iron, &c., $27,500; cap., $5,000; emp., 10.

Furnaces for m. of hollow ware and castings other than pig iron, 3; Hollow Ware and other Castings m'd., 3,134 tons; val. of hollow ware and castings, $156,936; cap., $35,000; emp., 67.

Establishments for m. of cotton, woollen and other machinery, 3; val. of machinery m'd., $215,000; cap., $120,000; emp., 172.

Establishments for m. of steam-engines and boilers, 2; val. of steam-engines and boilers, $160,000; cap., $30,000; emp., 135.

Manufactories of mechanics' tools, 2; val., $54,000; cap., $37,000; emp., 55.

Brass Founderies, 1; val. of articles m'd., $3,000; cap., $500; emp., 1.

Establishments for m. of chemical preparations, 1; val. of chemical preparations, $54,000; cap., $15,000; emp., 12.

Paper Manufactories, 1; Stock made use of, 150 tons; Paper

m'd., 52,500 reams; val. of paper, $60,000; cap., $30,000; emp., 20.

Piano-Forte Manufactories, –; all other musical instrument manufactories, 1; val. of musical instruments m'd., $6,000; cap., $1,000; emp., 2.

Sewing Machine Manufactories, 1; Sewing Machines m'd., 100; cap., $4,000; emp., 6.

Daguerreotype Artists, 5; Daguerreotypes taken, 9,300; cap., $3,550; emp., 12.

Establishments for m. of chronometers, watches, gold and silver ware and jewelry, 2; val. of m's., $155,000; cap., $51,000; emp., 77.

Saddle, Harness and Trunk Manufactories, 2; val. of saddles, &c., $10,000; cap., $3,200; emp., 14.

Upholstery Manufactories, 2; val. of upholstery, $2,000; cap., $1,200; emp., 2.

Hat and Cap Manufactories, 1; Hats and Caps m'd., 1,600; cap., $2,000; emp., 5.

Cordage Manufactories, 1; not in operation the past year.

Establishments for m. of railroad cars, coaches, chaises, wagons, sleighs, and other vehicles, 6; val. of railroad cars, &c., m'd., $339,000; cap., $46,500; emp., 201.

Establishments for m. of soap and tallow candles, 2; Soap m'd., 1,350 bbls. soft, 30 tons hard; val. of soap, $9,600; Tallow Candles m'd., 160,000 lbs.; val. of tallow candles, $22,400; cap., $5,600; emp., 10.

Establishments for m. of fire arms, 1; Fire Arms m'd., pistols, 3,000, rifles, 1,000; val. of fire arms, $40,000; cap., $24,000; emp., 35.

Chair and Cabinet Manufactories, 4; val. of chairs and cabinet ware, $26,000; cap., $6,800; emp., 22.

Tin Ware Manufactories, 3; val. of tin ware, (including tin roofing, $45,000,) $70,000; cap., $14,000; emp., 39.

Flour Mills, 1; Flour m'd., 6,000 bbls.; val. of flour m'd., $50,000; cap., $18,000; emp., 3.

Boots of all kinds m'd., 18,500 pairs; Shoes of all kinds m'd.,

10,000 pairs; val. of boots and shoes, $59,000; m. emp., 75; f. emp., 21.

Bricks m'd., 2,900,000; val. of bricks, $29,500; emp., 62.

Val. of snuff, tobacco and cigars, $65,000; m. emp., 36; f. emp., 10.

Val. of building stone quarried and prepared for building, $13,900; emp., 26.

Val. of marble prepared for market, $12,000; emp., 13.

Val. of mechanics' tools m'd., $54,000; emp., 55.

Firewood prepared for market, 815 cords; val. of firewood, $4,225; emp., 16.

Saxony Sheep, of different grades, –; Merino Sheep, of different grades, –; all other kinds of Sheep, 100; val. of all sheep, $250; Wool produced from Saxony sheep, – lbs.; Merino Wool produced, – lbs.; all other Wool produced, 390 lbs.

Horses, 775; val. of horses, $75,745; Oxen over three years old, 132; Steers under three years old, 41; val. of oxen and steers, $9,645; Milch Cows, 495; Heifers, 31; val. of cows and heifers, $18,550.

Butter, 14,085 lbs.; val. of butter, $3,100; Honey, 650 lbs.; val. of honey, $100.

Indian Corn, 1,232 acres; Indian Corn, per acre, 19 bush.; val., $23,408; Broom Corn, 2½ acres; Broom Bush, per acre, 1,560 lbs.; val., $390; Broom Seed, per acre, 36 bush.; val., $30.

Rye, 1,360 acres; Rye, per acre, 8½ bush.; val., $12,920.

Barley, 3 acres; Barley, per acre, 33 bush.; val., $6,700.

Oats, 176 acres; Oats, per acre, 17 bush.; val., $1,855.

Potatoes, 268 acres; Potatoes, per acre, 99 bush.; val., $15,990.

Onions, ¾ acre; Onions, per acre, 400 bush.; val., $300.

Turnips, cultivated as a field crop, 3 acres; Turnips, per acre, 400 bush.; val., $300.

Carrots, 18 acres; Carrots, per acre, 300 bush.; val., $1,800.

Beets and other esculent vegetables, 56¾ acres; val., $14,716; all other Grain or Root Crops, 173 acres; val., $2,000.

Millet, 27 acres; val., $304.

English Mowing, 841 acres; English Hay, 1,032 tons; val., $15,480.

Wet Meadow or Swale Hay, 131 tons; val., $917.

Apple Trees, cultivated for their fruit, 6,791; val., $2,620.

Pear Trees, cultivated for their fruit, (young trees,) 672; val., $123.

Tobacco, 17 acres; val., $1,690.

Establishments for m. of sashes, doors and blinds, 3; val. m'd., $105,000; cap., $29,000; emp., 105.

Establishments for m. of gas, 1; val. m'd., $21,000; cap., $50,000; emp., 6.

Establishments for m. of India-rubber goods, 1; val. of goods m'd., $18,000; cap., $8,000; m. emp., 5; f. emp., 18.

Bakeries, 1; cap., $3,100; Flour consumed, 1,000 bbls.; val. of bread m'd., $20,000; emp., 12.

Type and Stereotype Founderies, 1; val. of type, &c., m'd., $1,200; cap., $300; m. emp., 1.

Establishments for m. of boxes, (paper,) 2; val. of boxes m'd., $6,000; cap., $600; emp., 6.

Swine raised, 1,037; val. of same, $9,860.

Percussion Cap Manufactories, 1; val. of caps m'd., $6,000; cap., $2,000; emp., 5.

Optical Instrument Manufactories, 1; val. of instruments m'd., $1,000; cap., $300; emp., 1.

Plumbing Manufactories, 2; val. of work done, $5,500; cap., $3,000; emp., 7.

Electro-plating Manufactories, 1; val. of work done, $2,000; cap., $1,000; emp., 3.

Wooden Leg Manufactories, 1; val. of legs m'd., $9,000; cap., $1,500; emp., 5.

Clothing Manufactories, 6; val. of clothing m'd., $176,000; cap., $57,250; emp., 365.

Silver Platers, 2; val. of work done, $2,400; cap., $800; emp., 4.

Gas and Steam Fitting Manufactories, 1; val. of fittings m'd., $80,000; cap., $6,000; emp., 12.

Confectionery Manufactories, 1; val. of confectionery m'd., $75,000; cap., $8,000; emp., 40.

Flask Manufactories, 1; val. of flasks m'd., $4,000; cap., $3,000; emp., 7.

Lumber Dressing Establishments, 1; val. of lumber dressed, $20,000; cap., $10,000; emp., 15.

Establishments for m. of wire cloth and sieves, 1; val. of wire cloth, &c., m'd., $10,000; cap., $4,000; emp., 18.

Establishments for m. of hair-cloth, 1; val. of hair-cloth m'd., $1,000; cap., $500; emp., 2.

Establishments for m. of hydraulic pumps, 1; val. of pumps m'd., $11,000; cap., $4,500; emp., 10.

United States Armory.—Percussion Muskets m'd., 11,000; val. of muskets, $116,875; Cavalry Musketoons m'd., 2,000; val. of musketoons, $21,700; Extra Cones m'd., 22,388; Hammers for altering muskets, m'd., 14,003; Wipers m'd., 20,206; Compound Screw Drivers m'd., 13,331; Ball Screws m'd., 6,970; Spring Vises m'd., 7,879; Arm Chests m'd., 563; Packing Boxes m'd., 11.

TOLLAND.

Manufactories of forks, 1; Forks m'd., 19,000; cap., $700; emp., 2.

Tanneries, 1; Hides of all kinds tanned, 3,201; val. of leather tanned, $9,000; cap., $6,000; emp., 4.

Currying Establishments, 1; val. of leather curried, $500; cap., $100; emp., 1.

Boots of all kinds m'd., 100 pairs; Shoes of all kinds m'd., 50 pairs; val. of boots and shoes, $300; m. emp., 2.

Charcoal m'd., 2,400 bush.; val. of same, $140; emp., 3.

Lumber prepared for market, 675,000 ft.; val. of lumber, $4,550; emp., 16.

Firewood prepared for market, 200 cords; val. of firewood, $250; emp., 2.

Saxony Sheep, of different grades, –; Merino Sheep, of different grades, 41; all other kinds of Sheep, 320; val. of all sheep, $887; Wool produced from Saxony sheep, – lbs.; Merino Wool produced, 123 lbs.; all other Wool produced, 1,020 lbs.

Horses, 114; val. of horses, $8,975; Oxen over three years old, 202; Steers under three years old, 106; val. of oxen and steers, $13,279; Milch Cows, 627; Heifers, 213; val. of cows and heifers, $18,579.

Butter, 16,244 lbs.; val. of butter, $3,660; Cheese, 83,500 lbs.; val. of cheese, $7,854; Honey, 110 lbs.; val. of honey, $22.

Indian Corn, 100 acres; Indian Corn, per acre, 25 bush.; val., $2,500.

Wheat, 2 acres; Wheat, per acre, 18 bush.; val., $45.

Rye, 5 acres; Rye, per acre, 15 bush.; val., $75.

Barley, 5 acres; Barley, per acre, 18 bush.; val., $90.

Oats, 50 acres; Oats, per acre, 25 bush.; val., $750.

Potatoes, 84 acres; Potatoes, per acre, 100 bush.; val., $2,920.

Onions, ½ acre; Onions, per acre, 100 bush.; val., $31.

Turnips, cultivated as a field crop, 8 acres; Turnips, per acre, 100 bush; val., $200.

Carrots, ½ acre; Carrots, per acre, 351 bush.; val., $87.

English Mowing, 2,270 acres; English Hay, 1,963 tons; val., $14,543.

Wet Meadow or Swale Hay, 384 tons; val., $1,920.

Apple Trees, cultivated for their fruit, 7,415; val., $1,287.

Pear Trees, cultivated for their fruit, 50; val., $25.

Tobacco, 1 acre; val., $130.

Cranberries, 1 acre; val., $100.

Establishments for m. of casks, 2; cap., $200; Casks m'd., 700; val., $500; emp., 2.

Maple Sugar m'd., 233,000 lbs.; val., $26,700; emp., 40.

Shovel Handles m'd., 20,000; val., $2,500.

Val. of saw handles m'd., $100.

Hemlock Shingles m'd., 5,000; val., $45.

Baskets m'd., 100; val., $50.

Val. of wagon rims m'd., $2,000.

Hemlock Bark prepared for market, 175 cords; val., $700.

Saw Mills, 5; val. of lumber sawed, $5,000; emp., 5.

WALES.

Woollen Mills, 2; Sets of Machinery, 4; Wool consumed, 148,403 lbs.; Satinet m'd., 220,573 yds.; val. of satinet, $125,696; cap., $33,000; m. emp., 30; f. emp., 26.

Tanneries, 1; Hides of all kinds tanned, 320; val. of leather tanned, $650; cap., $500; emp., 1.

Currying Establishments, 1; val. of leather curried, $7,900; cap., $1,000; emp., 3.

Boots of all kinds m'd., 255 pairs; Shoes of all kinds m'd., 32,970 pairs; val. of boots and shoes, $27,735; m. emp., 31; f. emp., 11.

Charcoal m'd., 23,000 bush.; val. of same, $1,772; emp., 4.

Lumber prepared for market, 100,000 ft.; val. of lumber, $1,300; emp., 3.

Firewood prepared for market, 1,880 cords; val. of firewood, $4,800; emp., 4.

Merino Sheep, of different grades, 500; val. of all sheep, $1,146; Wool produced from Merino sheep, 972 lbs.

Horses, 83; val. of horses, $5,475; Oxen over three years old, 134; Steers under three years old, 47; val. of oxen and steers, $7,415; Milch Cows, 206; Heifers, 57; val. of cows and heifers, $6,125.

Butter, 12,035 lbs.; val. of butter, $2,407; Cheese, 7,155 lbs.; val. of cheese, $572.

Indian Corn, 99 acres, Indian Corn, per acre, 23 bush.; val. $2,550.

Wheat, 1 acre; Wheat, per acre, 15 bush.; val., $30.

Rye, 9 acres; Rye, per acre, 9 bush.; val., $124.

Barley, 2 acres; Barley, per acre, 15 bush.; val., $30.

Oats, 81 acres; Oats, per acre, 17 bush.; val., $815.

Potatoes, 90 acres; Potatoes, per acre, 82 bush.; val., $3,690.

Turnips, cultivated as a field crop, 2 acres; Turnips, per acre, 250 bush.; val., $125.

Carrots, ½ acre; Carrots, per acre, 386 bush.; val., $64.

English Mowing, 844 acres; English Hay, 618 tons; val., $7,416.

Wet Meadow or Swale Hay, 368 tons; val., $2,676.

Apple Trees, cultivated for their fruit, 1,135; val., $914.

Pear Trees, cultivated for their fruit, 38; val., $25.

Railroad Ties m'd., 12,760; val., $3,769.

WESTFIELD.

Cotton Mills, 1; Spindles, 156; Cotton consumed, 50,000 lbs.; val. of twine, batting, and carpet warp, $7,500; val. of batting, $200; m. emp., 4; f. emp., 4.

Furnaces for m. of hollow ware and castings other than pig iron, 1; val. of hollow ware and castings, $10,000; cap., $8,000; emp., 8.

Establishments for m. of steam-engines and boilers, 2; val. of steam-engines and boilers, $15,000; cap., $9,000; emp., 13.

Paper Manufactories, 1; Stock made use of, 270 tons; Paper m'd., 180 tons; val. of paper, $75,000; cap., $50,000; emp., 40.

Organ Manufactories, 1; val. of musical instruments m'd., $30,000; cap., $10,000; emp., 25.

Daguerreotype Artists, 1; Daguerreotypes taken, 1,000; cap., $400; emp., 1.

Saddle, Harness, and Trunk Manufactories, 2; val. of saddles, &c., $2,500; cap., $400; emp., 6.

Establishments for m. of railroad cars, coaches, chaises,

wagons, sleighs, and other vehicles, 2; val. of railroad cars, &c., m'd., $2,500; cap., $1,000; emp., 4.

Establishments for m. of soap and tallow candles, 1; Soap m'd., 100 bbls.; val. of soap, $350; cap., $150; emp., 1.

Powder Mills, 2; Powder m'd., 10,000 kegs; val. of powder, $24,000; cap., $17,000; emp., 7.

Chair and Cabinet Manufactories, 2; val. of chairs and cabinet ware, $3,000; cap., $1,500; emp., 4.

Tin Ware Manufactories, 2; val. of tin ware, $4,000; cap., $2,500; emp., 7.

Flour Mills, 3; Flour m'd., 1,800 bbls.; val. of flour m'd., $10,000; cap., $450; emp., 5.

Tanneries, 2; Hides of all kinds tanned, 3,000; val. of leather tanned, $6,000; cap., $2,500; emp., 4.

Boots of all kinds m'd., 600 pairs; Shoes of all kinds m'd., 400 pairs; val. of boots and shoes, $1,900; m. emp., 9.

Bricks m'd., 800,000; val. of bricks, $4,000; emp., 12.

Val. of snuff, tobacco and cigars, $49,900; m. emp., 42; f. emp., 20.

Val. of building stone quarried and prepared for building, $500; emp., 4.

Val. of whips m'd., $420,000; emp., 263.

Val. of wooden ware not otherwise enumerated, including farming utensils m'd, $800; emp., 2.

Lumber prepared for market, 263,000 ft.; val. of lumber, $3,500; emp., 5.

Firewood prepared for market, 1,083 cords; val. of firewood, $4,012; emp., 20.

Saxony Sheep, of different grades, –; Merino Sheep, of different grades, –; all other kinds of Sheep, 200; val. of all sheep, $300; Wool produced from Saxony sheep, – lbs.; Merino Wool produced, – lbs.; all other Wool produced, 600 lbs.

Horses, 455; val. of horses, $33,550; Oxen over three years old, 244; Steers under three years old, 213; val. of oxen and steers, $17,015; Milch Cows, 657; Heifers, 240; val. of cows and heifers, $19,778.

Butter, 65,160 lbs.; val. of butter, $13,032; Cheese, 2,540

lbs.; val. of cheese, $254; Honey, 1,503 lbs.; val. of honey, $210.

Indian Corn, 1,048 acres; Indian Corn, per acre, 24 bush.; val., $25,236; Broom Corn, 8 acres; Broom Bush, per acre, 750 lbs.; val., $480; Broom Seed, per acre, 30 bush.; val., $72.

Wheat, 21 acres; Wheat, per acre, 18 bush.; val., $760.

Rye, 1,992 acres; Rye, per acre, 7 bush.; val., $13,944.

Buckwheat, 346 acres; Buckwheat, per acre, 15 bush.; val., $2,595.

Oats, 214 acres; Oats, per acre, 24 bush.; val., $2,568.

Potatoes, 182 acres; Potatoes, per acre, 125 bush.; val., $9,250.

Turnips, cultivated as a field crop, 10 acres; Turnips, per acre, 200 bush.; val., $500.

Carrots, 2 acres; Carrots, per acre, 300 bush.; val., $180.

Beets and other esculent vegetables, – acres; all other Grain or Root Crops, 225 acres; val., $2,250.

English Mowing, 1,733 acres; English Hay, 2,614 tons; val., $41,824.

Wet Meadow or Swale Hay, 310 tons; val., $1,860.

Apple Trees, cultivated for their fruit, 6,192; val., $6,592.

Pear Trees, cultivated for their fruit, 232; val., $216.

Tobacco, 54 acres; val., $6,458.

Cranberries, 2 acres; val., $69.

Establishments for m. of casks, 5; cap., $60; Casks m'd., 3,000; val., $700; emp., 5.

Establishments for m. of cigar boxes, 1; whip boxes, 1; paper and fancy boxes, 1; cap., $10,000; val. of boxes m'd., $20,000, emp., 7.

WEST SPRINGFIELD.

Cotton Mills, 1; Spindles, 19,500; Cotton consumed, 1,083,279 lbs.; Cloth m'd., 3,500,000 yds., Sheetings and Drillings, Nos. 18—35; val. of cloth, $289,006.42; cap., $406,000; m. emp., 125; f. emp., 225.

Blacksmith Forges, 4; Bar Iron, Anchors, Chain Cables, and other articles of wrought iron m'd., 6 tons; val. of bar iron, &c., $2,400; cap., $1,200; emp., 4.

Paper Manufactories, 2; Stock made use of, 430 tons; Paper m'd., 130 tons of Brown Paper, 70,000 reams of White Paper; val. of paper, $149,000; cap. $67,000; emp., 85.

Piano-Forte Manufactories, 1; Piano-Fortes m'd., 4; cap., $400; emp., 1.

Establishments for m. of wagons, sleighs, and other vehicles, 1; val. of wagons, &c., m'd., $8,000; cap., $5,000; emp., 13.

Flour Mills, 1; Flour m'd., 4,000 bbls; val. of flour m'd., $52,000; cap., $10,000; emp. 2.

Tanneries, 2; Hides of all kinds tanned, 10,300; val. of leather tanned $3,900; cap., $3,200; emp., 3.

Currying Establishments, 2; val. of leather curried, $12,900; cap., $5,000; emp., 5.

Boots of all kinds m'd., 650 pairs; Shoes of all kinds m'd., 300 pairs; val. of boots and shoes, $2,640; m. emp., 4.

Val. of cigars, $3,120; m. emp., 5; f. emp., 1.

Lumber prepared for market, 150,000 ft.; val. of lumber, $2,700; emp., 2.

Firewood prepared for market, 1,515 cords; val. of firewood, $9,090; emp., 8.

Shad taken, 6,300; val. of same, $1,260; emp. 15.

Saxony Sheep, of different grades, –; Merino Sheep, of different grades, –; all other kinds of Sheep, 242; val. of all sheep, $605; Wool produced from Saxony sheep, – lbs.; Merino Wool produced, – lbs.; all other Wool produced, 605 lbs.

Horses, 232; val. of horses, $23,200; Oxen over three years old, 118; Steers under three years old, 111; val. of oxen and steers, $8,120; Milch Cows, 471; Heifers, 148; val. of cows and heifers, $18,705.

Butter, 56,188 lbs.; val. of butter, $12,361.36; Cheese, 870 lbs.; val. of cheese, $87; Honey, 176 lbs.; val. of honey, $44.

Indian Corn, 492 acres; Indian Corn, per acre, 35 bush.; val., $17,220; Broom Corn, $2\frac{5}{8}$ acres; Broom Bush, per acre,

700 lbs.; val., $183.75; Broom Seed, per acre, 60 bush.; val., $63.

Wheat, 23¼ acres; Wheat, per acre, 6 bush.; val., $279.

Rye, 595 acres; Rye, per acre, 12 bush.; val., $7,040.

Barley, 1 acre; Barley, per acre, 20 bush.; val., $20.

Oats, 105 acres; Oats, per acre, 30 bush.; val., $1,575.

Potatoes, 253 acres; Potatoes, per acre, 150 bush.; val. $18,975.

Onions, 5 acres; Onions, per acre, 300 bush.; val., $1,125.

Turnips, cultivated as a field crop, 27½ acres; Turnips, per acre, 300 bush.; val., $1,320.

Carrots, 3¾ acres; Carrots, per acre, 400 bush.; val., $495.

Beets and other esculent vegetables, 60 acres; val., 5,483; all other Grain or Root Crops, 115¼ acres; val., $1,661.

English Mowing, 1,404 acres; English Hay, 2,808 tons; val., $42,120.

Wet Meadow or Swale Hay, 430 tons; val., $4,300.

Apple Trees, cultivated for their fruit, 11,707; val., $5,853.

Pear Trees, cultivated for their fruit, 815; val., $815.

Tobacco, 23 acres; val., $4,600.

Beeswax, 25 lbs.; val. $10.

Milk Business—Cows, 95; val. of milk sold, $6,750; val. of each cow's product, $71.

Establishments for pulling wool, 1; cap., 1,200; skins pulled, 8,000; val. of skins after pulling, $1,000; wool, 6,000 lbs.; val. of wool, $2,100.

WILBRAHAM.

Woollen Mills, 2; Sets of Machinery, 3; Wool consumed, 35,000 lbs.; Cassimere m'd., $30,000 yds.; val. of cassimere, $21,000; Satinet m'd., 39,500 yds.; val. of satinet, $16,250; cap., $13,000; m. emp., 28; f. emp., 19.

Plough Manufactories, 1; Ploughs and other Agricultural Tools m'd., 3,600; val., $11,400; cap., $6,000; emp., 20.

Paper Manufactories, 1; Stock made use of, 40 tons; Paper m'd., 30 tons; val. of paper, $1,500; cap., $700; emp., 2.

Daguerreotype Artists, 1; Daguerreotypes taken, $250; emp., 1.

Tanneries, 1; Hides of all kinds tanned, 300; val. of leather tanned, $700; cap., $800; emp., 2.

Straw Hats m'd., 70.

Val. of building stone quarried and prepared for building, $3,000; emp., 9.

Charcoal m'd., 13,200 bush.; val. of same, $984.

Corn and other Brooms m'd., 2,000; val. of brooms, $360; emp., 1.

Lumber prepared for market, 229,700 ft.; val. of lumber, $3,300; emp., 13.

Firewood prepared for market, 4,332 cords; val. of firewood, $14,075; emp., 50.

Saxony Sheep, of different grades, –; Merino Sheep, of different grades, 22; all other kinds of Sheep, 687; val. of all sheep, $3,063; Wool produced from Saxony sheep, – lbs.; Merino Wool produced, 75 lbs.; all other Wool produced, 2,428 lbs.

Horses, 256; val. of horses, $22,375; Oxen over three years old, 302; Steers under three years old, 221; val. of oxen and steers, $22,976; Milch Cows, 699; Heifers, 238; val. of cows and heifers, $24,545.

Butter, 65,347 lbs.; val. of butter, $13,069.40; Cheese, 16,385 lbs.; val. of cheese, $1,638.50; Honey, 761 lbs.; val. of honey, $126.

Indian Corn, 784 acres; Indian Corn, per acre, 20 bush.; val., $17,248; Broom Corn, 5 acres; Broom Bush, per acre, 533 lbs.; val., $186.55; Broom Seed, per acre, 50 bush.; val., $62.50.

Wheat, 3 acres; Wheat, per acre, 9 bush.; val., $54.

Rye, 896 acres; Rye, per acre, 9 bush.; val., $10,886.40.

Oats, 362 acres; Oats, per acre, 21 bush.; val., $4,713.24.

Potatoes, 278 acres; Potatoes, per acre, 68 bush.; val., $12,287.60.

Turnips, cultivated as a field crop, 7 acres; Turnips, per acre, 155 bush.; val., $135.62.

Beets and other esculent vegetables, – acres; all other Grain or Root Crops, 176 acres; val., $1,444.

Millet, 1 acre; val., $20.

English Mowing, 2,165 acres; English Hay, 2,483 tons; val., $32,279.

Wet Meadow or Swale Hay, 713 tons; val., $4,991.

Apple Trees, cultivated for their fruit, 44,445; val., $3,588.

Pear Trees, cultivated for their fruit, 299; val., $57.

Tobacco, 7½ acres; val., $757.

Beeswax, 27 lbs.; val., $8.

All other articles manufactured are as follows: Overalls, 6,250 doz. pairs; Shirts and Bosoms, 400 doz.; Collars, 500 doz.; Cravats, 300 doz.; gross val., $35,950; cap., $6,000; emp., 75.

HAMPSHIRE COUNTY.

AMHERST.

Cotton Wicking Mills, 1; Cotton consumed, 50,000 lbs.; Wicking m'd., amount not stated; val. of wicking, $7,000; m. emp., 4; f. emp., 1.

Woollen Mills, 1; Sets of Machinery, 2; Wool consumed, 16,000 lbs., Cotton, 20,000 lbs.; Kentucky Jeans m'd., 145,600 yds.; val. of jeans, $28,000; m. emp., 10; f. emp., 10.

Paper Manufactories, 2; Stock made use of, 600 tons; Paper m'd., 300 tons; val. of paper, $24,000; cap., $15,000; emp., 25.

Daguerreotype Artists, 1; Daguerreotypes taken, 1,000; cap., $400; emp., 1.

Saddle, Harness and Trunk Manufactories, 3; val. of saddles, &c., $3,650; cap., $1,350; emp., 8.

Establishments for m. of railroad cars, coaches, chaises, wagons, sleighs, and other vehicles, 1; val. of railroad cars, &c., m'd., $2,000; cap., $800; emp., 3.

Chair and Cabinet Manufactories, 1; val. of chairs and cabinet ware, $3,000; cap., $2,000; emp., 3.

Tin Ware Manufactories, 1; val. of tin ware, $3,000; cap., $2,000; emp., 4.

Boots of all kinds m'd., 3,650 pairs; Shoes of all kinds m'd., 2,700 pairs; val. of boots and shoes, $13,500; m. emp., 24; f. emp., 5.

Establishments for m. of straw bonnets and hats, 2; val. of palm leaf hats, $32,000; m. emp., 3; f. emp., 170.

Bricks m'd., 250,000; val. of bricks, $1,125; emp., 2.

Val. of mechanics' tools m'd., $18,000; emp. 20.

Corn and other Brooms m'd., 55,000; val. of brooms, $8,280; emp., 8.

Lumber prepared for market, 500,000 ft.; val. of lumber, $60,000; emp., 20.

Firewood prepared for market, 1,738 cords; val. of firewood, $4,694; emp., 4.

Saxony Sheep, of different grades, –; Merino Sheep, of different grades, –; all other kinds of Sheep, 741; val. of all sheep, $1,417.50; Wool produced from Saxony Sheep, – lbs.; Merino Wool produced, – lbs.; all other Wool produced, 2,209 lbs.

Horses, 429; val. of horses, $33,900; Oxen over three years old, 321; Steers under three years old, 220; val. of oxen and steers, $23,448; Milch Cows, 835; Heifers, 292; val. of cows and heifers, $27,691.

Butter, 62,875 lbs.; val. of butter, $12,575; Cheese, 30,750 lbs.; val. of cheese, $3,075; Honey, 220 lbs.; val. of honey, $44.

Indian Corn, 873 acres; Indian Corn, per acre, 33 bush.;

val., $28,512; Broom Corn, 84 acres; Broom Bush, per acre, 600 lbs.; val., $5,040; Broom Seed, per acre, 50 bush.; val., $1,260.

Wheat, 19 acres; Wheat, per acre, 11½ bush.; val., $648.

Rye, 593 acres; Rye, per acre, 9 bush.; val., $6,685.

Barley, 2 acres; Barley, per acre, 40 bush.; val., $63.

Oats, 310 acres; Oats, per acre, 27 bush.; val., $4,090.

Potatoes, 238 acres; Potatoes, per acre, 95 bush.; val., $11,348.

Onions, 1 acre; Onions, per acre, 420 bush.; val., $315.

Turnips, cultivated as a field crop, 1½ acre; Turnips, per acre, 50 bush.; val., $19.

Carrots, 3½ acres; Carrots, per acre, 400 bush.; val., $467.

English Mowing, 2,405 acres; English Hay, 3,090 tons; val., $33,990.

Wet Meadow or Swale Hay, 913 tons; val., $5,478.

Apple Trees, cultivated for their fruit, 6,193; val., $2,522.

Pear Trees, cultivated for their fruit, 16; val., $26.

Hops, 3 acres; Hops, per acre, 2,400 lbs.; val., $480.

Tobacco, 7 acres; val., $800.

Establishments for m. of children's wagons and sleds, –; cap., $2,800; Wagons and Sleds m'd., 74,900; val., $14,985; emp., 18.

Number of wire covers and riddles, m'd., 4,000; cap., $1,000; m. emp., 5; f. emp., 8.

Axe Handles, &c., m'd., 30,000; cap., $12,000; emp., 10.

Swine raised, 525; val., $4,500.

BELCHERTOWN.

Woollen Mills, 1; Sets of Machinery, 1; Wool consumed, 40,000 lbs.; Satinet m'd., 60,000 yds.; val. of satinet, $30,000; cap., $15,000; m. emp., 12; f. emp., 6.

Axe Manufactories, 1; Axes m'd., 300; val., $375; cap., $300; emp., 1.

Manufactories of shovels, spades, forks and hoes, 1; Forks m'd., 250 doz.; val. of forks m'd., $1,500; cap., $500; emp., 2.

Paper Manufactories, 2; Stock made use of, 820 tons; Paper m'd., 318 tons; val. of paper, $33,440; cap., $20,000; emp., 22.

Harness Manufactories, 2; Harnesses m'd., 130; val. of harnesses m'd., $2,750; cap., $700; emp., 5.

Establishments for m. of railroad cars, coaches, chaises, wagons, sleighs, and other vehicles, 8; val. of 1,019 top carriages and wagons, and 91 sleighs m'd., $90,750; cap., $28,500; emp., 166.

Lumber prepared for market, 1,576,000 ft.; val. of lumber, $13,768.50; emp., 25.

Firewood prepared for market, 6,712 cords; val. of firewood, $15,886; emp., 112.

Saxony Sheep, of different grades, –; Merino Sheep, of different grades, 215; all other kinds of Sheep, 871; val. of all sheep, $2,348; Wool produced from Saxony sheep, – lbs.; Merino Wool produced, 655 lbs.; all other Wool produced, 2,178 lbs.

Horses, 489; val. of horses, $40,905; Oxen over three years old, 393; Steers under three years old, 498; val. of oxen and steers, $34,877; Milch Cows, 1,066; Heifers, 497; val. of cows and heifers, $37,212.

Butter, 91,520 lbs.; val. of butter, $18,304; Cheese, 45,519 lbs.; val. of cheese, $3,641; Honey, 1,228 lbs.; val. of honey, $200.

Indian Corn, 1,123 acres; Indian Corn, per acre, 25 bush.; val., $35,093.75.

Wheat, 6 acres; Wheat, per acre, 10$\frac{1}{16}$ bush.; val., $151.25.

Rye, 924 acres; Rye, per acre, 9 bush.; val., $12,474.

Barley, 1 acre; Barley, per acre, 16 bush.; val., $20.

Oats, 446 acres; Oats, per acre, 20 bush.; val., $5,798.

Potatoes, 327 acres; Potatoes, per acre, 85 bush.; val., $18,066.75.

English Mowing, 2,849 acres ; English Hay, 3,320 tons ; val., $49,800.

Wet Meadow or Swale Hay, 1,406 tons ; val., $9,842.

Apple Trees, cultivated for their fruit, 8,567 ; val., $4,807.

Pear Trees, cultivated for their fruit, 268 ; val., $57.

Swine raised, 839 ; val. of swine, $4,704 ; Pork, 96 tons ; val. of pork, $13,440.

Chickens, 7,331 ; val., $1,466.

Turkeys, 1,575 ; val., $1,381.

Eggs, 16,606 doz. ; val., $2,768.

CHESTERFIELD.

Furnaces for m. of hollow ware and castings other than pig iron, 1 ; Hollow Ware and other Castings m'd., 35 tons ; val. of hollow ware and castings, $3,150 ; cap., $2,000 ; emp., 3.

Tanneries, 1 ; Hides of all kinds tanned, 1,800 ; val. of leather tanned, $12,000 ; cap., $2,000 ; emp., 3.

Lumber prepared for market, 305,000 ft. ; val. of lumber, $2,464.

Firewood prepared for market, 300 cords ; val. of firewood, $600.

No men are regularly employed in the above branches of industry.

Merino Sheep, of different grades, 2,989 ; val. of all sheep, $4,483.

Horses, 178 ; val. of horses, $13,350 ; Oxen over three years old, 106 ; Steers under three years old, 140 ; val. of oxen and steers, $9,145 ; Milch Cows, 424 ; Heifers, 206 ; val. of cows and heifers, $15,710.

Butter, 42,200 lbs. ; val. of butter, $7,174 ; Cheese, 8,525 lbs. ; val. of cheese, $682.

Indian Corn, 184 acres ; Indian Corn, per acre, 30 bush. ; val., $5,520.

Wheat, 13 acres; Wheat, per acre, 15 bush.; val., $292.50.

Rye, 32 acres; Rye, per acre, 25 bush.; val., $1,000.

Barley, 28 acres; Barley, per acre, 30 bush.; val., $697.20.

Oats, 94 acres; Oats, per acre, 35 bush.; val., $1,480.50.

Potatoes, 125 acres; Potatoes, per acre, 100 bush.; val., $6,250.

Carrots, 6 acres; Carrots, per acre, 600 bush.; val., $900.

English Mowing, 3,127 acres; English Hay, 1,753 tons; val., not given.

Wet Meadow or Swale Hay, 154 tons; val., $770.

Apple Trees, cultivated for their fruit, 1,500; val., $1,000.

Maple Sugar m'd., 31,870 lbs.; val. of sugar, $800.

Saw Mills, 8.

Grist Mills, 3.

Swine raised, 172; val. of swine, $1,720.

CUMMINGTON.

Woollen Mills, –; Satinet m'd., 30,000 yds.; val. of satinet, $4,800; cap., $1,000; m. emp., 6; f. emp., 8.

Chair and Cabinet Manufactories, 2; val. of chairs and cabinet ware, $1,500; emp., 3.

Tanneries, 3; Hides of all kinds tanned, 10,000; val. of leather tanned, $44,000; cap., $20,000; emp., 17.

Val. of palm leaf hats, $2,200.

Lumber prepared for market, 995,000 ft.; val. of lumber, $9,000; emp., 5.

Saxony Sheep, of different grades, –; Merino Sheep, of different grades, –; all other kinds of Sheep, 1,225; val. of all sheep, $3,500; Wool produced from Saxony Sheep, – lbs.; Merino Wool produced, – lbs.; all other Wool produced, 4,478 lbs.

Horses, 227; val. of horses, $17,405; Oxen over three years old, 94; Steers under three years old, 134; val. of oxen and steers, $9,033; Milch Cows, 435; Heifers, 162; val. of cows and heifers, $12,000.

Butter, 31,560 lbs.; val. of butter, $5,680; Cheese, 18,145 lbs.; val. of cheese, $1,500.

Indian Corn, 138 acres; Indian Corn per acre, 38 bush.; val., $5,730.

Wheat, 7 acres; Wheat, per acre, $15\frac{3}{7}$ bush.; val., $162.

Rye, 7 acres; Rye, per acre, 13 bush.; val., $112.

Barley, 26 acres; Barley, per acre, 23 bush.; val., $2,300.

Oats, 41 acres; Oats, per acre, 29 bush.; val., $713.

Potatoes, 100 acres; Potatoes, per acre, 100 bush.; val., $5,000.

English Mowing, 3,166 acres; English Hay, 2,145 tons; val., $23,600.

Scythe Snathes m'd., 16,000; val., $2,000.

Scythe Stones m'd., 4,000 boxes; val., $8,000.

Towel Racks m'd., 300 doz.; val., $900.

Val. of toy bedsteads, &c., $1,000.

EASTHAMPTON.

Saddle, Harness and Trunk Manufactories, 1; val. of saddles, &c., $500; cap., $300; emp., 1.

Establishments for m. of railroad cars, coaches, chaises, wagons, sleighs, and other vehicles, 1; val. of railroad cars, &c., m'd., $1,500; cap., $2,000; emp., 2.

Tin Ware Manufactories, 1; val. of tin ware, $1,500; cap., $500; emp., 1.

Flour Mills, 2; val. of flour m'd., $18,000; cap., $8,000; emp., 3.

Tanneries, 1; Hides of all kinds tanned, 400; val. of leather tanned, $1,000; cap., $1,500; emp., 2.

Boots of all kinds m'd., 500 pairs; Shoes of all kinds m'd., 500 pairs; val. of boots and shoes, $2,050; m. emp., 6; f. emp., 1.

Val. of wooden ware not otherwise enumerated, including farming utensils m'd., $1,500; emp., 2.

Lumber prepared for market, 220,000 ft.; val. of lumber, $2,860; emp., 5.

Firewood prepared for market, 1,588 cords; val. of firewood, $5,742; emp., 12.

Saxony Sheep, of different grades, –; Merino Sheep, of different grades, –; all other kinds of Sheep, 138; val. of all sheep, $296; Wool produced from Saxony sheep, – lbs.; Merino Wool produced, – lbs.; all other Wool produced, 524 lbs.

Horses, 166; val. of horses, $14,678; Oxen over three years old, 96; Steers under three years old, 197; val. of oxen and steers, $8,699; Milch Cows, 302; Heifers, 152; val. of cows and heifers, $11,199.

Butter, 28,321 lbs.; val. of butter, $5,957.41; Cheese, 600 lbs.; val. of cheese, $72; Honey, 300 lbs.; val. of honey, $37.50.

Indian Corn, 444 acres; Indian Corn, per acre, 25½ bush.; val., $11,870; Broom Corn, 24 acres; Broom Bush, per acre, 303 lbs.; val., $727.20; Broom Seed, per acre, 31 bush.; val., $360.

Wheat, 24 acres; Wheat, per acre, 9 bush.; val., $432.

Rye, 609 acres; Rye, per acre, 8½ bush.; val., $6,470.

Oats, 100 acres; Oats, per acre, 21 bush.; val., $1,176.

Potatoes, 91 acres; Potatoes, per acre, 100 bush.; val., $5,005.

English Mowing, 669 acres; English Hay, 896 tons; val., $13,440.

Wet Meadow or Swale Hay, 414 tons; val., $4,140.

Apple Trees, cultivated for their fruit, 976; val., $874.

Tobacco, 1 acre; val., $100.

Establishments for m. of India-rubber goods, 1; cap., $110,000; val. of goods m'd., $150,000; m. emp., 60; f. emp., 70.

Establishments for m. of covered buttons, 1; cap., $140,000; Buttons m'd., 350,000 gross; val. of buttons m'd., $175,000; m. emp., 25; f. emp., 100.

ENFIELD.

Cotton Mills, 2; Spindles, 1,452; Cotton consumed, 100,000 lbs.; Cloth m'd., 600,000 yds., Satinet Warps; val., $20,000; cap., $7,000; m. emp., 7; f. emp., 16.

Woollen Mills, 2; Sets of Machinery, 7; Wool consumed, 230,000 lbs.; Satinet m'd., 330,000 yds.; val. of satinet, $150,000; cap., $129,000; m. emp., 53; f. emp., 41.

Daguerreotype Artists, 1; Daguerreotypes taken, 600; cap., $500; emp., 1.

Saddle, Harness and Trunk Manufactories, 1; val. of saddles, &c., $700; cap., $200; emp., 1.

Tin Ware Manufactories, 1; val. of tin ware, $2,000; cap., $800; emp., 2.

Boots of all kinds m'd., 400 pairs; Shoes of all kinds m'd., 2,160 pairs; val. of boots and shoes, $1,728; m. emp., 7.

Val. of palm leaf hats, $7,000.

Lumber prepared for market, 435,000 ft.; val. of lumber, $4,350; emp., 6.

Firewood prepared for market, 929 cords; val. of firewood, $1,625; emp., 9.

Saxony Sheep, of different grades, –; Merino Sheep, of different grades, –; all other kinds of Sheep, 173; val. of all sheep, $346; Wool produced from Saxony sheep, – lbs.; Merino Wool produced, – lbs.; all other Wool produced, 519 lbs.

Horses, 149; val. of horses, $9,935; Oxen over three years old, 82; Steers under three years old, 64; val. of oxen and steers, $5,775; Milch Cows, 286; Heifers, 60; val. of cows and heifers, $8,167.

Butter, 15,614 lbs.; val. of butter, $3,122.80; Cheese, 22,925 lbs.; val. of cheese, $2,292.50; Honey, 50 lbs.; val. of honey, $8.33.

Indian Corn, 379 acres; Indian Corn, per acre, 20 bush.; val., $8,420.

Wheat, 2 acres; Wheat, per acre, 23 bush.; val., $69.

Rye, 186 acres; Rye, per acre, 8 bush.; val., $2,106.

Oats, 112 acres; Oats, per acre, 26 bush.; val., $1,434.

Potatoes, 105 acres; Potatoes, per acre, 92 bush.; val., $4,815.

Onions, 20 bush.; val., $16.

Turnips, 20 bush.; val., $5.

English Mowing, 867 acres; English Hay, 857 tons; val., $11,998.

Wet Meadow or Swale Hay, 336 tons; val., $2,352.

Apple Trees, cultivated for their fruit, 920; val., $500.

Shingle Mills m'd., 15; val., $1,000; emp., 1.

GOSHEN.

Val. of mechanics' tools m'd., $9,500; emp., 14.

Val. of wooden ware not otherwise enumerated, including farming utensils m'd., $300.

Lumber prepared for market, 429,000 ft.; val. of lumber, $4,090; emp., 12.

Firewood prepared for market, 1,164 cords; val. of firewood, $2,900; emp., 4.

Saxony Sheep, of different grades, 254; Merino Sheep, of different grades, 210; val. of all sheep, $730; Wool produced from Saxony sheep, 720 lbs.; Merino Wool produced, 798 lbs.

Horses, 87; val. of horses, $7,145; Oxen, over three years old, 76; Steers under three years old, 67; val. of oxen and steers, $6,168; Milch Cows, 223; Heifers, 52; val. of cows and heifers, $6,690.

Butter, 19,315 lbs.; val. of butter, $3,863; Cheese, 8,280 lbs.; val. of cheese, $828.

Indian Corn, 98 acres; Indian Corn, per acre, 30 bush.; val., $2,940.

Wheat, 8 acres; Wheat, per acre, 20 bush.; val., $320.

Rye, 11 acres; Rye, per acre, 15 bush.; val., $206.

Barley, 7 acres; Barley, per acre, 22 bush.; val., $154.

Oats, 25 acres; Oats, per acre, 30 bush.; val., $375.

Potatoes, 76 acres; Potatoes, per acre, 100 bush.; val., $3,800.

Buckwheat, 20 acres; Buckwheat, per acre, $450 bush.; val., $338.

English Mowing, 1,285 acres; English Hay, 930 tons; val., $10,160.

Wet Meadow or Swale Hay, 110 tons; val., $660.

Apple Trees, cultivated for their fruit, 800; val., $500.

Maple Sugar m'd., 5,850 lbs.; val., $585.

Val. of ladders m'd., $300.

Val. of baby wagons and cabs m'd., $1,400.

Val. of broom handles m'd., $1,000.

GRANBY.

Woollen Mills, 1; Sets of Machinery, 2; Wool consumed, 75,000 lbs.; Satinet m'd., 100,000 yds.; val. of satinet, $50,000; cap., $25,000; m. emp., 15; f. emp., 12.

Paper Manufactories, 1; Stock made use of, 112 tons; Paper m'd., 80 tons; val. of paper, $5,500; cap., $4,000; emp., 7.

Val. of 2,350 palm leaf hats m'd., $330; f. emp., 9.

Lumber prepared for market, 117,350 ft.; val. of lumber, $14,082; emp., 14.

Firewood prepared for market, 2,239 cords; val. of firewood, $7,836; emp., 6.

Saxony Sheep, of different grades, –; Merino Sheep, of different grades, 387; all other kinds of Sheep, 170; val. of all sheep, $1,114; Wool produced from Saxony sheep, – lbs.; Merino Wool produced, 1,174 lbs.; all other Wool produced, 604 lbs.

Horses, 206; val. of horses, $12,772; Oxen over three years old, 193; Steers under three years old, 254; val. of oxen and steers, $16,721; Milch Cows, 473; Heifers, 181; val. of cows and heifers, $15,778.

Butter, 56,600 lbs.; val. of butter, $11,320; Cheese, 6,685 lbs.; val. of cheese, $668.50; Honey, 345 lbs.; val. of honey, $57.50.

Indian Corn, 565 acres; Indian Corn, per acre, 25 bush.; val., $15,652; Broom Corn, 1½ acre; Broom Bush, per acre, 667 lbs.; val., $100; Broom Seed, per acre, 67 bush.; val., $30.

Wheat, 9½ acres; Wheat, per acre, 12 bush.; val., $270.

Rye, 928 acres; Rye, per acre, 8½ bush.; val., $9,860.

Oats, 81 acres; Oats, per acre, 21 bush.; val., $850.50.

Potatoes, 169 acres; Potatoes, per acre, 90 bush.; val., $10,647.

Turnips, cultivated as a field crop, 1½ acre; Turnips, per acre, 140 bush.; val., $52.50.

Carrots, ¼ acre; Carrots, per acre, 1,000 bush.; val., $83.33.

English Mowing, 897 acres; English Hay, 1,312½ tons; val., $18,375.

Wet Meadow or Swale Hay, 902 tons; val., $6,314.

Apple Trees, cultivated for their fruit, 3,361; val., $800.

Tobacco, 2½ acres; val., $368.

Swine raised, 275; val., $1,374.

Buckwheat, 53 acres; 663 bush.; val., $663.

Beans, 1 acre; 8 bush.; val., $16.

Quinces, 150 bush.; val., $120.

GREENWICH.

Scythe Manufactories, 1; Scythes m'd., 6,000; val. of scythes, $2,500; cap., $1,500; emp., 6.

Brush Manufactories, 1; val. of brushes, $400; cap., $100; emp., 1.

Val. of palm leaf hats, $3,000; f. emp., almost all in the town, when occupied with nothing else of more importance.

Saxony Sheep, of different grades, –; Merino Sheep, of different grades, –; all other kinds of Sheep, 250; val. of all sheep, $675; Wool produced from Saxony sheep, – lbs.; Merino Wool produced, – lbs.; all other Wool produced, 875 lbs.

Horses, 126; val. of horses, $8,915; Oxen, over three years old, 137; Steers under three years old, 54; val. of oxen and steers, $7,775; Milch Cows, 296; Heifers, 93; val. of cows and and heifers, $8,585.

Butter, 13,723 lbs.; val. of butter, $2,744.60; Cheese, 20,850 lbs.; val. of cheese, $2,085.

Indian Corn, 350 acres; Indian Corn, per acre, 17 bush.; val., $5,950.

Wheat, 2½ acres; Wheat, per acre, 12 bush.; val., $30.

Rye, 397 acres; Rye, per acre, 7 bush.; val., $3,251.43.

Oats, 100 acres; Oats, per acre, 26 bush.; val., $1,000.

Potatoes, 133 acres; Potatoes, per acre, 76 bush.; val., $2,527.

English Mowing, 679 acres; English Hay, 622 tons; val., $7,775.

Wet Meadow or Swale Hay, 530 tons; val., $2,650.

Apple Trees, cultivated for their fruit, 674; val., $317.

Establishments for m. of boxes, (match boxes,) 1; val. of boxes m'd., $600; cap., $200; emp., 1.

Establishments for m. of silver plated trimmings for harnesses, 1; val., $6,000; cap., $2,000; emp., 6.

Buckwheat, 80 acres; 640 bush.; val., $530.

HADLEY.

Paper Manufactories, 1; Stock made use of, 225 tons; Paper m'd., 150 tons; val. of paper, $33,000; cap., $6,000; emp., 20.

Saddle, Harness and Trunk Manufactories, 1; val. of saddles, &c., $175; cap., $200; emp., 2.

Establishments for m. of railroad cars, coaches, chaises, wagons, sleighs, and other vehicles, 1; val. of railroad cars, &c., m'd., $1,200; cap., $300; emp., 1.

Tanneries, 1; Hides of all kinds tanned, 400; val. of leather tanned, $2,000; cap., $1,200; emp., 2.

Boots of all kinds m'd., 477 pairs; Shoes of all kinds m'd., 1,046 pairs; val. of boots and shoes, $3,138; m. emp., 5; f. emp., 1.

Val. of palm leaf hats m'd., $1,077; f. emp., 7.

Val. of blocks and pumps m'd., $175; emp., 1, during seven months.

Val. of mechanics' tools m'd., $300; emp., 1, during two months.

Corn and other Brooms m'd., 641,120; val. of brooms, $118,550; emp., 80.

Lumber prepared for market, 1,185,000 ft.; val. of lumber, $15,500; emp., 14.

Firewood prepared for market, 1,979 cords; val. of firewood, $5,249; emp., 5.

Saxony Sheep, of different grades, –; Merino Sheep, of different grades, 75; all other kinds of Sheep, 719; val. of all sheep, $1,603; Wool produced from Saxony sheep, – lbs.; Merino Wool produced, 250 lbs.; all other Wool produced, 1,709 lbs.

Horses, 317; val. of horses, $28,129; Oxen over three years old, 150; Steers under three years old, 230; val. of oxen and steers, $1,514; Milch Cows, 538; Heifers, 237; val. of cows and heifers, $22,638.

Butter, 70,890 lbs.; val. of butter, $14,178; Cheese, 7,760 lbs.; val. of cheese, $776; Honey, 328 lbs.; val. of honey, $61.

Indian Corn, 1,142 acres; Indian Corn, per acre, 37 bush.; val., $52,817; Broom Corn, 906 acres; Broom Bush, per acre, 700 lbs.; val., $63,420; Broom Seed, per acre, 60 bush.; val., $21,744.

Wheat, 47 acres; Wheat, per acre, 12 bush.; val., $1,128.

Rye, 805 acres; Rye, per acre, 13 bush.; val., $15,697.

Oats, 253 acres; Oats, per acre, 35 bush.; val., $5,932.

Potatoes, 153 acres; Potatoes, per acre, 110 bush.; val., $12,622.

Onions, ½ acre; Onions, per acre, 500 bush.; val., $187.50.

Turnips, cultivated as a field crop, $2\frac{3}{4}$ acres; Turnips, per acre, 400 bush.; val., $275.

Carrots, $3\frac{1}{2}$ acres; Carrots, per acre, 500 bush.; val., $577.50.

Beets and other esculent vegetables, 3 acres; val., $500; all other Grain or Root Crops, 15 acres; val., $150.

English Mowing, 1,925 acres; English Hay, 2,887 tons; val., $43,805.

Wet Meadow or Swale Hay, 332 tons; val., $2,490.

Apple Trees, cultivated for their fruit, 4,727; val., $3,545.

Pear Trees, cultivated for their fruit, 152; val., $120.

Tobacco, 57 acres; val., $9,690.

Establishments for m. of tobacco and dry goods boxes, 1; val. of boxes m'd., $2,000; cap., $500; emp., 1.

Corn Brushes, 35,000; val., $2,625.

Axe Handles, 450; val., $112.

Establishments for m. of wire, 1; Broom Wire m'd., 18 tons; val., $5,400; Piano Wire, $1\frac{1}{2}$ ton; val., $800; Sieve Wire, 1 ton; val., $400; emp., 2.

Bent Felloes, 800 sets; val., $1,000; Cut Felloes, 1,000 sets; val., $1,250.

Broom Handles m'd., 20,000; val., $250.

Sets of wheels m'd., 25; val., $200.

Val. of court plaster m'd., $1,500.

Val. of essence of life m'd., $2,500; m. emp., 1; f. emp., 2.

HATFIELD.

Flour Mills, (Custom Mill,) 1.

Corn and other Brooms m'd., 558,800; val. of brooms, $94,830; emp., 70.

Lumber prepared for market, 834,000 ft.; val. of lumber, $4,314; emp., 8.

Firewood prepared for market, 1,607 cords; val. of firewood, $4,035; emp., 4.

Saxony Sheep, of different grades, –; Merino Sheep, of dif-

ferent grades, –; all other kinds of Sheep, 21; val. of all sheep, $42; Wool produced from Saxony sheep, – lbs.; Merino Wool produced, – lbs.; all other Wool produced, 60 lbs.

Horses, 205; val. of horses, $14,350; Oxen over three years old, 124; Steers under three years old, 70; val. of oxen and steers, $10,050; Milch Cows, 252; Heifers 69; val. of cows and heifers, $9,732; Beef Cows, 242; gross val., $7,640.

Butter, 40,792 lbs.; val. of butter, $8,160; Cheese, 1,100 lbs.; val. of cheese, $132.

Indian Corn, 700 acres; Indian Corn, per acre, 30⅔ bush.; val., $23,630.20; Broom Corn, 499 acres; Broom Bush, per acre, 750 lbs.; val., $37,494; Broom Seed, per acre, 45 bush.; val., $8,420.

Wheat, 143 acres; Wheat, per acre, 6½ bush.; val., $1,886.

Rye, 330 acres; Rye, per acre, 9 bush.; val., $3,656.

Oats, 90 acres; Oats, per acre, 16½ bush.; val., $892.80.

Potatoes, 52 acres; Potatoes, per acre, 130 bush.; val., $3,365.

Millet, 7 acres; val., $35.

English Mowing, 1,043 acres; English Hay, 1,473 tons; val. $12,516.

Wet Meadow or Swale Hay, 674 tons; val., $5,392.

Apples, 1,665 bush.; val., $832.50.

Tobacco, 54 acres; val., $8,542.

HUNTINGTON.

Woollen Mills, 1; Satinet m'd., 1,500 yds.; val. of satinet, $1,245; cap., $500; m. emp., 1; f. emp., 1.

Axe Manufactories, 2; Axes, Hatchets and other Edge Tools m'd., 800 doz.; val., $8,800; cap., $2,200; emp., 9.

Paper Manufactories, 1; Stock made use of, 500,000 lbs.; val. of paper, $50,000; cap., $15,000; m. emp., 12; f. emp., 14.

Saddle, Harness and Trunk Manufactories, 1; val. of saddles, &c., $1,000; cap., $500; emp., 1.

Tanneries, 1; Hides of all kinds tanned, 75; val. of leather tanned, $400; cap., $200; emp., 1.

Boots of all kinds m'd., 200 pairs; Shoes of all kinds m'd., 150 pairs; val. of boots and shoes, $900; m. emp., 2.

Val. of palm leaf hats, $60; emp., 2 or 3 children.

Charcoal m'd., 3,000 bush.; val. of same, $270.

Val. of mechanics' tools m'd., $12,000; emp., 15.

Lumber prepared for market, 356,000 ft.; val. of lumber, $3,560.

Firewood prepared for market, 2,550 cords; val. of firewood, $3,825.; emp., 8.

Saxony Sheep, of different grades, –; Merino Sheep, of different grades, –; all other kinds of Sheep, 484; val. of all sheep, $968; Wool produced from Saxony sheep, – lbs.; Merino Wool produced, – lbs.; all other Wool produced, 1,600 lbs.

Horses, 154; val. of horses, $15,400; Oxen over three years old, 142; Steers under three years old, 170; val. of oxen and steers, $12,275; Milch Cows, 344; Heifers, 189; val. of cows and heifers, $12,966.

Butter, 32,950 lbs.; val. of butter, $6,950; Cheese, 12,275 lbs.; val. of cheese, $1,227.50.

Indian Corn, 133 acres; Indian Corn, per acre, 35 bush.; val., $5,818.75.

Wheat, 4 acres; Wheat, per acre, 17 bush.; val., $187.

Rye, 54 acres; Rye, per acre, 16 bush.; val., $1,080.

Oats, 46 acres; Oats, per acre, 15 bush.; val., $517.50.

Potatoes, 62 acres; Potatoes, per acre, 100 bush.; val., $3,720.

Turnips, cultivated as a field crop, 4 acres; Turnips, per acre, 170 bush.; val., $204.

English Mowing, 1,680 acres; English Hay, 1,600 tons; val., $16,000.

Apple Trees, cultivated for their fruit, 4,560; val., of apples, 50 cts. per bush.

Pear Trees, cultivated for their fruit, 202; val. of pears, not given.

Establishments for m. of sashes, doors and blinds, 1; cap., $1,000; val. m'd., $2,500; emp., 3.

Distilleries, 2, cider stills only.

Farrow Cows, 73; val., $1,825.

Basket Manufactories, 1; cap., $12,000; val. of stock used $2,500; val. of baskets m'd., $18,000; emp., 45.

Bedstead Manufactories, 1; cap., $10,000; val. of stock used, $8,000; val. of bedsteads m'd., $24,000; emp., 15.

Children's Cab and Wagon Manufactories, 1; cap., $4,000; val. of stock used, $2,500; val. of wagons, &c., m'd., $12,000; emp., 12.

Scythe Stone Manufactories, 1; cap., $800; val. of stock used, $300; val. of scythe stones m'd., $2,500; emp., 3.

MIDDLEFIELD.

Woollen Mills, 2; Sets of Machinery, 3; Wool consumed, 50,000 lbs.; Broadcloth m'd., 40,000 yds.; val. of broadcloth $42,000; cap., $16,000; m. emp., 25; f. emp., 20.

Paper Manufactories, 1; Stock made use of, 525,000 lbs.; Paper m'd., 350,270 lbs.; val. of paper, $28,021.60; cap., $20,000; emp., 14.

Daguerreotype Artists, 1; Daguerreotypes taken, 35; cap., $50; emp., 1.

Charcoal m'd., 52,500 bush.; val. of same, $4,200; emp., 2.

Lumber prepared for market, 498,500 ft.; val. of lumber, $3,565; emp., 21.

Firewood prepared for market, 1,115 cords; val. of firewood, $1,897; emp., 5.

Saxony Sheep, of different grades, 1,045; Merino Sheep, of different grades, 2,452; all other kinds of Sheep, 1,352; val. of all sheep, $7,276; Wool produced from Saxony sheep, 2,230 lbs.; Merino Wool produced, 7,907 lbs.; all other Wool produced, 4,336 lbs.

Horses, 110; val. of horses, $8,377; Oxen over three years old, 104; Steers under three years old, 202; val. of oxen and steers, $12,284; Milch Cows, 212; Heifers, 148; val. of cows and heifers, $9,193.

Butter, 14,965 lbs.; val. of butter, $2,993; Cheese, 5,430 lbs.; val. of cheese, $433; Honey, 580 lbs.; val. of honey, $92.

Indian Corn, 71 acres; Indian Corn, per acre, 40 bush.; val., $2,867.

Wheat, 3 acres; Wheat, per acre, 15 bush.; val., $90.

Rye, 3 acres; Rye, per acre, 15 bush.; val., $57.

Barley, 9 acres; Barley, per acre, 29 bush.; val., $203.

Oats, 43 acres; Oats, per acre, 27 bush.; val., $712.

Potatoes, 69 acres; Potatoes, per acre, 132 bush.; val., $3,255.

Onions, $\frac{1}{3}$ acre; Onions, per acre, 600 bush.; val., $150.

Turnips, cultivated as a field crop, $1\frac{1}{2}$ acre; Turnips, per acre, 191 bush.; val., $71.

Carrots, $3\frac{3}{4}$ acres; Carrots, per acre, 526 bush.; val., $493.

Beets and other esculent vegetables, – acres; all other Grain or Root Crops, 4 acres; val., $75.

English Mowing, 2,738 acres; English Hay, 2,065 tons; val., $20,650.

Wet Meadow or Swale Hay, 59 tons; val., $295.

Apple Trees, cultivated for their fruit, 9,036; val., $1,152.

Pear Trees, cultivated for their fruit, 137; val, $10.

Beeswax, 39 lbs.; val., $15.

Swine raised, 115; val. of swine, $801.

Bark, 256 cords; val., $768.

NORTHAMPTON.

Cotton Mills, 1; Spindles, 3,300; Cotton consumed, 160,000 lbs.; Cloth m'd., 700,000 yds. 33 inch Shirtings; val. of cloth, $42,000; m. emp., 25; f. emp., 50.

Woollen Mills, 4; Sets of Machinery, 11; Wool consumed, 275,000 lbs.; Satinet m'd., 200,000 yds.; val. of satinet, $100,-000; cap., $120,000; m. emp., 110; f. emp., 70.

Silk Manufactories, 2; Sewing Silk m'd., 17,000 lbs.; val. of sewing silk, $110,000; cap., $21,000; m. emp., 14; f. emp., 41.

Furnaces for m. of hollow ware and castings other than pig iron, 1; Hollow Ware and other Castings m'd., 100 tons; val. of hollow ware and castings, $7,000; cap., $6,000; emp., 6.

Establishments for m. of steam-engines and boilers, 1; val. of steam-engines and boilers, $12,000; cap., $20,000; emp., 15.

Manufactories of shovels, spades, forks and hoes, 1; val. of shovels, &c., $100,000; cap., $100,000; emp., 150.

Paper Manufactories, 3; Stock made use of, 600,000 tons; Paper m'd., 60,000 reams of writing, and 175 tons of wrapping; val. of paper, $100,000; cap., $100,000; emp., 100.

Establishments for m. of wagons and other vehicles, 2; val. of wagons, &c., m'd., $1,500; cap., $3,000; emp., 4.

Establishments for m. of soap and tallow candles, 1; Soap m'd., 300 bbls., and 10 tons hard soap; val. of soap, $2,600; Tallow Candles m'd., 4,000 lbs.; val. of tallow candles, $580; cap., $1,000; emp., 2.

Chair and Cabinet Manufactories, 2; val. of chairs and cabinet ware, $10,000; cap., $10,000; emp., 10.

Tin Ware Manufactories, 3; val. of tin ware, $15,000; cap., $5,000; emp., 18.

Bricks m'd., 1,400,000; val. of bricks, $7,000; emp., 22.

Corn and other Brooms m'd., 60,000; val. of brooms, $12,000; emp., 10.

Lumber prepared for market, 1,500,000 ft.; val. of lumber, $18,000; emp., 12.

Firewood prepared for market, 2,857 cords; val. of firewood, $11,428.

Saxony Sheep, of different grades, –; Merino Sheep, of different grades, –; all other kinds of Sheep, 591; val. of all sheep, $1,773; Wool produced from Saxony sheep, – lbs.; Merino Wool produced, – lbs.; all other Wool produced, 2,274 lbs.

Horses, 582; val. of horses, $57,985; Oxen over three years old, 144; Steers under three years old, 180; val. of oxen and steers, $15,000; Milch Cows, 634; Heifers, 186; val. of cows and heifers, $25,985.

Butter, 75,215 lbs.; val. of butter, $15,043.

Indian Corn, 1,175 acres; Indian Corn, per acre, 35 bush.; val., $1 per bush.; Broom Corn, 422 acres; Broom Bush, per acre, 700 lbs.; val., $29,540; Broom Seed, per acre, 50 bush.; val., $8,440.

Wheat, 50 acres; Wheat, per acre, 20 bush.; val., $2 per bush.

Rye, 665 acres; Rye, per acre, 15 bush.; val., $1.25 per bush.

Oats, 145 acres; Oats, per acre, 35 bush.; val., 65 cts. per bush.

Potatoes, 202 acres; Potatoes, per acre, 250 bush.; val., 75 cts. per bush.

English Mowing, 2,404 acres; English Hay, 3,575 tons; val., $16 per ton.

Apple Trees, cultivated for their fruit, 5,394; val., $5,026.

Pear Trees, cultivated for their fruit, 261; val., $423.

Tobacco, 25 acres; val., $2,500.

Establishments for m. of sashes, doors and blinds, 1; cap., $15,000; val. m'd., $40,000; emp., 9.

Establishments for m. of steam saw mills, 2; cap., $16,000; val. of m's., $30,000; emp., 18.

PELHAM.

Boots of all kinds m'd., 559 pairs; Shoes of all kinds m'd., 235 pairs; val. of boots and shoes, $1,683; m. emp., 9.

Val. of palm leaf hats m'd., $4,020; m. emp., 171.

Val. of building stone quarried and prepared for building, $1,240; emp., 4.

Charcoal m'd., 10,500 bush.; val. of same, $624; emp., 7.

Val. of mechanics' tools m'd., $150; emp., 1.

Lumber prepared for market, 486,700 ft.; val. of lumber, $6,816; emp., 19.

Firewood prepared for market, 623 cords; val. of firewood, $1,122; emp., 23.

Saxony Sheep, of different grades, – ; Merino Sheep, of different grades, –; all other kinds of Sheep, 140; val. of all sheep, $373; Wool produced from Saxony sheep, – lbs.; Merino Wool produced, – lbs.; all other Wool produced, 548 lbs.

Horses, 111; val. of horses, $7,640; Oxen over three years old, 146; Steers under three years old, 55; val. of oxen and steers, $9,072; Milch Cows, 281; Heifers, 89; val. of cows and heifers, $8,477.

Butter, 16,716 lbs.; val. of butter, $3,343.20; Cheese, 7,600 lbs.; val. of cheese, $836; Honey, 25 lbs.; val. of honey, $4.

Indian Corn, 243 acres; Indian Corn, per acre, 19 bush.; val., $6,184.

Rye, 103 acres; Rye, per acre, 7 bush.; val., $1,093.

Barley, 2 acres; Barley, per acre, 23 bush.; val., $57.50.

Oats, 70 acres; Oats, per acre, 16 bush.; val., $583.50.

Potatoes, 128 acres; Potatoes, per acre, 66 bush.; val., $5,206.14.

Onions, ½ acre; Onions, per acre, 100 bush.; val., $100.

English Mowing, 1,300 acres; English Hay, 734 tons; val., $8,808.

Wet Meadow or Swale Hay, 400 tons; val., $2,400.

Apple Trees, cultivated for their fruit, 2,657; val., $1,014.

Pear Trees, cultivated for their fruit, 21; val., $17.

PLAINFIELD.

Woollen Mills, 1; Sets of Machinery, 1; Wool consumed, 1,000 lbs.; Satinet m'd., 1,000 yds.; val. of satinet, $750; cap., $500; m. emp., 1.

Daguerreotype Artists, 2; Daguerreotypes taken, 1,200; cap., $1,000; emp., 2.

Saddle, Harness and Trunk Manufactories, 2; val. of saddles, &c., $500; cap., $150; emp., 3.

Establishments for m. of railroad cars, coaches, chaises, wagons, sleighs, and other vehicles, 1; val. of railroad cars, &c., m'd., $300; cap., $200; emp., 1.

Chair and Cabinet Manufactories, 1; val. of chairs and cabinet ware, $400; cap., $200; emp., 1.

Boots of all kinds m'd., 175 pairs; Shoes of all kinds m'd., 100 pairs; val. of boots and shoes, $650; m. emp., 2.

Val. of palm leaf hats m'd., $3,300; f. emp., 125.

Charcoal m'd., 1,000 bush.; val. of same, $70; emp., 1.

Val. of whips m'd., $50; emp., 1.

Lumber prepared for market, 315,000 ft.; val. of lumber, $2,362.50; emp., 10.

Firewood prepared for market, 1,500 cords; val. of firewood, $1,900; emp., 25.

Merino Sheep, of different grades, 700; val. of all sheep, $1,050; Merino Wool produced, 2,450 lbs.

Horses, 132; val. of horses, $8,860; Oxen over three years old, 100; Steers under three years old, 129; val. of oxen and steers, $6,515; Milch Cows, 334; Heifers, 106; val. of cows and heifers, $9,738.

Butter, 23,380 lbs.; val. of butter, $4,208.40; Cheese, 8,016 lbs.; val. of cheese, $721.44.

Indian Corn, 111 acres; Indian Corn, per acre, $32\frac{21}{111}$ bush.; val., $3,573.

Rye, 7 acres; Rye, per acre, $14\frac{3}{7}$ bush.; val., $150.

Barley, 23 acres; Barley, per acre, $21\frac{10}{23}$ bush.; val., $410.83.

Oats, 56 acres; Oats, per acre, $22\frac{9}{26}$ bush.; val., $625.

Potatoes, 93 acres; Potatoes, per acre, $104\frac{39}{93}$ bush.; val., $4,855.50.

Carrots, ½ acre; Carrots, per acre, 800 bush.; val., $133.33.

English Mowing, 2,158 acres; English Hay, 1,382 tons; val., $16,584.

Wet Meadow or Swale Hay, 250 tons; val., $1,500.

Apple Trees, cultivated for their fruit, 3,039; val., $1,445.

Pear Trees, cultivated for their fruit, 20; val., $50.

Type and Stereotype Founderies, 1; val. of type, &c., m'd., $1,200; cap., $1,000; m. emp., 2; f. emp., 1.

Establishments for m. of boxes, (butter and bail,) 3; val. of boxes m'd., $1,400; cap., $500; emp., 5.

All other articles m'd. in the town during the year:—20,175 lbs. Maple Sugar, 250 Corn Planters, 155,000 Broom Handles, 600 Bottles of Medicines; val., $4,614.

PRESCOTT.

Val. of palm leaf hats, $2,509; f. emp., 125.

Lumber prepared for market, 1,075,000 ft.; val. of lumber, $10,750; emp., 30.

Firewood prepared for market, 300 cords; val. of firewood, $300; emp., 1.

Saxony Sheep, of different grades, –; Merino Sheep, of different grades, –; all other kinds of Sheep, 167; val. of all sheep, $371; Wool produced from Saxony sheep, – lbs.; Merino Wool produced, – lbs.; all other Wool produced, 652 lbs.

Horses, 110; val., of horses, $8,550; Oxen over three years old, 118; Steers under three years old, 86; val. of oxen and steers, $8,861; Milch Cows, 336; Heifers, 73; val. of cows and heifers, $9,390.

Butter, 13,164 lbs.; val. of butter, $2,632.80; Cheese, 49,030 lbs.; val. of cheese, $4,576.

Indian Corn, 241 acres; Indian Corn, per acre, 24 bush.; val., $5,784.

Wheat, 3 acres; Wheat, per acre, 15 bush.; val., $135.

Rye, 85 acres; Rye, per acre, 8 bush.; val., $850.

Barley, 20 acres; Barley, per acre, 23 bush.; val., $368.

Oats, 92 acres; Oats, per acre, 22 bush.; val., $1,012.

Potatoes, 135 acres; Potatoes, per acre, 80 bush.; val., $5,400.

English Mowing, 1,248 acres; English Hay, 1,081 tons; val., $12,962.

Wet Meadow or Swale Hay, 220 tons; val., $1,080

Apple Trees, cultivated for their fruit, 2,564; val., $1,080.

Pear Trees, cultivated for their fruit, 53; val., $38.

Swine raised, 125; val., $936.

Buckwheat, 60 acres; Buckwheat, per acre, 10 bush.; val., $600.

SOUTH HADLEY.

Cotton Mills, 1; Spindles, 9,000; Cotton consumed, 386,900 lbs; Cloth, m'd., 2,378,475½ yds., Ginghams; val. of cloth, $256,000; Batting, m'd., 4,000 lbs.; val. of batting, $400; cap., $251,400; m. emp., 150; f. emp., 275.

Woollen Mills, 1; Sets of Machinery, 4, not running.

Forges, 7; cap., $1,000; emp., 3.

Paper Manufactories, 2; Stock made use of, 500 tons; Paper m'd., 90,000 reams; val. of paper, $100,000; cap., $75,000; emp., 62.

Cordage Manufactories, 1; Cordage m'd., 5,000; cap., $400; emp., 1.

Establishments for m. of boats, –; Boats built, 2.

Establishments for m. of railroad cars, coaches, chaises, wagons, sleighs, and other vehicles, 1; val. of railroad cars, &c., m'd., $4,000; cap., $500; emp., 8.

Tin Ware Manufactories, 1; val. of tin ware, $1,500; cap., $500; emp., 1.

Tanneries, 1; Hides tanned, 1,200.

Boots of all kinds m'd., 600 pairs; Shoes of all kinds m'd., 1,400 pairs; val. of boots and shoes, $2,500; m. emp., 11; f. emp., 3.

Lumber prepared for market, 300,000 ft.; val. of lumber, $5,000; emp., 5.

Firewood, prepared for market, 3,778 cords; val. of firewood, $19,990; emp., 68.

Shad, taken, 40,000; val. of same, $6,000; emp., 30.

Saxony Sheep, of different grades, –; Merino Sheep of different grades, –; all other kinds of Sheep, 221; val. of all sheep, $442; Wool produced from Saxony sheep, – lbs.; Merino Wool produced, – lbs.; all other wool produced, 663 lbs.

Horses, 197; val. of horses, $14,475; Oxen over three years old, 91; Steers under three years old, 88; val. of oxen and steers, $14,470; Milch Cows, 434; Heifers, 106; val. of cows and heifers, $18,310.

Butter, 80,360 lbs.; val. of butter, $16,072; Cheese, 4,500 lbs.; val. of cheese, $450; Honey, 661 lbs; val. of honey, $112.

Indian Corn, 491 acres; Indian Corn, per acre, 35 bush.; val., $17,185; Broom Corn, 2 acres; val. of Broom Bush, $14; val. of Broom Seed, $14.

Wheat, 1½ acre; Wheat, per acre, 15 bush.; val., $40.

Rye, 375 acres; Rye, per acre, 8 bush.; val., $3,000.

Oats, 185 acres; Oats, per acre, 40 bush.; val., $3,700.

Potatoes, 215 acres; Potatoes, per acre, 75 bush.; val., $4,837.50.

Onions, 5 acres; Onions, per acre, 500 bush.; val., $1,250.

Turnips, cultivated as a field crop, 15 acres; Turnips per acre, 300 bush.; val., $600.

Carrots, 1 acre; Carrots per acre, 550 bush.; val., $165.

Beets and other esculent vegetables, 40 acres; val., $800; all other Grain or Root Crops, 60 acres; val., $300.

English Mowing, 715 acres; English Hay, 1,000 tons; val., $12,000.

Wet Meadow or Swale Hay, 109 tons; val., $545.

Apple Trees, cultivated for their fruit, 4,979; val., $3,734.

Pear Trees, cultivated for their fruit, 508; val., $100.

Tobacco, 8½ acres; val., $1,600.

Beeswax, 100 lbs.; val., $35.

Establishments for m. of casks, 2; cap., $300; val., $800; emp., 3.

Establishments for m. of sashes, doors and blinds, 1; cap., $2,800; val. m'd., $7,000; emp., 8.

Establishments for m. of gas, 1; cap., $2,800; val. m'd., $1,200; emp., 1.

Establishments for m. of boxes, for cloth and tobacco, 1; cap., $1,000; val. of boxes m'd., $3,000; emp., 3.

SOUTHAMPTON.

Plough Manufactories, 1; Ploughs and other Agricultural Tools m'd., 30; val., $210; cap., $200; emp., 1.

Saddle, Harness and Trunk Manufactories, 1; val. of saddles, &c., $300; cap., $150; emp., 1.

Establishments for m. of railroad cars, coaches, chaises, wagons, sleighs, and other vehicles, 1; val. of railroad cars, &c., m'd., $500; cap., $200; emp., 1.

Boots of all kinds m'd., 200 pairs; Shoes of all kinds m'd., 250 pairs; val. of boots and shoes, $600; emp., 3.

Bricks, m'd., 350,000; val. of bricks, $1,575; emp., 3.

Val. of whips, m'd., $3,000; emp., 5.

Firewood, prepared for market, 3,403 cords; val. of firewood, $7,192; emp., 10.

Saxony Sheep, of different grades, –; Merino Sheep of different grades, –; all other kinds of Sheep, 624; val. of all sheep, $1,504; Wool produced from Saxony sheep, – lbs; Merino Wool produced, – lbs.; all other Wool produced, 1,750 lbs.

Horses, 223; val. of horses, $1,950; Oxen over three years old, 218; Steers under three years old, 190; val. of oxen and steers, $14,485; Milch Cows, 455; Heifers, 225; val. of cows and heifers, $11,925.

Butter, 47,650 lbs.; val. of butter, $9,530; Cheese, 3,450 lbs.; val. of cheese, $345.

Indian Corn, 567 acres; Indian Corn, per acre, 24 bush.; val., $16,956.

Wheat, 6 acres; Wheat, per acre, 15 bush.; val., $200.

Rye, 1,019 acres; Rye, per acre, 7 bush.; val., $10,729.

Oats, 192 acres; Oats, per acre, 25 bush.; val., $2,802.

Potatoes, 178 acres; Potatoes, per acre, 90 bush.; val., $9,455.40.

Turnips, cultivated as a field crop, 5 acres; Turnips, per acre, 100 bush.; val., $125.

English Mowing, 934 acres; English Hay, 1,230 tons; val., $18,450.

Wet Meadow or Swale Hay, 654 tons; val., $6,540.

Apple Trees, cultivated for their fruit, 1,711; val., $1,598.

Establishments for m. of friction matches, 1; cap., $400; Matches, m'd., 2,500 gross; val., $1,250; emp., 2.

Lumber, prepared for market; 392,000 Shingles; 747,000 ft. of Boards; 100,000 Staves; 200,000 Laths; val., $9,675; emp., 15.

WARE.

Cotton Mills, 4; Spindles, 20,000; Cotton consumed, 4,500 bales; Cloth m'd., 6,000,000 yds., consisting of 5,700,000 yds. Denims, and 300,000 yds. common cotton cloth; val. of cloth, $471,000; cap., $500,000; m. emp., 250; f. emp., 350.

Woollen Mills, 2; Sets of Machinery, 14; Wool consumed, 400,000 lbs.; Flannel or Blanketing, 800,000 yds.; val. of flannel or blanketing, $250,000; cap., $130,000; m. emp., 140; f. emp., 80.

Daguerreotype Artists, 2; Daguerreotypes taken, 1,075; cap., $350; emp., 3.

Saddle, Harness and Trunk Manufactories, 1; val. of saddles, &c., $1,300; cap., $500; emp., 2.

Establishments for m. of railroad cars, coaches, chaises, wagons, sleighs, and other vehicles, 1; val. of railroad cars, &c., m'd., $800.

Establishments for m. of soap and tallow candles, 2; Soap, m,d., 500 bbls.; val. of Soap, $2,000; Tallow Candles m'd., 15,000 lbs.; val. of tallow candles, $2,250, cap., $1,000; emp., 5.

Tin Ware Manufactories, 1; val. of tin ware, $1,500; cap., $900; emp., 2.

Currying Establishments, 1; val. of leather curried, $18,000; cap., $2,000; emp., 6.

Boots of all kinds m,d., 6,960 pairs; Shoes of all kinds m'd., 5,610 pairs; val., of boots and shoes, $2,850, (for bottoming); m. emp., 30; Stock owned out of town.

Establishments for m. of straw bonnets and hats, 2; Straw Bonnets m'd., 68,850; Straw Hats, m'd., 3,525; val. of palm leaf hats, $1,060; m. emp., 37; f. emp., 288.

Bricks m'd., 500,000; val. of bricks, $2,500; emp., 3.

Lumber prepared for market, 186,000 ft.; val. of lumber, $1,747; emp. 17.

Firewood prepared for market, 1,027 cords; val. of firewood, $2,475; emp., 27.

Saxony Sheep, of different grades, –; Merino Sheep, of different grades, –; all other kinds of Sheep, 271; val. of all sheep, $625; Wool produced from Saxony sheep, – lbs.; Merino Wool produced, – lbs.; all other Wool produced, 871 lbs.

Horses, 294; val. of horses, $20,660; Oxen over three years old, 252; Steers under three years old, 104; val. of oxen and steers, $14,937; Milch Cows, 714; Heifers, 158; val. of cows and heifers, $22,739.

Butter, 34,810 lbs.; val. of butter, $7,658$\frac{20}{100}$; Cheese, 58,350 lbs.; val. of cheese, $5,835; Honey, 1000 lbs.; val. of honey, $150.

Indian Corn, 424 acres; Indian Corn, per acre, 30 bush.; val., $12,847.

Wheat, 4 acres; Wheat, per acre, 18 bush.; val., $150.

Rye, 272 acres; Rye, per acre, 10½ bush.; val., $3,400.

Oats, 254 acres; Oats, per acre, 21 bush.; val., $3,177.

Potatoes, 184 acres; Potatoes, per acre, 75 bush.; val., $6,903.

Onions, ½ acre; Onions, per acre, 300 bush.; val., $75.

Turnips, cultivated as a field crop, 3 acres; Turnips, per acre, 250 bush.; val., $180.

Carrots, 1 acre; Carrots, per acre, 425 bush.; val., $127.

Beets and other esculent vegetables, – acres; all other Grain or Root Crops, mostly Buckwheat, 135 acres; val., $1,200.

Millet, 7 acres; val., $140.

English Mowing, 1,580 acres; English Hay, 1,741 tons; val., $24,374.

Wet Meadow or Swale Hay, 971 tons; val., $5,826.

Apple Trees, cultivated for their fruit, 4,029; val., $2,074.

Pear Trees, cultivated for their fruit, 200; val., $35

Cranberries, 2½ acres; val., $40.

Establishments for m. of gas, 1; cap., $20,000; val. m'd., $5,000; emp., 2.

Bakeries, 1; cap., $3,000; Flour consumed, 1,200 bbls.; val. of bread m'd., $18,000; emp., 8.

WESTHAMPTON.

Chair and Cabinet Manufactories, 1; val. of chairs and cabinet ware, $1,200; cap., $300; emp., 2.

Tanneries, 1; Hides of all kinds tanned and curried, 300; val. of leather tanned, $600; cap., $250; emp., 2.

Boots of all kinds m'd., 110 pairs; Shoes of all kinds m'd., 125 pairs; val. of boots and shoes, $580; m. emp., 2.

Charcoal m'd., 6,300 bush.; val. of same, $378; emp., 1.

Val. of wooden ware not otherwise enumerated, including farming utensils m'd., $1,090; emp., 1

Lumber prepared for market, 367,000 ft.; val. of lumber, $3,494; emp., 4.

Firewood prepared for market, 1,457 cords; val. of firewood, $3,567; emp., 8.

Saxony Sheep, of different grades, –; Merino Sheep, of different grades, 270; all other kinds of Sheep, 809; val. of all sheep, $3,500; Wool produced from Saxony sheep, – lbs.; Merino Wool produced, 675 lbs.; all other Wool produced, 2,427 lbs.

Horses, 140; val. of horses, $11,427; Oxen over three years old, 103; Steers under three years old, 93; val. of oxen and steers, $7,073; Milch Cows, 325; Heifers, 56; val. of cows and heifers, $11,049.

Butter, 39,220 lbs.; val. of butter, $7,844; Cheese, 1,725 lbs.; val. of cheese, $172.50; Honey, 1,200 lbs.; val. of honey, $204.

Indian Corn, 184 acres; Indian Corn, per acre, 30 bush.; val., $6,182.40.

Wheat, 1 acre; Wheat, per acre, 20 bush.; val., $40.

Rye, 116 acres; Rye, per acre, 6 bush.; val., $4,144.50.

Oats, 21 acres; Oats, per acre, 21$\frac{2}{3}$ bush.; val., $218.

Potatoes, 89 acres; Potatoes, per acre, 91 bush.; val., $4,852.20.

Onions, – acres; Onions raised, 40 bush.; val., $36.

Carrots, – acres; Carrots raised, 589 bush.; val., $29.45.

English Mowing, 961 acres; English Hay, 912 tons; val., $16,416.

Wet Meadow or Swale Hay, 353 tons; val., $3,530.

Apple Trees, cultivated for their fruit, 2,887; val., $2,849.

Pear Trees, cultivated for their fruit, 101; val., $190.

Beeswax, 20 lbs.; val., $8.

Establishments for m. of boxes for tooth powder, 1; cap., $150; val. of boxes m'd., $775; emp., 2.

Grass-fed Beef Cattle, 135; val., $3,545.

Quinces, 350 bush.; val., $350.

Maple Sugar produced, 4,025 lbs.; val., $483.

WILLIAMSBURG.

Cotton Mills, 1; Spindles, 4,000; Cotton consumed, 30,000 lbs.; Cloth m'd., 1,000,000 yds.; val. of cloth, $80,000; cap. $45,000; m. emp., 30; f. emp., 50.

Woollen Mills, 2; Sets of Machinery, 2; Wool consumed, 70,000 lbs.; Satinet m'd., 100,000 yds.; val. of satinet, $40,000; cap. $20,000; m. emp. 13; f. emp. 7; Flannel or Blanketing, 14,000 yds.; val. of flannel or blanketing, $5,600; cap., $3,000; m. emp., 4; f. emp., 2.

Establishments for m. of hosiery, –; Yarn m'd., and not made into hosiery, 4,000 lbs.; val. of yarn, $3,500; cap., $1,000; m. emp., 3; f. emp., 3.

Silk Manufactories, 1; Sewing Silk m'd., 6,000 lbs. val. of sewing silk, $30,000; cap., $7,000; m. emp., 5; f. emp., 17.

Furnaces for m. of hollow ware and castings other than pig iron, 1; Hollow Ware and other Castings m'd., 150 tons; val. of hollow ware and castings, $10,500; cap., $6,000; emp., 6.

Establishments for m. of cotton, woollen and other machinery, 1; val. of machinery m'd., $6,000; cap., $4,000; emp., 6.

Axe Manufactories, –; Edge Tools m'd.—Chisels—3,500 doz.; val., $11,500; cap., $2,500; emp., 8.

Brass Founderies, 1; val. of articles m'd., $60,000; cap., $20,000; emp., 75.

Harness Manufactories, 18; Trunk Manufactories, 4; val. of harnesses m'd., repaired, &c., $700; cap., $400; emp., 1.

Chair and Cabinet Manufactories, 1; val. of chairs and cabinet ware, $3,000; cap., $1,500; emp., 5.

Tin Ware Manufactories, 2; val. of tin ware, $8,000; cap., $4,500; emp., 15.

Grist Mills, 1; Runs of stones, 3; val. of grinding done, $36,000; cap., $6,000; emp., 2.

Tanneries, 1; Hides of all kinds tanned, 3,500; val. of leather tanned, $12,000; cap., $5,000; emp., 5.

Currying Establishments, 1; val. of leather curried, $10,000; connected with tanning establishment.

Boots of all kinds m'd., 575 pairs; Shoes of all kinds m'd., 400 pairs; val. of boots and shoes m'd., and mending done, $2,500; m. emp., 5.

Val. of building stone quarried and prepared for building, $1,000; emp., 2.

Val. of mechanics' tools m'd., (Bench Planes and Mouldings,) $25,000; emp., 43.

Val. of chisels, screw drivers, chopping knives, &c., m'd., $5,000.

Gold and Steel Pen Manufactories, 1; Gold Pens m'd., 80,000; cap., $25,000; m. emp., 13; f. emp., 12; Pencil Cases, gold and silver, m'd., 40,000; cap., $12,000; m. emp., 24; f. emp., 11; Steel Penholders m'd., 6,000 gross; cap., $3,000; m. emp., 2; f. emp., 2.

Lumber prepared for market, 125,000 ft.; val. of lumber, $1,600; emp., 8.

Firewood prepared for market, 2,500 cords; val. of firewood, $5,000; emp., 8.

Saxony Sheep, of different grades, –; Merino Sheep, of different grades, 708; all other kinds of Sheep, 609; val. of all sheep, $1,970; Wool produced from Saxony sheep, – lbs.; Merino Wool produced, 2,154 lbs.; all other Wool produced, 2,084 lbs.

Horses, 207; val. of horses, $17,445; Oxen over three years old, 168; Steers under three years old, 62; val. of oxen and steers, $9,243; Milch Cows, 544; Heifers, 386; val. of cows and heifers, $22,393.

Butter, 38,335 lbs.; val. of butter, $7,667; Cheese, 10,450 lbs.; val. of cheese, $1,045.

Indian Corn, 271 acres; Indian Corn, per acre, 30 bush.; val., $8,130.

Wheat, 4 acres; Wheat, per acre, 15 bush.; val., $120.

Rye, 109 acres; Rye, per acre, 12 bush.; val., $1,635.

Barley, 1 acre; Barley, per acre, 12 bush.; val., $15.

Oats, 27 acres; Oats, per acre, 25 bush.; val., $337.

Potatoes, 100 acres; Potatoes, per acre, 80 bush.; val., $3,200.

Onions, 100 bush.; val., $75.

Turnips, 350 bush.; val., $87.

Carrots, 350 bush.; val., $175.

English Mowing, 1,670 acres; English Hay, 1,676 tons; val., $20,112.

Wet Meadow or Swale Hay, 364 tons; val., $2,912.

Apple Trees, cultivated for their fruit, 4,798; val., $2,883.

Pear Trees, cultivated for their fruit, 34; val., $36.

Cranberries, 2½ acres; not commenced bearing.

Paper Button Boxes m'd., $3,000 gross; cap., $500; val. of boxes m'd., $1,000; m. emp., 1; f. emp., 3.

Saw Mills, 6; cap., $5,000; Lumber sawed, 565,000 ft.; val., $2,475; Shingles sawed, 100,000 ft.; val., $250; Laths sawed, 45,000 ft.; val., $247; emp., 5.

Tin-faced Suspender Buttons m'd., 13,000 gross; val., $12,000; cap., $8,000; m. emp., 10; f. emp., 10.

Val. of wood moulds and buttons, $10,000; Suspender Buttons, 90,000 gross; val., $5,000; Peacoat Buttons, 10,000; val., $1,500; cap., $12,000; emp., 22.

Vest and Pant. Buckles m'd., 30,000 gross; val., $6,000; cap., $3,000; m. emp., 1; f. emp., 5.

Val. of teaming done, $3,000; emp., 3.

Val. of blacksmithing, mostly custom-work, $2,000; emp., 4.

Val. of tailoring done, mostly custom-work, $1,800; emp., 6.

Val. of carriage-work done, mostly repairing, $600; emp., 1.

Garden Implements m'd., 1,100 doz.; val., $4,000; cap., $1,500; emp., 5.

Val. of dentistry done, $1,000; emp., 1.

Val. of brick masonry, $500; emp., 2.

About 15 men support their families by carpentering and joinering, which business amounts to $5,000.

Much more of all kinds of breadstuffs are consumed in the town than is produced.

WORTHINGTON.

Saddle, Harness and Trunk Manufactories, 1 ; val. of saddles, &c., $300 ; cap., $50 ; emp., 1.

Chair and Cabinet Manufactories, 1 ; val. of chairs and cabinet ware, $500 ; cap., $50 ; emp., 1.

Boots of all kinds m'd., 12,480 pairs ; Shoes of all kinds m'd., 7,800 pairs ; val. of boots and shoes, $27,690 ; m. emp., 25 ; f. emp., 20.

Val. of mechanics' tools m'd., $4,000 ; emp., 8.

Val. of wooden ware not otherwise enumerated, including farming utensils m'd., $5,000 ; emp., 11.

Lumber prepared for market, 550,000 ft. ; val. of lumber, $3,850 ; emp., 4.

Firewood prepared for market, 500 cords ; val. of firewood, $750 ; emp., 2.

Saxony Sheep, of different grades, – ; Merino Sheep, of different grades, 3,000 ; all other kinds of Sheep, 246 ; val. of all sheep, $8,115 ; Wool produced from Saxony sheep, – lbs. ; Merino Wool produced, 9,000 lbs. ; all other Wool produced, 984 lbs.

Horses, 190 ; val. of horses, $13,185 ; Oxen over three years old, 146 ; Steers under three years old, 112 ; val. of oxen and steers, $10,267 ; Milch Cows, 319 ; Heifers, 251 ; val. of cows and heifers, $11,680.

Butter, 41,120 lbs. ; val. of butter, $7,401.60 ; Cheese, 4,050 lbs. ; val. of cheese, $364.50.

Indian Corn, 134 acres ; Indian Corn, per acre, 35 bush. ; val., $4,690.

Wheat, 13 acres ; Wheat, per acre, 20 bush. ; val., $520.

Rye, 5 acres ; Rye, per acre, 20 bush. ; val., $125.

Barley, 18 acres ; Barley, per acre, 30 bush. ; val., $432.

Oats, 83 acres ; Oats, per acre, 40 bush. ; val., $1,992.

Potatoes, 132 acres ; Potatoes, per acre, 100 bush. ; val., $8,712.

Onions, 1 acre ; Onions, per acre, 525 bush. ; val., $250.

Turnips, cultivated as a field crop, 500 acres; Turnips, per acre, 200 bush.; val., $1,700.

Carrots, 2 acres; Carrots, per acre, 750 bush.; val., $187.50.

English Mowing, 4,970 acres; English Hay, 2,419 tons; val., $19,352.

Wet Meadow or Swale Hay, 345 tons; val., $1,725.

Apple Trees, cultivated for their fruit, 5,520; val., $1,840.

Pear Trees, cultivated for their fruit, 100; val., $100.

Beeswax, 50 lbs.; val., $20.

Establishments for the m. of childrens' wagons and sleds, 1; val., $15,000; cap., $5,000; emp., 12.

Establishments for the m. of baskets, 1; val., $700; cap., $100; emp., 2.

Grist Mills, 2; all kinds of grain ground, 1,300 bush.; val., $1,105; emp., 2.

MIDDLESEX COUNTY.

ACTON.

Saddle, Harness and Trunk Manufactories, 1; val. of saddles, &c., $300; cap., $300; emp., 1.

Hat and Cap Manufactories, 1; Hats and Caps m'd., 1,200; cap., $400; emp., 5.

Establishments for m. of railroad cars, coaches, chaises, wagons, sleighs, and other vehicles, 1; val. of railroad cars, &c., m'd., $1,500; cap., $500; emp., 2.

Powder Mills, 1; Powder m'd., 500,000 lbs.; val. of powder, $55,000; cap., $35,000; emp., 12.

Tin Ware Manufactories, 1; val. of tin ware, $10,000; cap., $4,000; emp., 12.

Flour Mills, 1; Flour m'd., 200 bbls.; val. of flour m'd., $1,800; cap., $1,000; emp., 2.

Boots of all kinds m'd., 7,000 pairs; Shoes of all kinds m'd., 15,500 pairs; val. of boots and shoes, $27,000; m. emp., 42; f. emp., 16.

Val. of building stone quarried and prepared for building, $1,400; emp., 3, during seven and one-half months.

Lumber prepared for market, 863,000 ft.; val. of lumber, $12,089; emp., 33, during three months.

Firewood prepared for market, 3,400 cords; val. of firewood, $11,900; emp., 45, during three months.

Saxony Sheep, of different grades, –; Merino Sheep, of different grades, –; all other kinds of Sheep, 4; val. of all sheep, $14; Wool produced from Saxony sheep, – lbs.; Merino Wool produced, – lbs.; all other Wool produced, 10 lbs.

Horses, 215; val. of horses, $17,320; Oxen over three years old, 183; Steers under three years old, 29; val. of oxen and steers, $10,226; Milch Cows, 835; Heifers, 64; val. of cows and heifers, $24,383.

Butter, 23,590 lbs.; val. of butter, $5,661.60; Cheese, 1,650 lbs.; val. of cheese, $115.50; Honey, 25 lbs.; val. of honey, $4.59.

Indian Corn, 370 acres; Indian Corn, per acre, 25¼ bush.; val., $9,809.10.

Wheat, 1 acre; Wheat, per acre, 12 bush.; val., $24.

Rye, 76 acres; Rye, per acre, 7½ bush.; val., $837.90.

Barley, 10 acres; Barley, per acre, 11½ bush.; val., $115.

Oats, 187 acres; Oats, per acre, 16 bush.; val., $1,795.20.

Potatoes, 146 acres; Potatoes, per acre, 80 bush.; val., $8,760.

Onions, ⅝ acre; Onions, per acre, 312 bush.; val., $120.90.

Turnips, cultivated as a field crop, 6¾ acres; Turnips, per acre, 150 bush.; val., $151.87½.

Carrots, 5¾ acres; Carrots, per acre, 465 bush.; val., $695.11.

English Mowing, 1,769 acres; English Hay, 1,619 tons; val., $29,142.

Wet Meadow or Swale Hay, 871 tons; val., $8,710.

Apple Trees, cultivated for their fruit, 24,080; val., $9,674.50.

Pear Trees, cultivated for their fruit, 601; val., $64.

Hops, 3 acres; Hops, per acre, 369 lbs.; val., $277.

Cranberries, 63 acres; val., $742.

Beeswax, 8 lbs.; val., $2.64.

Establishments for m. of casks, 4; cap., $1,500; Casks m'd., $3,600; val., 3,926; emp., 9.

Establishments for m. of sashes, doors and blinds, 1; cap., $5,000; val. m'd., $4,000; emp., 8.

Establishments for m. of mast hoops, 3; val., $4,000; cap., $1,000; emp., 8.

Establishments for m. of wheel hubs, 1; val., $300; cap., $75; emp., 1.

Establishments for m. of razor strops, 1; val., $600; cap., $50; emp., 2.

Establishments for m. of flannel printing, 1; val., $8,000; cap., $3,500; emp., 8.

Establishments for grinding plaster, 2; quantity ground, 500 tons; val., $750; cap., $2,000; emp., 5, three months.

Establishments for m. of bellows, 1; val., $300; cap., $200; emp., 2, three months.

Establishments for printing kerseymere, &c., 1; val., $11,000; cap., $7,000; emp., 4.

Establishments for tailoring, 2; val., $35,000; cap., $12,000; m. emp., 7; f. emp., 103.

Swine raised, 164; val., $1,478.

Peach Trees, 5,687; val., $649.

Beans, 210 bush.; val., $420.

Val. of milk sold, $12,037.

ASHBY.

Establishments for m. of railroad cars, coaches, chaises, wagons, sleighs, and other vehicles, 1; val. of railroad cars, &c., m'd., $500; cap., $100; emp., 2.

Tanneries, 1; Hides of all kinds tanned, 750; val. of leather tanned, $2,250; cap., $2,000; emp., 2.

Currying Establishments, 1; val. of leather curried, $1,000; cap., $1,000; emp., 1.

Boots m'd., 250 pairs; Shoes m'd., 275 pairs; val. of boots and shoes, $1,025; m. emp., 3.

Val. of building stone quarried and prepared for building, $2,000; emp., 3.

Val. of wooden ware, (tubs and pails,) not otherwise enumerated, including farming utensils m'd., $189,000; emp., 24.

Firewood prepared for market, 2,500 cords; val. of firewood, $6,250; emp., 8.

Saxony Sheep, of different grades, –; Merino Sheep, of different grades, –; all other kinds of Sheep, 96; val. of all sheep, $384; Wool produced from Saxony sheep, – lbs.; Merino Wool produced, – lbs.; all other Wool produced, 384 lbs.

Horses, 230; val. of horses, $1,800; Oxen over three years old, 194; Steers under three years old, 116; val. of oxen and steers, $12,917; Milch Cows, 598; Heifers, 174; val. of cows and heifers, $18,092.

Butter, 50,555 lbs.; val. of butter, $10,100; Cheese, 3,080 lbs.; val. of cheese, $308; Honey, 40 lbs.; val. of honey, $10.

Indian Corn, 207 acres; Indian Corn, per acre, 32 bush.; val., $7,286.40.

Wheat, 70 acres; Wheat, per acre, 18 bush.; val., $2,520.

Rye, 77 acres; Rye, per acre, 10 bush.; val., $770.

Barley, 15 acres; Barley, per acre, 25 bush.; val., $375.

Oats, 140 acres; Oats, per acre, 30 bush.; val., $2,100.

Potatoes, 125 acres; Potatoes, per acre, 100 bush.; val., $6,250.

Carrots, 10 acres; Carrots, per acre, 800 bush.; val., $2,000.

Beets and other esculent vegetables, – acres; all other Grain or Root Crops, 10 acres; val., $500.

English Mowing, 2,434 acres; English Hay, 1,525 tons; val., $27,450.

Wet Meadow or Swale Hay, 403 tons; val., $4,030.

Apple Trees, cultivated for their fruit, 9,405; val., $4,000.
Pear Trees, cultivated for their fruit, 100; val., $50.
Beeswax, 10 lbs.; val., $2.80.

ASHLAND.

Establishments for m. of cotton, woollen and other machinery, 1; val. of machinery m'd., $10,000; cap., $15,000; emp., 15.

Paper Manufactories, 1; Stock made use of, 40 tons; Paper m'd., 35 tons; val. of paper, $7,500; cap., $1,000; emp., 3.

Tin Ware Manufactories, 1; val. of tin ware, $22,000; cap., $8,000; emp., 17.

Boots of all kinds m'd., 101,444 pairs; Shoes of all kinds m'd., 3,000 pairs; val. of boots and shoes, $143,500; m. emp., 238; f. emp., 35.

Establishments for m. of straw bonnets and hats, –; Straw Bonnets m'd., 500; Straw Hats m'd., 500; val. of straw braid m'd. and not made into bonnets and hats, $461; m. emp., 15.

Bricks m'd., 200,000; val. of bricks, $1,400; emp., 3.

Val. of building stone quarried and prepared for building, $4,000; emp., 4.

Charcoal m'd., 11,600 bush.; val. of same, $1,933; emp., 3.

Val. of wooden ware not otherwise enumerated, including farming utensils m'd., $800; emp., 1.

Corn and other Brooms m'd., 850; val. of brooms, $100; emp., 1.

Lumber prepared for market, 81,500 ft.; val. of lumber, $1,422.50; emp., 1.

Firewood prepared for market, 1,236 cords; val. of firewood, $6,500; emp., 5.

Horses, 112; val. of horses, $9,143; Oxen over three years old, 82; Steers under three years old, 15; val. of oxen and steers, $4,800; Milch Cows, 273; Heifers, 33; val. of cows and heifers, $7,963.

Butter, 17,460 lbs.; val. of butter, $4,152; Cheese, 1,965 lbs.; val. of cheese, $182.80; Honey, 185 lbs.; val. of honey, $36.

Indian Corn, 154 acres, Indian Corn, per acre, 30 bush.; val., $4,620.

Wheat, 1¼ acre; Wheat, per acre, 20½ bush.; val., $37.

Rye, 6 acres; Rye, per acre, 12 bush.; val., $108.

Barley, 2 acres; Barley, per acre, 18 bush.; val., $36.

Oats, 74 acres; Oats, per acre, 30 bush.; val., $1,332.

Potatoes, 76½ acres; Potatoes, per acre, 80 bush.; val., $4,590.

Onions, 1 acre; Onions, per acre, 200 bush.; val., $150.

Turnips, cultivated as a field crop, 2 acres; Turnips, per acre, 350 bush.; val., $175.

Carrots, 2 acres; Carrots, per acre, 350 bush.; val., $259.

Beets and other esculent vegetables, – acres; val., $100, in gardens.

English Mowing, 927 acres; English Hay, 727 tons; val., $14,540.

Wet Meadow or Swale Hay, 402 tons; val., $4,020.

Apple Trees, cultivated for their fruit, 8,473; val., $3,431.

Pear Trees, cultivated for their fruit, 459; val., $137.

Cranberries, 4 acres; val., $250.

Establishments for m. of boxes, 2; cap., $7,500; val. of boxes m'd., $24,000; emp., 10.

Swine raised, 241; val., $2,410.

Peach Trees, 6,329; val., $519.

Plum Trees, 250; val., $148.

Tailoring capital invested, $1,300; amount of clothing m'd., $4,000.

Val. of patent medicines m'd., $1,600.

Val. of all other articles m'd. in the town during said year, $237.

BEDFORD.

Paper Manufactories, 1; Stock made use of, 200 tons; Paper m'd., 165 tons; val. of paper, $13,200; cap., $15,000; emp., 6.

Saddle, Harness and Trunk Manufactories, 2; val. of saddles, &c., $1,000; cap., $850; emp., 4.

Establishments for m. of railroad cars, coaches, chaises, wagons, sleighs, and other vehicles, 1; val. of railroad cars, &c., m'd., $1,750; cap., $500; emp., 1.

Tin Ware Manufactories, 1; val. of tin ware, $2,000; cap., $1,000; emp., 2.

Boots of all kinds m'd., 900 pairs; Shoes of all kinds m'd., 63,000 pairs; val. of boots and shoes, $34,700; m. emp., 54; f. emp., 66.

Lumber prepared for market, 85 ft.; val. of lumber, $1,530; emp., 10.

Firewood prepared for market, 1,266 cords; val. of firewood, $4,431; emp., 25.

Horses, 128; val. of horses, $14,080; Oxen over three years old, 90; Steers under three years old, 6; val. of oxen and steers, $5,775; Milch Cows, 454; Heifers, 76; val. of cows and heifers, $14,760.

Butter, 3,466 lbs.; val. of butter, $866.50; Cheese, 350 lbs.; val. of cheese, $35; Honey, 78 lbs.; val. of honey, $10.

Indian Corn, 204 acres; Indian Corn, per acre, 30 bush.; val., $6,120.

Rye, 26 acres; Rye, per acre, 10 bush.; val., $260.

Barley, 5 acres; Barley, per acre, 25 bush.; val., $105.

Oats, 95 acres; Oats, per acre, 25 bush.; val., $1,583.33.

Potatoes, 116 acres; Potatoes, per acre, 90 bush.; val., $8,700.

Turnips, cultivated as a field crop, 3 acres; Turnips, per acre, 300 bush.; val., $112.50.

Beets and other esculent vegetables, – acres; all other Grain or Root Crops, 4 acres; val., $1,620.

English Mowing, 1,088 acres; English Hay, 975 tons; val., $19,500.

Wet Meadow or Swale Hay, 718 tons; val., $7,180.

Apple Trees, cultivated for their fruit, 4,684; val., $4,492.50.

Pear Trees, cultivated for their fruit, 312; val., $118.

Cranberries, 82 acres; val., $870.

Swine raised, 148; val., $888.

Milk produced, 122,062 galls.; val., $17,437.50.

Hair Cloth Manufactories, 1; Stock used, 5,000 lbs.; Cloth m'd., 20,000 yds.; val., $15,000; cap., $10,000; emp., 25.

Gold Leaf Manufactories, 1; Gold Leaf m'd., 1,500 packs; val., $12,000; cap., $2,500; m. emp., 3; f. emp., 3.

Sash Angle Manufactories, 1; Sash Angles m'd., 1,800 gross; cap., $500; emp., 2.

Blind Fast Manufactories, 1; Blind Fasts m'd., 250 gross; val., $3,420; cap., $700; emp., 2.

BILLERICA.

Woollen Mills, 1; Sets of Machinery, 4; Wool consumed, 110,000 lbs.; Flannel or Blanketing m'd., 42,000 yds.; val. of flannel or blanketing, $84,000; cap., $30,000; m. emp., 23; f. emp., 13.

Establishments for m. of cotton, woollen and other machinery, 2; val. of machinery m'd., $40,000; cap., $6,000; emp., 13.

Establishments for m. of chemical preparations, 1; val. of chemical preparations, $40,000; cap., $10,000; emp., 8.

Chair and Cabinet Manufactories, 1; val. of chairs and cabinet ware, $10,000; cap., $2,500; emp., 15.

Boots of all kinds m'd., – pairs; Shoes of all kinds m'd., 5,320 pairs; val. of boots and shoes, $3,027; m. emp., 9; f. emp., 6.

Val. of building stone quarried and prepared for building, $700; emp., 2.

Firewood prepared for market, 2,130 cords; val. of firewood, $8,520; emp., 23.

Saxony Sheep, of different grades, –; Merino Sheep, of different grades, –; all other kinds of Sheep, 41; val. of all sheep, $123; Wool produced from Saxony sheep, – lbs.; Merino Wool produced, – lbs.; all other Wool produced, 93 lbs.

Horses, 237; val. of horses, $16,465; Oxen over three years old, 121; Steers under three years old, –; val. of oxen and steers, $7,135; Milch Cows, 531; Heifers, 142; val. of cows and heifers, $16,995.

Butter, 20,000 lbs.; val. of butter, $5,000.

Indian Corn, 331 acres; Indian Corn, per acre, 32 bush.; val., $10,592.

Rye, 116 acres; Rye, per acre, 10 bush.; val., $1,740.

Barley, 11 acres; Barley, per acre, 15 bush.; val., $165.

Oats, 46 acres; Oats, per acre, 15 bush.; val., $414.

Potatoes, 265 acres; Potatoes, per acre, 75 bush.; val., $19,875.

Onions, 1 acre; Onions, per acre, 300 bush.; val., $180.

Turnips, cultivated as a field crop, 15 acres; Turnips, per acre, 150 bush.; val., $450.

Carrots, 6 acres; Carrots, per acre, 350 bush.; val., $600.

Beets and other esculent vegetables, 140 acres; val., $13,000.

English Mowing, 1,592 acres; English Hay, 1,350 tons; val., $24,300.

Wet Meadow or Swale Hay, 772 tons; val., $9,264.

Apple Trees, cultivated for their fruit, 19,793; val., $10,619.

Pear Trees, cultivated for their fruit, 745; val., $233.

Cranberries, 211 acres; val., $4,104.

Swine raised, 315; val., $1,890.

Dyewood and Drug Manufactories, 1; val., $150,000; cap., $50,000; emp., 20.

BOXBOROUGH.

Val. of railroad cars, &c., m'd., $500 ; cap., $1,000 ; emp., 1.

Boots of all kinds m'd., 250 pairs ; Shoes of all kinds m'd., 4,600 pairs ; val. of boots and shoes, $4,000 ; m. emp., 4 ; f. emp., 12.

Charcoal m'd., 3,500 bush. ; val. of same, $525 ; emp., 1.

Lumber prepared for market, 14,000 ft. ; val. of lumber, $150 ; emp., 1.

Firewood prepared for market, 381 cords ; val. of firewood, $1,524 ; emp., 10, in part.

Saxony Sheep, of different grades, – ; Merino Sheep, of different grades, – ; all other kinds of Sheep, 6 ; val. of all sheep, $30 ; Wool produced from Saxony sheep, – lbs. ; Merino Wool produced, – lbs. ; all other Wool produced, 30 lbs.

Horses, 80 ; val. of horses, $6,580 ; Oxen over three years old, 62 ; Steers under three years old, 7 ; val. of oxen and steers, $3,100 ; Milch Cows, 374 ; Heifers, 34 ; val. of cows and heifers, $11,900.

Butter, 13,640 lbs. ; val. of butter, $3,410.

Indian Corn, 140 acres ; Indian Corn, per acre, 30 bush. ; val., $5,250.

Wheat, 1 acre ; Wheat, per acre, 15 bush. ; val., $30.

Rye, 38 acres ; Rye, per acre, 10½ bush. ; val., $600.

Oats, 60 acres ; Oats, per acre, 25 bush. ; val., $1,110.

Potatoes, 45 acres ; Potatoes, per acre, 60 bush. ; val., $2,700.

Carrots, 2 acres ; Carrots, per acre, 150 bush. ; val., $64.

English Mowing, 620 acres ; English Hay, 775 tons ; val., $13,950.

Wet Meadow or Swale Hay, 613 tons ; val., $6,130.

Apple Trees, cultivated for their fruit, 7,851 ; val., $4,167.

Pear Trees, cultivated for their fruit, 109 ; val., $41.

Hops, 14½ acres ; Hops, per acre, 700 lbs. ; val., $2,556.

Cranberries, 21 acres ; val., $512.

Milk, 42,390 cans ; val., $10,599.

Straw, 50 tons; val., $500.

White Beans, 100 bush.; val., $300.

Whortleberries and Blueberries raised, 400 bush.; val., $1,000.

BRIGHTON.

Saddle, Harness and Trunk Manufactories, 1; val. of saddles, &c., $3,000; cap., $1,000; emp., 3.

Establishments for m. of railroad cars, coaches, chaises, wagons, sleighs, and other vehicles, 2; val. of railroad cars, &c., m'd., $2,000; cap., $500; emp., 4.

Establishments for m. of oil and sperm candles, 1; Oil m'd., 150,000 galls.; val. of oil m'd., $150,000; Sperm Candles m'd., 8,000 lbs.; val. of sperm candles, $25,000; cap., $40,000; emp., 9.

Establishments for m. of soap and tallow candles, 1; Soap m'd., 250,000 lbs.; val. of soap, $15,000; emp., 3.

Tin Ware Manufactories, 1; val. of tin ware, $2,000; cap., $500; emp., 3.

Boots of all kinds m'd., 500 pairs; Shoes of all kinds m'd., 300 pairs; val. of boots and shoes, $2,000; m. emp., 4.

Horses, 307; val. of horses, $38,375; Oxen over three years old, 12; steers under three years old, –; val. of oxen and steers, $900; Milch Cows, 90; Heifers, –; val. of cows and heifers, $3,150.

Butter, 1,000 lbs.; val. of butter, $250.

Indian Corn, 40 acres; Indian Corn, per acre, 1,200 bush.

Rye, 21 acres; Rye, per acre, 25 bush.; val., $656.25.

Potatoes, 63 acres; Potatoes, per acre, 100 bush.; val., $6,300.

Onions, 2 acres; Onions, per acre, 200 bush.; val., $300.

Turnips, cultivated as a field crop, 10 acres; Turnips, per acre, 200 bush.; val., $500.

Carrots, 5 acres; Carrots, per acre, 500 bush.; val., $600.

Beets and other esculent vegetables, 100 acres; val., $20,000.

English Mowing, 600 acres; English Hay, 600 tons; val. $15,000.

Wet Meadow or Swale Hay, 20 tons; val., $200.

Salt Hay, 416 tons; val., $6,240.

Apple Trees, cultivated for their fruit, 18,000; val., $9,000.

Pear Trees, cultivated for their fruit, 5,000; val., $500.

Establishments for m. of sashes, doors and blinds, 1; cap., $700; val. m'd., $3,000; emp., 5.

Breweries, 1; cap., $5,000; Beer m'd., 5,000 bbls.; val., $25,000; emp., 7.

Strawberries raised, 22,000 boxes; val., $5,500.

Raspberries raised, 2,600 boxes; val, $650.

Currants raised, 100 bush.; val., $200.

Varnish m'd., 10,000 galls.; Japan, 9,000 galls.; val., $26,500; cap., $5,000; emp., 1.

BURLINGTON.

Chair and Cabinet Manufactories, 1; val. of chairs and cabinet ware, $1,200; cap., $300; emp., 2.

Boots of all kinds m'd., – pairs; Shoes of all kinds m'd., 4,000 pairs; val. of boots and shoes, $4,000; m. emp., 8; f. emp., 6.

Firewood prepared for market, 1,890 cords; val. of firewood, $6,609.

Horses, 112; val. of horses, $9,699; Oxen over three years old, 64; Steers under three years old, –; val. of oxen and steers, $3,720; Milch Cows, 331; Heifers, 25; val. of cows and heifers, $8,570.

Butter, 2,000 lbs.; val. of butter, $500.

Indian Corn, 149 acres; Indian Corn, per acre, 24 bush.; val., $3,576.

Rye, 14 acres; Rye, per acre, 10 bush.; val., $175.

Barley, 9 acres; Barley, per acre, 15 bush.; val., $135.

Oats, 11 acres; Oats, per acre, 20 bush.; val., $165.

Potatoes, 42 acres; Potatoes, per acre, 32 bush.; val., $1,075.

Turnips, cultivated as a field crop, 12 acres; Turnips, per acre, 120 bush.; val., $960.

Carrots, $\frac{3}{4}$ acre; Carrots, per acre, 560 bush.; val., $126.

English Mowing, 531 acres; English Hay, 444 tons; val., $8,703.

Wet Meadow or Swale Hay, 200 tons; val., $1,600.

Apple Trees, cultivated for their fruit, 3,358; val., $3,141.

Pear Trees, cultivated for their fruit, 100; val., $50.

Hops, 3 acres; Hops, per acre, 650 lbs.; val., $390.

Cranberries, 5 acres; val., $300.

Mules, 2; val., $300.

Val. of milk sold, $18,000.

Val. of veal sold, $1,000.

Cucumbers, 2 acres; val., $450.

CAMBRIDGE.

Shops for m. of iron railing, iron fences and iron safes, 1; val. of iron railing, &c., $1,200; cap., $1,000; emp., 4.

Establishments for m. of britannia ware, 1; val. of britannia ware, $40,000; cap., $25,000; emp., 25.

Glass Manufactories, 2; val. of glass m'd., $620,000; cap., $575,000; emp., 531.

Starch Manufactories, 1; Starch m'd. from wheat or flour, 70 tons; val. of starch, $14,000; cap., $4,000; emp., 4.

Establishments for m. of chemical preparations, 2; val. of chemical preparations, $4,600; cap., $2,500; emp., 4.

Piano-Forte Action Manufactories, 3; cap., $4,000; val. of m's., $10,000; emp., 10.

Church Organ Manufactories, 1; val. of musical instruments m'd., $12,000; cap., $4,000; emp., 8.

Daguerreotype Artists, 1; Daguerreotypes taken, 1,000; cap., $500; emp., 2.

Brush Manufactories, 3; val. of brushes, $191,000; cap., $113,600; m. emp., 143; f. emp., 93.

Saddle, Harness, and Trunk Manufactories, 4; val. of saddles, &c., $15,300; cap., $5,200; emp., 14.

Upholstery Manufactories, 1; val. of upholstery, $3,000; cap., $2,000; emp., 3.

Hat and Cap Manufactories, 4; Hats and Caps m'd., 161,600; cap., $13,500; emp., 52.

Cordage Manufactories, 1; Cordage m'd., 100,000 lbs.; cap., $6,000; emp., 10.

Establishments for m. of railroad cars, coaches, chaises, wagons, sleighs, and other vehicles, 5; val. of railroad cars, &c., m'd., $134,200; cap., $16,400; emp., 90.

Establishments for m. of oil and sperm candles, 2; Oil m'd., 180,000 galls.; val. of oil m'd., $126,000; cap., $30,000; emp., 7.

Establishments for m. of soap and tallow candles, 16; Soap m'd., 8,154,200 lbs.; val. of soap, $6,802,000; Tallow Candles m'd., 484,000 lbs.; val. of tallow candles, $94,000; cap., $1,300,000; emp., 140.

Chair and Cabinet Manufactories, 5; val. of chairs and cabinet ware, $128,500; cap., $68,000; emp., 168.

Tin Ware Manufactories, 6; val. of tin ware, $25,700; cap., $14,000; emp., 22.

Mills for m. of linseed oil, 1; Oil m'd., 100,000 galls.; val. of oil m'd., $90,000; cap., $50,000; emp., 10.

Tanneries, 1; Hides of all kinds tanned, 1,800; val. of leather tanned, $2,500; cap., $1,500; emp., 3.

Currying Establishments, 2; val. of leather curried, $90,000; cap., $20,000; emp., 18.

Boots of all kinds m'd., 7,780 pairs; Shoes of all kinds m'd., 3,500 pairs; val. of boots and shoes, $17,075; m. emp., 41.

Bricks m'd., 26,200,000; val. of bricks, $1,834,000.

Val. of snuff, tobacco, and cigars, $388,700; m. emp., 21; f. emp., 21.

Val. of building stone quarried and prepared for building, $67,000; emp., 72.

Val. of blocks and pumps m'd., $10,000; emp., 4.

Alewives taken, 275,000; val. of same, $1,000; emp., 5.

Horses, 603; val. of horses, $66,000; Oxen over three years old, 6; Steers under three years old, –; val. of oxen and steers, $400; Milch Cows, 115; Heifers, 20; val. of cows and heifers, $4,250.

Indian Corn, 4 acres; Indian Corn, per acre, 50 bush.; val., $200.

Rye, 15 acres; Rye, per acre, 17 bush.; val., $335.

Potatoes, 21 acres; Potatoes, per acre, 100 bush.; val., $1,825.

Turnips, cultivated as a field crop, 2 acres; Turnips, per acre, 500 bush.; val., $450.

Beets and other esculent vegetables, 1 acre; val., $200.

English Mowing, 300 acres; English Hay, 340 tons; val. $6,860.

Salt Hay, 329 tons; val., $4,935.

Apple Trees, cultivated for their fruit, 3,000; val., $2,500. No value this year.

Pear Trees, cultivated for their fruit, 749; val., $1,015.

Establishments for m. of sashes, doors and blinds, 1; val. m'd., $7,000; cap., $2,000; emp., 7.

Establishments for m. of gas, 1; val. m'd., $20,000; cap., $100,000; emp., 6.

Bakeries, 6; cap., $11,800; Flour consumed, 7,000 bbls.; val. of bread m'd., $117,500; emp., 39.

Type and Stereotype Founderies, 2; val. of type, &c., m'd., $71,000; cap., $17,000; m. emp., 95.

Establishments for m. of boxes, 4; Soap, Candle and Paper Boxes; cap., $34,000; val. of boxes m'd., $64,000; emp., 36.

Establishments for m. of ladders, 1; cap., $3,000; val. of ladders m'd., $8,000; emp., 20.

Establishments for m. of feather dusters, 1; cap., $1,000; val. of dusters m'd., $5,000; m. emp., 3; f. emp., 2.

Ice Business, 60,000 tons; val., $30,000; cap., $40,000; emp., 40.

Establishments for printing and book-binding, 3; cap., $41,000; val., $175,000; emp., 120.

Establishments for m. confectionery, 2; cap., $30,000; val., $110,000; emp., 18.

Establishments for leather dressing, 1; cap., $5,000; val., $10,000; emp., 3.

Establishments for wood turning, 1; cap., 10,000; val., $25,000; emp., 2.

Establishments for sweep sawing, 1; cap., $20,000; val., $45,000; emp., 4.

Planing Mills, 1; cap., $4,000; val., $12,000; emp., 6.

Establishments for m. of cigar boxes, 1; cap., $2,000; val., $8,000; emp., 2.

Establishments for m. of bacon, 2; cap., $23,000; val., $60,000; emp., 30.

Establishments for m. Penrhyn marble, 1; cap., $60,000; val., $125,000; emp., 35.

Establishments for m. of wash leather, 1; cap., $2,500; val., $6,000; emp., 4.

Establishments for m. of shovels and ladders, 1; cap., $2,000; val., $5,000; emp., 4.

Establishments for m. of clothes and fish lines, 1; cap., $2,000; val., $5,000; emp., 6.

Plumbers, 2; cap., $3,500; val., $7,000; emp., 6.

Marble Works, 1; cap., $4,000; val., $10,000; emp., 6.

Manufactories of Persian sherbet, 1; cap., $10,000; val., $7,000; emp., 3.

Manufactories of pulpits, 1; cap., $2,500; amount m'd., $6,000; emp., 5.

Manufactories of cement, 1; cap., 1,000; amount m'd., 10 tons; emp., 2.

CARLISLE.

Boots of all kinds m'd., 250 pairs; Shoes of all kinds m'd., 5,000 pairs; val. of boots and shoes, $4,500; m. emp., 4; f. emp., 4.

Lumber prepared for market, 112,000 ft.; val. of lumber, $1,568; emp., 50.

Firewood prepared for market, 1,500 cords; val. of firewood, $5,625; emp., 40.

Horses, 83; val. of horses, $5,800; Oxen over three years old, 126; Steers under three years old, 70; val. of oxen and steers, $7,030; Milch Cows, 290; Heifers, 72; val. of cows and heifers, $8,535.

Butter, 8,575 lbs.; val. of butter, $1,715.

Indian Corn, 175 acres; Indian Corn, per acre, 20 bush.; val., $3,500.

Rye, 28 acres; Rye, per acre, 12 bush.; val., $380.

Oats, 20 acres; Oats, per acre, 25 bush.; val., $250.

Potatoes, 121 acres; Potatoes, per acre, 66 bush.; val., $7,986.

English Mowing, 762 acres; English Hay, 650 tons; val., $13,000.

Wet Meadow or Swale Hay, 600 tons; val., $4,800.

Apple Trees, cultivated for their fruit, 1,300; val., $2,000.

Cranberries, 32 acres; val., $1,600.

Swine raised, 73; val., $500.

Beans, 12 acres; 100 bush.; val., $200.

Val. of turnips, onions, carrots and beets, $300.

Val. of milk sold, $800.

Val. of hand screws m'd., $400.

Val. of blacksmithing, $2,000; cap., $1,000; emp., 2.

CHARLESTOWN.

Establishments for m. of steam-engines and boilers, 2; val. of steam-engines and boilers, $65,000; cap., $50,000; emp., 37.

Shops for m. of iron railing, iron fences and iron safes, 1; val. of iron railing, &c., $10,000; cap., $1,000; emp., 6.

Copper Manufactories, 1; Copper m'd., 3,000; val., $9,000; cap., $800; emp., 3.

Brass Founderies, 1; val. of articles m'd., $40,000; cap., $5,000; emp., 5.

Establishments for m. of chemical preparations, 2; val. of chemical preparations, $60,000; cap., $20,000; emp., 7.

Daguerreotype Artists, 2; Daguerreotypes taken, $3,900; cap., $1,000; emp., 2.

Establishments for m. of chronometers, watches, gold and silver ware and jewelry, 1; val. of m.'s., $600; cap., $200; emp., 2.

Brush Manufactories, 2; val. of brushes, $40,000; cap., $20,000; emp., 35.

Saddle, Harness and Trunk Manufactories, 5; val. of saddles, &c., $6,000; cap., $1,700; emp., 13.

Upholstery Manufactories, 4; val. of upholstery, $200,000; cap., $62,000; emp., 68.

Vessels launched during said year, 2; Tonnage, 600 tons; cap., $8,000; emp., 30.

Establishments for m. of boats, 2; Boats built, 20; cap., $800; emp., 5.

Masts and Spar Sheds, 5; Masts and Spars m'd., 2,700; cap., $18,000; emp., 32.

Establishments for m. of railroad cars, coaches, chaises, wagons, sleighs, and other vehicles, 3; val. of railroad cars, &c., m'd., $17,000; cap., $5,200; emp., 9.

Lead Manufactories, 1; val. of lead m'd., $175,000; cap., $45,000; emp., 8.

Establishments for m. of oil and sperm candles, 2; Oil m'd.,

115,000 galls., viz.: 90,000 galls. whale oil, 18,000 galls. sperm oil, and 7,000 galls. lard oil; val. of oil m'd., $90,000; Sperm Candles m'd., 2,000 lbs.; val. of sperm candles, $5,600; cap., $16,000; emp., 12.

Establishments for m. of soap and tallow candles, 4; Soap m'd., 1,600,000 lbs.; val. of soap, $85,000; cap., $16,000; emp., 26.

Chair and Cabinet Manufactories, 5; val. of chairs and cabinet ware, $200,000; cap., $48,000; emp., 200.

Tin Ware Manufactories, 10; val. of tin ware, $30,000; cap., $7,000; emp., 44.

Comb Manufactories, 1; val. of combs m'd., $2,500; cap., $600; emp., 1.

Tanneries, 1; Hides of all kinds tanned, 14,000; val. of leather tanned, $120,000; cap., $75,000; emp., 40.

Currying Establishments, 5; val. of leather curried, $148,000; cap., $65,000; emp., 75.

Boots of all kinds m'd., 12,400 pairs; Shoes of all kinds m'd., 26,800 pairs; val. of boots and shoes, $32,810; m. emp., 75; f. emp., 41.

Val. of snuff, tobacco and cigars, $10,000; m. emp., 4; f. emp., 8.

Val. of building stone quarried and prepared for building, $30,000; emp., 55.

Casks of Lime m'd., 1,000; emp., 2; val. of lime, $800.

Val. of whips m'd., $60,000; emp., 40.

Val. of blocks and pumps m'd., $5,000; emp., 8.

Val. of mechanics' tools m'd., $6,000; emp., 4.

Lumber prepared for market, 345,000 ft.; val. of lumber, $517,000; emp., 10.

Horses, 846; val. of horses, $85,000; Oxen over three years old, 2; Steers under three years old, –; val. of oxen and steers, $225; Milch Cows, 15; val. of cows and heifers, $700.

Establishments for m. of casks, 6; cap., $3,600; Casks m'd., 27,000; val., $23,100; emp., 30.

Establishments for m. of stone and earthenware, 2; val. of stone and earthenware, $31,500; cap., $10,500; emp., 21.

Establishments for m. of gas, 1; cap., $100,000; val. m'd., $21,300.

Establishments for m. of pickles and preserves, 2; val. m'd., $200,000; cap., $80,000; emp., 60.

Distilleries, 1; cap., $8,000.

Breweries, 3; Beer m'd., 4,000 bbls.; val., $14,500; cap., $9,600; emp., 10.

Bakeries, 11; Flour consumed, 12,000 bbls.; val. of bread m'd., $205,000; cap., $32,000; emp., 59.

Ice Shops, 4; number of tons of ice, 186,000; val., $465,000; cap., $600,000; emp., 300.

Morocco Manufactories, 12; val., $378,000; cap., $40,700; emp., 96.

Blacksmiths, 11; val., $75,000; cap., $12,000; emp., 44.

Tailors, 12; val., $208,500; cap., $65,000; m. emp., 31; f. emp., 130.

Silver Plating, 1; val., $2,000; cap., $500; emp., 3.

Willow Ware, 1; val., $10,000; cap., $800; emp., 7.

Planing and Sawing, 1; Lumber planed, 6,000,000 ft.; Lumber sawed, 500,000 ft.; emp., 8.

CHELMSFORD.

Woollen Mills, 1; Sets of Machinery, 12; Wool consumed, 411,756 lbs.; "Eagle Ladies' Cloths" m'd., 55,000 yds.; val. of cloth, $52,250; Mixed Coating m'd., 77,000 yds.; val. of mixed coating, $35,000; Yarn m'd. and not made into cloth, 17,185 lbs.; val. of yarn, $34,299; cap., $63,000; m. emp., 66; f. emp., 44.

Establishments for m. of worsted goods, or goods of which worsted is a component part, –; Yarn m'd. and not made into cloth, 174,900 lbs.; val. of yarn, $80,456; cap., $39,000; m. emp., 10; f. emp., 34.

Furnaces for m. of hollow ware and castings other than pig

iron, 4; Hollow Ware and other Castings m'd., 1,810 tons; val. of hollow ware and castings, $118,000; cap., $84,000; emp., 120.

Establishments for m. of cotton, woollen and other machinery, 1; val. m'd., $60,000; cap., $44,000; emp., 60.

Scythe Manufactories, 1; Scythes m'd., 24,000; val. of scythes, $15,000; cap., $6,000; emp., 14.

Plough Manufactories, 1; Ploughs and other Agricultural Tools m'd., (Ploughs 50); val., $6,000; cap., $2,000; emp., 4.

Establishments for m. of wagons, sleighs, and other vehicles, 3; val. of wagons, sleighs, &c., m'd., $3,000; cap., $1,500.

Establishments for m. of soap and tallow candles, 2; val. of soap, $2,986; cap., $800; emp., 3.

Boots of all kinds m'd., 200 pairs; Shoes of all kinds m'd., 800 pairs; val. of boots and shoes, $1,500; m. emp., 7.

Val. of building stone quarried and prepared for building, $3,000; emp., 6.

Lumber prepared for market, 165,000 ft.; val. of lumber, $1,670.

Firewood prepared for market, 4,758 cords; val. of firewood, $17,880; emp., 35.

Saxony Sheep, of different grades, –; Merino Sheep, of different grades, –; all other kinds of Sheep, 13; val. of all sheep, $39.

Horses, 232; val. of horses, $21,506; Oxen over three years old, 136; Steers under three years old, 36; val. of oxen and steers, $8,473; Milch Cows, 556; Heifers, 45; val. of cows and heifers, $16,646.

Butter, 14,509 lbs.; val. of butter, $3,627.25; Cheese, 800 lbs.; val. of cheese, $64; Honey, 135 lbs.; val. of honey, $33.75.

Indian Corn, 368 acres; Indian Corn, per acre, 37 bush.; val., $12,761.

Wheat, 7½ acres; Wheat, per acre, 14 bush.; val., $186.

Rye, 144 acres; Rye, 1,419 bush.; val., $1,419.

Barley, 16 acres; Barley, per acre, 19 bush.; val., $271.80.

Oats, 141 acres; Oats, per acre, 23 bush.; val., $1,570.

Potatoes, 212 acres; Potatoes, per acre, 93 bush.; val., $14,951.25.

Onions, 2 acres; Onions, per acre, 400 bush.; val., $400.

Turnips, cultivated as a field crop, 10 acres; Turnips, per acre, 350 bush.; val., $700.

Carrots, 6½ acres; Carrots, per acre, 500 bush.; val., $812.50.

Beets and other esculent vegetables, 43 acres; val., $2,631.

Millet, 9½ acres; val., $171.

English Mowing, 1,876 acres; English Hay, 1,763 tons; val., $31,724.

Wet Meadow or Swale Hay, 1,600 tons; val., $14,400.

Apple Trees, cultivated for their fruit, 31,344; val., $6,685.25.

Pear Trees, cultivated for their fruit, 375; val., $1,125.

Cranberries, 41 acres; val., $1,230.

Beans, 42 acres; Beans, per acre, 9 bush.; val., $756.

Milk produced for market, 122,261 galls.; val., $15,282.62.

Val. of poultry, $1,200.

Corn cut for fodder, 40 acres; val., $800.

Oats cut for fodder, 25 acres; val., $375.

Cattle slaughtered, $1,750.

Vinegar m'd., 1,500 bbls.; val., $4,500.

CONCORD.

Cotton and Woollen Mills, 1; Spindles, 800; Cotton consumed, 40,000 lbs.

Woollen and Cotton Mills, 1; Sets of Machinery, 4; Wool consumed, 85,000 lbs.; Flannel or Blanketing m'd., 270,000 yds.; val. of flannel or blanketing, $54,000; cap., $20,000: m. emp., 25; f. emp., 30.

Harness Manufactories, 1; val. of harnesses, &c., $2,000; cap., $1,000; emp., 3.

Establishments for m. of wagons, sleighs, and other vehicles, 2; val. of wagons, sleighs, &c., m'd., $3,000; cap., $1,000; emp., 5.

Establishments for m. of fire arms, 1; Fire Arms m'd., rifles, 50; val. of fire arms, $1,000; cap., $500; emp., 1.

Tin Ware Manufactories, 1; val. of tin ware, $1,200; cap., $800; emp., 3.

Boots of all kinds m'd., 1,100 pairs; Shoes of all kinds m'd., 8,200 pairs; val. of boots and shoes, $13,350; m. emp., 15; f. emp., 5.

Val. of blocks and pumps m'd., $3,000; emp., 4.

Val. of wooden ware not otherwise enumerated, including farming utensils, pails and tubs m'd., $12,000; emp., 15.

Lumber prepared for market, 60,000 ft.; val. of lumber, $1,000; emp., 10.

Firewood prepared for market, 3,000 cords; val. of firewood, $12,000; emp., 30.

Saxony Sheep, of different grades, –; Merino Sheep, of different grades, 5; all other kinds of Sheep, 6; val. of all sheep, $100.

Horses, 272; val. of horses, $20,927; Oxen over three years old, 226; Steers under three years old, 161; val. of oxen and steers, $15,756; Milch Cows, 1,075; Heifers, 123; val. of cows and heifers, $24,875.

Butter, 11,080 lbs.; val. of butter, $2,770; Cheese, 1,200 lbs.; val. of cheese, $72; Honey, 220 lbs.; val. of honey, $40.

Indian Corn, 463 acres; Indian Corn, per acre, 35 bush.; val., $16,205.

Wheat, 6 acres; Wheat, per acre, 13 bush.; val., $200.

Rye, 120 acres; Rye, per acre, 11⅓ bush.; val., $1,700.

Barley, 7 acres; Barley, per acre, 12 bush.; val., $84.

Oats, 152 acres; Oats, per acre, 24 bush.; val., $1,813.

Potatoes, 306 acres; Potatoes, per acre, 76 bush.; val., $23,475.

Onions, 4 acres; Onions, per acre, 300 bush.; val., $900.

Turnips, cultivated as a field crop, 52 acres; Turnips, per acre, 150 bush.; val., $1,550.

Carrots, 13 acres; Carrots, per acre, 288 bush.; val., $1,023.

Beets and other esculent vegetables, 3 acres; val., $500.

Millet, 8 acres; val., $200.

English Mowing, 1,689 acres; English Hay, 1,900 tons; val., $38,000.

Wet Meadow or Swale Hay, 1,025 tons; val., $10,250.

Apple Trees, cultivated for their fruit, 6,808; val., $4,866.

Pear Trees, cultivated for their fruit, 856; val., $300.

Cranberries, 50 acres; val., $2,000.

Val. of Potter's hair balm m'd., $3,000; cap., $500; emp., 2.

Val. of milk sold, $27,490.

Val. of lead pencils m'd., $12,000.

Val. of garden seeds sold, $2,370.

DRACUT.

Cotton Mills, 1; Spindles, 2,350; Cotton consumed, 360,000 lbs.; Cloth m'd., 350,000 yds., Sail Duck; val. of cloth, $60,000; Twine m'd., 1,000 lbs.; val. of twine, $2,000; cap., $25,000; m. emp., 18; f. emp., 50.

Woollen Mills, 1; Sets of Machinery, 8; Wool consumed, 250,000 lbs.; Cassimere m'd., 250,000 yds.; Satinet m'd., 225,000 yds; cap., $75,000; m. emp., 120; f. emp., 60.

Paper Manufactories, 2; Stock made use of, 210,000 lbs.; Paper m'd., 150,000 lbs.; val. of paper, $10,500; cap., $10,000; emp., 4.

Lumber prepared for market, 98,500 ft.; val. of lumber, $1,203; emp., 16.

Firewood prepared for market, 2,622 cords; val. of firewood, $11,539; emp., 37.

Horses, 197; val. of horses, $14,775; Oxen over three years old, 229; Steers under three years old, 8; val. of oxen and steers, $11,850; Milch Cows, 765; Heifers, 76; val. of cows and heifers, $21,025.

Butter, 6,508 lbs.; val. of butter, $2,427; Cheese, 525 lbs.; val. of cheese, $82.50.

Indian Corn, 398 acres; Indian Corn, per acre, 30 bush.; val., $11,760.

Wheat, $2\frac{1}{2}$ acres; Wheat, per acre, 12 bush.; val., $54.

Rye, 83 acres; Rye, per acre, $10\frac{1}{3}$ bush.; val., $2,498.

Barley, 13 acres; Barley, per acre, $18\frac{2}{3}$ bush.; val., $242.

Oats, 131 acres; Oats, per acre, $30\frac{1}{3}$ bush.; val., $1,977.50.

Potatoes, 227 acres; Potatoes, per acre, 67 bush.; val., $8,515.70.

Onions, $5\frac{1}{2}$ acres; Onions, per acre, 350 bush.; val., $1,020.

Turnips, cultivated as a field crop, $15\frac{1}{2}$ acres; Turnips, per acre, 423 bush; val., $1,326.60.

Carrots, 5 acres; Carrots, per acre, 415 bush.; val., $825.80.

Beets and other esculent vegetables, 9 acres; val., $1,800.

English Mowing, 1,930 acres; English Hay, 2,040 tons; val., $40,800.

Wet Meadow or Swale Hay, 694 tons; val., $7,120.

Apple Trees, cultivated for their fruit, 19,774; val., $4,258.

Pear Trees, cultivated for their fruit, 382; val., $222.50.

Cranberries, 5 acres; val., $500.

Val. of cabbages raised, $1,500.

Squashes, 20 tons; val., $400.

Val. of buckwheat raised, $200.

Val. of milk produced, $25,291.88.

DUNSTABLE.

Establishments for m. of railroad cars, coaches, chaises, wagons, sleighs, and other vehicles, 2; val. of railroad cars, &c., m'd., $700; cap., $300.

Boots of all kinds m'd., 75 pairs; Shoes of all kinds m'd., 100 pairs; val. of boots and shoes, $350; m. emp., 1.

Charcoal m'd., 8,300 bush.; val. of same, $748.

Lumber prepared for market, 126,500 ft.; val. of lumber, $12,650.

Firewood prepared for market, 531 cords; val. of firewood, $2,124.

Saxony Sheep, of different grades, –; Merino Sheep, of different grades, –; all other kinds of Sheep, 164; val. of all sheep, $410; Wool produced from Saxony sheep, – lbs.; Merino Wool produced, – lbs.; all other Wool produced, 460 lbs.

Horses, 96; val. of horses, $6,322; Oxen over three years old, 125; Steers under three years old, 71; val. of oxen and steers, $8,605; Milch Cows, 355; Heifers, 108; val. of cows and heifers, $12,425.

Butter, 18,212 lbs.; val. of butter, $4,006.60; Cheese, 5,122 lbs.; val. of cheese, $512.20.

Indian Corn, 204 acres; Indian Corn, per acre, 25 bush.; val., $5,100.

Wheat, 5 acres; Wheat, per acre, 12 bush.; val., $135.

Rye, 178 acres; Rye, per acre, 10 bush.; val., $1,780.

Barley, 2 acres; Barley, per acre, 19 bush.; val., $38.

Oats, 68 acres; Oats, per acre, 20 bush.; val., $680.

Potatoes, 88 acres; Potatoes, per acre, 100 bush.; val., $4,400.

Onions, ¼ acre; Onions, per acre, 160 bush.; val., $30.

Carrots, 1 acre; Carrots, per acre, 400 bush.; val., $100.

English Mowing, 868 acres; English Hay, 868 tons; val., $13,020.

Wet Meadow or Swale Hay, 533 tons; val., $3,731.

Apple Trees, cultivated for their fruit, 1,436; val., $1,243.

Cranberries, 13 acres; val., $210.

Establishments for m. of casks, 2; Casks m'd., 150; val., $135; cap., $140; emp., 2, during part of the time.

Milk, 30,387 galls.; val., $3,646.44.

Swine raised, 97; val., $889.

Beans, 15 acres; Beans, per acre, 11 bush.; val., $330.

Buckwheat, 25 acres; Buckwheat, per acre, 5 bush.; val., $125.

FRAMINGHAM.

Woollen Mills, 3; Sets of Machinery, 39; Wool consumed, 1,632,132 lbs.; Flannel or Blanketing, 334,854 yds.; val. of flannel or blanketing, $331,368.60; Yarn m'd., and not made into cloth, 444,272 lbs.; val. of yarn, $133,281.60; cap., $300,000; m. emp., 126; f. emp., 148.

Establishments for m. of worsted goods, or goods of which worsted is a component part, – ; Yarn m'd., and not made into cloth; 624,000 lbs.; val. of yarn, $312,000; cap., $200,000; m. emp., 64; f. emp., 75.

Saddle, Harness and Trunk Manufactories, 3; val., of saddles, &c., $8,340; cap., $2,500; emp., 12; amount of capital in one of the manufactories not given.

Establishments for m. of railroad cars, coaches, chaises, wagons, sleighs, and other vehicles, 5; val. of railroad cars, &c., m'd., $5,710; emp., in two establishments, 8.

Tin Ware Manufactories, 2; val. of tin ware, $6,200; cap., $2,000; emp., 4.

Boots of all kinds m'd., 397 pairs; Shoes of all kinds m'd., 64,400 pairs; val. of boots and shoes, $57,000; m. emp., 57; f. emp., 40.

Establishments for m. of straw bonnets and hats, 2; Straw Bonnets, m'd., 107,000; Straw Hats, m'd., 60,000; m. emp., 25; f. emp., 300.

Val. of building stone quarried and prepared for building, $2,000; emp., 3.

Val. of lumber, $1,577.

Firewood prepared for market, 1,981 cords; val. of firewood, $9,569.

Merino Sheep, of different grades, 32; val. of all sheep, $128; Merino Wool produced, 100 lbs.

Horses, 330; val. of horses, $35,863; Oxen over three years old, 165; Steers under three years old, 21; val. of oxen and steers, $10,969; Milch Cows, 860; Heifers 129; val. of cows and heifers, $28,216.

Butter, 89,300 lbs.; val. of butter, $22,315; Cheese, 3,600 lbs.; val. of cheese, $222; Honey, 273 lbs.; val. of honey, $67.50.

Indian Corn, 658 acres; Indian Corn, per acre, 40⅔ bush.; val., $26,684.

Wheat, 15 acres; Wheat, per acre, 17½ bush.; val., $548.

Rye, 167 acres; Rye, per acre, 15 bush.; val., $3,130.

Barley, 14¼ acres; Barley, per acre, 25⅓ bush.; val., $428.

Oats, 347 acres; Oats, per acre, 30 bush.; val., $5,220.

Potatoes, 415 acres; Potatoes, per acre, 100 bush.; val., $41,500.

Onions, 230 acres; Onions, 210 bush. The val. of 75 bush. ($70,) only, is returned.

Turnips, 4,569 bush.; val., $671.

Carrots, 20 acres; Carrots, per acre, 528⅔ bush.; val., $4,400.

Beets, 112 bush.; val., $56; Buckwheat, 16½ acres; val., $252.

Millet, 20½ acres; val., $373.

English Mowing, 2,680 acres; English Hay, 2,779 tons; val., $55,580.

Wet Meadow or Swale Hay, 1,531 tons; val., $15,242.

Apple Trees, cultivated for their fruit, 30,768; val., $12,266.

Basket Willow cultivated, 1,128 acres; val., $1,090.

Cranberries, 10½ acres; val., $405.

Beeswax, 65 lbs.; val., $27.80.

Val. of whalebone m'd., $3,000; cap., $500; emp., 4.

Beans, 214 bush.; val., $428.

Val. of garden vegetables produced, $5,509.

Val. of animals slaughtered, $26,426.

Swine raised, 388; val., $3,065.

Grapes produced, 1,500 lbs.; val., $2,150.

Vinegar m'd., 200 bbls.; val., $700; cap., $1,800; emp., 1.

Ice housed, 400 tons; val., $500; cap., $700; emp., 2.

Peaches raised, 100 bush.; val., $200.

Strawberries raised, 15 bush.; val., $100.

GROTON.

Plough Manufactories, 1; Ploughs and other Agricultural Tools m'd., 6,000; val., $51,303; cap., $25,000; emp., 35.

Paper Manufactories, 2; Stock made use of, 2,250,000 lbs.; Paper m'd., 1,080,000 lbs.; val. of paper, $168,000; cap., $82,000; emp., 43.

Tin Ware Manufactories, 1; val. of tin ware, $15,000; cap., $8,000; emp., 8.

Tanneries, 1; Hides of all kinds tanned, 250; val. of leather tanned, $1,000; cap., $3,000; emp., 2.

Boots of all kinds, m'd., – pairs; Shoes of all kinds m'd., 117,500 pairs; val. of boots and shoes, $108,000; m. emp., 84; f. emp., 50.

Lumber prepared for market, 283,000 ft.; val. of lumber, $4,348.

Firewood prepared for market, 2,650 cords; val. of firewood, $8,798; prepared by farmers.

Saxony Sheep, of different grades, –; Merino Sheep of different grades, –; all other kinds of Sheep, 131; val. of all sheep, $344; Wool produced from Saxony sheep, – lbs.; Merino Wool produced, – lbs.; all other Wool produced, 361 lbs.

Horses, 288; val. of horses, $24,313; Oxen over three years old, 294; Steers under three years old, 106; val. of oxen and steers, 20,068; Milch Cows, 782; Heifers, 175; val. of cows and heifers, $24,681.

Butter, 42,006 lbs.; val. of butter, $9,215; Cheese, 3,840 lbs.; val. of cheese, $335; Honey, 400 lbs.; val. of honey, $80.

Indian Corn, 486 acres; Indian Corn, per acre, 24 bush.; val., $12,153.

Wheat, 5½ acres; Wheat, per acre, 7 bush.; val., $92.

Rye, 247 acres; Rye, per acre, 7 bush.; val., $2,573.

Barley, 9 acres; Barley, per acre, 15 bush.; val., $135.

Oats, 136 acres; Oats, per acre, 18½ bush.; val., $1,518.

Potatoes, 216 acres; Potatoes, per acre, 90 bush.; val., $12,510.

Onions, $\frac{7}{8}$ acre; Onions, per acre, 211 bush.; val., $157. Turnips, cultivated as a field crop, 1 acre; Turnips, per acre, 450 bush.; val., $90.

Carrots, 1 acre; Carrots, per acre, 650 bush.; val., $260.

English Mowing, 2,662 acres; English Hay, 2,698 tons; val., $43,279.

Wet Meadow or Swale Hay, 757 tons; val., $6,572.

Apple Trees, cultivated for their fruit, 11,578; val., $12,115.

Pear Trees, cultivated for their fruit, 91; val., $105.

Hops, 20 acres; Hops, per acre, 650 lbs; val., $3,411.

Cranberries, 1 acre; val., $253.

Bakeries, 1; cap., $2,000; Flour consumed, 1,100 bbls.; val. of bread m'd., $17,600; emp., 8.

Chestnuts, 271 bush; val., $923.

Val. of milk sold, $7,850.

HOLLISTON.

Cotton Mills, 1; Spindles, 2,000; Cotton consumed, 100,000 lbs.; Cloth m'd., 600,000 yds. of 52 by 56 Prints; val. of cloth, $30,000; cap., $30,000; m. emp., 12; f. emp., 18.

Harness Manufactories, 2; val. of harnesses, $24; cap., $800; emp., 2.

Establishments for m. of soap, 1; Soap m'd., 27,000 galls.; val. of soap, $3,240; emp., 3.

Chair and Cabinet Manufactories, 1; val. of chairs and cabinet ware, $1,000; cap., $2,000; emp., 2.

Tin Ware Manufactories, 1; val. of tin ware, $5,000; cap., $3,000; emp., 4.

Comb Manufactories, 1; val. of combs m'd., $75,000; cap., $50,000; emp., 70.

Boots of all kinds m'd., 277,439 pairs; Shoes of all kinds m'd., 67,820 pairs; val. of boots and shoes, $414,484; m. emp., 471; f. emp., 112.

Establishments for m. of straw bonnets and hats, 2; Straw Bonnets m'd., 76,250; Straw Hats m'd., 5,000; m. emp., 12; f. emp., 160.

Charcoal m'd., 800 bush.; val. of same, $132; emp., 1.

Val. of copper pumps m'd., $12,000; emp., 7.

Firewood prepared for market, 2,702 cords; val. of firewood, $13,510; emp., 27.

Saxony Sheep, of different grades, –; Merino Sheep, of different grades, –; all other kinds of Sheep, 3; val. of all sheep, $7.50; Wool produced from Saxony sheep, – lbs.; Merino Wool produced, – lbs.; all other Wool produced, 15 lbs.

Horses, 163; val. of horses, $12,952; Oxen over three years old, 119; Steers under three years old, 60; val. of oxen and steers, $8,105; Milch Cows, 364; Heifers, 40; val. of cows and heifers, $13,341.

Butter, 40,740 lbs.; val. of butter, $1,146; Cheese, 1,975 lbs.; val. of cheese, $157; Honey, 200 lbs.; val. of honey, $33.

Indian Corn, 262 acres; Indian Corn, per acre, 28 bush.; val., $7,336.

Wheat, 5 acres; Wheat, per acre, 13 bush.; val., $162.50.

Rye, 27 acres; Rye, per acre, 12 bush.; val., $486.

Barley, 9 acres; Barley, per acre, 19 bush.; val., $171.

Oats, 104 acres; Oats, per acre, 23 bush.; val., $1,435.

Potatoes, 106 acres; Potatoes, per acre, 98 bush.; val., $7,791.

Turnips, cultivated as a field crop, 8 acres; Turnips, per acre, 1,600 bush.; val., $400.

Carrots, 2 acres; Carrots, per acre, 1,200 bush.; val., $480.

English Mowing, 1,247 acres; English Hay, 1,095 tons; val., $21,900.

Wet Meadow or Swale Hay, 278 tons; val., $2,224.

Apple Trees, cultivated for their fruit, 9,152; val., $3,850.

Pear Trees, cultivated for their fruit, 148; val., $213.

Cranberries, 77 acres; val., $4,003.

Bakeries, 1; Flour consumed, 500 bbls.; val. of bread m'd., $9,000; cap., $1,500; emp., 6.

Establishments for m. of boxes for boots, shoes and bonnets, 2; val. of boxes m'd., $17,216; cap., $2,500; emp., 5.

Cider Refineries, 1; val., $3,500; Bbls. refined, 950; cap., $7,000; emp., 6.

Corn Planters m'd., 100; val., $500.

Washing Machines m'd., 200; val., $2,000; emp., 2.

HOPKINTON.

Cotton Mills, 2; Spindles, 1,523. [These Mills are owned in Boston, and have not been in operation for eight years.]

Plough Manufactories, 1; Ploughs and other Agricultural Tools m'd., 80; val., $450; cap., $100; emp., 1.

Saddle, Harness and Trunk Manufactories, 1; val. of saddles, &c., $300; cap., $200; emp., 1, part time.

Establishments for m. of boats, 2; Boats built, 24; cap., $100; emp., 2, part time.

Establishments for m. of railroad cars, coaches, chaises, wagons, sleighs, and other vehicles, 1; val. of railroad cars, &c., m'd., $1,125; cap., $500; emp., 3.

Tin Ware Manufactories, 1; val. of tin ware, $2,500; cap., $1,000; emp., 2.

Boots of all kinds m'd., 600,474 pairs; Shoes of all kinds m'd., – pairs; val. of boots and shoes, $1,058,820; m. emp., 1,233; f. emp., 88.

Val. of straw braid m'd. and not made into bonnets and hats, $400; f. emp., 4.

Val. of building stone quarried and prepared for building, $700; emp., 2.

Charcoal m'd., 5,000 bush.; val. of same, $375; emp., 1, part time.

Corn and other Brooms m'd., 960; val. of brooms, $100; emp., 2, part time.

Lumber prepared for market, 219,000 ft.; val. of lumber, $2,750; emp., 8.

Firewood prepared for market, 3,695 cords; val. of firewood, $12,800; emp., 16.

Saxony Sheep, of different grades, –; Merino Sheep, of different grades, –; all other kinds of Sheep, 8; val. of all sheep, $32.

Horses, 269; val. of horses, $25,080; Oxen over three years old, 140; Steers under three years old, 14; val. of oxen and steers, $7,636; Milch Cows, 546; Heifers, 68; val. of cows and heifers, $16,648.

Butter, 24,316 lbs.; val. of butter, $6,079; Cheese, 2,050 lbs.; val. of cheese, $164; Honey, 180 lbs.; val. of honey, $36.

Indian Corn, 267 acres; Indian Corn, per acre, $29\frac{4}{267}$ bush.; val., $8,720.

Wheat, $1\frac{1}{4}$ acre; Wheat, per acre, $12\frac{4}{5}$ bush.; val., $40.

Rye, $31\frac{1}{2}$ acres; Rye, per acre, $6\frac{88}{100}$ bush.; val., $325.

Barley, $2\frac{3}{4}$ acres; Barley, per acre, $14\frac{54}{100}$ bush.; val., $40.

Oats, $109\frac{1}{2}$ acres; Oats, per acre, $22\frac{96}{100}$ bush.; val., $1,509.

Potatoes, $205\frac{1}{2}$ acres; Potatoes, per acre, $82\frac{48}{100}$ bush.; val., $12,717.

Onions, $\frac{1}{4}$ acre; Onions, per acre, 120 bush.; val., $25.

Carrots, $1\frac{1}{2}$ acre; Carrots, per acre, 550 bush.; val., $232.

Beets and other esculent vegetables, $3\frac{1}{2}$ acres; val., $775; all other Grain or Root Crops, 3 acres; val., $30.

English Mowing, $1,734\frac{1}{2}$ acres; English Hay, 1,262 tons; val., $21,454.

Wet Meadow or Swale Hay, 541 tons; val., $4,328.

Apple Trees, cultivated for their fruit, 6,169; val., $4,883.

Pear Trees, cultivated for their fruit, 62; val., $85.

Cranberries, $46\frac{5}{8}$ acres; val., $778.

Establishments for m. of boot boxes, 2; cap., $4,000; val. boxes m'd., $30,000; emp., 10.

Establishments for m. of clothing, 2; cap., $6,000; val. of clothing m'd., $25,000; emp., 27.

Val. of cider vinegar, $760.

Val. of milk sold, $3,060.

Val. of peaches, $156.

Val. of whortleberries sent to market, $3,291.

Swine raised, 222; val., $1,917.

There have also been m'd. during the year, 25 sets of boot trees, and 110,000 hoops for boot and dry goods boxes; val., $1,450; emp., 3.

LEXINGTON.

Tin Ware Manufactories, 2; val. of tin ware, $8,000; cap., $3,000; emp., 7.

Firewood prepared for market, 950 cords; val. of firewood, $5,700.

Horses, 348; val. of horses, $36,440; Oxen over three years old, 122; Steers under three years old, –; val. of oxen and steers, $7,355; Milch Cows, 1,090; Heifers, 99; val. of cows and heifers, $33,888.

Butter, 400 lbs.; val. of butter, $100; Cheese, 100 lbs.; val. of cheese, $10.

Indian Corn, 323 acres; Indian Corn, per acre, 31 bush.; val., $10,021.

Rye, 62 acres; Rye, per acre, 11$\frac{25}{62}$ bush.; val., $4,805.

Oats, 3$\frac{1}{3}$ acres; Oats, per acre, 30 bush.; val., $62.

Potatoes, 177$\frac{1}{4}$ acres; Potatoes, per acre, 89$\frac{27}{177}$ bush.; val., $19,712.50.

Turnips, cultivated as a field crop, 24$\frac{1}{2}$ acres; Turnips, per acre, 447 bush.; val., $3,285.

Carrots, 12$\frac{3}{4}$ acres; Carrots, per acre, 600 bush.; val., $3,150.

Beets and other esculent vegetables, – acres; all other Grain or Root Crops, 244 acres; val., $18,840.

English Mowing, 1,958$\frac{3}{4}$ acres; English Hay, 2,521$\frac{1}{2}$ tons; val., $63,037.50.

Wet Meadow or Swale Hay, 608$\frac{1}{2}$ tons; val., $7,606.

Apple Trees, cultivated for their fruit, 25,109; val., $14,986.

Pear Trees, cultivated for their fruit, 347; val., $560.

Cranberries, – acres; val., $151.

Fur Manufactories, 2; amount m'd., $28,865.92; cap., $15,000; emp., 32.

Establishments for m. of Manilla and Jute mats, 1; amount m'd., $4,750; cap., $1,000; emp., 5.

Val. of 800 tons of ice cut, $2,400.

Val. of 350,846 galls. of milk produced, $52,626.90.

LINCOLN.

Firewood prepared for market, 1,173 cords; val. of firewood, $4,994.

Horses, 122; val. of horses, $12,925; Oxen over three years old, 105; Steers under three years old, 2; val. of oxen and steers, $6,650; Milch Cows, 535; Heifers, 59; val. of cows and heifers, $21,028.

Butter, 6,680 lbs.; val. of butter, $1,670; Cheese, 1,350 lbs.; val. of cheese, $109.

Indian Corn, 335 acres; Indian Corn, per acre, 30 bush.; val., $10,050.

Wheat, 1 acre; Wheat, per acre, 20 bush.; val., $40.

Rye, 45 acres; Rye, per acre, 17 bush.; val., $1,020.

Barley, 8 acres; Barley, per acre, 20 bush.; val., $160.

Oats, 52 acres; Oats, per acre, – bush.; val., $1,108.

Potatoes, 114 acres; Potatoes, per acre, 56 bush.; val., $5,609.

Turnips, cultivated as a field crop, 15 acres; Turnips, per acre, 317 bush.; val., $1,189.

English Mowing, 1,089 acres; English Hay, 1,089 tons; val., $21,195.

Wet Meadow or Swale Hay, 809 tons; val., $8,090.

Apple Trees, cultivated for their fruit, 15,195; val., $7,084.

Pear Trees, cultivated for their fruit, 2,283; val, $349.

Cranberries, 52 acres; val., $1,325.

Swine raised, 138; val., $1,314.
Val. of milk sold, $18,727.
Asparagus, 2½ acres; val. of crop, $580.
Strawberries, 2 acres; val. of crop., $600.
Pickles, 17 acres; val., $1,510.

LITTLETON.

Saddle, Harness and Trunk Manufactories, 1; val. of saddles, &c., $1,000; cap., $500; emp., 2.

Currying Establishments, 1; val. of leather curried, $700; cap., $600; emp., 1.

Boots of all kinds m'd., 80 pairs; Shoes of all kinds m'd., 1,522 pairs; val. of boots and shoes, $854; m. emp., 2; f. emp., 1.

Corn and other Brooms m'd., 270; val. of brooms, $75; emp., 1.

Lumber prepared for market, 108,000 ft.; val. of lumber, $1,512.

Firewood prepared for market, 1,659 cords; val. of firewood, $5,805.

Horses, 165; val. of horses, $13,046; Oxen, over three years old, 121; Steers under three years old, 10; val. of oxen and steers, $6,793; Milch Cows, 533; Heifers, 83; val. of cows and heifers, $17,020.

Butter, 10,957 lbs.; val. of butter, $2,410; Cheese, 75 lbs.; val. of cheese, $7.50; Honey, 25 lbs.; val. of honey, $4.

Indian Corn, 294½ acres; Indian Corn, per acre, 30 bush.; val., $8,835.

Wheat, 6¼ acres; Wheat, per acre, 9 bush.; val., $112.

Rye, 110¾ acres; Rye, per acre, 10 bush.; val., $1,388.

Barley, 20½ acres; Barley, per acre, 19 bush.; val., $355.

Oats, 98½ acres; Oats, per acre, 22 bush.; val., $1,137.

Potatoes, 133¾ acres; Potatoes, per acre, 82 bush.; val., $6,031.

Onions, ⅞ acre; Onions, per acre, 500 bush.; val., $262.

Turnips, cultivated as a field crop, 7 acres; Turnips, per acre, 100 bush.; val., $140.

Carrots, 6 acres; Carrots, per acre, 250 bush.; val., $375.

Beets and other esculent vegetables, 20 acres; val., $1,075.

Millet, ½ acre; val., $10.

English Mowing, 1,412 acres; English Hay, 1,511 tons; val., $24,176.

Wet Meadow or Swale Hay, 499 tons; val., $3,992.

Apple Trees, cultivated for their fruit, 11,690; val., $8,377.

Hops, 10½ acres; Hops, per acre, 385 lbs.; val., $1,185.

Cranberries, 36¾ acres; val., $625.

Milk sold, 92,050 cans; val., $21,171.

LOWELL.

Cotton Mills, 35; Spindles, 350,348; Cotton consumed, 37,431,724 lbs.; Cloth m'd., 98,647,359 yds. Sheetings, Shirtings, Printing Cloths, Drillings, Tickings and Osnaburgs; val. of cloth, $7,494,229; Yarn m'd., 23,000 lbs.; val. of yarn, $5,000; Batting m'd., 962,000 lbs.; val. of batting, $61,600; Pelisse Wadding m'd., 370,000 lbs.; val. of wadding, $53,000; cap., $9,490,000; m. emp., 2,105; f. emp., 7,349.

Calico Manufactories, 2; Calico printed, 21,900,000 yds.; val. of calico, $1,890,000; cap., $1,000,000; m. emp., 343; f. emp., 29.

Establishments for bleaching or coloring cotton, silk and woollen goods, not connected with calico establishments, 5; Goods bleached or colored, 28,000,000 yds.; val. of goods, $2,000,000; cap., $314,000; emp., 350.

Woollen Mills, 5; Sets of Machinery, 56; Wool consumed, 1,914,935 lbs.; Broadcloth m'd., 126,279 yds.; val. of broadcloth, $138,924; Cassimere m'd., 670,500 yds.; val. of cassimere, $737,550; Satinet m'd., 564,974 yds.; val. of satinet, $225,990; Shawls m'd., 10,167; val. of shawls, $35,000; Flannel or Blanketing, 600,000 yds.; val. of flannel or blanketing, $132,000; cap., $1,050,000; m. emp., 610; f. emp., 748.

Mills for m. of carpeting, 2; Wool consumed, 1,994,000 lbs.; Carpeting m'd., 1,223,654 yds.; val. of carpeting, including rags and mats, $900,000; cap., $1,400,000; m. emp., 365; f. emp., 595.

Establishments for m. of worsted goods, or goods of which worsted is a component part, 2; Yarn m'd., and not made into cloth, 75,000 lbs.; val. of yarn, $27,000; cap., $12,000; m. emp., 11; f. emp., 7.

Furnaces for m. of hollow ware and castings other than pig iron, 2; Hollow Ware and other Castings m'd., 3,625 tons; val. of hollow ware and castings, $243,000; cap., $24,500; emp., 180.

Establishments for m. of cotton, woollen and other machinery, 8; val. of machinery m'd., $748,000; cap., $551,000; emp., 761.

Establishments for m. of steam-engines and boilers, 2; val. of steam-engines and boilers, $117,000; cap., $77,500; emp., 126.

Shops for m. of iron railing, iron fences and iron safes, 2; val. of iron railing, &c., $5,500; cap., $2,800; emp., 8.

Copper Manufactories, 1; Copper m'd., 62,000 lbs.; val., $20,000; cap., $2,000; emp., 4.

Brass Founderies, 2; val. of articles m'd., $7,000; cap., $700; emp., 6.

Establishments for m. of chemical preparations, 1; val. of chemical preparations, $100,000; cap., $50,000; m. emp., 30; f. emp., 30.

Paper Manufactories, 1; Stock made use of, 300,000 lbs.; Paper m'd., 225,000 lbs.; val. of paper, $13,500; cap., $10,000; emp., 6.

Daguerreotype Artists, 7; Daguerreotypes taken, 17,000; cap., $9,500; emp., 17.

Establishments for m. of chronometers, watches, gold and

silver ware and jewelry, 2; val. of m's., $30,000; cap., $11,000; emp., 11.

Saddle, Harness and Trunk Manufactories, 7; val. of saddles, &c., $14,625; cap., $6,500; emp., 19.

Upholstery Manufactories, 4; val. of upholstery, $10,000; cap., $2,450; emp., 9.

Hat and Cap Manufactories, 2; Hats and Caps m'd., 15,400; cap., $11,400; emp., 30.

Cordage Manufactories, 1; Cordage m'd., 25 tons; cap., $1,000; emp., 8.

Card Manufactories, 1; val. of machine cards m'd., $20,000; cap., $12,000; emp., 8.

Establishments for m. of railroad cars, coaches, chaises, wagons, sleighs, and other vehicles, 4; val. of railroad cars, &c., m'd., $22,900; cap., $23,000; emp., 56.

Establishments for m. of soap and tallow candles, 3; Soap m'd., soft soap, 6,000 bbls., hard soap, 226,000 lbs.; val. of soap, $35,000; Tallow Candles m'd., 240,000 lbs.; val. of tallow candles, $32,100; cap., $33,000; emp., 18.

Powder Mills, 1; Powder m'd., 750,000 lbs.; val. of powder, $75,000; cap., $12,000; emp., 18.

Establishments for m. of fire arms, 2; Fire Arms m'd., rifles, single and double shot guns, and pistols; val. of fire arms, $5,000; cap., $1,700; emp., 8.

Tin Ware Manufactories, 10; val. of tin ware, $42,500; cap., $17,000; emp., 36.

Tanneries, 1; Hides of all kinds tanned, $12,000; val. of leather tanned, $90,000; cap., $30,000; emp., 30.

Currying Establishments, 2; val. of leather curried, $160,000; cap., $21,000; emp., 35.

Manufactories of patent and enamelled leather, 1; val. of leather m'd., $80,000; cap., $10,000; emp., 35.

Boots of all kinds m'd., 35,695 pairs; Shoes of all kinds m'd., 61,060 pairs; val. of boots and shoes, $131,852; m. emp., 148; f. emp., 102.

Val. of snuff, tobacco, and cigars, $19,200; m. emp., 11; f. emp., 5.

Charcoal m'd., 12,000 bush.; val. of same, $1,200; emp., 1.

Val. of blocks and pumps m'd., $1,500; emp., 2.

Lumber prepared for market, 13,500,000 ft.; val. of lumber, $250,000; emp., 340.

Horses, 945; val. of horses, $94,500; Oxen over three years old, 60; Steers under three years old, –; val. of oxen and steers, $3,300; Milch Cows, 500; Heifers, –; val. of cows and heifers, $1,500.

Butter, 2,000 lbs.; val. of butter, $500.

Indian Corn, 50 acres; Indian Corn, per acre, 40 bush.; val., $2,500.

Rye, 6 acres; Rye, per acre, 20 bush.; val., $120.

Oats, 16 acres; Oats, per acre, 25 bush.; val., $400.

Potatoes, 50 acres; Potatoes, per acre, 125 bush.; val., $3,125.

Onions, 7 acres; Onions, per acre, 200 bush.; val., $700.

Carrots, 5 acres; Carrots, per acre, 300 bush.; val., $500.

English Mowing, 378 acres; English Hay, 440 tons; val., $7,530.

Wet Meadow or Swale Hay, 62 tons; val., $725.

Apple Trees, cultivated for their fruit, 4,000; val., $3,000.

Pear Trees, cultivated for their fruit, 2,500; val., $1,500.

Cranberries, 18 acres; val., $2,500.

Establishments for m. of sashes, doors and blinds, 7; val. m'd., $111,400; cap., $30,000; emp., 115.

Establishments for m. of gas, 1; val. m'd., $66,200; cap., $200,000; emp., 35.

Bakeries, 4; Flour consumed, 5,820 bbls.; val. of bread m'd., $66,560; cap., $29,500; emp., 30.

Establishments for m. of boxes, (packing boxes,) 2; val. of boxes m'd., $46,000; cap., $32,000; emp., 21.

Establishments for m. of wire fence, 1; val., $10,000; cap., $20,000; emp., 6.

Establishments for m. of pyroligneous acid, 1; galls. m'd., 40,000; val., $3,200; emp., 4.

Establishments for m. of "excelsior" for mattresses, 1; quantity m'd., 100 tons; val., $4,000; cap., $2,000; emp., 6.

Establishments for m. of cotton bagging, 1; Bags m'd., 124,800; val., $26,000; cap., $14,000; m. emp., 7; f. emp., 20.

Establishments for m. of bedsteads, 1; Bedsteads m'd., 10,000; val., $30,000; cap., $20,000; emp., 40.

Establishments for m. of power loom harnesses, 3; val., $25,000; cap., $14,000; m. emp., 13; f. emp., 35.

Establishments for m. of weavers' reeds, 1; val., $4,000; cap., $2,000; emp., 5.

Establishments for m. of shuttles, 1; val., $8,000; cap., $5,000; emp., 5.

Establishments for m. of belting, 2; val., $88,000; cap., $22,000; emp., 13.

Establishments for m. of bobbins, 1; val., $18,000; cap., $12,000; emp., 28.

Establishments for m. of pickers, 1; val., $15,400; cap., $10,000; emp., 10.

Establishments for m. of scales, 1; val., $8,000; cap., $6,000; emp., 6.

Establishments for plumbing, 1; val. of lead used, $4,000; cap., $500; emp., 3.

Establishments for m. of cotton carpeting, 1; Carpeting m'd., 120,000 yds.; Cotton consumed, 40,000 lbs.; cap., $50,000; m. emp., 30; f. emp., 19.

Establishments for m. of screws, bolts and nuts, –; Iron used, 300 tons; val. of bolts and nuts m'd., $30,000; cap., $15,000; emp., 30.

Establishments for m. of mattresses, 1; number m'd., 1,000; val., $2,000; cap., $400; emp., 1.

Establishments for m. of picture-frames, 1; val., $3,100; cap., $1,150; emp., 1.

Establishments for m. of bird cages, seives, &c., 1; val., $5,000; cap., $1,400; emp., 6.

Establishments for m. of parasols and umbrellas, 1; val., $12,000; cap., $4,000; emp., 12.

Establishments for m. of clothing, 15; val., $450,200; cap., $34,900; emp., 211.

MALDEN.

Establishments for m. of linen, 1 ; not in operation.

Establishments for m. of britannia ware, 1 ; val. of britannia ware, $18,000 ; cap., $10,000 ; emp., 18.

Saddle, Harness and Trunk Manufactories, 1 ; val. of saddles, &c., $500 ; cap., $300 ; emp., 2.

Cordage Manufactories, 1 ; Cordage m'd., 6 tons ; cap., $400 ; emp., 3.

Establishments for m. of railroad cars, coaches, chaises, wagons, sleighs, and other vehicles, 3 ; val. of railroad cars, &c., m'd., $4,000 ; cap., $500 ; emp., 7.

Tin Ware Manufactories, 3 ; val. of tin ware, $10,000 ; cap., $5,000 ; emp., 10.

Flour Mills, 1 ; Flour m'd., 7,800 bbls. ; val. of flour m'd. $78,000 ; cap., $10,000 ; emp., 7.

Tanneries, 1 ; Hides of all kinds tanned, 11,751 ; val. of leather tanned, $74,616 ; cap., $9,000 ; emp., 20.

Currying Establishments, 3 ; val. of leather curried, $121,252 ; cap., $16,000 ; emp., 34.

Manufactories of patent and enamelled leather, 1 ; val. of leather m'd., $103,122 ; cap., $13,000 ; emp., 18.

Bricks m'd., 2,890,000 ; val. of bricks, $22,500 ; emp., 48.

Val. of snuff, tobacco and cigars, $9,100 ; m. emp., 10 ; f. emp., 3.

Val. of blocks and pumps m'd., $1,800 ; emp., 2.

Lasts m'd., 125,000 ; val., $30,000.

Horses, 310 ; val. of horses, $30,710 ; Oxen over three years old, 16 ; Steers under three years old, – ; val. of oxen and steers, $1,090 ; Milch Cows, 252 ; Heifers, – ; val. of cows and heifers, $7,903.

Indian Corn, 52 acres ; Indian Corn, per acre, 30 bush. ; val., $1,560.

Rye, $38\frac{1}{4}$ acres ; Rye, per acre, 20 bush. ; val., $956.

Potatoes, 59 acres; Potatoes, per acre, 95 bush.; val., $2,803.

English Mowing, 816 acres; English Hay, 830 tons; val., $20,750.

Wet Meadow or Swale Hay, 30 tons; val., $300.

Salt Hay, 742 tons; val., $8,904.

Apple Trees, cultivated for their fruit, 8,233; val., $3,027.

Pear Trees, cultivated for their fruit, 2,407; val., $550.

Establishments for m. of fringe and tassels, 1; cap., $4,000; val. of fringe and tassels, $6,000; m. emp., 8; f. emp., 6.

Establishments for m. of India-rubber goods, 1; cap., $100,-000; val. of goods m'd., $225,000; m. emp., 65; f. emp., 75.

Bakeries, 1; cap., $6,000; Flour consumed, 3,240 bbls.; val. of bread m'd., $40,000; emp., 10.

Swine raised, 107; val., $1,605.

Val. of crops produced from 162 acres of "garden land," for the market, $14,160.

Quinces raised, 75 bush.; val., $150.

Milk produced, 94,500 qts.; val., $11,340.

Dye Houses, 1; cap., $20,000; val., $50,000; m. emp., 40; f. emp., 20.

Paper Stainery, 1; quantity stained, 150 tons; val., $112,000.

Land devoted to nurseries, 15 acres; sales per year, $1,500.

Grist Mills, 1; Grain ground, 150,000 bush.

MARLBOROUGH.

Saddle, Harness and Trunk Manufactories, 1; val. of sad dles, &c., $5,000; cap., $1,500; emp., 4.

Tin Ware Manufactories, 2; val. of tin ware, $5,800; cap., $2,000; emp., 4.

Tanneries, 1; Hides of all kinds tanned, 2,000; val. of leather tanned, $3,500; cap., $2,000; emp., 2.

Boots of all kinds m'd., 103,500 pairs; Shoes of all kinds m'd., 1,971,500 pairs; val. of boots and shoes, $1,156,975; m. emp., 969; f. emp., 973.

Val. of whips m'd., $150; emp., 1.

Lumber prepared for market, 300,000 ft.; val. of lumber, $4,200; emp., 6.

Firewood, prepared for market, 3,134 cords; val. of firewood, $14,003; emp., 6.

Horses, 441; val. of horses, $36,957; Oxen and Steers, 409; val. of oxen and steers, $19,861; Milch Cows and Heifers, 1,062; val. of cows and heifers, $33,568.

Butter, 49,916 lbs.; val. of butter, $12,474; Cheese, 9,180 lbs.; val. of cheese, $734.

Indian Corn, 636 acres; Indian Corn, per acre, 34½ bush.; val., $26,396.40.

Rye, 98 acres; Rye, per acre, 11½ bush.; val., $1,714.

Barley, 43 acres; Barley, per acre, 22¾ bush.; val., $973.

Oats, 157 acres; Oats, per acre, 27 bush.; val., $2,763.80.

Potatoes, 506 acres; Potatoes, per acre, 60 bush.; val., $22,628.

Carrots, 10 acres; Carrots, per acre, 420 bush.; val., $1,260.

Beets and other esculent vegetables, 10 acres; val., $200.

Millet, 4 acres; val., $60.

English Mowing, 3,229 acres; English Hay, 4,130 tons; val., $82,600.

Wet Meadow or Swale Hay, 770 tons; val., $7,700.

Apple Trees, cultivated for their fruit, 25,003; val., $16,015.

Pear Trees, cultivated for their fruit, 307; val., $302.

Cranberries, 50 acres; val. 468.

Bakeries, 1; cap., $2,000; Flour consumed, 750 bbls.; val. of bread m'd., $15,000; emp., 5.

Establishments for m. of boxes, 1; cap., $500; val. of boxes m'd., $2,000; emp., 3.

Swine raised, 211; val. of swine, $2,114.

Val. of peaches, $1,564.

Val. of quinces, $302.

Organ Manufactories, 1; val. of organs m'd., $2,000.

Milk sent to market, 49,702 galls.; val. of same, at 12 cts. per gall., $6,212.

MEDFORD.

Daguerreotype Artists, 1 ; Daguerreotypes taken, 1,500 ; cap., $300 ; emp., 1.

Saddle, Harness and Trunk Manufactories, 2 ; val. of saddles, &c., $7,000 ; cap., $2,000; emp., 10.

Hat and Cap Manufactories, 2 ; Hats and Caps m'd., $5,000 ; cap., $3,000 ; emp., 7.

Vessels launched during said year, 12 ; Tonnage, 11,882 tons ; cap., $108,000 ; emp., 1,005.

Establishments for m. of railroad cars, coaches, chaises, wagons, sleighs, and other vehicles, 2 ; val. of railroad cars, &c., m'd., $13,750 ; cap., $2,000 ; emp., 16.

Chair and Cabinet Manufactories, 1 ; val. of chairs and cabinet ware, $3,000 ; cap., $500 ; emp., 3.

Tin Ware Manufactories, 1 ; val. of tin ware, $12,000 ; cap., $4,000 ; emp., 5.

Currying Establishments, 1 ; val. of leather curried, $40,000 ; cap., $10,000 ; emp., 10.

Boots of all kinds m'd., – pairs ; Shoes of all kinds m'd., 30,000 pairs ; val., of boots and shoes, $30,000 ; m. emp., 30 ; f. emp., 15.

Bricks m'd., 1,800,000 ; val. of bricks, $14,400 ; emp., 24.

Val. of building stone quarried and prepared for building, $8,000 ; emp., 10.

Val. of blocks and pumps m'd., $400 ; emp., 1.

Firewood prepared for market, 475 cords ; val. of firewood, $2,375 ; emp., 8.

Alewives, Shad and Salmon taken, 45,000 bbls. ; val. of same, $13,500 ; emp., 40.

Horses, 251 ; val. of horses, $3,500 ; Oxen over three years old, 40 ; Steers under three years old, – ; val. of oxen and steers, $3,000 ; Milch Cows, 131 ; Heifers, 8 ; val. of cows and heifers, $1,750.

Butter, 600 lbs. ; val. of butter, $180.

Indian Corn, 75 acres; Indian Corn, per acre, 450 bush.; val., $500.

Rye, 65 acres; Rye, per acre, 235 bush.; val., $300.

Potatoes, 95 acres; Potatoes, per acre, 1,900 bush.; val., $1,710.

Turnips, cultivated as a field crop, 30 acres; Turnips, per acre, 200 bush.; val., $1,500.

Carrots, 20 acres; Carrots, per acre, 300 bush.; val., $1,800.

English Mowing, 1,000 acres; English Hay, 1,000 tons; val., $25,000.

Salt Hay, 540 tons; val., $800.

Apple Trees, cultivated for their fruit, 9,432; val., $2,358.

Pear Trees, cultivated for their fruit, 2,358; val., $4,716.

Establishments for m. of casks, 1; cap., $500; Casks m'd., 175; val., $1,800; emp., 2.

Establishments for m. of sashes, doors, and blinds, 2; cap., $55,000; val. m'd., $200,000; emp., 70.

Distilleries, 1; cap., $20,000; Alcohol distilled, – bbls.; all other Liquors distilled, 1,200 bbls.; val., $135,000; emp., 6.

Bakeries, 2; cap., $7,500; Flour consumed, 2,800 bbls.; val. of bread m'd., $70,000; emp., 16.

MELROSE.

Daguerreotype Artists, 1; Daguerreotypes taken, 850; emp., 1.

Establishments for m. of railroad cars, coaches, chaises, wagons, sleighs, and other vehicles, 2; val. of railroad cars, &c., md., $600; emp., 2.

Tin Ware Manufactories, 1; val. of tin ware, $2,500; emp., 2.

Currying Establishments, 1.

Boots of all kinds m'd., – pairs; Shoes of all kinds m'd., 130,186 pairs; val. of boots and shoes, $99,428; m. emp., 144; f. emp., 130.

Firewood prepared for market, 197 cords; val. of firewood, $837.

Horses, 94; val. of horses, $7,460; Oxen over three years old, 16; Steers under three years old, 10; val. of oxen and steers, $980; Milch Cows, 103; Heifers, 10; val. of cows and heifers, $2,603.

Butter, 1,000 lbs.; val. of butter, $200.

Indian Corn, 35½ acres; Indian Corn, per acre, 30 bush.; val., $1,066.

Rye, 9 acres; Rye, per acre, 12 bush.; val., $108.

Oats, 3⅝ acres; Oats, per acre, 20 bush.; val., $54.37.

Potatoes, 13 acres; Potatoes, per acre, 94 bush.; val., $1,222.

Onions, 1 acre; Onions, per acre, 200 bush.; val., $120.

Turnips, cultivated as a field crop, 2¾ acres; val., $500.

Beets and other esculent vegetables, 2½ acres; val., $400.

English Mowing, 328 acres; English Hay, 244¼ tons; val., $4,885.

Wet Meadow or Swale Hay, 90 tons; val., $9,000.

Apple Trees, cultivated for their fruit, 7,635; val., $961.

Pear Trees, cultivated for their fruit, 1,827; val., $101.

Val. of counting room desks m'd., $1,800; cap., unknown; emp., 1.

NATICK.

Daguerreotype Artists, 1; Daguerreotypes taken, 2,191; cap., $500; emp., 1.

Saddle and Harness Manufactories, 2; val., $2,100; cap., $500; emp., 3.

Cap Manufactories, 1; val. of caps m'd., $413; cap., $25; emp., 1.

Establishments for m. of railroad cars, coaches, chaises, wagons, sleighs and other vehicles, 3; val. of railroad cars, &c., m'd., $5,960; cap. $1,550; emp., 10.

Boots of all kinds m'd., 570 pairs ; Shoes of all kinds m'd., 1,281,295 pairs ; val. of boots and shoes, $1,163,808 ; m. emp., 1,070 ; f. emp., 497.

Firewood prepared for market, 1,001 cords ; val. of firewood, $4,246 ; emp., 3.

Saxony Sheep, of different grades, – ; Merino Sheep, of different grades, – ; all other kinds of Sheep, 2 ; val. of all sheep, $18 ; Wool produced from Saxony sheep, – lbs ; Merino Wool produced, – lbs. ; all other Wool produced, 11 lbs.

Horses, 256 ; val. of horses, $28,160 ; Oxen over three years old, 80 ; Steers under three years old, 10 ; val. of oxen and steers, $5,878 ; Milch Cows, 291 ; Heifers, 25 ; val. of cows and heifers, $9,975.

Butter, 18,159 lbs. ; val. of butter, $4,539 ; Cheese, 625 lbs. ; val. of cheese, $62 ; Honey, 92 lbs. ; val. of honey, $19.

Indian Corn, 271 acres ; Indian Corn, per acre, 31⅓ bush ; val., $8,491.

Rye, 51 acres ; Rye, per acre, 17 16/17 bush. ; val., $1,189.

Barley, 14½ acres ; Barley, per acre, 18½ bush. ; val., $268.

Oats, 56 acres ; Oats, per acre, 24 bush. ; val., $1,008.

Potatoes, 136 acres ; Potatoes, per acre, 91 bush. ; val., $10,625.

Onions, ⅞ acre ; Onions, per acre, 500 bush. ; val., $217.

Turnips, cultivated as a field crop, 2 acres ; Turnips, per acre, 295 bush. ; val., $218.

Carrots, 3¼ acres ; Carrots, per acre, 636 bush., val., $689.

Beets and other esculent vegetables, 61 acres ; val., $4,878 ; all other Grain or Root crops, 2 acres ; val., $31.

English Mowing, 1,226 acres ; English Hay, 1,312 tons ; val., $25,580.

Wet Meadow or Swale Hay, 375 tons ; val., $3,715.

Apple Trees, cultivated for their fruit, 5,580 ; val., $2,830.

Pear Trees, cultivated for their fruit, 310 ; val., $428.

Cranberries, 810 bush. ; val., $1,620.

Bakeries, 1 ; cap., $1,100 ; Flour consumed, 620 bbls. ; val. of bread m'd., $9,110 ; emp., 4.

Establishments for m. of shoe boxes, 2; cap., $5,500; val. of boxes m'd., $19,100; emp., 10.

Val. of fruit, $810.

White Beans, 253 bush.; val., $525.

Milk, 50,380 galls.; val., $7,035.

Swine raised, 68; val., $1,507.

Establishments for m. of Pulp for Paper, 1; Stock used, 490 tons; cap., $16,500; val. of pulp m'd., $70,475; emp., 12.

Establishments for m. of Shoe Fillings, 2; cap., $500; val., $1,500; emp., 3.

Establishments for m. of Clothing, 5; val. of clothing m'd., $30,800; cap., 5,500; emp., 61.

Val. of treenails or ship pins, $4,136.

Val. of ship timber, $1,730.

Val. of ship plank, $260; cap., $1,250; emp., 5.

NEWTON.

Cotton Mills, 1; Spindles, 12,000; Cotton consumed, 420,000 lbs.; Cloth m'd., 2,000,000 yds., Printing Cloth 3-4 yd. wide; val. of cloth, $100,000; cap., $100,000; m. emp., 75; f. emp., 85.

Mills for m. of painted carpeting, 1; Carpeting m'd., 65,000 yds.; val. of carpeting, $25,000; cap., $6,000; m. emp., 15.

Establishments for m. of hosiery, 4; Hosiery m'd., 4,912 doz. pairs; val. of hosiery, $24,828; cap., $11,200; m. emp., 25; f. emp., 19.

Rolling, Slitting and Nail Mills, 1; Iron m'd. and not made into nails, 2,244½ tons; val. of iron, $200,000; cap., $35,000; emp., 20.

Furnaces for m. of hollow ware and castings other than pig iron, 1; Hollow Ware and other Castings m'd., 200 tons; val. of hollow ware and castings, $15,000; cap., $5,000; emp., 8.

Establishments for m. of cotton, woollen and other machinery, 1; val. of machinery m'd., $74,890; cap., $50,000; emp., 80.

Paper Manufactories, 5; Stock made use of, 2,452,000 lbs.; Paper m'd., 1,676,000 lbs.; val. of paper,. $204,349; cap., $171,000; emp., 59.

Saddle, Harness and Trunk Manufactories, 2; val. of saddles, &c., $3,300; cap., $2,800; emp., 3.

Establishments for m. of railroad cars, coaches, chaises, wagons, sleighs, and other vehicles, 2; val. of railroad cars, &c., m'd., $1,900; cap., $900; emp., 3.

Establishments for m. of soap and tallow candles, 2; Soap, m,d., 120,000 lbs.; val. of soap, $8,000; Tallow Candles m'd., 520,752 lbs.; val. of tallow candles, $75,000; cap., $39,000; emp., 10.

Chair and Cabinet Manufactories, 1; val. of chairs and cabinet ware, $90,000; cap., $15,000; emp., 70.

Tin Ware Manufactories, 3; val. of tin ware, $7,200; cap., $3,500; emp., 9.

Glue Manufactories, and Manufactories for the preparation of Gums, 3; val. of glue and gums m'd., $16,800; cap., $4,300; emp., 10.

Tanneries, 1; Hides tanned, 65,000 goat skins; val. of leather tanned, $32,500; cap., $6,000; emp., 8.

Currying Establishments, 1; val. of morocco leather curried, $43,000; cap., $4,000; emp., 17.

Boots of all kinds m'd., 800 pairs; Shoes of all kinds m'd., 15,570 pairs; val. of boots and shoes $16,370; m. emp., 14; f. emp., 5.

Firewood prepared for market, 547 cords; val. of firewood, $2,336; emp., 2.

Saxony Sheep, of different grades, –; Merino Sheep, of different grades, –; all other kinds of Sheep, 4; val. of all sheep, $6.

Horses, 522; val. of horses, $60,036; Oxen over three years old, 100; Steers under three years old, –; val. of oxen and steers, $5,285; Milch Cows, 529; Heifers, 3; val. of cows and heifers, $17,235.

Butter, 6,766 lbs.; val. of butter, $1,827; Honey, 750 lbs.; val. of honey, $125; val. of milk sold, $16,587.

Indian Corn, 271 acres ; Indian Corn, per acre, $30\frac{20}{271}$ bush. ; val., $9,168.

Wheat, 1 acre ; Wheat, per acre, 10 bush. ; val., $25.

Rye, 143 acres ; Rye, per acre, $16\frac{95}{143}$ bush. ; val., $3,574.

Barley, $7\frac{1}{2}$ acres ; Barley, per acre, $19\frac{1}{3}$ bush. ; val., $163.

Oats, $5\frac{1}{4}$ acres ; Oats, per acre, $17\frac{11}{21}$ bush. ; val., $92.

Potatoes, 211 acres ; Potatoes, per acre, $84\frac{81}{211}$ bush. ; val., $17,805.

Onions, 4 acres ; Onions, per acre, $241\frac{3}{4}$ bush. ; val., $967.

Turnips, cultivated as a field crop, 47 acres ; Turnips, per acre, $137\frac{32}{47}$ bush. ; val., $2,157.

Carrots, 27 acres ; Carrots, per acre, $391\frac{16}{27}$ bush. ; val., $3,523.

Beets and other esculent vegetables, 167 acres ; val., $8,890.

Millet, 8 acres ; val., $160.

English Mowing, 1,923 acres ; English Hay, 2,191 tons ; val., $46,206.

Wet Meadow or Swale Hay, 362 tons ; val., $4,992.

Apple Trees, cultivated for their fruit, 21,461 ; val., $14,064 ; Apples, 23,440 bush.

Pear Trees, cultivated for their fruit, 2,263 ; val., $1,624 ; Pears, 812 bush.

Cranberries, 5 acres ; val., $224 ; Cranberries, 112 bush.

Establishments for m. of casks, 1 ; cap., $300 ; Casks m'd., 1,100 ; val., $900 ; emp., 1.

Bakeries, 1 ; cap., $4,500 ; Flour consumed, 650 bbls. ; val. of bread m'd., $14,000 ; emp., 6.

Swine raised, 399 ; val., $5,040.

Val. of corn fodder, $7\frac{1}{2}$ acres, $350.

Val. of corn fodder from field corn, 260 tons, $3,120.

Val. of oat and barley fodder, 24 tons, $432.

Val. of rye, oat and barley straw, 116 tons, $9,280.

Strawberries, 7,353 boxes ; val., $2,208.

Quinces, 30 bush. ; val., $40.

Cherries, 294 bush. ; val., $748.

Val. of blackberries, $114.

Val. of raspberries, $455.

Currants, 167 bush. ; val., $334.

Val. of grapes, $2,605.

Plums, 47 bush.; val., $155.

Establishments for m. of clothing, 2; val. of clothing m'd., $7,500; cap., $2,000; m. emp., 2; f. emp., 8.

Establishments for m. of horse shoes, 1; val. m'd., $1,425; cap., $500; emp., 1.

Establishments for grinding dye woods, 1; Wood ground, 1,200 tons; val., $48,000; cap., $12,000; emp., 12.

Establishments for m. of architectural ornaments, 1; val. m'd., from November, 1854, to June, 1855, $500; average val. m'd. per year, $4,000; cap., $1,500; emp., from November, 1854, to June, 1855, 1; usual number emp., 4.

Establishments for m. of tripe, –; val. of tripe prepared, $20,000; cap., $7,000; emp., 6.

Nurseries, 6; val. of trees sold, $3,750.

Cider m'd., 600 bbls.; val., $1,200.

Vinegar m'd., 125 bbls.; val., $500.

Tomatoes, 10½ acres; val., $2,625.

Lettuce, 1⅛ acre, a portion raised under glass; val., $775.

Asparagus, 2½ acres; val., $475.

Squashes, 103,000 lbs.; val., $1,242.

Cabbages, 35 acres; val., $4,222.

Beets, 9 acres; 1,590 bush.; val., $1,036.

Peas, 23 acres; val., $1,945.

Sweet Corn, 12 acres; val., $935.

Pickles, 10½ acres; val., $1,835.

Melons, 3¼ acres; val., $283.

String Beans, 6½ acres; val., $620.

Field Beans, 30 bush.; val., $60.

Parsnips, 5½ acres; val., $1,557.

Val. of rhubarb, $293.

Val. of garden seeds raised for market, $300.

Establishments for m. of ribbons and trimmings, 1; val. of ribbons m'd., $6,000; Fringes, $7,000; Dress and Cloak Trimmings, $25,000; cap., $20,000; m. emp., 16; f. emp., 35.

Establishments for m. of window and door frames, brackets and mouldings, 1; cap., $1,000; val. m'd., $2,500; emp., 2.

NORTH READING.

Chair and Cabinet Manufactories, 1; val. of chairs and cabinet ware, $3,500; cap., $1,000; emp., 4.

Boots of all kinds m'd., – pairs; Shoes of all kinds m'd., 127,000 pairs; val. of boots and shoes, $144,000; m. emp., 141; f. emp., 190.

Lumber prepared for market, 900,000 ft.; val. of lumber, $12,600; emp., 43.

Firewood prepared for market, 2,700 cords; val. of firewood, $13,500; emp. 32.

Horses, 73; val. of horses, $5,565; Oxen over three years old, 114; Steers under three years old, 18; val. of oxen and steers, $6,430; Milch Cows, 280; Heifers, 28; val. of cows and heifers, $7,781.

Butter, 11,295 lbs.; val. of butter, $2,824.

Indian Corn, 113 acres; Indian Corn, per acre, 36 bush.; val., $4,068.

Rye, 34 acres; Rye, per acre, 11 bush.; val., $561.

Barley, 7 acres; Barley, per acre, 18 bush.; val., $126.

Oats, 20 acres; Oats, per acre, 24 bush.; val., $362.

Potatoes, 77 acres; Potatoes, per acre, 93 bush.; val., $7,161.

Onions, ½ acre; Onions, per acre, 250 bush.; val., $62.

Turnips, cultivated as a field crop, ½ acre; Turnips per acre, 100 bush.; val., $12.

Beets and other esculent vegetables, 10 acres; val., $1,000.

English Mowing, 574 acres; English Hay, 516 tons; val., $10,320.

Wet Meadow or Swale Hay, 377 tons; val., $3,770.

Apple Trees, cultivated for their fruit, 3,491; val., $1,227.

Pear Trees, cultivated for their fruit, 168; val., $63.

Hops, 8 acres; Hops, per acre, 500 lbs.; val., $800.

Cranberries, 46¼ acres; val., $1,500.

PEPPERELL.

Woollen Mills, 1; Satinet m'd., 30,000 yds.; val. of satinet, $10,000.

Paper Manufactories, 4; Stock made use of, 1,725 tons; Paper m'd., 962 tons; val. of paper, $85,600; cap., $68,000; emp., 78.

Saddle, Harness and Trunk Manufactories, 1; val. of saddles, &c., $1,000; cap., $1,000; emp., 2.

Establishments for m. of chaises, wagons, sleighs, and other vehicles, 3; val. of chaises, wagons, &c., m'd., $5,500; cap., $3,000; emp., 10.

Chair and Cabinet Manufactories, 1; val. of chairs and cabinet ware, $600; cap., $500.

Boots and Shoes of all kinds m'd., 53,100 pairs; val. of boots and shoes, $53,100; m. emp., 60; f. emp., 50.

Lumber prepared for market, 301,000 ft. of boards; val. of lumber, $3,612.

Firewood, prepared for market, 595 cords; val. of firewood, $2,380.

Saxony Sheep, of different grades, –; Merino Sheep of different grades, –; all other kinds of Sheep, 100; val. of all sheep, $300; Wool produced, 300 lbs.

Horses, 225; val. of horses, $18,778; Oxen and Steers, 313; val. of oxen and steers, $14,385.50; Milch Cows and Heifers, 771; val. of cows and heifers, $18,974.31.

Butter, 48,405 lbs.; val. of butter, $12,112.25; Cheese, 11,075 lbs.; val. of cheese, $1,107; Honey, 2,000 lbs; val. of honey, $250.

Indian Corn, 379 acres; Indian Corn, per acre, 28 bush.; val., $13,336.25.

Wheat, 17 acres; Wheat, per acre, 13 bush.; val., $555.

Rye, 120 acres; Rye, per acre, $9\frac{1}{3}$ bush.; val., $1,698.

Barley, 3 acres; Barley, per acre, $16\frac{2}{3}$ bush.; val., $50.

Oats, 256 acres; Oats, per acre, $27\frac{3}{4}$ bush.; val., $4,311,60.

Carrots, $\frac{1}{8}$ acre; Carrots, per acre, 320 lbs. seed; val., $120.

Potatoes, 196 acres; Potatoes, per acre, 99 bush.; val., $11,692.20.

Millet, 4 acres; val., $60.

English Mowing, 1,854 acres; English Hay, 1,734 tons; val., $31,213.

Wet Meadow or Swale Hay, 653 tons; val., $5,877.

Apple Trees, cultivated for their fruit, 10,365; val., $2,776.25.

Pear Trees, cultivated for their fruit, 1,000.

Hops, 3,500 lbs; val., $875.

Establishments for m. of casks, 5; cap. $3,000; Casks m'd., 2,000; val., $1,600.

Establishments for m. of sashes, doors and blinds, 3; cap., $4,000; val. m'd., $3,000; emp., 4.

Cider m'd., 795 bbls.; val., $1,590.

Swine raised, 372; val., $8,184.

Val. of milk sold, $2,259.

Tobacco—"do not raise the filthy weed. It is of no value if we do."

READING.

Chair and Cabinet Manufactories, 13; val. of chairs and cabinet ware, $205,000; cap., $68,000; emp., 179.

Tin Ware Manufactories, 2; val. of tin ware, $10,000; cap., $2,500; emp., 7.

Boots of all kinds m'd., – pairs; Shoes of all kinds m'd., 287,000 pairs; val. of boots and shoes, $191,500; m. emp., 267; f. emp., 156.

Lumber prepared for market, 789,000 ft.; val. of lumber, $11,273; emp., 10.

Firewood prepared for market, 2,303 cords; val. of firewood, $10,643; emp., 8.

Horses, 169; val. of horses, $18,209; Oxen over three years old, 44; Steers under three years old, –; val. of oxen and

steers, $2,495; Milch Cows, 264; Heifers, 21; val. of cows and heifers, $8,295.

Butter, 15,110 lbs.; val. of butter, $3,777.50; Honey, 100 lbs.; val. of honey, $20.

Indian Corn, 106 acres; Indian Corn, per acre, 32½ bush.; val. $3,961.75.

Rye, 17 acres; Rye, per acre, 12½ bush.; val., $267.50.

Barley, 3 acres; Barley, per acre, 19 bush.; val., $57.

Oats, 6 acres; Oats, per acre, 23½ bush.; val., $84.60.

Potatoes, 46 acres; Potatoes, per acre, 80 bush.; val., $3,680.

Turnips, cultivated as a field crop, 2 acres; Turnips, per acre, 265 bush.; val., $198.75.

Carrots, 1 acre; Carrots, per acre, 480 bush.; val., $96.

Beets and other esculent vegetables, 6 acres; val., $750; all other Grain or Root Crops, 6 acres; val., $500.

English Mowing, 548 acres; English Hay, 630 tons; val., $13,860.

Wet Meadow or Swale Hay, 449 tons; val., $4,490

Apple Trees, cultivated for their fruit, 11,466; val., $5,892.

Pear Trees, cultivated for their fruit, 812; val., $275.

Cranberries, 44 acres; val., $1,833.

Establishments for m. of coach lace, 1; val. m'd., $4,000; cap., $2,000; f. emp., 10.

Establishments for m. of organ pipe, 1; val. m'd., $10,000; cap., $3,000; emp., 10.

Milk sold, 30,405 galls.; val., $4,864.80.

Quince Trees, 200; val. of quinces, $100.

Swine raised, 288; val., $7,200.

SHERBORN.

Establishments for m. of Shoe Knives, 2; val. of cutlery, $375; cap., $200; emp., 2.

Establishments for m. of wagons, 1; val. of wagons m'd., $1,800; cap., $3,000; emp., 4.

Boots of all kinds m'd., 40 pairs; Shoes of all kinds m'd., 97,445 pairs; val. of boots and shoes, $83,375; m. emp., 111; f. emp., 94.

Val. of straw braid m'd. and not made into bonnets and hats, $110; f. emp., 2.

Val. of whips m'd., $1,250; emp., 3.

Lumber prepared for market, 131,000 ft.; val. of lumber, $2,170; emp., 26.

Firewood prepared for market, 1,669 cords; val. of firewood, $15,353; emp., 45.

Horses, 148; val. of horses, $9,406; Oxen over three years old, 162; Steers under three years old, 25; val. of oxen and steers, $10,817; Milch Cows, 470; Heifers, 9; val. of cows and heifers, $13,489.

Butter, 28,186 lbs.; val of butter, 6,482; Cheese, 900 lbs.; val. of cheese, $72.

Indian Corn, 362 acres; Indian Corn, per acre, 30 bush.; val., $12,163.

Wheat, 15 acres; Wheat, per acre, 15 bush.; val., $450.

Rye, 53 acres; Rye, per acre, 17 bush.; val., $1,351.50.

Barley, 22 acres; Barley, per acre, 17 bush.; val., $299.20.

Oats, 91 acres; Oats, per acre, 30 bush.; val., $2,184.

Potatoes, 87 acres; Potatoes, per acre, 92 bush.; val., $8,004.

Carrots, 3 acres; Carrots, per acre, 520 bush.; val., $514.80.

Beets and other esculent vegetables, – acres; all other Grain or Root Crops, 24 acres; val., $1,482.

English Mowing, 1,366 acres; English Hay, 1,436 tons; val., $25,848.

Wet Meadow or Swale Hay, 681 tons; val., $6,810.

Apple Trees, cultivated for their fruit, 16,386; val., $7,427.

Pear Trees, cultivated for their fruit, 71; val., $105.

Basket Willow cultivated, 2 acres; val., $200.

Cranberries, 488½ acres; val., $2,228.

Val. of vinegar m'd., $7,090; cap., $8,500; emp., 12.

Val. of milk produced, $1,685.

Val. of beef raised, $9,795.

Val. of pork raised, $2,843.
Val. of peaches raised, $620.
Val. of plums raised, $162.
Val. of cherries raised, $220.

SHIRLEY.

Cotton Mills, 4; Spindles, 15,868; Cotton consumed, 723,332 lbs.; Cloth m'd., 2,000,000 yds., Sheetings 1 yd. wide; val. of cloth, $110,000; cap., $64,500; m. emp., 88; f. emp., 89.

Manufactories of shovels, spades, forks and hoes, 1; val. of shovels, &c., $27,000; cap., $300; emp., 12.

Paper Manufactories, 2; Paper m'd., 400 tons; val. of paper, $53,000; emp., 15.

Saddle, Harness and Trunk Manufactories, 1; val., of saddles, &c., given with the carriages.

Establishments for m. of wagons, sleighs, and other vehicles, 1; val. of wagons, sleighs, &c., m'd., $15,000; emp., 26.

Tin Ware Manufactories, 1; val. of tin ware, $300.

Boots of all kinds m'd., 120 pairs; Shoes of all kinds m'd., 3,600 pairs; val. of boots and shoes, $4,900; m. emp., 5.

Establishments for m. of straw bonnets and hats, 1; val. of straw bonnets m'd., $200; val. of palm leaf hats, $3,000.

Bricks, m'd., 300,000; val. of bricks, $1,500.

Val. of wooden ware not otherwise enumerated, including hand-spikes, m'd., $1,600; emp., 2.

Brooms m'd., 720 doz.; val., $2,160.

Lumber and Wood prepared for market, – ft.; val. of lumber and wood, $16,759.

Saxony Sheep, of different grades, –; Merino Sheep of different grades, –; all other kinds of Sheep, 17; val. of all sheep, $34; Wool produced from Saxony sheep, – lbs.; Merino Wool produced, – lbs.; all other wool produced, 100 lbs.

Horses, 145; val. of horses, $10,900; Oxen over three years old, 84; Steers under three years old, –; val. of oxen and

steers, $5,170; Milch Cows and Heifers, 261; val. of cows and heifers, $14,370.

Butter, 13,970 lbs.; val. of butter, $3,484; Cheese, 3,600 lbs.; val. of cheese, $293; Honey, 115 lbs.; val. of honey, $23.

Indian Corn, 231 acres; Indian Corn, per acre, 20 bush.; val., $4,625.

Wheat, 16½ acres; Wheat, per acre, 9 bush.; val., $297.

Rye, 57 acres; Rye, per acre, 6½ bush.; val., $569.

Oats, 37 acres; Oats, per acre, 19 bush.; val., $376.

Potatoes, 84½ acres; Potatoes, per acre, 70 bush.; val., $3,459.

Turnips and Carrots, cultivated as a field crop, – acres; Turnips and Carrots, per acre, 70 bush.; val., $360.

English Mowing and Meadow, 1,279 acres; English Hay and Meadow, 1,218 tons; val., $17,291.

Apple Trees, cultivated for their fruit, –; val., $2,231.

Hops, 37 acres; Hops, per acre, 481 lbs; val., $7,999.

Strawberries, 20 rods; val., $120.

Establishments for m. of sashes, doors and blinds, 1; val. m'd., $313; emp., 1.

Establishments for m. of pickles and preserves, 1; val. m'd., $1,000.

There are 15 machines in this town for making horse nails, put in operation last May.

Val. of rakes m'd., $1,500.

Val. of milk sold, $6,170.

Val. of garden seeds raised, $500.

SOMERVILLE.

Establishments for bleaching or coloring cotton goods, not connected with calico establishments, 2; Goods bleached and colored, 21,600,000 yds.; val. of goods, $1,728,000, after they are finished; the goods are m'd. and owned in other towns; cap., $87,500; emp., 80.

Rolling, Slitting and Spike Mills, 2, one of which commenced operation in March, 1855; val. of iron m'd., $84,000; Machines for m. of spikes, 5; Spikes m'd., 1,200 tons; val. of spikes, $108,000; cap., $15,000; emp., 50.

Establishments for m. of steam-engines and boilers, 1; val. of steam-engines and boilers, $20,000; cap., $12,000; emp., 30.

Brass Founderies, 1; val of articles m'd, (Brass Tubes,) $200,000, "rather unwilling to answer Assessors' questions"; cap., $100,000; emp., 40.

Glass Manufactories, 1; val. of glass m'd., $120,000; cap., $60,000; emp., 100.

Saddle, Harness and Trunk Manufactories, 1; val. of saddles, &c., $5,000; cap., $2,000; emp., 5.

Cordage Manufactories, 2; Cordage m'd., 54 tons; cap., $4,000; emp., 12.

Currying Establishments, 1; val. of leather curried, $16,000; cap., $1,500; emp., 4.

Bricks m'd., 17,000,000; val. of bricks, $220,000; emp., 220, about half of the year.*

Val. of building stone quarried and prepared for building, $15,000; emp., 16.

Val. of pumps m'd., $5,000; emp., 3.

Alewives taken, 300 bbls.; val. of same, $900; emp., 7, about two months.

Horses, 408; val. of horses, $36,720; Oxen over three years old, 14; Steers under three years old, –; val. of oxen and steers, $700; Milch Cows, 170; Heifers, 8; val. of cows and heifers, $5,180.

Indian Corn, 12 acres; Indian Corn, per acre, 50 bush.; val., $600.

Rye, 23 acres; Rye, per acre, 30 bush.; val., $600.

Potatoes, 20 acres; Potatoes, per acre, 70 bush.; val., $1,400.

* Of the foregoing Bricks m'd. in this town, the last year, 5,500,000 were by the Boston Press Brick Company, incorporated in 1853, cap., $150,000; using two steam-engines, and five patent presses. Many of the other establishments use horses for grinding the clay.

Beets and other esculent vegetables, 150 acres; val., $15,000; all other Grain or Root Crops, 28 acres; val., $2,500.

English Mowing, 350 acres; English Hay, 400 tons; val., $8,000.

Wet Meadow or Swale Hay, 10 tons; val., $100.

Salt Hay, 220 tons; val., $3,000.

Apple Trees, cultivated for their fruit, 4,000; val., $2,400.

Pear Trees, cultivated for their fruit, 1,000; val., $700.

Establishments for m. of stone and earthenware, 1; cap., $3,000; val. of stone and earthenware, $7,000; emp., 8.

Bakeries, 1; Flour consumed, 1,000 bbls.; val. of bread m'd., $20,000; cap., $2,000; emp., 7.

Establishments for preparing hair for sofas, chairs and cushions, 1; quantity prepared, 50 tons; val. of hair before preparation, $24,000; weight of hair after preparation, 45 tons; val. of hair after preparation, $28,000; cap., $2,000; emp., 9.

Establishments for m. of vinegar, –; quantity m'd., 3,000 bbls.; val., $15,000; cap., $12,000; emp., 6.

Steam Planing Mills, 1; Boards and Clapboards planed, 10,000,000 ft.; val., $200,000; cap., $7,500; emp., 4.

Two blacksmiths and two shoemakers only in town, and they are employed mostly on repairs.

Nurseries, 3; val. of trees, shrubs and flowers sold, $4,200; cap., $8,000; emp., 10.

A large part of the farms in this town have been cut up into house and building lots, within a few years, some of which lie common at this time, and many others are used for pasturing horses, cows, &c.

SOUTH READING.

Cordage Manufactories, 1; Cordage m'd., 5,500; cap., $800; emp., 5.

Tin Ware Manufactories, 3; val. of tin ware, $7,325; cap., $8,000; emp., 6.

Currying Establishments, 1; val. of leather curried, $8,000; cap., $1,000; emp. 3.

Boots of all kinds, m'd., 167,500 pairs; Shoes of all kinds m'd., 175,208 pairs; val. of boots and shoes, $318,013; m. emp., 366; f. emp., 334.

Val. of mechanics' tools m'd., $2,600; emp., 5.

Lumber prepared for market, 47,000 ft.; val. of lumber, $1,525; emp., 4.

Firewood prepared for market, 874 cords; val. of firewood, $4,335; emp., 19.

Horses, 165; val. of horses, $17,135; Oxen over three years old, 10; Steers under three years old, –; val. of oxen and steers, $750; Milch Cows, 209; Heifers, 20; val. of cows and heifers, $7,136.

Butter, 6,053 lbs.; val. of butter, $1,469; Cheese, 60 lbs.; val. of cheese, $10; Honey, 142 lbs.; val. of honey, $24.

Indian Corn, 69 acres; Indian Corn, per acre, 29½ bush.; val., $2,029.

Rye, 7½ acres; Rye, per acre, 20 bush.; val., $173.

Barley, 1½ acre; Barley, per acre, 24 bush.; val., $36.

Oats, 9 acres; Oats, per acre, 25 bush.; val., $153.

Potatoes, 52 acres; Potatoes, per acre, 64 bush.; val., $3,287.

Onions, – acre; Onions, per acre, – bush.; val., $40.

Turnips, cultivated as a field crop, 6½ acres; Turnips, per acre, 40 bush.; val., $150.

Carrots, 1½ acre; Carrots, per acre, 150 bush.; val., $172.

English Mowing, 458 acres; English Hay, 488 tons; val., $10,031.

Wet Meadow or Swale Hay, 288 tons; val., $1,708.

Apple Trees, cultivated for their fruit, 10,740; val., $5,277.

Pear Trees, cultivated for their fruit, 1,511; val., $295.

Cranberries, 73 acres; val., $735.

Establishments for m. of sashes, doors and blinds, 1; cap., $6,000; val. m'd., $9,000; emp., 6.

Bakeries, 1; cap., $1,000; Flour consumed, 500 bbls.; val. of bread m'd., $4,000; emp., 4.

Establishments for m. of boxes for shoes, 2; cap., $1,700; val. of boxes m'd., $2,700; emp., 3.

Val. of bitters m'd., $16,000; cap., $30,000; emp., 2.

Val. of razor strops m'd., $6,000; cap., $1,500; emp., 4.

Ice cut, 27,500 tons; val. of ice cut, $13,500; cap., $20,000; emp., 20.

STONEHAM.

Furnaces for m. of hollow ware and castings other than pig iron, 1; Hollow Ware and other Castings m'd., – tons; val. of hollow ware and castings, chiefly stoves, $30,000; cap., $10,000; emp., 40.

Brass Founderies, 1; val. of articles m'd., $12,000; cap., $5,000; emp., 15.

Establishments for m. of chemical preparations, 1; val. of chemical preparations, $100,000; cap., $25,000; emp., 12.

Saddle, Harness and Trunk Manufactories, 1; val. of saddles, &c., $1,200; cap., $300; emp., 1.

Tin Ware Manufactories, 1; val. of tin ware, $5,000; cap., $1,000; emp., 2.

Tanneries, 1; Hides of all kinds tanned, 5,000; val. of leather tanned, $30,000; cap. $6,000; emp., 7.

Currying Establishments, 3; val. of leather curried, $171,000; cap., $61,000; emp., 58.

Manufactories of patent and enamelled leather, 1; val. of leather m'd., $30,000; cap., $8,000; emp., 15.

Boots of all kinds m'd., – pairs; Shoes of all kinds m'd., 1,392,000 pairs; val. of boots and shoes, $729,160; m. emp., 1,106; f. emp., 651.

Sewing Machines for the m. of shoes, 43.

Blocks and Pumps m'd. [An establishment just commenced operation.]

Lumber prepared for market, 20 tons; val. of lumber, $240.

Firewood prepared for market, 328 cords; val. of firewood, $2,318. Work done by farmers, at intervals.

Horses, 97 ; val. of horses, $9,960 ; Oxen over three years old, 22 ; Steers under three years old, – ; val. of oxen and steers, $1,510 ; Milch Cows, 155 ; Heifers, 3 ; val. of cows and heifers, $5,715.

Butter, 2,600 lbs. ; val. of butter, $657 ; Honey, 12 lbs. ; val. of honey, $2.

Indian Corn, 57 acres ; Indian Corn, per acre, 29 bush. ; val., $1,662.

Rye, 12½ acres ; Rye, per acre, 14½ bush. ; val., $189.75.

Barley, 2 acres ; Barley, per acre, 16 bush. ; val., $19.

Potatoes, 46 acres ; Potatoes, per acre, 68 bush. ; val., $2,797.

Turnips, cultivated as a field crop, 1¼ acre ; Turnips, per acre, 192 bush ; val., $59.

Carrots, 2 acres ; Carrots, per acre, 242 bush. ; val., $109.

Beets and other esculent vegetables, white beans, – acres ; val., $191.

English Mowing, 636 acres ; English Hay, 560 tons ; val., $9,850.

Wet Meadow or Swale Hay, 154 tons ; val., $1,304.

Salt Hay, 64 tons ; val., $960.

Apple Trees, cultivated for their fruit, 8,466 ; val., $3,182.

Pear Trees, cultivated for their fruit, 1,671 ; val., $479.

Cranberries, 12 acres ; val., $44.

Establishments for m. of boxes, for shoes, 1 ; just commenced.

Val. of milk sold, $2,725.

Beef Cattle slaughtered, 350.

An establishment for the m. of razor strops has just commenced operations.

Shoe Bench Manufactories, 2 ; cap., $700 ; val. m'd., $1,500 ; emp., 4.

STOWE.

Woollen Mills, 1 ; Sets of Machinery, 6 ; Wool consumed, 150,000 lbs. ; Flannel or Blanketing, 600,000 yds. ; val. of flannel or blanketing, $125,000 ; cap., $60,000 ; m. emp., 43 ; f. mep., 32.

Saddle, Harness and Trunk Manufactories, 1; val. of saddles, &c., $1,500; cap., $400; emp., 3.

Tanneries, 1; Hides of all kinds tanned, 3,000; val. of leather tanned, $15,000; cap., $10,000; emp., 10.

Currying Establishments, 1.

Boots of all kinds m'd., – pairs; Shoes of all kinds m'd., 62,000 pairs; val. of boots and shoes, $27,200; m. emp., 25; f. emp., 36.

Lumber prepared for market, 190,000 ft.; val. of lumber, $3,040; emp., 2.

Firewood prepared for market, 1,586 cords; val. of firewood, $5,790; emp., 5.

Horses, 167; val. of horses, $12,576; Oxen over three years old, 188; Steers under three years old, 42; val. of oxen and steers, $11,505; Milch Cows, 592; Heifers, 28; val. of cows and heifers, $17,835.

Butter, 22,690 lbs.; val. of butter, $5,219; Cheese, 3,460 lbs.; val. of cheese, $277; Honey, 360 lbs.; val. of honey, $72.

Indian Corn, 316 acres; Indian Corn, per acre, 31 bush.; val., $11,265.40.

Rye, 85 acres; Rye, per acre, 11 bush.; val., $1,168.85.

Barley, 28 acres; Barley, per acre, 21 bush.; val., $588.

Oats, 132 acres; Oats, per acre, $25\frac{1}{2}$ bush.; val., $4,851.30.

Potatoes, 213 acres; Potatoes, per acre, 74 bush.; val., $11,821.50.

Turnips, cultivated as a field crop, 8 acres; Turnips, per acre, 250 bush.; val., $400.

Carrots, 4 acres; Carrots, per acre, 480 bush.; val., $480.

Millet, 18 acres; val., $258.

English Mowing, 1,387 acres; English Hay, 1,280 tons; val., $23,040.

Wet Meadow or Swale Hay, 758 tons; val., $7,580.

Apple Trees, cultivated for their fruit, 13,275; val., $6,125.

Hops, 4 acres; Hops, per acre, 650 lbs.; val., $650.

Cranberries, 42 acres; val., $1,119.

Milk produced, 55,404 cans; val., $13,851.

SUDBURY.

Mills for m. of carpeting. 1; Wool consumed, 240,000 lbs.; Carpeting m'd., 120,000 yds.; m. emp., 60; f. emp., 7.

Establishments for m. of worsted yarn, 1; Goods m'd., * yds.; val. of goods, *; Yarn m'd., and not made into cloth, 150,000 lbs.; val. of yarn, *; cap., *; m. emp., 12; f. emp., 35.

Paper Manufactories, 1; Stock made use of, 405,000 lbs.; Paper m'd., 270,000 lbs.; val. of paper, $30,000; cap., $13,000; emp., 12.

Boots of all kinds m'd., 800 pairs; Shoes of all kinds m'd., 5,700 pairs; val. of boots and shoes, $7,000; m. emp., 7.

Val. of straw braid m'd. and not made into bonnets and hats, $50.

Lumber prepared for market, 600,000 ft.; val. of lumber, $7,200; emp., 3.

Firewood prepared for market, 1,377 cords; val. of firewood, $4,820; emp., 3.

Horses, 213; val. of horses, $15,975; Oxen over three years old, 217; Steers under three years old, –; val. of oxen and steers, $10,850; Milch Cows, 629; Heifers –; val. of cows and heifers, $18,870.

Butter, 33,200 lbs.; val. of butter, $7,968; Cheese, 6,025 lbs.; val. of cheese, $421.75; Honey, 155 lbs.; val. of honey, $26.

Indian Corn, 9,472 bush.; val., $9,472.

Rye, 1,335 bush.; val., $1,669.

Barley, 62 bush.

Oats, 4,071 bush.; val., $2,442.

Potatoes, 20,414 bush.; val., $20,414.

Carrots, 767 bush.

* The Assessors report that the owner of this Mill declined answering the above questions. The value of the real estate, machinery and stock of the concern, on the first day of May last, by the Assessors' books, was $52,000.

English Hay, 1,393 tons; val., $27,860.

Wet Meadow or Swale Hay, 1,311 tons; val., $10,488.

Cranberries, 898 bush.; val., $1,796.

Swine raised, 268; val., $2,680.

Apples, raised for market, 6,903 bush.; val., $2,761.

Apples, of inferior quality, given to cattle, 9,832 bush.; val., $688.24.

Other kinds of fruit are cultivated only for domestic use, except in quantities not worth mentioning.

Milk sold, 10,398 galls.; val., $1,351.74.

Ice cut by Russell, Harrington & Co., at the establishment of Nathaniel J. Wyeth, Assabet Pond, 30,000 tons.

The Assessors report that the quantity per acre of grain and potatoes, in 1854, was less than usual, because of drought. On more than half the acres cultivated, the yield was not over 25 bush. of corn, 20 of oats, and 50 bush. of potatoes to the acre.

TEWKSBURY.

Chair and Cabinet Manufactories, 2; val. of chairs and cabinet ware, $29,000; cap., $10,400; emp., 21.

Tanneries, 4; Hides of all kinds tanned, 44,200; val. of leather tanned, $34,300; cap., $10,800; emp., 14.

Currying Establishments, 2; val. of leather curried, $40,000; cap., $4,000; emp., 6.

Charcoal m'd., 500 bush.; val. of same, $100.

Lumber prepared for market, 110,700 ft.; val. of lumber, $1,314; emp., 2.

Firewood prepared for market, 1,847 cords; val. of firewood, $7,848; emp., 12.

Saxony Sheep, of different grades, –; Merino Sheep, of different grades, –; all other kinds of Sheep, 17; val. of all sheep, $61; Wool produced from Saxony sheep, – lbs.; Merino Wool produced, – lbs.; all other Wool produced, 84 lbs.

Horses, 172; val. of horses, $5,012; Oxen over three years old, 127; Steers under three years old, 10; val. of oxen and steers, 7,550; Milch Cows, 394; Heifers, 94; val. of cows and heifers, $3,251.

Butter, 12,575 lbs.; val. of butter, $3,143.75; Honey, 250 lbs.; val. of honey, $37.50.

Indian Corn, 287$\frac{1}{2}$ acres; Indian Corn, per acre, 29$\frac{4}{115}$ bush.; val., $8,347.

Wheat, 1$\frac{1}{2}$ acre; Wheat, per acre, 14 bush.; val., $40.

Rye, 229$\frac{1}{2}$ acres; Rye, per acre, 9$\frac{15}{23}$ bush.; val., $2,780.

Barley, 6$\frac{1}{2}$ acres; Barley, per acre, 27 bush.; val., $157.50.

Oats, 108 acres; Oats, per acre, 22$\frac{17}{27}$ bush.; val., $1,466.40.

Potatoes, 194 acres; Potatoes, per acre, 71$\frac{78}{97}$ bush.; val., $11,144.

Onions, 4$\frac{1}{4}$ acres; Onions, per acre, 273 bush.; val., $696.

Turnips cultivated as a field crop, 24$\frac{1}{4}$ acres; Turnips, per acre, 187$\frac{61}{97}$ bush.; val., $1,365.

Carrots, 9$\frac{3}{4}$ acres; Carrots, per acre, 260 bush.; val., $633.75.

Beets and other esculent vegetables, 24$\frac{3}{4}$ acres; val., $3,135; all other Grain or Root Crops, 35 acres; val., $675.

English Mowing, 1,123 acres; English Hay, 1,184 tons; val., $23,680.

Wet Meadow or Swale Hay, 523 tons; val., $4,184.

Apple Trees, cultivated for their fruit, 4,530; val., $2,696.

Pear Trees, cultivated for their fruit, 48; val., $67.

Hops, 1$\frac{1}{2}$ acre; Hops, per acre, 800 lbs.; val., $300.

Cranberries, 57 acres; val., $841.

Breweries, 1; cap., $1,000; Beer m'd., sold by the bottle; val., $5,000; emp., 2.

Swine raised, 255; val., $1,530.

Establishments for m. of ladders, 1; cap., $600; val., $3,000; emp., 3.

Establishments for m. of buckskin gloves, 1; cap., $1,000; val., $2,800; m. emp., 1; f. emp., 6.

TOWNSEND.

Musical Instrument Manufactories, 2; val. of musical instruments m'd., (Melodeons and Reed Organs,) $34,000; cap., $4,600; emp., 26.

Saddle, Harness and Trunk Manufactories, 1; val. of saddles, &c., $2,500; cap., $800; emp., 2.

Establishments for m. of wagons, sleighs, and other vehicles, 2; val. of wagons, sleighs, &c., m'd., $2,500; cap., $1,200; emp., 3.

Cabinet Manufactories, 1; val. of cabinet ware, (Sofa frames,) $8,000; cap., $2,500; emp., 6.

Tin Ware Manufactories, 1; val. of tin ware, $3,000; cap., $700; emp., 3.

Flour Mills, 1; Flour m'd., 2,000 bbls.; val. of flour m'd., $24,000; cap., $3,000; emp., 1.

Tanneries, 1; Hides of all kinds tanned, morocco, 7,200; val. of leather tanned, $3,000; cap., $1,000; emp., 2.

Boots of all kinds m'd., 125 pairs; Shoes of all kinds m'd., 175 pairs; val. of boots and shoes, $674; f. emp., 2.

Val. of palm leaf hats m'd., $5,000.

Bricks m'd., 100,000; val. of bricks, $4,000; emp., 4, six weeks.

Val. of building stone quarried and prepared for building, $1,800; emp., 4.

Charcoal m'd., 2,000 bush.; val. of same, $180; emp., 2.

Val. of wooden ware not otherwise enumerated, including farming utensils m'd., $15,000; emp., 12.

Lumber prepared for market, 1,580,000 ft.; val. of lumber, $18,683; emp., 35.

Firewood prepared for market, 3,937 cords; val. of firewood, $11,822; emp., 25.

Saxony Sheep, of different grades, – ; Merino Sheep, of different grades, –; all other kinds of Sheep, 39; val. of all sheep, $82; Wool produced from Saxony sheep, – lbs.; Merino Wool produced, – lbs.; all other Wool produced, 136 lbs.

Horses, 235; val. of horses, $19,489; Oxen over three years old, 200; Steers under three years old, 45; val. of oxen and steers, $11,183; Milch Cows, 523; Heifers, 85; val. of cows and heifers, $15,824.

Butter, 36,950 lbs.; val. of butter, $7,390; Cheese, 4,175 lbs.; val. of cheese, $334.

Indian Corn, 377 acres; Indian Corn, per acre, 21 bush.; val., $7,917.

Wheat, 13 acres; Wheat, per acre, 13 bush.; val., $425.

Rye, 169¾ acres; Rye, per acre, 8 bush.; val., $2,037.

Barley, 11 acres; Barley, per acre, 18 bush.; val., $198.

Oats, 54 acres; Oats, per acre, 17 bush.; val., $550.80.

Potatoes, 185 acres; Potatoes, per acre, 73 bush.; val., $7,103.

Onions, ¼ acre; Onions, per acre, 400 bush.; val., $83.

Turnips, cultivated as a field crop, ½ acre; Turnips, per acre, 400 bush.; val., $50.

Carrots, 2 acres; Carrots, per acre, 426 bush.; val., $264.

English Mowing, 1,342 acres; English Hay, 1,242 tons; val., $21,114.

Wet Meadow or Swale Hay, 668 tons; val., $6,680.

Apple Trees, cultivated for their fruit, 6,048; val., $4,384.

Pear Trees, cultivated for their fruit, 373; val., $60.

Hops, 6 acres; Hops, per acre, 400 lbs.; val., $820.

Establishments for m. of casks, 6; cap., $16,700; Casks m'd., 367,550; val., $82,892; emp., 117.

Establishments for m. of sashes, doors and blinds, 1; cap., $300; val. m'd., $600; emp., 1.

Establishments for m. of bread boxes, 1; cap., $200; val. of boxes m'd., $600; emp., 1.

Book Binderies, 1; val. of books bound, $8,000; cap., $2,500; m. emp., 4; f. emp., 5.

Keg Staves and Headings m'd., 700,000; val., $4,500.

TYNGSBOROUGH.

Brushes m'd., 51,000; val. of brushes, $9,000; cap., $6,000; emp., 12.

Lumber prepared for market, 280,000 ft.; val. of lumber, $3,360.

Firewood prepared for market, 1,957 cords; val. of firewood, $8,096; emp., 6.

Saxony Sheep, of different grades, –; Merino Sheep of different grades, –; all other kinds of Sheep, 69; val. of all sheep, $207; Wool produced from Saxony sheep, – lbs.; Merino Wool produced, – lbs.; all other Wool produced, 158 lbs.

Horses, 105; val. of horses, $6,995; Oxen over three years old, 120; Steers under three years old, 71; val. of oxen and steers, $7,525; Milch Cows, 282; Heifers, 73; val. of cows and heifers, $9,722.

Butter, 16,530 lbs.; val. of butter, $4,131.50; Cheese, 2,668 lbs.; val. of cheese, $320.16.

Indian Corn, 158 acres; Indian Corn, per acre, 29 bush.; val., $5,817.50.

Wheat, 5¾ acres; Wheat, per acre, 8½ bush.; val., $122.

Rye, 85 acres; Rye, per acre, 8½ bush.; val., $1,119.

Barley, 1 acre; Barley, per acre, 6 bush.; val., $7.25.

Oats, 57 acres; Oats, per acre, 30 bush.; val., $1,033.80.

Potatoes, 84 acres; Potatoes, per acre, 105½ bush.; val., $8,418.

Onions, ½ acre; Onions, per acre, 200 bush.; val., $50.

Turnips cultivated as a field crop, ¾ acre; Turnips, per acre, 87½ bush.; val., $43.75.

Carrots, 1 acre; Carrots, per acre, 227½ bush.; val., $150.15.

English Mowing, 945 acres; English Hay, 903 tons; val., $18,060.

Wet Meadow or Swale Hay, 682 tons; val., $5,820.

Apple Trees, cultivated for their fruit, 6,881; val., $2,932.

Cranberries, 2 acres; val., $82.

WALTHAM.

Cotton Mills, 3; Spindles, 22,000; Cotton consumed, 1,181,-349 lbs.; Cloth m'd., 3,608,328 yds., Shirtings and Sheetings; val. of cloth, not given; cap., $350,000; m. emp., 185; f. emp., 428.

Establishments for bleaching cotton goods, not connected with calico establishments, 1; Goods bleached, 16,800,000 yds.; val. of goods, $1,300,000; cap., $100,000; emp., 140.

Furnaces for m. of hollow ware and castings other than pig iron, 1; Hollow Ware and other Castings m'd., 1,000 tons; val. of hollow ware and castings, $65,000; cap., $50,000; emp., 30.

Establishments for m. of cotton, woollen and other machinery, 1; val. of machinery m'd., $15,000; cap., $12,000; emp., 15.

Establishments for m. of chemical preparations, 2; val. of chemical preparations, $162,000; cap., $110,000; emp., 85.

Paper Manufactories, 1; Stock made use of, 400 tons; Paper m'd., 300 tons; val. of paper, $21,000; cap., $10,000; emp., 8.

Musical Instrument Manufactories, 1; val. of musical instruments m'd., $1,300; cap., $500; emp., 2.

Daguerreotype Artists, 2; Daguerreotypes taken, 2,700; cap., $1,000; emp., 4.

Establishments for m. of watches, 1; val. of watches, $80,000; cap., $80,000; emp., 70.

Harness Manufactories, 1; val. of harnesses, $2,000; cap., $1,000; emp., 2.

Hat Manufactories, 1; Hats and Caps m'd., 2,000; cap., $2,000; emp., 10.

Cordage Manufactories, 1; Cordage m'd., 1,000; cap., $200; emp., 1.

Establishments for m. of chaises, wagons, sleighs, and other vehicles, 2; val. of chaises, &c., m'd., $19,000; cap., $7,000; emp., 19.

Cabinet Manufactories, 2; val. of cabinet ware, $36,500 cap., $15,500; emp., 37.

Tin Ware Manufactories, 1; val. of tin ware, $6,000; cap., $1,000; emp., 4.

Boots of all kinds m'd., 2,500 pairs; Shoes of all kinds m'd., 56,450 pairs; val. of boots, $9,800; val. of shoes, $52,475; m. emp., 50; f. emp., 20.

Charcoal m'd., 6,200 bush.; val. of same, $1,000; emp., 1.

Val. of pumps m'd., $3,500; emp., 3.

Lumber prepared for market, 500,000 ft.; val. of lumber, $8,000; emp., 2.

Firewood prepared for market, 3,000 cords; val. of firewood, $18,000; emp., 10.

Horses, 332; val. of horses, $36,520; Oxen over three years old, 68; Steers under three years old, –; val. of oxen and steers, $4,250; Milch Cows, 561; Heifers, 26; val. of cows and heifers, $17,350.

Butter, 5,200 lbs.; val. of butter, $1,300.

Indian Corn, 284 acres; Indian Corn, per acre, 32½ bush.; val., $9,199.

Rye, 70 acres; Rye, per acre, 22 bush.; val., $1,931.25.

Barley, 29 acres; Barley, per acre, 23 bush.; val., $806.25.

Potatoes, 176 acres; Potatoes, per acre, 99½ bush.; val., $17,532.

Turnips, cultivated as a field crop, 33 acres; Turnips, per acre, 300 bush.; val., $1,962.

Carrots, 17 acres; Carrots, per acre, 400 bush.; val., $2,082.

Beets and other esculent vegetables, 10 acres; val., $1,308.

English Mowing, 1,761 acres; English Hay, 1,617 tons; val., $38,808.

Wet Meadow or Swale Hay, 429 tons; val., $5,148.

Apple Trees, cultivated for their fruit, 15,173; val., $5,775.20.

Pear Trees, cultivated for their fruit, 2,021; val., $579.

Cranberries, 20 acres; val., $400.

Establishments for m. of gas, 1; cap., $30,000; val. m'd., $7,500; emp., 2.

Bakeries, 1; cap., $5,000; Flour consumed, 725 bbls.; val. of bread m'd., $18,000; emp., 6.

Establishments for m. of boxes, (shoe and dry goods cases,) 1; cap., $8,000; val. of boxes m'd., $10,500; emp., 4.

Val. of school and tailors' crayons m'd., $3,800; val. of fancy iron furniture m'd., $2,000; val. of clothing m'd., $45,200; val. of books, $6,000; cap. invested in the above branches of industry, $9,000; emp., 94.

Squashes produced, 178,000 lbs.; val., $1,780.

Cherries produced, 735 bush.; val., $1,470.

Currants produced, 402 bush.; val., $804.

Quinces produced, 450 bush.; val., $675.

Cabbages produced, 90,350; val., $2,710.50.

Val. of milk sold, $33,270.

Pickles, 4,742,000; val., $5,927.50.

Val. of peas and beans, $2,732.

Tomatoes, 1,660 bush.; val., $830.

Val. of melons, $500.

Val. of strawberries, $1,470.

Val. of other cultivated berries, $420.

Val. of herbs, $1,050.

WATERTOWN.

Woollen Mills, 1; Sets of Machinery, 3; Wool consumed, 100,000 lbs.; Yarn m'd. and not made into cloth, 72,000 lbs.; val. of yarn, $50,400; cap., $30,000; m. emp., 20; f. emp., 4.

Establishments for m. of hosiery, 1; Hosiery m'd., 200 doz. shirts and drawers; val. of hosiery, $1,400; cap., $1,000; f. emp., 7.

Furnaces for m. of hollow ware and castings other than pig iron, 1; Hollow Ware and other Castings m'd., 480 tons; val. of hollow ware and castings, $36,000; cap., $30,000; emp., 30.

Axe Manufactories, 1; Axes, Hatchets and other Edge Tools m'd., 2,000; val., $2,000; cap., $1,000; emp., 3.

Starch Manufactories, 1; not in operation during the year.

Establishments for m. of chemical preparations, 1; val. of chemical preparations, $50,000; cap., $30,000; emp., 12.

Paper Manufactori s, 1; Stock made use of, 150 tons; Paper m'd., 105 tons; val. of paper, $10,500; cap., $6,000; emp., 7

Saddle, Harness and Trunk Manufactories, 1; val. of saddles, &c., $800; cap., $300; emp., 1.

Upholstery Manufactories, 3; val. of upholstery, $8,500; cap., $3,200; m. emp., 3; f. emp., 5.

Carriage Builders, 3; val. of carriages m'd., $8,700; cap., $3,000; emp., 9.

Chair and Cabinet Manufactories, 2; val. of chairs and cabinet ware, $4,000; cap., $2,200; emp., 3.

Tin Ware Manufactories, 2; val. of tin ware, $3,800; cap., $1,600; emp., 5.

Boots of all kinds m'd., 250 pairs; Shoes of all kinds m'd., 150 pairs; val. of boots and shoes, $1,300; m. emp., 4.

Val. of snuff, tobacco and cigars, $1,200; m. emp., 2.

Alewives taken, 100,000; val. of same, $300; emp., 5; val. of other fish taken, $1,200.

Horses, 360; val. of horses, $50,985; Oxen over three years old, 29; Steers under three years old, –; val. of oxen and steers, $1,780; Milch Cows, 235; Heifers, 15; val. of cows and heifers, $9,860; Swine raised, 394.

Indian Corn, 81½ acres; Indian Corn, per acre, 50 bush.; val., $4,830.

Wheat, 1 acre; Wheat, per acre, 20 bush.; val., $55.

Rye, 110 acres; Rye, per acre, 20 bush.; val., $2,750.

Barley, 5 acres; Barley, per acre, 20 bush.; val., $125.

Oats, 5 acres; Oats, per acre, 35 bush.; val., $131.25.

Potatoes, 113 acres; Potatoes, per acre, 160 bush.; val., $14,464.

Turnips, cultivated as a field crop, 25⅓ acres; Turnips, per acre, 300 bush.; val., $3,040.

Carrots, 18 acres; Carrots, per acre, 800 bush.; val., $3,600.

Beets and other esculent vegetables, 388 acres; val., $58,200.

English Mowing, 1,340 acres; English Hay, 1,415 tons; val., $28,300.

Wet Meadow or Swale Hay, 54 tons; val., $648.

Salt Hay, 45½ tons; val., $455.

Apple Trees, cultivated for their fruit, 14,602; val., $8,915.

Pear Trees, cultivated for their fruit, 1,560; val., $3,226.

Establishments for m. of sashes, doors and blinds, 2; cap., $8,000; val. m'd., $20,000; emp., 17.

Bakeries, 1; cap., $4,000; Flour consumed, 800 bbls.; val. of bread m'd., $16,000; m. emp., 6; f. emp., 2.

Establishments for m. of boot and shoe boxes, 1; cap., $800; val. of boxes m'd., $2,500; emp., 3.

Book Binding Establishments, 1; val. of binding done, $1,600; cap., $300; m. emp., 2; f. emp., 2.

Horse Collar Manufactories, 1; val. of collars m'd., $1,800; cap., $500; emp., 2.

Clothing Manufactories, 2; val. of clothing m'd., $3,000; cap., $750; m. emp., 2; f. emp., 3.

Shirt and Bosom Manufactories, 2; val. of shirts, &c., m'd., $90,000; cap., $45,000; m. emp., 5; f. emp., 398.

WAYLAND.

Forges, 2; Bar Iron, Anchors, Chain Cables, and other articles of wrought iron m'd., 8 tons; val. of bar iron, &c., $800; cap., $600; emp., 6.

Boots of all kinds m'd., - pairs; Shoes of all kinds m'd., 98,500 pairs; val. of boots and shoes, $82,600; m. emp., 87; f. emp., 42.

Firewood prepared for market, 534 cords; val. of firewood, $2,136; emp., 20.

Horses, 162; val. of horses, $14,434; Oxen over three years old, 121; Steers under three years old, 35; val. of oxen and steers, $4,473; Milch Cows, 387; Heifers, 32; val. of cows and heifers, $12,096.

Butter, 14,060 lbs.; val. of butter, $3,515; Cheese, 775 lbs.; val. of cheese, $67.75; Honey, 90 lbs.; val. of honey, $16.

Indian Corn, 312 acres; Indian Corn, per acre, 30 bush.; val., $10,296.

Rye, 104 acres; Rye, per acre, 12 bush.; val., $1,872.

Barley, 22 acres; Barley, per acre, 14 bush.; val., $308.

Oats, 55 acres; Oats, per acre, 22 bush.; val., $726.

Potatoes, 214 acres; Potatoes, per acre, 60 bush.; val., $12,840.

English Mowing, 1,223 acres; English Hay, 1,140 tons; val., $22,800.

Wet Meadow or Swale Hay, 1,078 tons; val., $8,624.

Apple Trees, cultivated for their fruit, 6,434; val., $4,518.

Pear Trees, cultivated for their fruit, 431; val., $609.

Cranberries, 44 acres; val., $1,263.

Breweries, 1; cap., $500; Beer m'd., 400 bbls.; val., $2,800; emp., 4.

WEST CAMBRIDGE.

Establishments for bleaching or coloring woollen goods, 1; val. of goods, $18,600; emp., 25.

Saddle, Harness and Trunk Manufactories, 2; val. of saddles, &c., $1,200; cap., $400; emp., 2.

Hat and Cap Manufactories, 1; Hats and Caps m'd., 1,800; cap., $3,000; emp., 6.

Card Manufactories, 1; val. of hand cards m'd., $2,000; cap., $1,000; emp., 2.

Establishments for m. of railroad cars, coaches, chaises, wagons, sleighs, and other vehicles, 2; val. of railroad cars, &c., m'd., $3,500; cap., $1,400; emp., 3.

Tin Ware Manufactories, 1; val. of tin ware, $2,000; cap., $1,200; emp., 1.

Boots of all kinds m'd., 550 pairs; Shoes of all kinds m'd., 3,100 pairs; val. of boots and shoes, $6,525; m. emp., 7; f. emp., 3.

Val. of mechanics' tools m'd., $1,000; emp., 1.

Horses, 401; val. of horses, $38,780; Oxen over three years old, 44; Steers under three years old, –; val. of oxen and

steers, $2,200 ; Milch Cows, 277 ; Heifers, 20 ; val. of cows and heifers, $7,225.

Indian Corn, 82 acres; Indian Corn, per acre, 25 bush. ; val., $2,050.

Rye, 36 acres ; Rye, per acre, 25 bush. ; val., $1,350.

Barley, 3 acres ; Barley, per acre, 25 bush. ; val., $75.

Potatoes, 57 acres ; Potatoes, per acre, 150 bush. ; val., $8,550.

Onions, 2 acres ; Onions, per acre, 500 bush. ; val., $750.

Turnips, cultivated as a field crop, 20 acres ; Turnips, per acre, 600 bush. ; val., $2,400.

Carrots, 9 acres ; Carrots, per acre, 500 bush. ; val., $1,350.

Beets and other esculent vegetables, 673 acres ; val., $122,335.

English Mowing, 950 acres ; English Hay, 1,145 tons ; val., $22,900.

Wet Meadow or Swale Hay, 259 tons ; val., $2,590.

Apple Trees, cultivated for their fruit, 13,667 ; val., $14,707.

Pear Trees, cultivated for their fruit, 757 ; val., $1,874.

Bakeries, 1 ; Flour consumed, 3,000 bbls. ; val. of bread m'd., $50,000 ; cap., $3,000 ; emp., 5.

Saw Manufactories, 1 ; val. of saws m'd., $40,000 ; cap., $30,000 ; emp., 35.

Ice cut, 61,500 tons ; val., $24,600.

WESTFORD.

Val. of building stone quarried and prepared for building, $25,000 ; emp., 50.

Lumber prepared for market, 200,000 ft. ; val. of lumber, $6,000 ; emp., 30.

Firewood prepared for market, 3,300 cords ; val. of firewood, $11,550 ; emp., 50.

Saxony Sheep, of different grades, – ; Merino Sheep, of different grades, – ; all other kinds of Sheep, 30 ; val. of all sheep, $100; Wool produced from Saxony sheep, - lbs.; Merino Wool produced, - lbs.; all other Wool produced, 120 lbs.

Horses, 194; val. of horses, $14,000; Oxen over three years old, 240; Steers under three years old, 48; val. of oxen and steers, $12,960; Milch Cows, 630; Heifers, 88; val. of cows and heifers, $20,124.

Butter, 36,000 lbs.; val. of butter, $9,000; Cheese, 2,470 lbs.; val. of cheese, $247; Honey, 20 lbs.; val. of honey, $3.60.

Indian Corn, 363 acres; Indian Corn, per acre, 20 bush.; val., $7,260.

Rye, 236 acres; Rye, per acre, 8 bush.; val., $2,078.

Barley, 20 acres; Barley, per acre, 20 bush.; val., $400.

Oats, 104 acres; Oats, per acre, 20 bush.; val., $1,248.

Potatoes, 118 acres; Potatoes, per acre, 75 bush.; val., $6,637.

Onions, 1 acre; Onions, per acre, 300 bush.; val., $150.

Carrots, 2 acres; Carrots, per acre, 500 bush.; val., $400.

Beets and other esculent vegetables, 2 acres; val., $1,000.

English Mowing, 1,788 acres; English Hay, 1,541 tons; val., $30,820.

Wet Meadow or Swale Hay, 1,074 tons; val., $12,888.

Apple Trees, cultivated for their fruit, 10,000; val., $10,000; Nursery Apple Trees, 30,000.

Pear Trees, cultivated for their fruit, 300; val, $100.

Hops, 4½ acres; Hops, per acre, 500 lbs.; val., $678.

Cranberries, 43 acres; val., $1,088.

Beeswax, 4 lbs.; val., $1.50.

Establishments for m. of boxes, 1; cap., $10,000; val. of boxes m'd., $9,000; emp., 6.

Swine raised, 374; val., $2,578.

Val. of milk sold, $10,000.

WESTON.

Establishments for m. of cotton, woollen and other machinery, 1; val. m'd., $26,000; cap., $10,000; emp., 26.

Manufactories of shovels, spades, forks and hoes, 1; val. of shovels, &c., $2,000; cap., $300; emp., 2.

Saddle, Harness and Trunk Manufactories, 1; val. of saddles, &c., $2,000; cap., $5,000; emp., 2.

Establishments for m. of wagons and other vehicles, 1; val. of wagons, &c., m'd., $1,500; cap., $500; emp., 2.

Chair and Cabinet Manufactories, 1; val. of chairs and cabinet ware, $5,000; cap., $1,000; emp., 8.

Tanneries, 1; Hides of all kinds tanned, 800; val. of leather tanned, $3,000; cap., $2,000; emp., 3.

Boots of all kinds m'd., 1,875 pairs; Shoes of all kinds m'd., -; val. of boots and shoes, $5,737.50; m. emp., 17.

Val. of mechanics' tools m'd., $3,300; emp., 7.

Firewood prepared for market, 1,000 cords; val. of firewood, $5,500; emp., 50, part the year.

Horses, 195; val. of horses, $13,650; Oxen over three years old, 154; Steers under three years old, 50; val. of oxen and steers, $7,160; Milch Cows, 463; Heifers, 100; val. of cows and heifers, $14,500.

Butter, 26,300 lbs.; val. of butter, $6,575.

Indian Corn, 339 acres; Indian Corn, per acre, 30 bush.; val., $12,204.

Wheat, 1 acre; Wheat, per acre, 25 bush.; val., $62.25.

Rye, 54 acres; Rye, per acre, 12 bush.; val., $972.

Barley, 40 acres; Barley, per acre, 15 bush.; val., $731.

Oats, 37 acres; Oats, per acre, 20 bush.; val., $518.

Potatoes, 206 acres; Potatoes, per acre, 75 bush.; val., $15,450.

Turnips, cultivated as a field crop, 2 acres; Turnips, per acre, 500 bush.; val., $500.

Carrots, 11 acres; Carrots, per acre, 450 bush.; val., $1,485.

Beets and other esculent vegetables, 2 acres; val., $200.

English Mowing, 1,607 acres; English Hay, 1,085 tons; val., $22,785.

Wet Meadow or Swale Hay, 570 tons; val., $7,410.

Apple Trees, cultivated for their fruit, 13,322; val., $6,471.

Pear Trees, cultivated for their fruit, 700; val., $229.

Cranberries, – acres; val., $370.

Establishments for m. of stone and earthenware, 1; val. of stone and earthenware, $1,500; cap., $1,000; emp., 4.

Bakeries, 1; cap., $4,000; Flour consumed, 600 bbls.; val. of bread m'd., $11,000; emp., 6.

Val. of strawberries, $800.

Val. of raspberries and other berries cultivated, $250.

Val. of grapes cultivated, $285.

Milk, 40,000 galls.; val., $5,600.

Val. of pickles, $1,000.

WILMINGTON.

Manufactories of patent and enamelled leather, 1; just commenced.

Val. of house pumps m'd., $2,000; emp., 2, part of the time.

Lumber prepared for market, 316,000 ft.; val. of lumber, $4,561.

Firewood prepared for market, 3,639 cords; val. of firewood, $13,533.

Saxony Sheep, of different grades, –; Merino Sheep, of different grades, –; all other kinds of Sheep, 2; val. of all sheep, $3.

Horses, 121; val. of horses, $8,790; Oxen, over three years old, 63; Steers under three years old, –; val. of oxen and steers, $3,660; Milch Cows, 259; Heifers, 7; val. of cows and heifers, $7,219.

Butter, 15,533 lbs.; val. of butter, $3,883.25.

Indian Corn, 115 acres; Indian Corn, per acre, 28½ bush.; val., $3,277.50.

Rye, 20 acres; Rye, per acre, 13 bush.; val., $390.

Barley, raised during the year, 32 bush.

Oats, 8 acres; Oats, per acre, 32½ bush.; val., $130.

Potatoes, 80 acres; Potatoes, per acre, 72½ bush.; val., $5,800.

Carrots, 3 acres; Carrots, per acre, 235 bush.; val., $176.25.

English Mowing, 553 acres; English Hay, 502 tons; val., $10,040.

Wet Meadow or Swale Hay, 523 tons; val., $4,184.

Apple Trees, cultivated for their fruit, 5,520; val., $1,800.

Hops, 5,680 lbs.; val., $1,684.

Cranberries, 887 bush.; val., $1,774.

Bakeries, 2; Flour consumed, 11,640 bbls.; val. of bread m'd., $220,000; emp., 32.

There are about twenty persons who butcher and sell meat a part of the time. About 2,000 head of cattle slaughtered.

WINCHESTER.

Establishments for m. of machinery, 1; val. of machinery m'd., $17,500; cap., $4,000; emp., 20.

Piano-Forte Manufactories, 5; Piano-Fortes m'd., 700 cases; cap., $23,700; val. of musical instruments m'd., $73,700; emp., 46.

Establishments for m. of railroad cars and other vehicles, 1; val. of vehicles m'd., $4,000; cap., $1,000; emp., 3.

Tin Ware Manufactories, 1; val. of tin ware, $500; cap., $600; emp., 1.

Tanneries, 1; Hides of all kinds tanned, $5,000; val. of leather tanned, $30,000; cap., $10,000; emp., in tanning and currying, 25.

Currying Establishments, 3, one connected with tannery; val. of leather curried, $120,000; cap., $25,000; emp., 25.

Horses, 142; val. of horses, $12,805; Oxen over three years

old, 58; Steers under three years old, –; val. of oxen and steers, $3,205; Milch Cows, 134; Heifers, 26; val. of cows and heifers, $4,427.

Butter, 1,225 lbs.; val. of butter, $306.

Indian Corn, 35 acres; Indian Corn, per acre, 31 bush.; val., $1,078.

Rye, 12 acres; Rye, per acre, 15 bush.; val., $225.

Potatoes, 33 acres; Potatoes, per acre, 100 bush.; val., $3,300.

Beets and other esculent vegetables, 52 acres; val., $10,365.

English Mowing, 450½ acres; English Hay, 403 tons; val., $8,060.

Wet Meadow or Swale Hay, 50 tons; val., $500.

Apple Trees, cultivated for their fruit, 10,447; val., $8,025.

Pear Trees, cultivated for their fruit, 3,818; val., $696.

Establishments for m. of felting, wadding, &c., 1; val. m'd., $10,000; cap., $10,000; emp., 3.

WOBURN.

Establishments for m. of hosiery, 1; Hosiery m'd., (Hose, Drawers and Shirts,) – pairs; val. of hosiery, $6,000; cap., $800; m. emp., 4; f. emp., 8.

Establishments for m. of cotton, woollen and other machinery, 2; val. of machinery m'd. and repairing done, $4,000; cap., $3,000; emp., 4.

Smiths' Shops, 4; val. of work done, $9,300; cap., $2,100; emp., 9.

Glass Manufactories, 1; val. of glass m'd., (Watch, Spectacle and Miniature Glass,) $16,000; cap., $8,000; m. emp., 8; f. emp., 6.

Establishments for m. of chemical preparations, 1; val. of chemical preparations, $50,000; cap., $20,000; emp., 10.

Establishments for m. of chronometers, watches, gold and

silver ware and jewelry, 1; val. of m's., $1,500; cap., $500; emp., 2.

Saddle, Harness and Trunk Manufactories, 3; val. of saddles, carriage trimmings, &c., $7,000; cap., $1,050; emp., 7.

Upholstery Manufactories, 1; val. of upholstery, $7,500; cap., $500; emp., 6.

Hat and Cap Manufactories, 1; Hats and Caps m'd., 3,600; val., $8,000; cap., $1,600; emp., 7.

Establishments for m. of sleighs and other vehicles, 3; val. of sleighs, &c., m'd., $7,000; cap., $3,500; emp., 10.

Establishments for m. of soap and tallow candles, 1; Soap m'd., 1,500 bbls. soft; val., $6,000; Hard Soap, 12 tons; val., $1,500; cap., $2,100; emp., 3.

Chair and Cabinet Manufactories, 2; val. of chairs and cabinet ware, $7,000; cap., $2,000; emp., 6.

Tin Ware Manufactories, 2; val. of tin ware and stove pipe, $6,000; cap., $2,700; emp., 2.

Comb Manufactories, 1; Combs m'd., 60,000 doz; val., $25,000; cap., $8,000; emp., 30.

Tanneries, 6; Hides of all kinds tanned and curried, 64,000; val. of leather tanned, $543,000; cap., $280,000; emp., 209.

Currying Establishments, 12; val. of leather curried, $203,048; cap., $55,100; emp., 71.

Manufactories of patent and enamelled leather, 6; val. of leather m'd., $314,200; cap., $61,700; emp., 110.

Establishments for m. of boots and shoes, 26; Boots of all kinds m'd., 70,255 pairs; Shoes of all kinds m'd., 284,429 pairs; val. of boots and shoes, $279,287; cap., $58,700; m. emp., 405; f. emp., 475.

Establishments for m. of straw bonnets and hats, 3; Straw Bonnets m'd., 720; val. of same, $2,160; f. emp., 8.

Val. of mechanics' tools m'd., $7,000; emp., 3.

Val. of saws, squares, bevels, and currier's tools, $35,000; emp., 18.

Val. of wooden ware not otherwise enumerated, including farming utensils m'd., (480 ships' buckets,) $240; emp., 1.

Lasts m'd., 1,250; val., $250.

Lumber prepared for market, 80,000 ft.; val. of lumber, $800; emp., 1.

Firewood prepared for market, 1,235 cords; val. of firewood, $6,670; emp., 20.

Horses, 229; val. of horses, $20,535; Oxen over three years old, 60; Steers under three years old, 2; val. of oxen and steers, $3,330; Milch Cows, 382; Heifers, 14; val. of cows and heifers, $11,161.

Butter, 9,431 lbs.; val. of butter, $2,357; Honey, 42 lbs.; val. of honey, $10.50.

Indian Corn, 144 acres; Indian Corn, per acre, 22 bush.; val., $3,168.

Wheat, 1 acre; Wheat, per acre, 7 bush.; val., $14.

Rye, 24 acres; Rye, per acre, 9½ bush.; val., $285.

Barley, 10 acres; Barley, per acre, 16 bush.; val., $160.

Oats, 2½ acres; Oats, per acre, 20 bush.; val., $35.

Potatoes, 106 acres; Potatoes, per acre, 67 bush.; val., $7,102.

Onions, 3 acres; Onions, per acre, 59 bush.; val., $106.20.

Turnips, cultivated as a field crop, 16 acres; Turnips, per acre, 400 bush.; val., $3,200.

Carrots, 10 acres; Carrots, per acre, 298 bush.; val., $1,490.

Beets and other esculent vegetables, 36 acres; val., $7,840; all other Grain or Root Crops, 25 acres; val., $1,850.

Marrow Squashes raised, 87,250 lbs.; val., $1,745.

English Mowing, 1,249 acres; English Hay, 1,068 tons; val., $23,496.

Wet Meadow or Swale Hay, 236 tons; val., $2,596.

Apple Trees, cultivated for their fruit, 16,462; val., $11,293.20.

Pear Trees, cultivated for their fruit, 2,752; val., $1,207.

Cranberries, 9 acres; val., $531.

Establishments for m. of sashes, doors and blinds, 1; val. m'd., $600; cap., $500; emp., 1.

Bakeries, 1; cap., $4,000; Flour consumed, 1,000 bbls.; val. of bread m'd., $22,000; emp., 11.

Establishments for m. of boxes, (fancy pasteboard,) 1; val. of boxes m'd., $2,000; cap., $500; m. emp., 2; f. emp., 2.

Swine raised, 1,014; val., $15,182.

Milk, 244,455 galls.; val., $8,555.92.

Peach Trees, 4,091; val. of peaches, $1,218.

Plum Trees, 522; val. of plums, $135.

Cherry Trees, 1,577; val. of cherries, $965.

Quince Trees, 1,949; val. of quinces, $542.

Grapes raised, 4,485 lbs.; val., $645.10; of these, 400 lbs. were raised in a green-house, and sold for $1 per lb.

Val. of currants, strawberries and raspberries, $480.

Establishments for m. of currier's tables and frames, 1; val. m'd., $2,000; cap., $200; emp., 1.

Establishments for dressing morocco and goat skins, 1; Skins dressed, 36,400; val., $27,297; cap., $5,000; emp., 16.

Establishments for m. of heel stiffening and soles, or boot and shoe counters, 1; val. m'd., $2,500; cap., $500; m. emp., 2; f. emp., 2.

Establishments for m. of clothing, 3; val. of clothing m'd., $20,000; cap., $3,400; m. emp., 9; f. emp., 24.

Establishments for m. of shoe patterns, 1; Patterns m'd., 1,250; val., $125; emp., 1.

NANTUCKET COUNTY.

NANTUCKET.

Shops for m. of rag carpeting, 2; Carpeting m'd., 2,392 yds.; val. of carpeting, $1,196; cap., $972; m. emp., 2; f. emp., 16.

Forges, 11; Bar Iron, Anchors, Chain Cables, and other articles of wrought iron, m'd., 36 tons; val. of bar iron, &c., $12,000; cap. $7,500; emp., 20.

Brass Founderies, 1; val. of articles m'd., $700; cap., $1,100; emp., 4.

Daguerreotype Artists, 1; Daguerreotypes taken, 1,200; cap., $700; emp., 2.

Saddle, Harness and Trunk Manufactories, 2; val. of saddles, &c., $1,200; cap., $900; emp., 4.

Hat and Cap Manufactories, 1; Hats and Caps m'd., $2,000; cap., $1,000; emp., 2.

Establishments for m. of boats, 4; Boats built, 99; cap., $3,480; emp., 12.

Masts and Spar Sheds, 1; Masts and Spars m'd., 89; cap., $600; emp., 2.

Sail Lofts, 3; Sails made of Am. fabric, 202; of For. fabric, 157; val. of sails m'd. of Am. fabric, $12,170; val. of sails of For. fabric, $6,405; cap., $750; emp., 15.

Establishments for m. of carts and wagons, 3; val. of carts and wagons m'd., $800; cap., $650; emp., 3.

Establishments for m. of oil and sperm candles, 7; Oil m'd., 1,038,344 galls., (970,828 whale and 67,516 sperm); val. of oil m'd., $768,529.40; Sperm Candles m'd., 142,450 lbs.; val. of sperm candles, $17,405; cap., $736,013; emp., 50.

Establishments for m. of soap and tallow candles, 2; Soap m'd., 32,000 lbs.; val. of soap, $2,170; cap., $900; emp., 3.

Chair and Cabinet Manufactories, 2; val. of chairs and cabinet ware, $250; cap., $500; emp., 4.

Tin Ware Manufactories, 5; val. of tin ware, $4,000; cap., $2,500; emp., 7.

Boots of all kinds m'd., 1,150 pairs; Shoes of all kinds m'd., 4,895 pairs; val. of boots and shoes, $10,275; m. emp., 11; f. emp., 20.

Establishments for m. of straw bonnets and hats, 1; Straw Bonnets m'd., 9,000; Straw Hats m'd, 138,000; m. emp., 2; f. emp., 237.

Val. of blocks and pumps m'd, $1,800; emp., 7.

Vessels employed in the whale fishery, 44; Tonnage, 14,266 tons; Sperm Oil imported, 175,700 galls.; val. of sperm oil imported, $251,512.55; Whale Oil imported, 261,739 galls.; val.

of whale oil imported, $146,049.82; Whalebone imported, 81,752 lbs.; val. of whalebone imported, $32,306.86; cap. in the whale fishery, $1,432,600; emp., 1,100.

Codfish taken in boats, 763 quintals; val. of codfish taken, $4,228; Salt consumed, 700 bush.; cap., $1,200; emp., 94.

Alewives taken, 70,000; val. of same, $700; emp., 20.

Saxony Sheep, of different grades, –; Merino Sheep, of different grades, –; all other kinds of Sheep, 1,201; val. of all sheep, $3,483; Wool produced from Saxony sheep, – lbs.; Merino Wool produced, – lbs.; all other Wool produced, 3,029 lbs.

Horses, 346; val. of horses, $34,665; Oxen over three years old, 62; Steers under three years old, 59; val. of oxen and steers, $4,512; Milch Cows, 548; Heifers, 205; val. of cows and heifers, $17,928.

Butter, 24,152 lbs.; val. of butter, $7,155.60.

Indian Corn, 380 acres; Indian Corn, per acre, 21 bush.; val., $7,895.70.

Wheat, 2½ acres; Wheat, per acre, 10 bush.; val., $37.50.

Rye, 13 acres; Rye, per acre, 9 bush.; val., $117.

Barley, 23 acres; Barley, per acre, 24 bush.; val., $644.

Oats, 66 acres; Oats, per acre, 19½ bush.; val., $772.20.

Potatoes, 72 acres; Potatoes, per acre, 108 bush.; val., $7,776.

Onions, 5 acres; Onions, per acre, 187 bush.; val., $561.

Turnips, cultivated as a field crop, 51 acres; Turnips, per acre, 152 bush.; val., $3,100.40.

Carrots, 17 acres; Carrots, per acre, 331½ bush.; val., $1,690.65.

Beets and other esculent vegetables, 95 acres; val., $9,535.

English Mowing, 1,425 acres; English Hay, 2,463 tons; val., $39,328.

Wet Meadow or Swale Hay, 179 tons; val., $1,790.

Salt Hay, 209 tons; val., $1,463.

Pear Trees, cultivated for their fruit, 6; val., $40.

Cranberries, 19¾ acres; val., $1,140.

Establishments for m. of casks, 9; cap., $11,500; Casks m'd., 20,250; val., $25,312; emp., 26.

Establishments for m. of gas, 1; cap., $40,000; val. m'd., $3,030.68; emp., 4.

Bakeries, 2; cap., $1,100; Flour consumed, 1,200 bbls; val. of bread m'd., $14,600; emp., 6.

Establishments for m. of candle and soap boxes, 2; cap., $640; val. of boxes m'd., $1,170; emp., 3.

Pollock taken, 700 quintals; val., $2,450; Salt consumed, 700 bush.

Oil from cod, pollock, and sharks, 65 bbls.; val., $1,300.

Bluefish taken, 700 bbls.; val., $4,900; Salt consumed, 1,050 bush.

Swordfish taken, 26 bbls.; val., $208.

Val. of fresh cod for market, $3,024; all other fish sold fresh, $3,235.

Quince Trees, 90; Quinces produced, 90 bush.; val., $135.

Cherry Trees, 21; Cherries produced, 10 bush; val., $44.

Strawberries, 1¼ acre; val., $310.

Swine raised, 541; val., $10,112.

Lambs sold for market, 130; val., $650.

Mules, 1; val., $50.

NORFOLK COUNTY.

BELLINGHAM.

Cotton Mills, 2; Spindles, 3,132; Cotton consumed, 117,000 lbs.; Cloth m'd., 284,000 yds. Superior 4 quartered Sheeting, between coarse and fine; val. of cloth, $22,700; Yarn m'd., 22,360 lbs.; val. of yarn, $3,577.60; cap., $3,000; m. emp., 20; f. emp., 20.

Woollen Mills, 1.

Brush Manufactories, 1; val. of brushes, $2,000; cap., $1,000; emp., 3.

Establishments for m. of boats, 2; Boats built, 66; cap., $500; emp., 4.

Glue Manufactories, and Manufactories for the preparation of Gums, 2; val. of glue and gums m'd., $2,000; cap., $800; emp., 7.

Boots of all kinds m'd., 61,900 pairs; Shoes of all kinds m'd., – pairs; val., of boots and shoes, $116,675; m. emp., 132; f. emp., 11.

Val. of straw braid m'd. and not made into bonnets and hats, $1,470; f. emp., 58.

Val. of wooden ware not otherwise enumerated, including arming utensils, m'd., $18,000; emp., 20.

Lumber prepared for market, 1,166,700 ft.; val. of lumber, $12,144.50; emp., 50.

Firewood prepared for market, 1,972 cords; val. of firewood, $6,883.50; emp., 30.

Horses, 156; val. of horses, $10,760; Oxen over three years old, 118; Steers under three years old, 28; val. of oxen and steers, $10,403; Milch Cows, 364; Heifers, 47; val. of cows and heifers, $11,860.

Butter, 21,170 lbs.; val. of butter, $5,267; Cheese, 2,855 lbs.; val. of cheese, $171.30; Honey, 505 lbs.; val. of honey, $84.

Indian Corn, 241 acres; Indian Corn, per acre, 24 bush; val., $5,784.

Rye, 94 acres; Rye, per acre, 9 bush.; val., $1,057.

Barley, 7 acres; Barley, per acre, 12 bush.; val., $84.

Oats, 100 acres; Oats, per acre, 24 bush.; val., $1,200.

Potatoes, 156 acres; Potatoes, per acre, 77 bush.; val., $6,000.

Turnips, cultivated as a field crop, 3 acres; Turnips, per acre, 40 bush.; val., $35.

Carrots, ¾ acre; Carrots, per acre, 120 bush., val., $50.

Beets and other esculent vegetables, 1 acre; val., $100.

English Mowing, 1,447 acres; English Hay, 858 tons; val., $17,160.

Wet Meadow or Swale Hay, 431 tons; val., $4,310.

Apple Trees, cultivated for their fruit, 6,005; val., $2,000.

Pear Trees, cultivated for their fruit, 260; val., $73.

All other kinds of fruit trees, 1,000; val., $300.

Val. of hops, $10.

Cranberries, 33 acres; val., $1,059.

Beeswax, 20 lbs.; val., $10.

Establishments for m. of boot, bonnet and hat boxes, 3; cap., $4,500; val. of boxes m'd., $12,400; emp., 10.

Swine raised, 273; val., $3,169.11.

BRAINTREE.

Woollen Mills, 1; Sets of Machinery, 4; Wool consumed, 52,000 lbs; Yarn m'd. and not made into cloth, 39,000 lbs.; val. of yarn, $32,000; cap., $15,000; m. emp., 9; f. emp., 7.

Mills for m. of carpeting, 1; Wool consumed, 16,000 lbs.; Carpeting m'd., 18,000 yds.; val. of carpeting, $20,500; cap., $25,000; m. emp., 45; f. emp., 8.

Tack Manufactories, 2; Coffin Tacks, &c., m'd., 108 tons; val. of tacks, $33,000; cap., $15,000; emp., 45.

Paper Manufactories, 1; Stock made use of, 350 tons; Paper m'd., 230 tons; val. of paper, $30,000; cap., $12,000; emp., 13.

Establishments for m. of railroad cars, coaches, chaises, wagons, sleighs, and other vehicles, 2; val. of railroad cars, &c., m'd., $16,000; cap., $6,000; emp., 20.

Chocolate Mills, 1; Chocolate m'd., 55,000 lbs.; cap., $3,000; emp., 3.

Tin Ware Manufactories, 1; val. of tin ware, $3,000; cap., $1,000; emp., 3.

Boots of all kinds m'd., 107,210 pairs; Shoes of all kinds m'd., 17,503 pairs; val. of boots and shoes, $237,252; m. emp., 281; f. emp., 185.

Val. of building stone quarried and prepared for building, $46,000 ; emp., 57.

Firewood prepared for market, 939 cords ; val. of firewood, $5,581.

Horses, 194 ; val. of horses, $16,591 ; Oxen over three years old, 78 ; Steers under three years old, – ; val. of oxen and steers, $5,473 ; Milch Cows, 423 ; Heifers, 48 ; val. of cows and heifers, $15,382.

Butter, 7,928 lbs. ; val. of butter, $1,924 ; Cheese, 525 lbs. ; val. of cheese, $57.

Indian Corn, 96 acres ; Indian Corn, per acre, 38½ bush. ; val., $3,548.

Rye, 10½ acres ; Rye, per acre, 15 bush. ; val., $219.

Potatoes, 76 acres ; Potatoes, per acre, 109 bush. ; val., $4,172.

Onions, 1 acre ; Onions, per acre, 150 bush. ; val., $110.

Turnips, cultivated as a field crop, 5 acres ; Turnips, per acre, 300 bush. ; val., $187.

Carrots, 3¼ acres ; Carrots, per acre, 450 bushels.

Beets and other esculent vegetables, 3 acres ; val., $220.

English Mowing, 1,214 acres ; English Hay, 1,008 tons ; val., $18,160.

Wet Meadow or Swale Hay, 355 tons ; val., $2,840.

Salt Hay, 175 tons ; val., $2,625.

Apple Trees, cultivated for their fruit, 5,328 ; val., $4,862.

Pear Trees, cultivated for their fruit, 813 ; val., $260.

Establishments for m. of twine and webbing, 1 ; Twine, &c., m'd., 3,000,000 lbs. ; cap., $50,000 ; m. emp., 25 ; f. emp., 50.

BROOKLINE.

Establishments for m. of hosiery, 1 ; Hosiery m'd., woollen ; val. of hosiery, $780 ; cap., $980 ; m. emp., 2.

Saddle, Harness and Trunk Manufactories, 2 ; val. of saddles, &c., $600 ; cap., $1,500 ; emp., 4.

Establishments for m. of railroad cars, coaches, chaises, wagons, sleighs, and other vehicles, 2; val. of railroad cars, &c., m'd., $5,000; cap., $1,800; emp., 6.

Tin Ware Manufactories, 1; val. of tin ware, $1,500; cap., $3,000; emp., 3.

Tanneries, 1; Hides of all kinds tanned, 3,500; val. of leather tanned, $12,000; cap., $12,000; emp., 4.

Currying Establishments, 1; val. of leather curried, $8,000; cap., $8,000; emp., 4.

Boots m'd., 540 pairs; shoes m'd., 250 pairs; val., $2,400; m. emp., 8.

Firewood prepared for market, 50 cords; val. of firewood, $400; emp., 2.

Horses, 453; val. of horses, $87,503; Oxen over three years old, 73; Steers under three years old, –; val. of oxen and steers, $4,548; Milch Cows, 239; Heifers, 31; val. of cows and heifers, $13,660.

Butter, 6,000 lbs.; val. of butter, $1,500.

Indian Corn, 69½ acres; Indian Corn, per acre, 40 bush.; val., $2,780.

Rye, 47½ acres; Rye, per acre, 30 bush.; val., $1,425.

Barley, 5 acres; Barley, per acre, 20 bush.; val., $100.

Potatoes, 70 acres; Potatoes, per acre, 204 bush.; val., $7,140.

Onions, 4¼ acres; Onions, per acre, 32 bush.; val., $652.

Turnips, cultivated as a field crop, 23 acres; Turnips, per acre, 210 bush.; val., $1,616.

Carrots, 29 acres; Carrots, per acre, 220 bush.; val., $2,112.

Beets and other esculent vegetables, 15½ acres; val., $1,000.

English Mowing, 958 acres; English Hay, 1,437 tons; val., $28,780.

Salt Hay, 153 tons; val., $1,530.

Apple Trees, cultivated for their fruit, 15,650; val., $8,450.

Pear Trees, cultivated for their fruit, 6,355; val., $4,673.

Establishments for m. of gas, 1; val. m'd., $5,000; cap., $50,000; emp., 3.

CANTON.

Cotton Mills, 5; Spindles, 11,448; Cotton consumed, 811,246 lbs.; Cloth m'd., 2,873,132 yds. of Printing Cloth; val. of cloth, $112,637.52; Yarn m'd., 37,500 lbs.; val. of yarn, $12,000; Twine m'd., $145,000 lbs.; val. of twine, $42,000; cap. $174,600; m. emp., 93; f. emp., 106.

Establishments for m. of worsted goods, or goods of which worsted is a component part, 1; Goods m'd., Fancy Worsted; val. of goods, $20,000; cap., $10,000; m. emp., 13; f. emp., 14.

Silk Manufactories, 1; Sewing Silk m'd., 13,000 lbs.; val. of sewing silk, $75,000; cap., $20,000; m. emp., 8; f. emp., 40.

Rolling, Slitting and Nail Mills, 1; Iron m'd. and not made into nails, 2,000 tons; val. of iron, $160,000; cap., $85,000; emp., 50.

Forges, 2; Bar Iron, Anchors, Chain Cables, and other articles of wrought iron m'd., 700 tons; val. of bar iron, &c., $77,000; cap., $80,000; emp., 40.

Furnaces for m. of hollow ware and castings other than pig iron, 1; Hollow Ware and other Castings m'd., 1,000 tons; val. of hollow ware and castings, $65,000; cap., $35,000; emp., 30.

Establishments for m. of cotton, woollen and other machinery, 2; val. of machinery m'd., $5,500; cap., $7,200; emp., 7.

Establishments for m. of cutlery, 2; val. of cutlery, $30,000; cap., $12,000; emp., 40.

Copper Manufactories, 1; Copper m'd., 1,000 tons; val., $10,000,000; cap., $90,000; emp., 60.

Piano-Forte Key Manufactories, 3; cap., $5,500; all other musical instrument manufactories, 1; val. of musical instruments m'd., $2,000; cap., $2,000; emp., 14.

Saddle, Harness and Trunk Manufactories, 2; val. of saddles, &c., $2,000; cap., $2,000; emp., 5.

Tin Ware Manufactories, 2; val. of tin ware, $6,000; cap., $6,000; emp., 5.

Boots of all kinds m'd., 500 pairs; Shoes of all kinds m'd., 1,000 pairs; val. of boots and shoes, $2,800; m. emp., 5; f. emp., 1.

Bricks m'd., 60,000; val. of bricks, $360; emp., 2.

Val. of mechanics' tools m'd., $500; emp., 1.

Firewood prepared for market, 2,674 cords; val. of firewood, $8,494; emp., 10.

Saxony Sheep, of different grades, –; Merino Sheep, of different grades, –; all other kinds of Sheep, 14; val. of all sheep, $45; Wool produced from Saxony sheep, – lbs; Merino Wool produced, – lbs.; all other Wool produced, 50 lbs.

Horses, 261; val. of horses, $23,900; Oxen over three years old, 51; Steers under three years old, 4; val. of oxen and steers, $2,875; Milch Cows, 406; Heifers, 72; val. of cows and heifers, $13,849.

Butter, 10,440 lbs.; val. of butter, $2,610; Cheese, 2,412 lbs.; val. of cheese, $147.70.

Indian Corn, 141 acres; Indian Corn, per acre, 23 bush.; val., $3,211.

Rye, 17 acres; Rye, per acre, 13 bush.; val., $175.

Barley, 14 acres; Barley, per acre, 10 bush.; val., $175.

Potatoes, 117 acres; Potatoes, per acre, 116 bush.; val., $13,616.

Onions, $\frac{1}{3}$ acre; Onions, per acre, 315 bush.; val., $96.

Turnips, cultivated as a field crop, 11$\frac{1}{2}$ acres; Turnips, per acre, 118 bush.; val., $339.

Carrots, 3 acres; Carrots, per acre, 386 bush.; val., $356.

English Mowing, 1,089 acres; English Hay, 836 tons; val., $17,540.

Wet Meadow or Swale Hay, 573 tons; val., $6,000.

Salt Hay, 8 tons; val., $125.

Apple Trees, cultivated for their fruit, 3,107; val., $2,668.

Pear Trees, cultivated for their fruit, 631; val., $316.

Cranberries, 94 acres; val., $4,716.

Establishments for m. of sashes, doors, and blinds, 1; cap., $5,000; val. m'd., $4,100; emp., 6.

Bakeries, 1; cap., $2,000; Flour consumed, 1,000 bbls.; val. of bread m'd., $2,000; emp., 7.

Establishments for m. of paper boxes, 1; cap., $1,000; val. of boxes m'd., $12,000; emp., 15.

Val. of printing presses m'd., $40,000; val. of curtain fixtures m'd., $4,000; cap., $17,000; emp., in both establishments, 36.

Swine raised, 327; val., $2,693.

COHASSET.

Daguerreotype Artists, 1; Daguerreotypes taken, 600; cap., $100; emp., 1.

Sail Lofts, 1; Sails made of Am. fabric, 12; val. of sails m'd. of Am. fabric, $753.70; cap., $100; emp., 1.

Establishments for m. of salt, 1; Salt m'd., 1,000 bush.; val. of salt, $500; cap., $700; emp., 1.

Establishments for m. of soap and tallow candles, 1; Soap m'd., 12 tons; val. of soap, $1,200; emp., 2.

Tin Ware Manufactories, 2; val. of tin ware, $4,500; emp., 3.

Boots of all kinds m'd., 500 pairs; Shoes of all kinds m'd., 1,000 pairs; val. of boots and shoes, $2,500; m. emp., 116; f. emp., 5.

Firewood prepared for market, 221 cords; val. of firewood, $1,371; emp., 25.

Vessels employed in the mackerel and cod fisheries, 26; Tonnage, 1,749 tons; Mackerel taken, 7,592¼ bbls.; val. of mackerel taken, $60,738.25; Salt consumed, 11,388⅜ bush.; cap., $76,245; emp., 331.

Saxony Sheep, of different grades, –; Merino Sheep, of different grades, –; all other kinds of Sheep, 150; val. of all sheep, $579; Wool produced from Saxony sheep, – lbs.; Merino Wool produced, – lbs.; all other Wool produced, 525 lbs.

Horses, 108; val. of horses, $7,955; Oxen over three years old, 91; Steers under three years old, 25; val. of oxen and steers, $4,630; Milch Cows, 187; Heifers, 11; val. of cows and heifers, $7,150.

Butter, 9,835 lbs.; val. of butter, $2,458.75; Cheese, 820 lbs.; val. of cheese, $82; Honey, 490 lbs.; val. of honey, $98.

Indian Corn, 80 acres; Indian Corn, per acre, 42 bush.; val., $3,360.

Wheat, 3¼ acres; Wheat, per acre, 15 bush.; val., $97.50.

Rye, 15 acres; Rye, per acre, 15 bush.; val., $281.25.

Barley, 10 acres; Barley, per acre, 20 bush.; val., $200.

Potatoes, 30 acres; Potatoes, per acre, 100 bush.; val., $3,000.

Onions, 4 acres; Onions, per acre, 160 bush.; val., $640.

Carrots, 5 acres; Carrots, per acre, 500 bush.; val., $630.

English Mowing, 612 acres; English Hay, 692 tons; val., $12,456.

Wet Meadow or Swale Hay, 120 tons; val., $1,100.

Salt Hay, 27 tons; val., $270.

Apple Trees, cultivated for their fruit, 4,934; val., $3,231.

Pear Trees, cultivated for their fruit, 252; val., $104.

Cranberries, 8 acres; val., $263.

Swine raised, 115; val., $870.

DEDHAM.

Cotton Mills, 2; Spindles, 4,972; Cotton consumed, 227,000 lbs.; Cloth m'd., 1,160,000 yds., Printing Cloth, Sheeting and Shirting; val. of cloth, $57,000; cap., $68,000; m. emp., 30; f. emp., 72.

Woollen Mills, 1; Sets of Machinery, 18; Wool consumed, 600,000 lbs.; Cassimere and Satinet m'd., 600,000 yds.; val. of cassimere and satinet, $400,000; cap., $200,000; m. emp., 100; f. mep., 200.

Furnaces for m. of hollow ware and castings other than pig iron, 2; Hollow Ware and other Castings m'd., 680 tons; val.

of hollow ware and castings, $43,000; cap., $21,000; emp., 23.

Establishments for m. of cotton, woollen and other machinery, 1; val. of machinery m'd., $10,000; cap., $3,000; emp., 4.

Saddle, Harness and Trunk Manufactories, 2; val. of saddles, &c., $3,000; cap., $1,000; emp., 4.

Hat and Cap Manufactories, 1; Hats and Caps m'd., 60; cap., $200; emp., 1.

Card Manufactories, 1; val. of playing cards m'd., $30,000; cap., $20,000; emp., 25.

Establishments for m. of railroad cars, coaches, chaises, wagons, sleighs, and other vehicles, 5; val. of railroad cars, &c., m'd., $9,500; cap., $3,400; emp., 22.

Sugar Refineries, 1; Sugar refined, 750 tons; val. of sugar, $56,250; emp., 20.

Establishments for m. of soap and tallow candles, 1; Soap, m'd., – lbs.; val. of soap, $8,000; cap., $2,000; emp., 2.

Chair and Cabinet Manufactories, 4; val. of chairs and cabinet ware, $185,000; cap., $82,800; emp., 235.

Tin Ware Manufactories, 3; val. of tin ware, $8,500; cap., $3,000; emp., 9.

Tanneries, 2; Hides of all kinds tanned, 300,000; val. of leather tanned, $78,750; cap., $30,000; emp., 22.

Currying Establishments, 1; val. of leather curried, $25,000; cap., $7,000; emp., 15.

Boots of all kinds m'd., 7,000 pairs; Shoes of all kinds m'd., 13,000 pairs; val. of boots and shoes, $20,000; m. emp., 55; f. emp., 13; 36 of the emp. are in the House of Correction.

Establishments for m. of straw bonnets and hats, 1; Straw Bonnets, m'd., 10,000; Straw Hats, m'd., 10,000; val. of straw braid m'd. and not made into bonnets and hats, $22,500; m. emp., 2; f. emp., 100.

Val. of whips m'd., $500; emp., 1.

Lumber prepared for market, 15,000 ft.; val. of lumber, $450.

Firewood prepared for market, 2,487 cords; val. of firewood, $9,111.

Saxony Sheep, of different grades, –; Merino Sheep, of different grades, –; all other kinds of Sheep, 3; val. of all sheep, $10.

Horses, 519; val. of horses, $42,526; Oxen over three years old, 125; Steers under three years old, 2; val. of oxen and steers, $7,155; Milch Cows, 965; Heifers, 26; val. of cows and heifers, $27,804.

Butter, 8,970 lbs.; val. of butter, $1,794; Cheese, 650 lbs.; val. of cheese, $81.25.

Indian Corn, 266 acres; Indian Corn, per acre, 40 bush.; val., $13,300.

Rye, 54½ acres; Rye, per acre, 15 bush.; val., $1,430.

Barley, 22 acres; Barley, per acre, 20 bush.; val., $605.

Oats, 2 acres; Oats, per acre, 45 bush.; val., $81.

Potatoes, 137 acres; Potatoes, per acre, 100 bush.; val., $13,700.

Onions, ½ acre; Onions, per acre, 360 bush.; val., $180.

Turnips, cultivated as a field crop, 16 acres; Turnips, per acre, 100 bush.; val., $320.

Carrots, 14¾ acres; Carrots, per acre, 420 bush; val., $1,548.75.

Beets and other esculent vegetables, 20 acres; val., $2,375.

English Mowing, 2,210 acres; English Hay, 2,082 tons; val., $45,804.

Wet Meadow or Swale Hay, 1,854 tons; val., $18,540.

Salt Hay, 30 tons; val., $420.

Apple Trees, cultivated for their fruit, 12,850; val., $5,891.

Pear Trees, cultivated for their fruit, 657; val., $284.

Cranberries, 76 acres; val., $1,634.

Establishments for m. of gas, 1; cap., $40,000; val. m'd., $6,000; emp., 3.

Bakeries, 1; cap., $1,500; Flour consumed, 1,300 bbls.; val. of bread m'd., $15,000; emp., 6.

Establishments for m. of painted carpets, 1; cap., $5,000; val. of carpets m'd., $20,000; emp., 8.

Milk, 249,035 galls.; val., $31,129.37.

Strawberries raised, 10,600 boxes; val., $2,120.

Peaches raised, 1,070 bush.; val., $2,140.

Beans raised, 100 bush.; val., $200.

DORCHESTER.

Cotton Mills, 1; Spindles, 5,376; Cotton consumed, 492,813 lbs.; Cloth m'd., 644,381 yds. of ticking; val. of cloth, $69,188; Yarn m'd., 206,937 lbs.; val. of yarn, $69,103; Warp m'd., 51,780 lbs.; val. of warp, $15,534. This Mill was burnt when it had been in operation 6 months.

Forges, 1; Bar Iron, Anchors, Chain Cables, and other articles of wrought iron m'd., 1,200 tons; val. of bar iron, &c., $96,000; cap., $35,000; emp., 54.

Furnaces for m. of hollow ware and castings other than pig iron, 1; Hollow Ware and other Castings m'd., 800 tons; val. of hollow ware and castings, $48,000; cap., $15,000; emp., 36.

Establishments for m. of britannia ware, 1; val. of britannia ware, $100,000; cap., $50,000; emp., 100.

Starch Manufactories, 1; Starch m'd. from wheat or flour, 722,000 lbs.; val. of starch, $64,800; cap., $45,000; emp., 25.

Paper Manufactories, 3; Stock made use of, 600,000 lbs.; Paper m'd., 20,000 reams; val. of paper, $75,000; cap., $25,000; emp., 41.

Saddle, Harness and Trunk Manufactories, 3; val. of saddles, &c., $5,900; cap., $1,600; emp., 6.

Cordage Manufactories, 1; Cordage m'd., 50,000; cap., $500; emp., 7.

Establishments for m. of railroad cars, coaches, chaises, wagons, sleighs, and other vehicles, 3; val. of railroad cars, &c., m'd., $51,400; cap., $8,500; emp., 32.

Establishments for m. of soap and tallow candles, 2; Soap m'd., 180,000 lbs.; val. of soap, $30,000; Tallow Candles m'd., 350,000 lbs.; val. of tallow candles, $35,000; cap., $10,000; emp., 9.

Chocolate Mills, 3; Chocolate m'd., 976,333 lbs.; cap., $30,000; emp., 40.

Chair and Cabinet Manufactories, 14; val. of chairs and cabinet ware, $193,600; cap., $62,250; emp., 204.

Tin Ware Manufactories, 3; val. of tin ware, $8,000; cap., $3,000; emp., 8.

Currying Establishments, 4; val. of leather curried, $19,200; cap., $4,800; emp., 9.

Boots of all kinds m'd., 800 pairs; Shoes of all kinds m'd., 825 pairs; val. of boots and shoes, $4,637; m. emp., 7.

Val. of building stone quarried and prepared for building, $12,000; emp., 20.

Val. of blocks and pumps m'd., $1,000; emp., 2.

Saxony Sheep, of different grades, 6; Merino Sheep, of different grades, –; all other kinds of Sheep and Lambs, 3; val. of all sheep, $105.

Horses, 747; val. of horses, $95,410; Oxen over three years old, 66; Steers under three years old, 6; val. of oxen and steers, $4,679; Milch Cows, 506; Heifers, 24; val. of cows and heifers, $21,013.

Indian Corn, 100¾ acres; Indian Corn, per acre, 68 bush.; val., $6,847.

Rye, 36 acres; Rye, per acre, 27 bush.; val., $1,191.

Barley, 10 acres; Barley, per acre, 32 bush.; val., $400.

Potatoes, 140 acres; Potatoes, per acre, 157 bush.; val., $23,992.

Turnips, cultivated as a field crop, 19 acres; Turnips, per acre, 813 bush.; val., $3,862.25.

Carrots, 20½ acres; Carrots, per acre, 800 bush.; val., $4,375.

Beets and other esculent vegetables, 78⅝ acres; val., $18,438.

English Mowing, 1,325 acres; English Hay, 1,917 tons; val., $38,340.

Wet Meadow or Swale Hay, 255 tons; val., $3,060.

Salt Hay, 416 tons; $4,992.

Apple Trees, cultivated for their fruit, 15,839; val., $11,262.

Pear Trees, cultivated for their fruit, 19,282; val., $8,019.

Establishments for m. of sashes, doors and blinds, 1; cap., $2,000; val. m'd., $12,000; emp., 15.

Bakeries, 2; cap., $3,400; Flour consumed, 850 bbls.; val. of bread m'd., $18,600; emp., 10.

Peach Trees, 1,842; val., of peaches, $736.

Cherries, 3,115 bush.; val., $6,230.

Strawberries, 4,495 boxes; val., $1,618,50.

Val. of raspberries, $30.

Plums, 222 bush.; val., $444.

Currants, 888 bush.; val., $1,776.

Swine raised, 877; val., $8,045.

Establishments for m. of refrigerators, 1; val. of refrigerators sold, $18,900; cap., $5,000; emp., 7.

Establishments for m. of clothing, 1; amount of sales, $7,000; cap., $1,000; emp., 10.

Establishments for m. of confectionery, 1; amount of sales, $30,000; cap., $5,000; emp., 13.

Establishments for m. of piano-forte hammers, 1; amount of sales, $6,000; cap., $500; emp., 6.

Flower Establishments, 5; amount of sales, $14,000; cap., $6,400; emp., 11.

Nurseries, 2; amount of sales, $4,200; emp., 4.

DOVER.

Brush Manufactories, 1; val. of brushes, $2,000; cap., $700; emp., 1.

Boots of all kinds m'd., 7,488 pairs; Shoes of all kinds m'd., 300 pairs; val. of boots and shoes, $14,000; m. emp., 15; f. emp., 4.

Val. of snuff, tobacco and cigars, $3,000; m. emp., 3; f. emp., 1.

Val. of building stone quarried and prepared for building, $200; emp., 1.

Charcoal m'd., 12,000 bush.; val. of same, $2,374; emp., 8.

Val. of whips m'd., $450; emp., 3.

Val. of wooden ware not otherwise enumerated, including farming utensils m'd., $1,000; emp., 2.

Lumber prepared for market, 5,182 ft.; val. of lumber, $81; emp., 1, one month.

Firewood prepared for market, 1,379 cords; val. of firewood, $4,705; emp., 5.

Saxony Sheep, of different grades, –; Merino Sheep, of different grades, –; all other kinds of Sheep, 10; val. of all sheep, $52; Wool produced from Saxony sheep, – lbs.; Merino Wool produced, – lbs.; all other Wool produced, 24 lbs.

Horses, 94; val. of horses, $7,525; Oxen over three years old, 58; Steers under three years old, –; val. of oxen and steers, $3,472; Milch Cows, 250; Heifers, 31; val. of cows and heifers, $7,726.

Butter, 11,299 lbs.; val. of butter, $2,706.50; Cheese, 1,340 lbs.; val. of cheese, $133.30; Honey, 124 lbs.; val. of honey, $23.33.

Indian Corn, 137 acres; Indian Corn, per acre, $34\frac{24}{137}$ bush.; val., $4,753.75.

Wheat, $\frac{3}{4}$ acre; Wheat, per acre, 17 bush.; val., $34.

Rye, $31\frac{1}{2}$ acres; Rye, per acre, $10\frac{1}{4}$ bush.; val., $416.

Barley, $10\frac{3}{4}$ acres; Barley, per acre, $18\frac{1}{4}$ bush.; val., $180.25.

Oats, 28 acres; Oats, per acre, $19\frac{1}{4}$ bush.; val., $331.70.

Potatoes, 64 acres; Potatoes, per acre, $81\frac{1}{6}$ bush.; val., $4,554.90.

Onions, $\frac{1}{8}$ acre; Onions, 120 bush.; val., $96.

Turnips, cultivated as a field crop, $1\frac{3}{4}$ acre; Turnips, per acre, 193 bush.; val., $48.

Carrots, $1\frac{1}{8}$ acre; Carrots, per acre, $293\frac{1}{3}$ bush.; val., $79.12.

Millet, $\frac{1}{2}$ acre; val., $4.

English Mowing, 840 acres; English Hay, 633 tons; val., $11,762.

Wet Meadow or Swale Hay, 356 tons; val., $3,450.

Apple Trees, cultivated for their fruit, 5,730; val., $2,414.

Pear Trees, cultivated for their fruit, 100; val., $40.

Cranberries, $34\frac{3}{4}$ acres; val., $767.

Beeswax, 20 lbs.; val., $8.

Establishments for m. of casks, 1; cap., $1,000; Casks m'd., 26,000; val., $5,000; emp., 7.

Swine raised, 76; val., $687.

Beans, 12 acres; 120 bush.; val., $300.

Milk sold, 20,787 galls.; val., $2,286.57.

FOXBOROUGH.

Cotton Mills, 2; Spindles, 800; Cotton consumed, 68,000 lbs.; Yarn m'd., 40,000 lbs.; val. of yarn not given; Thread m'd., 16,000 lbs.; val. of thread, $7,000; Batting m'd., 3,000 lbs.; val. of batting, $250; cap., $10,500; m. emp., 6; f. emp., 10.

Establishments for bleaching or coloring cotton goods, not connected with calico establishments, 1; Goods bleached or colored, 20,000 lbs.; val. of goods, not known; cap., $2,500; emp., 3.

Furnaces for m. of hollow ware and castings other than pig iron, 1; Hollow Ware and other Castings m'd., 350 tons; val. of hollow ware and castings, $27,000; cap., $7,000; emp., 25.

Saddle, Harness and Trunk Manufactories, 1; val. of saddles, &c., $1,000; cap., $500; emp., 2.

Establishments for m. of railroad cars, coaches, chaises, wagons, sleighs, and other vehicles, 1; val. of railroad cars, &c., m'd., $4,500; cap., $1,500; emp., 6.

Tin Ware Manufactories, 1; val. of tin ware, $800; cap., $500; emp., 1.

Boots of all kinds m'd., 250 pairs; Shoes of all kinds m'd., 800 pairs; val. of boots and shoes, $1,425; m. emp., 2.

Establishments for m. of straw bonnets and hats, 1; Straw Bonnets m'd., 1,100,000; Straw Hats m'd., 900,000; m. emp., 250; f. em. 3,000.

Val. of building stone quarried and prepared for building, $1,300; emp., 4.

Charcoal m'd., 22,300 bush.; val. of same, $2,398; emp., not known.

Lumber prepared for market, 277,000 ft.; val. of lumber, $3,926.

Firewood prepared for market, 2,134 cords; val. of firewood, $7,669.

Saxony Sheep, of different grades, –; Merino Sheep of different grades, –; all other kinds of Sheep, 9; val. of all sheep, $27; Wool produced from Saxony sheep, – lbs.; Merino Wool produced, – lbs.; all other wool produced, 36 lbs.

Horses, 226; val. of horses, $22,245; Oxen over three years old, 88; Steers under three years old, 13; val. of oxen and steers, $5,073; Milch Cows, 351; Heifers, 34; val. of cows and heifers, $10,922.

Butter, 15,635 lbs.; val. of butter, $3,909; Cheese, 1,840 lbs.; val. of cheese, $184; Honey, 419 lbs.; val. of honey, $52.

Indian Corn, 180 acres; Indian Corn, per acre, 28 bush.; val., $5,040.

Rye, 17 acres; Rye, per acre, 12 bush.; val., $300.

Barley, 5 acres; Barley, per acre, 17 bush.; val., $85.

Oats, 10 acres; Oats, per acre, 20 bush.; val., $130.

Potatoes, 90 acres; Potatoes, per acre, 95 bush.; val., $6,450.

Turnips, cultivated as a field crop, 5 acres; Turnips, per acre, 200 bush.; val., $333.

Carrots, 1½ acre; Carrots, per acre, 600 bush.; val., $225.

English Mowing, 1,312 acres; English Hay, 843 tons; val., $16,860.

Wet Meadow or Swale Hay, 392 tons; val., $4,704.

Apple Trees, cultivated for their fruit, 10,000; val., $2,600.

Pear Trees, cultivated for their fruit, 630; val., $142.

Cranberries, 48 acres; val., $1,113.

Bakeries, 1; cap., $3,000; Flour consumed, 650 bbls.; val. of bread m'd., $11,000; emp., 7.

Establishments for m. of boxes, principally for bonnets and hats, 2; cap., $15,200; val. of boxes m'd., $14,500; emp., 15.

Hoops m'd., 470,000; val., $9,600.

Val. of baskets m'd., $505.

Val. of milk sold, $3,300.

Val. of ice sold, $500.

Val. of clothes dryers m'd. and sold, $375.

Val. of jewelry m'd., $45,000.

Straw Braid trimmed and pressed, 1,092,000 yds.; val of labor on the same, $855.

FRANKLIN.

Cotton Mills, 4—3 not in operation; Spindles, 3,724; Cotton consumed, 15,672 lbs.; Thread m'd., 12,000 lbs.; val. of thread, $3,840; Batting m'd., 40,000 lbs.; val. of batting, $4,000; cap., $2,500; m. emp., 5; f. emp., 3.

Establishments for m. of boats, –; Boats built, 88; cap., $550; emp., 5.

Establishments for m. of wagons, sleighs, and other vehicles, 2; val. of wagons, &c., m'd., $800; cap., $400; emp., 3.

Tin Ware Manufactories, 1; val. of tin ware, $1,000; cap., $1,000; emp., 2.

Boots of all kinds m'd., 20,000 pairs; Shoes of all kinds m'd., – pairs; val. of boots and shoes, $35,000; m. emp., 70.

Establishments for m. of straw bonnets and hats, 6; Straw Bonnets and Hats m'd., 579,160; val. of straw braid m'd. and not made into bonnets and hats, $2,000; val. of straw bonnets and hats, $405,000; m. emp., 96; f. emp., 1,578.

Lumber prepared for market, 752,416 ft.; val. of lumber, $9,000; emp., 55.

Firewood prepared for market, 1,979 cords; val. of firewood, $7,748; emp., 69.

Saxony Sheep, of different grades, –; Merino Sheep, of different grades, –; all other kinds of Sheep, 19; val. of all sheep, $53; Wool produced from Saxony sheep, – lbs.; Merino Wool produced, – lbs.; all other Wool produced, 57 lbs.

Horses, 206; val. of horses, $14,503; Oxen over three years old, 172; Steers under three years old, 56; val. of oxen and steers, $10,265; Milch Cows, 485; Heifers, 76; val. of cows and heifers, $13,738.

Butter, 21,325 lbs.; val. of butter, $5,311; Cheese, 3,990 lbs.; val. of cheese, $317; Honey, 65 lbs; val. of honey, $13.

Indian Corn, 386 acres; Indian Corn, per acre, 20 bush.; val., $8,496.

Wheat, $1\frac{1}{4}$ acre; Wheat, per acre, 12 bush.; val., $18.75.

Rye, 107 acres; Rye, per acre, 8 bush.; val., $1,284.

Barley, 7 acres; Barley, per acre, 19 bush.; val., $133.

Oats, 149 acres; Oats, per acre, 20 bush.; val., $1,728.

Potatoes, 166 acres; Potatoes, per acre, 95 bush.; val., $9,604.

Turnips, cultivated as a field crop, 11 acres; Turnips, per acre, 50 bush.; val., $137.50.

Carrots, 2½ acres; Carrots, per acre, 254 bush.; val., $315.

Millet, 8 acres; val., $102.

English Mowing, 1,879 acres; English Hay, 1,030 tons; val., $20,600.

Wet Meadow or Swale Hay, 701 tons; val., $5,608.

Apple Trees, cultivated for their fruit, 6,644; val., $3,322.

Pear Trees, cultivated for their fruit, 70; val., $45.

Cranberries, 105 acres; val., $3,175.

Beeswax, 3 lbs.; val., $1.

Establishments for m. of boot, bonnet and thread boxes, 4; cap., $4,000; val. of boxes m'd., $6,836.83; emp., 10.

Swine raised, 307; val., $3,124.

Val. of bonnet wire m'd., $10,000; cap., $1,000; emp., 3.

White Beans, 25 acres; Beans, per acre, 8½ bush.; val., $540.

MEDFIELD.

Manufactories of shovels, spades, forks and hoes, 1; val. of shovels, &c., $6,000; cap., $1,000; emp., 8.

Brush Manufactories, 2; val. of brushes, $6,500; cap., $6,000; emp., 5.

Establishments for m. of railroad cars, coaches, chaises, wagons, sleighs and other vehicles, 2; val. of railroad cars, &c., m'd., $11,000; cap. $2,700; emp., 8.

Tin Ware Manufactories, 1; val. of tin ware, $7,800; cap., $2,000; emp., 6.

Tanneries, 1; Hides of all kinds tanned, 1,400; val. of leather tanned, $5,000; cap. $1,000; emp., 2.

Establishments for m. of straw bonnets and hats, 2; Straw Bonnets m'd., 360,000; Straw Hats m'd., 408,000; val. of straw braid m'd. and not made into bonnets and hats, $60,000; m. emp., 165; f. emp., 570.

Firewood prepared for market, 850 cords; val. of firewood, $3,825; emp., 20.

Horses, 129; val. of horses, $11,000; Oxen over three years old, 96; Steers under three years old, 24; val. of oxen and steers, $5,795; Milch Cows, 363; Heifers, 39; val. of cows and heifers, $11,305.

Butter, 10,566 lbs.; val. of butter, $2,642.

Indian Corn, 175 acres; Indian Corn, per acre, 30 bush.; val., $5,250.

Wheat, 6 acres; Wheat, per acre, 15 bush.; val., $180.

Rye, 47 acres; Rye, per acre, 12 bush.; val., $700.

Barley, 33 acres; Barley, per acre, 20 bush.; val., $660.

Oats, 26 acres; Oats, per acre, 12 bush.; val., $187.

Potatoes, 75 acres; Potatoes, per acre, 80 bush.; val., $5,000.

English Mowing, 674 acres; English Hay, 674 tons; val., $13,480.

Wet Meadow or Swale Hay, 684 tons; val., $5,472.

Apple Trees, cultivated for their fruit, 3,275; val., $1,386.

Cranberries, 110 acres; val., $3,750.

Establishments for m. of sashes, doors and blinds, 1; val. m'd., $600; cap., $200; emp., 1.

Bakeries, 1; cap., $2,000; Flour consumed, 200 bbls.; val. of bread m'd., $20,000; emp., 8.

Swine raised, 110; val., $1,400.

MEDWAY.

Cotton Mills, 4, (one other Mill, burned Dec. last, containing 1,200 spindles); Spindles, 2,424; Cotton consumed, 3,555,000 lbs.; Thread m'd., 35,000 lbs.; val. of thread, $21,500; Batting m'd., 1,630,000 lbs.; val. of batting, $163,000; Pelisse

Wadding m'd., 24,000 bales; val. of wadding, $36,640; Flannel m'd., 450,000 yds.; val. of flannel, $38,250; cap., $175,000; m. emp., 64; f. emp., 60.

Establishments for bleaching or coloring cotton goods, not connected with calico establishments, 1; Goods bleached or colored, 23,400 lbs.; val. of goods, $8,200; emp., 2. This establishment has been destroyed by fire. The above returns are for six months only.

Establishments for m. of hosiery, –; Yarn m'd., and not made into hosiery, 6,240 lbs.; val. of yarn, $2,500; m. emp., 3; f. emp., 2, six months.

Establishments for m. of cotton, woollen and other machinery, 1; val. of machinery m'd., $2,000; cap., $3,000; emp., 3.

Paper Manufactories, 2; Stock made use of, 1,475,000 lbs.; Paper m'd., 1,200,000 lbs.; val. of paper, $55,125; cap., $22,000; emp., 15.

Piano-Forte Manufactories, 1; Piano-Fortes m'd., 2; all other musical instrument manufactories, 2; val. of musical instruments m'd., $7,000; emp., 9.

Upholstery Manufactories, 2; val. of upholstery, $13,600; cap., $2,000; emp., 13.

Establishments for m. of railroad cars, coaches, chaises, wagons, sleighs, and other vehicles, 2; val. of railroad cars, &c., m'd., $1,100; cap., $1,600; emp., 3.

Chair and Cabinet Manufactories, 2; val. of chairs and cabinet ware, $1,000; cap., $2,000; emp., 4, part of time.

Tin Ware Manufactories, 1; val. of tin ware, $300; emp., 2, part of time.

Boots of all kinds m'd., 100,275 pairs; Shoes of all kinds m'd., 2,000 pairs; val. of boots and shoes, $155,000; m. emp., 246; f. emp., 61.

Establishments for m. of straw bonnets and hats, 2; Straw Bonnets m'd., 100,000; m. emp., 20; f. emp., 180.

Bricks, m'd., 450,000; val. of bricks, $2,700; emp., 6.

Lumber prepared for market, 975,000 ft.; val. of lumber, $13,500; emp., 16.

Firewood prepared for market, 2,765 cords; val. of firewood, $11,280; emp. 16.

Horses, 331; val. of horses, $29,580; Oxen over three years old, 198; Steers under three years old, 26; val. of oxen and steers, $12,230; Milch Cows, 640; Heifers, 24; val. of cows and heifers, $18,580.

Butter, 30,480 lbs.; val. of butter, $7,620; Cheese, 4,090 lbs.; val. of cheese, $409; Honey, 280 lbs.; val. of honey, $56.

Indian Corn, 379 acres; Indian Corn, per acre, 26 bush.; val., $12,100.

Wheat, 4 acres; Wheat, per acre, 15 bush.; val., $150.

Rye, 52 acres; Rye, per acre, 11 bush.; val., $846.

Barley, 8 acres; Barley, per acre, 16 bush.; val., $96.

Oats, 101 acres; Oats, per acre, 24 bush.; val., $1,595.

Potatoes, 129 acres; Potatoes, per acre, 102 bush.; val., $13,160.

Onions, 28 bush.; val., $21.

Turnips, cultivated as a field crop, 270 bush; val., $67.

Carrots, –; Carrots, per acre, 210 bush.; val., $420.

Beets and other esculent vegetables, – acres; val., $50.

English Mowing, 1,776 acres; English Hay, 1,573 tons; val., $31,460.

Wet Meadow or Swale Hay, 1,060 tons; val., $10,600.

Apple Trees, cultivated for their fruit, 11,500; val., $4,080; Apples, 10,300 bush.

Pear Trees, cultivated for their fruit, 387; val., $112.

Cranberries, 73 acres; val., $2,600.

Bakeries, 1; Flour consumed, 250 bbls.; val. of bread m'd., $3,000; cap., $600; emp., 5.

Establishments for m. of boot and bonnet boxes, 3; val. of boxes m'd., $13,000; emp., 9.

Swine raised, 434; val., $5,090.

Church Bells m'd., 50,000 lbs.; val., $16,000; emp., 2.

Bonnet Wire m'd., 1,000,000 yds.; val., $4,000; emp., 3.

Milk sold from 100 cows; val., $2,500.

MILTON.

Paper Manufactories, 1; Stock made use of, 150 tons; Paper m'd., 100 tons; val. of paper, $25,000; cap., $50,000; emp., 30.

Saddle, Harness and Trunk Manufactories, 1; val. of saddles, &c., $600; cap., $400; emp., 2.

Chocolate Mills, 1; Chocolate m'd., 120,000 lbs.; cap., $30,000; emp., 6.

Chair and Cabinet Manufactories, 3; val. of chairs and cabinet ware, $24,000; cap., $13,500; emp., 26.

Tanneries, 1; Hides of all kinds tanned, 4,000; val. of leather tanned, $8,000; cap., $5,000; emp., 7.

Boots of all kinds m'd., 1,400 pairs; Shoes of all kinds m'd., 800 pairs; val. of boots and shoes, $4,500; m. emp., 4; f. emp., 1.

Val. of building stone quarried and prepared for building, $50,000; emp., 70.

Lumber prepared for market, 6,000 ft.; val. of lumber, $275; emp., 1.

Firewood prepared for market, 1,050 cords; val. of firewood, $4,700; emp., 14.

Horses, 374; val. of horses, $37,400; Oxen over three years old, 70; Steers under three years old, –; val. of oxen and steers, $5,000; Milch Cows, 491; Heifers, 70; val. of cows and heifers, $18,000.

Butter, 3,600 lbs.; val. of butter, $1,000; Cheese, – lbs.; val. of cheese, $500; Honey, 100 lbs.

Indian Corn, 150 acres; Indian Corn, per acre, 40 bush.; val., $6,000.

Rye, 50 acres; Rye, per acre, 20 bush.; val., $1,250.

Barley, 17 acres; Barley, per acre, 20 bush.; val., $300.

Oats, 15 acres; Oats, per acre, 25 bush.; val., $225.

Potatoes, 130 acres; Potatoes, per acre, 100 bush.; val., $13,000.

Turnips, cultivated as a field crop, 20 acres; Turnips, per acre, 250 bush.; val., $1,250.

Carrots, 19 acres; Carrots, per acre, 300 bush.; val., $1,200.

English Mowing, 1,395 acres; English Hay, 1,400 tons; val., $28,000.

Wet Meadow or Swale Hay, 325 tons; val., $3,000.

Salt Hay, 320 tons; val., $4,000.

Apple Trees, cultivated for their fruit, 8,700; val., $7,500.

Pear Trees, cultivated for their fruit, 1,417; val., $600.

Cranberries, 25 acres; val., $350.

Establishments for m. of preserves, 1; cap., $800; val. m'd., $2,000; emp., 2.

Bakeries, 3; cap., $19,000; Flour consumed, 2,600 bbls.; val. of bread m'd., $59,000; emp., 25.

Swine raised, 443; val., $2,600.

Wool pulled, 225,000 lbs.; val., $75,000; emp., 12.

Sheep Skins m'd. for boot and shoe linings, 275,000; val., $220,000; cap., $40,000; emp., 45.

NEEDHAM.

Cotton Mills, 1; Batting m'd., 88,800 lbs.; val. of batting, $8,000; cap., $5,000; m. emp., 10.

Establishments, for m. of hosiery, 5; Hosiery m'd., (Stockings, Shirts and Drawers,) 7,000 doz.; val. of hosiery, $20,000; cap., $10,000; m. emp., 20; f. emp., 30.

Rolling, Slitting and Nail Mills, 1.; Machines for m. of nails, 19; Nails m'd., 600 tons; val. of nails, $42,000; cap., $10,000; emp., 25.

Establishments for m. of cotton, woollen and other machinery, 1; val. of paper mill machinery m'd., $50,000; cap., $25,000; emp., 35.

Establishments for m. of butts or hinges, 1; val. of brass or composition butts or hinges, $8,000; cap., $7,000; emp., 16.

Paper Manufactories, 6; Stock made use of, 1,500 tons; Paper m'd., 1,225 tons; val. of paper, $235,600; cap., $152,000; emp., 60.

Tin Ware Manufactories, 1; val. of tin ware, $150; emp., 2.

Val. of white lead, chrome green and vermillion, m'd., $18,000; cap., $5,000; emp., 4.

Glue Manufactories, and Manufactories for the preparation of gums, 4; val. of glue and gums m'd., $18,300; cap., $13,000; emp., 18.

Boots of all kinds m'd., 24,000 pairs; Shoes of all kinds m'd., 89,400 pairs; val. of boots and shoes, $118,120; m. emp., 105; f. emp., 55.

Firewood prepared for market, 2,110 cords; val. of firewood, $10,200; emp., 21 during four months.

Horses, 259; val. of horses, $21,385; Oxen over three years old, 54; Steers under three years old, 8; val. of oxen and steers, $3,200; Milch Cows, 486; Heifers, 49; val. of cows and heifers, $14,819.

Butter, 15,800 lbs.; val. of butter, $3,950; Cheese, 300 lbs.; val. of cheese, $16; Honey, 100 lbs.; val. of honey, $20.

Indian Corn, 328 acres; Indian Corn, per acre, 35 bush.; val., $11,480.

Rye, 90 acres; Rye, per acre, 14 bush.; val., $1,572.

Barley, 48 acres; Barley, per acre, 17 bush.; val., $1,729.

Potatoes, 202 acres; Potatoes, per acre, 82 bush.; val., $13,251.

Onions, 1 acre; Onions per acre, 300 bush.; val., $225.

Turnips, cultivated as a field crop, 16 acres; Turnips, per acre, 250 bush.; val., $1,000.

Carrots, 17 acres; Carrots, per acre, 400 bush.; val., $2,267.

Beets, and other esculent vegetables, 38 acres; val., $2,400;

Buckwheat, 1 acre; val., $12.

Millet, 16 acres; val., $425.

English Mowing, 1,500 acres; English Hay, 1,425 tons; val., $28,500.

Wet Meadow or Swale Hay, 727 tons; val., $7,997.
Apple Trees, cultivated for their fruit, 12,000; val., $3,437.
Pear Trees, cultivated for their fruit, 1,125; val., $425.
Cranberries, 42 acres; val., $1,060.
Swine raised, 640; val., $8,983.
Milk produced, 44,031 galls; val., $6,164.

QUINCY.

Harness Manufactories, 2; (business principally repairing.)

Vessels launched during said year, 1; Tonnage, 1,500 tons; cap., $30,000; emp., 50.

Establishments for m. of boats, 1; Boats built, 20; cap., $250; emp., 2.

Establishments for m. of wagons, sleighs and other vehicles, 2; val. of wagons &c., m'd., $7,500; cap., $2,000; emp., 7.

Chair and Cabinet Manufactories, 2; val. of chairs and cabinet ware, $9,000; cap., $2,500; emp., 6.

Tin Ware, Sheet Iron ware, and Stove Manufactories. 2; val of tin ware, &c., $14,500; cap., $3,500; emp., 4.

Tanneries, 2; val., of leather tanned, $10,000; cap., $4,000; emp., 4.

Currying Establishments, 5; val. of leather curried, $45,000; cap., $12,000; emp., 18.

Manufactories of patent and enamelled leather, 1; val., of leather m'd., $10,000; cap., $2,000; emp., 6.

Boots of all kinds m'd., 79,925 pairs; Shoes of all kinds m'd., 6,000 pairs; val. of boots and shoes, $309,500; m. emp., 425; f. emp., 146.

Val. of building stone quarried and prepared for building, $238,000; emp., 324.

Firewood prepared for market, 250 cords; val. of firewood, $1,500.

Horses, 302; val. of horses, $35,695; Oxen over three years old, 76; Steers under three years old, –; val. of oxen and steers, $5,960; Milch Cows, 442; Heifers, 5; val. of cows and heifers, $15,650.

Indian Corn, 109 acres; Indian Corn, per acre, 43 bush.; val., $5,155.70.

Rye, 38 acres; Rye, per acre, 24 bush.; val., $1,140.

Barley, 35 acres; Barley, per acre, 25 bush.; val., $875.

Potatoes, 50 acres; Potatoes, per acre, 110 bush.; val., $5,500.

Turnips, cultivated as a field crop, $1\frac{3}{4}$ acre; Turnips, per acre, 400 bush.; val., $175.

Carrots, 8 acres; Carrots, per acre, 400 bush.; val., $1,056.

English Mowing, 1,309 acres; English Hay, 1,450 tons; val., $29,000.

Wet Meadow or Swale Hay, 18 tons; val., $144.

Salt Hay, 780 tons; val., $7,800.

Apple Trees, cultivated for their fruit, 4,160; val., $4,565.

Pear Trees, cultivated for their fruit, 1,875; val., $450.

Swine raised, 340; val., $6,350.

Milk produced, 176,800 galls.; val., $24,752.

Stores, (English and W. I. Goods, Apothecaries', Jewelry, and Variety,) 18; val. of business, $213,000.

Establishments, for m. of boot and shoe makers' ink, 1; val. of ink m'd., $6,000.

Establishments for melting and preparing lead for market, 1; val. of lead prepared, $7,000.

Sloops emp. in freighting stone and other articles, 10; emp., 45 men and boys.

RANDOLPH.

Saddle, Harness and Trunk Manufactories, 1; val. of saddles, &c., $1,500; cap., $500; emp., 2.

Establishments for m. of railroad cars, coaches, chaises, wagons, sleighs, and other vehicles, 1; val. of railroad cars, &c., m'd., $1,000; cap., $500; emp., 2.

Establishments for m. of soap and tallow candles, 1; Soap m'd., 1,000 bbls.; val. of soap, $4000; cap., $1,000; emp., 3.

Tin Ware Manufactories, 1; val. of tin ware, $4,500; cap., $1,000; emp., 2.

Boots of all kinds m'd., 345,100 pairs; Shoes of all kinds m'd., 363,300 pairs; val. of boots and shoes, $1,269,400; m. emp., 1,110; f. emp., 422.

Val. of building stone quarried and prepared for building, $800; emp., 2.

Val. of blocks and pumps m'd., $600; emp., 1.

Lumber prepared for market, 700,000 ft.; val. of lumber, $7,700; emp., 4.

Firewood prepared for market, 3,470 cords; val. of firewood, $17,050; emp., 8.

Horses, 270; val. of horses, $29,300; Oxen over three years old, 57; Steers under three years old, 4; val. of oxen and steers, $3,535; Milch Cows, 294; Heifers 15; val. of cows and heifers, $11,645.

Butter, 7,649 lbs.; val. of butter, $1,912; Cheese, 3,750 lbs.; val. of cheese, $350; Honey, 440 lbs.; val. of honey, $75.

Indian Corn, 71 acres; Indian Corn, per acre, 28¼ bush.; val., $2,005.

Rye, 7 acres; Rye, per acre, 15 bush.; val., $157.

Barley, 1½ acre; Barley, per acre, 10 bush.; val., $20.

Potatoes, 96 acres; Potatoes, per acre, 110 bush.; val., $8,976.

Turnips, cultivated as a field crop, 6 acres; Turnips, per acre, 150 bush.; val., $180.

Carrots, 2 acres; Carrots, per acre, 450 bush.; val., $270.

English Mowing, 1,000 acres; English Hay, 1,060 tons; val., $21,200.

Wet Meadow or Swale Hay, 341 tons; val., $2,728.

Apple Trees, cultivated for their fruit, 1,614; val., $2,162.

Pear Trees, cultivated for their fruit, 575; val., $600.

Cranberries, 51¼ acres; val., $2,650.

Bakeries, 1; cap., $400; Flour consumed, 250 bbls.; val. of bread m'd., $6,000; emp., 4.

Establishments for m. of boxes, 2; cap., $6,000; val. of boxes m'd., $13,000; emp., 11.

Swine raised, 505; val., $7,675.

Grapes, 450 lbs.; val., $600.

ROXBURY.

Establishments for m. of hosiery, 1; Hosiery m'd., 3,000 doz.; val. of hosiery, $10,000; Yarn m'd. and not make into hosiery, 75,000 lbs.; val. of yarn, $28,000; cap., $4,000; m. emp., 10; f. emp., 20.

Rolling, Slitting and Nail Mills, 1; Nails m'd., 200 tons; val. of nails and spikes, $25,000; cap., $10,000; emp., 22.

Forges, 28; Bar Iron, Anchors, Chain Cables, and other articles of wrought iron m'd., 110 tons; val. of bar iron, &c., $34,000; cap., $28,000; emp., 39.

Furnaces for m. of hollow ware and castings other than pig iron, 3; Hollow Ware and other Castings m'd., 2,380 tons; val. of hollow ware and castings, $178,000; cap., $165,000; emp., 140.

Establishments for m. of cotton, woollen and other machinery, 1; val. of machinery m'd., $3,000; cap., $1,000; emp., 5.

Establishments for m. of steam-engines and boilers, 4; val. of steam-engines and boilers, $168,000; cap., $32,000; emp., 129.

Shops for m. of fire engines, 1; Fire Engines m'd., 40; val. of fire engines, $50,000; emp., 45.

Establishments for m. of cutlery, 1; val. of cutlery, $10,000; cap., $2,000; emp., 4.

Establishments for m. of butts or hinges, 1; Iron and Brass Butts or Hinges m'd., 15,000 doz.; val. of butts or hinges, $9,000; cap., $5,000; emp., 15.

Brass Founderies, 1; val. of articles m'd, $3,000; cap., $1,000; emp., 6.

Starch Manufactories, 4 ; Starch m'd. from wheat or flour, 6,625 bbls. ; val. of starch, $117,000 ; cap., $112,000 ; emp., 19.

Establishments for m. of chemical preparations, 1 ; val. of chemical preparations, $150,000 ; cap., $50,000 ; emp., 45.

Piano-Forte Manufactories, 1 ; Piano-Forte Cases m'd., 80 ; cap., $8,000 ; all other musical instrument manufactories, 1, (Organ Factory) ; val. of musical instruments m'd., $40,000 ; cap., $8,000 ; emp., 36.

Clock Manufactories, 1 ; Clocks m'd., 1,000 ; cap., $15,000 ; emp., 22.

Sewing Machine Manufactories, 1 ; Sewing Machines m'd., 500 ; cap., $10,000 ; emp., 10.

Daguerreotype Artists, 2 ; Daguerreotypes taken, 3,000 ; cap., $1,000 ; emp., 2.

Saddle, Harness and Trunk Manufactories, 2 ; val. of saddles, &c., $4,000 ; cap., $1,600 ; emp., 3.

Cordage Manufactories, 2 ; Cordage m'd., 3,100 tons ; cap., $125,000 ; emp., 285.

Card Manufactories, 1 ; val. of cards of all kinds m'd., (Business and Visiting Cards,) $75,000 ; cap., $10,000 ; emp., 10.

Establishments for m. of railroad cars, coaches, chaises, wagons, sleighs, and other vehicles, 6 ; val. of railroad cars, &c., m'd., $49,500 ; cap., $25,000 ; emp., 58.

Lead Manufactories, 1 ; val. of lead m'd., $150,000 ; cap., $50,000 ; emp., 30.

Establishments for m. of oil and sperm candles, 1 ; Oil m'd., 37,000 galls. rosin oil ; val. of oil m'd., $37,000 ; cap., $150,000 ; emp., 10.

Establishments for m. of soap and tallow candles, 2 ; Soap m'd., 170 tons ; val. of soap, $20,000 ; Tallow Candles m'd., 25,000 lbs. ; val. of tallow candles, $2,500 ; cap., $10,000 ; emp., 10.

Chair and Cabinet Manufactories, 4 ; val. of chairs and cabinet ware, $12,000 ; cap., $3,000 ; emp., 16.

Tin Ware Manufactories, 5 ; val. of tin ware, $39,000 ; cap., $10,000 ; emp., 29.

Establishments for m. of white lead and other paints, 1; White Lead m'd., 500 tons; val. of white lead m'd., $150,000; emp., 30.

Establishments for m. of camphene or burning fluid, 1; Camphene m'd., 175,000 galls.; cap., $20,000; emp., 5.

Glue Manufactories, and Manufactories for the preparation of Gums, 1; val. of glue and gums m'd., $100,000; cap., $20,000; emp., 10.

Tanneries, 1; Hides of all kinds tanned, 5,000; val. of leather tanned, $30,000; cap., $15,000; emp., 10.

Currying Establishments, 8; val. of leather curried, $372,000; cap., $110,000; emp., 106.

Manufactories of patent and enamelled leather, 2; val. of leather m'd., $400,000; cap., $56,000; emp., 135.

Boots of all kinds m'd., 1,000 pairs; Shoes of all kinds m'd., 3,000 pairs; val. of boots and shoes, $8,000; m. emp., 30.

Bricks m'd., 2,500,000; val. of bricks, $17,500; emp., 35.

Val. of snuff, tobacco and cigars, $15,000; m. emp., 25; f. emp., 20.

Val. of building stone quarried and prepared for building, $100,000; emp., 200.

Horses, 937; val. of horses, $93,700; Oxen over three years old, 18; Steers under three years old, –; val. of oxen and steers, $900; Milch Cows, 254; Heifers, 38; val. of cows and heifers, $9,000.

Butter, 1,000 lbs.; val. of butter, $200; Honey, 1,000 lbs.; val. of honey, $200.

Indian Corn, 96 acres; Indian Corn, per acre, 40 bush.; val., $3,840.

Rye, 20 acres; Rye, per acre, 30 bush.; val., $600.

Barley, 20 acres; Barley, per acre, 30 bush.; val., $400.

Potatoes, 153 acres; Potatoes, per acre, 150 bush.; val., $11,000.

Onions, 50 acres; Onions, per acre, 100 bush.; val., $4,000.

Turnips, cultivated as a field crop, 50 acres; Turnips, per acre, 200 bush.; val., $2,000.

Carrots, 100 acres; Carrots, per acre, 300 bush.; val., $6,000.

Beets and other esculent vegetables, 100 acres; val., $5,000; all other Grain or Root Crops, 100 acres; val., $3,000.

English Mowing, 755 acres; English Hay, 755 tons; val., $15,000.

Salt Hay, 224 tons; val., $2,240.

Apple Trees, cultivated for their fruit, 1,825; val., $9,125.

Pear Trees, cultivated for their fruit, 2,255; val., $4,510.

Beeswax, 500 lbs.; val., $250.

Establishments for m. of casks, 1; cap. $5,000; Casks m'd., 60,000; val., $60,000; emp., 20.

Establishments for m. of fringe and tassels, 2; cap., $53,000; val. of fringe and tassels, $362,000; m. emp., 66; f. emp., 56.

Establishments for m. of sashes, doors and blinds, 2; cap., $5,000; val. m'd., $23,000; emp., 9.

Establishments for m. of gas, 1; cap., $80,000; val. m'd., $15,000; emp., 3.

Distilleries, 1; cap., $60,000; Alcohol distilled, 20,000 bbls.; val., $450,000; emp., 14.

Breweries, 3; cap., $25,000; Beer m'd., 7,800 bbls.; val., $50,000; emp., 18.

Establishments for m. of India-rubber goods, 2; cap., $160,-000; val. of goods m'd., $450,000; m. emp., 110; f. emp., 10.

Bakeries, 11; cap., $50,000; Flour consumed, 16,250 bbls.; val. of bread m'd., $236,000; emp., 66.

Establishments for m. of wooden boxes, 3; cap., $5,000; val. of boxes m'd., $25,000; emp., 14.

Plumbing Manufactories, 4; val. m'd., $10,500; cap., $4,000; emp., 11.

Morocco Manufactories, 2; val. m'd., $60,000; cap,, $12,000; emp., 37.

Refrigerator Manufactories, 1; val. m'd., $12,000; cap., $3,000; emp., 12.

Gas Fixture Manufactories, 1; val. m'd., $15,000; cap., $2,000; emp., 5.

Copal Varnish Manufactories, 1; val. m'd., $35,000; cap., $3,000; emp., 2.

Spirits Turpentine Manufactories, 1; val. m'd., $25,000; cap., $5,000; emp., 5.

Rosin Manufactories, 1; val. m'd., $20,000; cap., $5,000; emp., 5.

Turning Manufactories, 2; val. m'd., $2,700; cap., $600; emp., 4.

Oakum Manufactories, 1; val. m'd., $60,000; cap., $5,000; emp., 14.

Paper Stamp Manufactories, 1; val. m'd., $7,000; cap., $1,000; emp., 39.

Pitch and Naptha Manufactories, 1; val. m'd., $8,000; cap., $50,000; emp., 10.

Iron Bedstead Manufactories, 1; val. m'd., $4,000; cap., $1,000 emp., 3.

Mat Manufactories, 1; val. m'd., $3,000; cap, $600; emp., 8.

Bone Mill and Tallow Manufactories, 1; val. m'd., $75,000; cap., $20,000; emp., 20.

Mantel Slate Manufactories, 1; val. m'd., $20,000; cap., $10,000; emp., 14.

Hose Machinery, 1; val. m'd., $25,000.

Papier Mache Manufactories, 1; val. m'd., $29,000; cap., $5,000; emp., 50.

Gold Beating Manufactories, 1; val. m'd., $10,000; cap., $1,000; emp., 1.

Marble Working Manufactories, 1; val. m'd., $15,000; cap., $1,000; emp., 8.

Grist Mills, 2; val. of grain ground, $350,000; cap., $20,000; emp., 10.

Carpentering Establishments, 20; val. of labor, $200,000; cap., $10,000; emp., 100.

Boss Masons, 10; val. of labor, $100,000; cap., $10,000; emp., 50.

Painting Establishments, 10; val. of labor, $100,000; cap., $5,000; emp., 50.

SHARON.

Cotton Mills, 1; Spindles, 608; Cotton consumed, 103,552 lbs.; Cloth m'd., 48,247 yds., Belting Duck, for Machine Belting, 37½ inches wide; val. of cloth, $23,411.70; cap., $10,000; m. emp., 9; f. emp., 11.

Axe Manufactories, 1; Axes, Hatchets and other Edge Tools m'd., –; val., $300; emp., 1.

Establishments for m. of cutlery, shoe and butcher knives, 1; val. of cutlery, $40,000; cap., $20,000; emp., 40.

Boots of all kinds, m'd., 29,604 pairs; Shoes of all kinds m'd., 1,000 pairs; val. of boots and shoes, $74,976; m. emp., 84; f. emp., 16.

Charcoal m'd., 20,480 bush.; val. of same, $2,560; emp., 12.

Lumber prepared for market, 40,000 ft. of boards, and 100,000 shingles; val. of lumber, $830; emp., 1.

Firewood prepared for market, 2,750 cords; val. of firewood, $10,758; emp., 43.

Saxony Sheep, of different grades, –; Merino Sheep, of different grades, –; all other kinds of Sheep, 3; val. of all sheep, $12; Wool produced from Saxony sheep, – lbs.; Me rino Wool produced, – lbs.; all other Wool produced, 9 lbs.

Horses, 147; val. of horses, $11,088; Oxen over three years old, 76; Steers under three years old, 17; val. of oxen and steers, 4,865; Milch Cows, 399; Heifers, 57; val. of cows and heifers, $12,634.

Butter, 21,492 lbs.; val. of butter, $5,373; Cheese, 1,750 lbs.; val. of cheese, $175; Honey, 50 lbs.; val. of honey, $8.33.

Indian Corn, 256 acres; Indian Corn, per acre, 30 bush.; val., $7,680.

Wheat, 1 acre; Wheat, per acre, 18 bush.; val., $36.

Rye, 21 acres; Rye, per acre, 12 bush.; val., $378.

Barley, 30 acres; Barley, per acre, 17 bush.; val., $637.50.

Oats, 6½ acres; Oats, per acre, 12½ bush.; val., $40.62½.

Potatoes, 109 acres; Potatoes, per acre, 100 bush.; val., $8,720.

Onions, $\frac{1}{4}$ acre; Onions, per acre, 400 bush.; val., $80.

Turnips, cultivated as a field crop, $2\frac{3}{4}$ acres; Turnips, per acre, 350 bush.; val., $288.50.

Carrots, 1 acre; Carrots, per acre, 985 bush.; val., $295.50.

Millet, 2 acres; val., $30.

English Mowing, 971 acres; English Hay, 731 tons; val., $14,620.

Wet Meadow or Swale Hay, 600 tons; val., $6,000.

Apple Trees, cultivated for their fruit, 1,008; val., $944.

Cranberries, 17 acres; val., $1,117.

Establishments for m. of boot, shoe, bitters, and corn starch boxes, 1; cap., $350; val. of boxes m'd., $630; emp., 1.

Swine raised, 241; val., $2,884.

Milk sold, 19,448 galls.; val., $2,333.76.

Establishments for m. of trowels, 1; val. m'd., $30,000; cap., $15,000; emp., 20.

Establishments for m. of bitters and corn starch, 1; val., $30,000; emp., 7.

Establishments for m. of boot webbing, 1; val. m'd., $3,250; emp., 3.

Hoops m'd., 225,000; val. of hoops, $6,634; emp., 25.

STOUGHTON.

Cotton Mills, 1; Spindles, 320; Cotton consumed, 18,000 lbs.; Thread m'd., 12,000 lbs.; val. of thread, $12,000; cap., $5,000; m. emp., 5; f. emp., 5.

Woollen Mills, 1; Sets of Machinery, 2; Wool consumed, 40,000 lbs.; Yarn m'd. and not made into cloth, 22,800 lbs.; val. of yarn, $20,000; cap., $4,000; m. emp., 9; f. emp., 3.

Saddle, Harness and Trunk Manufactories, 2; val. of saddles, &c., $1,500; cap., $700; emp., 3.

Establishments for m. of railroad cars, coaches, chaises, wagons, sleighs, and other vehicles, 2; val. of railroad cars, &c., m'd., $1,000; cap., $3,300; emp., 14.

Tin Ware Manufactories, 2; val. of tin ware, $6,500; cap., $2,500; emp., 5.

Currying Establishments, 2; val. of leather curried, $13,500; cap., $3,000; emp., 8.

Boots of all kinds m'd., 355,212 pairs; Shoes of all kinds m'd., 15,800 pairs; val. of boots and shoes, $938,935; m. emp., 1,234; f. emp., 769.

Val. of building stone quarried and prepared for building, $1,000; emp., 2.

Charcoal m'd., 2,000 bush.; val. of same, $340; emp., 1.

Val. of mechanics' tools m'd., $12,000; emp., 15.

Lasts m'd., 15,000 pairs; val., $8,250.

Firewood prepared for market, 3,411 cords; val. of firewood, $8,678; emp., 12.

Horses, 244; val. of horses, $28,773; Oxen over three years old, 66; Steers under three years old, 20; val. of oxen and steers, $4,833; Milch Cows, 414; Heifers, 30; val. of cows and heifers, $14,220.

Butter, 16,380 lbs.; val. of butter, $4,050; Cheese, 6,725 lbs.; val. of cheese, $792.

Indian Corn, 131 acres; Indian Corn, per acre, 30 bush.; val., $3,930.

Rye, 9 acres; Rye, per acre, 8 bush.; val., $108.

Barley, 10 acres; Barley, per acre, 15 bush.; val., $145.

Potatoes, 87 acres; Potatoes, per acre, 100 bush.; val., $8,700.

English Mowing, 1,103 acres; English Hay, 910 tons; val., $17,270.

Wet Meadow or Swale Hay, 462 tons; val., $4,158.

Apple Trees, cultivated for their fruit, 6,234; val., $2,613.

Pear Trees, cultivated for their fruit, 332; val., $116.

Cranberries, 14 acres; val., $862.

Establishments for m. of boxes, 1; cap., $6,000; val. of boxes m'd., $4,625; emp., 3.

WALPOLE.

Cotton Mills, 3; Spindles, 3,050; Cotton consumed, 67,000 lbs.; Cloth m'd., 120,000 yds., (Sheeting and Printing Cloths); val. of cloth, $6,000; Thread m'd., 5,000 lbs.; val. of thread, $1,500; Batting m'd., 48,000 lbs.; val. of batting, $4,800; cap., $14,000; m. emp., 48; f. emp., 30.

Establishments for bleaching or coloring cotton goods, not connected with calico establishments, 1; Goods bleached or colored, 120 tons of thread, yarn, and knitting cotton; val. of goods, $75,000; cap., $5,000; emp., 9.

Woollen Mills, 1; Sets of Machinery, 3; Wool consumed, 55,000 lbs.

Mills for m. of carpeting, 1; Wool List consumed, 3,000 lbs.; Carpeting m'd., 12,000 yds.; val. of carpeting, $4,350; cap., $1,500; m. emp., 2; f. emp., 3.

Establishments for m. of hosiery, –; Yarn m'd. and not made into hosiery, 36,000 lbs.; val. of yarn, $30,000; cap., $15,000; m. emp., 12; f. emp., 16.

Forges, 4; Bar Iron, Anchors, Chain Cables, and other articles of wrought iron m'd., 350 tons; val. of bar iron, &c., $56,000; cap., $25,000; emp., 12.

Furnaces for m. of hollow ware and castings other than pig iron, 1; Hollow Ware and other Castings m'd., 200 tons; val. of hollow ware and castings, $6,000; cap., $5,000; emp., 12.

Manufactories of shovels, spades, forks and hoes, 1; val. of shovels, &c., $6,000; cap., $500; emp., 12.

Paper Manufactories, 3; Stock made use of, 1,100 tons; Paper m'd., 850 tons; val. of paper, $100,000; cap., $27,000; emp., 50.

Saddle, Harness and Trunk Manufactories, 2; val. of saddles, &c., $1,500; cap., $300; emp., 4.

Hat and Cap Manufactories, 1; Hats and Caps m'd., 3,000; cap., $1,000; emp., 4.

Cordage Manufactories, 2; Cordage m'd., 10,000; cap., $1,000; emp., 8.

Card Manufactories, 1; val. of machine cards m'd., $25,000; cap., $5,000; emp., 7.

Establishments for m. of railroad cars, coaches, chaises, wagons and other vehicles, 2; val. of railroad cars, &c., m'd., $2,000; cap., $1,000; emp., 3.

Boots of all kinds m'd., 1,600 pairs; Shoes of all kinds m'd., – pairs; val. of boots and shoes, $31,500; m. emp., 48; f. emp., 7.

Establishments for m. of straw bonnets and hats, 1; Straw Bonnets m'd., 50,000; Straw Hats m'd., 10,000; m. emp., 10; f. emp., 175.

Lumber prepared for market, 200,000 ft.; val. of lumber, $3,600; emp., 3.

Firewood prepared for market, 1,200 cords; val. of firewood, $4,500; emp., 10.

Horses, 180; val. of horses, $15,000; Oxen over three years old, 78; Steers under three years old, 7; val. of oxen and steers, $4,560; Milch Cows, 480; Heifers, 35; val. of cows and heifers, $1,700.

Butter, 43,000 lbs.; val. of butter, $9,890; Cheese, 1,000 lbs.; val. of cheese, $80.

Indian Corn, 247 acres; Indian Corn, per acre, 30 bush.; val., $7,800.

Wheat, $\frac{3}{4}$ acre; Wheat, per acre, 20 bush.; val., $30.

Rye, 45 acres; Rye, per acre, 14 bush.; val., $700.

Barley, 43 acres; Barley, per acre, 20 bush.; val., $775.

Oats, 30 acres; Oats, per acre, 25 bush.; val., $330.

Potatoes, 140 acres; Potatoes, per acre, 90 bush.; val., $945.

Onions, $\frac{3}{8}$ acre; Onions, per acre, 320 bush.; val., $90.

Turnips, cultivated as a field crop, $3\frac{3}{4}$ acres; Turnips, per acre, 225 bush.; val., $109.

Carrots, $1\frac{1}{2}$ acre; Carrots, per acre, 350 bush.; val., $94.50.

Beets and other esculent vegetables, $1\frac{1}{2}$ acre.

Millet, $\frac{1}{2}$ acre; val., $10.

English Mowing, 992 acres; English Hay, 1,644 tons; val., $32,880.

Wet Meadow or Swale Hay, 612 tons; val., $1,720.

Apple Trees, cultivated for their fruit, 2,500; val., $2,000.

Cranberries, 68 acres; val., $1,374.

Val. of hair mattresses m'd., $20,000; val. of wicking m'd., $15,000; cap., $15,000; emp., 20.

Val. of swine, $6,900.

Val. of peaches, $700.

Val. of strawberries, $250.

Val. of beans, $150.

WEYMOUTH.

Rolling, Slitting and Nail Mills, 3; Machines for m. of nails, 85; Nails m'd., 80,000 casks; val. of nails, $350,000; cap., $130,000; emp., 200 to 250.

Forges, 1; (connected with the Nail Mills.)

Piano-Forte Manufactories, 1; Piano-Fortes m'd., 6; val. of musical instruments m'd., $1,500; cap., $300; emp., 1.

Establishments for m. of railroad cars, coaches, chaises, wagons, sleighs, and other vehicles, 1; val. of railroad cars, &c., m'd., $2,000; cap., $500; emp., 2.

Chair and Cabinet Manufactories, 1; val. of chairs and cabinet ware, $10,000; cap., $2,500; emp., 10.

Tin Ware manufactories, 3; val. of tin ware, $14,300; cap., $2,600; emp., 9.

Tanneries, 1; Hides of all kinds tanned, 6,000; val. of leather tanned, $9,000; cap., $4,000; emp., 3.

Currying Establishments, 2; val. of leather curried, $54,200; cap., $4,500; emp., 12.

Boots of all kinds m'd., 297,692 pairs; Shoes of all kinds m'd., 689,630 pairs; val. of boots and shoes, $1,593,080; m. emp., 1,781; f. emp., 866.

Val. of building stone quarried and prepared for building, $2,700; emp., 11.

Val. of mechanics' tools m'd., $2,500.

Val. of wooden ware not otherwise enumerated, including farming utensils m'd., $1,400 ; emp., 14.

Firewood prepared for market, 1,652 cords ; val., $9,650 ; emp., 17.

Alewives, Shad, and Salmon taken, 100,000 ; val. of same, $252 ; emp., 6.

Horses, 422 ; val. of horses, $43,945 ; Oxen over three years old, 30 ; Steers under three years old, 6 ; val. of oxen and steers, $2,015 ; Milch Cows, 426 ; Heifers, 79 ; val. of cows and heifers, $17,806.

Butter, 15,070 lbs. ; val. of butter, $3,767 ; Cheese, 1,350 lbs. ; val. of cheese, $135 ; Honey, 1,500 lbs. ; val. of honey, $300.

Indian Corn, 93 acres ; Indian Corn, per acre, 38 bush. ; val., $3,515.

Rye, 12 acres ; Rye, per acre, 16 bush. ; val., $240.

Barley, 9 acres ; Barley, per acre, 16 bush. ; val., $172.

Potatoes, 129 acres ; Potatoes, per acre, 101 bush. ; val., $13,029.

Onions, 1 acre ; Onions, per acre, 400 bush ; val., $300.

Turnips, cultivated as a field crop, 2 acres ; Turnips, per acre, 500 bush. ; val., $400.

Carrots, 2 acres ; Carrots, per acre, 707 bush. ; val., $565.

English Mowing, 1,302 acres ; English Hay, 1,385 tons ; val., $27,700.

Wet Meadow or Swale Hay, 217 tons ; val., $2,170.

Salt Hay, 241 tons ; val., $2,892.

Apple Trees, cultivated for their fruit, 15,088 ; val., $5,429.

Pear Trees, cultivated for their fruit, 2,287 ; val., $985.

Cranberries, 8 acres ; val., $400.

Establishments for m. of casks, 1 ; cap. embraced in the Rolling and Nail Mill ; Casks m'd., 80,000 ; val., $12,000 ; emp., 6.

Bakeries, 1 ; Flour consumed, 1,200 bbls.; Meal consumed, 1,500 bush. ; val. of bread m'd., $20,000 ; cap., $2,500 ; emp., 8.

Boot and shoe boxes m'd., 40,000 ; cap., $1,500 ; val. of boxes m'd., $13,000 ; emp., 10.

Milk, 136,000 galls.; val. of milk, $21,760.
Swine raised, 828; val., $18,187.
Ice, 800 tons; val., $2,000.
Cherries, 190 bush.; val., $570.
Grapes, 75 bush.; val., $150.
Peaches, 643 bush.; val., $1,286.
Squashes and Pumpkins, 65,290 lbs.; val., $657.
Val. of confectionery m'd., $6,000; cap., $500; emp., 3.

WEST ROXBURY.

Establishments for m. of hosiery, 1; Hosiery m'd., woollen hosiery and shirts; val. of hosiery, $2,432; m. emp., 3; f. emp., 2.

Saddle, Harness and Trunk Manufactories, 1; val. of saddles, &c., $5,000; cap., $1,500; emp., 3.

Establishments for m. of soap and tallow candles, 1; Soap m'd., 100,000 lbs.; val. of soap, $12,000; cap., $1,000; emp., 2.

Tin Ware Manufactories, 1; val. of tin ware, $2,000; cap., $2,500; emp., 4.

Tanneries, 1; Hides of all kinds tanned, 7,000; val. of leather tanned, $49,000; cap., $20,000; emp., 5.

Currying Establishments, 1; val. of leather curried, $75,000; emp., 20. The capital employed in this establishment comes from Boston.

Manufactories of patent and enamelled leather, 1; val. of leather m'd., $10,000; cap., $5,000; emp., 7.

Horses, 521; val. of horses, $59,500; Oxen over three years old, 96; val. of oxen, $6,150; Milch Cows, 349; Heifers, 31; val. of cows and heifers, $14,118.

Indian Corn, 81 acres; Indian Corn, per acre, 45⅓ bush.; val., $3,521.

Rye, 61 acres; Rye, per acre, 26⅔ bush.; val., $1,699.50.

Potatoes, 76 acres; Potatoes, per acre, 101 bush.; val., $9,380.

Turnips, cultivated as a field crop, (Ruta Baga,) 13 acres; Turnips, per acre, 411⅓ bush.; val., $2,177.

Carrots, 14 acres; Carrots, per acre, 396⅔ bush.; val., $1,935.

Beets and other esculent vegetables, 145 acres; val., $15,985.

English Mowing, 1,720 acres; English Hay, 2,193 tons; val., $43,860.

Wet Meadow or Swale Hay, 464 tons; val., $4,640.

Salt Hay, 71 tons; val., $568.

Apple Trees, cultivated for their fruit, 9,871; val., $7,696.

Pear Trees, cultivated for their fruit, 2,638; val., $1,662.

Establishments for m. of gas, 1; cap., $36,000; val. m'd., $7,000; emp., 3.

Wool Pulling Establishments, 1; cap., $10,000; Wool pulled, 200,000 lbs.; emp., 10.

Swine raised, 770; val., $5,803.

WRENTHAM.

Cotton Mills, 3; Spindles, 1,912; Cotton consumed, 1,321, 700 lbs.; Yarn m'd., 118,000 lbs.; val. of yarn, $22,350; Thread m'd., 8,800 lbs.; val. of thread, $3,960; Batting m'd., 1,075,000 lbs.; val. of batting, $75,250; cap., $35,000; m. emp., 38; f. emp., 13.

Mills for m. of carpeting, 1; Wool consumed, 16,645 lbs.; Carpeting m'd., 81,952 yds.; val. of carpeting, $45,073; cap., $2,000; m. emp., 33; f. emp., 6.

Axe Manufactories, 1; Axes, Hatchets and other Edge Tools m'd., 313; val., $389; cap., $500; emp., 1.

Establishments for m. of chronometers, watches, gold and silver ware and jewelry, 3; val. of m's., $189,000; cap., $6,700; emp., 134.

Establishments for m. of boats, 2; Boats built, 310; cap., $2,000; emp., 17.

Establishments for m. of railroad cars, coaches, chaises, wagons, sleighs, and other vehicles, 2; val. of railroad cars, &c., m'd., $2,900; cap., $1,000; emp., 4.

Chair and Cabinet Manufactories, 1; val. of chairs and cabinet ware, $8,000; cap., $3,000; emp., 9.

Boots of all kinds m'd., 45,200 pairs; Shoes of all kinds m'd., –; val. of boots and shoes, $51,000; m. emp., 65; f. emp., 20.

Establishments for m. of straw bonnets and hats, 3; Straw Bonnets m'd., 168,500; Straw Hats m'd., 252,000; val. of straw braid m'd. and not made into bonnets and hats, $850; m. emp., 50; f. emp., 530.

Lumber prepared for market, 616,850 ft.; val. of lumber, $6,651; prepared by farmers in winter.

Firewood prepared for market, 4,312 cords; val. of firewood, $13,101; prepared by farmers in winter.

Saxony Sheep, of different grades, –; Merino Sheep, of different grades, –; all other kinds of Sheep, 59; val. of all sheep, $118; Wool produced from Saxony sheep, – lbs.; Merino Wool produced, – lbs.; all other Wool produced, 180 lbs.

Horses, 310; val. of horses, $24,132; Oxen over three years old, 244; Steers under three years old, 46; val. of oxen and steers, $13,853; Milch Cows, 781; Heifers, 113; val. of cows and heifers, $25,134.

Butter, 38,615 lbs.; val. of butter, $9,654; Cheese, 3,880 lbs.; val. of cheese, $353.

Indian Corn, 486 acres; Indian Corn, per acre, 29 bush.; val., $14,124.

Rye, 110 acres; Rye, per acre, 8 bush.; val., $1,354.

Barley, 20 acres; Barley, per acre, 19 bush.; val., $287.

Oats, 114 acres; Oats, per acre, 17 bush.; val., $1,134.

Potatoes, 222 acres; Potatoes, per acre, 90 bush.; val., $11,601.

English Mowing, 2,659 acres; English Hay, 1,908 tons; val., $38,160.

Wet Meadow or Swale Hay, 1,185 tons; val., $593.

Apple Trees, cultivated for their fruit, 11,861; val., $4,048.

Cranberries, 90 acres; val., $3,110.
Swine raised, 477; val., $4,770.
White Beans, 574 bush.; val., $1,722.
Val. of hoops m'd., $3,380.
Val. of baskets m'd., $4,575.

PLYMOUTH COUNTY.

ABINGTON.

Tack and Brad Manufactories, 2; Tacks and Brads m'd., 740,300 lbs., or 1,405,300,000 tacks; val. of tacks and brads, $61,350; cap., $28,000; m. emp., 46; f. emp., 16.

Saddle, Harness and Trunk Manufactories, 4; val. of saddles, &c., $2,400; cap., $700; emp., 3, in three establishments.

Establishments for m. of railroad cars, coaches, chaises, wagons, sleighs, and other vehicles, 4; val. of railroad cars, &c., m'd., $2,900; cap. of 1 establishment, $500; emp., 5.

Establishments for m. of soap and tallow candles, 1; Soap m'd., – lbs.; val. of soap, $4,800; emp., 3.

Chair and Cabinet Manufactories, 1; val. of chairs and cabinet ware, $1,000; emp., 1.

Tin Ware Manufactories, 2; val. of tin ware, $4,500; cap., $1,300; emp., 3.

Currying Establishments, 1; val. of leather curried, $3,000; cap., $500; emp., 2.

Boots of all kinds m'd., 552,307 pairs; Shoes of all kinds m'd., 1,265,317 pairs; val. of boots and shoes, $2,167,355.50; m. emp., 2,417; f. emp., 691.

Val. of mechanics' tools m'd., $200; emp., 1.

Lumber prepared for market, 1,489,100 ft.; val. of lumber, $17,550; emp., 28.

Firewood prepared for market, 3,913 cords ; val. of firewood, $17,815 ; emp., 31.

Saxony Sheep, of different grades, 1 ; Merino Sheep, of different grades, – ; all other kinds of Sheep, 36 ; val. of all sheep, $78.

Horses, 435 ; val. of horses, $50,777 ; Oxen over three years old, 70 ; Steers under three years old, 10 ; val. of oxen and steers, $4,620 ; Milch Cows, 474 ; Heifers, 51 ; val. of cows and heifers, $17,069.

Butter, 14,343 lbs. ; val. of butter, $4,490 ; Cheese, 3,460 lbs. ; val. of cheese, $346 ; Honey, 320 lbs. ; val. of honey, $44.

Indian Corn, 84$\frac{2}{3}$ acres ; Indian Corn, per acre, 27$\frac{5}{12}$ bush. ; val., $2,115.

Wheat, 1 acre ; Wheat, per acre, 30 bush.

Rye, 12$\frac{1}{6}$ acres ; Rye, per acre, 17$\frac{2}{3}$ bush. ; val., $294.

Oats, 1^{1} acre ; Oats, per acre, 40 bush. ; val., $35.

Potatoes, 118$\frac{1}{2}$ acres ; Potatoes, per acre, 102$\frac{1}{3}$ bush. ; val., $9,600.

Val. of Onions raised, $18.

Turnips, cultivated as a field crop, 4$\frac{1}{4}$ acres ; Turnips, per acre, 250 bush. ; val., $278.

Carrots, 1$\frac{1}{4}$ acre ; Carrots, per acre, 434 bush. ; val., $175.

English Mowing, 1,094$\frac{1}{4}$ acres ; English Hay, 1,119$\frac{1}{2}$ tons ; val., $17,736.

Wet Meadow or Swale Hay, 395 tons ; val., $2,366.

Apple Trees, cultivated for their fruit, 15,929 ; val., $3,818.

Pear Trees, cultivated for their fruit, 1,974 ; val., $369.

Cranberries, – acres ; val., $266.

Beeswax, 25 lbs. ; val., $8.50.

Establishments for m. of boot and shoe boxes, 3 ; Shoe and Tack Boxes, 2 ; cap., $3,700 ; val. of boxes m'd., $10,500 ; emp., 10.

Milk sold, 121,240 qts. ; val. of 105,865 qts., $3,131.

Swine raised, 154 ; val., $1,533.

Hungarian Nectar, 2,940 bottles ; val., $450.

Establishments for m. of confectionery, 1 ; Confectionery m'd., 15 tons ; val., $4,500.

Printing Presses, 1 ; cap., $1,000.

BRIDGEWATER.

Rolling, Slitting and Nail Mills, 4; Iron m'd. and not made into nails, 1,000 tons; val. of iron, $80,000; Machines for m. of nails, 52; Nails m'd., 62,500 casks; val. of nails, $250,000; cap., $77,000; emp., 207.

Forges, 2; Bar Iron, Anchors, Chain Cables, and other articles of wrought iron m'd., 70 tons; val. of bar iron, &c., $10,500; cap., $6,000; emp., 20.

Furnaces for m. of hollow ware and castings other than pig iron, 1; Hollow Ware and other Castings m'd., 600 tons; val. of hollow ware and castings, $40,000; cap., $18,000; emp., 30.

Paper Manufactories, 2; Stock made use of, 270 tons; Paper m'd., 210 tons; val. of paper, $30,000; cap., $18,000; emp., 20.

Establishments for m. of railroad cars, coaches, chaises, wagons, sleighs, and other vehicles, 2; val. of railroad cars, &c., m'd., $5,800; cap., $2,000; emp., 7.

Establishments for m. of soap, 2; Soap m'd., 25,120 galls.; val. of soap, $2,540; cap., $1,500; emp., 3.

Tin Ware Manufactories, 1; val. of tin ware, $500; cap., $500; emp., 2.

Establishments for m. of cotton gins, 1; val. of cotton gins m'd., $14,000; cap., $30,000; emp., 40.

Boots of all kinds m'd., 600 pairs; Shoes of all kinds m'd., 166,000 pairs; val. of boots and shoes, $125,700; m. emp., 55; f. emp., 35.

Bricks m'd., 3,000,000; val. of bricks, $12,000; emp., 30.

Charcoal m'd., 63,600 bush.; val. of same, $4,000; emp., 20.

Lumber prepared for market, 900,000 ft.; val. of lumber, $7,600; emp., 30.

Firewood prepared for market, 2,217 cords; val. of firewood, $6,651; emp., 30.

Horses, 229; val. of horses, $16,472; Oxen over three years old, 151; Steers under three years old, 18; val. of oxen and

steers, $7,557; Milch Cows, 444; Heifers, 51; val. of cows and heifers, $14,228.

Butter, 25,836 lbs.; val. of butter, $6,459; Cheese, 6,670 lbs.; val. of cheese, $834; Honey, 130 lbs.; val. of honey, $26.

Indian Corn, 283 acres; Indian Corn, per acre, 29 bush; val., $8,136.

Wheat, 1½ acre; Wheat, per acre, 16 bush.; val., $48.

Rye, 57 acres; Rye, per acre, 11 bush.; val., $857.

Barley, 3½ acres; Barley, per acre, 24 bush.; val., $80.

Oats, 129 acres; Oats, per acre, 23 bush.; val., $1,898.

Potatoes, 157 acres; Potatoes, per acre, 86 bush.; val., $6,786.

Onions, 1 acre; Onions, per acre, 380 bush.; val., $190.

Turnips, cultivated as a field crop, 4½ acres; Turnips, per acre, 325 bush.; val., $450.

Carrots, ½ acre; Carrots, per acre, 416 bush., val., $62.

Beets and other esculent vegetables, ¾ acre; val., $42.

English Mowing, 1,540 acres; English Hay, 1,128 tons; val., $20,304.

Wet Meadow or Swale Hay, 414 tons; val., $4,140.

Apple Trees, cultivated for their fruit, 9,299; val., $3,902.

Pear Trees, cultivated for their fruit, 1,180; val., $128.

Cranberries, 14 acres; val., $520.

Establishments for m. of shingle and box board mills, 1; Mills m'd., 12; val., $4,000; cap., $3,000; emp., 5.

CARVER.

Cotton Mills, 1; Spindles, 1,728; Cotton consumed, 50,000 lbs.; Shoe and Boot Lacings m'd., 150,000 gross; val. of lacings, $20,000; cap., $35,000; m. emp., 10; f. emp., 40.

Furnaces for m. of hollow ware and castings other than pig iron, 4; Hollow Ware and other Castings m'd., 575 tons; val. of hollow ware and castings, $45,160; cap., $25,500; emp., 64.

Charcoal m'd., 4,950 bush.; val. of same, $381; emp., 1.

Lumber prepared for market, 178,500 ft.; val. of lumber, $14,581.50; emp., 12.

Firewood prepared for market, 1,612 cords; val. of firewood, $4,345; emp., 6.

Saxony Sheep, of different grades, –; Merino Sheep, of different grades, –; all other kinds of Sheep, 183; val. of all sheep, $372; Wool produced from Saxony sheep, – lbs; Merino Wool produced, – lbs.; all other Wool produced, 395 lbs.

Horses, 140; val. of horses, $10,235; Oxen over three years old, 86; Steers under three years old, 25; val. of oxen and steers, $4,165; Milch Cows, 280; Heifers, 70; val. of cows and heifers, $8,438.

Butter, 7,285 lbs.; val. of butter, $1,821.25; Cheese, 869 lbs.; val. of cheese, $104.28; Honey, 50 lbs.; val. of honey, $10.

Indian Corn, 198 acres; Indian Corn, per acre, 23 bush.; val., $4,783.90.

Rye, 97 acres; Rye, per acre, 6 bush.; val., $873.

Oats, 17 acres; Oats, per acre, 16 bush.; val., $195.84.

Potatoes, 85 acres; Potatoes, per acre, 55 bush.; val., $3,740.

Millet, 1¼ acre; val., $21.

English Mowing, 475 acres; English Hay, 435 tons; val., $7,830.

Wet Meadow or Swale Hay, 581 tons; val., $5,229.

Salt Hay, 40 tons; val., $360.

Apple Trees, cultivated for their fruit, 4,186; val., $1,781.

Pear Trees, cultivated for their fruit, 7; val., $4.01.

Basket Willow cultivated, 1 acre; val., $202.08.

Cranberries, 70 acres; val., $1,622.50.

Establishments for m. of shoe boxes, 1; cap., $400; val. of boxes m'd., $3,600; emp., 5.

Establishments for m. of cast iron grates, 1; Grates m'd., 25 tons; val. of grates, $5,000; cap., $3,000; emp., 8.

DUXBURY.

Tack and Brad Manufactories, –; Tacks and Brads m'd., 1,000,000 per day, 50 tons annually; val. of tacks, $8,000; cap., $3,000; emp., 15.

Saddle, Harness and Trunk Manufactories, 1; val. of saddles, &c., $600; cap., $432; emp., 1.

Vessels launched during said year, 3; Tonnage, 650 tons; cap., $28,000; emp., 30.

Establishments for m. of boats, 1; Boats built, 4; cap., $200; emp., 2.

Tin Ware Manufactories, 1; val. of tin ware, $2,000; cap., $200; emp., 2.

Boots of all kinds m'd., 900 pairs; Shoes of all kinds m'd., 202,105 pairs; val. of boots and shoes, $153,598; m. emp., 156; f. emp., 57.

Bricks m'd., 125,000; val. of bricks, $750; emp., 7.

Lumber prepared for market, 117,000 ft.; val. of lumber, $10,800; emp., 9.

Firewood prepared for market, 242,300 cords; val. of firewood, $661,100; emp., 8.

Vessels employed in the mackerel and cod fisheries, 11; Tonnage, 447 tons; Mackerel taken, – bbls.; Codfish taken, 1,625 quintals; val. of mackerel taken, $14,960; val. of codfish taken, $6.811; Salt consumed, 2,000 bush.; cap., $11,800; emp., 64.

Saxony Sheep, of different grades, –; Merino Sheep, of different grades, –; all other kinds of Sheep, 18; val. of all sheep, $43; Wool produced from Saxony sheep, – lbs.; Merino Wool produced, – lbs.; all other Wool produced, 67 lbs.

Horses, 264; val. of horses, $24,624; Oxen over three years old, 86; Steers under three years old, 47; val. of oxen and steers, $5,655; Milch Cows, 237; Heifers, 32; val. of cows and heifers, $10,447.

Butter, 13,842 lbs.; val. of butter, $3,460.

Indian Corn, 207 acres; Indian Corn, per acre, $25\frac{1}{2}$ bush.; val., $5,279.

Wheat, $\frac{1}{2}$ acre; Wheat, per acre, 16 bush.; val., $18.

Rye, 50 acres; Rye, per acre, 8 bush.; val., $615.

Barley, $1\frac{3}{4}$ acre; Barley, per acre, 16 bush.; val., $29.

Oats, 19 acres; Oats, per acre, 24 bush.; val., $274.

Potatoes, 113 acres; Potatoes, per acre, 69 bush.; val., $3,938.

Onions, 1 acre; Onions, per acre, 155 bush.; val., $87.

Turnips, cultivated as a field crop, 7 acres; Turnips, per acre, 300 bush.; val., $842.

Carrots, 12 acres; Carrots, per acre, 351 bush.; val., $1,899.

Beets and other esculent vegetables, $\frac{1}{2}$ acre; val., $30.

English Mowing, 638 acres; English Hay, 772 tons; val., $11,580.

Wet Meadow or Swale Hay, 128 tons; val., $896.

Salt Hay, 715 tons; val., $5,720.

Apple Trees, cultivated for their fruit, 6,280; val., $2,572.

Pear Trees, cultivated for their fruit, 126; val., $19.

Cranberries, 4 acres; val., $244.

Establishments for m. of boxes, 1; cap., $3,000; val. of boxes m'd., $7,000; emp., 4.

Swine raised, 449; val., $3,601.

Poultry raised, 4,041; val. $1,347.

Eggs produced, 13,133 doz.; val., $2,188.

EAST BRIDGEWATER.

Rolling, Slitting and Nail Mills, 1; Iron m'd. and not made into nails, 1,000 tons; val. of iron, $70,000; Machines for m. of nails, 29; Nails m'd., 24,000 kegs; val. of nails, $96,000; cap., $50,000; emp., 75.

Forges, 1; Bar Iron, Anchors, Chain Cables, and other articles of wrought iron, m'd., 468 tons; val. of bar iron, &c., $32,760; cap. $2,000; emp., 5.

Furnaces for m. of hollow ware and castings other than pig iron, 1; Hollow Ware and other Castings m'd., 100 tons; val. of hollow ware and castings, $7,000; cap., $8,000; emp., 8.

Establishments for m. of cotton, woollen and other machinery, 1; val. of machinery m'd., $10,000; cap., $8,000; emp., 10.

Establishments for m. of steam-engines and boilers, 1; val. of steam-engines and boilers, $51,000; cap., $50,000; emp., 35.

Tack and Brad Manufactories, 2; Tacks and Brads m'd., 450 tons; val. of tacks and brads, $70,000; cap., $15,000; m. emp., 56; f. emp., 12.

Brass Founderies, 1; val. of articles m'd., $600; cap., $500; emp., 2.

Saddle, Harness and Trunk Manufactories, 2; val. of saddles, &c., $2,000; cap., $1,400; emp., 2.

Establishments for m. of boats, 1; Boats built, 6; cap., $300; emp., 1.

Establishments for m. of railroad cars, coaches, chaises, wagons, sleighs, and other vehicles, 3; val. of railroad cars, &c., m'd., $4,000; cap., $1,700; emp., 6.

Establishments for m. of fire arms, 1; Fire Arms m'd., sporting rifles, double and single barrel guns; val. of fire arms, $1,000; cap., $800; emp., 1.

Tin Ware Manufactories, 2; val. of tin ware, $4,000; cap., $1,500; emp., 5.

Establishments for m. of cotton gins, 2; val. of cotton gins m'd., $85,000; cap., $84,000; emp., 60.

Boots of all kinds m'd., 3,120 pairs; Shoes of all kinds m'd., 442,200 pairs; val. of boots and shoes, $399,200; m. emp., 235; f. emp., 134.

Bricks m'd., 500,000; val. of bricks, $2,500; emp., 9.

Val. of snuff, tobacco, and cigars, $4,400; m. emp., 5; f. emp., 2.

Val. of mechanics' tools m'd., $3,000; emp., 2.

Lumber prepared for market, 608,000 ft.; val. of lumber, $6,530; emp., 21; Shingles m'd., 379,000; val. of shingles, $947.50.

Firewood prepared for market, 2,175 cords; val. of firewood, $6,990; emp. 7.

Saxony Sheep, of different grades, –; Merino Sheep, of different grades, –; all other kinds of Sheep, 11; val. of all sheep, $33; Wool produced from Saxony sheep, – lbs.; Merino Wool produced, – lbs.; all other Wool produced, 36 lbs.

Horses, 214; val. of horses, $19,250; Oxen, over three years old, 104; Steers under three years old, 33; val. of oxen and steers, $6,121; Milch Cows, 359; Heifers, 63; val. of cows and heifers, $14,246.

Butter, 22,752 lbs.; val. of butter, $6,825.60; Cheese, 4,310 lbs.; val. of cheese, $603.40.

Indian Corn, 209¾ acres; Indian Corn, per acre, 30 bush.; val., $7,046.48.

Wheat, 3¼ acres; Wheat, per acre, 20 bush.; val., $130.

Rye, 33¼ acres; Rye, per acre, 20 bush.; val., $997.50.

Barley, 6¼ acres; Barley, per acre, 25 bush.; val., $195.41¼.

Oats, 29¾ acres; Oats, per acre, 25 bush.; val., $371.87½.

Potatoes, 252½ acres; Potatoes, per acre, 100 bush.; val., $252.50.

Turnips, cultivated as a field crop, 6½ acres; Turnips, per acre, 300 bush.; val., $780.

Carrots, 4 acres; Carrots, per acre, 400 bush.; val., $960.

English Mowing, 1,314½ acres; English Hay, 728½ tons; val., $14,570.

Wet Meadow or Swale Hay, 510 tons; val., $5,100.

Apple Trees, cultivated for their fruit, 8,042; val., $1,657.

Pear Trees, cultivated for their fruit, 1,021; val., $173.

Cranberries, 7 acres; val., $250.

Establishments for m. of boxes for packing boots, shoes, tacks, brads, inks, pickles and preserves, 2; val. of boxes m'd., $15,450; cap., $9,100; emp., 9.

Establishments for m. of cap tubes, 1; Tubes m'd., 4,800,000; val. of tubes, $4,800; cap., $3,000; emp., 3.

Nurseries, 2; val. sold, $2,000; cap., $4,100; emp., 3.

Establishments for m. of patterns, 1; val. of patterns m'd., $2,000; emp., 1.

HALIFAX.

Establishments for m. of soap and tallow candles, 1; Soap m'd., 6,337 galls.; val., $792; emp., 1.

Boots of all kinds m'd., 500 pairs; shoes of all kinds m'd., 15,000 pairs; val. of boots and shoes, $16,500; m. emp., 20; f. emp., 12.

Charcoal m'd., 26,700 bush; val. of same, $1,544; emp., 15.

Lumber prepared for market, 1,138,000 ft.; val. of lumber, $11,334; emp., 51.

Firewood prepared for market, 1,519 cords; val. of firewood, $7,019; emp., 58.

Saxony Sheep, of different grades, –; Merino Sheep, of different grades, –; all other kinds of Sheep, 82; val. of all sheep, $185; Wool produced from Saxony sheep, – lbs.; Merino Wool produced, – lbs.; all other Wool produced, 272 lbs.

Horses, 91; val. of horses, $6,000; Oxen over three years old, 97; Steers under three years old, 200; val. of oxen and steers, $6,145; Milch Cows, 207; Heifers, 29; val. of cows and heifers, $6,534.

Butter, 8,580 lbs.; val. of butter, $2,145; Cheese, 5,920 lbs.; val. of cheese, $592; Honey, 125 lbs.; val. of honey, $18.75.

Indian Corn, 200 acres; Indian Corn, per acre, 20 bush.; val., $4,500.

Rye, 29 acres; Rye, per acre, 6 bush.; val., $261.

Barley, 4 acres; Barley, per acre, 8 bush.; val., $32.

Oats, 50 acres; Oats, per acre, 12 bush.; val., $300.

Potatoes, 78 acres; Potatoes, per acre, 60 bush.; val., $2,340.

Turnips, cultivated as a field crop, 5 acres; Turnips, per acre, 180 bush.; val., $225.

Carrots, 1 acre; Carrots, per acre, 300 bush.; val., $150.

English Mowing, 503 acres; English Hay, 365 tons; val., $6,570.

Wet Meadow or Swale Hay, 312 tons; val., $2,496.

Apple Trees, cultivated for their fruit, 5,304; val., $1,145.

Pear Trees, cultivated for their fruit, 160; val., $25.

Cranberries, 4 acres; val., $200.

Beeswax, 7 lbs.; val., $2.80.

Men's Garments m'd., 57,600; amount paid for making, $15,400; f. emp., 700.

Churches, 3; School-houses, 5; Unoccupied Dwelling-houses, 5.

HANOVER.

Forges, 2; Bar Iron, Anchors, Chain Cables, and other articles of wrought iron m'd., 352 tons; val. of bar iron, &c., $50,120; cap., $51,000; emp., 15.

Furnaces for m. of hollow ware and castings other than pig iron, 1; not in operation.

Establishments for m. of railroad cars, coaches, chaises, wagons, sleighs, and other vehicles, 2; val. of railroad cars, &c., m'd., $8,800; cap., $5,400; emp., 13.

Establishments for m. of soap and tallow candles, –; Soap m'd., 2 tons hard, 50 bbls. soft; val. of soap, $350; emp., 1.

Tanneries, 2; Hides of all kinds tanned, 1,280; val. of leather tanned, $7,040; cap., $6,000; emp., 6.

Boots of all kinds m'd., 88,078 pairs; Shoes of all kinds m'd., 57,126 pairs; val. of boots and shoes, $233,282; m. emp., 169; f. emp., 99.

Charcoal m'd., 3,400 bush.; val. of same, $845; emp., 3.

Lumber prepared for market, cooper's timber, 230 cords; Ship Timber, 43 tons; Ranging Timber, 2,600 ft.; Shingles, 27,000; Boards, 363,000 ft.; val. of lumber, $4,786; emp., 5.

Firewood prepared for market, 1,381 cords; val. of firewood, $3,735; emp., 12.

Saxony Sheep, of different grades, –; Merino Sheep, of different grades, –; all other kinds of Sheep, 169; val. of all

sheep, $676; Wool produced from Saxony sheep, – lbs.; Merino Wool produced, – lbs.; all other Wool produced, 507 lbs.

Horses, 164; val. of horses, $14,760; Oxen over three years old, 112; Steers under three years old, 22; val. of oxen and steers, $11,095; Milch Cows, 273; Heifers, 49; val. of cows and heifers, $9,170.

Butter, 20,475 lbs.; val. of butter, $5,118.75; Cheese, 5,232 lbs; val. of cheese, $523.20; Honey, 175 lbs.; val. of honey, $29.75.

Indian Corn, 205 acres; Indian Corn, per acre, 30 bush.; val., $6,150.

Wheat, ½ acre; Wheat, per acre, 16 bush.; val., $16.

Rye, 72 acres; Rye, per acre, 12 bush.; val., $1,080.

Barley, 4 acres; Barley, per acre, 15 bush.; val., $75.

Oats, 5 acres; Oats, per acre, 16 bush.; val., $32.

Potatoes, 169 acres; Potatoes, per acre, 80 bush.; val., $6,760.

Onions, 1 acre; Onions, per acre, 600 bush.; val., $420.

Turnips, cultivated as a field crop, 2 acres; Turnips, per acre, 206 bush.; val., $164.80.

Carrots, 4 acres; Carrots, per acre, 300 bush.; val., $360.

Beets and other esculent vegetables, 7 acres; val., $609.

English Mowing, 772 acres; English Hay, 604 tons; val., $12,080.

Wet Meadow or Swale Hay, 350 tons; val., $2,800.

Salt Hay, 82 tons; val., $820.

Apple Trees, cultivated for their fruit, 7,437; val., $3,025.

Pear Trees, cultivated for their fruit, 566; val., $90.

Cranberries, 5 acres; val., $170.

Beeswax, 15 lbs.; val., $750.

Swine raised, 285; val., $4,275.

Beans, 4½ acres; 70 bush.

Garments (coats, pants and vests), m'd., 1,409.

Fowls, 1,527; Turkeys, 62.

Pumpkins, 50 tons.

HANSON.

Tack and Brad Manufactories, 2; Tacks and Brads m'd., 187 tons; val. of tacks and brads, $37,000; cap., $10,000; emp., 37.

Tanneries, 1; Hides of all kinds tanned, $150; val. of leather tanned, $500; cap., $500; emp., 1.

Boots of all kinds m'd., 14,398 pairs; Shoes of all kinds m'd., 133,160 pairs; val. of boots and shoes, $158,230; m. emp., 158; f. emp., 150. These boots and shoes are m'd. for manufacturers in other towns.

Val. of building stone quarried and prepared for building, $2,230; emp., 5.

Charcoal m'd., 5,580 bush.; val. of same, $4,911; emp., 6.

Lumber prepared for market, 392,260 ft.; val. of lumber, $4,672; emp., 6.

Firewood prepared for market, 2,713 cords; val. of firewood, $8,185; emp., 10.

Saxony Sheep, of different grades, –; Merino Sheep, of different grades, –; all other kinds of Sheep, 63; val. of all sheep, $189; Wool produced from Saxony sheep, – lbs.; Merino Wool produced, – lbs.; all other Wool produced, 158 lbs.

Horses, 155; val. of horses, $10,045; Oxen over three years old, 78; Steers under three years old, 23; val. of oxen and steers, $5,230; Milch Cows, 225; Heifers, 43; val. of cows and heifers, $8,201.

Butter, 22,500 lbs.; val. of butter, $5,625; Cheese, 2,675 lbs.; val. of cheese, $334; Honey, 225 lbs.; val. of honey, $28.

Indian Corn, 144 acres; Indian Corn, per acre, 24 bush. val., $3,442.

Wheat, 1 acre; Wheat, per acre, 13 bush.; val., $22.

Rye, 29 acres; Rye, per acre, 8 bush.; val., $348.

Barley, 4½ acres; Barley, per acre, 11½ bush.; val., $52.

Oats, 30 acres; Oats, per acre, 20 bush.; val., $360.

Potatoes, 103 acres; Potatoes, per acre, 60 bush.; val., $4,635.

Onions, ¼ acre; Onions, per acre, 344 bush.; val., $64.

Turnips, cultivated as a field crop, 4¾ acres; Turnips, per acre, 160 bush.; val., $285.

Carrots, 2½ acres; Carrots, per acre, 220 bush.; val., $137.

English Mowing, 669 acres; English Hay, 586 tons; val., $10,548.

Wet Meadow or Swale Hay, 225 tons; val., $2,250.

Salt Hay, 156 tons; val., $1,560.

Apple Trees, cultivated for their fruit, 6,861; val., $1,594.

Pear Trees, cultivated for their fruit, 295; val., $35.

Cranberries, 8 acres; val., $552.

Beeswax, 12 lbs.; val., $5.

Establishments for m. of boxes for boots and shoes, 3; val. of boxes m'd., $8,200; cap., $12,000; emp., 9.

HINGHAM.

Rolling, Slitting and Nail Mills, 1; Machines for m. of nails, 8; Nails m'd., 240,000 lbs.; val. of nails, $10,000; cap., $2,250; emp., 8.

Forges, 13; Bar Iron, Anchors, Chain Cables, and other articles of wrought iron m'd., 23 tons; val. of bar iron, &c., $11,900; cap., $5,400; emp., 21.

Furnaces for m. of hollow ware and castings other than pig iron, 2; Hollow Ware and other Castings m'd., 260 tons; val. of hollow ware and castings, $19,000; cap., $9,000; emp., 16.

Axe Manufactories, 2; Axes, Hatchets and other Edge Tools m'd., 62,000; val., $24,800; cap., $8,000; emp., 21.

Plough Manufactories, 1; Ploughs and other Agricultural Tools m'd., 25; val., $200; cap., $100; emp., 1.

Establishments for m. of chronometers, watches, gold and silver ware and jewelry, 1; val. of m's., $400; cap., $100; emp., 1.

Saddle, Harness and Trunk Manufactories, 4; val. of saddles, &c., $4,950; cap., $1,300; emp., 7.

Hat and Cap Manufactories, 3; Hats and Caps m'd., 8,500; cap., $2,000; emp., 15.

Cordage Manufactories, 1; Cordage m'd., 722 tons; cap., $40,000; emp., 60.

Masts and Spar Sheds, 1; val. of masts and spars m'd., $2,000; cap., $500; emp., 2.

Sail Lofts, 1; Sails made of Am. fabric, 100; val. of sails m'd. of Am. fabric, $10,000; cap., $2,000; emp., 5.

Establishments for m. of salt, 2; Salt m'd., 1,500 bush.; val. of salt, $562.50; cap., $1,050; emp., 2.

Establishments for m. of railroad cars, coaches, chaises, wagons, sleighs and other vehicles, 2; val. of railroad cars, &c., m'd., $4,500; cap., 1,000; emp., 5.

Chair and Cabinet Manufactories, 2; val. of chairs and cabinet ware, $29,000; cap., $5,555; emp., 34.

Tin Ware Manufactories, 1; val. of tin ware, $3,000; cap., $2,000; emp., 3.

Tanneries, 2; Hides of all kinds tanned, 10,100; val. of leather tanned, $47,000; cap., $10,000; emp., 7.

Currying Establishments, 3; val. of leather curried, $86,000; cap., $4,800; emp., 19.

Boots of all kinds m'd., 300 pairs; Shoes of all kinds m'd., 69,317 pairs; val. of boots and shoes, $95,480; m. emp., 205; f. emp., 31.

Val. of building stone quarried and prepared for building, $3,750; emp., 8.

Gross val. of all wooden ware m'd. in the town during the year, $35,100; emp., 65.

Lumber prepared for market, 66,500 ft.; val. of lumber, $804; emp., 1.

Firewood prepared for market, 2,726 cords; val. of firewood, $12,020; emp., 10.

Vessels employed in the mackerel and cod fisheries, 20; Tonnage, 1,495 tons; Mackerel taken, 5,415 bbls.; Codfish taken, 1,250 quintals; val. of mackerel taken, $44,364; val. of codfish taken, $4,500; Salt consumed, 8,533 bush.; cap., $59,785; emp., 264.

Saxony Sheep, of different grades, –; Merino Sheep, of different grades, –; all other kinds of Sheep, 299; val. of all sheep, $1,164; Wool produced from Saxony sheep, – lbs.; Merino Wool produced, – lbs.; all other Wool produced, 1,196 lbs.

Horses, 318; val. of horses, $27,587; Oxen over three years old, 80; Steers under three years old, 44; val. of oxen and steers, $5,870; Milch Cows, 368; Heifers, 73; val. of cows and heifers, $13,428.

Butter, 21,777 lbs.; val. of butter, $6,748; Cheese, 1,645 lbs.; val. of cheese, $165; Honey, 479 lbs.; val. of honey, $90.10.

Indian Corn, 153 acres; Indian Corn, per acre, 37 bush.; val., $4,988.

Wheat, (Indian) 2 acres; Wheat, per acre, 14 bush.; val., $56.

Rye, 45 acres; Rye, per acre, 11 bush.; val., $1,032.

Barley, 11 acres; Barley, per acre, 22 bush.; val., $455.

Oats, 4 acres; Oats, per acre, 18 bush.; val., $54.

Potatoes, 104½ acres; Potatoes, per acre, 76 bush.; val., $6,006.38.

Onions, 2 acres; Onions, per acre, 450 bush.; val., $600.

Turnips, cultivated as a field crop, 4 acres; Turnips, per acre, 240 bush.; val., $80.

Carrots, 9 acres; Carrots, per acre, 600 bush.; val., $1,312.

Beets and other esculent vegetables, 11 acres; val., $650; all other Grain or Root Crops, 62 acres; val., $3,075.

English Mowing, 1,575 acres; English Hay, 1,370 tons; val., $24,680.

Wet Meadow or Swale Hay, 297 tons; val., $2,230.

Salt Hay, 200 tons; val., $2,000.

Apple Trees, cultivated for their fruit, 12,474; val., $4,796.85.

Pear Trees, cultivated for their fruit, 3,607; val., $669.

Cranberries, 6 acres; val., $351.

Beeswax, 22 lbs.; val., $7.50.

Establishments for m. of casks, 3; cap., $300; Casks m'd., 1,000; val., $650; emp., 4.

Establishments for m. of fringe and tassels, 2; cap., $9,500; val. of fringe and tassels, $65,000; m. emp., 41; f. emp., 114.

Establishments for m. of sashes, doors and blinds, 1; val. m'd., $4,000; cap., $3,500; emp., 7.

Bakeries, 1; cap., $4,000; Flour consumed, 1,000 bbls.; val. of bread m'd., $14,000; emp., 9.

Establishments for m. of boxes (4 pill, and 1 fish), 5; cap., $150; val. of boxes m'd., $800; emp., 5.

Val. of all other articles m'd., (wrought spikes, ships' wheels, bait mills, and balance frames, bobbins, and other wood turning,) $55,500; cap. $4,800; emp., 50.

HULL.

Vessels employed in the mackerel and cod fisheries, 2; Tonnage, 158 tons; Mackerel taken, 140 bbls.; Codfish taken, 2,175 quintals; val. of mackerel taken, $2,175; val. of perch and codfish taken, $600; Salt consumed, 140 bush.; cap., $2,000; emp., 15.

Val. of perch and codfish taken for the market, $600.

Saxony Sheep, of different grades, –; Merino Sheep, of different grades, –; all other kinds of Sheep, 70; val. of all sheep, $210; Wool produced from Saxony sheep, – lbs.; Merino Wool produced, – lbs.; all other Wool produced, 290 lbs.

Horses, 15; val. of horses, $900; Oxen over three years old, 10; Steers under three years old, 7; val. of oxen and steers, $584; Milch Cows, 33; Heifers, 8; val. of cows and heifers, $1,540.

Butter, 1,275 lbs.; val. of butter, $208.75.

Indian Corn, 14 acres; Indian Corn, per acre, 40 bush.; val., $560.

Potatoes, 8 acres; Potatoes, per acre, 85 bush.; val., $680.

English Mowing, 172 acres; English Hay, 168 tons; val., $2,836.

Wet Meadow or Swale Hay, 45 tons; val., $272.

Salt Hay, 45 tons; val., $270.

Apple Trees, cultivated for their fruit, 762; val., $575.

Pear Trees, cultivated for their fruit, 185; val., $215.

Lobsters taken, 116,000; val., $6,380; cap., $1,890; emp., 27.

Irish Moss, 362 bbls.; val., $543; emp., 3.

KINGSTON.

Cotton Mills, 1; Spindles, 750; Cotton consumed, 25,000 lbs.; Yarn m'd., 21,000 lbs.; val. of yarn, $20,000; cap., $15,000; m. emp., 4; f. emp., 11.

Rolling, Slitting and Nail Mills, 2; Machines for m. of nails, 8; Nails m'd., 75 tons; val. of nails, $8,800; cap., $4,000; emp., 7.

Forges, 2; Bar Iron, Anchors, Chain Cables, and other articles of wrought iron m'd., 150 tons; val. of bar iron, &c., $24,000; cap., $10,000; emp., 10.

Furnaces for m. of hollow ware and castings other than pig iron, 1; Hollow Ware and other Castings m'd., 60 tons; val. of hollow ware and castings, $4,200; cap., $5,000; emp., 7.

Tack and Brad Manufactories, 3; Tacks and Brads m'd., 55 tons; val. of tacks and brads, $9,000; cap., $7,000; emp., 6.

Saddle, Harness and Trunk Manufactories, 1; val. of saddles, &c., $350; cap., $300; emp., 1.

Vessels launched during said year, 1; Tonnage, 175 tons; cap., $10,000; emp., 16.

Sail Lofts, 1; Sails made of Am. fabric, 73; of For. fabric, –; val. of sails m'd. of Am. fabric, –; val. of sails of For. fabric, $3,500; cap., $1,500; emp., 2.

Establishments for m. of soap and tallow candles, 1; Soap, m'd., 100,000 lbs.; val. of soap, $6,000; cap., $2,000; emp., 3.

Tin Ware Manufactories, 1; val. of tin ware m'd., $600; cap., $1,500; emp., 4.

Boots of all kinds m'd., – pairs; Shoes of all kinds m'd., 80,000 pairs; val. of boots and shoes, $80,000; m. emp., 85; f. emp., 40.

Bricks m'd., 60,000; val. of bricks, $480; emp., 2.

Val. of mechanics' tools, augers, m'd., $7,200; emp., 8.

Lumber prepared for market, 320,000 ft.; val. of lumber, $2,000; emp., 15.

Firewood prepared for market, 4,700 cords; val. of firewood, $18,250; emp., 100.

Vessels employed in the mackerel and cod fisheries, 10; Tonnage, 1,040 tons; Codfish taken, 7,000 quintals; val. of codfish taken, $22,700; Salt consumed, 8,000 bush.; cap., $40,000; emp., 86.

Saxony Sheep, of different grades, –; Merino Sheep of different grades, –; all other kinds of Sheep, 60; val. of all sheep, $200; Wool produced from Saxony sheep, – lbs.; Merino Wool produced, – lbs.; all other wool produced, 190 lbs.

Horses, 156; val. of horses, $13,500; Oxen over three years old, 70; Steers under three years old, 14; val. of oxen and steers, $4,500; Milch Cows, 220; Heifers, 40; val. of cows and heifers, $7,900.

Butter, 11,000 lbs.; val. of butter, $2,500; Cheese, 600 lbs.; val. of cheese, $60; Honey, 250 lbs.; val. of honey, $42.

Indian Corn, 120 acres; Indian Corn, per acre, 30 bush.; val., $4,000.

Wheat, 2 acres; Wheat, per acre, 20 bush.; val., $85.

Rye, 22 acres; Rye, per acre, 11 bush.; val., $300.

Barley, 2 acres; Barley, per acre, 18 bush.; val., $45.

Oats, 15 acres; Oats, per acre, 20 bush.; val., $200.

Potatoes, 65 acres; Potatoes, per acre, 75 bush.; val., $4,000.

Carrots, 5 acres; Carrots, per acre, 125 bush; val., $300.

Beets and other esculent vegetables, – acres; all other Grain or Root Crops, 10 acres; val., $250.

English Mowing, 450 acres; English Hay, 500 tons; val., $8,500.

Wet Meadow or Swale Hay, 130 tons; val., $940.

Salt Hay, 220 tons; val., $1,900.

Apple Trees, cultivated for their fruit, 4,100; val., $1,500.

Pear Trees, cultivated for their fruit, 190; val., $125.

Bakeries, 1; cap., $1,000; Flour consumed, 300 bbls.; val. of bread m'd., $4,800; emp., 4.

LAKEVILLE.

Rolling, Slitting and Nail Mills, 1; Machines for m. of nails, 6; Nails m'd., 130 tons; val. of nails, $15,600; cap., $1,500; emp., 8.

Boots of all kinds m'd., – pairs; Shoes of all kinds m'd., 60,000 pairs; val. of boots and shoes, $50,500; m. emp., 60; f. emp., 33.

Val. of building stone quarried and prepared for building, $3,000; emp., 8.

Firewood prepared for market, 1,220 cords; val. of firewood, $6,000; emp., 7.

Saxony Sheep, of different grades, –; Merino Sheep, of different grades, –; all other kinds of Sheep, 220; val. of all sheep, $660; Wool produced from Saxony sheep, – lbs.; Merino Wool produced, – lbs.; all other Wool produced, 600 lbs.

Horses, 124; val. of horses, $8,000; Oxen over three years old, 128; Steers under three years old, 68; val. of oxen and steers, $8,600; Milch Cows, 260; Heifers, 52; val. of cows and heifers, $3,500.

Butter, 13,600 lbs.; val. of butter, $3,400; Cheese, 10,400 lbs.; val. of cheese, $1,248; Honey, 300 lbs.; val. of honey, $60.

Indian Corn, 430 acres; Indian Corn, per acre, 23½ bush.; val., $10,100.

Rye, 61 acres; Rye, per acre, 8 bush.; val., $732.

Oats, 67 acres; Oats, per acre, 32 bush.; val., $1,430.

Potatoes, 92 acres; Potatoes, per acre, 55 bush.; val., $5,000.

English Mowing, 1,015 acres; English Hay, 671 tons; val., $13,420.

Wet Meadow or Swale Hay, 193 tons; val., $1,544.

Apple Trees, cultivated for their fruit, 4,200; val., $3,400.

Pear Trees, cultivated for their fruit, 540; val., $125.

Cranberries, 3½ acres; val., $125.

Val. of porte-monnaies m'd., $3,000; cap., $1,500; emp., 5.

MARION.

Vessels launched during said year, 1; Tonnage, 300 tons; val., $18,000; emp., 25.

Sail Lofts, 1; Sails made of Am. fabric, 7; val. of sails m'd. of Am. fabric, $564; cap., $400; emp., 1.

Establishments for m. of salt, 1; Salt m'd., 275 bush.; val. of salt, $137.50; cap., $200; emp., 1.

Establishments for m. of railroad cars, coaches, chaises, wagons, sleighs, and other vehicles, 1; val. of railroad cars, &c., m'd., $650; cap., $100; emp., 2.

Lumber prepared for market, 174,000 ft.; val. of lumber, $2,191; emp., 5.

Firewood prepared for market, 1,576 cords; val. of firewood, $5,910; emp., 15.

Vessels employed in the whale fishery, 2; Tonnage, 250 tons; Sperm Oil imported, 8,127 galls.; val. of sperm oil imported, $12,190; Blackfish Oil imported, 315 galls.; val. of Blackfish oil imported, $204.75; cap. in the whale fishery, $12,000; emp., 31.

Saxony Sheep, of different grades, –; Merino Sheep, of

different grades, –; all other kinds of Sheep, 65; val. of all sheep, $195; Wool produced from Saxony sheep, – lbs.; Merino Wool produced, – lbs.; all other Wool produced, 193 lbs.

Horses, 66; val. of horses, $2,090; Oxen over three years old, 32; Steers under three years old, 10; val. of oxen and steers, $1,858; Milch Cows, 122; Heifers, 32; val. of cows and heifers, $4,088.

Butter, 2,785 lbs.; val. of butter, $696.25; Honey, 200 lbs.; val. of honey, $40.

Indian Corn, 64½ acres; Indian Corn, per acre, 22½ bush.; val., $1,439.

Rye, 30 acres; Rye, per acre, 8 bush.; val., $358.

Barley, 4 acres; Barley, per acre, 14 bush.; val., $56.

Oats, 7 acres; Oats, per acre, 16 bush.; val., $55.

Potatoes, 36 acres; Potatoes, per acre, 82 bush.; val., $2,377.

Onions, – acre; Onions, per acre, 48 bush.; val., $28.80.

Turnips, cultivated as a field crop, – acre; Turnips, per acre, 402 bush.; val., $160.80.

Carrots, – acre; Carrots, per acre, 85 bush.; val., $25.50.

English Mowing, 291 acres; English Hay, 269½ tons; val., $4,851.

Wet Meadow or Swale Hay, 51 tons; val., $432.

Salt Hay, 255 tons; $2,040.

Apple Trees, cultivated for their fruit, 2,855; val., $574.

Pear Trees, cultivated for their fruit, 98; val., $10, (small trees.)

Cranberries, – acres; val., $134.

Beeswax, 50 lbs.; val., $16.

Breweries, 1; cap., $225; Beer m'd., 100 bbls.; val., $520; emp., 2.

Oak Ship Timber, 55 tons; val., $550.

P. Pine Ship Timber, 39 tons; val., $273.

MARSHFIELD.

Daguerreotype Artists, 1; Daguerreotypes taken, 700; cap., $150; emp., 1.

Boots of all kinds m'd., 4,000 pairs; Shoes of all kinds m'd., 69,170 pairs; val. of boots and shoes, $79,170; m. emp., 105; f. emp., 25.

Charcoal m'd., 1,500 bush.; val. of same, $750; emp., 3.

Val. of wooden ware not otherwise enumerated, including farming utensils m'd., $3,000; emp., 5.

Lumber prepared for market, 1,250,000 ft.; val. of lumber, $13,450; emp., cannot say.

Firewood prepared for market, 941 cords; val. of firewood, $3,764; emp., cannot say.

Val. of codfish taken, $1,500; emp., 8, three months.

Alewives, Shad and Salmon taken, 322,000; val. of same, $2,415; emp., 28, one month.

Saxony Sheep, of different grades, –; Merino Sheep, of different grades, –; all other kinds of Sheep, 306; val. of all sheep, $918; Wool produced from Saxony sheep, – lbs.; Merino Wool produced, – lbs.; all other Wool produced, 994 lbs.

Horses, 248; val. of horses, $20,305; Oxen over three years old, 204; Steers under three years old, 67; val. of oxen and steers, $12,916; Milch Cows, 420; Heifers, 104; val. of cows and heifers, $15,308.

Butter, 22,349 lbs.; val. of butter, $5,587; Cheese, 3,971 lbs.; val. of cheese, $397; Honey, 404 lbs.; val. of honey, $50.

Indian Corn, 280 acres; Indian Corn, per acre, 26 bush.; val., $7,339.

Wheat, 4¾ acres; Wheat, per acre, 14 bush.; val., $140.

Rye, 59 acres; Rye, per acre, 10 bush.; val., $862.

Barley, 2 acres; Barley, per acre, 20 bush.; val., $32.

Oats, 55 acres; Oats, per acre, 23 bush.; val., $950.

Potatoes, 124 acres; Potatoes, per acre, 92 bush.; val., $5,718.

Turnips, cultivated as a field crop, 9 acres; Turnips, per acre, 300 bush.; val., $663.

Carrots, 6 acres; Carrots, per acre, 485 bush.; val., $970.

Beets and other esculent vegetables, 50 acres; val., $2,000.

English Mowing, 1,059 acres; English Hay, 1,045 tons; val., $15,696.

Wet Meadow or Swale Hay, 636 tons; val., $5,724.

Salt Hay, 1,444 tons; val., $10,108.

Apple Trees, cultivated for their fruit, 13,728; val., $2,777.

Pear Trees, cultivated for their fruit, 942; val., $380.

Cranberries, 10 acres; val., $230.

Establishments for m. of boxes, for shoes and hats, 3; cap., $1,000; val. of boxes m'd., $5,981; emp., 4.

Swine raised, 400; val., $3,939.

Val. of lobsters taken, $2,250.

Val. of labor in making clothing, $4,982; val. of labor in fitting shoes, $1,500; done by females.

Peach Trees, 1,253; Peaches, 360 bush.; val., $360.

Val. of whortleberries sold, $1,500.

Quinces, 125 bush.; val., $187.

MIDDLEBOROUGH.

Cotton Mills, 1; Spindles, 2,272; Cotton consumed, 70,000 lbs.; Cloth m'd., 315,000 yds., Printing Cloths; val. of cloth, $16,000; Batting m'd., 40,000 lbs.; val. of batting, $3,200; cap., $20,000; m. emp., 15; f. emp., 20.

Furnaces for m. of hollow ware and castings other than pig iron, 1; not in operation.

Manufactories of shovels, spades, forks and hoes, 3; val. of shovels, &c., $49,500; cap., $19,000; emp., 46.

Daguerreotype Artists, 1; Daguerreotypes taken, 400; cap., $250; emp., 1.

Saddle, Harness and Trunk Manufactories, 2; val. of saddles, &c., $1,100; cap., $400; emp., 2.

Establishments for m. of railroad cars, coaches, chaises, wagons, sleighs, and other vehicles, 7; val. of railroad cars, &c., m'd., $7,230; cap., $2,800; emp., 8.

Establishments for m. of soap and tallow candles, 2; Soap m'd., hard, 7 tons; Soft, 484 lbs.; val. of soap, $2,190.

Tin Ware Manufactories, 1; val. of tin ware, $900; cap., $400; emp., 2.

Boots of all kinds m'd., 1,000 pairs; Shoes of all kinds m'd., 160,285 pairs; val. of boots and shoes, $161,336; m. emp., 153; f. emp., 127.

Establishments for m. of straw bonnets and hats, 1; Straw Bonnets, m'd., 2,000; Straw Hats, m'd., 40,000; val. of bonnets and hats, $25,000; m. emp., 8; f. emp., 150.

Bricks, m'd., 70,000; val. of bricks, $2,800; emp., 3.

Charcoal m'd., 4,000 bush.; val. of same, $400; emp., 1.

Lumber prepared for market, 2,715,000 ft.; val. of lumber, $21,500; emp., 50.

Firewood prepared for market, 4,299 cords; val. of firewood, $17,196; emp., 30.

Alewives taken, 350,000; val. of same, $1,800; emp., 5.

Saxony Sheep, of different grades, –; Merino Sheep, of different grades, –; all other kinds of Sheep, 359; val. of all sheep, $695; Wool produced from Saxony sheep, – lbs.; Merino Wool produced, – lbs.; all other Wool produced, 847 lbs.

Horses, 417; val. of horses, $32,051; Oxen over three years old, 340; Steers under three years old, 145; val. of oxen and steers, $15,063; Milch Cows, 853; Heifers, 163; val. of cows and heifers, $23,351.

Butter, 27,485 lbs.; val. of butter, $6,871; Cheese, 9,515 lbs.; val. of cheese, $951.50.

Indian Corn, 616 acres; Indian Corn, per acre, 22 bush.; val., $13,552.

Wheat, 1 acre; Wheat, per acre, 12 bush.; val., $24.

Rye, 136 acres; Rye, per acre, 8 bush.; val., $1,629.

Oats, 156 acres; Oats, per acre, 20 bush.; val., $1,872.

Potatoes, 295 acres; Potatoes, per acre, 40 bush.; val., $7,080.

Onions, ½ acre; Onions, per acre, 200 bush.; val., $67.

Turnips, cultivated as a field crop, 13 acres; Turnips, per acre, 100 bush.; val., $325.

English Mowing, 2,964 acres; English Hay, 2,087 tons; val., $41,740.

Wet Meadow or Swale Hay, 973 tons; val., $6,811.

Apple Trees, cultivated for their fruit, 14,119; val., $2,836.

Pear Trees, cultivated for their fruit, 394; val., $100.

Cranberries, 50 acres; val., $800.

Establishments for m. of casks, 1; cap., $200; Casks m'd., 4,500; val., $660; emp., 1.

Bakeries, 1; cap., $550; Flour consumed, 376 bbls.; val. of bread m'd., $9,600; emp., 6.

Establishments for m. of shoe, bonnet, hat, spice, yeast and trunk boxes, 2; cap., $10,000; val. of boxes m'd., $15,000; emp., 17.

Swine raised, 794; val., $15,880.

NORTH BRIDGEWATER.

Musical Instrument Manufactories, 112; val. of musical instruments m'd., $8,780; cap., $2,000; emp., 9.

Daguerreotype Artists, 1; Daguerreotypes taken, 800; cap., $450; emp., 1.

Brush Manufactories, 2; val. of brushes, $8,000; cap., $3,000; emp., 11.

Saddle, Harness and Trunk Manufactories, 1; val. of saddles, &c., $6,000; cap., $2,000; emp., 4.

Establishments for m. of railroad cars, coaches, chaises, wagons, sleighs, and other vehicles, 3; val. of railroad cars, &c., m'd., $5,200; cap., $1,600; emp., 8.

Establishments for m. of soap and tallow candles, 2; Soap m'd., 280 bbls.; val. of soap, $1,120.

Chair and Cabinet Manufactories, 1; val. of chairs and cabinet ware, $20,000; cap., $10,000; emp., 32.

Tin Ware Manufactories, 2; val. of tin ware, $13,000; cap., $4,600; emp., 7.

Boots of all kinds m'd., 66,956 pairs; Shoes of all kinds m'd., 694,760 pairs; val. of boots and shoes, $724,847; m. emp., 692; f. emp., 484.

Val. of building stone quarried and prepared for building, $500; emp., 4.

Val. of blacking, $8,000; emp., 4.

Val. of blocks and pumps m'd., $50; emp., 1.

Val. of mechanics' tools m'd., $2,540; emp., 44.

Lasts m'd., 40,000; val., $10,000.

Lumber prepared for market, 213,000 ft.; val. of lumber, $32,025.

Firewood prepared for market, 3,348 cords; val. of firewood, $13,796; emp., 60.

Saxony Sheep, of different grades, –; Merino Sheep, of different grades, –; all other kinds of Sheep, 5; val. of all sheep, $10; Wool produced from Saxony sheep, – lbs.; Merino Wool produced, – lbs.; all other Wool produced, 20 lbs.

Horses, 343; val. of horses, $29,880; Oxen over three years old, 74; Steers under three years old, 26; val. of oxen and steers, $5,760; Milch Cows, 420; Heifers, 36; val. of cows and heifers, $17,068.

Butter, 20,075 lbs.; val. of butter, $5,018.75; Cheese, 6,505 lbs.; val. of cheese, $650.50; Honey, 620 lbs.; val. of honey, $155.

Indian Corn, 216 acres; Indian Corn, per acre, 28 bush.; val., $6,075.

Rye, 25 acres; Rye, per acre, 15 bush.; val., $567.

Barley, 7 acres; Barley, per acre, 23 bush.; val., $240.

Oats, 20 acres; Oats, per acre, 19 bush.; val., $225.60.

Potatoes, 310 acres; Potatoes, per acre, 90 bush.; val., $27,667.

Turnips, cultivated as a field crop, 5 acres; Turnips, per acre, 200 bush.; val., $250.

Carrots, $\frac{1}{2}$ acre; Carrots, per acre, 400 bush.; val., $50.

Beets and other esculent vegetables, 20 acres; val., $5,000.

English Mowing, 1,550 acres; English Hay, 1,266 tons; val., $25,320.

Wet Meadow or Swale Hay, 375 tons; val., $3,750.

Apple Trees, cultivated for their fruit, 7,700; val., $3,000.

Pear Trees, cultivated for their fruit, 818; val., $100.

Cranberries, 16 acres; val., $3,200.

Beeswax, 100 lbs.; val., $73.

Bakeries, 1; Flour consumed, 200 bbls.; val. of bread m'd., $5,000; cap., $4,000; emp., 6.

Establishments for m. of shoe boxes, 1; val. of boxes m'd., $1,500; cap., $1,000; emp., 1.

Val. of boot trees and forms m'd., $2,000.

Peat, 500 cords; val., $2,000.

Swine raised, 526; val., $4,208.

PEMBROKE.

Boots of all kinds m'd., 700 pairs; Shoes of all kinds m'd., 35,350 pairs; val. of boots and shoes, $31,000; m. emp., 27; f. emp., 64.

Charcoal m'd., 8,000 bush.; val. of same, $800; emp., 2.

Lumber prepared for market, 1,721,000 ft.; emp., 17.

Firewood prepared for market, 2,229 cords; val. of firewood, $6,015; emp., 14.

Alewives, Shad and Salmon taken, 143,100; val. of same, $894; emp., 7.

Saxony Sheep, of different grades, –; Merino Sheep, of different grades, –; all other kinds of Sheep, 145; val. of all sheep, $396; Wool produced from Saxony sheep, –; Merino Wool produced, –; all other Wool produced, 362 lbs.

Horses, 210; val. of horses, $15,874; Oxen over three years old, 99; Steers under three years old, 54; val. of oxen and

steers, $6,167 ; Milch Cows, 295 ; Heifers, 42 ; val. of cows and heifers, $10,296.

Butter, 18,785 lbs. ; val. of butter, $4,733 ; Cheese, 1,881 lbs. ; val. of cheese, $195 ; Honey, 227 lbs. ; val. of honey, $33.

Indian Corn, 143 acres ; Indian Corn, per acre, 27 bush. ; val., $3,853.

Wheat, $\frac{1}{2}$ acre ; Wheat, per acre, 24 bush. ; val., $20.

Rye, 27 acres ; Rye, per acre, 14 bush. ; val., $465.

Barley, 3$\frac{1}{2}$ acres ; Barley, per acre, 17 bush. ; val., $60.

Oats, 19 acres ; Oats, per acre, 25 bush. ; val., $294.

Potatoes, 80 acres ; Potatoes, per acre, 89 bush. ; val., $3,939.

Onions, $\frac{1}{32}$ acre. ; Onions, per acre, 320 bush. ; val., $10.

Turnips, cultivated as a field crop, 4 acres ; Turnips, per acre, 263 bush. ; val., $367.

Carrots, $\frac{3}{4}$ acre ; Carrots, per acre, 630 bush. ; val., $97.

English Mowing, 682 acres ; English Hay, 621 tons ; val., $10,856.

Wet Meadow or Swale Hay, 272 tons ; val., $1,682.

Apple Trees, cultivated for their fruit, 10,059 ; val., $2,330.

Pear Trees, cultivated for their fruit, 53 ; val., $36.

Cranberries, 9 acres ; val., $1,067.

Establishments for m. of boxes for packing boots, shoes, &c., 4 ; cap., $29,500 ; val. of boxes m'd., $28,000 ; emp., 33.

PLYMOUTH.

Cotton Mills, 1 ; Spindles, 1,500 ; Cotton consumed, 285,000 lbs. ; Cloth m'd., 280,000 yds. cotton duck ; val. of cloth, $56,000 , cap., $23,000 ; m. emp., 30 ; f. emp., 26.

Rolling, Slitting and Nail Mills, 1 ; Machines for m. of nails, 12 ; Nails m'd., 650 tons ; val. of nails, $52,000 ; cap., $30,000 ; emp., 38.

Furnaces for m. of hollow ware and castings other than pig

iron, 1; Hollow Ware and other castings m'd., 90 tons; val. of hollow ware and castings, $20,000; cap., $24,000; emp., 28.

Daguerreotype Artists, 2; Daguerreotypes taken, 1,000; cap., $600; emp., 2.

Saddle, Harness and Trunk Manufactories, 3; val. of saddles, &c., $2,700; cap., $1,800; emp., 3.

Cordage Manufactories, 6; cordage m'd., 2,406 tons; cap., $169,500; emp., 241.

Vessels launched during said year, 2; Tonnage, 445 tons; cap., $26,700; emp., 14.

Sail Lofts, 2; Sails made of Am. fabric, 294; val. of sails m'd. of Am. fabric, $14,600; emp., 8.

Establishments for m. of wagons, sleighs and other vehicles, 2; val. of wagons, &c., m'd., $1,000; cap., $700; emp., 3.

Establishments for m. of soap, 1; Soap m'd., 2,000 lbs.; val. of soap, $140; cap., $200; emp., 1.

Tin Ware Manufactories, 2; val. of tin ware, $6,800; cap., $7,000; emp., 10.

Boots of all kinds m'd, 750 pairs; Shoes of all kinds m'd., 175,300 pairs; val. of boots and shoes, $155,000; m. emp.. 232; f. emp., 210.

Bricks m'd., 200,000; val. of bricks, $10,000; emp., 5.

Val. of building stone quarried and prepared for building, $4,000; emp., 20.

Charcoal m'd., 20,000 bush.; val. of same, $2,000; emp., 6.

Val. of blocks and pumps m'd., $400; emp., 1.

Lumber prepared for market, 400,000 staves; val. of lumber, $12,000; emp., 5.

Firewood prepared for market, 5,306 cords; val. of firewood, $26,530; emp., 103.

Vessels employed in the cod fishery, 53; Tonnage, 3,778 tons; Codfish taken, 30,942 quintals; val. of codfish taken, $90,606; val. of cod liver oil sold, $5,300; Salt consumed, 34,700 bush.; cap., $195,000; emp., 412.

Alewives taken, 622 bbls.; val. of same $118; emp., 5.

Saxony Sheep, of different grades, –; Merino Sheep, of different grades, –; all other kinds of sheep, 186; val. of all sheep., $418; Wool produced from Saxony sheep, – lbs.; Merino Wool produced, – lbs.; all other Wool produced, 425 lbs.

Horses, 237; val. of horses, $15,400; Oxen over three years old, 102; Steers under three years old, 35; val. of oxen and steers, $5,904; Milch Cows, 411; Heifers, 56; val. of cows and heifers, $9,779.

Butter, 9,165 lbs.; val. of butter, $2,291.25; Honey, 155 lbs.; val. of honey, $31.

Indian Corn, 184 acres; Indian Corn, per acre, 30 bush.; val., $5,847.90; Rye, 44 acres; Rye, per acre, 12 bush.; val., $777.

Barley, 10½ acres; Barley, per acre, 20 bush.; val., $210.

Oats, 28½ acres; Oats, per acre, 30 bush.; val., $427.50.

Potatoes, 79 acres; Potatoes, per acre, 78 bush.; val., $6,187.

Onions, 1⅛ acres; Onions, per acre, 400 bush.; val., $337.50.

Turnips, cultivated as a field crop, 15 acres; Turnips, per acre, 400 bush.; val., $2,400.

Carrots, 3¼ acres; Carrots, per acre, 600 bush.; val., $585.

Beets and other esculent vegetables, 30 acres; val., $2,000; all other Grain or Root Crops, 20 acres; val., $1,500.

English Mowing, 970 acres; English Hay, 1,212 tons; val., $18,180.

Wet Meadow or Swale Hay, 107 tons; val., $856.

Salt Hay, 153 tons; val., $1,224.

Apple Trees, cultivated for their fruit, 12,350; val., $4,523.

Pear Trees, cultivated for their fruit, 1,300; val., $391.

Cranberries, 1½ acres; val., $15.

Beeswax, 100 lbs.; val., $40.

Establishments for m. of casks, 3; cap., $2,510; Casks, m'd., 10,650; val., $15,850; emp., 12.

Establishments for m. of sashes, doors and blinds, 1; cap., $1,500; val. m'd., $1,000; emp., 6; not been in operation a year.

Establishments for m. of gas, 1; cap., $40,000; emp., 4; just commenced.

Bakeries, 1; cap., $7,000; Flour consumed, 800 bbls.; val., of bread m'd., $14,000; emp., 6.

Establishments for m. of Zinc, Nails and Brads, 1; No. of machines, 8; quantity m'd., 50 tons; val. of zinc m'd., $8,500; val. of nails, and brads m'd., $10,000; cap., $10,000; emp., 15.

Establishments for m. of rivets, 2; No. of machines, 18; quantity m'd., 500 tons; val. m'd., $50,000; cap., $40,000; emp., 26.

Val. of clothing m'd., not including what is made for Boston people, $3,500. There are large quantities of shop work taken from clothing establishments in Boston, and made up in this town.

Establishments for m. of thimbles, for sails, 2; val. of stock used, $2,000; val. of thimbles m'd., $3,200; emp., 4.

Swine raised, 559; val. of swine, $8,944.

Val. of milk sold, $6,355.

Establishments for m. of neck stocks, 3; val. of stocks m'd., $82,500; emp., 245.

PLYMPTON.

Cotton Mills, 1; Spindles, 1,088; Cotton consumed, 50,000 lbs.; Cloth m'd., 212,000 yds., Print Goods, 60-64; val. of cloth, $9,540; Batting m'd., 2,000 lbs.; val. of batting, $200; cap., $5,000; m. emp., 6; f. emp., 15.

Rolling, Slitting and Nail Mills, –; Machines for m. of nails, 2, in tack manufactory; Nails m'd., 30,000 lbs.; val. of nails, $1,500; emp., 3.

Tack and Brad Manufactories, 1; Tacks and Brads m'd., 170,100,000; val. of tacks and brads, 4,252.50; cap., $2,000 emp., 4.

Manufactories of shovels, spades, forks and hoes, 1; val. of shovels, &c., $28,000; cap., $25,000; emp., 20.

Establishments for m. of railroad cars, coaches, chaises, wagons, sleighs and other vehicles, 1; val. of railroad cars, &c., m'd., $500; cap. $100; emp., 1.

Val. of building stone quarried and prepared for building, $300; emp., 4.

Charcoal m'd., 16,570 bush.; val. of same, $1,128.60; emp., 8.

Lumber prepared for market, 779,000 ft.; val. of lumber, $10,161.50; emp., 40.

Firewood prepared for market, 1,735 cords; val. of firewood, $6,213; emp., 42.

Saxony Sheep, of different grades, –; Merino Sheep, of different grades, –; all other kinds of Sheep, 40; val. of all sheep, $98; Wool produced from Saxony sheep, – lbs.; Merino Wool produced, – lbs.; all other Wool produced, 128½ lbs.

Horses, 107; val. of horses, $9,375; Oxen over three years old, 122; Steers under three years old, 33; val. of oxen and steers, $6,481; Milch Cows, 257; Heifers, 85; val. of cows and heifers, $7,729.

Butter, 10,529 lbs.; val. of butter, $2,657.25; Cheese, 2,320 lbs.; val. of cheese, $278.40; Honey, 81 lbs.; val. of honey, $12.40.

Indian Corn, 205 acres; Indian Corn, per acre, $23\frac{44}{205}$ bush.; val., $5,234.90.

Rye, 26 acres; Rye, per acre, 7 bush.; val., $259.50.

Barley, 2¼ acres; Barley, per acre, $11\frac{5}{9}$ bush.; val., $34.66⅔.

Oats, 65 acres; Oats, per acre, 17⅕ bush.; val., $715.52.

Potatoes, 78 acres; Potatoes, per acre, $63\frac{11}{78}$ bush.; val., $2,462.50.

Turnips, cultivated as a field crop, 2 acres; Turnips, per acre, 160 bush.; val., $192.

Carrots, ¾ acre; Carrots, per acre, 150 bush.; val., $83.

Millet, ¾ acre; val., $7.

English Mowing, 677 acres; English Hay, 600¼ tons; val., $10,804.50.

Wet Meadow or Swale Hay, 518 tons; val., $3,108.

Apple Trees, cultivated for their fruit, 6,315; val., $2,447.

Pear Trees, cultivated for their fruit, 178; val., $61.50.

Cranberries, 18 acres; val., $157.

Beeswax, 5 lbs.; val., $2.50.

Establishments for m. of boot, shoe and packing boxes, 2; cap., $2,500; val. of boxes m'd., $3,800; emp., 4.

Boots Bottomed, 1,020 pairs; val. of labor, $519; emp., 3.

Shoes Bottomed, 70,400 pairs; val. of labor, $12,342; emp., 108.

Shoes Stitched or Fitted, 63,415 pairs; val. of labor, $2,695.13; f. emp., 75.

Saw, Shingle and Box Board Mills, 8; val. of mills, privileges and machinery, $2,000; Lumber sawed, 1,460,000 ft.

Grist Mills, 2.

Codfish taken, 3,800 quintals; val., $11,400; emp., 25.

Boots and Shoes, custom-work, m'd., 262 pairs; val., $144.

ROCHESTER.

Vessels launched during said year, 5; Tonnage, 2,170 tons; cap., $54,000; emp., 175.

Sail Lofts, 1; Sails made of Am. fabric, 58; val. of sails m'd. of Am. fabric, $5,700; cap., $1,000; emp., 2.

Establishments for m. of salt, 1; Salt m'd, 300 bush.; val. of salt, $150; cap., $400; emp., 1.

Charcoal m'd., 24,100 bush.; val. of same, $2,410.

Lumber prepared for market, 2,121,000 ft.; val. of lumber, $19,524; emp., 15.

Firewood prepared for market, 1,817 cords; val. of firewood, $5,677; emp., 8.

Vessels employed in the whale fishery, 16; Tonnage, 3,269; Sperm Oil imported, 100,629 galls.; val. of sperm oil imported, $176,100.75; Whale Oil imported, 45,108 galls.; val. of whale oil imported, $33,831; Whalebone imported, 11,000 lbs.; val.

of whalebone imported, $4,950; cap. in the whale fishery, $225,800; emp., 368.

Alewives taken, 720,000; val. of same, $1,800; emp., 10.

Saxony Sheep, of different grades, –; Merino Sheep, of different grades, –; all other kinds of Sheep, 331; val. of all sheep, $662; Wool produced from Saxony sheep, – lbs.; Merino Wool produced, – lbs.; all other Wool produced, 930 lbs.

Horses, 225; val. of horses, $16,780; Oxen over three years old, 182; Steers under three years old, 69; val. of oxen and steers, $11,072; Milch Cows, 518; Heifers, 136; val. of cows and heifers, $16,392.

Butter, 26,468 lbs.; val. of butter, $6,617; Cheese, 2,270 lbs.; val. of cheese, $227; Honey, 330 lbs.; val. of honey, $82.50.

Indian Corn, 445 acres; Indian Corn, per acre, 22 bush.; val., $9,790.

Wheat, 8 acres; Wheat, per acre, 12½ bush.; val., $150.

Rye, 200 acres; Rye, per acre, 6½ bush.; val., $1,876.

Barley, 6 acres; Barley, per acre, 14 bush.; val., $68.80.

Oats, 116 acres; Oats, per acre, 18½ bush.; val., $1,075.

Potatoes, 155 acres; Potatoes, per acre, 79 bush.; val., $9,179.

Turnips, cultivated as a field crop, 13½ acres; Turnips, per acre, 200 bush.; val., $1,080.

Carrots, 2½ acres; Carrots, per acre, 300 bush.; val., $375.

English Mowing, 1,629 acres; English Hay, 1,243 tons; val., $22,374.

Wet Meadow or Swale Hay, 433 tons; val., $3,464.

Salt Hay, 249 tons; val., $2,490.

Apple Trees, cultivated for their fruit, 11,034; val., $2,580.

Pear Trees, cultivated for their fruit, 150; val., $51.

Cranberries, 34½ acres; val., $949.

Establishments for m. of casks, 1; cap., $1,200; Casks m'd., 1,000; val., $2,926; emp., 3.

Swine raised, 484; val., $5,487.

Shingles, 896,000; Staves, 685,000; val., $4,650.50; cap., $1,500; emp., 6.

SCITUATE.

Vessels launched during said year, 2; Tonnage, 572 tons; cap., $5,000; emp., 40.

Establishments for m. of boats, 1; Boats built, 18; cap., $300; emp., 2.

Sail Lofts, 1; Sails made of Am. fabric, 55; val. of sails m'd. of Am. fabric, $2,520; cap., $1,000; emp., 2.

Establishments for m. of railroad cars, coaches, chaises, wagons, sleighs, and other vehicles, 1; val. of railroad cars, &c., m'd., $500; cap., $200; emp., 1.

Chair and Cabinet Manufactories, 1; val. of chairs and cabinet ware, $175; cap., $50; emp., 1.

Tin Ware Manufactories, 1; val. of tin ware, $400; cap., $300; emp., 1.

Mills for grinding Indian corn and rye meal, (foreign,) 2; Meal m'd., 26,000 bush.; val. of meal m'd., $29.250; cap., $11,000; emp., 3.

Boots of all kinds, m'd., 8,922 pairs; Shoes of all kinds m'd., 19,080 pairs; val. of boots and shoes, $35,254; m. emp., 38; f. emp., 29.

Val. of building stone quarried and prepared for building, $3,000; emp., 6.

Lumber prepared for market, 1,000,000 ft.; val. of lumber, $15,000; emp., 4.

Firewood prepared for market, 275 cords; val. of firewood, $1,539; emp., 2.

Alewives, Shad and Salmon taken, 68,000; val. of same, $600; emp., 4.

Saxony Sheep, of different grades, –; Merino Sheep, of different grades, –; all other kinds of sheep, 238; val. of all sheep, $740; Wool produced from Saxony sheep, – lbs.; Merino Wool produced, – lbs.; all other Wool produced, 702 lbs.

Horses, 233; val. of horses, $15,811; Oxen over three years old, 185; Steers under three years old, 68; val. of oxen and

steers, 11,635; Milch Cows, 385; Heifers, 120; val. of cows and heifers, $15,752.

Butter, 27,844 lbs.; val. of butter, $6,796; Cheese, 4,633 lbs.; val. of cheese, $525; Honey, 280 lbs.; val. of honey, $50.

Indian Corn, 248 acres; Indian Corn, per acre, 36 bush.; val., $9,045.

Wheat, 1 acre; Wheat, per acre, 10 bush.; val., $20.

Rye, 51½ acres; Rye, per acre, 681 bush.; val., $952.

Barley, 28¼ acres; Barley, per acre, 19½ bush.; val., $457.

Oats, 6¾ acres; Oats, per acre, 17 bush.; val., $88.

Potatoes, 67 acres; Potatoes, per acre, $101\frac{8}{67}$ bush.; val., $4,936.

Carrots, 1½ acre; bush. per acre, 400; val., $80.

English Mowing, 1,170½ acres; English Hay, 1,181¾ tons; val., $18,905.

Wet Meadow or Swale Hay, 194 tons; val., $1,161.

Salt Hay, 589 tons; val., $4,468.

Apple Trees, cultivated for their fruit, 9,527; val., $4,350.

Pear Trees, cultivated for their fruit, 785; val. of fruit raised, $126.50.

Cranberries, 9½ acres; val., $257.

Val. of slop-work done by females for Boston clothing establishments, $4,164.

Val. of Irish moss collected, $4,855.

Swine raised, 377; val., $7,896.

Val. of fowls raised, $3,377.

Val. of shoe heels m'd., $312.

Vegetable Gardens, 343; val. of produce, $2,744.

Val. of berries sold in Boston, $950.

Val. of lobsters taken, $900.

Val. of fresh and salt fish sold, $2,000; emp., 11 boats, 15 men, and 8 boys.

Val. of peaches, cherries and currants raised, $747.

SOUTH SCITUATE.

Tack Manufactories, 2; Tacks m'd., 375,000,000; val. of tacks and brads, $15,000; cap., $7,500; emp., 17.

Vessels launched during said year, 1; Tonnage, 180 tons; cap., $1,500; emp., 5.

Boots of all kinds m'd., 2,500 pairs; Shoes of all kinds m'd., 5,000 pairs; val. of boots and shoes, $9,700; m. emp., 44; f. emp., 28.

Bricks m'd., 200,000; val. of bricks, $1,800; emp., 5.

Val. of mechanics' tools m'd., $3,000; emp., 3.

Val. of wooden ware not otherwise enumerated, (Buckets,) $2,000; emp., 4.

Lumber prepared for market, 226,000 ft.; val. of lumber, $22,600; emp., 8.

Firewood prepared for market, 1,223 cords; val. of firewood, $4,892.

Alewives taken, 59,000; val. of same, $443; emp., 6.

Saxony Sheep, of different grades, –; Merino Sheep, of different grades, –; all other kinds of Sheep, 44; val. of all sheep, $88; Wool produced from Saxony sheep, – lbs.; Merino Wool produced, – lbs.; all other Wool produced, 160 lbs.

Horses, 182; val. of horses, $13,200; Oxen over three years old, 138; Steers under three years old, 49; val. of oxen and steers, $13,800; Milch Cows, 309; Heifers, 82; val. of cows and heifers, $10,910.

Butter, 22,350 lbs.; val. of butter, $4,470; Cheese, 3,985 lbs.; val. of cheese, $398.50; Honey, 421 lbs.; val. of honey, $84.20.

Indian Corn, 193 acres; Indian Corn, per acre, 25 bush.; val., $4,825.

Rye, 46 acres; Rye, per acre, 10 bush.; val., $460.

Barley, 10 acres; Barley, per acre, 20 bush.; val., $160.

Oats, 20 acres; Oats, per acre, 20 bush.; val., $100.

Potatoes, 146 acres; Potatoes, per acre, 75 bush.; val., $4,380.

Turnips, cultivated as a field crop, 1 acre; Turnips, per acre, 200 bush.; val., $24.

Carrots, 2 acres; Carrots, per acre, 600 bush.; val., $28.80.

English Mowing, 1,116 acres; English Hay, 762 tons; val., $11,430.

Wet Meadow or Swale Hay, 278 tons; val., $1,650.

Salt Hay, 414 tons; val., $3,312.

Apple Trees, cultivated for their fruit, 6,100; val., $2,962.

Pear Trees, cultivated for their fruit, 147; val., $135.

Cranberries, 6 acres; val., $120.

Beeswax, 5 lbs.; val., $1.

Establishments for m. of shoe and trunk boxes, 3; cap., $13,000; val. of boxes m'd., $12,417; emp., 23.

Saw Mills, 5; Lumber sawed, 250,000 ft.

Grist Mills, 4; Grain ground, 4,500 bush.

Swine raised, 225; val., $1,350.

Val. of "sale work" m'd., $5,000.

WAREHAM.

Rolling, Slitting and Nail Mills, 12; Iron m'd. and not made into nails, 275 tons; val. of iron, $21,000; Machines for m. of nails, 290; Nails m'd., 211,152 casks; val. of nails, $846,152; cap., $650,000; emp., 860.

Furnaces for m. of hollow ware and castings other than pig iron, 1; Hollow Ware and other Castings m'd., 313 tons; val. of hollow ware and castings, $40,000; cap., $30,000; emp., 30.

Saddle, Harness and Trunk Manufactories, 2; val. of saddles, &c., $600; cap., $500; emp., 3.

Establishments for m. of railroad cars, coaches, chaises, wagons, sleighs, and other vehicles, 1; val. of railroad cars, &c., m'd., $1,000; cap., $2,000; emp., 4.

Chair and Cabinet Manufactories, 1; val. of chairs and cabinet ware, $1,200; cap., $2,500; emp., 2.

Tin Ware Manufactories, 1; val. of tin ware, $300; cap., $200; emp., 1.

Tanneries, 1; Hides of all kinds tanned, 100; val. of leather tanned, $300; cap., $200; emp., 1.

Boots of all kinds m'd., 100 pairs; Shoes of all kinds m'd., 500 pairs; val. of boots and shoes, $1,000; m. emp., 3.

Charcoal m'd., 6,000 bush.; val. of same, $600; emp., 4.

Lumber prepared for market, 45,000 ft.; val. of lumber, $675; emp., 3.

Firewood prepared for market, 4,000 cords; val. of firewood, $16,000; emp., 50.

Alewives, Shad and Salmon taken, 1,100 bbls.; val. of same, $1,100; emp., 4.

Saxony Sheep, of different grades, –; Merino Sheep, of different grades, –; all other kinds of Sheep, 45; val. of all sheep, $90; Wool produced from Saxony sheep, – lbs.; Merino Wool produced, – lbs.; all other Wool produced, 90 lbs.

Horses, 179; val. of horses, $10,000; Oxen over three years old, 74; Steers under three years old, 36; val. of oxen and steers, $4,420; Milch Cows, 287; Heifers, 39; val. of cows and heifers, $9,078.

Butter, 8,190 lbs.; val. of butter, $2,040; Honey, 100 lbs.; val. of honey, $20.

Indian Corn, 136 acres; Indian Corn, per acre, 26 bush.; val., $3,162.

Rye, 92 acres; Rye, per acre, 7 bush.; val., $954.

Barley, 1 acre; Barley, per acre, 10 bush.; val., $12.

Oats, 8 acres; Oats, per acre, 16 bush.; val., $92.

Potatoes, 87 acres; Potatoes, per acre, 75 bush.; val., $4,400.

Onions, 2 acres; Onions, per acre, 240 bush; val., $240.

Turnips, cultivated as a field crop, 2 acres; Turnips, per acre, 200 bush.; val., $160.

Carrots, 2¼ acres; Carrots, per acre, 300 bush.; val., $200.

English Mowing, 331 acres; English Hay, 409 tons; val., $8,180.

Wet Meadow or Swale Hay, 116 tons; val., $928.

Salt Hay, 526 tons; val., $4,208.

Apple Trees, cultivated for their fruit, 3,780; val., $500.

Pear Trees, cultivated for their fruit, 500; val., $50.

Beeswax, 8 lbs.; val., $4.

Establishments for m. of nail casks, 5; cap., $10,000; Casks m'd., 300,000; val., $45,000; emp., 34.

WEST BRIDGEWATER.

Furnaces for m. of hollow ware and castings other than pig iron, 4; Hollow Ware and other Castings m'd., 295 tons; val. of hollow ware and castings, $16,900; cap., $21,000; emp., 29.

Manufactories of shovels and spades, 1; (Partly m'd., in this town and finished in Easton); cap., $10,000; emp., 9.

Establishments for m. of wagons, sleighs and other vehicles, 4; val. of wagons, &c., m'd., $4,680; cap., $1,800; emp., 8.

Cabinet Manufactories, 1; val. of chairs and cabinet ware, $1,000; cap., $200; emp., 3.

Boots of all kinds m'd., 27,600 pairs; Shoes of all kinds m'd., 141,700 pairs; val. of boots and shoes, $178,460; m. emp., 204; f. emp., 96.

Val. of straw braid m'd., and not made into bonnets and hats, $383.95; f. emp., 24.

Charcoal m'd., 1,840 bush.; val. of same, $1,018.60; emp., 4.

Lumber prepared for market, 189,833 ft.; val. of lumber, $2,970.50; emp., 3, part of the time.

Firewood prepared for market, 985 cords; val. of firewood, $4,633.50; emp., 57, part of the time.

Saxony Sheep, of different grades, – ; Merino Sheep, of different grades, – ; all other kinds of sheep, 11 ; val. of all sheep, $33 ; Wool produced from Saxony sheep, – lbs. ; Merino Wool produced, – lbs. ; all other wool produced, 61 lbs.

Horses, 144 ; val. of horses, $9,194 ; Oxen over three years old, 151 ; Steers under three years old, 21 ; val. of oxen and steers, $8.821 ; Milch Cows, 347 ; Heifers, 63 ; val. of cows and heifers, $13,346.

Butter, 20,588 lbs. ; val. of butter, $5,147 ; Cheese, 5,590 lbs. ; val. of cheese, $698.75 ; Honey, 174 lbs. ; val. of honey, $35.34.

Indian Corn, 192 acres ; Indian Corn, per acre, $27\frac{182}{192}$ bush. ; val., $5,386.

Wheat, 3 acres ; Wheat, per acre, $16\frac{2}{3}$ bush. ; val., $125.

Rye, 28 acres ; Rye, per acre, $15\frac{2}{2}$ bush. ; val., $666.

Barley, 9 acres ; Barley, per acre, $19\frac{8}{9}$ bush. ; val., $179.

Oats, 55 acres ; Oats, per acre, $22\frac{7}{55}$ bush. ; val., $791.05.

Potatoes, 133 acres ; Potatoes, per acre, $87\frac{33}{133}$ bush. ; val., $8,703.

Beets, and other esculent vegetables, 8 acres ; val., $690.

English Mowing, $953\frac{1}{2}$ acres ; English Hay, $844\frac{3}{4}$ tons.

Wet Meadow or Swale Hay, 16,995 tons.

Salt Hay, 858 tons ; val., $8,580.

Apple Trees, cultivated for their fruit, 7,980 ; val., $3,424.50.

Pear Trees, cultivated for their fruit, 356 ; val., $53.75.

Cranberries, 86 acres ; val., $969.35.

Beeswax, 1 lb. ; val., $1.

Establishments for m. of boot and shoe boxes, 1 ; cap., $3,000 ; val. of boxes m'd., $4,000 ; emp., 3.

Val. of vanes m'd., $4,000 ; cap., $1,500 ; emp., 3.

Onions, Turnips, Carrots and Beets raised, 1,380 bush. ; val., $690.

SUFFOLK COUNTY.

BOSTON.

Mills for m. of carpeting, 1; Woollen Yarn consumed, 14,000 lbs.; Cotton Yarn, 13,000 lbs.; Carpeting m'd., 28,000 yds.; val. of carpeting, $21,000; cap., $100,000; m. emp., 80; f. emp., 25.

Rolling, Slitting and Nail Mills, 3; Iron m'd. and not made into nails, 22,000 tons; val. of iron, $1,525,000; cap., $657,000; emp., 600.

Forges, 3; Bar Iron, Anchors, Chain Cables, and other articles of wrought iron m'd., 1,750 tons; val. of bar iron, &c., $232,000; cap., $400,000; emp., 195.

Furnaces for m. of hollow ware and castings other than pig iron, 7; Hollow Ware and other Castings m'd., 6,922 tons; val. of hollow ware and castings, $443,500; cap., $317,500; emp., 346.

Establishments for m. of cotton, woollen and other machinery, 21; val. of machinery m'd., $247,000; cap., $122,500; emp., 198.

Establishments for m. of steam-engines and boilers, 17; val. of steam-engines and boilers, $1,835,000; cap., $1,274,000; emp., 1,437.

Axe Manufactories, 1; Axes, Hatchets and other Edge Tools m'd., 2,000; val., $10,000; cap., $2,500; emp., 6.

Establishments for m. of cutlery, 2; val. of cutlery, $17,000; cap., $6,000; emp., 12.

Establishments for m. of butts or hinges, 1; Brass or Composition Butts or Hinges m'd., 1,000 doz.; val. of brass or composition butts or hinges, $5,000; cap., $3,000; emp., 7.

Establishments for m. of latches and door handles, 4; Door

Handles and Latches m'd., 3,783 doz.; val. of door handles and latches, $39,100; cap., $12,500; emp., 29.

Lock Manufactories, 7; Locks m'd., 26,250; val. of locks, $66,700; cap., $24,500; emp., 84.

Plough Manufactories, 1; Ploughs and other Agricultural Tools m'd., 2,200; val., $100,000; cap., $24,500; emp., 45.

Shops for m. of iron railing, iron fences, iron safes, and other iron ware, 13; val. of iron railing, &c., $562,500; cap, $192,300; emp., 302.

Brass Founderies, 13; val. of articles m'd, $984,000; cap., $314,000; emp., 310.

Establishments for m. of britannia ware, 1; val. of britannia ware, $40,000; cap., $15,000; emp., 25.

Glass Manufactories, 3; val. of glass m'd., $1,190,000; cap., $615,000; emp., 586.

Establishments for m. of chemical preparations, 7; val. of chemical preparations, $270,500; cap., $146,500; emp., 52.

Piano-Forte Manufactories, 20; Piano-Fortes m'd., 6,122; cap., $941,000; all other musical instrument manufactories, 10; val. of musical instruments m'd., $1,984,700; cap., $102,100; emp., 1,248.

Sewing Machine Manufactories, 5; Sewing Machines m'd., 3,385; cap., $83,000; emp., 168.

Daguerreotype Artists, 34; Daguerreotypes taken, 227,408; cap., $82,500; emp., 108.

Establishments for m. of chronometers, watches, gold and silver ware and jewelry, 22; val. of m's., $617,000; cap., $185,500; emp., 208.

Brush Manufactories, 2; val. of brushes, $225,000; cap., $120,000; emp., 125.

Saddle, Harness and Trunk Manufactories, 39; val. of saddles, &c., $757,200; cap., $169,100; emp., 378.

Upholstery Manufactories, 51; val. of upholstery, $1,550,800; cap., $455,300; emp., 416.

Hat and Cap Manufactories, 37; Hats and Caps m'd., 727,300; cap., $143,200; emp., 500.

Cordage Manufactories, 2; Cordage m'd., 2,023 tons; cap., $150,000; emp., 135.

Vessels launched during said year, 35; Tonnage, 44,300 tons; cap., $905,000; emp., 922.

Establishments for m. of boats, 7; Boats built, 115; cap., $10,700; emp., 35.

Masts and Spar Sheds, 7; Masts and Spars m'd. 3,160; cap., $158,000; emp., 72.

Sail Lofts, 33; Sails made of Am. fabric, 6,767; of For. fabric, 42; val. of sails m'd. of Am. fabric, $431,172; val. of sails of For. fabric, $2,695; cap., $70,000; emp., 203.

Establishments for m. of salt, 2; Salt m'd., 110,000 bush.; val. of salt, $75,000; cap., $40,000; emp., 22.

Establishments for m. of railroad cars, coaches, chaises, wagons, sleighs and other vehicles, 28; val. of railroad cars, &c., m'd., $279,035; cap., $102,400; emp., 302.

Sugar Refineries, 2; Sugar refined, 28,000,000 lbs.; val. of sugar, $2,000,000; emp., 290.

Establishments for m. of oil and sperm candles, 7; Oil m'd., (whale, 730,000 galls.; Sperm, 150,000; Lard, 180,000; Rosin, 120,000; Palm, 40,000) 1,220,000 galls.; val. of stearine m'd., $1,236,000; Sperm Candles m'd., 111,000 lbs.; Palm Candles m'd., 1,125,498 lbs.; val. of sperm candles, $34,000; val. of palm candles, $255,000; cap., $730,000; emp., 141.

Establishments for m. of soap and tallow candles, 4; Soap m'd., 900,000 lbs.; val. of soap, $47,000; Tallow Candles m'd., 200,000 lbs.; val. of tallow candles, $28,000; cap., $49,500; emp., 24.

Establishments for m. of fire arms, 2; Fire Arms m'd., (250 fowling-pieces, 100 rifles,) 350; val. of fire arms, $7,500; cap., $2,500; emp., 7.

Establishments for m. of cannon, 1; Cannon m'd., (39 iron guns, 10 and 8 inch, Columbiads; 6 iron guns, 9 and 11 inch, navy; 25 iron guns, 4, 6 and 9 pounders; 49 bronze guns, 6, 12 and 32 pounders,) 119; val. of cannon, $54,151; cap., $50,000; emp., 40.

Chair and Cabinet Manufactories, 36; val. of chairs and cabinet ware, $1,063,800; cap., $360,700; emp., 600.

Tin Ware manufactories, 47; val. of tin ware, $416,500; cap., $195,200; emp., 218.

Comb Manufactories, 3; val. of combs m'd., $6,500; cap., $2,500; emp., 9.

Establishments for m. of white lead and other paints, 3; White Lead m'd., 1,570 tons; val. of white lead m'd., $253,850; other paints m'd, (French zinc, 1,226,000 lbs.; American, 100,000 lbs.; other paints, 25,000 lbs,) 603 tons; Japan, 3,000 galls.; val. of other paints, $115,340; cap., $116,000; emp., 23.

Mills for m. of linseed oil, 1; Oil m'd., 525,000 galls.; val. of oil m'd., $500,000; cap., $400,000; emp., 45.

Establishments for m. of camphene or burning fluid, 6; Camphene m'd., 820,000 galls.; cap., $114,500; emp., 27.

Flour Mills, 2; Flour m'd., 87,000 bbls.; val. of flour m'd., $870,000; cap., $300,000; emp., 80.

Currying Establishments, 19; val. of leather curried, $829,200; cap., $86,200; emp., 152.

Boots of all kinds m'd., 35,100 pairs; Shoes of all kinds m'd., 177,100 pairs; val. of boots and shoes, $193,900; m. emp., 145; f. emp., 155.

Val. of mathematical, magnetical, and other instruments, $101,000; emp., 69.

Val. of snuff, tobacco and cigars, $56,750; m. emp., 25; f. emp., 41.

Val. of building stone prepared for building, $323,000; emp., 287.

Val. of marble prepared for market, $311,000; emp., 286.

Charcoal m'd., 30,000 bush.; val. of same, $5,000; emp., 8.

Val. of whips m'd., $3,000; emp., 2.

Val. of blacking, $28,000; emp., 30.

Val. of blocks and pumps m'd., $115,300; emp., 84.

Val. of mechanics' tools m'd., $112,000; emp., 106.

Val. of wooden ware not otherwise enumerated, including farming utensils, m'd., $36,000; emp., 29.

Gold and Steel Pen Manufactories, 2; Gold Pens m'd., 6,500; cap., $3,500; emp., 6.

Lasts m'd., 280,000 pairs; val., $56,000.

Sperm Oil imported, 121,241 galls.; val. of sperm oil imported, $130,357; Whale Oil imported, 2,294 galls.; val. of whale oil imported, $1,605; Whalebone imported, 21,800 lbs.; val. of whalebone imported, $8,720.

Vessels employed in the mackerel and cod fisheries, 89; Tonnage, 7,100 tons; Mackerel taken, 28,599 bbls.; Codfish taken, 1,000 quintals; val. of mackerel taken, $287,000; val. of cod liver oil sold for medicinal purposes, $30,000; Salt consumed, 45,000 bush.; cap., $260,000; emp., 1,000.

Horses, 4,800; val. of horses, $761,625; Milch Cows, 132, val. of cows, $5,405.

Establishments for m. of casks, 16; cap., $48,700; Casks m'd., 122,000; val., $158,000; emp., 140.

Establishments for m. of stone and earthenware, 1; cap., $15,000; val. of stone and earthenware, $20,000; emp., 29.

Establishments for m. of sashes, doors and blinds, 7; val. m'd., $44,500; cap., $12,800; emp., 33.

Establishments for m. of gas, 3; cap., $941,000; val. m'd., $431,000; emp., 171.

Establishments for m. of pickles and preserves, 3; cap., $65,000; val. m'd., $130,000; emp., 87.

Distilleries, 9; cap., $850,000; Alcohol distilled, 55,612 bbls.; all other Liquors distilled, 79,397 bbls.; val., $2,495,000; emp., 107.

Breweries, 7; cap., $67,600; Beer m'd., 47,800 bbls.; val., $238,408; emp., 56.

Establishments for m. of friction matches, 1; cap., $10,000; Matches m'd., 110,000 gross; val., $50,000; emp., 60.

Bakeries, 51; cap., $126,700; Flour consumed, 62,619 bbls.; val. of bread m'd., $935,810; emp., 220.

Type and Stereotype Founderies, 6; cap., $96,000; val. of type, &c., m'd., $230,000; m. emp., 160; f. emp., 54.

Establishments for m. of boxes, 7; cap., $15,900; val. of

boxes m'd., (wooden boxes, $25,500; Paper boxes, $40,500,) $66,000; emp., 63.

Rivet Manufactories, 1; val. m'd., $4,000; cap., $1,000; emp., 4.

Horse Shoe Nail Manufactories, 2; val. m'd., $4,500; cap., $1,000; emp., 6.

File Manufactories, 2; val. m'd., $28,000; cap., $2,500; emp., 15.

Saw Manufactories, 1; val. m'd., $2,500; cap., $1,000; emp., 5.

Portable Grist Mill Manufactories, 1; val. m'd., $15,000; cap., $6,000; emp., 10.

Mineral and Soda Water Manufactories, 2; val. m'd., $47,600; cap., $12,000; emp., 27.

Wrought Iron Tube Manufactories, 1; val. m'd., $60,000; cap., $30,000; emp., 15.

Sewing Machine Needle Manufactories, 1; val. m'd., $15,000; cap., $2,000; emp., 14.

Plane Manufactories, 2; val. m'd., $4,000; cap, $1,000; emp., 4.

Spirit Level Manufactories, 1; val. m'd., $20,000; cap., $5,000; emp., 12.

Fur Manufactories, 9; val. m'd., $342,000; cap., $123,000; emp., 162.

Copper Manufactories, 9; val. m'd., $256,500; cap., $93,500; emp., 103.

Soap-stone Manufactories, 6; val. m'd., $60,000; cap., $20,000; emp., 24.

Lamp and Gas Fixture Manufactories, 3; val. m'd., $233,000; cap., $113,000; emp., 225.

Picture Frame and Looking Glass Manufactories, 8; val. m'd., $150,000; cap., $40,000; emp., 90.

Perfumery Manufactories, 1; val. m'd., $20,000; cap., $5,000; emp., 10.

Yeast Powder Manufactories, 1; val. m'd., $100,000; cap., $15,000; emp., 20.

Leather Belting Manufactories, 1; val. m'd., $100,000; cap., $40,000; emp., 8.

Cork Manufactories, 3; val. m'd., $11,000; cap., $3,500; emp., 17.

Scale Manufactories, 3; val. m'd., $45,000; cap., $21,000; emp., 21.

Chain Manufactories, 1; val. m'd., $15,000; cap., $5,000; emp., 6.

Pocket Book Manufactories, 2; val. m'd., $6,000; cap., $2,000; emp., 4.

Steam and Gas Fitting Manufactories, 5; val. m'd., $209,000; cap., $123,000; emp., 110.

Show Case Manufactories, 4; val. m'd., $55,000; cap., $20,000; emp., 27.

Clothing Manufactories, –; val. m'd., $8,500,000; cap., $2,500,000. Number of establishments, and hands employed, not reported.

Paint Mill Manufactories, 1; val. m'd., $3,000; cap., $1,500; emp., 2.

Piano-Forte Hardware Manufactories, 2; val. m'd., $17,500; cap., $10,000; emp., 17.

Wood Moulding Manufactories, 1; val. m'd., $20,000; cap., 18,000; emp., 12.

Paper Hanging Manufactories, 4; val. m'd., $177,000; cap., $46,500; emp., 68.

Planing Machine Manufactories, 1; val. m'd., $10,000; cap., $3,000; emp., 10.

Axle-tree Manufactories, 2; val. m'd., $150,000; cap., $50,000; emp., 50.

Buckle Manufactories, 1; val. m'd., $9,000; cap., $3,000; emp., 25.

Blacksmiths' Bellows Manufactories, 1; val. m'd., $6,000; cap., $2,000; emp., 3.

Wire Work Manufactories, 2; val. m'd., $33,000; cap., $9,500; emp., 19.

Benzole Gas Machine Manufactories, 1; val. m'd., $3,000; cap., $1,000; emp., 2.

Truss and Shoulder Brace Manufactories, 4; val. m'd., $42,000; cap., $13,300; emp., 55.

Umbrella Manufactories, 2; val. m'd., $60,000; cap., $19,000; emp., 58.

Saddlery Hardware Manufactories, 1; val. m'd., $15,000; cap., $10,000; emp., 8.

Iron Bedstead Manufactories, 1; val. m'd., $4,000; cap., $2,000; emp., 3.

Vise Manufactories, 1; val. m'd., $800; cap., $400; emp., 3.

Piano-Forte Key Manufactories, 1; val. m'd., $30,000; cap., $5,000; emp., 28.

Forcing Pump Manufactories, 1; val. m'd., $6,000; cap., $2,000; emp., 4.

Canvas Stretcher Manufactories, 1; val. m'd., $1,000; cap., $300; emp., 1.

Essence Manufactories, 2; val. m'd., $25,000; cap., $5,000; emp., 5.

Grindstone Manufactories, 1; val. m'd., $20,000; cap., $5,000; emp., 5.

Vinegar Manufactories, 4; val. m'd., $28,300; emp., $7,000; emp., 7.

Saleratus Manufactories, 1; val. m'd., $8,000; cap., $1,500; emp., 1.

Spirits Turpentine Manufactories, 1; val. m'd., $60,000; cap., $50,000; emp., 8.

Carriage Spring Manufactories, 2; val. m'd., $13,500; cap., $2,000; emp., 10.

Spike Manufactories, 1; val. m'd., $172,000; cap., $40,000; emp., 13.

Lard Manufactories, 1; val. m'd., $500,000; cap., $15,000; emp., 15.

Daguerreotype Stock Manufactories, 2; val. m'd., $20,000; cap., $2,000; emp., 20.

French Burr Mill Stone Manufactories, 2; val. m'd., $12,500; cap., $3,800; emp., 11.

Steamboat Manufactories, 1; cap., $10,000; emp., 15.

Lithographic Press Manufactories, 1; val. m'd., $2,500; cap., $1,500; emp., 2.

Bag Manufactories, 2; val. m'd., $40,000; cap., $16,000; emp., 20.

CHELSEA.

Furnaces for m. of hollow ware and castings other than pig iron, 1; Hollow Ware and other Castings m'd., 800 tons; val. of hollow ware and castings, $48,000; cap., $10,000; emp., 31.

Establishments for m. of cotton, woollen and other machinery, 1; val. of machinery m'd., $20,000; cap.,$10,000; emp., 18.

Shops for m. of iron safes, 2; val. of iron safes, &c., $45,000; cap., $35,000; emp., 33.

Brass Founderies, 1; val. of articles m'd., $20,000; cap., $3,000; emp., 4.

Piano-Forte Manufactories, – ; all other musical instrument manufactories, 1; val. of horizontal organs m'd., $20,000; cap., $10,000; emp., 4.

Daguerreotype Artists, 1; Daguerreotypes taken, 3,000; cap., $600; emp., 2.

Brush Manufactories, 1; val. of brushes, $2,000; cap., $400; emp., 2.

Saddle, Harness and Trunk Manufactories, 3; val. of saddles, &c., $1,000; cap., $500; emp., 4.

Upholstery Manufactories, 1; val. of upholstery, $6,500; cap., $500; emp., 3.

Establishments for m. of boats, 2; Boats built, 89; cap., $3,000; emp., 16.

Establishments for m. of salt, 1; Salt m'd., 48,000 bush.; val. of salt, $31,000; cap., $10,000; emp., 9.

Establishments for m. of oil, 2; Rosin oil m'd., 112,000 galls.; Lard oil m'd., 75,000 galls.; val. of oil m'd., $100,000; emp., 16.

Tin Ware Manufactories, 4; val. of tin ware, $2,500; cap., $500; emp., 5.

Establishments for m. of white lead and other paints, 1; White Lead m'd., 400 tons; val. of white lead m'd., $64,000; other paints, &c., m'd., (Zinc Paint,) 700 tons; val., $105,000;

Putty, 400 tons; val., $24,000; Whiting, 800 tons; val., $16,000; val. of Ship's Paints, $20,000; cap., $50,000; emp., 14.

Mills for m. of linseed oil, 1; Oil m'd., 320,000 galls.; val., of oil, m'd., $300,000; cap., $150,000; emp., 38.

Tanneries, 1; Hides of all kinds tanned, 15,000; val. of leather tanned, $120,000; cap., $40,000; emp., 35.

Currying Establishments, 1; val. of leather curried, $7,000; cap., $300; emp., 4.

Bricks m'd., 300,000; val. of bricks m'd., $1,650; emp., 5.

Val. of snuff, tobacco and cigars, $14,000; m. emp., 11; f. emp., 7.

Val. of mechanics' tools m'd., $6,000; emp., 4.

Corn and other Brooms m'd., 150,000; val. of brooms, $30,000; emp., 18.

Horses, 200; val. of horses, $20,000; Oxen over three years old, 4; Steers under three years old, –; val. of oxen and steers, $160; Milch Cows, 50; Heifers, –; val. of cows and heifers, $1,500.

Honey, 100 lbs.; val. of honey, $15.

Indian Corn, 5 acres; Indian Corn, per acre, 25 bush.; val., $125.

Barley, 1 acre; Barley, per acre, 30 bush.; val., $30.

Potatoes, 15 acres; Potatoes, per acre, 100 bush.; val., $1,500.

Turnips, cultivated as a field crop, 1 acre; Turnips, per acre, 300 bush.; val., $120.

Beets and other esculent vegetables, 1 acre; val., $80.

English Mowing, 85 acres; English Hay, 78 tons; val., $1,950.

Salt Hay, 85 tons; val., $1,190.

Apple Trees, cultivated for their fruit, 1,000; val., $2,000.

Pear Trees, cultivated for their fruit, 500; val., $2,500.

Establishments for m. of casks, 1; cap., $1,500; Casks m'd., 36,000; val., $10,000; emp., 8.

Establishments for m. of gas, 1; cap., $100,000; val. m'd., $14,000; emp., 5.

Bakeries, 2; cap., $5,000; Flour consumed, 1,900 bbls;; val. of bread m'd., $30,000; emp., 10.

Establishments for m. of boxes, (Merchandise Packing), 2; val. of boxes m'd., $6,000; cap., $1,500; emp., 8.

Varnish Manufactories, 3; Varnish m'd., 29,000 galls.; val. of varnish, $57,000; cap., $8,000 ; emp., 6.

Laundry and Dyeing Establishments, 1; val. of goods dyed, $35,900; cap., $25,000; emp., 100.

Paper Stainery, 1; val. of paper hangings m'd., $60,000; cap., $30,000; emp., 30.

Shoe Lining Manufactories, 1; val. of shoe linings m'd., $20,000; cap., $2,000; emp., 3.

NORTH CHELSEA.

Bricks m'd., 1,700,000; val. of bricks, $11,900; emp., 22.

Horses, 77; val. of horses, $6,350; Oxen over three years old, 32; Steers under three years old, –; val. of oxen and steers, $2,000; Milch Cows, 261; Heifers, –; val. of cows and heifers, $6,525.

Indian Corn, 53 acres; Indian Corn, per acre, 50 bush.; val., $2,663.

Rye, 78 acres; Rye, per acre, 20 bush.; val., $1,575.

Barley, 12 acres; Barley, per acre, 15 bush.; val., $182.

Potatoes, 39 acres; Potatoes, per acre, 100 bush.; val., $3,867.

Turnips, cultivated as a field crop, 20 acres; Turnips, per acre, 100 bush.; val., $1,000.

Carrots, 15 acres; Carrots, per acre, 600 bush.; val., $2,700.

Beets and other esculent vegetables, 60 acres; 15,510 bush.; val., $3,877.50.

English Mowing, 505 acres; English Hay, 824 tons; val., $18,952.

Salt Hay, 895 tons; val., $12,530.

Apple Trees, cultivated for their fruit, 1,500; producing 1,909 bbls. of apples; val., $3,818.

Pear Trees, cultivated for their fruit, 220; producing 110 bush. of pears; val., $330; nearly all young trees.

Milk produced from 261 cows, 119,055 galls., sold at the farms at 16 cts. per gall., [$19,048.80,] and at market, 25 cts. per gall., [$29,763.75.]

WINTHROP.

Copper Manufactories, 1; Copper m'd., 1,000 tons; val., $400,000; cap., $200,000; emp., $60.

Horses, 54; val. of horses, $2,640; Oxen over three years old, 14; Steers under three years old, 1; val. of oxen and steers, $700; Milch Cows, 76; Heifers, 6; val. of cows and heifers, $2,025.

Butter, 500 lbs.; val. of butter, $100.

Indian Corn, 30 acres; Indian Corn, per acre, 35 bush.; val., $1,050.

Wheat, 1 acre; Wheat, per acre, 30 bush.; val., $78.00.

Rye, 30 acres; Rye, per acre, 20 bush.; val., $600.

Barley, 10 acres; Barley, per acre, 25 bush.

Potatoes, 45 acres; Potatoes, per acre, 70 bush.; val., $2,835.

Onions, ½ acre.

Carrots, 3 acres; Carrots, per acre, 400 bush.; val., $180.

Beets and other esculent vegetables, 1 to 2 acres; val., $30.

English Mowing, 150 acres; English Hay, 140 tons; val., $2,800.

Salt Hay, 200 tons; val., $3,000.

Apple Trees, cultivated for their fruit, 2,000.

Pear Trees, cultivated for their fruit, 300.

Lighters, 3; val., $1,200.

Milk Carts, 11; val. of milk sold, $2,500; Milkmen, 11.

WORCESTER COUNTY.

ASHBURNHAM.

Cotton Mills, 2; Spindles, 4,840; Cotton consumed, 190,000 lbs.; Cloth m'd., 360,000 yds., common Coarse Sheeting; val. of cloth, $30,000; Yarn m'd., 100,000 lbs.; val. of yarn, $32,000; cap., $40,000; m. emp., 22; f. emp., 33.

Chair and Cabinet Manufactories, 4; val. of chairs and cabinet ware, $300,000; cap., $125,000; emp., 300, $\frac{1}{6}$ females.

Tin Ware Manufactories, 1; val. of tin ware, $1,000; cap., $400; emp., 2.

Tanneries, 2; Hides of all kinds tanned, 50,000, sheep and goat skins; val. of leather tanned, $25,000; cap., $8,000; emp., 18.

Boots of all kinds m'd., 1,000 pairs; Shoes of all kinds m'd., 1,500 pairs; val. of boots and shoes, $4,000; m. emp., 6.

Bricks m'd., 300,000; val. of bricks, $1,500; emp., 4.

Charcoal m'd., 1,500 bush.; val. of same, $120.

Val. of wooden ware not otherwise enumerated, including farming utensils m'd., $25,000; emp., 12.

Lumber prepared for market, 1,500,000 ft.; val. of lumber, $13,500; emp., 30.

Firewood prepared for market, 4,500 cords; val. of firewood, $13,500; emp., 65.

Saxony Sheep, of different grades, –; Merino Sheep, of different grades, –; all other kinds of Sheep, 159; val. of all sheep, $477; Wool produced from Saxony sheep, – lbs.; Merino Wool produced, – lbs.; all other Wool produced, 600 lbs.

Horses, 196; val. of horses, $11,760; Oxen over three years old, 184; Steers under three years old, 120; val. of oxen and steers, $11,600; Milch Cows, 454; Heifers, 254; val. of cows and heifers, $17,295.

Butter, 34,000 lbs.; val. of butter, $8,500; Cheese, 8,000 lbs.; val. of cheese, $800.

Indian Corn, 175 acres; Indian Corn, per acre, 32 bush; val., $5,500.

Wheat, 20 acres; Wheat, per acre, 15 bush.; val., $475.

Rye, 20 acres; Rye, per acre, 16 bush.; val., $400.

Barley, 37 acres; Barley, per acre, 20 bush.; val., $740.

Oats, 130 acres; Oats, per acre, 30 bush.; val., $2,000.

Potatoes, 125 acres; Potatoes, per acre, 100 bush.; val., $6,250.

Onions, 150 bush.; val., $150.

Carrots, 4 acres; Carrots, per acre, 400 bush., val., $500.

English Mowing, 2,100 acres; English Hay, 1,600 tons; val., $22,400.

Wet Meadow or Swale Hay, 500 tons; val., $4,000.

Apple Trees, cultivated for their fruit, could not ascertain the number; Apples, 10,000 bush.; val., $3,200.

Friction Match Woods m'd., 2,500 cases; val., $9,500; emp., 9.

Val. of friction match boxes, $3,000; emp., 3.

Val. of mattress filling m'd., $5,000; emp., 5.

Domestic wine m'd., 2,500 galls.; val. of domestic wine m'd., $2,500; emp., 2.

Val. of cotton thread spools m'd., $3,500; emp., 10.

Val. of palm leaf hats, $2,500.

ATHOL.

Cotton Mills, 1; Spindles, 1,400; Cotton consumed, 300 bales; Cloth m'd., 300,000 yds.; val. of cloth, $25,400; Batting m'd., 40,000 lbs.; val. of batting, $4,000; cap., $6,500; m. emp., 12; f. emp., 20.

Furnaces for m. of hollow ware and castings other than

pig iron, 1; Hollow Ware and other Castings m'd., 20 tons; val. of hollow ware and castings, $2,000; cap., $500; emp., 2.

Establishments for m. of cotton, woollen and other machinery, 3; val. of machinery m'd., $15,500; cap., $3,500; emp., 10.

Scythe Manufactories, 1; Scythes m'd., 6,000; val. of scythes, $3,500; cap., $2,000; emp., 5.

Paper Manufactories, 1; Stock made use of, 13,000 lbs.; val. of paper, $6,000; cap., $4,500; emp., 4.

Daguerreotype Artists, 1; Daguerreotypes taken, 400; cap., $300; emp., 1.

Saddle, Harness and Trunk Manufactories, 1; val. of saddles, &c., $1,200; cap., $500; emp., 2.

Establishments for m. of railroad cars, coaches, chaises, wagons, sleighs, and other vehicles, 2; val. of railroad cars, &c., m'd., $5,700; cap., $1,200; emp., 7.

Chair and Cabinet Manufactories, 5; val. of chairs and cabinet ware, $18,200; cap., $6,700; emp., 26.

Tin Ware Manufactories, 1; val. of tin ware, $12,000; cap., $2,500; emp., 4.

Tanneries, 1; Hides of all kinds tanned, 3,200; val. of leather tanned, $18,000; cap., $15,000; emp., 4.

Currying Establishments, 1; val. of leather curried, $20,000; cap., $1,000; emp., 4.

Boots of all kinds m'd., 51,000 pairs; Shoes of all kinds m'd., 20,000 pairs; val. of boots and shoes, $100,000; m. emp., 114; f. emp., 36.

Val. of palm leaf hats, $20,000; m. emp., 15; f. emp., 700.

Bricks m'd., 300,000; val. of bricks, $1,500; emp., 4.

Val. of building stone quarried and prepared for building, $500; emp., 2.

Val. of wooden ware not otherwise enumerated, including farming utensils m'd., $8,600; emp., 9.

Shoe Pegs m'd., 10,000 bush.; val., $7,500.

Lumber prepared for market, 2,590,000 ft.; val. of lumber, $30,400; emp., 72.

Firewood prepared for market, 1,868 cords; val. of firewood, $4,390; emp., 20.

Saxony Sheep, of different grades, –; Merino Sheep, of different grades, –; all other kinds of Sheep, 95; val. of all sheep, $325; Wool produced from Saxony sheep, – lbs.; Merino Wool produced, – lbs.; all other Wool produced, 332 lbs.

Horses, 253; val. of horses, $20,130; Oxen over three years old, 249; Steers under three years old, 103; val. of oxen and steers, $14,822; Milch Cows, 488; Heifers, 127; val. of cows and heifers, $15,800.

Butter, 27,660 lbs.; val. of butter, $6,085.20; Cheese, 19,770 lbs.; val. of cheese, $1,571.60; Honey, 100 lbs.; val. of honey, $20.

Indian Corn, 228 acres; Indian Corn, per acre, 22 bush.; val., $5,483.

Wheat, 2 acres; Wheat, per acre, 10 bush.; val., $90.

Rye, 57 acres; Rye, per acre, 16 bush.; val., $1,368.

Barley, 47 acres; Barley, per acre, 21 bush.; val., $1,034.

Oats, 107 acres; Oats, per acre, 24 bush.; val., $1,540.80.

Potatoes, 162 acres; Potatoes, per acre, 83 bush.; val., $6,723.

Onions, ½ acre; Onions, per acre, 300 bush.; val., $150.

Carrots, ½ acre; Carrots, per acre, 536 bush.; val., $89.

English Mowing, 1,684 acres; English Hay, 1,261 tons; val., $18,915.

Wet Meadow or Swale Hay, 490 tons; val., $3,920.

Apple Trees, cultivated for their fruit, 4,235; val., $3,263.

Pear Trees, cultivated for their fruit, 144; val., $125.

Hops, 1½ acre; Hops, per acre, 400 lbs.; val., $200.

Establishments for m. of casks, 1; cap., $50; Casks m'd., 100; emp., 1.

Establishments for m. of sashes, doors, and blinds, 5; cap., $6,000; val. m'd., $22,000; emp., 33.

Establishments for m. of friction matches, 2; cap., $2,500; Matches m'd., 35,000 gross; val., $17,000; emp., 22.

Establishments for m. of boxes, 8; cap., $12,300; val. of boxes m'd., $37,765; emp., 35.

Swine raised, 137; val., $1,156.

Establishments for m. of pails, 3; cap., $12,000; val. of pails m'd., $37,250.

Saw Mills, 20.

Grist Mills, 3.

AUBURN.

Cotton Mills, 2; Spindles, 4,104; Cotton consumed, 244,000 lbs.; Cloth m'd., 840,000 yds., (Sheeting, 5 yds. to the lb., 4-4 wide); val. of cloth, $46,000; Batting m'd., 55,000 lbs.; val. of batting, $4,400; cap., $60,000; m. emp., 40; f. emp., 30.

Establishments for m. of cotton, woollen and other machinery, 1; not in operation; cap., $8,000.

Tanneries, 1; Hides of all kinds tanned, 1,000; val. of leather tanned, $5,000; cap., $2,500; emp., 5.

Lumber prepared for market, 191,000 ft.; val. of lumber, $2,864; emp., 6.

Firewood prepared for market, 3,825 cords; val. of firewood, $10,439; emp., 40.

Saxony Sheep, of different grades, –; Merino Sheep, of different grades, –; all other kinds of Sheep, 63; val. of all sheep, $260; Wool produced from Saxony sheep, – lbs.; Merino Wool produced, – lbs.; all other Wool produced, 216 lbs.

Horses, 95; val. of horses, $7,050; Oxen over three years old, 152; Steers under three years old, 64; val. of oxen and steers, $9,718; Milch Cows, 312; Heifers, 91; val. of cows and heifers, $10,700.

Butter, 15,565 lbs.; val. of butter, $3,891.25; Cheese, 4,500 lbs.; val. of cheese, $450; Honey, 300 lbs.; val. of honey, $75.

Indian Corn, 306 acres; Indian Corn, per acre, 32 bush.; val., $7,246.80.

Rye, 53 acres; Rye, per acre, 18 bush.; val., $1,417.50.

Barley, 4 acres; Barley, per acre, 16 bush.; val., $64.

Oats, 181 acres; Oats, per acre, 25 bush.; val., $2,262.50.

Potatoes, 110 acres; Potatoes, per acre, 98 bush.; val., $8,624.

Onions, 1 acre; Onions, per acre, 450 bush.; val., $337.50.

Turnips, cultivated as a field crop, 1 acre; Turnips, per acre, 225 bush.; val., $46.

Carrots, 3 acres; Carrots, per acre, 655 bush.; val., $589.80.

Beets and other esculent vegetables, – acres; val., $1,200; all other Grain or Root crops, 5 acres; val., $125.

English Mowing, 1,396 acres; English Hay, 1,340 tons; val., $24,120.

Wet Meadow or Swale Hay, 277 tons; val., $2,216.

Apple Trees, cultivated for their fruit, 5,175; val., $3,105.

Pear Trees, cultivated for their fruit, 30; val., $45.

Establishments for m. of woods for ploughs, cultivators, &c., 1; cap., $2,000; val. m'd., $7,000; emp., 10.

Swine raised, 198; val., $1,444.

BARRE.

Cotton Mills, 1; Spindles, 4,096; Cotton consumed, 400,400 lbs.; Cloth m'd., 1,196,000 yds., No. 16 Sheeting; val. of cloth, $83,720; cap., $75,000; m. emp., 30; f. emp., 35.

Woollen Mills, 2; Sets of Machinery, 5; Wool consumed, 150,000 lbs.; Cassimere m'd., $1,000 yds.; val. of cassimere, $700; Flannel or Blanketing, 304,000 yds.; val. of flannel or blanketing, $77,480; Yarn m'd. and not made into cloth, 2,000 lbs.; val. of yarn, $1,667; cap., $106,000; m. emp., 34; f. emp., 27.

Furnaces for m. of hollow ware and castings other than pig iron, 1; Hollow Ware and other Castings m'd., 100 tons; val. of hollow ware and castings, $7,000; cap., $2,000; emp., 8.

Establishments for m. of cotton, woollen and other machinery, 1; val. of machinery m'd., $5,000; cap., $1,000; emp., 4.

Plough Manufactories, 1; Ploughs and other Agricultural Tools m'd., 50; val., $400; cap., $100; emp., 2.

Saddle, Harness and Trunk Manufactories, 1; val. of saddles, &c., $1,500; cap., $500; emp., 4.

Upholstery Manufactories, 1; val. of upholstery, $5,000; cap., $1,500; emp., 8.

Hat and Cap Manufactories, 1; Hats and Caps m'd., 700; cap., $700; emp., 2.

Tin Ware Manufactories, 2; val. of tin ware, $8,000; cap., $2,500; emp., 12.

Boots of all kinds m'd., 14,500 pairs; Shoes of all kinds m'd., 300 pairs; val. of boots and shoes, $26,500; m. emp., 28; f. emp., 5.

Val. of palm leaf hats, $70,000; m. emp., 5; f. emp., 600.

Lumber prepared for market, 256,000 ft.; val. of lumber, $2,573; emp., 5.

Firewood prepared for market, 3,000 cords; val. of firewood, $8,250; emp., 25.

Saxony Sheep, of different grades, –; Merino Sheep, of different grades, –; all other kinds of Sheep, 202; val. of all sheep, $505; Wool produced from Saxony sheep, – lbs.; Merino Wool produced, – lbs.; all other Wool produced, 628 lbs.

Horses, 452; val. of horses, $3,905; Oxen over three years old, 369; Steers under three years old, 119; val. of oxen and steers, $24,992; Milch Cows, 1,587; Heifers, 468; val. of cows and heifers, $62,312.

Butter, 35,700 lbs.; val. of butter, $8,925; Cheese, 323,830 lbs.; val. of cheese, $32,383.

Indian Corn, 606 acres; Indian Corn, per acre, 35 bush.; val., $23,972.

Wheat, 2 acres; Wheat, per acre, 27 bush.; val., $67.

Rye, 137 acres; Rye, per acre, 15 bush.; val., $2,571.

Barley, 202 acres; Barley, per acre, 20 bush.; val., $4,037.

Oats, 521 acres; Oats, per acre, 30 bush.; val., $7,820.

Potatoes, 297 acres; Potatoes, per acre, 100 bush.; val., $17,645.

Carrots, 6½ acres; Carrots, per acre, 500 bush.; val., $811.

English Mowing, 4,065 acres; English Hay, 3,919 tons; val., $58,785.

Wet Meadow or Swale Hay, 1,065 tons; val., $8,496.

Apple Trees, cultivated for their fruit, 10,495; val., $6,249.

Hops, ¾ acre; Hops, per acre, 403 lbs.; val., $112.

Establishments for m. of casks, 1; cap., $1,500; Casks m'd., 25,000; val., $450; emp., 4.

Establishments for m. of sashes, doors and blinds, 1; cap., $300; val. m'd., $2,000; emp., 2.

Bakeries, 1; cap., $1,500; Flour consumed, 4,000 bbls.; val. of bread m'd., $5,500; emp., 3.

Establishments for m. of boxes for cloth, boots, shoes and hats, 2; cap., $3,000; val. of boxes m'd., $14,000; emp., 10.

Pork raised, 150,000 lbs.; val., $10,500.

Val. of beef raised, $14,000.

BERLIN.

Boots of all kinds m'd., 9,340 pairs; shoes of all kinds m'd., 34,340 pairs; val. of boots and shoes, $35,275; m. emp., 34; f. emp., 24.

Lumber prepared for market, 64,500 ft.; val. of lumber, $818; emp., 2.

Firewood prepared for market, 880 cords; val. of firewood, $3,175; emp., 3.

Saxony Sheep, of different grades, –; Merino Sheep, of different grades, –; all other kinds of Sheep, 87; val. of all sheep, $256; Wool produced from Saxony sheep, – lbs; Merino Wool produced, – lbs.; all other Wool produced, 223 lbs.

Horses, 143; val. of horses, $10,215; Oxen over three years

old, 150; Steers under three years old, 74; val. of oxen and steers, $9,287; Milch Cows, 350; Heifers, 77; val. of cows and heifers, $10,489.

Butter, 28,800 lbs.; val. of butter, $7,200; Cheese, 2,130 lbs.; val. of cheese, $170; Honey, 87 lbs.; val. of honey, $14.

Indian Corn, 193 acres; Indian Corn, per acre, 29 bush.; val., $5,728.

Wheat, 2½ acres; Wheat, per acre, 9 bush.; val., $45.

Rye, 53 acres; Rye, per acre, 10½ bush.; val., $858.

Barley, 8 acres; Barley, per acre, 17½ bush.; val., $140.

Oats, 59 acres; Oats, per acre, 25 bush.; val., $885.

Potatoes, 96 acres; Potatoes, per acre, 74 bush.; val., $4,418.

Turnips, cultivated as a field crop, 2½ acres; Turnips, per acre, 110 bush.; val., $55.

Carrots, 3 acres; Carrots, per acre, 277 bush.; val., $69.

Beets and other esculent vegetables, beans, 10 acres; val., $300.

English Mowing, 902 acres; English Hay, 943 tons; val., $14,145.

Wet Meadow or Swale Hay, 454 tons; val., $3,632.

Apple Trees, cultivated for their fruit, 6,349; val., $3,800.

Pear Trees, cultivated for their fruit, 344; val., $59.

Hops, 5 acres; Hops, per acre, 350 lbs.; val., $437.

Cranberries, 9 acres; val., $102.

Beeswax, 7 lbs.; val., $3.50.

Swine raised, 218; val., $2,054.

Val. of peaches and quinces, $303.

BLACKSTONE.

Cotton Mills, 4; Spindles, 43,440; Cotton consumed, 1,241,-400 lbs.; Cloth m'd., 5,368,500 yds. Fine Sheetings and Printing Cloths; in consequence of repairs, not more than half the usual quantity was made during the year; val. of cloth,

$365,940; Yarn m'd., 15,000 lbs.; val. of yarn, $4,000; Batting m'd., 42,600 lbs.; val. of batting, $3,425; Flannel m'd., 44,700 yds.; val. of flannel, $3,800; cap., $1,026,500; m. emp., 546; f. emp., 544.

Woollen Mills, 4; Sets of Machinery, 39; Wool consumed, 1,210,000 lbs; Cassimere m'd., 1,085,000 yds.; val. of cassimere, $1,150,000; Satinet m'd., 140,500 yds.; val. of satinet, $60,000; cap., $246,000; m. emp., 400; f. emp., 207.

Scythe Manufactories, 1; Scythes m'd., 2,000 doz.; val. of scythes, $14,000; cap., $14,000; emp., 20.

Saddle, Harness and Trunk Manufactories, 2; val. of saddles, &c., $1,120; cap., $1,100; emp., 11.

Cordage Manufactories, 2; Cordage m'd., 69,000 lbs.; cap., $3,500; emp., 12.

Establishments for m. of wagons and other vehicles, 2; val. of wagons, &c., m'd., $6,200; cap., $6,000; emp., 18.

Establishments for m. of soap, 1; Soap m'd., 1,400 bbls., 14 tons; val. of soap, $5,600; cap., $800; emp., 3.

Glue Manufactories, and Manufactories for the preparation of Gums, 1; val. of glue and gums m'd., $250; cap., $350; emp., 2.

Boots of all kinds m'd., 1,400 pairs; Shoes of all kinds m'd., 320 pairs; val. of boots and shoes, $4,800; m. emp., 8; f. emp., 3.

Val. of building stone quarried and prepared for building, $400; emp., 1.

Lumber prepared for market, 311,500 ft.; val. of lumber, $4,200; emp., 9, three months each.

Firewood prepared for market, 3,200 cords; val. of firewood, $11,000; emp., 38, three months each.

Horses, 215; val. of horses, $21,130; Oxen over three years old, 114; Steers under three years old, 16; val. of oxen and steers, $7,550; Milch Cows, 350; Heifers, 35; val. of cows and heifers, $11,800.

Butter, 10,000 lbs.; val. of butter, $2,500; Cheese, 1,200 lbs.; val. of cheese, $85; Honey, 200 lbs.; val. of honey, $43.

Indian Corn, 180 acres; Indian Corn, per acre, 30 bush.; val., $6,000.

Wheat, 10 acres ; Wheat, per acre, 12 bush. ; val., $240.

Rye, 70 acres ; Rye, per acre, 9 bush. ; val., $790.

Barley, $\frac{1}{4}$ acre ; Barley, per acre, 16 bush. ; val., $4.

Oats, 38 acres ; Oats, per acre, 18 bush. ; val., $450.

Potatoes, 153 acres ; Potatoes, per acre, 86 bush. ; val., $9,200.

Onions, $\frac{1}{2}$ acre ; Onions, per acre, 140 bush. ; val., $70.

Turnips, cultivated as a field crop, $5\frac{2}{3}$ acres ; Turnips, per acre, 260 bush. ; val., $255.

Carrots, $\frac{1}{4}$ acre ; Carrots, per acre, 500 bush. ; val., $50.

Beets and other esculent vegetables, – acres ; all other Grain or Root Crops, 28 acres ; val., $2,000.

Millet, 1 acre ; val., $18.

English Mowing, 1,350 acres ; English Hay, 1,025 tons ; val., $18,450.

Wet Meadow or Swale Hay, 280 tons ; val., $2,370.

Apple Trees, cultivated for their fruit, 8,000 ; val., $1,600.

Pear Trees, cultivated for their fruit, 200 ; val., $35.

Cranberries, 57 acres ; val., $1,650.

Establishments for m. of sashes, doors and blinds, 1 ; val. m'd., $325 ; cap., $80 ; emp., 1.

Bakeries, 2 ; cap., $5,300 ; Flour consumed, 2,680 bbls. ; val. of bread m'd., $43,600 ; emp., 10.

Establishments for m. of boxes for cassimere and satinet, 1 ; cap., $1,100 ; val. of boxes m'd., $1,500 ; emp., 1.

Woollen Rags m'd. into Wool, 88,400 lbs. ; val., $3,550 ; cap., $6,500 ; m. emp., 2 ; f. emp., 1.

Val. of milk sold, $6,000.

BOLTON.

Comb Manufactories, 1 ; val. of combs m'd., $1,247 ; cap., $200 ; emp., 2.

Boots of all kinds m'd., – pairs ; Shoes of all kinds m'd.,

56,060 pairs; val. of boots and shoes, $48,236; m. emp., 57; f. emp., 57.

Val. of cigars, $3,000; m. emp., 1; f. emp., 1.

Casks of Lime m'd., 480; val. of lime, $600; emp., 1.

Val. of pumps m'd., $800; emp., 1.

Lumber prepared for market, 427,000 ft.; val. of lumber, $6,316; emp., 3.

Firewood prepared for market, 2,585 cords; val. of firewood, $8,500; emp., 5.

Saxony Sheep, of different grades, –; Merino Sheep, of different grades, –; all other kinds of Sheep, 22; val. of all sheep, $66.

Horses, 191; val. of horses, $16,330; Oxen over three years old, 184; Steers under three years old, 28; val. of oxen and steers, $9,945; Milch Cows, 621; Heifers, 67; val. of cows and heifers, $20.778.

Butter, 29,004 lbs.; val. of butter, $7,226; Cheese, 2,490 lbs.; val. of cheese, $243; Honey, 50 lbs.; val. of honey, $10.

Indian Corn, 285 acres; Indian Corn, per acre, 30 bush.; val., $7,795.

Wheat, 14 acres; Wheat, per acre, 12 bush.; val., $387.

Rye, 86 acres; Rye, per acre, 15 bush.; val., $1,404.

Barley, 10 acres; Barley, per acre, 17 bush.; val., $154.

Oats, 70 acres; Oats, per acre, 20 bush.; val., $818.

Potatoes, 144 acres; Potatoes, per acre, 71 bush.; val., $7,952.

Turnips, cultivated as a field crop, 19 acres; Turnips, per acre, 267 bush.; val., $1,189.

Carrots, 30 acres; Carrots, per acre, 425 bush.; val., $3,460.

Beets and other esculent vegetables, – acres; val., $1,217; all other Grain or Root Crops, Buckwheat, 6 acres; val., $72.

English Mowing, 1,463 acres; English Hay, 1,486 tons; val., $25,975.

Wet Meadow or Swale Hay, 608 tons; val., $5,475.

Apple Trees, cultivated for their fruit, 14,497; val., $5,834.

Pear Trees, cultivated for their fruit, 104; val., $105.

Hops, 2 acres; Hops, per acre, 1,150 lbs.; val., 500.

Cranberries, 27 acres; val., $520.

Establishments for m. of boxes for shoes, 1; cap., $1,500; val. of boxes m'd., $1,900; emp., 1.

Swine raised, 196; val., $2,929.

Val. of comb wash m'd., $200.

Hames m'd., 900 pairs; val., $500.

Val. of milk sold, $6,971.

Val. of jackass, $20.

BOYLSTON.

Cotton Mills, 1; Spindles, 4,500; Cotton consumed, 275,000 lbs.; Cloth m'd., am't. not given; val. of cloth, $33,000; Yarn m'd., 225,000 lbs; val. of yarn, $37,500; m. emp., 17; f. emp., 33.

Lumber prepared for market, 153,000 ft.; val. of lumber, $2,295; emp., 10.

Firewood prepared for market, 3,882 cords; val. of firewood $10,701; emp., 10.

Saxony Sheep, of different grades, –; Merino Sheep, of different grades, –; all other kinds of sheep, 18; val. of all sheep, $85; Wool produced from Saxony sheep, – lbs.; Merino Wool produced, – lbs.; all other Wool produced, 96 lbs.

Horses, 111; val. of horses, $6,770; Oxen over three years old, 148; Steers under three years old, 136; val. of oxen and steers, $8,704; Milch Cows, 490; Heifers 65; val. of cows and heifers, $15,150.

Butter, 35,120 lbs.; val. of butter, $7,726.20; Cheese, 4,165 lbs.; val. of cheese, $333.20.

Indian Corn, 234 acres; Indian Corn, per acre, $27\frac{27}{32}$ bush.; val., $6,949.80.

Buckwheat, 15 acres; Buckwheat, per acre, 8 bush.; val., $108.

Rye, $59\frac{1}{2}$ acres; Rye, per acre, 9 bush.; val., $803.25.

Barley, $2\frac{1}{2}$ acres; Barley, per acre, $15\frac{1}{2}$ bush.; val., $38.75.

Oats, 170 acres ; Oats, per acre, $24\frac{25}{32}$ bush. ; val., $2,325.60.

Potatoes, $97\frac{3}{4}$ acres ; Potatoes, per acre, $72\frac{10}{32}$ bush. ; val., $5,298.05.

Turnips, cultivated as a field crop, $\frac{1}{2}$ acre ; Turnips, per acre, 50 bush. ; val., $12.50.

English Mowing, 1,010 acres ; English Hay, 960 tons ; val., $11,520,

Wet Meadow or Swale Hay, 380 tons ; val., $2,660.

Apple Trees, cultivated for their fruit, 8,600 ; val., $2,630.

Pear Trees, cultivated for their fruit, 150 ; val., $8.

Hops, 5 acres; Hops, per acre, 526 lbs. ; val., $657.50.

BROOKFIELD.

Cotton Mills, 1 ; Spindles, 3,300 ; Cotton consumed, 270,000 lbs.; Cloth m'd., 900,000 yds. Denims ; val. of cloth, $90,000 ; m. emp., 30 ; f. emp., 43.

Furnaces for m. of hollow ware and castings other than pig iron, 1 ; Hollow Ware and other Castings m'd., 150 tons ; val. of hollow ware and castings, $9,000 ; cap., $2,000 ; emp., 8.

Establishments for m. of railroad cars, coaches, chaises, wagons, sleighs, and other vehicles, 1 ; val. of railroad cars, &c., m'd., $2,576 ; cap., $1,500 ; emp., 4.

Establishments for m. of soap and tallow candles, 1 ; Soap m'd., 225 bbls. ; val. of soap, $900 ; cap., $200 ; emp., 2.

Currying Establishments, 3 ; val. of leather curried, $55,000 ; cap., $7,000 ; emp., 14.

Boots of all kinds m'd., 69,000 pairs ; Shoes of all kinds m'd., 156,000 pairs ; val. of boots and shoes, $272,000 ; m. emp., 305 ; f. emp., 207.

Bricks m'd., 400,000 ; val. of bricks, $2,000 ; emp., 9.

Lumber prepared for market, 715,000 ft. ; val. of lumber, $7,939 ; emp., 6.

Firewood prepared for market, 4,149 cords ; val. of firewood, $12,440 ; emp., 7.

Saxony Sheep, of different grades, –; Merino Sheep, of different grades, –; all other kinds of Sheep, 367; val. of all sheep, $1,099; Wool produced from Saxony sheep, – lbs.; Merino Wool produced, – lbs.; all other Wool produced, 1,202 lbs.

Horses, 188; val. of horses, $14,845; Oxen over three years old, 213; Steers under three years old, 246; val. of oxen and steers, $17,680; Milch Cows, 447; Heifers, 161; val. of cows and heifers, $15,798.

Butter, 23,425 lbs.; val. of butter, $5,387.75; Cheese, 11,035 lbs.; val. of cheese, $971.50; Honey, 67 lbs.; val. of honey, $13.40.

Indian Corn, 203½ acres; Indian Corn, per acre, 28$\frac{8}{10}$ bush.; val., $5,872.50.

Wheat, 1 acre; Wheat, per acre, 8 bush.; val., $12.

Rye, 118 acres; Rye, per acre, 12$\frac{4}{10}$ bush.; val., $1,889.

Barley, 30 acres; Barley, per acre, 17$\frac{14}{15}$ bush.; val., $538.

Oats, 143 acres; Oats, per acre, 25⅛ bush.; val., $1,795.50.

Potatoes, 139 acres; Potatoes, per acre, 86$\frac{1}{10}$ bush.; val., $5,983.50.

Carrots, 2½ acres; Carrots, per acre, 525⅗ bush.; val., $328.50.

English Mowing, 1,378¼ acres; English Hay, 1,473¼ tons; val., $17,679.

Wet Meadow or Swale Hay, 737 tons; val., $5,963.

Apple Trees, cultivated for their fruit, 4,752; val., $2,358.

Pear Trees, cultivated for their fruit, 138; val., $55.

Cranberries, 98 acres; val., $701.

Beeswax, 7 lbs.; val., $3.50.

Establishments for m. of casks, –; cap., $780; Nail Casks m'd., 6,000.

Carriage Wheels m'd., 4,000 sets; val., $40,000; cap., $12,000; Hay Cutters m'd., 2,000; val. m'd., $12,000; cap., $3,000; emp., 45.

CHARLTON.

Chair and Cabinet Manufactories, 1; val. of chairs and cabinet ware, $1,000; cap., $500; emp., 2.

Boots of all kinds m'd., 31,500 pairs; Shoes of all kinds m'd., 56,600 pairs; val. of boots and shoes, $96,086; m. emp., 121; f. emp., 48.

Val. of marble quarried and prepared for market, $1,800; emp., 7.

Val. of mechanics' tools m'd., $16,000; emp., 20.

Lumber prepared for market, 1,050,000 ft.; val. of lumber, $9,164; emp., 12.

Firewood prepared for market, 5,363 cords; val. of firewood, $12,700; emp., 10.

Saxony Sheep, of different grades, –; Merino Sheep, of different grades, –; all other kinds of Sheep, 334; val. of all sheep, $832; Wool produced from Saxony sheep, – lbs.; Merino Wool produced, – lbs.; all other Wool produced, 1,047 lbs.

Horses, 316; val. of horses, $26,443; Oxen over three years old, 562; Steers under three years old, 236; val. of oxen and steers, $36,800; Milch Cows, 875; Heifers, 316; val. of cows and heifers, $31,177.

Butter, 48,015 lbs.; val. of butter, $9,603; Cheese, 38,485 lbs.; val. of cheese, $3,848; Honey, 352 lbs.; val. of honey, $88.

Indian Corn, 487 acres; Indian Corn, per acre, 31 bush.; val., $16,984.

Wheat, 5 acres; Wheat, per acre, 14 bush.; val., $150.

Rye, 34 acres; Rye, per acre, 15 bush.; val., $765.

Barley, 19 acres; Barley, per acre, 24 bush.; val., $456.

Oats, 475 acres; Oats, per acre, 30 bush.; val., $8,550.

Potatoes, 211 acres; Potatoes, per acre, 100 bush.; val., $10,550.

Carrots, 1½ acre; Carrots, per acre, 333⅓ bush.; val., $125.

English Mowing, 3,713 acres; English Hay, 3,394 tons; val., $42,425.

Wet Meadow or Swale Hay, 1,093 tons; val., $7,651.

Apple Trees, cultivated for their fruit, 3,845; val., $2,124.

Pear Trees, cultivated for their fruit, 153; val., $40.

Beeswax, 25 lbs.; val., $10.

Establishments for m. of sashes, doors and blinds, 1; cap., $800; val. m'd., $1,000; emp., 1.

Establishments for m. of boxes for shoes, 1; cap., $2,000; val. of boxes m'd., $6,500; emp., 6.

Swine raised, 218; val., $2,000.

Buckwheat, 25 acres; 300 bush.; val., $300.

CLINTON.

Cotton Mills,* 3; Spindles, 27,384; Cotton consumed, 1,295,125 lbs.; Cloth m'd., 5,390,365 yds.; Ginghams, 5,195,722; Counterpanes, 394,643; val. of cloth, $632,392; cap., $1,475,000; m. emp., 424; f. emp., 683.

Woollen Mills, 1; Sets of Machinery, 2; Wool consumed, 37,500 lbs.; Fancy Twist Cassimere m'd., 75,000 yds.; val. of cassimere, $45,000; cap., $20,000; m. emp., 20; f. emp., 8.

Mills for m. of carpeting, 1; Worsted bought, 270,329 lbs.; Carpeting m'd., 207,462 yds.; val. of carpeting, $270,700; cap., $200,000; m. emp., 53; f. emp., 100.

Establishments for m. of worsted goods, or goods of which worsted is a component part, 1; Goods m'd., 572,932 yds. of Coach Lace; val. of goods, $53,284; cap., included in Cotton Mills; m. emp., 10; f. emp., 36. In this concern, 689 lbs. of silk are used for the m. of silk coach lace.

* The Assessors make the following additional return:—" Lancaster Quilt Company, 1st September, 1855; cap., $125,000; Cotton consumed per year, 249,493 lbs.; Spindles, 1,600; Square yds. m'd. per year, 394,643; m. emp., 40; f. emp., 62.

Furnaces for m. of hollow ware and castings other than pig iron, 1; Hollow Ware and other Castings m'd., 150 tons; val. of hollow ware and castings, $10,500; cap., $10,000; emp., 8.

Establishments for m. of cotton, woollen and other machinery, 2; val. of machinery m'd., $37,800; cap., $15,000; emp., 30.

Establishments for m. of railroad cars, coaches, chaises, wagons, sleighs, and other vehicles, 1; val. of railroad cars, &c., m'd., $2,000; cap., $3,000; emp., 3. Just commenced operation.

Establishments for m. of soap and tallow candles, –; Soap m'd., 780 bbls.; val. of soap, $3,120; cap., $1,200; emp., 2.

Tin Ware Manufactories, 1; val. of tin ware, $3,000; cap., $4,500; emp., 4.

Comb Manufactories, 2; val. of combs m'd., $28,000; cap., $8,400; emp., 50.

Boots of all kinds m'd., 2,772 pairs; Shoes of all kinds m'd., 9,988 pairs; val. of boots and shoes, $21,331; m. emp., 12; f. emp., 7.

Bricks m'd., 400,000; val. of bricks, $2,400; emp., 5.

Horses, 109; val. of horses, $10,900; Oxen over three years old, 26; Steers under three years old, –; val. of oxen and steers, $2,020; Milch Cows, 109; Heifers, 22; val. of cows and heifers, $4,033.

Butter, 3,375 lbs.; val. of butter, $810.

Indian Corn, 46 acres; Indian Corn, 1,236 bush.; val., $1,236.

Rye, 18 acres; Rye, 255 bush.; val., $340.

Oats, 17 acres; Oats, 532 bush.; val., $319.

Potatoes, 33 acres; Potatoes, per acre, 2,645 bush.; val., $1,763.

Carrots, – acres; Carrots, 392 bush; val., $98.

English Mowing, 286 acres; English Hay, 330 tons; val., $5,940.

Apples, 2,351 bush.; val., $1,417.

Establishments, for m. of sashes, doors and blinds, 1; cap., $800; val. m'd., $2,000; emp., 2.

Establishments for m. of gas, 1; cap., $24,000; val. m'd., $10,330; emp., 4.

Bakeries, 1; cap., $6,000; Flour consumed, 1,040 bbls.; val. of bread m'd., $20,000; emp., 7.

Gross value of all other articles m'd. in the town, viz.: cloth-cases, belts, loom-harnesses, and roll-coverings, $8,475; cap., $6,000; emp., 12.

DANA.

Val. of palm leaf hats m'd., $7,350; f. emp., 214.

Corn and other Brooms m'd., 900; val. of brooms, $150; emp., 1.

Lumber prepared for market, 580,000 ft.; val. of lumber, $6,940; emp., 16.

Firewood prepared for market, 163 cords; val. of firewood, $326; emp., 4.

Saxony Sheep, of different grades, –; Merino Sheep, of different grades, –; all other kinds of Sheep, 211; val. of all sheep, $585; Wool produced from Saxony sheep, – lbs.; Merino Wool produced, – lbs.; all other Wool produced, 712 lbs.

Horses, 146; val. of horses, $11,244; Oxen over three years old, 163; Steers under three years old, 72; val. of oxen and steers, $9,375; Milch Cows, 251; Heifers, 80; val. of cows and heifers, $8,541.

Butter, 12,270 lbs.; val. of butter, $2,699.40; Cheese, 12,345 lbs.; val. of cheese, $864.15; Honey, 30 lbs.; val. of honey, $5.

Indian Corn, 214 acres; Indian Corn, per acre, 24 bush.; val., $6,420.

Rye, 95 acres; Rye, per acre, 8 bush.; val., $950.

Barley, 8 acres; Barley, per acre, 17 bush.; val., $136.

Oats, 105 acres; Oats, per acre, 14 bush.; val., $882.

Potatoes, 99 acres; Potatoes, per acre, 78 bush.; val., $3,875.

Turnips, cultivated as a field crop, $\frac{1}{4}$ acre; Turnips, per acre, 120 bush.; val., $7.50.

Carrots, $1\frac{1}{8}$ acre; Carrots, per acre, 214 bush.; val., $85.

English Mowing, 698 acres; English Hay, 639 tons; val., $8,946.

Wet Meadow or Swale Hay, 476 tons; val., $3,808.

Apple Trees, cultivated for their fruit, 1,079; val., $944.

Cranberries, 5 acres; val., $50.

Establishments for m. of sashes, doors and blinds, 1; cap., $200; val. m'd., $500; emp., 1.

Swine raised, 84; val., $659.

Staves, 100,000; val., $4,000; emp., 4.

White Beans, 60 bush.; val., $120.

Buckwheat, 281 bush.; val., $210.75.

Bulls, 7; val. $175.

Piano-Forte Leg Manufactories, 2; Legs m'd., 5,200 sets; val., $46,800; Melodeon Legs m'd., 700 sets; val., $3,150; cap., $12,000; emp., 30.

DOUGLAS.

Cotton Mills, 1; Spindles, 4,480; Cotton consumed, 200,000 lbs.; Cloth m'd., 1,000,000 yds. Print Goods, 52 by 58, Nos. 23, 28; val. of cloth, $35,000, cap., $50,000; m. emp., 36; f. emp., 35.

Axe Manufactories, 2; Axes, Hatchets and other Edge Tools m'd., 477,000; val., $396,950; cap., $312,000; emp., 270.

Chair and Cabinet Manufactories, 1; val., $500; cap., $2,000; emp., 2.

Tin Ware and Sheet Iron Manufactories, 1; val. of tin ware, $800; cap., $1,000; emp., 2.

Boots of all kinds m'd., 5,000 pairs; Shoes of all kinds m'd., 34,370 pairs; val. of boots and shoes, $36,036; m. emp., 50; f. emp., 50.

Charcoal m'd., 18,700 bush.; val. of same, $1,870; emp., 12.

Lasts m'd., 20,000; val., $4,600.

Lumber prepared for market, 664,000 ft.; val. of lumber, $8,853.33; emp., 30.

Firewood prepared for market, 3,295 cords; val. of firewood, $12,355; emp., 21.

Saxony Sheep, of different grades, –; Merino Sheep, of different grades, –; all other kinds of Sheep, 78; val. of all sheep, $140; Wool produced from Saxony sheep, – lbs.; Merino Wool produced, – lbs.; all other Wool produced, 200 lbs.

Horses, 170; val. of horses, $12,149; Oxen over three years old, 169; Steers under three years old, 63; val. of oxen and steers, $8,285; Milch Cows, 396; Heifers, 71; val. of cows and heifers, $10,836.

Butter, 14,930 lbs.; val. of butter, $3,732.50; Cheese, 3,790 lbs.; val. of cheese, $303.20; Honey, 850 lbs.; val. of honey, $85.

Indian Corn, 256 acres; Indian Corn, per acre, 24 bush.; val., $6,912.

Rye, 51 acres; Rye, per acre, 15 bush.; val., $1,147.

Oats, 158 acres; Oats, per acre, 22 bush.; val., $1,781.

Potatoes, 169 acres; Potatoes, per acre, 55 bush.; val., $6,972.

English Mowing, 1,593 acres; English Hay, 814 tons; val., $16,280.

Wet Meadow or Swale Hay, 199 tons; val., $1,592.

Apple Trees, cultivated for their fruit, 1,096; val., $780.

Pear Trees, cultivated for their fruit, 74; val., $93.

Cranberries, 3½ acres; val., $100.

Establishments for m. of boxes for shoes and boots, 1; cap., $850; val. of boxes m'd., $650; emp., 2.

Mills for planing, ploughing, matching and jointing boards, 1; Planed, 30,000 ft.; val. of labor, $174.

Swine raised, 275; val., $1,428.

DUDLEY.

Woollen Mills, 2; Sets of Machinery, 6; Wool consumed, 85,000 lbs.; Broadcloth m'd., 32,500 yds.; val. of broadcloth, $65,000; Satinet m'd., 100,000 yds; val. of satinet, $50,000; Yarn m'd., and not m'd. into cloth, 8,000 lbs.; val. of yarn. $6,400; cap., $7,500; m. emp., 51; f. emp., 39.

Establishments for m. of linen 1; Linen m'd., 1,000,000 yds.; val. of linen, $1,000,000; cap., $100,000; m. emp., 65; f. emp., 75.

Saddle, Harness and Trunk Manufactories, 1; val. of saddles, &c., $800; cap., $500; emp., 1.

Establishments for m. of fire arms, 1; Fire Arms m'd., 2,300 Rifles and Pistols; val. of fire arms, $13,400; cap., $3,000; emp., 10.

Tanneries, 1; Hides of all kinds tanned, 1,000; val. of leather tanned, $4,200; cap., $3,000; emp., 6.

Boots of all kinds m'd., – pairs; Shoes of all kinds m'd., 9,000 pairs; val. of boots and shoes, $6,000; m. emp., 20; f. emp., 25.

Lumber prepared for market, 30,000 ft.; val. of lumber, $450; emp., 3.

Firewood prepared for market, 1,325 cords; val. of firewood, $3,320; emp., 9.

Merino Sheep raised, 175; val. of all sheep, $565; Merino Wool produced, 570 lbs.

Horses, 161; val. of horses, $11,912; Oxen over three years old, 186; Steers under three years old, 164; val. of oxen and steers, $14,500; Milch Cows, 534; Heifers, 262; val. of cows and heifers, $22,430.

Butter, 32,860 lbs.; val. of butter, $8,215; Cheese, 21,950 lbs.; val. of cheese, $2,195; Honey, 200 lbs.; val. of honey, $40.

Indian Corn, 332 acres; Indian Corn, per acre, 33 bush.; val., $13,250.

Rye, 94 acres; Rye, per acre, 12 bush.; val., $1,725.

Barley, 6 acres; Barley, per acre, 30 bush.; val., $180.

Oats, 273 acres; Oats, per acre, 32 bush.; val., $4,417.

Potatoes, 160 acres; Potatoes, per acre, 100 bush.; val., $8,155.

Onions, 2¼ acres; Onions, per acre, 250 bush.; val., $345.

Carrots, 2 acres; Carrots, per acre, 460 bush.; val., $368.

Buckwheat, 57 acres; val., $684.

English Mowing, 2,300 acres; English Hay, 2,234 tons; val., $31,276.

Wet Meadow or Swale Hay, 418 tons; val., $2,508.

Apple Trees, cultivated for their fruit, 3,940; val., $2,342.

Pear Trees, cultivated for their fruit, 48; val., $48.

Cranberries, 7¼ acres; val., $120.

Swine raised, 196; val., $1,568.

FITCHBURG.

Cotton Mills, 4; Spindles, 6,944; Cotton consumed, 985,233 lbs.; Cloth m'd., 1,249,000 yds. Cotton Duck and Shirtings; val. of cloth, $252,025; cap., $151,000; m. emp., 97; f. emp., 105.

Woollen Mills, 1; Sets of Machinery, 3; Wool consumed, 100,000 lbs.; Cassimere m'd., 75,000 yds.; val. of cassimere, $75,000; cap., $50,000; m. emp., 34; f. emp., 16.

Establishments for m. of hosiery, 1; Hosiery m'd., 1,566 doz. shirts and drawers; val. of hosiery, $12,480; cap., $15,000; m. emp., 13; f. emp., 12.

Furnaces for m. of hollow ware and castings other than pig iron, 2; Hollow Ware and other Castings m'd., 880 tons; val. of hollow ware and castings, $55,000; cap., $23,000; emp., 48.

Establishments for m. of cotton, woollen and other machinery, 4; val. of machinery m'd., $85,400; cap., $43,500; emp., 129.

Establishments for m. of steam-engines and boilers, 1; val. of steam-engines and boilers, $40,000; cap., $20,000; emp., 20.

Scythe Manufactories, 3; Scythes m'd., 7,925 doz.; val. of scythes, $62,072; cap., $26,500; emp., 58.

Axe Manufactories, 3; Axes, Hatchets and other Edge Tools m'd., 100,000; val., $52,000; cap., $27,760; emp., 40.

Brass Founderies, 1; val. of articles m'd., $10,000; cap., $1,000; emp., 3.

Paper Manufactories, 8; Stock made use of, 2,359 tons; Paper m'd., 1,332 tons; val. of paper, $287,533; cap., $137,500; emp., 121.

Piano-Forte Manufactories, 1; Piano-Fortes m'd., 152; cap., $5,000; all other musical instruments m'd., 1,000; val. of musical instruments m'd., $7,500; cap., $1,000; emp., 6.

Daguerreotype Artists, 2; Daguerreotypes taken, 2,700; cap., $500; emp., 3.

Establishments for m. of chronometers, watches, gold and silver ware and jewelry, 2; val. of m's., $27,000; cap., $18,000; emp., 7.

Saddle, Harness and Trunk Manufactories, 2; val. of saddles, &c., $6,000; cap., $1,700; emp., 10.

Establishments for m. of railroad cars, coaches, chaises, wagons, sleighs and other vehicles, 3; val. of railroad cars, &c., m'd., $14,000; cap., $4,000; emp., 10.

Establishments for m. of soap and tallow candles, 1; Soap m'd., soft, 600 bbls.; Hard, 25 tons; val. of soap, $5,000; Tallow Candles m'd., 10 tons; val. of tallow candles, $2,800; cap., $4,000; emp., 4.

Establishments for m. of fire arms, 1; Fire Arms m'd., rifles and fowling guns; val. of fire arms, $1,000; cap., $600; emp., 1.

Chair and Cabinet Manufactories, 4; val. of chairs and cabinet ware, $204,000; cap., $62,600; emp., 144.

Tin Ware Manufactories, 5; val. of tin ware, $12,800; cap., $5,500; emp., 14.

Boots of all kinds m'd., 3,200 pairs; Shoes of all kinds m'd., 33,350 pairs; val. of boots and shoes, $31,950; m. emp., 39; f. emp., 18.

Val. of palm leaf hats, $30,000; m. emp., 6.

Bricks, m'd., 1,050,000; val. of bricks, $5,600; emp., 10.

Val. of building stone quarried and prepared for building, $75,000; emp., 98.

Charcoal m'd., 1,000 bush.; val. of same, $80; emp., 1.

Val. of blocks and pumps m'd., $4,000; emp., 4.

Lumber prepared for market, 2,289,000 ft.; val. of lumber, $119,805; emp., 37.

Firewood prepared for market, 9,537 cords; val. of firewood, $25,111; emp., 38.

Saxony Sheep, of different grades, –; Merino Sheep, of different grades, –; all other kinds of Sheep, 82; val. of all sheep, $328; Wool produced from Saxony sheep, – lbs.; Merino Wool produced, – lbs.; all other Wool produced, 358 lbs.

Horses, 378; val. of horses, $35,898; Oxen over three years old, 221; Steers under three years old, 70; val. of oxen and steers, $6,480; Milch Cows, 534; Heifers, 145; val. of cows and heifers, $19,819.

Butter, 31,391 lbs.; val. of butter, $7,847.75; Cheese, 7,814 lbs.; val. of cheese, $992.30; Honey, 200 lbs.; val. of honey, $40.

Indian Corn, 300 acres; Indian Corn, per acre, 27⅓ bush.; val., $9,410.

Wheat, 28 acres; Wheat, per acre, 17 bush.; val., $826.

Rye, 88 acres; Rye, per acre, 14 bush.; val., $1,552.50.

Barley, 8¼ acres; Barley, per acre, 18 bush.; val., $110.50.

Oats, 112 acres; Oats, per acre, 17 bush.; val., $1,194.

Potatoes, 145¼ acres; Potatoes, per acre, 99 bush.; val., $10,779.75.

Onions, ¾ acre; Onions, per acre, 357 bush.; val., $202.25.

Carrots, 5 acres; Carrots, per acre, 712 bush.; val., $1,068.90.

Beets and other esculent vegetables, 6 acres; val., $1,000; all other Grain or Root Crops, 10 acres; val., $500.

English Mowing, 2,699 acres; English Hay, 2,254 tons; val., $40,572.

Wet Meadow or Swale Hay, 367 tons; val., $3,303.

Apple Trees, cultivated for their fruit, 22,583; val., $7,749.

Pear Trees, cultivated for their fruit, 1,871; val., $150.

Hops, 3 acres; Hops, per acre, 516½ lbs.; val., $387.50.

Establishments for m. of casks, 1; cap., $500; Casks m'd., 1,000; val., $1,000; emp., 2.

Establishments for m. of sashes, doors and blinds, 3; cap., $5,500; val. m'd., $10,000; emp., 8.

Establishments for m. of gas, 1; cap., $20,000; val. m'd., $5,000; emp., 2.

Bakeries, 1; cap., $3,000; Flour consumed, 1,500 bbls.; val. of bread m'd., $25,000; emp., 8.

Establishments for m. of boxes (different varieties), 1; cap., $1,500; val. of boxes m'd., $3,000; emp., 4.

Swine raised, 600; val., $4,800.

Tailoring Establishments, 6; cap., $17,500; val. m'd., $54,000; emp., 100.

Rattan Manufactories, 1; cap., $25,000; val. m'd., $50,000; emp., 22.

Sieve Manufactories, 1; val. m'd., $2,600; emp., 1.

Bellows Manufactories, 1; val. m'd., $1,000; emp., 1.

Fan Blower Manufactories, 1; cap., $200; val. m'd., $1,500; emp., 1.

Scythe Snathe Manufactories, 1; cap., $1,500; val. m'd., $14,200; emp., 6.

Silk and Satin Bonnet Manufactories, 4; cap., $7,000; val. m'd., $8,500; emp., 31.

Reed Manufactories, 1; cap., 1,500; val. m'd., $4,000; emp., 4.

Spool and Bobbin Manufactories, 1; cap., $2,000; val. m'd., $5,000; emp., 6.

Paper Hanging Manufactories, 1; cap., $2,000; val. m'd., $6,000; emp., 6.

Piano Case Manufactories, 1; cap., $6,000; val. m'd., $33,000; emp., 35.

GARDNER.

Chair and Cabinet Manufactories, 14; val. of chairs and cabinet ware, $483,350; cap., $224,850; emp., 441.

Bricks m'd., 200,000; val. of bricks, $1,000; emp., 3.

Lumber prepared for market, 1,417,000 ft.; val. of lumber, $14,460; emp., 17.

Firewood prepared for market, 3,971 cords; val. of firewood, $13,813; emp., 183.

Saxony Sheep, of different grades, 58; Merino Sheep, of different grades, –; all other kinds of Sheep, –; val. of all sheep, $249.

Horses, 170; val. of horses, $14,420; Oxen over three years old, 154; Steers under three years old, 111; val. of oxen and steers, $10,743; Milch Cows, 356; Heifers, 110; val. of cows and heifers, $12,379.

Butter, 15,158 lbs.; val. of butter, $2,091.05; Cheese, 5,045 lbs.; val. of cheese, $504.50; Honey, 330 lbs.; val. of honey, $82.

Indian Corn, 81 acres; Indian Corn, per acre, 30 bush.; val., $2,144.

Wheat, 7 acres; Wheat, per acre, 15 bush.; val., $210.

Rye, 9 acres; Rye, per acre, 20 bush.; val., $270.

Barley, 34 acres; Barley, per acre, 20 bush.; val., $612.

Oats, 15 acres; Oats, per acre, 25 bush.; val., $375.

Potatoes, 112 acres; Potatoes, per acre, 80 bush.; val., $4,480.

Onions, ½ acre; Onions, per acre, 128 bush.; val., $64.

Turnips, cultivated as a field crop, 2 acres; Turnips, per acre, 82 bush.; val., $54.

Carrots, 3 acres; Carrots, per acre, 200 bush.; val., $300.

English Mowing, 1,364 acres; English Hay, 1,055 tons; val., $18,990.

Wet Meadow or Swale Hay, 295 tons; val., $2,655.

Apple Trees, cultivated for their fruit, 3,134; val., $1,417.

Pear Trees, cultivated for their fruit, 38; val., $22.

Bark, 165 cords; val., $825.

Females emp. in caning chairs, 1,671.

GRAFTON.

Cotton Mills, 7; Spindles, 28,904; Cotton consumed, 1,547,656 lbs.; Cloth, m'd., 6,589,882 yds., 4-4 Sheeting, 7-8 Shirting, 26 in. Print Cloths, 60 in. Table Covers; val. of cloth, $397,113; Yarn, m'd., 10,000 lbs.; val. of yarn, $2,500; cap., $526,500; m. emp., 259; f. emp., 241.

Establishments for m. of cotton, woollen and other machinery, 1; val. of machinery m'd., $500; cap., $2,000; emp., 2.

Manufactories of shovels, spades, forks and hoes, 1; val. of shovels, &c., $1,500; cap., $400; emp., 2.

Saddle, Harness and Trunk Manufactories, 1; val. of saddles, &c., m'd., $160; cap., $25; emp., 1.

Establishments for m. of railroad cars, coaches, chaises, wagons, sleighs and other vehicles, 1; val. of railroad cars, &c., m'd., $4,000; cap., $2,000; emp., 3.

Tin Ware Manufactories, 2; val. of tin ware, $1,500; cap., $500; emp., 2.

Boots of all kinds m'd., 136,424 pairs; Shoes of all kinds m'd., 554,720 pairs; val. of boots and shoes, $580,856; m. emp., 495; f. emp., 327.

Val. of building stone quarried and prepared for building, $300; emp., 2.

Val. of mechanics' tools m'd., $500; emp,. 3.

Lumber prepared for market, 62,000 ft.; val. of lumber, $982; emp., 6.

Firewood prepared for market, 1,600 cords; val. of firewood, $6,800; emp., 20.

Saxony Sheep, of different grades, –; Merino Sheep, of different grades, –; all other kinds of sheep, 14; val. of all sheep, $50; Wool produced from Saxony sheep, – lbs.; Merino Wool produced, – lbs; all other Wool produced, 35 lbs.

Horses, 271; val. of horses, $18,840; Oxen over three years old, 224; Steers under three years old, 56; val. of oxen and steers, $12,800; Milch Cows 762; Heifers, 94; val. of cows and heifers, $28,248.

Butter, 19,800 lbs.; val. of butter, $4,950; Cheese, 2,500 lbs.; val. of cheese, $200; Honey, 40 lbs.; val. of honey, $8.

Indian Corn, 455 acres; Indian Corn, per acre, 33 bush.; val., $16,891.87½.

Rye, 73 acres; Rye, per acre, 16 bush.; val., $1,580.04.

Barley, 31 acres; Barley, per acre, 15 bush.; val., $465.

Oats, 205 acres; Oats, per acre, 32 bush.; val., $4,067.20.

Potatoes, 208 acres; Potatoes, per acre, 125 bush; val., $19,500.

Carrots, 8 acres; Carrots, per acre, 600 bush.; val., $1,200.

Beets and other esculent vegetables, 5 acres; val., $250; all other Grain or Root Crops, 3 acres; val., $175.

English Mowing. 2,259 acres; English Hay, 2,414 tons; val., $43,452.

Wet Meadow or Swale Hay, 635 tons; val., $4,445.

Apple Trees, cultivated for their fruit, 16,326; val., $4,520.

Pear Trees, cultivated for their fruit, 455; val., $180.

Cranberries, 20 acres; val., $650.

Establishments for m. of boxes, (Boot and Shoe) 1; cap., $100; val. of boxes m'd., $1,800; emp., 2.

Val. of milk sold, $12,000.

Val. of peaches, $1,200.

Val. of quinces, $300.

Swine raised, 525; val., $10,000.

HARDWICK.

Plough Manufactories, 1; Ploughs and other Agricultural Tools m'd., 12; val., $100.

Saddle, Harness and Trunk Manufactories, –; val. of saddles, &c., $1,000; cap., $500; emp., 1.

Establishments for m. of railroad cars, coaches, chaises, wagons, sleighs, and other vehicles, 4; val. of railroad cars, &c., m'd., $3,700; cap., $2,000; emp., 7.

Tanneries, 1; Hides of all kinds tanned, 1,700; val. of leather tanned, $7,000; cap., $4,000; emp., 2.

Boots of all kinds m'd., – pairs; Shoes of all kinds m'd., – pairs; val. of boots and shoes, $1,600; m. emp., 4.

Val. of palm leaf hats, $3,000.

Lumber prepared for market, 65,000 ft.; val. of lumber, $9,800.

Firewood prepared for market, 1,548 cords; val. of firewood, $2,812.

Saxony Sheep, of different grades, –; Merino Sheep, of different grades, –; all other kinds of Sheep, 217; val. of all sheep, $776; Wool produced from Saxony sheep, – lbs.; Merino Wool produced, – lbs.; all other Wool produced, 712 lbs.

Horses, 232; val. of horses, $18,080; Oxen over three years old, 360; Steers under three years old, 92; val. of oxen and steers, $25,951; Milch Cows, 1,389; Heifers, 256; val. of cows and heifers, $41,926.

Butter, 33,725 lbs.; val. of butter, $6,745; Cheese, 310,540 lbs.; val. of cheese, $31,054; Honey, 80 lbs.; val. of honey, $14.

Indian Corn, 471 acres; Indian Corn, per acre, 33 bush.; val., $15,373.

Wheat, 15 acres; Wheat, per acre, 17 bush.; val., $496.

Rye, 146 acres; Rye, per acre, 12½ bush.; val., $1,844.

Barley, 51 acres; Barley, per acre, 23 bush.; val., $953.

Oats, 391 acres; Oats, per acre, 21 bush.; val., $4,129.

Potatoes, 254 acres; Potatoes, per acre, 98 bush.; val., $12,516.

Turnips, cultivated as a field crop, 1½ acre; Turnips, per acre, 300 bush.; val., $40.

Carrots, 2 acres; Carrots, per acre, 420 bush.; val., $210.

English Mowing, 2,788 acres; English Hay, 3,139 tons; val., $37,468.

Wet Meadow or Swale Hay, 1,000 tons; val., $5,000.

Apple Trees, cultivated for their fruit, 4,878; val., $3,467.

Pear Trees, cultivated for their fruit, 336; val., $52.

Beeswax, 9 lbs.; val., $3.

Establishments for m. of casks, 2; val., $200; emp., 2.

Establishments for m. of boxes for packing cloth and tools, 1; cap., $5,000; val. of boxes m'd., $9,000; emp., 2.

Swine raised, 412; val., $3,435.

HARVARD.

Establishments for m. of horse power, broomcorn machines, shafting, pulleys, &c., machinery, 1; val. of machinery m'd., $6,000; cap., $3,000; emp., 8.

Paper Manufactories, 1; Stock made use of, 60 tons; Paper m'd., 40 tons; val. of paper, $4,000; cap., $2,000; emp., 4.

Boots of all kinds m'd., 350 pairs; Shoes of all kinds m'd., 17,800 pairs; val. of boots and shoes, $8,612; m. emp., 12; f. emp., 10.

Bricks m'd., 1,500,000; val. of bricks, $7,000; emp., 16.

Val. of marble prepared for market, $15,450; emp., 15.

Val. of slate stone quarried and prepared for market, $1,400.

Corn and other Brooms m'd., 24,600; val. of brooms, $6,150; emp., 11.

Lumber prepared for market, 229,000 ft.; val. of lumber, $2,961; emp., 17.

Firewood prepared for market, 1,611 cords; val. of firewood, $5,560; emp., 12, three months.

Horses, 224; val. of horses, $17,505; Oxen over three years old, 198; Steers under three years old, 42; val. of oxen and steers, $11,645; Milch Cows, 917; Heifers, 137; val. of cows and heifers, $28,155.

Butter, 43,730 lbs.; val. of butter, $10,932; Cheese, 1,350 lbs.; val. of cheese, $135; Honey, 200 lbs.; val. of honey, $40.

Indian Corn, 424 acres; Indian Corn, per acre, 37 bush.; val., $15,285.

Wheat, 46 acres; Wheat, per acre, 18 bush.; val., $1,679.

Rye, 133 acres; Rye, per acre, 13 bush.; val., $1,729.

Barley, 45 acres; Barley, per acre, 23½ bush.; val., $1,068.

Oats, 160 acres; Oats, per acre, 33 bush.; val., $2,609.

Potatoes, 194 acres; Potatoes, per acre, 100 bush.; val., $9,700.

Onions, ½ acre; Onions, per acre, 150 bush.; val., $60.

Turnips, cultivated as a field crop, 33½ acres; Turnips, per acre, 182 bush.; val., $749.

Carrots, 10½ acres; Carrots, per acre, 600 bush.; val., $1,641.

Beets and other esculent vegetables, – acres; all other Grain or Root Crops, Buckwheat, 27½ acres; val., $431.

Millet, 4 acres; val., $135.

English Mowing, 2,157 acres; English Hay, 2,254 tons; val., $33,810.

Wet Meadow or Swale Hay, 947 tons; val., $7,576.

Apple Trees, cultivated for their fruit, 21,694; val., $10,316.

Pear Trees, cultivated for their fruit, 1,342; val., $628.

Hops, 33½ acres; Hops, per acre, 600 lbs.; val., $5,000.

Cranberries, 31½ acres; val., $1,085.

Establishments for m. of pickles and preserves, 3; cap., $3,000; val. m'd., $8,858; emp., 24, three months.

Establishments for m. of boxes for shoes, 1; cap., $700; val. of boxes m'd., $1,400; emp., 1.

Milk, 81,575 cans; val., $19,578.

Peach Trees, 9,516; val., $2,123.

Quince Trees, 2,045; val., $476.

Swine raised, 413; val., $3,025.

Sieves m'd., 200 doz.; val., $300; emp., 3, three months.

Herbs prepared for market, 8 tons; val., $4,000; emp., 3.

Herbs pulverized, 1,400 doz.; val., $1,225; emp., 2, six months.

Val. of garden seeds, $1,500; emp., 1.

Horse Radish prepared, 10 tons; val., $1,200; emp., 3, six months.

Rose Water, 40 galls.; val., $50 emp., 1, one week.

Val. of sales from nursery, $1,500.

Calves marketed, 1,600; val., $11,200; gathered from this and neighboring towns.

Beef Cattle, 150; val. $6,000.

Val. of mutton and lamb, $400.

Squashes, 8 tons; val., $200.

Grapes, 66 bush.; val., $75.

Grass Seed, 196 bush.; val., $229.

Walnuts, 240 bush.; val., $360.

Chestnuts, 198 bush.; val., $396.

Milling Establishments for sawing lumber, shingles, laths, jointing, planing, and grist grinding, 1; val., $1,687; cap. $7,000; emp., 2.

Beans, 65 acres; val., $1,173.

Val. of berries sold, $1,500.

Stores, 2; amount of sales, $30,000.

Blacksmiths' Shops, 3; amount of business, $3,500.

HOLDEN.

Cotton Mills, 5; Spindles, 10,500; Cotton consumed, 435,000 lbs.; Cloth m'd., 1,850,000 yds.; 1,300,000 yds. for Prints, 400,000 yds. Drilling, and 150,000 yds. Bagging; val. of cloth, $109,000; Yarn m'd., 30,000 lbs.; val. of yarn, $10,000; cap., $52,750; m. emp., 120; f. emp., 80.

Woollen Mills, 2; Sets of Machinery, 3; Wool consumed, 70,000 lbs.; Cassimere m'd., 3,000 yds.; val. of cassimere, $3,000; Satinet m'd., 85,000 yds.; val. of satinet, $37,500; Flannel or Blanketing, 1,000 yds.; val. of flannel or blanketing, $750; Yarn m'd. and not made into cloth, 3,000 lbs.; val. of yarn, $3,000; cap., $5,500; m. emp., 24; f. emp., 6.

Saddle, Harness and Trunk Manufactories, 1; val. of saddles, &c., $1,000; cap., $400; emp., 2.

Establishments for m. of railroad cars, coaches, chaises, wagons, sleighs, and other vehicles, 1; val. of railroad cars, &c., m'd., $600; cap., $500; emp., 2.

Tin Ware Manufactories, 1; val. of tin ware, $3,000; cap., $600; emp., 5.

Tanneries, 1; Hides of all kinds tanned, 900; val. of leather tanned, $5,500; cap., $3,400; emp., 3.

Currying Establishments, 1; val. of leather curried, $5,500; cap., "same as above"; emp., 1.

Boots of all kinds bottomed, 53,500 pairs; val. of labor, $16,200; m. emp., 84. These boots were bottomed for manufacturers in adjoining towns.

Lumber prepared for market, 1,124,000 ft.; val. of lumber, $16,039; emp., 29.

Firewood prepared for market, 6,682 cords; val. of firewood, $27,880; emp., 44.

Saxony Sheep, of different grades, -; Merino Sheep, of different grades, -; all other kinds of Sheep, 160; val. of all sheep, $405; Wool produced from Saxony sheep, - lbs.; Merino Wool produced, - lbs.; all other Wool produced, 558 lbs.

Horses, 258; val. of horses, $21,600; Oxen over three years old, 212; Steers under three years old, 98; val. of oxen and steers, $14,605; Milch Cows, 543; Heifers, 137; val. of cows and heifers, $20,250.

Butter, 38,980 lbs.; val. of butter, $8,580; Cheese, 8,400 lbs.; val. of cheese, $750.

Indian Corn, 309 acres; Indian Corn, per acre, 30 bush.; val., $9,270.

Wheat, 19 acres; Wheat, per acre, 17 bush.; val., $727.

Rye, 88 acres; Rye, per acre, 12 bush.; val., $1,300.

Barley, 14 acres; Barley, per acre, 12 bush.; val., $168.

Oats, 165 acres; Oats, per acre, 27 bush.; val., $2,673.

Potatoes, 181 acres; Potatoes, per acre, 78 bush.; val., $8,470.

Turnips, cultivated as a field crop, 4 acres; Turnips, per acre, 125 bush.; val., $125.

Carrots, 6 acres; Carrots, per acre, 650 bush.; val., $1,170.

English Mowing, 2,186 acres; English Hay, 1,821 tons; val., $27,315.

Wet Meadow or Swale Hay, 672 tons; val., $6,720.

Apple Trees, cultivated for their fruit, 7,027; val., $5,475.

Pear Trees, cultivated for their fruit, 117; val., $258.

Establishments for m. of casks, 1; cap., $125; Casks m'd., $200; val., $200.

Establishments for m. of sashes, doors and blinds, 1; cap., $500; val. m'd., $400; emp., 1, three months.

Establishments for m. of baskets, 1; cap., $1,000; val. of baskets m'd., $2,000; emp., 5.

HUBBARDSTON.

Establishments for m. of railroad cars, coaches, chaises, wagons, sleighs, and other vehicles, 1; val. of railroad cars, &c., m'd., $1,000; cap., $200; emp., 2.

Chair and Cabinet Manufactories, 6; val. of chairs and cabinet ware, $25,835; cap., $8,000; emp., 44.

Tin Ware Manufactories, 1; val. of tin ware, $18,000; cap., $5,000; emp., 9.

Glue Manufactories, and Manufactories for the preparation of Gums; val. of glue and gums m'd., $3,000; cap., $800; emp., 4.

Tanneries, 1; Hides of all kinds tanned, 1,800; val. of leather tanned, $4,250; cap., $2,000; emp., 4.

Boots of all kinds m'd., $15,600 pairs; Shoes of all kinds m'd., – pairs; val. of boots and shoes, $20,250; m. emp., 39.

Val. of palm leaf hats, $2,700; f. emp., 200.

Val. of wooden ware not otherwise enumerated, including farming utensils m'd., $2,000; emp., 2.

Lumber prepared for market, 2,540,000 ft.; val. of lumber, $30,480; emp., 33.

Firewood prepared for market, 4,000 cords; val. of firewood, $10,000; emp., 25.

Saxony Sheep, of different grades, –; Merino Sheep, of different grades, –; all other kinds of Sheep, 157; val. of all sheep, $662; Wool produced from Saxony sheep, –; Merino Wool produced, –; all other Wool produced, 428 lbs.

Horses, 256; val. of horses, $20,760; Oxen over three years old, 200; Steers under three years old, 104; val. of oxen and steers, $17,890; Milch Cows, 681; Heifers, 211; val. of cows and heifers, $29,238.

Butter, 47,285 lbs.; val. of butter, $11,917; Cheese, 22,800 lbs.; val. of cheese, $1,931.

Indian Corn, 221 acres; Indian Corn, per acre, 35 bush.; val., $9,668.75.

Wheat, 13 acres; Wheat, per acre, 20 bush.; val., $520.

Rye, 34 acres; Rye, per acre, 20 bush.; val., $1,020.

Barley, 79 acres; Barley, per acre, 28 bush.; val., $2,212.

Oats, 141 acres; Oats, per acre, 47 bush.; val., $3,313.50.

Potatoes, 185 acres; Potatoes, per acre, 150 bush.; val., $13,875.

Onions, ½ acre; Onions, per acre, 270 bush; val., $102.

Carrots, 8½ acres; Carrots, per acre, 500 bush.; val., $1,062.50.

Beets, and other esculent vegetables, 4 acres; val., $500.

English Mowing, 2,465 acres; English Hay, 2,247 tons; val., $35,952.

Wet Meadow or Swale Hay, 622 tons; val., $4,976.

Apples, 12,184 bush.; val., $3,216.

Establishments for m. of boot, shoe and cloth boxes, 2; cap., $900; val. of boxes m'd., $2,000; emp., 8.

LANCASTER.

Cotton Mills, 1; Spindles, 1,600; Cotton consumed, 125,000 lbs.; Cloth m'd., 468,000 yds., middling quality; val. of cloth, $37,440; m. emp., 12; f. emp., 19.

Piano-Forte Manufactories, 1; Piano-Forte Keys m'd., 1,250; cap., $5,000; emp., 15.

Saddle, Harness and Trunk Manufactories, 1; val. of saddles, &c., $1,000; cap., $500; emp., 2.

Establishments for m. of soap and tallow candles, 1; Soap m'd., 832 bbls.; val. of soap, $3,328; Tallow Candles m'd., 500 lbs.; val. of tallow candles, $70; cap., $2,000; emp., 3.

Tin Ware Manufactories, 1; val. of tin ware, $400; emp., 2.

Comb Manufactories, 2; val. of combs m'd., $3,000; cap., $1,300; emp., 6.

Boots of all kinds m'd., – pairs; Shoes of all kinds m'd., 52,000 pairs; val. of boots and shoes, $52,000; m. emp., 31; f. emp., 17.

Bricks m'd., 1,550,000; val. of bricks, $6,975; emp., 19.

Val. of blocks and copper pumps m'd., $10,000; emp., 5.

Val. of mechanics' tools m'd., $300; emp., 1.

Lumber prepared for market, 925,000 ft.; val. of lumber, $12,950; emp., 18.

Firewood prepared for market, 22,680 cords; val. of firewood, $79,380.

Horses, 224; val. of horses, $17,100; Oxen over three years old, 127; Steers under three years old, 48; val. of oxen and steers, $6,845; Milch Cows, 559; Heifers, 103; val. of cows and heifers, $18,406.

Butter, 31,160 lbs.; val. of butter, $7,790; Cheese, 2,205 lbs.; val. of cheese, $175.

Indian Corn, 334 acres; Indian Corn, per acre, 30 bush.; val., $15,030; Broom Corn, 2 acres; Broom Bush, per acre, 400 lbs.

Wheat, 45 acres; Wheat, per acre, 15 bush.; val., $1,350.

Rye, 167 acres; Rye, per acre, 13 bush.; val., $3,258.

Barley, 12 acres; Barley, per acre, 10 bush.; val., $90.

Oats, 138 acres; Oats, per acre, 35 bush.; val., $3,622.

Potatoes, 201 acres; Potatoes, per acre, 125 bush.; val., $18,843.

Onions, 2 acres.

Turnips, cultivated as a field crop, 12 acres; Turnips, per acre, 100 bush.; val., $240.

Carrots, 17 acres; Carrots, per acre, 400 bush.; val., $1,450.

Beets and other esculent vegetables, 5 acres; all other Grain, Buckwheat crop, 15 acres; val., $112.50.

English Mowing, 1,889 acres; English Hay, 1,663 tons; val., $29,934.

Wet Meadow or Swale Hay, 250 tons; val., $2,250.

Apple Trees, cultivated for their fruit, 13,630; val., $3,384.

Pear Trees, cultivated for their fruit, 452; val., $146.

Hops, 11 acres; Hops, per acre, 700 lbs.; val., $2,550.

Establishments for m. of sashes, doors and blinds, 1; cap., $500; val. m'd., $2,000; emp., 2.

Establishments for m. of pocket books, 1; cap., $500; val. m'd., $6,400; emp., 20.

Establishments for m. of stoves, 1; cap., $800; val. m'd., $2,000; emp., 2.

Establishments for m. of mortising machines, 1; cap., $2,000; val. m'd., $3,000; emp., 8.

Milk sold, 36,500 galls.

LEICESTER.

Woollen Mills, 6; Sets of Machinery, 23; Wool consumed, 744,317 lbs.; Cassimere m'd., 470,000 yds.; val. of cassimere $367,500; Satinet m'd., 170,000 yds.; val. of satinet, $55,500; Flannel or Blanketing, 591,090 yds.; val. of flannel or blanketing, $137,600; cap., $250,000; m. emp., 228; f. emp., 114.

Card Manufactories, 12; val. of cards of all kinds m'd., $175,000 (machine, clothing, and hand cards); cap., $97,000; emp., 70.

Tanneries, 3; Hides of all kinds tanned, 8,500; val. of leather tanned, $14,800; cap., $49,000; emp., 5.

Currying Establishments, 4; val. of leather curried, $45,000; cap., $13,500; emp., 12.

Boots of all kinds m'd., 48,000 pairs; Shoes of all kinds m'd. – pairs; val. of boots and shoes, $85,000; m. emp., 58; f. emp., 12.

Charcoal m'd., 10,500 bush.; val. of same, $1,250; emp. 6.

Lumber prepared for market, 445,000 ft.; val. of lumber, $5,300; emp., 19.

Firewood prepared for market, 3,662 cords; val. of firewood, $11,140; emp., 30.

Saxony Sheep, of different grades, –; Merino Sheep, of different grades, –; all other kinds of sheep, 41; val. of all sheep, $135; Wool produced from Saxony sheep, – lbs.; Merino Wool produced, – lbs.; all other Wool produced, 170 lbs.

Horses, 256; val. of horses, $22,500; Oxen over three years old, 122; Steers under three years old, 45; val. of oxen and steers, $9,650; Milch Cows, 392; Heifers, 85; val. of cows and heifers, $12,800.

Butter, 18,440 lbs.; val. of butter, $4,610; Cheese, 13,250 lbs.; val. of cheese, $1,060.

Indian Corn, 142 acres; Indian Corn, per acre, 30 bush.; val., $4,260.

Rye, 5 acres; Rye, per acre, 15 bush.; val., $112.50.

Barley, 28½ acres; Barley, per acre, 20 bush.; val., $492.

Oats, 92 acres; Oats, per acre, 30 bush.; val., $1,350.

Potatoes, 137 acres; Potatoes, per acre, 100 bush.; val., $849.40.

English Mowing, 1,592 acres; English Hay, 1,640 tons; val., $24,600.

Wet Meadow or Swale Hay, 385 tons; val., $2,685.

Apple Trees, cultivated for their fruit, 3,156; val., $1,078.

Pear Trees, cultivated for their fruit, 325; val., $162.

Cranberries, 10 acres; val., $50.

Establishments for m. of card and boot boxes, 1; cap., $500; val. of boxes m'd., $2,000; emp., 1.

Buckwheat, 12 acres; Buckwheat, per acre, 22½ bush.; val., $200.

Establishments for m. of paper mill engines, boxes and plates, and planing knives, 1, (Stiles & Co.); val. of business, $31,000.

Establishments for m. of blind staples, 1; rat traps, 1; val. of business, $5,000.

Establishments for m. of horse nets and shoe strings, 1; Shoe counters, boot stiffenings, 1; val. of business, $300.

LEOMINSTER.

Paper Manufactories, 2. Stock made use of, 570 tons; Paper m'd., 440 tons; val. of paper, $52,800; cap., $40,000; emp., 26.

Piano-Forte Case Manufactories, 4; Piano-Forte Cases m'd., 1,536; cap., $30,000; val. of musical instruments m'd., $54,000; emp., 86.

Saddle, Harness and Trunk Manufactories, 1; val. of saddles, &c., $600; cap., $300; emp., 2.

Establishments for m. of railroad cars, coaches, chaises, wagons, sleighs and other vehicles, 1; val. of railroad cars, &c., m'd., $2,100; cap. $1,500; emp., 3.

Establishments for m. of fire arms, –; val. of fire arms, $100.

Chair and Cabinet Manufactories, 3; val. of chairs and cabinet ware, $21,000; cap., $7,000; emp., 23.

Tin Ware Manufactories, 1; val. of tin ware, $8,000; cap., $2,000; emp., 2.

Comb Manufactories, 20; val. of combs m'd., $130,375; cap., $28,000; emp., 182.

Flour Mills, 1; Flour m'd., 200 bbls.; val. of flour m'd., $2,000; cap., $1,000; emp., 1.

Tanneries, 1; Hides of all kinds tanned, 4,000; val. of leather tanned, $20,000; cap., $5,000; emp., 6.

Currying Establishments, 1; val. of leather curried, $30,000; cap., $4,000; emp., 13.

Manufactories of patent and enamelled leather, 1; val. of leather m'd., $55,000; cap., $5,000; emp., 10.

Boots of all kinds m'd., 6,275 pairs; Shoes of all kinds m'd., 35,000 pairs; val. of boots and shoes, $29,400; m. emp., 44; f. emp., 36.

Val. of palm leaf hats, $372.

Bricks m'd., 600,000; val. of bricks, $4,200; emp., 6.

Val. of building stone quarried and prepared for building, $2,000; emp., 2.

Charcoal m'd., 4,000 bush.; val. of same, $480.

Val. of mechanics' tools m'd., $6,000; emp., 8.

Val. of wooden ware not otherwise enumerated, (Tubs and Pails,) including farming utensils m'd., $20,000; emp., 8.

Lumber prepared for market, 1,700 ft.; val. of lumber, $22,100.

Firewood prepared for market, 3,230 cords; val. of firewood, $11,900.

Saxony Sheep, of different grades, –; Merino Sheep, of different grades, –; all other kinds of Sheep, 46; val. of all sheep, $187; Wool produced from Saxony sheep, – lbs.; Merino Wool produced, – lbs.; all other Wool produced, 184 lbs.

Horses, 286; val. of horses, $26,000; Oxen over three years old, 204; Steers under three years old, 122; val. of oxen and steers, $15,344; Milch Cows, 638; Heifers, 247; val. of cows and heifers, $28,797.

Butter, 50,000 lbs.; val. of butter, $12,500; Cheese, 8,955 lbs.; val. of cheese, $749; Honey, 419 lbs.; val. of honey, $83.50.

Indian Corn, 434 acres; Indian Corn, per acre, $32\frac{1}{2}$ bush.; val., $17,513.

Wheat, 68 acres; Wheat, per acre, 16 bush.; val., $2,176.

Rye, 130 acres; Rye, per acre, 13 bush.; val., $2,540.

Barley, 41 acres; Barley, per acre, 22 bush.; val., $900.

Oats, 130 acres; Oats, per acre, 30 bush.; val., $1,923.

Potatoes, 174 acres; Potatoes, per acre, 115 bush.; val., $9,943.

Onions, $\frac{1}{3}$ acre; Onions, per acre, 531 bush.; val., $177.

Turnips, cultivated as a field crop, 4 acres; Turnips, per acre, 509 bush.; val., $407.

Carrots, 13 acres; Carrots, per acre, 800 bush.; val., $2,751.

Beets and other esculent vegetables, 3 acres; val., $1,800.

English Mowing, 2,266 acres; English Hay, 2,293 tons; val., $34,395.

Wet Meadow or Swale Hay, 612 tons; val., $5,971.

Apple Trees, cultivated for their fruit, 14,890; val., $9,611.

Pear Trees, cultivated for their fruit, 500; val., $438.

Cranberries, 112 bush.; val., $224.

Establishments for m. of casks, 2; cap., $100; Casks m'd., 800; val., $500; emp., 2.

Establishments for m. of sashes, doors and blinds, 2; cap., $3,000; val. m'd., $6,500; emp., 6.

Breweries, 1; cap., $400; Beer m'd., 200 bbls; val., $1,200; emp., 1.

Establishments for m. of paper boxes, 2; cap., $600; val. of boxes m'd., $2,400; emp., 7.

Swine raised, 484; val., $5,946.

Quinces, 1,387 bush.; val., $1,387.

Bayberry Tallow, 445 lbs.; val., $89.

Baskets, 2,500; val., $1,150; emp., 5.

Corn Planters m'd., 5,000; val., $15,000; cap., $3,000; emp., 15.

Horn Buttons m'd., 7,500 gross; val., $6,000; cap., $1,500; emp., 11.

Beans, 303 bush.; val. $606.

Val. of peaches, $572.

Val. of plums, $220.

LUNENBURG.

Establishments for m. of railroad cars, coaches, chaises, wagons, sleighs, and other vehicles, 2; val. of railroad cars, &c., m'd., $950; cap., $225; emp., 5.

Tanneries, 1; Hides of all kinds tanned, 1,200; val. of leather tanned, $1,200; cap., $700; emp., 2.

Currying Establishments, 2; val. of leather curried, $2,500; cap., $1,200; emp., 2.

Boots of all kinds, m'd., 660 pairs; Shoes of all kinds m'd., 6,586 pairs; val. of boots and shoes, $4,286; m. emp., 13; f. emp., 12.

Val. of palm leaf hats, $2,458; f. emp., 130.

Lumber prepared for market, 581,000 ft.; val. of lumber, $8,668; emp., 40.

Firewood prepared for market, 2,938 cords; val. of firewood, $8,865; emp., 40.

Saxony Sheep, of different grades, –; Merino Sheep, of different grades, –; all other kinds of sheep, 140; val. of all sheep, $371; Wool produced from Saxony sheep, – lbs.; Merino Wool produced, – lbs.; all other Wool produced, 414 lbs.

Horses, 190; val. of horses, $13,350; Oxen over three years old, 246; Steers under three years old, 91; val. of oxen and steers, 15,678; Milch Cows, 543; Heifers, 177; val. of cows and heifers, $16,811.

Butter, 26,732 lbs.; val. of butter, $6,683; Cheese, 7,400 lbs.; val. of cheese, $740; Honey, 160 lbs.; val. of honey, $32.

Indian Corn, 315 acres; Indian Corn, per acre, 27½ bush.; val., $10,064.40.

Wheat, 68 acres; Wheat, per acre, 12 bush.; val., $2,244.

Rye, 53 acres; Rye, per acre, 10 bush.; val., $795.

Barley, 10 acres; Barley, per acre, 14 bush.; val., $175.

Oats, 70 acres; Oats, per acre, 22½ bush.; val., $1,102.

Potatoes, 160 acres; Potatoes, per acre, 89 bush.; val., $10,680.

Onions, $\frac{1}{12}$ acre; Onions, per acre, 900 bush.; val., $56.25.

Turnips, cultivated as a field crop, 6 acres; Turnips, per acre, 282 bush.; val., $282.

Carrots, 6 acres; Carrots, per acre, 337; val., $606.60.

English Mowing, 1,997 acres; English Hay, 1,764 tons; val., $31,752.

Wet Meadow or Swale Hay, 713 tons; val., $6,417.

Apple Trees, cultivated for their fruit, 7,713; val., $6,613; small trees, not in a bearing state, 4,337.

Pear Trees, cultivated for their fruit, 278; val., $233.

Hops, 28 acres; Hops, per acre, 479 lbs.; val., $3,755.36.

Cranberries, 6 acres; val., $245.

Establishments for m. of casks, 3; cap., $300; Casks m'd., 800; val., $300; emp., 3.

Swine raised, 138; val., $1,178.

Val. of milk, $2,217.

Val. of squashes, $200.

Buckwheat, 4 acres; 60 bush.; val., $75.

Val. of apples used for cider, vinegar, feeding stock, $1,000.

MENDON.

Saddle, Harness and Trunk Manufactories, 1; val. of saddles, &c., $1,500; cap., $700; emp., 1.

Boots of all kinds m'd, 94,640 pairs; Shoes of all kinds m'd.,

32,400 pairs; val. of boots and shoes, $209,200 ; m. emp., 182 ; f. emp., 93.

Val. of straw braid m'd. and not made into bonnets and hats, $1,740.

Bricks m'd., 175,000 ; val. of bricks, $875 ; emp., 4.

Lumber prepared for market, 340,000 ft.; val. of lumber, $4,250 ; emp., 15.

Firewood prepared for market, 1,377 cords; val. of firewood, $6,885 ; emp., 43.

Saxony Sheep, of different grades, – ; Merino Sheep, of different grades, – ; all other kinds of Sheep, 28 ; val. of all sheep, $135 ; Wool produced from Saxony sheep, – lbs.; Merino Wool produced, – lbs. ; all other Wool produced, 185 lbs.

Horses, 119 ; val. of horses, $10,175 ; Oxen over three years old, 136 ; Steers under three years old, 39 ; val. of oxen and steers, $9,131 ; Milch Cows, 404 ; Heifers, 43 ; val. of cows and heifers, $15,374.

Butter, 24,440 lbs.; val. of butter, $6,110 ; Cheese, 6,100 lbs.; val. of cheese, $610.

Indian Corn, 197 acres; Indian Corn, per acre, 36 bush.; val., $8,868.75.

Wheat, 12 acres ; Wheat, per acre, 14 bush.; val. $336.

Rye, 48 acres ; Rye, per acre, 12½ bush. ; val., $904.50.

Barley, 17 acres ; Barley, per acre, 42 bush. ; val., $892.50.

Oats, 64½ acres ; Oats, per acre, 29 bush. ; val., $1,126.80.

Potatoes, 103½ acres ; Potatoes, per acre, 108 bush. ; val., $6,706.80.

Onions, 4 acres ; Onions, per acre, 115 bush. ; val., $368.

Turnips, cultivated as a field crop, 5½ acres ; Turnips, per acre, 185 bush. ; val., $327.

Buckwheat, 5 acres ; val., $120.

English Mowing, 1,522 acres ; English Hay, 1,355 tons ; val., $37,100.

Wet Meadow or Swale Hay, 386 tons ; val., $3,860.

Apple Trees, cultivated for their fruit, 5,239 ; val., $2,845.30.

Pear Trees, cultivated for their fruit, 162 ; val., $175.

Cranberries, 39 acres ; val., $3,792.

Establishments for m. of sashes, doors and blinds, 1 ; val. m'd., $3,000 ; cap., $1,500 ; emp., 3.

Establishments for m. of boxes for boots, 3 ; cap., $2,960 ; val. of boxes m'd., $5,920 ; emp., 8.

Peach Trees raised, 1,555 ; val. of fruit, $640.

Cherry Trees raised, 102 ; val. of fruit, $340.

Quince Trees raised, 367 ; val. of fruit, $235.

Val. of beans raised, $236.

Val. of milk sold, $3,240.

Bulls, 7 ; val., $140.

MILFORD.

Establishments for m. of cotton, woollen and other machinery, 2 ; val. of machinery m'd., $15,000 ; cap., $5,000 ; emp., 17.

Axe Manufactories, – ; Axes, Hatchets and other Edge Tools m'd., 1,800 ; val., $875 ; cap., $300 ; emp., 2.

Daguerreotype Artists, 1; Daguerreotypes taken, 3,500 ; cap., $1,000 ; emp., 2.

Saddle, Harness and Trunk Manufactories, 2 ; val. of saddles, &c., $2,500 ; cap., $1,000 ; emp., 4.

Hat and Cap Manufactories, 1 ; Hats and Caps m'd., 936 ; cap., $2,573 ; emp., 3.

Establishments for m. of railroad cars, coaches, chaises, wagons, sleighs and other vehicles, 3 ; val. of railroad cars, &c., m'd., $22,340 ; cap., $12,000 ; emp., 17.

Establishments for m. of soap and tallow candles, 1 ; Soap m'd., 25,000 lbs. and 800 bbls. ; val. of soap, $4,100 ; Tallow Candles m'd., 2,000 lbs. ; val. of tallow candles, $280 ; cap., $2,000 ; emp., 3.

Chair and Cabinet Manufactories, 1 ; val. of chairs and cabinet ware, $7,700 ; cap., $2,200 ; emp., 6.

Tin Ware Manufactories, 2 ; val. of tin ware, $19,000 ; cap., $5,500 ; emp., 9.

Currying Establishments, 1 ; val. of leather curried, $18,000 ; cap., $6,000 ; emp., 7.

Boots of all kinds m'd., 1,042,944 pairs ; Shoes of all kinds m'd., 5,048 pairs ; val. of boots and shoes, $1,787,315.20 ; m. emp., 2,951 ; f. emp., 447.

Establishments for m. of straw bonnets and hats, 1 ; Straw Bonnets m'd., 3,000 ; val., $1,436.25 ; m. emp., 1 ; f. emp., 2.

Val. of building stone quarried and prepared for building, $7,423 ; emp., 16.

Val. of blocks and pumps m'd., $2,000 ; emp., 2.

Corn and other Brooms m'd., 6,780 ; val. of brooms, $850 ; emp., 2.

Lasts m'd., 43,720 ; val., $11,030.

Lumber prepared for market, 2,541,000 ft. ; val. of lumber, $33,281 ; emp., 6.

Firewood prepared for market, 3,119 cords ; val. of firewood, $15,600 ; emp., 50.

Horses, 365 ; val. of horses, $41,510 ; Oxen over three years old, 116 ; Steers under three years old, 56 ; val. of oxen and steers, $9,265 ; Milch Cows, 533 ; Heifers, 37 ; val. of cows and heifers, $18,666.

Butter, 19,467 lbs. ; val. of butter, $4,866.75 ; Cheese, 3,784 lbs. ; val. of cheese, $302.72 ; Honey, 583 lbs. ; val. of honey, $104.94.

Indian Corn, 287 acres ; Indian Corn, per acre, 24$\frac{7}{8}$ bush. ; val., $8,923.75.

Rye, 26 acres ; Rye, per acre, 11 bush. ; val., $429.

Barley, 9 acres ; Barley, per acre, 19 bush. ; val., $213.75.

Oats, 61 acres ; Oats, per acre, 22 bush. ; val., $805.20.

Potatoes, 208 acres ; Potatoes, per acre, 100 bush. ; val., $15,600.

Onions, $\frac{3}{4}$ acre ; Onions, per acre, 433 bush. ; val., $243.

Turnips, cultivated as a field crop, 5$\frac{1}{2}$ acres ; Turnips, per acre, 330 bush. ; val., $726.

Carrots, 3 acres ; Carrots, per acre, 698 bush. ; val., $523.50.

Beets and other esculent vegetables, 15 acres ; val., $5,365.50 ; all other Grain or Root Crops, 12 acres ; val., $1,200.

English Mowing, 1,782 acres ; English Hay, 1,582 tons ; val., $31,640.

Wet Meadow or Swale Hay, 479½ tons ; val., $4,795.

Apple Trees, cultivated for their fruit, 26,480 ; val., $6,345.

Pear Trees, cultivated for their fruit, 2,106 ; val., $446.

Cherry Trees, 2,682 ; val. of cherries, $1,108.

Peach Trees, 4,527 ; val. of peaches, $2,174.

Cranberries, 56½ acres ; val., $4,072.

Establishments for m. of sashes, doors, and blinds, 1 ; cap., $900 ; val. m'd., $1,500 ; emp., 2.

Establishments for m. of gas, 1 ; cap., $32,000 ; val. m'd., $6,000 ; emp., 4.

Breweries, 1 ; cap., $2,000 ; Beer m'd., 900 bbls. ; val., $4,500 ; emp., 3.

Bakeries, 1 ; cap., $6,000 ; Flour consumed, 1,100 bbls ; ; val. of bread m'd., $15,000 ; emp., 11.

Establishments for m. of boxes for boots, 3 ; cap., $4,500 ; val. of boxes m'd., $24,180 ; emp., 15.

Swine raised, 647 ; val., $6,750.

Val. of milk, $12,394.

MILLBURY.

Cotton Mills, 6 ; Spindles, 18,896 ; Cotton consumed, 913,866 lbs. ; Printing Cloth, m'd., 3,399,472 yds. ; Sheeting, 1,214,000 yds. ; Satinet Warps, 364,000 yds. ; val. of cloth, $1,236,851 ; cap., $205,000 ; m. emp., 160 ; f. emp., 186.

Woollen Mills, 3 ; Sets of Machinery, 15 ; Wool consumed, 405,000 lbs. ; Cassimere m'd., 119,208 yds. ; val. of cassimere, $110,920 ; Satinet m'd., 227,000 yds. ; val. of satinet, $61,290 ; Yarn m'd., and not made into cloth, 80,000 lbs. ; val. of yarn, $64,000 ; cap., $135,000 ; Guernsey Frocks m'd., 1,000 dozen ; val. $9,000 ; Ribbed Shirts and Drawers m'd., 100 dozen ; val., $1,200 ; m. emp., 125 ; f. emp., 110.

Furnaces for m. of hollow ware and castings other than pig iron, 1; val. of hollow ware and castings, $16,000; cap., $4,000; emp., 16.

Edge Tool Manufactories, 1; Chisels, Drawing Knives and other Edge Tools m'd,–; val., $70,000; cap., $25,000; emp., 60.

Manufactories of forks and hoes, 1; val, of forks and hoes, $10,000; cap., $3,000; emp., 10.

Paper Manufactories, 1; Stock made use of, 832,000 lbs.; Paper m'd., 437,543 lbs.; val. of paper, $45,942; cap., $28,000; emp., 17.

Upholstery Manufactories, 2; val. of upholstery, $6,000; cap., $1,800; emp., 9.

Establishments for m. of chaises, wagons and other vehicles, 3; val. m'd., $5,500; cap., $4,000; emp., 15.

Black Lead Manufactories, 1; val. of black lead m'd., $720; cap., $300; emp., 1.

Establishments for m. of fire arms, 1; Fire Arms m'd., Muskets and Pistols, 1,500; val. of fire arms, $9,000; cap., $2,000; emp., 10.

Cabinet Manufactories, 1; val. of cabinet ware, $800; cap., $500; emp., 2.

Tin Ware Manufactories, 1; val. of tin ware, $1,000.

Tanneries, 1; Hides of all kinds tanned, 63,250; val. of leather tanned, $27,815; cap., $6,000; emp., 6.

Currying Establishments, 4; val. of leather curried, $70,705; cap., $9,200; emp., 13.

Boots of all kinds m'd., 3,050 pairs; Shoes of all kinds m'd., 86,700 pairs; val. of boots and shoes, $95,250; m. emp., 110; f. emp., 60; cap., $23,850.

Bricks m'd., 350,000; val. of bricks, $1,925; emp., 3.

Val. of mechanics' tools m'd., $5,500; emp., 14.

Lumber prepared for market, 356,000 ft.; val. of lumber, $6,340; emp., 7.

Firewood prepared for market, 1,836 cords; val. of firewood, $9,180; emp., 8.

Horses, 204; val. of horses, $14,177; Oxen over three years old, 152; Steers under three years old, 97; val. of oxen and steers, $10,060; Milch Cows, 400; Heifers, 67; val. of cows and heifers, $13,340.

Butter, 14,915 lbs.; val. of butter, $3,728; Cheese, 6,210 lbs.; val. of cheese, $559.

Indian Corn, 229 acres; Indian Corn, per acre, 32$\frac{1}{3}$ bush.; val., $8,146.

Wheat, 2$\frac{1}{4}$ acres; Wheat, per acre, 30 bush.; val., $60.

Rye, 58 acres; Rye, per acre, 12$\frac{1}{8}$ bush.; val., $839.

Barley, 29$\frac{1}{2}$ acres; Barley, per acre, 14 bush; val., $283.

Oats, 197 acres; Oats, per acre, 25$\frac{2}{3}$ bush.; val., $2,779.

Potatoes, 110 acres; Potatoes, per acre, 117 bush.; val., $9,674.

Onions, 1 acre; Onions, per acre, 400 bush.; val., $268.

Turnips, cultivated as a field crop, raised among corn, 3,330 bush.; val., $832.

Carrots, 4 acres; Carrots, per acre, 636 bush.; val., $636.

Beets and other esculent vegetables, 1 acre; val., $100.

English Mowing, 1,709 acres; English Hay, 1,805 tons; val., $30,685.

Wet Meadow or Swale Hay, 270 tons; val., $2,700.

Apple Trees, cultivated for their fruit, 15,500; val., $7,479.

Pear Trees, cultivated for their fruit, 344; val., $240.

Cranberries, 12 acres; val., $204.

Establishments for m. of sashes, doors and blinds, 2; cap., $16,000; val., $36,000; emp., 32.

Val. of porte monnaies m'd., $30,000; cap., $10,000; m. emp., 8; f. emp., 16.

Val. of gilt jewelry m'd., $30,000; cap., $10,000; m. emp., 30; f. emp., 25.

Swine raised, 232; val., $2,500.

Cherry Trees, 500; val. of cherries, $200.

Peach Trees, 2,020; val. of peaches, $650.

Quinces, 150 bush.; val., $100.

Val. of grapes sold, $100.

White Beans, 325 bush.; val., $650.

Milk sold, 92,336 quarts; val., $3,693.

NEW BRAINTREE.

Establishments for m. of railroad cars, coaches, chaises, wagons, sleighs, and other vehicles, 1; val. of railroad cars, &c., m'd., $1,500; cap., $500; emp., 2.

Boots of all kinds m'd., 1,086 pairs; Shoes of all kinds m'd., 7,080 pairs; val. of boots and shoes, $7,155; m. emp., 8; f. emp., 5.

Val. of palm leaf hats, $70; f. emp., 2.

Lumber prepared for market, 100,000 ft.; val. of lumber, $1,400; emp., 4.

Firewood prepared for market, 500 cords; val. of firewood, $1,250.

Saxony Sheep, of different grades, –; Merino Sheep, of different grades, 50; all other kinds of Sheep, –; val. of all sheep, $168; Wool produced from Saxony sheep, – lbs.; Merino Wool produced, 179 lbs.

Horses, 115; val. of horses, $8,630; Oxen over three years old, 182; Steers under three years old, 40; val. of oxen and steers, $11,630; Milch Cows, 1,091; Heifers, 140; val. of cows and heifers, $34,830.

Butter, 12,635 lbs.; val. of butter, $3,158; Cheese, 265,650 lbs.; val. of cheese, $26,565.

Indian Corn, 257 acres; Indian Corn, per acre, 30 bush.; val., $8,674.

Wheat, 3 acres; Wheat, per acre, 16 bush.; val., $120.

Rye, 100 acres; Rye, per acre, 18 bush.; val., $2,250.

Barley, 97 acres; Barley, per acre, 26 bush.; val., $2,522.

Oats, 183 acres; Oats, per acre, 26 bush.; val., $2,379.

Potatoes, 130 acres; Potatoes, per acre, 100 bush.; val., $6,500.

English Mowing, 1,954 acres; English Hay, 2,100 tons; val., $29,400.

Wet Meadow or Swale Hay, 542 tons; val., $3,252.

Apple Trees, cultivated for their fruit, 3,200; val., $3,477.

Pear Trees, cultivated for their fruit, 43; val., $8.

Cranberries, 6 acres; val., $366.

Shoe Shaves m'd., 200 doz.; val., $800; cap., $500; emp., 2.

Buckwheat, 125 bush.; val., $94.

Swine raised, 238; val., $2,380.

NORTHBOROUGH.

Cotton Mills, 1; Spindles, 2,150; Cotton consumed, 100,000 lbs.; Cloth m'd., 387,000 yds. Calico, light cloths for printing; val. of cloth, $22,000; cap., $10,000; m. emp., 10; f. emp., 22.

Saddle, Harness and Trunk Manufactories, 1; val. of saddles, &c., $500; cap., $150; emp., 1.

Tin Ware Manufactories, 1; val. of tin ware, $500; cap., $700; emp., 1.

Comb Manufactories, 5; val. of combs m'd., $50,000; cap., $25,000; emp., 47.

Tanneries, 1; Hides of all kinds tanned, 3,000; val. of leather tanned, $20,000; cap., $10,000; emp., 5.

Currying Establishments, 1; val. of leather curried, $25,000; cap., $5,000; emp., 4.

Boots of all kinds m'd., 13,500 pairs; Shoes of all kinds m'd., 8,250 pairs; val. of boots and shoes, $27,590; m. emp., 34.

Bricks m'd., 2,100,000; val. of bricks, $12,000; emp., 20.

Charcoal m'd., 550 bush.; val. of same, $100; emp., 1.

Lumber prepared for market, 1,990,000 ft.; val. of lumber, $47,850; emp., 50.

Firewood prepared for market, 3,226 cords; val. of firewood, $12,824.

Saxony Sheep, of different grades, –; Merino Sheep, of different grades, –; all other kinds of Sheep, 30; val. of all sheep, $150; Wool produced from Saxony sheep, – lbs.; Merino Wool produced, – lbs.; all other Wool produced, 120 lbs.

Horses, 209; val. of horses, $16,130; Oxen over three years

old, 148; Steers under three years old, 74; val. of oxen and steers, $12,220; Milch Cows, 440; Heifers, 107; val. of cows and heifers, $18,118.

Butter, 26,545 lbs.; val. of butter, $6,636; Cheese, 1,825 lbs.; val. of cheese, $146; Honey, 60 lbs.; val. of honey, $12.

Indian Corn, 253 acres; Indian Corn, per acre, 35 bush.; val., $9,842.

Wheat, 8 acres; Wheat, per acre, 14½ bush.; val., $290.

Rye, 35 acres; Rye, per acre, 22 bush.; val., $290.

Barley, 7 acres; Barley, per acre, 15½ bush.; val., $108.

Oats, 65 acres; Oats, per acre, 23 bush.; val., $900.

Potatoes, 108 acres; Potatoes, per acre, 100 bush.; val., $6,831.

Turnips, cultivated as a field crop, 20 acres; Turnips, per acre, 400 bush.; val., $1,600.

Carrots, 8 acres; Carrots, per acre, 200 bush.; val., $480.

English Mowing, 1,418 acres; English Hay, 1,623 tons; val., $25,968.

Wet Meadow or Swale Hay, 545 tons; val., $5,510.

Apple Trees, cultivated for their fruit, 7,783; val., $4,928.

Pear Trees, cultivated for their fruit, 159; val., $107.

Cranberries, 3 acres; val., $200.

Val. of milk, $10,000.

NORTHBRIDGE.

Cotton Mills, 2; Spindles, 8,652; Cotton consumed, 722,000 lbs.; Cloth m'd., 2,700,000 yds., Sheetings; val. of cloth, $162,000; m. emp., 55; f. emp., 105.

Furnaces for m. of hollow ware and castings other than pig iron, 1; Hollow Ware and other Castings m'd., 880 tons; val. of hollow ware and castings, $68,992; cap., $10,000; emp., 25.

Establishments for m. of cotton, woollen and other machinery, 1; val. of machinery m'd., $300,000; cap., $100,000; emp., 300.

Scythe Manufactories, 1; Scythes m'd., 13,200; val. of scythes, $10,000; cap., $10,000; emp., 18, three months.

Chair and Cabinet Manufactories, 1; val. of chairs and cabinet ware, $500; cap., $200; emp., 1.

Currying Establishments, 2; val. of leather curried, $20,000; cap., $6,000; emp., 6.

Boots of all kinds m'd., 43,000 pairs; Shoes of all kinds m'd., 57,000 pairs; val. of boots and shoes, $120,000; m. emp., 120; f. emp., 40.

Val. of building stone quarried and prepared for building, $1,200; emp., 3.

Charcoal m'd., 1,000 bush.; val. of same, $80.

Lumber prepared for market, 765,000 ft.; val. of lumber, $11,475; emp., 20.

Firewood prepared for market, 3,700 cords; val. of firewood, $16,650; emp., 50.

Horses, 120; val. of horses, $8,400; Oxen over three years old, 256; Steers under three years old, 40; val. of oxen and steers, $13,600; Milch Cows, 239; Heifers, 40; val. of cows and heifers, $8,965.

Butter, 9,000 lbs.; val. of butter, $2,250; Cheese, 2,000 lbs.; val. of cheese, $180.

Indian Corn, 170 acres; Indian Corn, per acre, 30 bush.; val., $5,950.

Rye, 50 acres; Rye, per acre, 8 bush.; val., $500.

Oats, 120 acres; Oats, per acre, 25 bush.; val., $1,800.

Potatoes, 120 acres; Potatoes, per acre, 75 bush.; val., $5,400.

Turnips, cultivated as a field crop, 3 acres; Turnips, per acre, 200 bush.; val., $150.

English Mowing, 918 acres; English Hay, 690 tons; val., $12,420.

Wet Meadow or Swale Hay, 400 tons; val., $4,000.

Apple Trees, cultivated for their fruit, 3,000; val., $3,000.

Pear Trees, cultivated for their fruit, 100; val., $20.

Cranberries, 25 acres; val., $680.

Establishments for m. of boxes for machinery, 1; cap., $500; val. of boxes m'd., $3,000; emp., 3.

Swine raised, 100; val., $1,000.

Milk sold, 80,000 qts.; val., $3,200.

NORTH BROOKFIELD.

Woollen Mills, 1; not in operation.

Copper and Sheet Iron Ware Manufactories, 1; val. of copper and sheet iron ware, $2,000; emp., 1.

Currying Establishments, 1; val. of leather curried, $28,467.04; emp., 4. The business done is job work.

Boots of all kinds m'd., 230,000 pairs; Shoes of all kinds m'd., 395,500 pairs; val. of boots and shoes, $655,450; m. emp., 645; f. emp., 498.

Val. of marble quarried and prepared for market, $200; emp., 1.

Lasts m'd., 28,766; val., $6,000.

Firewood prepared for market, 915 cords; val. of firewood, $3,859; prepared in small lots by farmers.

Saxony Sheep, of different grades, – ; Merino Sheep, of different grades, –; all other kinds of Sheep, 93; val. of all sheep, $283; Wool produced from Saxony sheep, – lbs.; Merino Wool produced, – lbs.; all other Wool produced, 337 lbs.

Horses, 245; val. of horses, $17,131; Oxen over three years old, 268; Steers under three years old, 161; val. of oxen and steers, $18,029; Milch Cows, 434; Heifers, 193; val. of cows and heifers, $19,232.

Butter, 21,336 lbs.; val. of butter, $5,334; Cheese, 37,425 lbs.; val. of cheese, $3,742.50.

Indian Corn, 190 acres; Indian Corn, per acre, 32 bush.; val., $6,080.

Wheat, $\frac{1}{2}$ acre; Wheat, per acre, 12 bush.; val., $12.

Rye, 38$\frac{1}{2}$ acres; Rye, per acre, 9 bush.; val., $519.75.

Barley, 30$\frac{1}{2}$ acres; Barley, per acre, 20$\frac{1}{2}$ bush.; val., $500.

Oats, 139 acres; Oats, per acre, 20 bush.; val., $1,391.

Potatoes, 139 acres; Potatoes, per acre, 105 bush.; val., $7,297.50.

Carrots, 2 acres; Carrots, per acre, 400 bush., val., $200.

Beets and other esculent vegetables (raised in gardens); val., $5,000.

English Mowing, 2,072 acres; English Hay, 2,031 tons; val., $28,434.

Wet Meadow or Swale Hay, 682 tons; val., $4,092.

Apple Trees, cultivated for their fruit, 6,753; val., $3,795.

Pear Trees, cultivated for their fruit, 692; val., $224.

Swine raised, 208; val., $3,744.

Stock Shaves m'd., 1,812; val., $604; emp., 1.

Razor Strops, 1,200; val., $3,500; m. emp., 2; f. emp., 2.

Pocket Books, 27,000; val., $10,000; m. emp., 2; f. emp., 18.

OAKHAM.

Plough Manufactories, 1; Ploughs and other Agricultural Tools m'd., 100; val., $800; cap., $500; emp., 1.

Establishments for m. of railroad cars, coaches, chaises, wagons, sleighs and other vehicles, 1; val. of railroad cars, &c., m'd., $2,000; cap., $1,000; emp., 2.

Charcoal, m'd., 2,000 bush.; val. of same, $160; emp., 1.

Lumber prepared for market, 850,000 ft.; val. of lumber, $8,400; emp., 5.

Firewood prepared for market, 481 cords; val. of firewood, $1,443; emp., 1.

Saxony Sheep, of different grades, –; Merino Sheep, of different grades, –; all other kinds of sheep, 100; val. of all

sheep, $471; Wool produced from Saxony sheep, - lbs.; Merino Wool produced, - lbs.; all other wool produced, 423 lbs.

Horses, 139; val. of horses, $10,076; Oxen over three years old, 140; Steers under three years old, 88; val. of oxen and steers, $10,473; Milch Cows, 534; Heifers, 90; val. of cows and heifers, $17,725.

Butter, 16,906 lbs; val. of butter, $3,381.20; Cheese, 81,180 lbs.; val. of cheese, $8,118.

Indian Corn, 195 acres; Indian Corn, per acre, 27 bush.; val., $5,272.

Wheat, 23 acres; Wheat, per acre, 12 bush.; val., $220.80.

Rye, 11 acres; Rye, per acre, 13 bush.; val., $157.

Barley, 40 acres; Barley, per acre, 24 bush.; val., $772.

Oats, 184 acres; Oats, per acre, 26 bush.; val., $2,500.

Potatoes, 165 acres; Potatoes, per acre, 70 bush.; val., $6,930.

Carrots, 1 acre; Carrots, per acre, 412 bush.; val., $103.

English Mowing, 1,555 acres; English Hay, 1,487 tons; val., $11,000.

Wet Meadow or Swale Hay, 304 tons; val., $2,268.

Apple Trees, cultivated for their fruit, 2,836; val., $2,640.

Cranberries, 2 acres; val., $20.

Establishments for m. of casks, 1; cap., $500; Casks m'd., $7,500; val., $1,250; emp., 3.

Val. of dish covers, corn poppers, rat traps, &c., m'd., $20,000; cap., $5,000; emp., 25.

OXFORD.

Cotton Mills, 5; Spindles, 8,012; Cotton consumed, 650,000 lbs.; Cloth m'd., 2,187,300 yds.; val. of cloth, $131,000; cap., $85,000; m. emp., 68; f. emp., 90.

Woollen Mills, 2; Sets of Machinery, 9; Wool consumed, 150,000 lbs.; Flannel or Blanketing, 537,600 yds.; val. of flannel or blanketing, $134,400.

Establishments for m. of hosiery, 1; Hosiery m'd., 200,000 yds.; val. of hosiery, $28,000; cap., $6,000; m. emp., 25; f. emp., 5.

Forges, 7; Bar Iron, Anchors, Chain Cables, and other articles of wrought iron m'd., 10 tons; cap., $1,300; emp., 7.

Saddle, Harness and Trunk Manufactories, 2; val. of saddles, &c., $2,600; cap., $600; emp., 4.

Cordage Manufactories, 2; Cordage m'd., 300,000 lbs.; cap., $15,000; emp., 27.

Tin Ware Manufactories, 2; val. of tin ware, $2,500; cap., $1,500; emp., 3.

Boots of all kinds m'd., 6,200 pairs; Shoes of all kinds m'd., 421,000 pairs; val. of boots and shoes, $263,800; m. emp., 391; f. emp., 351.

Bricks m'd., 200,000; val. of bricks, $1,100; emp., 2.

Lumber prepared for market, 1,152,000 ft.; val. of lumber, $14,300; emp., 35.

Firewood prepared for market, 9,111 cords; val. of firewood, $33,853; emp., 104.

Saxony Sheep, of different grades, –; Merino Sheep, of different grades, –; all other kinds of Sheep, 110; val. of all sheep, $365; Wool produced from Saxony sheep, – lbs.; Merino Wool produced, – lbs.; all other Wool produced, 341 lbs.

Horses, 334; val. of horses, $27,070; Oxen over three years old, 308; Steers under three years old, 170; val. of oxen and steers, $25,504; Milch Cows, 686; Heifers, 207; val. of cows and heifers, $25,404.

Butter, 13,915 lbs.; val. of butter, $2,854.50; Cheese, 12,700 lbs.; val. of cheese, $1,146; Honey, 307 lbs.; val. of honey, $56.

Indian Corn, 419 acres; Indian Corn, per acre, 35⅔ bush.; val., $14,400.

Rye, 82 acres; Rye, per acre, 15⅓ bush.; val., $1,654.

Barley, 49 acres; Barley, per acre, 20 bush.; val., $1,000.

Oats, 446 acres; Oats, per acre, 31⅔ bush.; val., $8,788.

Potatoes, 241 acres; Potatoes, per acre, 99⅓ bush.; val., $14,700.

Turnips, cultivated as a field crop, 6 acres; Turnips, per acre, 200 bush.; val., $240.

Carrots, 13 acres; Carrots, per acre, 387½ bush.; val., $1,500.

Beets and other esculent vegetables, – acres; all other Grain or Root crops, 16 acres; val., $600.

English Mowing, 3,425 acres; English Hay, 3,928 tons; val., $61,278.

Wet Meadow or Swale Hay, 910 tons; val., $7,150.

Apple Trees, cultivated for their fruit, 11,350; val., $5,675.

Pear Trees, cultivated for their fruit, 68; val., $90.

Beeswax, 14 lbs.; val., $5.

Establishments for m. of boxes for boots and shoes, 1; cap., $1,000; val. of boxes m'd., $4,000; emp., 6.

Buckwheat, 115 acres; Buckwheat, per acre, 17 bush.; val., $1,800.

PAXTON.

Tanneries, 1; Hides of all kinds tanned, 374; val. of leather tanned, $1,850; cap., $1,000; emp., 1.

Boots of all kinds m'd., 58,100 pairs; Shoes of all kinds m'd., – pairs; val. of boots and shoes, $104,100; m. emp., 95; f. emp., 28.

Lumber prepared for market, 113,000 ft.; val. of lumber, $1,243.

Firewood prepared for market 1,752 cords; val. of firewood, $5,206.25.

Saxony Sheep, of different grades, –; Merino Sheep, of different grades, –; all other kinds of Sheep, 39; val. of all sheep, $111; Wool produced from Saxony sheep, – lbs.; Merino Wool produced, – lbs.; all other Wool produced, 146 lbs.

Horses, 111; val. of horses, $7,770; Oxen over three years old, 93; Steers under three years old, 97; val. of oxen and steers, $6,692; Milch Cows, 225; Heifers, 74; val. of cows and heifers, $6,808.

Butter, 8,610 lbs.; val. of butter, $2,152.50; Cheese, 9,130 lbs.; val. of cheese, $730.40.

Indian Corn, 90 acres; Indian Corn, per acre, 26 bush.; val., $2,956.

Rye, 6 acres; Rye, per acre, 18 bush.; val., $135.

Barley, 34½ acres; Barley, per acre, 20 bush.; val., $509.25.

Oats, 89 acres; Oats, per acre, 29 bush.; val., $1,300.50.

Potatoes, 102 acres; Potatoes, per acre, 104 bush.; val., $4,257.60.

Carrots, 1½ acre; Carrots, per acre, 412 bush.; val., $137.

English Mowing, 1,074 acres; English Hay, 810 tons; val., $11,340.

Wet Meadow or Swale Hay, 318 tons; val., $2,226.

Apple Trees, cultivated for their fruit, 2,534; val., $715.

Establishments for m. of boxes for boots, 1; cap., $200; val. of boxes m'd., 700; emp., 1.

PETERSHAM.

Tin Ware manufactories, 1; val. of tin ware, $100.

Tanneries, 2; Hides of all kinds tanned, 1,400; val. of leather tanned, $4,000; cap., $2,200; emp., 4.

Boots of all kinds m'd., 475 pairs; Shoes of all kinds m'd., 100 pairs; val. of boots and shoes, $887; m. emp., 1.

Val. of palm leaf hats, $14,926; made in families.

Bricks m'd., 50,000; val. of bricks, $250; emp., 1, three months.

Charcoal m'd., 13,600 bush.; val. of same, $952; emp., 3.

Lumber prepared for market, 1,195,000 ft.; val. of lumber, $10,502; emp., 12.

Firewood prepared for market, 1,218 cords; val. of firewood, $1,959; emp., 3.

Saxony Sheep, of different grades, –; Merino Sheep, of different grades, –; all other kinds of Sheep, 398; val. of all

sheep, $1,384; Wool produced from Saxony sheep, – lbs.; Merino Wool produced, – lbs.; all other Wool produced, 1,015 lbs.

Horses, 293; val. of horses, $26,295; Oxen over three years old, 381; Steers under three years old, 261; val. of oxen and steers, $27,694; Milch Cows, 817; Heifers, 329; val. of cows and heifers, $29,987.

Butter, 41,370 lbs.; val. of butter, $9,485; Cheese, 81,010 lbs.; val. of cheese, $8,049; Honey, 10 lbs.; val. of honey, $2.

Indian Corn, 355 acres; Indian Corn, per acre, 34 bush.; val., $13,881.

Wheat, 4 acres; Wheat, per acre, 15 bush.; val., $186.

Rye, 92 acres; Rye, per acre, 9 bush.; val., $1,072.

Barley, 112 acres; Barley, per acre, 22 bush.; val., $2,464.

Oats, 227 acres; Oats, per acre, 30 bush.; val., $3,403.

Potatoes, 177 acres; Potatoes, per acre, 100 bush.; val., $8,661.

English Mowing, 2,717 acres; English Hay, 2,911 tons; val., $43,665.

Wet Meadow or Swale Hay, 767 tons; val., $6,392.

Apple Trees, cultivated for their fruit, 5,904; val., $3,916.

Pear Trees, cultivated for their fruit, 241; val., $137.

Establishments for m. of casks, 1; cap., $3,000; ready to go into operation the first of June.

Establishments for m. of boxes for cloth and hats, 2; cap., $1,000; val. of boxes m'd., $5,000; emp., 3.

Ladders m'd., 300; val., $500; emp., 1.

Swine raised, 411; val., $3,139.

PHILLIPSTON.

Chair and Cabinet Manufactories, 2; val. of chairs and cabinet ware, $10,500; emp., 12.

Tanneries, 2; Hides of all kinds tanned, 2,800; val. of leather tanned, $11,500; cap., $3,000; emp., 5.

Charcoal m'd., 5,400 bush.; val. of same, $486.

Lumber prepared for market, 990,000 ft.; val. of lumber, $9,446; emp., in one establishment, 5.

Firewood prepared for market, 1,369 cords; val. of firewood, $3,600.

Saxony Sheep, of different grades, –; Merino Sheep, of different grades, –; all other kinds of Sheep, 74; val. of all sheep, $296.

Horses, 115; val. of horses, $9,515; Oxen over three years old, 144; Steers under three years old, 98; val. of oxen and steers, $11,660; Milch Cows, 230; Heifers, 93; val. of cows and heifers, $8,955.

Butter, 21,370 lbs.; val. of butter, $4,274; Cheese, 24,100 lbs.; val. of cheese, $2,219.

Indian Corn, 139 acres; Indian Corn, per acre, 43 bush.; val., $6,574.70.

Wheat, 9½ acres; Wheat, per acre, 15½ bush.; val., $330.75.

Rye, 32 acres; Rye, per acre, 11 bush.; val., $440.

Barley, 30 acres; Barley, per acre, 18½ bush.; val., $555.

Oats, 90 acres; Oats, per acre, 30 bush.; val., $1,350.

Potatoes, 102 acres; Potatoes, per acre, 103 bush.; val., $5,253.

Carrots, cultivated in gardens, 720 bush.; val., $180.

English Mowing, 1,541 acres; English Hay, 1,385 tons; val., $23,545.

Wet Meadow or Swale Hay, 388 tons; val., $3,104.

Apple Trees, cultivated for their fruit, –; val. of apples, $1,600.

Establishments for m. of boxes for boots, 1, in part; val. of boxes m'd., $900; emp., 2, in part.

Swine raised, 92; val., $971.

White Beans, 20 bush.; val., $40.

Pumpkins, 300 loads; val., $376.

Hogshead Staves, 20,000; val., $320.

Shingles, 150,000; val., $337.50.

Ox Bows, 144; val., $100.

Axe Helves, 125; val., $31.25.

Washstands, 600 ; val., $300.
Toilet Tables, 600 ; val., $300.
Knife Handles, 80,000 ; val., $144.
Churn Handles, 5,000 ; val., $14.
Ventilators, 5,000 ; val., $37.50.
Hemlock Bark, 104 cords ; val., $468.

PRINCETON.

Saddle, Harness and Trunk Manufactories, 1 ; val. of saddles, &c., $200; cap., $50 ; emp., 1.

Chair and Cabinet Manufactories, 2 ; val. of chairs and cabinet ware, $100,000 ; cap., $4,000 ; emp., 50.

Tanneries, 1 ; Hides of all kinds tanned, 300 ; val. of leather tanned, $1,500 ; cap., $1,000 ; emp., 1.

Boots of all kinds m'd., 300 pairs ; Shoes of all kinds m'd., 6,000 pairs ; val. of boots and shoes, $4,000 ; m. emp., 15 ; f. emp., 6.

Val. of straw braid m'd. and not made into bonnets and hats, $500 ; val. of palm leaf hats, $4,000 ; f. emp., 25.

Charcoal m'd., 3,000 bush. ; val. of same, $360.

Lumber prepared for market, 342,000 ft. ; val. of lumber, $5,047.

Firewood prepared for market, 2,020 cords ; val. of firewood, $4,385.

Saxony Sheep, of different grades, – ; Merino Sheep, of different grades, – ; all other kinds of sheep, 160 ; val. of all sheep., $513 ; Wool produced from Saxony sheep, – lbs. ; Merino Wool produced, – lbs. ; all other Wool produced, 598 lbs.

Horses, 200 ; val. of horses, $10,000 ; Oxen over three years old, 228 ; Steers under three years old, 106 ; val. of oxen and steers, $18,333 ; Milch Cows, 427 ; Heifers, 89 ; val. of cows and heifers, $13,500.

Butter, 42,735 lbs. ; val. of butter, $9,401 ; Cheese, 13,150 lbs.; val. of cheese, $1,088; Honey, 500 lbs.; val. of honey, $110.

Indian Corn, 220 acres; Indian Corn, per acre, 30 bush.; val., $7,420.

Black Sea Wheat, 29 acres; Wheat, per acre, 18 bush.; val., $1,044.

Rye, 29 acres; Rye, per acre, 15 bush.; val., $539.

Barley, 41 acres; Barley, per acre, 25 bush.; val., $1,005.

Oats, 84 acres; Oats, per acre, 30 bush.; val., $1,532.

Potatoes, 125 acres; Potatoes, per acre, 95 bush.; val., $6,000.

Onions, 100 bush; val., $70.

Val. of turnips, $50.

Val. of carrots raised in the town, $500.

Val. of beets, $100.

Val. of buckwheat, $50.

English Mowing, 1,900 acres; English Hay, 1,724 tons; val., $27,584.

Wet Meadow or Swale Hay, 604 tons; val., $6,644.

Apple Trees, cultivated for their fruit, 3,294; val., $3,116.

Pear Trees, cultivated for their fruit, 200; val., $100.

Hops, 2 acres; Hops, per acre, 300 lbs.; val., $100.

Cranberries, 4 acres; val., $50.

ROYALSTON.

Woollen Mills, 1; Sets of Machinery, 4; Wool consumed, 80,000 lbs.; Doeskin m'd., 40,000 yds.; val. of Doeskin, $35,000; Cassimere m'd., 35,000 yds.; val. of cassimere, $30,000; m. emp., 35; f. emp., 34.

Establishments for m. of chronometers, watches, gold and silver ware and jewelry, –; val. of m's., $1,500; cap., $500; emp., 1.

Brush Manufactories, 1; val. of brushes, $3,500; cap., $1,800; emp., 5.

Chair and Cabinet Manufactories, 5; val. of chairs and cabinet ware, $27,800; cap., $20,500; emp., 40.

Tanneries, 1; Hides of all kinds tanned, 300; val. of leather tanned, $400; cap., $800; emp., 1.

Currying Establishments, 1; val. of leather curried, $1,600; cap., $800; emp., 1.

Boots of all kinds m'd., 206 pairs; Shoes of all kinds m'd., 360 pairs; val. of boots and shoes, $1,151; m. emp., 3.

Val. of palm leaf hats, $10,000.

Charcoal m'd., 2,000 bush.; val. of same, $140; emp., 2.

Val. of wooden ware not otherwise enumerated, including farming utensils m'd., $11,100; emp., 3.

Shoe Pegs m'd., 7,000 bush.; val., $4,200.

Lumber prepared for market, 4,373,000 ft.; val. of lumber, $43,860; emp., 31.

Firewood prepared for market, 531 cords; val. of firewood, $1,100; emp., 2.

Saxony Sheep, of different grades, 6; Merino Sheep, of different grades, –; all other kinds of Sheep, 144; val. of all sheep, $603; Wool produced from Saxony sheep, 33 lbs.; Merino Wool produced, – lbs.; all other Wool produced, 475 lbs.

Horses, 236; val. of horses, $21,312; Oxen over three years old, 268; Steers under three years old, 279; val. of oxen and steers, $19,702; Milch Cows, 543; Heifers, 253; val. of cows and heifers, $19,607.

Butter, 33,905 lbs.; val. of butter, $7,798.15; Cheese, 17,735 lbs.; val. of cheese, $1,773.50; Honey, 50 lbs.; val. of honey, $10.

Indian Corn, 207 acres; Indian Corn, per acre, 31⅝ bush.; val., $7,374.

Wheat, 19 acres; Wheat, per acre, 11 bush.; val., $522.50.

Rye, 34 acres; Rye, per acre, 15 bush.; val., $891.

Barley, 85 acres; Barley, per acre, 24 bush.; val., $2,550.

Oats, 109 acres; Oats, per acre, 31 bush.; val., $1,689.50.

Potatoes, 117 acres; Potatoes, per acre, 103⅝ bush.; val., $7,277.40.

Onions, $\frac{1}{4}$ acre; Onions, per acre, 300 bush.; val., $75.

Turnips, cultivated as a field crop, $\frac{1}{2}$ acre; Turnips, per acre, 330 bush.; val., $41.25.

Carrots, 3 acres; Carrots, per acre, 1,123 bush.; val., $1,123.

English Mowing, 2,854 acres; English Hay, 1,813 tons; val., $30,821.

Wet Meadow or Swale Hay, 734 tons; val., $5,872.

Apple Trees, cultivated for their fruit, 8,417; val., $2,704.

Pear Trees, cultivated for their fruit, 103; val., $36.50.

Establishments for m. of pails, 3; Pails m'd., 210,000; val. of pails, $33,000; cap., $33,000; emp., 38.

Grape Wine m'd., 6 bbls.; val., $192.

Val. of milk sold, $600; emp., 1.

Saw Mills, 15.

Grist Mills, 2.

RUTLAND.

Establishments for m. of railroad cars, coaches, chaises, wagons, sleighs, and other vehicles, 3; cap., $3,500; emp., 7.

Val. of palm leaf hats m'd., $1,113; f. emp., 70.

Lumber prepared for market, 326,500 ft.; val. of lumber, $3,945; emp., 8.

Firewood prepared for market, 2,946 cords; val. of firewood, $7,876; emp., 6.

Saxony Sheep, of different grades, –; Merino Sheep, of different grades, –; all other kinds of Sheep, 152; val. of all sheep, $453; Wool produced from Saxony sheep, – lbs.; Merino Wool produced, – lbs.; all other Wool produced, 508 lbs.; val., $169.33.

Horses, 226; val. of horses, $15,480; Oxen over three years old, 332; Steers under three years old, 146; val. of oxen and steers, $18,208; Milch Cows, 691; Heifers, 196; val. of cows and heifers, $19,655.

Butter, 33,932 lbs.; val. of butter, $7,358; Cheese, 19,670 lbs.; val. of cheese, $1,876.

Indian Corn, 225 acres; Indian Corn, per acre, 26½ bush.; val., $6,638.40.

Wheat, 1½ acre; Wheat, per acre, 17 bush.; val., $75.

Rye, 24 acres; Rye, 9 bush.; val., $200.

Barley, 73 acres; Barley, per acre, 20½ bush.; val., $1,505.

Oats, 201 acres; Oats, per acre, 30 bush.; val., $3,646.

Potatoes, 189 acres; Potatoes, per acre, 96½ bush.; val., $10,970.

Carrots, 6¼ acres; Carrots, per acre, 427 bush; val., $1,325.

English Mowing, 2,129 acres; English Hay, 1,673 tons; val., $26,826.

Wet Meadow or Swale Hay, 680 tons; val., $5,440.

Apple Trees, cultivated for their fruit, 2,892; val., $2,034.

Pear Trees, cultivated for their fruit, 60; val., $10.

Cranberries, 5 acres; val., $300.

Swine raised, 125; val., $1,150.

Mules, 1; val., $50.

SHREWSBURY.

Saddle, Harness and Trunk Manufactories, 1; val. of saddles, &c., $1,300; cap., $300.

Establishments for m. of railroad cars, coaches, chaises, wagons, sleighs, and other vehicles, –; val. of railroad cars, &c., m'd., $3,000; cap., $900; two-thirds of this business is repairing carriages.

Establishments for m. of fire arms, 5; Fire Arms m'd., 167 Rifles, 513 Fowling Pieces, 50 Pistols, and $800 in repairs; val. of fire arms, $6,075; cap., $1,500; emp., 6.

Tanneries, 1; Hides of all kinds tanned, 14,356; val. of leather tanned, $40,582; cap., $15,000; emp., 8.

Currying Establishments, 1; val. of leather curried, $128,000; cap., $60,000; emp., 22.

Boots of all kinds m'd., 24,273 pairs; Shoes of all kinds m'd., 58,600 pairs; val. of boots and shoes, $80,300; cap., $16,900; m. emp., 110; f. emp., 66.

Lumber prepared for market, 24,000 ft.; val. of lumber, $360.

Firewood prepared for market, 1,586 cords; val. of firewood, $7,933.

Saxony Sheep, of different grades, –; Merino Sheep, of different grades, –; all other kinds of Sheep, 60; val. of all sheep, $613; Wool produced from Saxony sheep, – lbs.; Merino Wool produced, – lbs.; all other Wool produced, 125 lbs.

Horses, 241; val. of horses, $18,695; Oxen over three years old, 224; Steers under three years old, 40; val. of oxen and steers, $14,495; Milch Cows, 767; Heifers, 97; val. of cows and heifers, $18,790.

Butter, 69,340 lbs.; val. of butter, $16,843; Cheese, 3,900 lbs.; val. of cheese, $353.

Indian Corn, 316 acres; Indian Corn, per acre, 33 bush.; val., $10,428.

Wheat, 5 acres; Wheat, per acre, 11 bush.; val., $130.

Rye, 57 acres; Rye, per acre, 11 bush.; val., $627.

Barley, 6 acres; Barley, per acre, 22 bush.; val., $132.

Oats, 187 acres; Oats, per acre, 27 bush.; val., $3,029.

Potatoes, 101 acres; Potatoes, per acre, 100 bush.; val., $7,532.

Beets and other esculent vegetables, 20 acres; val., $3,345; all other Grain or Root Crops, 28 acres; val., $3,253.

Millet, 3 acres; val., $80.

English Mowing, 1,884 acres; English Hay, 1,703 tons; val., $26,444.

Wet Meadow or Swale Hay, 707 tons; val., $5,624.

Apple Trees, cultivated for their fruit, 19,360; Apples, 21,104 bush.; val., $10,454.

Pear Trees, cultivated for their fruit, 567; val., $200.

Val. of all other kinds of fruit, $1,008.

Swine raised, 252; val., $2,625.

Establishments for m. of boot counters and shoe stiffenings, 1; Boot Counters m'd., 12,000; val., $240; Shoe Stiffenings m'd., 100,000 pairs; val., $1,200; cap., $600; emp., 3.

"J. C. Stone & Co. have quite an extensive Nursery of Fruit Trees. They have probably fifteen or twenty thousand in cultivation, and gave us six thousand, which they called worth $1,500."

Shrewsbury has from two to three thousand peach trees, cultivated for their fruit, and about as many quince trees.

SOUTHBOROUGH.

Cotton Mills, 2; Spindles, 500; Cotton consumed, 480,000 lbs.; Cloth m'd., - yds., Kerseys, principally of cotton wool; val. of cloth, $123,000; Yarn m'd., 50,000 lbs.; val. of yarn, $6,750; cap., $70,000; m. emp., 49; f. emp., 47.

Woollen Mills, -; Sets of Machinery, 3; Wool consumed, 30,000 lbs.

Cordage Manufactories, 1; val. of cordage (cotton), m'd., $3,000; cap., $10,000; emp., 12.

Currying Establishments, 1; val. of leather curried, $2,600; cap., $500; emp., 4.

Boots of all kinds m'd., 15,800 pairs; Shoes of all kinds m'd., 234,000 pairs; val. of boots and shoes, $202,100; m. emp., 137; f. emp., 105.

Val. of blocks and pumps m'd., $300; emp., 1.

Lumber prepared for market, 184,000 ft.; val. of lumber, $2,654.

Firewood prepared for market, 2,044 cords; val. of firewood, $11,641; emp., 6.

Horses, 180; val. of horses, $15,182; Oxen over three years old, 64; Steers under three years old, -; val. of oxen and steers, $4,800; Milch Cows, 663; Heifers, 48; val. of cows and heifers, $21,330.

Butter, 33,273 lbs.; val. of butter, $8,515; Cheese, 580 lbs.; val. of cheese, $42; Honey, 40 lbs.; val. of honey, $5.

Indian Corn, 288 acres; Indian Corn, per acre, 30 bush.; val., $8,640.

Wheat, 2 acres; Wheat, per acre, 12 bush.; val., $48.

Rye, 21 acres; Rye, per acre, 10 bush.; val., $239.

Barley, 4 acres; Barley, per acre, 15 bush.; val., $60.

Oats, 145 acres; Oats, per acre, 25 bush.; val., $2,175.

Potatoes, 153 acres; Potatoes, per acre, 100 bush.; val., $9,558.

Turnips, cultivated as a field crop, 5 acres; Turnips, per acre, 400 bush.; val., $500.

Beets and other esculent vegetables, 40 acres; val., $1,400.

English Mowing, 2,300 acres; English Hay, 1,742 tons; val., $29,308.

Wet Meadow or Swale Hay, 574 tons; val., $5,740.

Apple Trees, cultivated for their fruit, 7,000; val., $8,694.

Pear Trees, cultivated for their fruit, 600; val., $50.

Cranberries, 20 acres; val., $200.

Establishments for m. of sashes, doors and blinds, 1; cap., $4,000; val. m'd., $500; emp., 2.

Whortleberries, 400 bush.; val., $600.

Vinegar, 3,000 galls.; val., $300.

SOUTHBRIDGE.

Cotton Mills, 3; Spindles, 17,144; Cotton consumed, 855,878 lbs.; Cloth m'd., 2,132,819 yds. 4-4 Sheetings; val. of cloth, $115,455; Yarn m'd., 281,750 lbs.; (275,000 lbs. of this yarn were used for warps for the m. of de laines, as given below); val. of yarn, $70,235; cap., $196,000; m. emp., 141; f. emp., 139.

Mousseline de Laine Printing Establishments, 1; Mousseline de Laine printed, 4,500,000 yds.; val. of mousseline de laines, $675,000; cap., $150,000; m. emp., 140; f. emp., 20.

Woollen Mills, 1; Sets of Machinery, 6; Wool consumed, 155,000 lbs.; Cassimere m'd., 14,800 yds.; val. of cassimere, $100,000; Roller Cloth m'd., 143 yds.; val. of roller cloth, $350; Woollen Shawls, 97 yds.; val. of shawls, $390; cap., $90,000; m. emp., 65; f. emp., 35.

Establishments for m. of worsted goods, or goods of which worsted is a component part (Mousseline de Laines), 1; Goods m'd., 4,400,000 yds.; val. of goods, $440,000; cap., $275,000; m. emp., 226; f. emp., 214. In this business, 18 sets of cards and 9,000 spindles are used, and 540,000 lbs. of wool consumed.

Establishments for m. of cutlery, 1; val. of cutlery, $9,000; cap., $2,500; emp., 5.

Daguerreotype Artists, 1; Daguerreotypes taken, 1,000; cap., $500; emp., 1.

Saddle and Harness Manufactories, 2; val. of saddles, &c., $3,000; cap., $1,000; emp., 4.

Hat and Cap Manufactories, 1; Hats and Caps m'd., 400; cap., $1,000; emp., 3.

Establishments for m. of soap and tallow candles, 1; Soap m'd., hard, 150,000 lbs.; Soft, 360 bbls.; val. of soap, $8,516; Tallow Candles m'd., 13,000 lbs.; val. of tallow candles, $1,900; cap., $2,000; emp., 3.

Cabinet Manufactories, 1; val. of cabinet ware, $2,300; cap., $1,200; emp., 3.

Tin Ware Manufactories, 1; val. of tin ware, $500.

Boots of all kinds m'd., 725 pairs; Shoes of all kinds m'd., 14,652 pairs; val. of boots and shoes, $12,759; m. emp., 34; f. emp., 20.

Bricks m'd., 500,000; val. of bricks, $2,250; emp., 4.

Lumber prepared for market, 976,500 ft.; val. of lumber, $10,450; emp., 25.

Firewood prepared for market, 4,520 cords; val. of firewood, $12,378; emp., 18.

Saxony Sheep, of different grades, –; Merino Sheep, of different grades, 18; all other kinds of Sheep, 216; val. of all sheep, $641; Wool produced from Saxony sheep, – lbs.; Merino Wool produced, 71 lbs.; all other Wool produced, 641 lbs.

Horses, 244 ; val. of horses, $22,830; Oxen over three years old, 250 ; Steers under three years old, 102; val. of oxen and steers, $15,669; Milch Cows, 462 ; Heifers, 169; val. of cows and heifers, $16,708.

Butter, 19,345 lbs.; val. of butter, $4,256; Cheese, 20,710 lbs.; val. of cheese, $1,864; Honey, 574 lbs.; val. of honey, $115.

Indian Corn, 217 acres; Indian Corn, per acre, 37 bush.; val., $8,825.

Wheat, 7 acres; Wheat, per acre, 18 bush.; val., $252.

Rye, 45 acres; Rye, per acre, 16 bush.; val., $902.

Barley, 35 acres; Barley, per acre, 22½ bush.; val., $787.

Oats, 130 acres; Oats, per acre, 26¾ bush.; val., $2,174.

Potatoes, 136 acres; Potatoes, per acre, 117½ bush.; val., $990.

Onions, 201 bush.; val., $151.

Turnips, 933 bush.; val., $187.

Carrots, 1,665 bush.; val., $500.

Beets and other esculent vegetables, - acres; val., $166; all other Grain or Root Crops, - acres; val., $150.

English Mowing, 1,579 acres; English Hay, 1,774 tons; val., $24,836.

Wet Meadow or Swale Hay, 497 tons; val., $2,982.

Apple Trees, cultivated for their fruit, 6,970; val., $2,264.

Pear Trees, cultivated for their fruit, 504; val., $86.

Establishments, for m. of sashes, doors and blinds, 1; cap., $2,000; val. m'd., $3,000; emp., 4.

Establishments for m. of gas, 1; cap., $5,000; val. m'd., $1,000; emp., 1.

Bakeries, 1; cap., $2,000; Flour consumed, 629 bbls.; val. of bread m'd., $10,700; emp., 5.

Establishments for m. of boxes for boots, shoes and cloth, 1; cap., $12,000; val. of boxes m'd., $16,750; emp., 11.

Swine raised, 233; val., $2,238.

Spectacles m'd., (Gold, 2,868 pairs; Silver, 11,276 pairs; Steel, 1,473 pairs; Plated Goggles, 720 pairs); val., $18,000; cap., $6,000; emp., 18.

Weavers' Shuttles m'd., 46,000; val., $16,000; cap., $10,000; emp., 22.

SPENCER.

Cotton Mills, 1; not running.

Woollen Mills, 3; Sets of Machinery, 3½; Satinet m'd., 112,000 yds.; val. of satinet, 33,600; cap., $15,000; m. emp., 20; f. emp., 12.

Establishments for m. of railroad cars, coaches, chaises, wagons, sleighs and other vehicles, 2; val. of railroad cars, &c., m'd., $20,000; cap., $6,000; emp., 16.

Powder Mills, 1; Powder m'd., 100,000 lbs.; val. of powder, $12,500; cap., $3,000; emp., 4.

Chair and Cabinet Manufactories, 2; val. of chairs and cabinet ware, $4,000; cap., $1,500; emp., 4.

Tin Ware Manufactories, 1; val. of tin ware, $2,000; cap., $1,000; emp., 2.

Currying establishments, 2; val. of leather curried, $58,800; cap., $5,000; emp., 10.

Boots of all kinds m'd., 205,102 pairs; Shoes of all kinds m'd., – pairs; val. of boots and shoes, $410,204; m. emp., 300; f. emp., 38.

Bricks m'd., 510,000; val. of bricks, $2,550; emp., 8.

Lumber prepared for market, 604,000 ft.; val. of lumber, $8,068; emp., 20.

Firewood prepared for market, 3,162 cords; val. of firewood, $8,796; emp., 10.

Saxony Sheep, of different grades, –; Merino Sheep, of different grades, –; all other kinds of sheep, 72; val. of all sheep, $354; Wool produced from Saxony Sheep, – lbs.; Merino Wool produced, – lbs.; all other Wool produced, 290 lbs.

Horses, 258; val. of horses, $24,616; Oxen over three years old, 346; Steers under three years old, 201; val. of oxen and steers, $25,715; Milch Cows, 650; Heifers, 361; val. of cows and heifers, $29,072.

Butter, 27,305 lbs.; val. of butter, $7,461; Cheese, 28,986 lbs.; val. of cheese, $2,318.88.

Indian Corn, 264 acres; Indian Corn, per acre, 31½ bush; val., $8,245.

Rye, 37 acres; Rye, per acre, 13¼ bush.; val., $611.

Barley, 50 acres; Barley, per acre, 19 bush; val., $959.

Oats, 241 acres; Oats, per acre, 22 bush.; val., $3,109.20.

Potatoes, 186 acres; Potatoes, per acre, 99 bush.; val., $9,187.

English Mowing, 2,532 acres; English Hay, 2,308 tons; val., $27,696.

Wet Meadow or Swale Hay, 634 tons; val., $3,804.

Apple Trees, cultivated for their fruit, 1,569; val., $1,273.

Establishments for m. of sashes, doors and blinds, 1; cap., $2,500, val. m'd., $5,000; emp., 4.

Establishments for m. of boxes for boots, 1; No. boxes m'd., 8,120; cap., $2,000; val. of boxes m'd., $2,842; emp., 6.

Establishments for m. of wire, 2; Wire m'd., 234,000 lbs.; val. of wire, $36,600; cap., $20,000.

Wheel Spokes, m'd., 75,000; val. of spokes, $2,250; emp., 4.

STERLING.

Chair and Cabinet Manufactories, 6; val. of chairs and cabinet ware, $52,650; cap., $15,500; emp., 47.

Tanneries, 1; Hides of all kinds tanned, 3,000; val. of leather tanned, $10,500; cap., $5,000; emp., 5.

Currying Establishments, 1; val. of leather curried, $8,000; cap., $5,000; emp., 2.

Val. of palm leaf hats m'd., $6,000; f. emp., 400.

Bricks m'd., 200,000; val. of bricks, $800; emp., 3.

Lumber prepared for market, 297,000 ft.; val. of lumber, $3,564; emp., 6.

Firewood prepared for market, 1,967 cords; val. of firewood, $6,884; emp., 12.

Saxony Sheep, of different grades, –; Merino Sheep, of different grades, –; all other kinds of sheep, 65; val. of all sheep, $200; Wool produced from Saxony sheep, – lbs.; Merino Wool produced, – lbs., all other Wool produced, 295 lbs.

Horses, 245; val. of horses, $17,605; Oxen over three years old, 382; Steers under three years old, 69; val. of oxen and steers, $21,910; Milch Cows, 637; Heifers, 122; val. of cows and heifers, $20,940.

Butter, 63,700 lbs.; val. of butter, $14,651; Cheese, 4,400 lbs.; val. of cheese, $352.

Indian Corn, 366 acres; Indian Corn per acre, 35 bush.; val., $12,810.

Wheat, 57 acres; Wheat, per acre, 15 bush.; val., $1,496.

Rye, 140 acres; Rye, per acre, 15 bush.; val., $2,100.

Barley, 21 acres; Barley, per acre, 30 bush.; val., $525.

Oats, 149 acres; Oats, per acre, 30 bush.; val., $2,235.

Potatoes, 190 acres; Potatoes, per acre, 125 bush.; val., $11,875.

English Mowing, 3,411 acres; English Hay, 3,411 tons; val., $54,576.

Wet Meadow or Swale Hay, 468 tons; val., $3,744.

Apple Trees, cultivated for their fruit, 18,564; val., $6,380.

Pear Trees, cultivated for their fruit, 357; val., $271.

Hops, 2 acres; Hops, per acre, 2,000 lbs.; val., $1,000.

Establishments for m. of stone and earthenware, 1; cap., $2,000; val. of stone and earthenware, $3,000; emp., 4.

Swine raised, 400; val., $3,200.

Establishments for m. of children's wagons, 1; wagons m'd., 4,000; val., $2,000; cap., $1,200; emp., 3.

Establishments for m. of Needles, 1; needles m'd., 10,000,000; val., $10,000; cap., $4,000; emp., 18.

STURBRIDGE.

Cotton Mills, 3; Spindles, 9,732; Cotton consumed, 445,900 lbs.; Cloth, m'd., 1,523,785 yds.; Printing Cloths, No. 30, 28 inches wide, 64 x 64; val. of cloth, $84,000; Yarn m'd., 110,000 lbs.; val. of yarn, $18,333; Batting m'd.,

5,000 lbs.; val. of batting, $500; cap., $105,000; m. emp., 76; f. emp., 125.

Woollen Mills, 1; Sets of Machinery, 3; Wool consumed, 71,300 lbs.; Satinet m'd., 46,480 yds.; val. of satinet, $9,300;

Yarn m'd., and not made into cloth., 15,000 lbs.; val. of yarn, $4,000; cap., $15,000; m. emp., 6; f. emp., 10.

Daguerreotype Artists, 2; Daguerreotypes taken, 300; cap., $500; emp., 2.

Saddle, Harness and Trunk Manufactories, 1; val. of saddles, &c., $600; cap., $250; emp., 1.

Establishments for m. of coaches, chaises, wagons and other vehicles, 2; val. m'd., $5,600; cap., $4,500; emp., 13.

Tin Ware Manufactories, 1; val. of tin ware, $400; cap., $1,000; emp., 1.

Tanneries, 2; Hides of kinds tanned, 2,200; val. of leather tanned, $7,500; cap., $4,000; emp., 6.

Currying Establishments, 3; val. of leather curried, $23,000; cap., $4,000; emp., 9.

Boots of all kinds m'd., 11,800 pairs; Shoes of all kinds m'd., 66,960 pairs; val., of boots and shoes, $75,000; m. emp., 105; f. emp., 85.

Val. of mechanics' tools m'd., $63,000; emp., 72; cap., $65,200.

Lumber prepared for market, 908,800 ft.; val. of lumber, $9,088; emp., 16.

Firewood prepared for market, 1,345 cords; val. of firewood, $4,035; emp., 8.

Saxony Sheep, of different grades, –; Merino Sheep, of different grades, –; all other kinds of sheep, 527; val. of all sheep, $1,581; Wool produced from Saxony sheep, – lbs.; Merino Wool produced, – lbs.; all other Wool produced, 1,714 lbs.

Horses, 199; val. of horses, $14,925; Oxen over three years old, 340; Steers under three years old, 242; val. of oxen and steers, $22,088; Milch Cows, 674; Heifers, 250; val. of cows and heifers, $22,372.

Butter, 37,285 lbs.; val. of butter, $8,575.55; Cheese,

14,320 lbs.; val. of cheese, $1,288; Honey, 300 lbs.; val. of honey, $60.

Indian Corn, 339 acres; Indian Corn, per acre, 28 bush.; val., $11,855.

Wheat, 7½ acres; Wheat, per acre, 18 bush.; val., $301.

Rye, 81 acres; Rye, per acre, 10 bush.; val., $1,215.

Barley, 37¼ acres; Barley, per acre, 25 bush.; val., $917.

Oats, 241 acres; Oats, per acre, 25 bush.; val., $3,615.

Potatoes, 176 acres; Potatoes, per acre, 96 bush.; val., $11,844.

Turnips, cultivated as a field crop, 1 acre; Turnips, per acre, 240 bush.; val., $48.

Carrots, ½ acre; Carrots, per acre, 333 bush.; val., $50.

Beets, and other esculent vegetables, – acres; all other Grain or Root Crops, 7 acres; val., $110.

English Mowing, 2,110½ acres; English Hay 2,171½ tons; val., $32,572.50.

Wet Meadow or Swale Hay, 1,010½ tons; val., $5,557.75.

Apple Trees, cultivated for their fruit, 3,395; val., $2,370; Apples produced, 6,425 bush.

Pear Trees, cultivated for their fruit 144; val., $47.50; Pears produced, 47½ bush.

Cranberries, 2 acres; val., $48.

Beeswax, 10 lbs.; val., $3.

Val. of grave stones m'd., $2,000; cap., $1,000; emp., 2.

Swine raised, 327; val. of swine, $2,338.

Quinces, 50 bush.; val., $25.

Peaches, 500 bush.; val., $250.

SUTTON.

Cotton Mills, 6; Spindles, 13,648; Cotton consumed, 579,729 lbs.; Cloth m'd., 2,633,484 yds. Print Goods; val. of cloth, $160,992.91; Batting m'd., 200,000 lbs.; val. of batting, $15,000; cap., $127,000; m. emp., 100; f. emp., 150.

Establishments for m. of cotton, woollen and other machinery, 4; val. of machinery m'd., $30,000; cap., $8,000; emp., 20.

Brush Manufactories, 1; val. of brushes, $600; cap., $200; emp., 1.

Establishments for m. of railroad cars, coaches, chaises, wagons, sleighs, and other vehicles, 3; val. of railroad cars, &c., m'd., $1,600; cap., $1,000; emp., 5.

Establishments for m. of soap and tallow candles, 3; Soft Soap m'd., 500 bbls.; Chemical Soap m'd., 16,000 lbs.; val. of soap, $2,500; cap., $500; emp., 3.

Boots of all kinds m'd., 500 pairs; Shoes of all kinds m'd., 229,000 pairs; val. of boots and shoes, $197,800; m. emp., 170; f. emp., 130.

Val. of building stone quarried and prepared for building, $300; emp., 1.

Charcoal m'd., 6,000 bush.; val. of same, $660; emp., 1.

Val of wooden ware not otherwise enumerated, including farming utensils m'd., $1,000; emp., 4.

Lumber prepared for market, 796,000 ft.; val. of lumber, $10,138; emp., 70.

Firewood prepared for market, 5,065 cords; val. of firewood $24,635; emp., 116.

Saxony Sheep, of different grades, 1; Merino Sheep, of different grades, 19; all other kinds of sheep, 275; val. of all sheep, $1,084; Wool produced from Saxony sheep, 5 lbs.; Merino Wool produced, 33 lbs.; all other Wool produced, 625 lbs.

Horses, 343; val. of horses, $29,250; Oxen over three years old, 288; Steers under three years old, 231; val. of oxen and steers, $15,843; Milch Cows, 713; Heifers, 215; val. of cows and heifers, $27,542.

Butter, 67,100 lbs.; val. of butter, $16,715; Cheese, 25,573 lbs.; val. of cheese, $2,626; Honey, 580 lbs.; val. of honey, $116.

Indian Corn, 496½ acres; Indian Corn, per acre, 38 bush.; val., $18,857.

Wheat, 10 acres; Wheat, per acre, 20 bush.; val., $250.

Rye, 121 acres; Rye, per acre, 20 bush.; val., $3,025.

Barley, 24 acres; Barley, per acre, 30 bush.; val., $900.

Oats, 372 acres; Oats, per acre, 40 bush.; val., $8,928.

Potatoes, 256 acres; Potatoes, per acre, 100 bush.; val., $12,800.

Onions, 2¼ acres; Onions, per acre, 450 bush.; val., $506.

Turnips, cultivated as a field crop, 6½ acres; Turnips, per acre, 150 bush.; val., $168.75.

Carrots, 11 acres; Carrots, per acre, 700 bush.; val., $1,028.25.

Beets and other esculent vegetables, 169 acres; val., $5,000.

English Mowing, 3,422 acres; English Hay, 4,302 tons; val., $68,832.

Wet Meadow or Swale Hay, 439 tons; val., $4,002.

Apple Trees, cultivated for their fruit, 25,569; val., $8,316.

Pear Trees, cultivated for their fruit, 547; val., $264.

Cranberries, 29 acres; val., $1,078.

Beeswax, 60 lbs.; val., $29.10.

Establishments for m. of casks, 1; val., $600; emp., 3.

Establishments for m. of baskets, 1; val. m'd., $600; cap., $100; emp., 2.

Livery Stables, 2; cap., $4,000; emp., 4.

Buckwheat, 33 acres; Buckwheat, per acre, 25 bush.; val., $693.

Winter Squashes, 1 acre; Squashes, per acre, 5,000 lbs.; val., $75.

Cabbages, 1¼ acre; Cabbages, per acre, 4,000 heads; val., $200.

Cider, 1,780 bbls., val., $2,225.

Wine, 32 bbls.; val., $800.

Vinegar, 525 bbls.; val., $1,575.

Lambs, for market, 234; val., $819.

Calves, for market, 502; val., $3,765.

Pork, for market, 75,000 lbs.; val., $6,750.

Pork, for home consumption, 90,000 lbs.; val., $8,100.

Beef, for home consumption, 70,000 lbs.; val., $4,900.

Beef, for market, 140,000 lbs.; val., $9,800.

Val. of chestnuts sold, 750.

Val. of hickory nuts sold, $200.
Val. of currants sold, $1,000.
Val. of whortleberries, sold, $1,500.
Swine raised, 552; val., $4,564.
Bulls raised, 12; val., $530.
Swarms of Bees, 127; val., $897.
Milk sold, 14,655 galls.; val., $2,233.
Val. of poultry, $2,210.
Val. of eggs, $3,728.
Sumach prepared for market, 20 tons; val. $500.
Rowen, 100 tons; val., $2,500.
Straw, 300 tons; val., $3,000.
Husks and Stalks, 1,482 tons; val., $8,892.

Corn, planted broadcast, 100 acres; tons, per acre, 3; val., $3,600.

White Beans, 10 acres; Beans, per acre, 20 bush.; Beans raised among corn, $500 bush.; val. of all beans, $1,400.

Val. of pumpkins raised, $1,482.
Turnips, raised among corn, 12,340 bush.; val., $1,542.50.
Cherry Trees, 291; val. of cherries, $239.
Plum Trees, 275; val. of plums, $141.
Peach Trees, 987; val. of peaches, $500.
Quince Trees, 890; val. of quinces, $372.

Establishments for m. of flocks, 1; val. m'd., $37,440; cap., $4,000; m. emp., 14; f. emp., 2.

TEMPLETON.

Woollen Mills, 1; Sets of Machinery, 7; Wool consumed, 275,000 lbs.; Cassimere m'd., 220,000 yds.; val. of cassimere, $198,000; cap., $50,000; m. emp., 85; f. emp., 45.

Furnaces for m. of hollow ware and castings other than pig iron, 1; Hollow Ware and other Castings m'd., 300 tons; val. of hollow ware and castings, $24,000; cap., $5,000; emp., 15.

Establishments for m. of cotton, woollen and other machinery, 3; val. of machinery m'd., $10,000; cap., $4,400; emp., 10.

Saddle, Harness and Trunk Manufactories, 1; val. of saddles, &c., $1,000; cap., $300; emp., 1.

Hat and Cap Manufactories, 1; Hats and Caps m'd., 750; cap., $300; emp., 1.

Establishments for m. of railroad cars, coaches, chaises, wagons, sleighs, and other vehicles, 1; val. of railroad cars, &c., m'd., $2,000; cap., $500; emp., 2.

Chair and Cabinet Manufactories, 10; val. of chairs and cabinet ware, $164,900; cap., $55,200; m. emp., 139; f. emp., 150.

Tin Ware Manufactories, 2; val. of tin ware, $36,000; cap., $12,000; emp., 21.

Tanneries, 2; Hides of all kinds tanned, 3,000; val. of leather tanned, $17,500; cap., $7,500; emp., 7.

Boots of all kinds m'd., 34,000 pairs; Shoes of all kinds m'd., 1,700 pairs; val. of boots and shoes, $46,400; m. emp., 92; f. emp., 20.

Val. of palm leaf hats, $2,000; f. emp., 100.

Bricks m'd., 225,000; val. of bricks, $1,125; emp., 3.

Charcoal m'd., 400 bush.; val. of same, $32; emp., 1.

Val. of wooden ware not otherwise enumerated, including farming utensils m'd., $50,300; cap., $31,000; emp., 61.

Lumber prepared for market, 1,000,000 ft.; val. of lumber, $18,700; emp., 25.

Firewood prepared for market, 3,000 cords; val. of firewood, $8,000; emp., 8.

Saxony Sheep, of different grades, –; Merino Sheep, of different grades, –; all other kinds of Sheep, 39; val. of all sheep, $195; Wool produced from Saxony sheep, – lbs; Merino Wool produced, – lbs.; all other Wool produced, 170 lbs.

Horses, 327; val. of horses, $28,980; Oxen over three years old, 193; Steers under three years old, 147; val. of oxen and steers, $15,071; Milch Cows, 530; Heifers, 198; val. of cows and heifers, $19,404.

Butter, 32,615 lbs.; val. of butter, $6,523; Cheese, 13,845 lbs.; val. of cheese, $1,207.

Indian Corn, 174 acres; Indian Corn, per acre, 35 bush.; val., $6,070.

Wheat, 14 acres; Wheat, per acre, 16 bush.; val., $448.

Rye, 20 acres; Rye, per acre, 10 bush.; val., $225.

Barley, 106 acres; Barley, per acre, 25 bush.; val., $2,000.

Oats, 87 acres; Oats, per acre, 30 bush.; val., $1,350.

Potatoes, 163 acres; Potatoes, per acre, 113 bush.; val., $9,440.

Carrots, 1 acre; Carrots, per acre, 600 bush.; val., $200.

English Mowing, 2,239 acres; English Hay, 1,690 tons; val., $27,040.

Wet Meadow or Swale Hay, 529 tons; val., $4,232.

Apple Trees, cultivated for their fruit, 4,318; val., $2,209.

Pear Trees, cultivated for their fruit, 100; val., $300.

Establishments for m. of friction matches, 2; Matches m'd., 50,000 gross; val., $27,000; cap., $14,000; emp., 43.

Establishments for m. of boxes for cloth and hats, 3; val. of boxes m'd., $7,000; cap., $5,000; emp., 5.

Winnowing Mills m'd., 75; val., $750.

Blacksmiths' Shops, 4; val. of business, $4,000; cap., $1,000; emp., 10.

Val. of tailoring business, $7,000; emp., 10.

Val. of millinery, $500.

Val. of sofa frames, $3,000; emp., 2.

Val. of chair-seat frames, $5,000; emp., 10.

Bark, 348 cords; val., $1,500.

Val. of ship timber prepared for market, $2,000.

Val. of work done in finishing palm leaf hats, $7,000; emp., 10.

Swine raised, 335; val., $2,659.

UPTON.

Saddle, Harness and Trunk Manufactories, 1; val. of saddles, &c., $3,000; cap., 500; emp., 2.

Establishments for m. of railroad cars, coaches, chaises, wagons, sleighs, and other vehicles, 2; val. of railroad cars, &c., m'd., $5,000; cap., $900; emp., 4.

Boots of all kinds m'd., 104,000 pairs; shoes of all kinds m'd., – pairs; val. of boots and shoes, $179,000; m. emp., 260; f. emp., 130.

Establishments for m. of straw bonnets and hats, 1; Straw Bonnets m'd., 335,000; val., $250,000; m. emp., 70; f. emp., 1,125.

Val. of mechanics' tools m'd., $1,000; emp., 2.

Lumber prepared for market, 688,000 ft.; val. of lumber, $9,632; emp., 10.

Firewood prepared for market, 1,803 cords; val. of firewood, $6,310; emp., 5.

Horses, 146; val. of horses, $9,769; Oxen over three years old, 136; Steers under three years old, 31; val. of oxen and steers, $8,832; Milch Cows, 394; Heifers, 57; val. of cows and heifers, $13,229.

Butter, 10,812 lbs.; val. of butter, $2,703; Cheese, 6,380 lbs.; val. of cheese, $638.

Indian Corn, 230 acres; Indian Corn, per acre, 25 bush.; val., $5,775.

Rye, 66 acres; Rye, per acre, 9 bush.; val., $1,025.

Barley, 8 acres; Barley, per acre, 16 bush.; val., $129.

Oats, 111 acres; Oats, per acre, 20 bush.; val., $1,454.70.

Potatoes, 176 acres; Potatoes, per acre, 86 bush.; val., $9,506.87.

Onions, 1 acre; Onions, per acre, 300 bush.; val., $300.

Carrots, 1 acre; Carrots, per acre, 400 bush.; val., $120.

Beets and other esculent vegetables, – acres; all other Grain or Root Crops, 40 acres; val., $4,000.

English Mowing, 1,264 acres; English Hay, 1,042 tons; val., $18,756.

Wet Meadow or Swale Hay, 380 tons; val., $3,040.

Apple Trees, cultivated for their fruit, 3,462; val., $2,481.

Pear Trees, cultivated for their fruit, 200; val., $100.

Cranberries, 48 acres; val., $2,766.

Establishments for m. of sashes, doors and blinds, 1; val. m'd., $8,350; cap., $5,000; emp., 8.

Establishments for m. of boxes for boots, shoes, and bonnets, -; cap., $1,700; val. of boxes m'd., $10,700; emp., 7.

Buckwheat, 4 acres; Buckwheat, per acre, 10½ bush.; val., $42.

Cider, 475 bbls.; val., $593.

White Beans, 200 bush.; val., $450.

Swine raised, 232; val., $857.

Peach Trees, 500; val., $750.

Plum Trees, 200; val., $75.

Cherry Trees, 450; val., $400.

Shingles, 350,000; val., $875; emp., 2.

UXBRIDGE.

Cotton Mills, 1; Spindles, 10,256; Cotton consumed, 478,000 lbs., 40,000 lbs. for satinet warps; Cloth m'd., 1,572,000 yds. 4-4 Sheeting, No. 33 yarn; val. of cloth, $141,480; cap., $128,000; m. emp., 90; f. emp., 96.

Woollen Mills, 6; Sets of Machinery, 28; Wool consumed, 738,000 lbs.; Cassimere m'd., 597,000 yds.; val. of cassimere, $530,000; Satinet m'd., 328,000 yds.; val. of satinet, $89,020; cap., $231,000; m. emp., 238; f. emp., 141.

Daguerreotype Artists, 1; Daguerreotypes taken, 500; cap., $200; emp., 1.

Saddle, Harness and Trunk Manufactories, 1; val. of saddles, &c., $300; cap., $1,000; emp., 1.

Upholstery Manufactories, 1; val. of upholstery, $600; cap., $400; emp., 6.

Establishments for m. of railroad cars, coaches, chaises, wagons, sleighs, and other vehicles, 1; val. of railroad cars, &c., m'd., $1,000; cap., $4,000; emp., 3.

Establishments for m. of soap and tallow candles, 2; Soap m'd., 464 bbls.; val. of soap, $1,450; cap., $800; emp., 3.

Chair and Cabinet Manufactories, 1; val. of chairs and cabinet ware, $1,500; cap., $1,800; emp., 2.

Tin Ware Manufactories, 2; val. of tin ware, $5,500; emp., 4.

Tanneries, 1; Hides of all kinds tanned, 500; val. of leather tanned, $3,000; cap., $5,000; emp., 2.

Currying Establishments, 1; val. of leather curried, $4,000; cap., $1,500; emp., 2.

Boots of all kinds m'd., 29,600 pairs; Shoes of all kinds m'd., – pairs; val. of boots and shoes, $75,700; m. emp., 82; f. emp., 16.

Bricks m'd., 800,000; val. of bricks, $4,800; emp., 10.

Val. of building stone quarried and prepared for building, $14,000; emp., 30.

Val. of mechanics' tools m'd., $10,000; emp., 10.

Lumber prepared for market, 762,000 ft.; val. of lumber, $10,287; emp., 26.

Firewood prepared for market, 5,737 cords; val. of firewood, $23,023; emp., 60, during winter.

Saxony Sheep, of different grades, –; Merino Sheep, of different grades, –; all other kinds of Sheep, 20; val. of all sheep, $60; Wool produced from Saxony sheep, – lbs.; Merino Wool produced, – lbs.; all other Wool produced, 83 lbs.

Horses, 178; val. of horses, $12,780; Oxen over three years old, 276; Steers under three years old, 30; val. of oxen and steers, $15,203; Milch Cows, 541; Heifers, 77; val. of cows and heifers, $17,696.

Butter, 27,290 lbs.; val. of butter, $6,917; Cheese, 3,835 lbs.; val. of cheese, $294; Honey, 325 lbs.; val. of honey, $66.

Indian Corn, 388 acres; Indian Corn, per acre, 30$\frac{1}{5}$ bush.; val., $11,141.

Wheat, 3$\frac{1}{4}$ acres; Wheat, per acre, 11$\frac{3}{8}$ bush.; val., $69.

Rye, 130 acres; Rye, per acre, 10$\frac{1}{5}$ bush.; val., $1,593.

Barley, 3$\frac{1}{2}$ acres; Barley, per acre, 13 bush.; val., $57.

Oats, 239 acres; Oats, per acre, 18$\frac{1}{2}$ bush.; val., $2,622.

Potatoes, 247 acres; Potatoes, per acre, 89$\frac{3}{4}$ bush.; val., $13,374.

Onions, 1$\frac{1}{20}$ acre; Onions, per acre, 457 bush; val., $292.

Turnips, cultivated as a field crop, 1 acre; Turnips, per acre, 166 bush.; val., $50.

Carrots, 2 acres; Carrots, per acre, 138 bush.; val., $163.

Beets and other esculent vegetables, 3 acres; val., $400; all other Grain or Root Crops, Buckwheat, 10 acres; val., $125.

Millet, 1$\frac{1}{2}$ acre; val., $30.

English Mowing, 2,626 acres; English Hay, 1,753 tons; val., $29,133.

Wet Meadow or Swale Hay, 647 tons; val., $5,231.

Apple Trees, cultivated for their fruit, 12,820; val., $3,236.

Pear Trees, cultivated for their fruit, 114; val., $78.

Cranberries, 83 acres; val., $1,991.

Beeswax, 21$\frac{1}{2}$ lbs.; val., $10.

Establishments for m. of sashes, doors and blinds, 1; not in operation now; cap., $2,000; val. m'd., $6,000; emp., 4.

Establishments for m. of boxes for satinet and cassimere, 2; cap., $700; val. of boxes m'd., $2,250; emp., 3.

Swine raised, 308; val., $2,442.

There are several dairies in town from which milk is sold, amounting annually to about $1,665.

WARREN.

Cotton Mills, 1; Spindles, 1,400; Cotton consumed, 90,000 lbs.; Yarn m'd., 75,000 lbs.; val. of yarn, $25,000; cap., $28,000; m. emp., 17; f. emp., 6.

Woollen Mills, 1; Sets of Machinery, 1; Wool consumed, 30,000 lbs.; Satinet m'd., 60,000 yds.; val. of satinet, $[illegible]0,000; Kentucky Jeans, 9 yds.; cap., $30,000; m. emp., 9; f. emp., 6.

Forges, 1; not in operation.

Establishments for m. of cotton, woollen and other machinery, 2; val. of machinery m'd., $15,000; cap., $13,000; emp., 30.

Scythe Manufactories, 1; Scythes m'd., 7,200 doz.; val. of scythes, $4,200; cap., $1,500; emp., 6.

Shave and Chisel Manufactories, 1; Shaves and Chisels m'd., 72,000; val., $30,000; cap., $10,000; emp., 35.

Saddle, Harness and Trunk Manufactories, 1; val. of saddles, &c., $1,500; cap., $300; emp., 2.

Tin Ware Manufactories, 1; val. of tin ware, $1,000; cap., $1,200; emp., 2.

Grist Mills, 3; Meal m'd., 69,000 bush.; cap., 12,000; emp., 5.

Tanneries, 2; Hides of all kinds tanned, 34,500; val. of leather tanned, $20,000; cap., $14,000; emp., 12.

Boots of all kinds m'd., 400 pairs; Shoes of all kinds m'd., 3,000 pairs; val. of boots and shoes, $4,000; m. emp., 5; f. emp., 10.

Charcoal m'd., 4,000 bush.; val. of same, $320; emp. 1.

Val. of blocks and pumps m'd., $10,000; emp., 4.

Val. of wooden ware not otherwise enumerated, including farming utensils m'd., $3,500; emp., 7.

Lasts m'd., 13,000; val., $4,000.

Lumber prepared for market, 932,000 ft.; val. of lumber, $15,435; emp., 16.

Firewood prepared for market, 3,469 cords; val. of firewood, $10,407; emp., 17.

Saxony Sheep, of different grades, 47; Merino Sheep, of different grades, 127; all other kinds of Sheep, 208; val. of all sheep, $955; Wool produced from Saxony sheep, 164; Merino Wool produced, 317; all other Wool produced, 624 lbs.

Horses, 195; val. of horses, $19,890; Oxen over three years old, 216; Steers under three years old, 150; val. of oxen and

steers, $15,330 ; Milch Cows, 1,136 ; Heifers, 323 ; val. of cows and heifers, $39,623.

Butter, 25,466 lbs. ; val. of butter, $6,366 ; Cheese, 122,285 lbs. ; val. of cheese, $11,005.

Indian Corn, 320 acres ; Indian Corn, per acre, 34 bush. ; val., $11,750.

Wheat, 6 acres ; Wheat, per acre, 17 bush. ; val., $184.

Rye, 80 acres ; Rye, per acre, 10 bush. ; val., $1,080.

Barley, 11 acres ; Barley, per acre, 20 bush. ; val., $220.

Oats, 359 acres ; Oats, per acre, 27 bush. ; val., $5,331.15.

Potatoes, 184 acres ; Potatoes, per acre, 85 bush. ; val., $7,820.

Onions, $\frac{1}{8}$ acre ; Onions, per acre, 50 bush. ; val., $25.

Turnips, cultivated as a field crop, 2 acres ; Turnips, per acre, 178 bush. ; val., $59.

Carrots, $\frac{1}{4}$ acres ; Carrots, per acre, 50 bush. ; val., $12.50.

Beets and other esculent vegetables, – acres ; all other Grain or Root Crops, 60 acres ; val., $1,200.

English Mowing, 1,788 acres ; English Hay, 2,324 tons ; val., $35,760.

Wet Meadow or Swale Hay, 800 tons ; val., $5,600.

Apple Trees, cultivated for their fruit, 5,971 ; val., $3,100.

Cranberries, 1 acre ; val., $25.

Milk, 172,080 galls. ; val., $18,929.

Swine raised, 291 ; val., $3,055.

WEBSTER.

Cotton Mills, 5 ; Spindles, 26,220 ; Cotton consumed, 847,168 lbs. ; Cloth, m'd., 3,500,000 yds. ; (Printing Cloth, 3,000,000 yds. ; Shoe Lining Cloth, 500,000 yds. ;) val. of cloth, $150,000 ; Yarn m'd., 250,000 lbs. ; val. of yarn, $62,500 ; Thread m'd., 65,113 lbs. ; val. of thread, $20,000 ; cap., $275,000 ; m. emp., 267 ; f. emp., 263.

Woollen Mills, 2 ; Sets of Machinery, 9, not all in operation ;

Wool consumed, 233,250 lbs.; Broadcloth m'd., 40,000 yds.; val. of broadcloth, $60,000; Cassimere m'd., 100,000 yds.; val. of cassimere, $85,000; cap., $175,000; m. emp., 170; f. emp., 50.

Establishments for m. of soap and tallow candles, 1; Soap m'd., 10,000 galls.; val. of soap, $1,200; cap., $1,200; emp., 2.

Chair and Cabinet Manufactories, 1; val. of chairs and cabinet ware, $1,600; cap., $500; emp., 2.

Tin Ware Manufactories, 1; val. of tin ware, $2,500; cap., $3,000; emp., 3.

Flour Mills, 1; cap., $1,000.

Boots of all kinds m'd., 400 pairs; Shoes of all kinds m'd., 141,300 pairs; val. of boots and shoes, $111,000; m. emp., 115; f. emp., 111.

Establishments for m. of straw bonnets and hats, 1; Straw Bonnets m'd., $8,000; m. emp., 2; f. emp., 30.

Charcoal m'd., 3,000 bush.; val. of same, $300; emp., 2.

Lumber prepared for market, 263,000 ft.; val. of lumber, $3,310; emp., 20.

Firewood prepared for market, 4,800 cords; val. of firewood, $14,400; emp., 64.

Saxony Sheep, of different grades, –; Merino Sheep, of different grades, 19; all other kinds of Sheep, –; val. of all sheep, $44; Wool produced from Saxony sheep, – lbs.; Merino Wool produced, 48 lbs.

Horses, 96; val. of horses, $6,925; Oxen over three years old, 64; Steers under three years old, 11; val. of oxen and steers, $3,650; Milch Cows, 202; Heifers, 32; val. of cows and heifers, $7,401.

Butter, 6,870 lbs.; val. of butter, $1,685; Cheese, 2,730 lbs.; val. of cheese, $224.

Indian Corn, 106 acres; Indian Corn, per acre, 27 bush.; val., $3,115.

Rye, 9 acres; Rye, per acre, 15 bush.; val., $162.

Oats, 91 acres; Oats, per acre, 22 bush.; val., $895.

Potatoes, 51 acres; Potatoes, per acre, 91 bush.; val., $2,421.

Carrots, 1 acre; Carrots, per acre, 450 bush.; val., $75.

70

English Mowing, 655 acres; English Hay, 727 tons; val., $8,388.

Wet Meadow or Swale Hay, 83 tons; val., $415.

Apple Trees, cultivated for their fruit, 2,253; val., $562.

Pear Trees, cultivated for their fruit, 175; val., $10.

Cranberries, 16 acres; val., $566.

Breweries, –; Beer m'd., 350 bbls.; val., $2,100; emp., 1.

Bakeries, 1; cap., $1,000; Flour consumed, 300 bbls; val. of bread m'd., $5,000; emp., 3.

Val. of loom harness twine m'd., $2,000; cap., $400; emp., 29.

Establishments for m. of marble, 1; val. m'd., $2,500; cap., $200; emp., 3.

WESTBOROUGH.

Establishments for m. of railroad cars, coaches, chaises, wagons, sleighs, and other vehicles, 15; val. of railroad cars, &c., m'd., $15,000; cap., $3,000; emp., 20.

Tin Ware Manufactories, 2; val. of tin ware, $5,000; cap., $2,500; emp., 5.

Currying Establishments, 1; val. of leather curried, $129,000; cap., $2,500; emp., 3.

Boots of all kinds m'd., 129,000 pairs; Shoes of all kinds m'd., 468,000 pairs; val. of boots and shoes, $421,000; m. emp., 400; f. emp., 100.

Val. of building stone quarried and prepared for building, $1,000; emp., 2.

Lumber prepared for market, 1,000,000 ft.; val. of lumber, $100,000; emp., 20.

Firewood prepared for market, 4,396 cords; val. of firewood, $20,881; emp., 30.

Horses, 242; val. of horses, $19,360; Oxen over three years old, 180; Steers under three years old, 48; val. of oxen and

steers, $12,750; Milch Cows, 897; Heifers, 170; val. of cows and heifers, $29,970.

Butter, 20,779 lbs.; val. of butter, $5,195; Cheese, 2,325 bs.; val. of cheese, $290; Honey, 255 lbs.; val. of honey, $42.

Indian Corn, 480 acres; Indian Corn, per acre, 35 bush.; val., $16,800.

Wheat, 2¾ acres; Wheat, per acre, 14 bush.; val., $78.

Rye, 94½ acres; Rye, per acre, 12 bush.; val., $1,508.

Barley, 14¼ acres; Barley, per acre, 18 bush.; val., $129.

Oats, 219 acres; Oats, per acre, 25 bush.; val., $3,285.

Potatoes, 192 acres; Potatoes, per acre, 100 bush.; val., $9,600.

Onions, 4 acres; Onions, per acre, 350 bush.; val., $1,050.

Turnips, cultivated as a field crop, 11 acres; Turnips, per acre, 200 bush.; val., $440.

Carrots, 4 acres; Carrots, per acre, 450 bush.; val., $450.

Beets, and other esculent vegetables, 1 acre; val., $100.

Millet, 18 acres; val., $540.

English Mowing, 1,883 acres; English Hay, 1,883 tons; val., $33,894.

Wet Meadow or Swale Hay, 688 tons; val., $4,816.

Apple Trees, cultivated for their fruit, young trees mostly, 12,879; val., $6,270.

Pear Trees, cultivated for their fruit, young trees mostly, 1,000; val., $500.

Cranberries, 7½ acres; val., $300.

Establishments for m. of sashes, doors and blinds, 1; val. m'd., $300; emp., 1.

Bakeries, 1; cap., $1,000; Flour consumed, $500 bbls.; val. of bread m'd., $8,000; emp., 8.

Establishments for m. of boxes, 2; cap., $500; val. of boxes m'd., $3,600; emp., 3.

Swine raised, 395; val., $3,950.

Milk, 193,736; val., $24,217.

Buckwheat, 11½ acres; Buckwheat, per acre, 15 bush.; val., $129.

Quinces, 98 bush.; val., $98.
Beans, 286 bush.; val., $572.
Squashes, 10 tons; val., $160.
Val. of cabbages, $500.
Val. of shoe knives m'd., $250.
Val. of shoe stamps and screws, $1,000.

WEST BOYLSTON.

Cotton Mills, 4; Spindles, 14,592; Cotton consumed, 1,178,000 lbs.; Cloth m'd., 2,007,816 yds.; Shirting, 72,600 yds.; Sheeting, 1,935,216 yds.; val. of cloth, $223,806.67; Yarn m'd., 2,750 lbs.; val. of yarn, $900; Batting m'd., 30,000 lbs.; val. of batting, $2,400; Flannel m'd., 411,840 yds.; val. of flannel, $35,006.40; cap., $181,000; m. emp., 141; f. emp., 177.

Tin Ware Manufactories, 1; val. of tin ware, $500; cap., $100; emp., 1.

Boots of all kinds m'd., 19,000 pairs; Shoes of all kinds m'd., 2,000 pairs; val. of boots and shoes, $41,200; m. emp., 51; f. emp., 6.

Lumber prepared for market, 31,000 ft.; val. of lumber, $465.

Firewood prepared for market, 2,130 cords; val. of firewood, $5,325.

Saxony Sheep, of different grades, –; Merino Sheep, of different grades, –; all other kinds of Sheep, 15; val. of all sheep, $77.

Horses, 171; val. of horses, $12,695; Oxen over three years old, 126; Steers under three years old, 36; val. of oxen and steers, $7,702; Milch Cows, 355; Heifers, 65; val. of cows and heifers, $12,671.

Butter, 31,195 lbs.; val. of butter, $7,794.75; Cheese, 1,575 lbs.; val. of cheese, $110.25.

Indian Corn, 204 acres; Indian Corn, per acre, $29\frac{1}{12}$ bush.; val., $6,526.30.

Wheat, 8 acres; Wheat, per acre, 13 bush.; val., $234.

Rye, 92 acres; Rye, per acre, $11\frac{6}{46}$ bush.; val., $1,536.

Barley, $4\frac{1}{2}$ acres; Barley, per acre, $13\frac{1}{3}$ bush.; val., $60.

Oats, 199 acres; Oats, per acre, $26\frac{78}{109}$ bush.; val., $1,747.20.

Potatoes, 96 acres; Potatoes, per acre, $106\frac{55}{96}$ bush.; val., $7,688.25.

Onions, $\frac{1}{4}$ acre; Onions, per acre, 200 bush.; val., $37.50.

Carrots, 4 acres; Carrots, per acre, 400 bush.; val., $320.

English Mowing, 1,416 acres; English Hay, 1,457 tons; val., $26,226.

Wet Meadow or Swale Hay, 213 tons; val., $1,065.

Apple Trees, cultivated for their fruit, 11,315; val., $3,173.62.

Pear Trees, cultivated for their fruit, 595; val., $69.

Val. of cranberries, $56.

Establishments for m. of sashes, doors, and blinds, 2; cap., $300; val. m'd., $2,800; emp., 6.

Fanning Mills m'd., 50; val., $600.

Val. of baskets m'd., $1,800; emp., 5.

Val. of school apparatus m'd., $4,000; emp., 4.

Milk sold, 7,200 galls.; val., $1,152.

Val. of palm leaf bonnets m'd., $700.

Cotton carpets m'd., 600 yds.; val., $270.

Cotton Counterpanes m'd., 52,000; val., $83,200.

WEST BROOKFIELD.

Saddle, Harness and Trunk Manufactories, 1; val. of saddles, &c., m'd., 48 harnesses; cap., $400; emp., 2.

Hat and Cap Manufactories, 1; Caps m'd., 100; cap., work, $75.

Establishments for m. of wagons, sleighs, and other vehicles,

2; val. m'd., about $3,000; cap., $800; emp., 4. Repairing is the principal work.

Chair and Cabinet Manufactories, 1; val. of chairs and cabinet ware, $800; cap., $500; emp., 2.

Tin Ware Manufactories, 1; val. of tin ware, $5,000; cap., $2,000; emp., 3.

Boots of all kinds m'd., 41,000 pairs; Shoes of all kinds m'd., 20,000 pairs; val. of boots and shoes, $81,988; cap., $22,000; m. emp., 131; f. emp., 17.

Charcoal m'd., 1,200 bush.; val. of same, $96.

Lumber prepared for market, 12,000 ft.; val. of lumber, $2,530; emp., 9.

Firewood prepared for market, 1,248 cords; val. of firewood, $4,814.

Saxony Sheep, of different grades, 24; Merino Sheep, of different grades, 66; all other kinds of Sheep, 42; val. of all sheep, $400; Wool produced from Saxony sheep, 106 lbs.; Merino Wool produced, 170 lbs.; all other Wool produced, 136 lbs.

Horses, 154; val. of horses, $12,750; Oxen over three years old, 132; Steers under three years old, 205; val. of oxen and steers, $13,021; Milch Cows, 689; Heifers, 225; val. of cows and heifers, $24,956.

Butter, 16,110 lbs.; val. of butter, $3,544.20; Cheese, 82,625 lbs.; val. of cheese, $7,849.37; Honey, 55 lbs.; val. of honey, $13.75.

Indian Corn, 268 acres; Indian Corn, per acre, 34½ bush.; val., $10,615.65.

Wheat, 7 acres; Wheat, per acre, 17 bush.; val., $238.

Rye, 96 acres; Rye, per acre, 14⅓ bush.; val., $1,938.

Barley, 25 acres; Barley, per acre, 25½ bush.; val., $635.

Oats, 157½ acres; Oats, per acre, 23¼ bush.; val., $2,119.32.

Potatoes, 173 acres; Potatoes, per acre, 94 bush.; val., $9,762.

Onions, 27 bush.; val., $18.90.

Turnips, cultivated as a field crop, 1½ acre; Turnips, per acre, 600 bush.; val., $150.

Carrots, 3 acres; Carrots, per acre, 320 bush.; val., $287.40.

English Mowing, 1,558 acres; English Hay, 1,889 tons; val., $28,335.

Wet Meadow or Swale Hay, 838 tons; val., $7,542.

Apple Trees, cultivated for their fruit, 5,309; val., $3,079.

Pear Trees, cultivated for their fruit, 42; val., $23.

Type and Stereotype Founderies, 1; cap., $500; val. of type, &c., m'd., $1,200; m. emp., 2.

Quinces, 16 bush.; val., $16.

Cherries, 2 bush.; val., $6.

Plums, 2 bush.; val., $3.

Swine raised, 280; val., $2,503.

Printing Offices, 1; cap., $5,000; m. emp., 8; f. emp., 4; business, job work.

The Neat Stock is a mixture of native and Durham.

Buckwheat, 18½ acres; Buckwheat, per acre, 10½ bush.; val., $187.

Peaches, 94 bush.; val., $189.

Grapes, 9 bush.; val., $9.

Milk sold, 13,353 galls.; val., $1,602.36.

Axe Handle Manufactories, 1.

WESTMINSTER.

Paper Manufactories, 3; Stock made use of, 535 tons; Paper m'd., 357 tons; val., of paper, $79,900; cap., $15,000; emp., 40.

Saddle, Harness and Trunk Manufactories, 1; emp., 1.

Chair and Cabinet Manufactories, 18; val. of chairs and cabinet ware, $95,380; cap., 39,210; emp., 138.

Tin Ware Manufactories, 1; val. of tin ware, $9,000; cap., $3,000; emp., 4.

Flour Mills, 1; Flour m'd., 2,800 bbls.; val. of flour m'd., $8,400; cap., $3,000; emp., 2.

Tanneries, 1; Hides of all kinds tanned, 700; val. of leather tanned, $3,500; cap., $2,000; emp., 2.

Boots of all kinds m'd., 230 pairs; Shoes of all kinds m'd., 155 pairs; val. of boots and shoes, $938; m. emp., 3.

Lumber prepared for market, 989,000 ft.; val. of lumber, $12,571; emp., 17.

Firewood prepared for market, 7,861 cords; val. of firewood, $20,469; emp., 29.

Saxony Sheep, of different grades, –; Merino Sheep, of different grades, –; all other kinds of Sheep, 108; val. of all sheep, $392; Wool produced from Saxony sheep, – lbs.; Merino Wool produced, – lbs.; all other Wool produced, 439 lbs.

Horses, 240; val. of horses, $16,500; Oxen over three years old, 264; Steers under three years old, 169; val. of oxen and steers, $17,843; Milch Cows, 563; Heifers, 150; val. of cows and heifers, $20,643.

Butter, 38,916 lbs.; val. of butter, $9,078.90; Cheese, 14,656 lbs.; val. of cheese, $1,285.

Indian Corn, 218 acres; Indian Corn, per acre, 32 bush.; val., $6,871.

Wheat, 38 acres; Wheat, per acre, 15⅓ bush.; val., $1,171.50.

Rye, 65 acres; Rye, per acre, 13⅔ bush.; val., $1,070.

Barley, 54 acres; Barley, per acre, 27⅓ bush.; val., $1,229.70.

Oats, 93 acres; Oats, per acre, 24½ bush.; val., $1,426.

Potatoes, 266 acres; Potatoes, per acre, 116⅓ bush.; val., $19,544.80.

Onions, $\frac{26}{160}$ acre; Onions, per acre, 445 bush.; val., $65.

Turnips cultivated as a field crop, 3 acres; Turnips, per acre, 216⅔ bush.; val., $160.50.

Carrots, 8½ acres; Carrots, per acre, 443 bush.; val., $1,195.50.

English Mowing, 2,697 acres; English Hay, 2,035 tons; val., $34,483.

Wet Meadow or Swale Hay, 633 tons; val., $5,164.

Apple Trees, cultivated for their fruit, 7,560; val., $3,785.

Pear Trees, cultivated for their fruit, 309; val., $86.

Cranberries, 8 acres; val., $434.

Establishments for m. of pickles and preserves, 1; cap., $2,500; val., m'd., $5,000; emp., 12.

Bakeries, 1; cap., $5,000; Flour consumed, 825 bbls.; val. of bread m'd., $15,000; emp., 8.

Swine raised, 94; val., $1,077.

Val. of boys' sleds m'd., $500.

Val. of wheelbarrows and hay cutters m'd., $1,400.

Paint Shops, 2; cap., $2,000; emp. 8.

WINCHENDON.

Cotton Mills, 1; Spindles, 8,600; Cotton consumed, 337,837 lbs; Cloth m'd., 1,649,984 yds.; Heavy Sheetings and Drillings; val. of cloth, $155,808.77; cap., $80,000; m. emp., 58; f. emp., 128.

Woollen Mills, 1; Sets of Machinery, 3; Satinet m'd., 24,000 yds.; val. of satinet, $7,000; Kentucky Jeans, 18,000 yds.; val. of jeans, $3,000; cap., $15,000; m. emp., 14; f. emp., 10.

Furnaces for m. of hollow ware and castings other than pig iron, 1; Hollow Ware and other Castings m'd., 180 tons; val. of hollow ware and other castings, $12,600; cap., $5,000; emp., 10.

Establishments for m. of cotton, woollen and other machinery, 2; val. of machinery m'd., $50,000; cap., $12,000; emp., 42.

Sand Paper Manufactories, 1; Paper m'd., 400 reams; val. of paper, $1,200; cap., $200; emp., 1; part of the time.

Daguerreotype Artists, 1; Daguerreotypes taken, 800; cap., $150; emp., 1.

Saddle, Harness and Trunk Manufactories, 1; val. of saddles, &c., $2,000; cap., $500; emp., 2.

Chair and Cabinet Manufactories, 2; val. of chairs and cabinet ware, $40,000; cap., $8,000; emp., 31.

Tin Ware Manufactories, 1; val. of tin ware, $1,500; cap., $300; emp., 1.

Establishments for m. of white lead and other paints, 1; White Lead, m'd., – lbs.; other paints m'd., Prussian Blue, 5,830 lbs.; Chrome Yellow, 2,000 lbs.; Varnish, 720 gallons; val. of other paints, $5,000; cap., $2,000; emp., 2.

Tanneries, 1; Hides of all kinds tanned, 8,000; val. of leather tanned, $40,000; cap., $6,000; emp., 11.

Boots of all kinds m'd., 75 pairs; Shoes of all kinds m'd., 250 pairs; val. of boots and shoes, $500; m. emp., 3.

Val. of wooden ware not otherwise enumerated, including farming utensils m'd., $250,000; emp., 221.

Lumber prepared for market, 2,509,000 ft.; val. of lumber, $30,108; emp., 70.

Firewood prepared for market, 5,036 cords; val. of firewood, $15,000; emp., 12.

Saxony Sheep, of different grades, –; Merino Sheep, of different grades, –; all other kinds of Sheep, 62; val. of all sheep, $170; Wool produced from Saxony sheep, – lbs.; Merino Wool produced, – lbs.; all other Wool produced, 376 lbs.

Horses, 266; val. of horses, $22,293; Oxen over three years old, 296; Steers under three years old, 140; val. of oxen and steers, $16,179; Milch Cows, 475; Heifers, 148; val. of cows and heifers, $16,343.

Butter, 22,745 lbs.; val. of butter, $5,000; Cheese, 7,047 lbs.; val. of cheese, $800; Honey, 75 lbs.; val. of honey, $18.

Indian Corn, 320 acres; Indian Corn, per acre, 15 bush.; val., $5,300.

Wheat, 4½ acres; Wheat, per acre, 12 bush.; val., $156.

Rye, 26 acres; Rye, per acre, 18 bush.; val., $585.

Barley, 87 acres; Barley, per acre, 20 bush.; val., $1,566.

Oats, 75 acres; Oats, per acre, 22 bush.; val., $1,650.

Potatoes, 204 acres; Potatoes, per acre, 80 bush.; val., $8,160.

Carrots, $5\frac{1}{2}$ acres; Carrots, per acre, 600 bush.; val., $975.

English Mowing, 2,976 acres; English Hay, 1,488 tons; val., $25,296;

Wet Meadow or Swale Hay, 744 tons; val., $6,700.

Apple Trees, cultivated for their fruit, 3,000; val., $1,300.

Establishments for m. of friction matches, 1; cap., $3,000; Matches m'd., 24,000 gross; val., $9,600; emp., 15.

Establishments for m. of boxes—Nest Boxes, and for packing pails and other ware, 4; cap., $3,000; val., of boxes m'd., $5,500; emp., 8.

Val. of baskets m'd., $10,000; cap., $1,000; emp., 12.

Val. of spools and bobbins m'd., $12,500; cap., $5,800; emp., 18.

WORCESTER.

Cotton Mills, 3; Spindles, 7,256; Cotton consumed, 456,000 lbs.; Cloth, m'd., 1,556,000 yds.; 4 qr. Brown Sheetings; val. of cloth, $104,120; m. emp., 74; f. emp., 65.

Woollen Mills, 6; Sets of Machinery, 19; Wool consumed, 578,000 lbs.; Cassimere m'd., 250,000 yds.; val. of cassimere, $187,500; Satinet m'd., 359,200 yds.; val. of satinet, $90,570.

Establishments for m. of hosiery, 1; Hosiery m'd., shirts, drawers and stockings, – pairs; val. of hosiery, $21,500; cap., $3,000; m. emp., 10; f. emp., 7.

Rolling, Slitting and Nail Mills, 3; Iron m'd. and not made into nails, 3,050 tons; val. of iron, $310,000; Machines for m. of nails, 5; Nails m'd., 120 tons; val. of nails, $22,500; cap., $83,000; emp., 82.

Furnaces for m. of hollow ware and castings other than pig iron, 5; Hollow Ware and other Castings m'd., 7,150 tons; val. of hollow ware and castings, $479,000; cap., $90,000; emp., 190.

Establishments for m. of cotton, woollen and other machinery,

7; val. of machinery m'd., $373,000; cap., $155,000; emp., 190.

Establishments for m. of cutlery, 1; val. of cutlery, $2,000; cap., $500; emp., 2.

Plough Manufactories, 1; Ploughs and other Agricultural Tools m'd., 130,000; val., $500,000; cap., $110,000; emp., 225.

Brass Founderies, 2; val. of articles m'd., $11,750; cap., $1,500; emp., 6.

Paper Manufactories, 1; Stock made use of, 195,000 lbs.; Paper m'd., 156,000 lbs.; val. of paper, $16,000; cap., $3,000; emp., 8.

Musical Instrument Manufactories, 4; val. of musical instruments m'd., $27,000; cap., $12,000; emp., 26.

Daguerreotype Artists, 7; Daguerreotypes taken, 30,077; cap., $7,000; emp., 14.

Establishments for m. of chronometers, watches, gold and silver ware and jewelry, 1; val. of m's., $10,000; cap., $3,000; emp., 3.

Saddle, Harness and Trunk Manufactories, 8; val. of saddles, &c., $39,800; cap., $8,800; emp., 50.

Upholstery Manufactories, 3; val. of upholstery, $12,000; cap., $4,600; emp., 11.

Hat and Cap Manufactories, 5; Hats and Caps m'd., 24,900; cap., $15,000; emp., 55.

Cordage Manufactories, 1; Cordage m'd., 10,000 lbs.; cap., $2,500; emp., 3.

Card Manufactories, 2; val. of cards of all kinds m'd., (Machine Cards,) $63,000; cap., $31,600; emp., 15.

Establishments for m. of railroad cars, coaches, chaises, wagons, sleighs and other vehicles, 6; val. of railroad cars, &c., m'd., $203,000; cap., $85,200; emp., 141.

Establishments for m. of soap and tallow candles, 4; Soap m'd., hard, 30,000 lbs.; Soft, 1,900 bbls.; val. of soap, $11,000; Tallow Candles m'd., 50,000 lbs.; val. of tallow candles, $7,000; cap., $6,500; emp., 22.

Establishments for m. of fire arms, barrels, 4; Fire Arms

m'd., Pistols, (revolvers,) 12,000; Rifles and Fowling Guns, 800; Rifle Barrels, 10,000; val. of fire arms, $130,000; cap., $55,000; emp., 194.

Chair and Cabinet Manufactories, 4; val. of chairs and cabinet ware, $20,000; cap., $7,000; emp., 20.

Tin Ware Manufactories, 9; val. of tin ware, $34,500; cap., $11,500; emp., 34.

Establishments for m. of camphene or burning fluid, 1; Camphene m'd., 33,000 galls; cap., $1,000; emp., 1.

Tanneries, 1; Hides of all kinds tanned, 1,500; val. of leather tanned, $8,000; cap., $4,000; emp., 5.

Currying Establishments, 3; val. of leather curried, $95,000; cap., $10,000; emp., 18.

Boots of all kinds m'd., 572,762 pairs; Shoes of all kinds m'd., 162,450 pairs; val. of boots and shoes, $1,160,970; cap., 176,000; m. emp., 1,198; f. emp., 248.

Bricks m'd., 5,900,000; val. of bricks, $32,450; emp., 55.

Val. of 575,000 cigars, $7,950; m. emp., 12; f. emp., 1.

Val. of building stone quarried and prepared for building, $16,310; emp., 36.

Val. of whips m'd., $3,000; emp., 2.

Val. of blacking, $2,000; emp., 2.

Val. of mechanics' tools m'd., $448,424; emp,. 334.

Lumber prepared for market, 740,000 ft.; val. of lumber, $11,100; emp., 5.

Firewood prepared for market, 5,380 cords; val. of firewood, $25,430; emp., 41.

Saxony Sheep, of different grades, –; Merino Sheep, of different grades, –; all other kinds of sheep, 72; val. of all sheep, $435; Wool produced from Saxony Sheep, – lbs.; Merino Wool produced, – lbs; all other Wool produced, 300 lbs.

Horses, 1,237; val. of horses, $160,715; Oxen over three years old, 468; Steers under three years old, 103; val. of oxen and steers, $33,565; Milch Cows 1,297; Heifers, 1,000; val. of cows and heifers, $51,321.

Butter, 39,626 lbs.; val. of butter, $9,906; Cheese, 9,650

lbs.; val. of cheese, $927; Honey, 531 lbs.; val. of honey, $106.

Indian Corn, 720 acres; Indian Corn, per acre, 38¾ bush.; val., $33,462.

Wheat, 30 acres; Wheat, per acre, 16 bush.; val., $1,071.

Rye, 250 acres; Rye, per acre, 13½ bush.; val., $5,025.

Barley, 18 acres; Barley, per acre, 19 bush.; val., $429.

Oats, 518 acres; Oats, per acre, 31½ bush.; val., $9,816.

Potatoes, 406 acres; Potatoes, per acre, 109½ bush.; val., $33,375.

Onions, 2,306 bush.; val., $1,153.

Turnips, 8,371 bush.; val., $2,093.

Carrots, 32½ acres; Carrots, per acre, 743 bush.; val., $6,043.

Beets and other esculent vegetables, 117 acres; val., $16,190.

Millet, 6 acres; val., $160.

English Mowing, 4,586 acres; English Hay, 5,241 tons; val., $104,780.

Wet Meadow or Swale Hay, 1,020 tons; val., $10,200.

Apple Trees, cultivated for their fruit, 22,150; val., $16,695.

Pear Trees, cultivated for their fruit, 6,156; val., $2,262.

Cranberries, 33 bush.; val., $75.

Establishments for m. of stone and earthenware, 1; cap., $8,000; val. of stone and earthenware, $18,000; emp., 16.

Establishments for m. of sashes, doors, and blinds, 2; cap., $4,000; val. m'd., $25,000; emp., 25.

Establishments for m. of gas, 1; cap., $90,000; val. m'd., $22,000; emp., 6.

Breweries, –; Beer m'd., 1,500 bbls.; val., $6,000; emp., 10.

Bakeries, 6; cap., $7,800; Flour consumed, 3,398 bbls.; val. of bread m'd., $74,500; emp., 29.

Establishments for m. of paper and wooden boxes, 4; cap., $3,500; val. of boxes m'd., $19,165; emp., 19.

Buckwheat, 60 acres; Buckwheat, per acre, 14¼ bush.; val., $1,669.

Milk sold, 241,508 galls.; val., $3,384.

Swine raised, 1,177; val., $14,747.

The Assessors report the following branches of business, as employing 1,701 persons; total value of articles manufactured, $939,500; capital, $237,800, viz.:—

Establishments for m. of lightning conductors, vanes, &c., 1.

Establishments for m. of steel and iron wire, 1.

Establishments for m. of water wheels, 1.

Establishments for m. of mowing and reaping machines, 1.

Establishments for m. of wrenches, shaves, chisels, and copying presses, 3.

Establishments for m. of shafting and gearing, 1.

Establishments for m. of hay and straw cutters, 1.

Establishments for m. of percussion presses and stencil cutting, 2.

Establishments for m. of porte monnaies, 1.

Establishments for m. of railroad turn tables, 1.

Establishments for m. of weavers' reeds and harnesses, 1.

Establishments for m. of umbrellas and parasols, 1.

Establishments for m. of wire sieves and netting, 4.

Establishments for m. of shuttles, 1.

Establishments for m. of shoe tools, kits, &c., 6.

Establishments for m. of carriage wheels, 1.

Establishments for m. of apple parers, 1.

Establishments for m. of perforated board, 1.

Establishments for m. of coffins, 2.

Establishments for m. of leather belting, 2.

Establishments for m. of card setting machines, 1.

Establishments for m. of bit stocks and window springs, 1.

Establishments for m. of saws, 1.

Establishments for m. of trusses, 1.

Establishments for m. of confectionery, 1.

Establishments for m. of files, 1.

Establishments for m. of letter envelopes (45,000,000), 1.

Establishments for m. of blank books, 2.

Establishments for m. of enamelled leather cloth, 1.

Establishments for m. of clothing, 14.

ABSTRACT BY COUNTIES.

COTTON.*

COUNTIES.	Cotton Mills.	Number of Spindles.	Pounds of Cotton consumed.	Yards of Cloth manufactured.	Value of Cotton Cloth.	Pounds of Cotton Yarn manufactured and not made into Cloth.	Value of Cotton Yarn.	Pounds of Cotton Thread manufactured.	Value of Cotton Thread.	Pounds of Cotton Batting manufactured.
Barnstable,	-	-	-	-	-	76	$76 00	-	-	-
Berkshire,	24	42,936	3,193,715	10,805,268	$561,688 00	625,876	205,440 00	-	-	53,900
Bristol,	51	216,799	9,424,555	35,234,724	2,382,621 00	768,720	155,850 00	183,700	$158,600 00	498,886
Dukes,	-	-	-	-	-	-	-	-	-	-
Essex,	20	239,073	12,996,005	38,851,372	3,579,131 66	199,677	38,131 22	-	-	-
Franklin,	6	9,354	750,387	3,007,542	126,867 00	-	-	-	-	7,500
Hampden,	24	229,070	15,879,107	51,361,332	3,725,654 08	108,000	27,300 00	-	-	-
Hampshire,	10	37,752	731,400	10,678,475½	869,000 00	-	-	-	-	4,000
Middlesex,	48	406,889	40,256,405	107,205,687	7,794,229 00	24,000	7,000 00	-	-	962,000
Nantucket,	-	-	-	-	-	-	-	-	-	-
Norfolk,	29	37,766	6,796,983	5,129,760	290,937 22	424,797	107,030 60	285,580	107,334 00	2,884,800
Plymouth,	5	7,338	480,000	807,000	81,540 00	21,000	20,000 00	-	-	42,000
Suffolk,	-	-	-	-	-	-	-	-	-	-
Worcester,	77	292,550	15,343,192	51,915,407	4,947,544 35	1,149,500	269,718 00	65,113	20,000 00	372,600
Totals,	294	1,519,527	105,851,749	314,996,567½	$24,359,212 31	3,321,146	$830,546 37	534,393	$285,934 00	4,825,686

* See Note (1.)

COTTON—Continued.

COUNTIES.	Value of Cotton Batting.	Pounds of Pelisse Wadding manufactured.	Value of Pelisse Wadding.	Yards of Cotton Flannel manufactured.	Value of Cotton Flannel.	Pounds of Wicking manufactured.	Value of Wick'g.	Capital invested in the manufacture of Cotton.	Males employed.	Females employed.
Barnstable,	-	-	-	-	-	-	-	-	-	-
Berkshire,	$4,350 00	-	$50,000 00	-	-	-	-	$854,000 00	475	624
Bristol,	39,649 24	-	225 00	693,504	-	-	-	3,066,050 00	1,696	2,170
Dukes,	-	-	-	-	-	-	-	-	-	-
Essex,	-	-	-	396,000	$43,000 00	-	-	5,932,000 00	1,457	3,491
Franklin,	750 00	-	-	-	-	15,000	$2,550 00	34,200 00	83	140
Hampden,	200 00	-	-	1,231,576	-	-	-	5,658,000 00	1,933	3,722
Hampshire,	400 00	-	-	-	-	-	7,000 00	803,400 00	466	742
Middlesex,	61,600 00	370,000	53,000 00	-	-	-	-	10,059,500 00	2,483	8,019
Nantucket,	-	-	-	-	-	-	-	-	-	-
Norfolk,	255,300 00	-	36,640 00	450,000	38,250 00	-	-	502,600 00	328	330
Plymouth,	3,400 00	-	-	-	-	-	-	98,000 00	65	112
Suffolk,	-	-	-	-	-	-	-	-	-	-
Worcester,	29,725 00	-	-	456,540	38,806 40	-	-	4,953,250 00	2,951	3,500
Totals,	$395,374 24	370,000	$139,865 00	3,227,620	$120,056 40	15,000	$9,550 00	$31,961,000 00	11,937	22,850

CALICO.

COUNTIES.	Calico Manufactories.	Yards of Calico Printed.	Value of Calico.	Yards of Goods Bleached and Colored in said Calico Factories, and not Printed.	Value of Goods Bleached and Colored.	Capital Invested in Calico Establishments.	Males employed.	Females employed.
Barnstable,	-	-	-	-	-	-	-	-
Berkshire,	1	3,640,000	$273,000 00	-	-	$50,000 00	55	5
Bristol,	3	35,500,000	2,980,000 00	1,000,000	$70,000 00	930,000 00	625	100
Dukes,	-	-	-	-	-	-	-	-
Essex,	-	-	-	-	-	-	-	-
Franklin,	-	-	-	-	-	-	-	-
Hampden,	-	-	-	-	-	-	-	-
Hampshire,	-	-	-	-	-	-	-	-
Middlesex,	2	21,900,000	1,890,000 00	-	-	1,000,000 00	343	29
Nantucket,	-	-	-	-	-	-	-	-
Norfolk,	-	-	-	-	-	-	-	-
Plymouth,	-	-	-	-	-	-	-	-
Suffolk,	-	-	-	-	-	-	-	-
Worcester,	-	-	-	-	-	-	-	-
Totals,	6	61,040,000	$5,143,000 00	1,000,000	$70,000 00	$1,980,000 00	1,023	134

COUNTIES.	BLEACHING AND COLORING.* Establishments for Bleaching or Colo'ing Cotton Goods, and not connected with Calico Estab'ts.	Goods Bleached or Colored.	Value of Goods Bleached or Colored.	Capital invested.	Hands employed.	WOOLLEN.† Woollen Mills.	Sets of Machinery.	Pounds of Wool consumed.	Yards of Broadcloth manuf'd.	Value of Broadcloth.	Yards of Cassimere.
Barnstable,	-	-	-	-	-	2	3	36,000	-	-	-
Berkshire,	-	-	-	-	-	23	97	3,383,500	382,900	$175,600 00	1,600,000
Bristol,	-	-	-	-	-	1	5	90,000	-	-	90,000
Dukes,	-	-	-	-	-	-	-	-	-	-	-
Essex,	-	200,000 lbs.	-	$150,000 00	60	33	216	4,411,140	132,227½	107,800 62	542,577
Franklin,	-	-	-	-	-	5	12	393,000	-	-	140,000
Hampden,	-	-	-	-	-	12	21	687,403	-	-	137,000
Hampshire,	-	-	-	-	-	18	47	1,157,000	40,000	42,000 00	-
Middlesex,	8	66,400,000 yds.	$5,028,000 00	501,500 00	570	10	76	2,738,888	132,000	87,250 00	250,000
Nantucket,	-	-	-	-	-	-	-	-	-	-	-
Norfolk,	3	283,400 lbs.	83,200 00	7,500 00	14	5	27	747,000	-	-	600,000
Plymouth,	-	-	-	-	-	-	-	-	-	-	-
Suffolk,	-	-	-	-	-	-	-	-	-	-	-
Worcester,	-	-	-	-	-	47	191	5,142,367	72,500	125,000 00	3,085,008
Totals,	11	483,400 lbs. 66,400,000 yds.	$5,111,200 00	$659,000 00	614	146	695	18,786,298	759,627½	$837,650 62	6,444,585

* See Note (2.)

† See Note (3.)

WOOLLEN—Continued.

COUNTIES.	Value of Cassimere.	Yards of Satinet.	Value of Satinet.	Yards of Kentucky Jeans.	Value of Jeans.	Yards of Flannel or Blanketing.	Value of Flannel or Blanketing.	Pounds of Woollen Yarn manufactur'd and not made into cloth.	Value of Woollen Yarn.
Barnstable,	- -	- -	- -	- -	- -	25,000	$7,000 00	- -	$16,000 00
Berkshire,	$980,000 00	2,486,200	$1,111,100 00	- -	- -	3,000	2,250 00	- -	- -
Bristol,	95,000 00	- -	- -	1,785,000	- -	- -	- -	- -	- -
Dukes,	- -	3,000	1,500 00	- -	- -	5,000 00	1,900 00	- -	- -
Essex,	370,321 65	271,629	110,064 40	- -	- -	6,749,883	1,913,700 47	- -	24,000 00
Franklin,	150,000 00	360,000	175,400 00	- -	- -	- -	- -	300	250 00
Hampden,	102,500 00	885,573	400,296 00	- -	- -	1,800	900 00	1,400	1,240 00
Hampshire,	- -	822,500	376,795 00	145,600	$28,000 00	814,000	255,600 00	- -	- -
Middlesex,	- -	255,000	10,000 00	- -	- -	1,246,854	594,368 60	533,457	217,980 60
Nantucket,	- -	- -	- -	- -	- -	- -	- -	- -	- -
Norfolk,	400,000 00	- -	- -	- -	- -	- -	- -	61,800	52,000 00
Plymouth,	- -	- -	- -	- -	- -	- -	- -	- -	- -
Suffolk,	- -	- -	- -	- -	- -	- -	- -	- -	- -
Worcester,	2,917,620 00	1,652,180	523,780 00	18,009	3,000 00	1,433,690	350,230 00	93,000	75,067 00
Totals,	$5,015,441 65	6,736,082	$2,708,935 40	1,918,609	$31,000 00	10,279,227	$3,125,949 07	689,957	$386,537 60

COUNTIES.	WOOLLEN—Continued.			CARPETING.*							
	Capital invested.	Males employed.	Females empl'd.	Carpet Mills.	Pounds of Cotton consumed.	Pounds of Wool consumed.	Yards of Carpeting manufact'd.	Value of Carpeting.	Capital invested.	Males employed.	Females empl'd.
Barnstable,	$22,000 00	13	8	-	-	-	-	-	-	-	-
Berkshire,	1,297,000 00	968	544	-	-	-	-	-	-	-	-
Bristol,	30,000 00	50	18	-	-	-	-	-	-	-	-
Dukes,	-	2	3	-	-	-	-	-	-	-	-
Essex,	2,973,000 00	2,130	1,715	2	-	330,000	175,000	$100,000 00	$35,000 00	110	55
Franklin,	161,500 00	129	84	-	-	-	-	-	-	-	-
Hampden,	159,000 00	184	121	-	-	-	-	-	-	-	-
Hampshire,	440,000 00	377	250	-	-	-	-	-	-	-	-
Middlesex,	578,000 00	423	331	4	40,000	2,234,000	1,463,654	900,000 00	1,900,000 00	455	621
Nantucket,	-	-	-	2	-	-	2,392	1,196 00	972 00	2	16
Norfolk,	219,000 00	118	210	3	-	32,645	111,952	69,923 00	28,200 00	80	17
Plymouth,	-	-	-	-	-	-	-	-	-	-	-
Suffolk,	-	-	-	1	13,000	14,000	28,000	21,000 00	100,000 00	80	25
Worcester,	1,426,000 00	1,552	860	1	-	270,329	207,462	270,700 00	200,000 00	53	100
Totals,	$7,305,500 00	5,946	4,144	13	53,000	2,880,974	1,988,460	$1,362,819 00	$2,264,172 00	780	834

* See Note (4.)

COUNTIES.	WORSTED.*								HOSIERY.†		
	Establishments for the manufact'e of Worsted Goods, or Goods of which Worsted is a component part	Yards of such Goods manufactured.	Value of the same.	Pounds of Worsted manufact'd and not made into cloth.	Value of Worsted Yarn.	Capital invested.	Males employed.	Females empl'd.	Establishments for the manufacture of Hosiery.	Quantity manufactured.	Description of Goods.
Barnstable,	–	–	–	–	–	–	–	–	–	–	–
Berkshire,	–	–	–	–	–	–	–	–	–	–	–
Bristol,	–	–	–	–	–	–	–	–	–	–	–
Dukes,	–	–	–	–	–	–	–	–	1	–	–
Essex,	1	3,216,998	$536,000 00	–	–	$700,000 00	109	192	–	3,800 doz. prs.	Ribbed Hose and Vests.
Franklin,	–	–	–	–	–	–	–	–	–	–	–
Hampden,	–	–	–	–	–	–	–	–	–	–	–
Hampshire,	–	–	–	–	–	–	–	–	1	–	–
Middlesex,	3	–	–	1,023,900	$419,456 00	251,000 00	97	151	6	4,912 doz. prs. 200 "	Hose. Shirts, Drawers.
Nantucket,	–	–	–	–	–	–	–	–	–	–	–
Norfolk,	1	–	–	–	–	10,000 00	13	14	9	–	Yarn, Hose, Shirts, Drawers.
Plymouth,	–	–	–	–	–	–	–	–	–	–	–
Suffolk,	–	–	–	–	–	–	–	–	–	–	–
Worcester,	2	4,972,932	493,284 00	–	–	275,000 00	236	250	3	1,568 doz. 200,000 yds.	Shirts and Drawers.
Totals,	7	8,189,930	$1,029,284 00	1,023,900	$419,456 00	$1,236,000 00	455	607	20		

* See Note (5.)

† See Note (6.)

COUNTIES.	HOSIERY—Continued.						LINEN.							
	Value.	Pounds of Yarn not made into Hosiery.	Value of Yarn.	Capital invested.	Males employed.	Females emplo'd.	Establishments for the manufacture of Linen.	Yards of Linen manufactured.	Value of Linen.	Pounds of Linen Thread manufactured.	Value of Linen Thread.	Capital invested.	Males employed.	Females emplo'd.
Barnstable,	-	-	-	-	-	-	-	-	-	-	-	-	-	-
Berkshire,	-	-	-	-	-	-	-	-	-	-	-	-	-	-
Bristol,	-	-	-	-	-	-	1	1,600,000	$240,000	-	-	$365,000	300	250
Dukes,	-	3,500	$3,040	-	2	3	-	-	-	-	-	-	-	-
Essex,	$13,700	-	-	-	9	6	1	-	-	1,150,000	$200,000	85,000	100	120
Franklin,	-	-	-	-	-	-	-	-	-	-	-	-	-	-
Hampden,	-	-	-	-	-	-	-	-	-	-	-	-	-	-
Hampshire,	-	4,000	3,500	$3,000	3	3	-	-	-	-	-	-	-	-
Middlesex,	32,228	-	-	13,000	4	34	1*	-	-	-	-	-	-	-
Nantucket,	-	-	-	-	-	-	-	-	-	-	-	-	-	-
Norfolk,	32,212	117,240	60,500	29,980	50	70	-	-	-	-	-	-	-	-
Plymouth,	-	-	-	-	-	-	-	-	-	-	-	-	-	-
Suffolk,	-	-	-	-	-	-	-	-	-	-	-	-	-	-
Worcester,	61,980	-	-	24,000	48	24	1	1,000,000	1,000,000	-	-	100,000	65	75
Totals,	$140,120	124,740	$67,040	$69,980	116	140	4	2,600,000	$1,240,000	1,150,000	$200,000	$550,000	465	445

* Not in operation.

COUNTIES.	SILK.*								ROLLING, SLITTING AND NAIL MACHINES.†								
	Silk manufactories.	Yards of Silk.	Value of same.	Pounds of Sewing Silk.	Value of same.	Capital invested.	Males employed.	Females empl'd.	Rolling, Slitting and Nail Mills.	Tons of iron manufactured and not made into Nails.	Value of same.	Number of Nail Machines.	Tons of Nails manufactured.	Value of Nails.	Capital invested.	Hands employed.
Barnstable, . .	-	-	-	-	-	-	-	-	2	-	-	15	200	$15,000	$12,000	10
Berkshire, . .	-	-	-	-	-	-	-	-	-	-	-	-	-	-	-	-
Bristol, . .	-	-	-	-	-	-	-	-	8	3,365	$275,850	246	11,365	944,414	491,075	727
Dukes, . .	-	-	-	-	-	-	-	-	-	-	-	-	-	-	-	-
Essex, . .	1	-	-	8,000	$85,000	$7,000	8	5	1	1,000	-	6	-	-	-	8
Franklin, . .	-	-	-	-	-	-	-	-	-	-	-	-	-	-	-	-
Hampden, . .	-	-	-	-	-	-	-	-	-	-	-	-	-	-	-	-
Hampshire, .	3	-	-	23,000	140,000	28,000	19	58	-	-	-	-	-	-	-	-
Middlesex, .	-	-	-	-	-	-	-	-	3	2,244	284,000	5	1,200	108,000	50,000	70
Nantucket, .	-	-	-	-	-	-	-	-	-	-	-	-	-	-	-	-
Norfolk, . .	1	-	-	13,000	75,000	20,000	8	40	6	2,000	160,000	104	4,800	417,000	235,000	322
Plymouth, . .	-	-	-	-	-	-	-	-	23	2,275	171,000	407	16,872	1,280,052	814,750	1,206
Suffolk, . .	-	-	-	-	-	-	-	-	3	22,000	1,525,000	-	-	-	657,000	600
Worcester, .	-	-	-	-	-	-	-	-	3	3,050	310,000	5	120	22,500	83,000	82
Totals, .	5	-	-	44,000	$300,000	$55,000	35	103	49	35,934	$2,725,850	788	34,557	$2,786,966	$2,342,825	3,025

* See Note (7.)

* See Note (8.)

COUNTIES.	FORGES.*					PIG-IRON.				
	Num'r of Forges.	Tons of Bar Iron, Anchors, Chain-Cables, and other articles wro't.	Val. of the same.	Capital invested.	Hands employed.	Number of Furnaces for the manufacture of Pig Iron.	Tons of Pig-Iron.	Value of Pig-Iron.	Capital Invested.	Hands employed.
Barnstable,	14	50	$9,700 00	$4,100 00	12	-	-	-	-	-
Berkshire,	-	-	-	-	-	8	21,816	$641,540 00	$567,400 00	323
Bristol,	1	250	35,000 00	20,000 00	15	-	-	-	-	-
Dukes,	-	-	-	-	-	-	-	-	-	-
Essex,	99	1,138	204,300 00	56,500 00	159	9†	-	-	-	-
Franklin,	-	-	-	-	-	-	-	-	-	-
Hampden,	5	81	29,900 00	6,200 00	14	-	-	-	-	-
Hampshire,	7	-	-	1,000 00	3	-	-	-	-	-
Middlesex,	2	8	800 00	600 00	6	-	-	-	-	-
Nantucket,	11	36	12,000 00	7,500 00	20	-	-	-	-	-
Norfolk,	36	2,360	263,000 00	168,000 00	45	-	-	-	-	-
Plymouth,	20	1,063	129,280 00	74,400 00	71	-	-	-	-	-
Suffolk,	3	1,750	232,000 00	400,000 00	195	-	-	-	-	-
Worcester,	8	10	-	1,300 00	7	-	-	-	-	-
Totals,	206	6,746	$915,980 00	$739,600 00	547	17	21,816	$641,540 00	$567,400 00	323

* See Note (9.)

† All in Beverly, but no particulars given.

COUNTIES.	HOLLOW WARE AND CASTINGS.					MACHINERY.			
	Number of Furnaces for the manufacture of Hollow Ware and Castings other than Pig-Iron.*	Tons of Hollow Ware and Castings other than Pig Iron.	Value of Hollow Ware and Castings.	Capital invested.	Hands employed.	Establishments for the manufacture of Cotton, Woollen and other machinery.	Gross value of Machin'y manufactured.	Capital invested.	Hands employed.
Barnstable,	1	350	$30,000 00	$20,000 00	35	1	$10,000 00	No return.	25
Berkshire,	10	590	43,800 00	26,600 00	38	7	82,500 00	$41,300 00	63
Bristol,	12	44,390	477,100 00	207,000 00	344	7	598,500 00	393,000 00	673
Dukes,	-	-	-	-	-	-	-	-	-
Essex,	7	3,510	236,200 00	199,000 00	155	8	537,500 00	345,600 00	408
Franklin,	2	250	20,000 00	9,000 00	8	-	-	-	-
Hampden,	6	3,384	186,936 00	47,000 00	89	5	575,000 00	455,000 00	507
Hampshire,	3	285	20,650 00	14,000 00	15	1	6,000 00	4,000 00	6
Middlesex,	10	7,115	507,000 00	203,500 00	408	18	995,390 00	695,000 00	994
Nantucket,	-	-	-	-	-	-	-	-	-
Norfolk,	9	5,410	367,000 00	268,000 00	265	6	70,500 00	39,200 00	54
Plymouth,	17	2,293	192,260 00	140,500 00	212	1	10,000 00	8,000 00	10
Suffolk,	8	7,722	491,500 00	327,500 00	377	22	267,000 00	132,500 00	216
Worcester,	15	9,810	684,092 00	151,500 00	330	33	937,200 00	370,400 00	784
Totals,	100	85,109	$3,256,538 00	$1,613,600 00	2,276	109	$4,089,590 00	$2,484,000 00	3,740

* See Note (10.)

COUNTIES.	STEAM ENGINES AND BOILERS.				FIRE ENGINES.				SCYTHES.				
	Establishments for the manufacture of St'm Engines and Boilers.	Value of Steam Engines and Boilers.	Capital invested.	Hands employ'd.	Shops for the manufacture of Fire Engines.	Fire Engines.	Value of Fire Engines.	Hands employed.	Scythe manufactories.	Scythes manufactured.	Value of Scythes.	Capital invested.	Hands employed.
Barnstable,	-	-	-	-	-	-	-	-	-	-	-	-	-
Berkshire,	1	$65,000 00	$20,000 00	50	-	-	-	-	-	-	-	-	-
Bristol,	2	325,000 00	275,000 00	400	-	-	-	-	-	-	-	-	-
Dukes,	-	-	-	-	-	-	-	-	-	-	-	-	-
Essex,	6	342,000 00	223,000 00	200	-	-	-	-	-	-	-	-	-
Franklin,	1	10,000 00	5,000 00	2	-	-	-	-	2	340	$260 00	$500 00	2
Hampden,	5	205,000 00	41,000 00	157	-	-	-	-	1	14,000	9,000 00	4,000 00	15
Hampshire,	1	12,000 00	20,000 00	15	-	-	-	-	1	6,000	2,500 00	1,500 00	6
Middlesex,	5	202,000 00	139,500 00	193	-	-	-	-	1	24,000	15,000 00	6,000 00	14
Nantucket,	-	-	-	-	-	-	-	-	-	-	-	-	-
Norfolk,	4	168,000 00	32,000 00	129	1	40	$50,000 00	45	-	-	-	-	-
Plymouth,	1	51,000 00	50,000 00	35	-	-	-	-	-	-	-	-	-
Suffolk,	17	1,835,000 00	1,274,000 00	1,437	-	-	-	-	-	-	-	-	-
Worcester,	1	40,000 00	20,000 00	20	-	-	-	-	7	137,940	93,772 00	54,000 00	107*
Totals,	44	$3,255,000 00	$2,099,500 00	2,638	1	40	$50,000 00	45	12	182,280	$120,532 00	$66,000 00	144

* Eighteen hands in Northbridge, are employed only three months.

COUNTIES.	AXES, HATCHETS AND EDGE TOOLS.*					CUTLERY.				SCREWS.				
	Axe Manufactories.	Axes, Hatchets and other Edge Tools manufactured.	Value of Tools.	Capital invested.	Hands employed.	Establishments for the manufac'e of Cutlery.	Value of Cutlery.	Capital invested.	Hands employed.	Screw Manufactories.	Number of Gross of Screws manufactured.	Value of Screws.	Capital invested.	Hands employed.
Barnstable,	1	3,000	$2,500 00	$1,800 00	6	-	-	-	-	-	-	-	-	-
Berkshire,	3	3,300	8,150 00	8,000 00	8	-	-	-	-	-	-	-	-	-
Bristol,	1	1,300	1,015 00	1,000 00	2	-	-	-	-	1	400,000	$150,000	$105,000	200
Dukes,	-	-	-	-	-	-	-	-	-	-	-	-	-	-
Essex,	1	6,000	-	2,000 00	5	-	-	-	-	-	-	-	-	-
Franklin,	1	7,600	7,000 00	5,000 00	6	3	$465,000	$355,000	600	-	-	-	-	-
Hampden,	-	-	-	-	-	-	-	-	-	-	-	-	-	-
Hampshire,	5	51,900	20,675 00	5,000 00	18	-	-	-	-	-	-	-	-	-
Middlesex,	1	2,000	2,000 00	1,000 00	3	2	375	200	2	1†	-	30,000	15,000	30
Nantucket,	-	-	-	-	-	-	-	-	-	-	-	-	-	-
Norfolk,	2	313	689 00	500 00	2	4	80,000	34,000	84	-	-	-	-	-
Plymouth,	2	62,000	24,800 00	8,000 00	21	-	-	-	-	-	-	-	-	-
Suffolk,	1	2,000	10,000 00	2,500 00	6	2	17,000	6,000	12	-	-	-	-	-
Worcester,	8	650,800	549,825 00	375,060 00	407	3	11,250	3,000	7	-	-	-	-	-
Totals,	26	790,213	$626,654 00	$409,860 00	484	14	$573,625	$398,200	705	2	400,000	$180,000	$120,000	230

* See Note (11.)

† This establishment manufactures Nuts and Screws.

COUNTIES.	BUTTS OR HINGES. Establishments for the manufacture of Butts or Hinges.	Dozens of Iron Butts or Hinges manufactured.	Dozens of Brass or Composition Butts or Hinges manufactured.	Value of Iron and Brass, and Composition Butts or Hinges.	Capital invested.	Hands employed.	DOOR HANDLES AND LATCHES. Establishments for the manufac're of Latches and Door Handles.	Dozens of Door Handles and Latches manufactured.	Value of Door Handles and Latches.	Capital invested.	Hands employed.
Barnstable,	-	-	-	-	-	-	-	-	-	-	-
Berkshire,	-	-	-	-	-	-	-	-	-	-	-
Bristol,	-	-	-	-	-	-	-	-	-	-	-
Dukes,	-	-	-	-	-	-	-	-	-	-	-
Essex,	-	-	-	-	-	-	-	-	-	-	-
Franklin,	-	-	-	-	-	-	-	-	-	-	-
Hampden,	-	-	-	-	-	-	-	-	-	-	-
Hampshire,	-	-	-	-	-	-	-	-	-	-	-
Middlesex,	-	-	-	-	-	-	-	-	-	-	-
Nantucket,	-	-	-	-	-	-	-	-	-	-	-
Norfolk,	2	-	15,000*	$17,000 00	$12,000 00	31	-	-	-	-	-
Plymouth,	-	-	-	-	-	-	-	-	-	-	-
Suffolk,	1	-	1,000	5,000 00	3,000 00	7	4	3,783	$39,100 00	$12,500 00	29
Worcester,	-	-	-	-	-	-	-	-	-	-	-
Totals,	3	-	16,000	$22,000 00	$15,000 00	38	4	3,783	$39,100 00	$12,500 00	29

* The number of Butts or Hinges manufactured at one establishment, in Needham, is not returned.

COUNTIES.	LOCKS.					TACKS AND BRADS.*				
	Lock Manufact'rs	Locks manufact'd	Value of Locks.	Capital invested.	Hands employed.	Number of Tack and Brad Manufactories.	Tons of Tacks and Brads manufactured.	Value of Tacks and Brads.	Capital invested.	Hands employed.
Barnstable,	-	- -	- -	- -	-	1	100	$20,000 00	$15,000 00	25
Berkshire,	-	- -	- -	- -	-	1	1	350 00	450 00	1
Bristol,	-	- -	- -	- -	-	11	1,940	361,760 00	188,000 00	221
Dukes,	-	- -	- -	- -	-	-	- -	- -	- -	-
Essex,	-	- -	- -	- -	-	-	- -	- -	- -	-
Franklin,	-	- -	- -	- -	-	-	- -	- -	- -	-
Hampden,	-	- -	- -	- -	-	1	9	1,500 00	1,000 00	1
Hampshire,	-	- -	- -	- -	-	-	- -	- -	- -	-
Middlesex,	-	- -	- -	- -	-	-	- -	- -	- -	-
Nantucket,	-	- -	- -	- -	-	-	- -	- -	- -	-
Norfolk,	-	- -	- -	- -	-	2	108	33,000 00	12,000 00	13
Plymouth,	-	- -	- -	- -	-	12	742	204,602 00	72,500 00	109
Suffolk,	7	26,250	$66,700 00	$24,500 00	84	-	- -	- -	- -	-
Worcester,	-	- -	- -	- -	-	-	- -	- -	- -	-
Totals,	7	26,250	$66,700 00	$24,500 00	84	28	2,900	$621,212 00	$288,950 00	370

* See Note (12.)

COUNTIES.	SHOVELS, SPADES, FORKS & HOES				PLOUGHS AND OTHER AGRICULTURAL IMPLEMENTS.†						
	Shovel, Spade, Fork and Hoe Manufactories.	Value of Shovels, Spades, Forks and Hoes.	Capital Invested.	Hands employed.	Plough Manufactories.	Ploughs manuf'd.	Val. of the same.	Other Agricultural implements manufactured.	Val. of the same.	Capital invested.	Hands employed.
Barnstable,	-	- -	- -	-	-	- -	- -	- -	- -	- -	-
Berkshire,	2	$2,665 00	$2,375 00	7	4	- -	- -	40,000	$4,400 00	$1,000 00	12
Bristol,	4	659,000 00	229,000 00	394	-	- -	- -	- -	- -	- -	-
Dukes,	-	- -	- -	-	-	- -	- -	- -	- -	- -	-
Essex,	-	- -	- -	-	-	- -	- -	- -	- -	- -	-
Franklin,	2	1,350 00	6,600 00	5	4	155	$900 00	109,330	14,705 00	3,800 00	13
Hampden,	1	No return.	700 00	2	2	13,984	39,812 86	20,000	2,500 00	14,000 00	57
Hampshire,	1	101,500 00	101,200 00	154	1	30	210 00	13,200	4,000 00	1,700 00	6
Middlesex,	2	29,000 00	3,300 00	14	3	6,130	57,753 00	100	2,000 00	27,100 00	40
Nantucket,	-	- -	- -	-	-	- -	- -	- -	- -	- -	-
Norfolk,	2	12,000 00	1,500 00	20	-	- -	- -	- -	- -	- -	-
Plymouth,	5*	77,500 00	60,000 00	75	1	25	200 00	- -	- -	100 00	1
Suffolk,	-	- -	- -	-	1	2,200	100,000 00	- -	- -	24,500 00	45
Worcester,	2	11,500 00	3,400 00	12	6	130,162	508,300 00	5,000	29,200 00	117,100 00	259
Totals,	21	$894,515 00	$408,075 00	683	22	152,686	$707,175 86	187,630	$56,805 00	$189,300 00	433

* One establishment in West Bridgewater is engaged on Shovels that are finished in Easton.

† See Note (13.)

Counties.	IRON RAIL'GS, FENCES & SAFES.				COPPER.*					BRASS FOUNDERIES.			
	Shops for manufacture of Iron Railing, Iron Fences, and Iron Safes.	Value of Iron Railing, Iron Fences and Iron Safes manuf'red.	Capital invested.	Hands employed.	Copper Manufactories.	Pounds of Copper manufactured.	Value of same.	Capital invested.	Hands employed	Number of Brass Founderies.	Value of articles manufact'ed in Brass Founder's	Capital invested.	Hands employed.
Barnstable,	-	-	-	-	-	-	-	-	-	-	-	-	-
Berkshire,	-	-	-	-	-	-	-	-	-	-	-	-	-
Bristol,	-	-	-	-	1	2,000,000	$500,000	$240,000	90	6	$127,000	$10,000	43
Dukes,	-	-	-	-	-	-	-	-	-	-	-	-	-
Essex,	4	$32,200	$7,500	18	-	-	-	-	-	3	25,000	15,000	10
Franklin,	-	-	-	-	-	-	-	-	-	-	-	-	-
Hampden,	-	-	-	-	-	-	-	-	-	2†	3,000	500	1
Hampshire,	-	-	-	-	-	-	-	-	-	1	60,000	20,000	75
Middlesex,	4	16,700	4,800	18	2	69,000	29,000	2,800	7	5	259,000	110,700	62
Nantucket,	-	-	-	-	-	-	-	-	-	1	700	1,100	4
Norfolk,	-	-	-	-	1	2,000,000	500,000	90,000	60	1	3,000	1,000	6
Plymouth,	-	-	-	-	-	-	-	-	-	1	600	500	2
Suffolk,	15	607,500	227,300	335	10	2,000,000	656,500	293,500	163	14	1,004,000	324,000	328
Worcester,	-	-	-	-	-	-	-	-	-	3	21,750	2,500	9
Totals,	23	$656,400	$239,600	371	14	6,069,000	$1,685,500	$626,300	320	37	$1,504,050	$515,300	540

* See Note (14.)

† See Note (15.)

COUNTIES.	BRITANNIA WARE.				BUTTONS.						
	Establishments for the manufacture of Britannia Ware.	Value of Britannia Ware.	Capital invested.	Hands employed.	Button Manufactories.	Gross of Metal Buttons manufactured.	Value of Metal Buttons.	Gross of other Buttons manufactured.	Val. of the same.	Capital invested.	Hands employed.
Barnstable, .	-	-	-	-	-	-	-	-	-	-	-
Berkshire, .	-	-	-	-	-	-	-	-	-	-	-
Bristol, .	4	$99,000 00	$56,000 00	160	2	1,538,000	$27,620 00	-	-	$8,000 00	26
Dukes, .	-	-	-	-	-	-	-	-	-	-	-
Essex, .	2	5,000 00	2,000 00	4	-	-	-	-	-	-	-
Franklin, .	-	-	-	-	-	-	-	-	-	-	-
Hampden, .	-	-	-	-	1	-	-	90,000	$30,000 00	3,000 00	25
Hampshire, .	-	-	-	-	3	-	-	563,000	203,500 00	160,000 00	167
Middlesex, .	2	58,000 00	35,000 00	43	-	-	-	-	-	-	-
Nantucket, .	-	-	-	-	-	-	-	-	-	-	-
Norfolk, .	1	100,000 00	50,000 00	100	-	-	-	-	-	-	-
Plymouth, .	-	-	-	-	-	-	-	-	-	-	-
Suffolk, .	1	40,000 00	15,000 00	25	-	-	-	-	-	-	-
Worcester, .	-	-	-	-	1	-	-	7,500	6,000 00	1,500 00	11
Totals, .	10	$302,000 00	$158,000 00	332	7	1,538,000	$27,620 00	660,500	$239,500 00	$172,500 00	229

COUNTIES.	GLASS. Glass Manufactories.	GLASS. Quantity of Window Glass manufactured.	GLASS. Value of Window Glass.	GLASS. Value of other Glass manufactured.	GLASS. Capital invested.	GLASS. Hands employed.	STARCH. Starch Manufactories.	STARCH. Quantity of St'ch manufactured from Wheat or Flour.	STARCH. Quant'ty of St'ch manuf'd from Potatoes.	STARCH. Value of all St'ch manufactured.	STARCH. Capital invested.	STARCH. Hands employed.
Barnstable,	1	-	-	$600,000 00	$400,000 00	500	-	-	-	-	-	-
Berkshire,	3	17,869	$48,125 00	45,000 00	145,000 00	150	-	-	-	-	-	-
Bristol,	2	-	-	9,000 00	2,500 00	6	-	-	-	-	-	-
Dukes,	-	-	-	-	-	-	-	-	-	-	-	-
Essex,	-	-	-	-	-	-	-	-	-	-	-	-
Franklin,	-	-	-	-	-	-	-	-	-	-	-	-
Hampden,	-	-	-	-	-	-	-	-	-	-	-	-
Hampshire,	-	-	-	-	-	-	-	-	-	-	-	-
Middlesex,	4*	-	-	756,000 00	643,000 00	645	2	140,000 lbs.	-	$14,000 00	$4,000 00	4
Nantucket,	-	-	-	-	-	-	-	-	-	-	-	-
Norfolk,	-	-	-	-	-	-	5	722,000 lbs. 6,625 bbls.	-	181,800 00	157,000 00	44
Plymouth,	-	-	-	-	-	-	-	-	-	-	-	-
Suffolk,	3	-	-	1,190,000 00	615,000 00	586	-	-	-	-	-	-
Worcester,	-	-	-	-	-	-	-	-	-	-	-	-
Totals,	13	17,869	$48,125 00	$2,600,000 00	$1,805,500 00	1,887	7	862,000 lbs. 6,625 bbls.	-	$195,800 00	$161,000 00	48

* The returns do not specify the description of Glass manufactured in Cambridge or Somerville.

COUNTIES.	CHEMICAL PREPARATIONS.				PAPER.*					
	Establishm'ts for the manufact'e Ch'mical Prep'n	Value of Chemical Preparat'ns.	Capital invested.	Hands employed.	Paper Manufactories.	Tons of Stock used.	Quantity of Paper made.	Value of Paper made.	Capital invested.	Hands employed.
Barnstable,	4	$3,165 00	$6,600 00	5	-	-	-	-	-	-
Berkshire,	-	-	-	-	37	11,595	4,513 tons. 169,453 reams.	$1,535,890 00	$961,200 00	1,156
Bristol,	1	14,000 00	10,000 00	8	3	1,030	525 tons. 250,000 reams.	78,568 00	17,600 00	50
Dukes,	-	-	-	-	-	-	-	-	-	-
Essex,	1	66,500 00	600,000 00	20	4	2,150	1,500	325,000 00	153,000 00	106
Franklin,	-	-	-	-	-	-	-	-	-	-
Hampden,	1	54,000 00	15,000 00	12	8	1,735	875 tons. 122,500 reams.	439,600 00	255,700 00	352
Hampshire,	-	-	-	-	13	602,769	1,198 tons. 150,000 reams.	373,940 00	255,000 00	276
Middlesex,	11	566,600 00	267,500 00	198	21	5,423	3,667	616,549 00	386,000 00	241
Nantucket,	-	-	-	-	-	-	-	-	-	-
Norfolk,	1	150,000 00	50,000 00	45	16	4,138	3,005 tons. 20,000 reams.	250,125 00	288,000 00	209
Plymouth,	-	-	-	-	2	270	210	30,000 00	18,000 00	20
Suffolk,	7	270,500 00	146,500 00	52	-	-	-	-	-	-
Worcester,	-	-	-	-	17	4,043	2,466	492,175 00	230,000 00	220
Totals,	26	$1,124,765 00	$1,095,600 00	340	121	633,153	17.959 tons. 711 953 reams.	$4,141,847 00	$2,564,500 00	2,630

* See Note (16.)

COUNTIES.	PIANO-FORTES AND OTHER MUSICAL INSTRUMENTS.*								CLOCKS.			
	Manufactories of Pianofortes and other Musical Instruments.	Number of Piano-fortes manufactured.	Capital invested.	No. of all other Musical Inst'nt Manufactories.	Value of Musical Instruments manufactured.	Value of Piano-forte and Melodeon Legs, Cases, Keys, Piano-forte Act'n and other detached parts of Musical Instruments.	Capital invested.	Hands employed.	No. of Clock Manufactories.	Clocks manufactured.	Capital invested.	Hands employed.
Barnstable,	-	-	-	-	-	-	-	-	-	-	-	-
Berkshire,	2	-	-	70	$15,000 00	-	$29,000 00	15	-	-	-	-
Bristol,	1	3	-	-	7,500 00	-	1,200 00	4	1	800	$2,000 00	4
Dukes,	-	-	-	-	-	-	-	-	-	-	-	-
Essex,	5	200	$30,000 00	12	5,700 00	$83,000 00	1,000 00	57	-	-	-	-
Franklin,	1	-	4,500 00	-	-	-	-	16	-	-	-	-
Hampden,	1	4	400 00	-	36,000 00	-	11,000 00	28	-	-	-	-
Hampshire,	-	-	-	-	-	-	-	-	-	-	-	-
Middlesex,	14	-	27,700 00	-	133,000 00	93,700 00	12,100 00	102	-	-	-	-
Nantucket,	-	-	-	-	-	-	-	-	-	-	-	-
Norfolk,	10	8	13,500 00	112	59,280 00	-	12,300 00	59	1	1,000	15,000	22
Plymouth,	-	-	-	-	-	-	-	-	-	-	-	-
Suffolk,	22	6,122	955,000 00	10	$2,004,700 00	47,500 00	112,000 00	1,297	-	-	-	-
Worcester,	13	152	46,000 00	1,000	34,500 00	136,950 00	25,000 00	187	-	-	-	-
Totals,	69	6,489	$1,077,100 00	1,204	$2,295,680 00	$361,150 00	$203,600 00	1,765	2	1,800	$17,000 00	26

* See Note (17.)

Counties.	SEWING MACHINES.				DAGUERREOTYPES.*				CHRONOMETERS, WATCHES, GOLD AND SILVER WARE, AND JEWELRY †			
	Sewing Machine Manufactories.	Number of Sewing Machines manufactured.	Capital invested.	Hands employed.	Number of Daguerreotype Artists.	Number of Daguerreotypes taken.	Capital invested.	Hands employed	Number of establishments for the manufacture of Chronomet's, Watches, Gold and Silver Ware and Jew'y	Value of the manufacture of said establishments.	Capital invested.	Hands employed.
Barnstable,	-	-	-	-	1	300	$100	1	-	-	-	-
Berkshire,	-	-	-	-	7	5,050	2,300	8	1	$16,000	$2,500	8
Bristol,	-	-	-	-	11	17,865	6,600	19	25	946,200	350,000	724
Dukes,	-	-	-	-	-	-	-	-	-	-	-	-
Essex,	-	-	-	-	17	54,800	12,650	29	7	31,000	11,500	15
Franklin,	-	-	-	-	5	3,325	2,375	4	-	-	-	-
Hampden,	1	100	$4,000	6	11	11,850	4,250	18	2	155,000	51,000	77
Hampshire,	-	-	-	-	7	3,910	2,300	8	-	-	-	-
Middlesex,	1	43	-	-	15	29,141	12,800	28	5	112,100	91,700	85
Nantucket,	-	-	-	-	1	1,200	700	2	-	-	-	-
Norfolk,	1	500	10,000	10	3	3,600	1,100	3	3	189,000	6,700	134
Plymouth,	-	-	-	-	5	2,900	1,450	5	1	400	100	1
Suffolk,	5	3,385	83,000	168	35	230,408	83,100	110	22	617,000	185,500	208
Worcester,	-	-	-	-	16	39,277	10,150	25	4	38,500	21,500	11
Totals,	8	4,028	$97,000	184	134	403,626	$139,875	260	70	2,105,200	$720,500	1,263

* See Note (18.)

† See Note (19.)

COUNTIES.	BRUSHES.				SADDLES, HARNESS & TRUNKS.*				UPHOLSTERY.			
	Brush Manufactories.	Value of Brushes	Capital invested.	Hands employed.	Saddle, Harness and Trunk Manufactories.	Value of Saddles, Harnesses and Trunks manufactured.	Capital invested.	Hands employed.	Upholst'y Manufactories.	Value of Upholstery manufactured.	Capital invested.	Hands employed.
Barnstable,	-	-	-	-	8	$4,955	$3,925	12	-	-	-	-
Berkshire,	-	-	-	-	24	37,430	14,350	51	-	-	-	-
Bristol,	-	-	-	-	18	100,473	19,550	79	8	$29,000	$8,700	23
Dukes,	-	-	-	-	-	-	-	-	-	-	-	-
Essex,	-	-	-	-	35	63,797	21,725	66	8	22,300	8,100	15
Franklin,	-	-	-	-	10	8,450	3,950	17	-	-	-	-
Hampden,	1	$3,500	$800	4	10	19,200	7,100	29	2	2,000	1,200	2
Hampshire,	1	400	100	1	36	11,875	4,500	26	-	-	-	-
Middlesex,	5	231,000	133,600	271	50	93,989	39,900	123	13	229,000	70,150	94
Nantucket,	-	-	-	-	2	1,200	900	4	-	-	-	-
Norfolk,	4	10,500	7,700	9	21	25,600	11,600	38	2	13,600	2,000	13
Plymouth,	2	8,000	3,000	11	20	20,700	8,832	26	-	-	-	-
Suffolk,	3	227,000	120,400	127	42	758,200	169,600	382	52	1,557,300	455,800	419
Worcester,	2	4,100	2,000	6	37	74,180	21,875	113	7	23,600	8,300	34
Totals,	18	$484,500	$267,600	429	313	$1,220,049	$327,807	966	92	$1,876,800	$554,250	600

* See Note (20.)

COUNTIES.	HATS AND CAPS.*				CORDAGE.†				BOATS.‡			
	Hat and Cap Manufactories.	Number of Hats and Caps manufactured.	Capital invested.	Hands employed	Cordage Manufactories.	Pounds of Cordage manufactured.	Capital invested.	Hands employed.	Establishments for the manufacture of Boats	Number of Boats built.	Capital invested.	Hands employed
Barnstable, . .	1	675	$200 00	1	-	- -	- -	-	8	140	$7,200	16
Berkshire, . .	3	8,100	6,000 00	14	1	1,000	$300 00	2	-	-	- -	-
Bristol, . .	2	16,350	2,500 00	9	1	2,000,000	75,000 00	60	19	490	16,160	50
Dukes, . .	-	- -	- -	-	-	- -	- -	-	2	30	500	4
Essex, . .	19	554,200	137,400 00	308	13	1,429,918	31,300 00	108	15	1,021	12,510	39
Franklin, . .	-	- -	- -	-	-	- -	- -	-	-	-	- -	-
Hampden, . .	2	1,900	2,300 00	6	1	- -	- -	-	-	-	- -	-
Hampshire, .	-	- -	- -	-	1	5,000	400 00	1	1	2	- -	-
Middlesex, .	13	191,013	34,925 00	118	7	276,500	12,400 00	39	4	44	900	7
Nantucket, .	1	2,000	1,000 00	2	-	- -	- -	-	4	99	3,480	12
Norfolk, . .	2	3,060	1,200 00	5	5	6,260,000	126,500 00	300	5	484	3,300	28
Plymouth, . .	3	8,500	2,000 00	15	7	6,256,000	209,500 00	301	3	28	800	5
Suffolk, . .	37	727,300	143,200 00	500	2	4,046,000	150,000 00	135	9	204	13,700	51
Worcester, .	10	27,786	19,648 00	61	6	379,000	31,000 00	54	-	-	- -	-
Totals, .	93	1,540,884	$350,373 00	1,042	44	20,653 418	$636,400 00	1.000	70	2,542	$58.550	212

* See Note (21.)

† See Note (22.)

‡ See Note (23.)

COUNTIES.	VESSELS LAUNCHED.*				MASTS AND SPARS.†				SAIL LOFTS.		
	Number of Vessels launched.	Tonnage of said Vessels.	Capital invested.	Hands employed.	Number of Mast and Spar Sheds.	Number of Masts and Spars manufactured.	Capital invested.	Hands employed.	Number of Sail Lofts.	Number of Sails made of American fabric.	Number of Sails maufactured of Foreign fabric.
Barnstable,	3	1,520	$90,000 00	68	3	300	$2,600 00	4	19	1,088	-
Berkshire,	-	-	-	-	-	-	-	-	-	-	-
Bristol,	21	8,319	365,000 00	379	6	1,610	8,800 00	28	14	2,783	507
Dukes,	1	192	11,000 00	7	-	-	-	-	1	100	-
Essex,	66	20,064	280,500 00	826	8	1,553	11,400 00	27	22	1,876	2
Franklin,	-	-	-	-	-	-	-	-	-	-	-
Hampden,	-	-	-	-	-	-	-	-	-	-	-
Hampshire,	-	-	-	-	-	-	-	-	-	-	-
Middlesex,	14	12,482	116,000 00	1,035	5	2,700	18,000 00	32	-	-	-
Nantucket,	-	-	-	-	1	89	600 00	2	3	202	157
Norfolk,	1	1,500	30,000 00	50	-	-	-	-	1	12	-
Plymouth,	15	4,492	143,200 00	305	1	-	500 00	2	7	587	-
Suffolk,	35	44,300	905,000 00	922	7	3,160	158,000 00	72	33	6,767	42
Worcester,	-	-	-	-	-	-	-	-	-	-	-
Totals,	156	92,869	$1,940,700 00	3,592	31	9,412	$199,900 00	167	100	13,415	708

* See Note (24.)

† See Note (25.)

COUNTIES.	SAIL-LOFTS—Continued.				CARDS.				SALT.				
	Value of Sails manufactured of Ame'can fabric.	Value of Sails manufactured of Foreign Fabric.	Capital invested.	Hands employed.	Card Manufactories.	Value of Cards of all kinds manufactured.	Capital invested.	Hands employed.	Establishments for the manufacture of Salt	Number of bushels of Salt manufactured.	Value of Salt.	Capital invested.	Hands employed
Barnstable, .	$63,830 00	- -	$30,500	47	-	- -	- -	-	181	143,669	$236,178	$101,312	207
Berkshire, .	- -	- -	- -	-	-	- -	- -	-	-	- -	- -	- -	-
Bristol, .	175,572 34	$18,582 75	5,250	125	-	- -	- -	-	5	14,811	7,406	33,562	9
Dukes, .	2,200 00	- -	200	2	-	- -	- -	-	1	75	37	100	1
Essex, .	170,814 00	241 00	55,250	105	1	$20,000	$10,000	6	-	- -	- -	- -	-
Franklin, .	- -	- -	- -	-	-	- -	- -	-	-	- -	- -	- -	-
Hampden, .	- -	- -	- -	-	1	30,240	10,000	11	-	- -	- -	- -	-
Hampshire, .	- -	- -	- -	-	-	- -	- -	-	-	- -	- -	- -	-
Middlesex, .	- -	- -	- -	-	2	22,000	13,000	10	-	- -	- -	- -	-
Nantucket, .	12,170 00	6,405 00	750	15	-	- -	- -	-	-	- -	- -	- -	-
Norfolk, .	753 70	- -	100	1	3	130,000	35,000	42	1	1,000	500	700	1
Plymouth, .	33,364 00	3,500 00	6,000	21	-	- -	- -	-	4	2,075	850	1,650	5
Suffolk, .	431,172 00	2,695 00	70,000	203	-	- -	- -	-	3	158,000	106,000	50,000	38
Worcester, .	- -	- -	- -	-	14	238,000	128,600	85	-	- -	- -	- -	-
Totals, .	$889,876 04	$31,423 75	$168,050	519	21	$440,240*	$196,600	154	195	319,630	$350,971	$187,324	261

* $105,000 of this amount comprises the value of blank and playing cards; the remainder is the value of machine cards, for factories.

COUNTIES.	RAILROAD CARS, COACHES, CHAISES, WAGONS, SLEIGHS AND OTHER VEHICLES.*				LEAD.				SUGAR REFINED.			
	Establishments for the manuf'e of Railr'd Cars, Coach's, Chai's, Wag'ns, Sleighs, & other vehicl's	Value of Railr'd Cars, Coaches, Chais's, Wag'ns, Sleighs and other vehicles manufactured.	Capital invested.	Hands employed.	Lead Manufactories.	Value of all manufact's of Lead.	Capital invested.	Hands employed.	Sugar Refineries	Pounds of Sugar refined.	Value of Sugar refined.	Hands employed.
Barnstable,	9	$11,820 00	$7,050 00	21	-	-	-	-	-	-	-	-
Berkshire,	27	112,281 00	62,700 00	157	-	-	-	-	-	1,700	$180 00	5
Bristol,	42	138,725 00	41,595 00	153	-	-	-	-	-	-	-	-
Dukes,	-	-	-	-	-	-	-	-	-	-	-	-
Essex,	78	461,408 00	317,500 00	487	1†	$15,000 00	$70,000 00	30	-	-	-	-
Franklin,	14	28,775 00	12,400 00	41	-	-	-	-	-	-	-	-
Hampden,	14	384,140 00	62,900 00	258	-	-	-	-	-	-	-	-
Hampshire,	17	102,550 00	35,500 00	186	-	-	-	-	-	-	-	-
Middlesex,	61	288,095 00	78,050 00	307	1	175,000 00	45,000 00	8	-	-	-	-
Nantucket,	3	800 00	650 00	3	-	-	-	-	-	-	-	-
Norfolk,	35	165,200 00	59,200 00	190	1	150,000 00	50,000 00	30	1	1,500,000	56,250 00	20
Plymouth,	33	46,760 00	19,900 00	71	-	-	-	-	-	-	-	-
Suffolk,	28	279,035 00	102,400 00	302	-	-	-	-	2	28,000,000	2,000,000 00	290
Worcester,	64	333,366 00	149,925 00	315	-	-	-	-	-	-	-	-
Totals,	425	$2,352,955 00	$949,770 00	2,491	3	$340,000 00	$165,000 00	68	3	29,501,700	$2,056,430 00	315

* See Note (26.)

† See Note (27.)

OIL AND SPERM CANDLES.

COUNTIES.	Establishments for the manufacture of Oil and Sp'm Candles	Number of gallons Oil manufactured.	Value of Oil manufactured.	Pounds of Sp'rm Candles manufactured.	Value of Sperm Candles.	Capital invested.	Hands employed.
Barnstable, .	1	1,200	$9,600 00	- -	- -	$6,000 00	No return.
Berkshire, .	- -	- -	- -	- -	- -	- -	- -
Bristol, . .	19	3,420,268	3,062,296 18	678,110	$189,970 80	1,410,000 00	128
Dukes, . .	1	459,380	448,215 00	68,800	20,640 00	100,000 00	12
Essex, . .	2	53,700	38,035 00	1,000,000	200,000 00	64,000 00	27
Franklin, . .	- -	- -	- -	- -	- -	- -	- -
Hampden, . .	- -	- -	- -	- -	- -	- -	- -
Hampshire, .	- -	- -	- -	- -	- -	- -	- -
Middlesex, .	5	445,000	366,000 00	10,000	30,600 00	86,000 00	28
Nantucket, .	7	1,038,344	768,529 40	142,450	17,405 00	736,013 00	50
Norfolk, . .	1	37,000	37,000 00	- -	- -	150,000 00	10
Plymouth, . .	- -	- -	- -	- -	- -	- -	- -
Suffolk, . .	9	407,000	1,336,000 00	1,236,498	289,000 00	730,000 00	157
Worcester, .	- -	- -	- -	- -	- -	- -	- -
Totals, .	45	5,861,892	$6,065,675 58	3,135,858	$747,615 80	$3,282,013 00	412

SOAP AND TALLOW CANDLES.

COUNTIES.	Establishments for the manufacture of Soap and Tall'w Candles.	Pounds of Hard, Soap manufactured.	Barrels of Soft Soap manufactured.	Value of Soap.	Pounds of Tallow Candles manufactured.	Value of Tallow Candles.	Capital invested.	Hands employed.
Barnstable,	-	-	-	-	4,000	$600 00	-	No ret'n
Berkshire,	2	1,050	-	$260 00	43,000	6,440 00	$3,100 00	4
Bristol,	9	774,551	-	158,401 58	80,000	10,800 00	19,100 00	27
Dukes,	-	-	-	-	-	-	-	-
Essex,	23	2,123,950	4,800	129,880 00	275,250	42,957 00	61,300 00	69
Franklin,	-	-	-	-	-	-	-	-
Hampden,	6	60,000	2,611	13,483 00	170,300	23,890 00	6,800 00	15
Hampshire,	3	20,000	800	4,600 00	19,000	2,830 00	2,000 00	7
Middlesex,	30	10,374,200	8,361	6,958,726 00	1,244,752	201,100 00	1,390,900 00	206
Nantucket,	2	32,000	-	2,170 00	-	-	900 00	3
Norfolk,	8	645,000	-	75,200 00	375,000	37,500 00	24,000 00	28
Plymouth,	10	30,484	1,336	17,932 00	-	-	3,700 00	12
Suffolk,	4	900,000	-	47,000 00	200,000	28,000 00	49,500 00	24
Worcester,	17	300,244	6,936	46,714 00	85,000	12,050 00	21,200 00	50
Totals,	114	15,261,479	24,844	$7,354,366 58	2,496,302	$366,167 00	$1,582,500 00	445

COUNTIES.	POWDER MILLS.					FIRE ARMS.					
	Powder Mills.	Pounds of Powder manufactured.	Value of Powder.	Capital invested.	Hands employed.	Establishm'ts for the manufacture of Fire Arms.	Description of Fire Arms manufactured.	Number of Fire Arms manufactured.	Val. of Fire Arms	Capital invested.	Hands employed.
Barnstable,	-	-	-	-	-	-	-	-	-	-	-
Berkshire,	2	450,000	$41,625	$10,500	10	2	Rifles.	60	$1,900	$600	2
Bristol,	-	-	-	-	-	1	Rifles & Carbines.	350	2,500	300	7
Dukes,	-	-	-	-	-	-	-	-	-	-	-
Essex,	-	-	-	-	-	-	-	-	-	-	-
Franklin,	-	-	-	-	-	-	-	-	-	-	-
Hampden,	3	440,000	44,000	25,000	10	2	Sporting-guns, Rifles, Pistols, Revolvers, Percussion Muskets, and Cavalry Musketoons.	20,000	213,000*	64,000	35
Hampshire,	-	-	-	-	-	-	-	-	-	-	-
Middlesex,	2	1,250,000	130,000	15,500	30	3	Rifles, single and double shot Guns and Pistols.	50	6,000	2,200	9
Nantucket,	-	-	-	-	-	-	-	-	-	-	-
Norfolk,	-	-	-	-	-	-	-	-	-	-	-
Plymouth,	-	-	-	-	-	1	Rifles, and double and single barrel Guns.	-	1,000	800	1
Suffolk,	-	-	-	-	-	2	Rifles and Fowling Pieces.	350	7,500	2,500	7
Worcester,	1	100,000	12,500	3,000	4	13	Rifles, Fowling Pieces and Pistols.	27,300	159,575	62,100	221
Totals,	8	2,240,000	$228,125	$54,000	54	24	-	48,110	$391,475	$132,500	282

* See Note (28.)

COUNTIES.	CANNON.						CHOCOLATE MILLS.			
	Establishm't for the manufacture of Cannon.	Description of Cannon.	Number of Cannon.	Value of Cannon.	Capital Invested.	Hands employed.	Number of Chocolate Mills.	Pounds of Chocolate manufactured.	Capital Invested.	Hands employed.
Barnstable,	-	- -	-	- -	- -	-	-	- -	- -	-
Berkshire,	-	- -	-	- -	- -	-	-	- -	- -	-
Bristol,	-	- -	-	- -	- -	-	-	- -	- -	-
Dukes,	-	- -	-	- -	- -	-	-	- -	- -	-
Essex,	-	- -	-	- -	- -	-	1	80,000	$10,000 00	2
Franklin,	-	- -	-	- -	- -	-	-	- -	- -	-
Hampden,	-	- -	-	- -	- -	-	-	- -	- -	-
Hampshire,	-	- -	-	- -	- -	-	-	- -	- -	-
Middlesex,	-	- -	-	- -	- -	-	-	- -	- -	-
Nantucket,	-	- -	-	- -	- -	-	-	- -	- -	-
Norfolk,	-	- -	-	- -	- -	-	5	1,151,333	93,000 00	49
Plymouth,	-	- -	-	- -	- -	-	-	- -	- -	-
Suffolk,	1	Columbiads, Navy Guns, & Pound'rs.	119	$54,151 00	$50,000 00	40	-	- -	- -	-
Worcester,	-	- -	-	- -	- -	-	-	- -	- -	-
Totals,	1	- -	119	$54,151 00	$50,000 00	40	6	1,231,333	$103,000 00	51

COUNTIES.	CHAIR AND CABINET MANUFACT'S.				TIN WARE.				COMB MANUFACTORIES.			
	Number of Chair and Cabinet Manufactories.	Value of Chairs and Cabinet Ware manufactured.	Capital invested.	Hands employed.	Tin Ware Manufactories.	Value of Tin Ware Manufactured.	Capital invested	Hands employed.	Number of Comb Manufactories.	Value of Combs manufactured.	Capital invested.	Hands employed.
Barnstable,	1	$100	$200	1	18	$9,900	$7,400	22	-	-	-	-
Berkshire,	21	34,842	22,200	56	13	58,200	25,600	47	2	$1,000	$160	7
Bristol,	4	12,030	9,300	15	27	133,300	44,800	85	1	8,300	2,000	5
Dukes,	-	-	-	-	1	200	500	1	-	-	-	-
Essex,	45	288,800	457,250	416	39	94,965	29,500	111	16	226,500	144,900	230
Franklin,	9	53,170	23,300	73	7	6,000	5,000	13	-	-	-	-
Hampden,	7	29,400	13,600	27	12	85,700*	21,975	65	-	-	-	-
Hampshire,	9	19,600	14,050	25	10	32,500	14,200	43	-	-	-	-
Middlesex,	40	732,300	229,000	724	63	253,525	103,100	225	3	102 500	58,600	73
Nantucket,	2	250	500	4	5	4,000	2,500	7	-	-	-	-
Norfolk,	31	92,600	170,750	510	31	122,350	41,600	97	-	-	-	-
Plymouth,	7	52,375	18,305	71	15	36,000	19,500	40	-	-	-	-
Suffolk,	36	1,063,800	360,700	600	51	419,000	195,500	223	3	6,500	2,500	9
Worcester,	97	1,590,715	594,460	1,721	48	195,600	59,800	152	30	212,622	62,900	287
Totals,	309	$3,969,982	$1,913,615	4,243	340	$1,451,240	$570,975	1,131	55	$557,422	$271,060	611

* $45,000 of the amount comprises the value of tin roofing.

COUNTIES.	WHITE LEAD AND OTHER PAINTS.*							LINSEED OIL.				
	Establishments for the manufacture of White Lead and other Paints.	Tons of White Lead manufactured.	Value of White Lead manufactured.	Tons of other Paints manufactured.	Value of other Paints.	Capital invested.	Hands employed.	Number of Mills for the manufacture of Linseed Oil.	Gallons of Oil manufactured.	Value of oil.	Capital invested.	Hands employ'd.
Barnstable,	-	-	-	-	-	-	-	-	-	-	-	-
Berkshire,	-	-	-	-	-	-	-	-	-	-	-	-
Bristol,	-	-	-	-	-	-	-	-	-	-	-	-
Dukes,	-	-	-	-	-	-	-	-	-	-	-	-
Essex,	1	900	$144,000 00	-	-	-	-	-	-	-	-	-
Franklin,	-	-	-	-	-	-	-	-	-	-	-	-
Hampden,	-	-	-	-	-	-	-	-	-	-	-	-
Hampshire,	-	-	-	-	-	-	-	-	-	-	-	-
Middlesex,	-	-	-	-	-	-	-	1	100,000	$90,000 00	$50,000 00	10
Nantucket,	-	-	-	-	-	-	-	-	-	-	-	-
Norfolk,	1	500	168,000 00	-	-	$5,000 00	34	-	-	-	-	-
Plymouth,	-	-	-	-	-	-	-	-	-	-	-	-
Suffolk,	4	1,970	317,850 00	2,503	$280,340 00	166,000 00	37	2	845,000	800,000 00	550,000 00	83
Worcester,	-	-	-	-	-	-	-	-	-	-	-	-
Totals,	6	3,370	$629,850 00	2,503	$280,340 00	$171,000 00	71	3	945,000	$890,000 00	$600,000 00	93

* See Note (29.)

COUNTIES.	CAMPHENE OR BURNING FLUID.				GLUE AND GUM MANUFACTORIES.				COTTON GINS.			
	Establishments for the manufacture of Camphene or burning fluid.	Gallons of Camphene manufactured.	Capital invested.	Hands employed.	Glue Manufactories, and manufactories for the preparation of Gum.	Value of Glue and Gums manufactured.	Capital invested.	Hands employed.	Establishments for the manufacture of Cotton Gins.	Value of Cotton Gins manufactured.	Capital invested.	Hands employed.
Barnstable,	-	-	-	-	-	-	-	-	-	-	-	-
Berkshire,	-	-	-	-	-	-	-	-	-	-	-	-
Bristol,	-	-	-	-	-	-	-	-	-	-	-	-
Dukes,	-	-	-	-	-	-	-	-	-	-	-	-
Essex,	-	-	-	-	9	$391,500	$84,400	85	-	-	-	-
Franklin,	-	-	-	-	1	800	800	2	-	-	-	-
Hampden,	-	-	-	-	-	-	-	-	-	-	-	-
Hampshire,	-	-	-	-	-	-	-	-	-	-	-	-
Middlesex,	-	-	-	-	3	16,800	4,300	10	-	-	-	-
Nantucket,	-	-	-	-	-	-	-	-	-	-	-	-
Norfolk,	1	175,000	$20,000	5	7	120,300	33,800	35	-	-	-	-
Plymouth,	-	-	-	-	-	-	-	-	3	$99,000	$114,000	100
Suffolk,	6	820,000	114,500	27	-	-	-	-	-	-	-	-
Worcester,	1	33,000	1,000	1	2	3,250	1,150	6	-	-	-	-
Totals,	8	1,028,000	$135,500	33	22	$532,650	$124,450	138	3	$99,000	$114,000	100

COUNTIES.	FLOUR MILLS.*					TANNERIES.				
	Number of Flour Mills.	Barrels of Flour manufactured.	Value of Flour manufactured.	Capital invested.	Hands employed	Number of Tanneries.	Number of Hides tanned.	Value of Leather tanned.	Capital invested.	Hands employed.
Barnstable,	-	-	-	-	-	2	1,700	$4,900 00	$2,100 00	3
Berkshire,	12	87,300	$251,840 00	$98,000 00	30	23	87,768	270,000 00	139,400 00	107
Bristol,	2	60,000	670,000 00	150,000 00	36	10	12,875	31,350 00	15,200 00	14
Dukes,	-	-	-	-	-	1	600	2,500 00	3,500 00	2
Essex,	-	-	-	-	-	99	1,093,564	2,386,635 00	1,173,560 00	618
Franklin,	1	500	4,000 00	4,000 00	1	26	35,020	156,600 00	251,783 00	59
Hampden,	6	15,300	112,000 00	28,450 00	10	21	52,209	178,531 00	83,200 00	86
Hampshire,	3	-	18,000 00	8,000 00	3	10	17,675	72,000 00	30,150 00	32
Middlesex,	3	10,000	103,800 00	14,000 00	10	23	236,751	984,666 00	448,300 00	377
Nantucket,	-	-	-	-	-	-	-	-	-	-
Norfolk,	-	-	-	-	-	10	326,900	201,750 00	91,000 00	57
Plymouth,	-	-	-	-	-	6	11,630	54,840 00	16,700 00	15
Suffolk,	2	87,000	870,000 00	300,000 00	80	1	15,000	120,000 00	40,000 00	35
Worcester,	3	3,000	10,400 00	5,000 00	3	34	212,480	321,597 00	159,100 00	136
Totals,	32	263,100	$2,040,040 00	$607,450 00	173	266	2,104,172	$4,785,369 00	$2,453,993 00	1,541

* See Note (30.)

COUNTIES.	CURRYING ESTABLISHMENTS.*				PATENT AND ENAMELLED LEATHER.†			
	Number of Currying Establishments.	Value of Leather Curried.	Capital Invested.	Hands employed.	Manufactories of Patent and Enamel'd Leather.	Value of Leather manufactured.	Capital invested.	Hands employed.
Barnstable,	3	$7,000 00	$3,700 00	6	-	-	-	-
Berkshire,	5	151,800 00	22,000 00	31	-	-	-	-
Bristol,	1	1,000 00	500 00	1	-	-	-	-
Dukes,	-	-	-	-	-	-	-	-
Essex,	97	2,434,075 00	943,500 00	623	7	$269,620 00	$67,000 00	64
Franklin,	10	34,306 00	14,833 00	18	-	-	-	-
Hampden,	10	132,300 00	41,100 00	43	-	-	-	-
Hampshire,	2	28,000 00	2,000 00	6	-	-	-	-
Middlesex,	39	1,161,300 00	284,600 00	357	10	527,322 00	92,700 00	178
Nantucket,	-	-	-	-	-	-	-	-
Norfolk,	24	604,900 00	148,800 00	189	4	420,000 00	63,000 00	148
Plymouth,	4	89,000 00	5,300 00	21	-	-	-	-
Suffolk,	20	836,200 00	86,500 00	156	-	-	-	-
Worcester,	35	770,172 00	145,600 00	151	1	55,000 00	5,000 00	10
Totals,	250	$6,250,047 00	$1,698,433 00	1,602	22	$1,271,942 00	$227,700 00	400

* See Note (31.)

† See Note (32.)

COUNTIES.	BOOTS AND SHOES.*					STRAW BONNETS AND HATS.†						
	Pairs of Boots manufactured.	Pairs of Shoes manufactured.	Value of Boots and Shoes manufactured.	Males employed.	Females employed.	Establishments for the manufacture of Straw Bonnets and Hats.	Number of Straw Bonnets manufactured.	Number of Straw Hats manufactured.	Value of Straw Braid manufactured and not made into Bonnets or Hats.	Value of Palm Leaf Hats.	Males employed.	Females employed.
Barnstable,	4,281	11,163	$19,240	56	18	–	–	–	–	–	–	–
Berkshire,	32,220	27,245	110,888	158	39	–	–	–	–	$790	–	14
Bristol,	48,880	409,330	498,083	494	212	4	190,255	67,840	$3,278	–	41	590
Dukes,	325	1,025	3,068	7	–	–	–	–	–	–	–	–
Essex,	4,893,519	17,342,118	12,190,936	15,104	19,595	–	–	–	–	–	–	–
Franklin,	31,213	9,168	62,306	92	8	–	–	–	–	43,212	16	986
Hampden,	27,800	79,795	124,091	201	41	3	158,295	10,270	–	–	29	462
Hampshire,	26,886	22,476	60,369	131	30	4	68,850	5,875	–	56,556	461	474
Middlesex,	1,388,119	6,527,105	6,522,074	7,385	4,257	9	184,470	65,500	560	8,461	52	474
Nantucket,	1,150	4,895	10,275	11	20	1	9,000	138,000	–	–	2	237
Norfolk,	1,494,396	1,205,608	4,990,700	6,623	2,582	16	2,367,160	1,580,000	87,675	–	593	6,191
Plymouth,	773,751	3,862,032	4,868,618	5,169	2,345	2	2,000	40,000	384	–	8	174
Suffolk,	35,100	177,100	193,900	145	155	–	–	–	–	–	–	–
Worcester,	3,133,689	3,499,439	7,847,175	9,425	3,524	3	346,000	–	2,240	184,189	99	3,608
Totals,	11,892,329	33,174,499	$37,501,723	45,001	32,826	42	3,326,030	1,907,485	$94,137	$293,208	1,301	13,210

* See Note (33.)

† See Note (34.)

COUNTIES.	BRICKS.			MATHEMATICAL INSTRUMENTS.		SNUFF, TOBACCO AND CIGARS.			BUILDING STONE.	
	Number of Bricks manufactured.	Value of Bricks.	Hands employed.	Value of Mathematical instruments manufactured.	Hands employed.	Value of Snuff, Tobacco and Cigars manufac'd.	Males employed in the business.	Females employed.	Value of building stone, quarried and prepared for market.	Hands employed.
Barnstable, .	550,000	$3,550 00	12	- -	-	- -	-	-	$500 00	2
Berkshire, . .	2,835,000	29,600 00	53	$50 00	1	$3,000 00	3	-	81,500 00	88
Bristol, . .	5,920,000	43,190 00	84	2,500 00	3	9,450 00	18	5	39,000 00	64
Dukes, . .	700,000	3,000 00	14	- -	-	- -	-	-	- -	-
Essex, . .	11,358,000	104,715 00	148	100,300 00	3	211,525 00	91	156	363,000 00	528
Franklin, . .	1,225,000	7,870 00	18	- -	-	- -	-	-	2,300 00	4
Hampden, . .	8,300,000	168,500 00	131	1,000 00	No ret'n.	207,515 00	153	59	53,100 00	113
Hampshire, .	2,500,000	12,200 00	30	- -	-	- -	-	-	- -	-
Middlesex, .	48,490,000	2,097,800 00	299	- -	-	453,200 00	98	37	135,600 00	180
Nantucket, .	- -	- -	-	- -	-	- -	-	-	- -	-
Norfolk, . .	3,010,000	20,560 00	43	- -	-	18,000 00	28	21	452,000 00	691
Plymouth, . .	4,155,000	30,330 00	61	- -	-	4,400 00	5	2	16,780 00	55
Suffolk, . .	2,000,000	13,550 00	27	101,000 00	69	70,750 00	36	48	323,000 00	287
Worcester, .	17,310,000	92,300 00	189	- -	-	10,950 00	13	2	118,433 00	193
Totals, .	108,353,000	$2,627,165 00	1,109	$204 850 00	76	$988,790 00	445	330	$1,585,213 00	2,205

COUNTIES.	MARBLE.		LIME.			MINERAL COAL AND IRON ORE.		CHARCOAL.*		
	Value of Marble quarried and prepared for market.	Hands employed.	Number of Casks of Lime manufactured.	Value of Lime manufactured.	Hands employed.	Value of Mineral Coal and Iron Ore manufactured.	Hands employed in the business.	Bushels of Charcoal manufactured.	Value of Charcoal manufactured.	Hands employed.
Barnstable,	-	-	-	-	-	-	-	-	-	-
Berkshire,	$82,800 00	83	87,932	$94,107 00	108	$111,475 00	225	1,663,904	$131,410 00	352
Bristol,	3,000 00	5	-	-	-	-	-	138,240	23,177 50	135
Dukes,	-	-	-	-	-	-	-	-	-	-
Essex,	8,400 00	7	-	-	-	-	-	-	-	-
Franklin,	2,000 00	3	-	-	-	-	-	248,650	19,183 50	27
Hampden,	12,000 00	13	-	-	-	-	-	132,348	11,016 88	21
Hampshire,	-	-	-	-	-	-	-	73,300	5,542 00	11
Middlesex,	125,000 00	35	1,000	800 00	2	-	-	49,900	6,193 00	10
Nantucket,	-	-	-	-	-	-	-	-	-	-
Norfolk,	-	-	-	-	-	-	-	56,780	7,672 00	21
Plymouth,	-	-	-	-	-	-	-	186,240	20,788 20	73
Suffolk,	311,000 00	286	-	-	-	-	-	30,000	5,000 00	8
Worcester,	17,450 00	23	-	-	-	-	-	77,850	7,486 00	31
Totals,	$561,650 00	455	88,932	$94,907 00	110	$111,475 00	225	2,[illegible]57,212	$237,469 08	689

* See Note (35.)

COUNTIES.	WHIPS.		BLACKING.*		BLOCKS & PUMPS.		MECHANICS' TOOLS.†		WOODEN WARE.‡	
	Value of Whips manufactured.	Hands employed.	Value of Blacking manufactured.	Hands employed.	Value of Blocks and P'mps manufactured.	Hands employed.	Value of Mechanics' Tools manufactured.	Hands employed.	Value of Wooden Ware manufactured.	Hands employed.
Barnstable,	-	-	-	-	$5,850 00	10	-	-	-	-
Berkshire,	$12,000 00	39	-	-	1,500 00	3	$3,500 00	6	$10,050 00	31
Bristol,	-	-	$22,000 00	6	28,540 00	27	122,000 00	128	4,400 00	7
Dukes,	-	-	-	-	300 00	2	-	-	-	-
Essex,	-	-	5,000 00	8	24,695 00	32	84,300 00	65	11,744 00	6
Franklin,	700 00	2	10,800 00	10	-	-	127,800 00	92	22,387 00	25
Hampden,	421,400 00	268	-	-	-	-	54,000 00	55	2,600 00	6
Hampshire,	3,050 00	6	-	-	175 00	1	59,450 00	88	7,890 00	14
Middlesex,	61,400 00	44	-	-	44,200 00	36	54,900 00	38	218,610 00	55
Nantucket,	-	-	-	-	1,800 00	7	-	-	-	-
Norfolk,	950 00	4	-	-	1,600 00	3	15,000 00	16	20,400 00	36
Plymouth,	-	-	8,000 00	4	450 00	2	15,940 00	58	40,100 00	74
Suffolk,	3,000 00	2	28,000 00	30	115,300 00	84	118,000 00	110	36,000 00	29
Worcester,	3,000 00	2	2,000 00	2	90,100 00	89	487,724 00	392	371,500 00	327
Totals,	$505,500 00	367	$75,800 00	60	$314,510 00	296	$1,142,614 00	1048	$745,711 00	610

* See Note (36.) † See Note (37.) ‡ See Note (38.)

COUNTIES.	CORN AND OTHER BROOMS.*			GOLD PENS.†				LASTS AND SHOE PEGS.			
	Number of Corn and other Br'ms manufactured.	Value of Brooms manufactured.	Hands employed.	Gold Pen Manufactories.	Gold Pens manufactured.	Capital invested.	Hands employed	Lasts manufactured	Value of same.	Bushels of Shoe Pegs manufactured.	Val. of same.
Barnstable,	-	-	-	-	-	-	-	-	-	-	-
Berkshire,	9,081	$1,900 00	6	-	-	-	-	44,000	$7,000	-	-
Bristol,	-	-	-	-	-	-	-	-	-	-	-
Dukes,	-	-	-	-	-	-	-	-	-	-	-
Essex,	3,250	630 00	3	-	-	-	-	193,600	42,320	-	-
Franklin,	192,200	35,250 00	37	-	-	-	-	-	-	-	-
Hampden,	59,500	12,110 00	10	-	-	-	-	-	-	800	$1,200
Hampshire,	1,314,920	233,660 00	168	1	80,000	$25,000 00	25	-	-	-	-
Middlesex,	10,720	2,435 00	4	-	-	-	-	126,250	30,250	-	-
Nantucket,	-	-		-	-	-	-	-	-	-	-
Norfolk,	-	-	-	-	-	-	-	30,000	8,250	-	-
Plymouth,	-	-	-	-	-	-	-	40,000	10,000	-	-
Suffolk,	150,000	30,000 00	18	2	6,500	3,500 00	6	560,000	56,000	-	-
Worcester,	40,380	7,150 00	14	-	-	-	-	105,486	25,630	17,000	11,700
Totals,	1,780,051	$323,135 00	260	3	86,500	$28,500 00	31	1,099,336	$179,450	17,800	$12,900

* See Note (39.)

† See Note (40.)

COUNTIES.	LUMBER.*				FIREWOOD.†		
	Feet of Lumber prepared for market.	Value of same.	Value of Lumber not expressed in feet.	Hands employed.	Cords of Firewood prepared for market.	Value of same.	Hands employed.
Barnstable, . .	- -	- -	- -	- -	12,634	$66,613 00	319
Berkshire, . .	18,625,806	$683,931 00	- -	395	94,226	233,930 00	446
Bristol, . .	5,017,500	116,950 00	- -	137	42,701	171,381 00	562
Dukes, . .	- -	- -	- -	- -	570	3,890 00	2
Essex, . .	10,282,263	205,915 23	- -	151	31,723	153,423 00	323
Franklin, . .	18,798,500	316,408 00	- -	306	27,493	61,212 00	124
Hampden, . .	7,643,700	129,811 00	- -	121	55,429	155,486 00	269
Hampshire, .	12,355,550	191,173 00	$12,647 00	239	39,866	108,013 00	341
Middlesex, .	22,085,200	894,607 50	16,999 00	637	77,259	324,099 00	625
Nantucket, .	- -	- -	- -	- -	- -	- -	- -
Norfolk, . .	5,254,148	58,157 50	- -	131	37,655	147,205 00	302
Plymouth, . .	15,643,193	227,973 50	8,233 50	323	54,210	864,275 00	660
Suffolk, . .	- -	- -	- -	- -	- -	- -	- -
Worcester, .	48,058,800	799,656 33	2,000 00	973	198,144	671,388 00	1,352
Totals, .	163,764,660	3,624,583 06	$39,879 50	3,413	671,910	$2,960,915 00	5,325

* See Note (41.)

† See Note (42.)

WHALE FISHERY.*

COUNTIES.	Vessels employed in the Whale Fishery.	Tonnage of the same.	Gallons of Sperm Oil imported.	Val. of the same.	Gall'ns of Whale Oil imported.	Val. of the same.	Pounds of Whale Bone imported	Val. of the same.	Capital invested.	Hands employed.
Barnstable,	24	3,601	81,756	$123,633 00	110,366	$68,470 00	12,000	$4,800 00	$280,654 00	535
Berkshire,	-	-	-	-	-	-	-	-	-	-
Bristol,	388	127,542	1,546,361	2,318,174 00	6,161,602	3,616,599 00	1,890,748	745,596 00	12,100,494 00	8,821
Dukes,	12	3,863	3,150	5,550 00	63,000	37,800 00	20,000	6,000 00	390,000 00	360
Essex,	6	1,310	26,845	41,500 00	1,575	1,250 00	No return.	No return.	105,000 00	149
Franklin,	-	-	-	-	-	-	-	-	-	-
Hampden,	-	-	-	-	-	-	-	-	-	-
Hampshire,	-	-	-	-	-	-	-	-	-	-
Middlesex,	-	-	-	-	-	-	-	-	-	-
Nantucket,	44	14,226	175,700	251,513 00	261,739	146,050 00	81,752	32,307 00	1,432,600 00	1,100
Norfolk,	-	-	-	-	-	-	-	-	-	-
Plymouth,	18	3,519	108,756	188,291 00	45,108	33,831 00	11,000	4,950 00	237,800 00	399
Suffolk,	No ret'n.	No ret'n.	121,241	130,357 00	2,294	1,605 00	21,800	8,720 00	No return.	No ret'n.
Worcester,	-	-	-	-	-	-	-	-	-	-
Totals,	492	154,061	2,063,809	$3,059,018 00	6,645,684	$3,905,605 00	2,037,300	$802,373 00	$14,546,548 00	11,364

* See Note (43.)

MACKEREL AND COD FISHERIES.*

COUNTIES.	Vessels employed in the Mackerel and Cod Fisheries.	Tonnage of vessels employed in the Mackerel and Cod Fish's.	Barrels of Mackerel taken.	Quintals of Cod Fish taken.	Value of Mackerel taken.	Value of Cod Fish taken.	Value of Cod Liver Oil sold for medicinal purposes.	Bushels of Salt consumed in the Mackerel and Cod Fisheries.	Capital invested.	Hands employed.
Barnstable,	376	26,757	43,068	127,468	$373,984 00	$429,869 00	2,533 00	157,056	$995,256 00	3,619
Berkshire,	-	-	-	-	-	-	-	-	-	-
Bristol,	2	159	No ret'n.	No return.	No return.	No return.	No return.	No return.	7,500 00	20
Dukes,	-	-	-	-	-	-	-	-	-	-
Essex,	556	34,803	61,650	270,357	572,111 00	850,599 00	23,062 00	157,032	2,047,650 00	4,613
Franklin,	-	-	-	-	-	-	-	-	-	-
Hampden,	-	-	-	-	-	-	-	-	-	-
Hampshire,	-	-	-	-	-	-	-	-	-	-
Middlesex,	-	-	-	-	-	-	-	-	-	-
Nantucket,	No ret'n.	No ret'n.	-	763	-	4,228 00	-	700	1,200 00	94
Norfolk,	26	1,749	7,592	-	60,738 00	-	-	11,388	76,245 00	331
Plymouth,	96	7,368	12,555	39,792	61,499 00	128,717 00	5,300 00	53,373	308,585 00	874
Suffolk,	89	7,100	28,599	1,000	287,000 00	No return.	30,000 00	45,000	260,000 00	1,000
Worcester,	-	-	-	-	-	-	-	-	-	-
Totals,	1,145	77,936	153,464	439,380	$1,355,332 00	$1,413,413 00	$60,895 00	424,549	$3,696,436 00	10,551

* See Note (44.)

COUNTIES.	ALEWIVES, SHAD AND SALMON.*				SHEEP AND WOOL.†							
	Alewives, Shad and Salmon taken.		Value of Alewives, Shad and Salmon taken.	Hands employed	Saxony Sheep, of different grades.	Merino Sheep, of different grades.	All other kinds of Sheep.	Val. of all Sheep.	Pounds of Wool produced from Saxony Sheep.	Pounds of Merino Wool.	Pounds of all other Wool.	Val. of all Wool.‡
Barnstable,	4,956 bbls.	312,000	$11,258	77	–	–	1,477	$3,287 00	–	–	3,578	$1,323 00
Berkshire,	–	–	–	–	4,296	43,122	16,405	116,678 00	8,243	129,640	50,400	69,664 00
Bristol,		1,335,672	18,266	83	217	588	5,545	14,247 00	192	1,326	14,221	6,823 00
Dukes,		600,000	3,000	65	–	1,351	7,781	21,607 00	–	3,650	16,241	7,359 00
Essex,	300 bbls.	295,000	6,500	50	9	181	2,027	6,263 00	27	528	5,920	2,396 00
Franklin,	–	–	–	–	303	7,396	11,408	44,613 00	1,212	23,616	34,765	22,039 00
Hampden,		12,800	2,310	33	539	1,429	7,421	23,204 00	1,617	3,293	22,977	10,402 00
Hampshire,		40,000	6,000	30	1,299	11,006	9,822	44,521 00	2,950	25,063	31,845	22,147 00
Middlesex,	45,300 bbls.	375,000	15,700	52	–	37	880	2,295 00	–	–	2,362	873 00
Nantucket,		70,000	700	20	–	–	1,201	3,483 00	–	–	3,209	1,187 00
Norfolk,		100,000	252	6	6	–	270	1,001 00	–	–	881	326 00
Plymouth,	1,722 bbls.	1,662,000	9,170	69	1	–	2,986	8,153 00	–	–	8,623	3,090 00
Suffolk,	–	–	–	–	–	–	–	–	–	–	–	–
Worcester,	–	–	–	–	136	474	5,602	20,491 00	308	1,388	18,081	7,417 00
Totals,	52,278 bbls.	4,802,472	$73,156	485	6,806	65,584	72,825	$309,843 00	14,549	188,504	213,103	$155,046 00

* See Note (45.)

† See Note (46.)

‡ Estimate.

HORSES, OXEN, COWS AND CALVES.*

COUNTIES.	Horses.	Value of Horses.	Oxen over three years old.	Steers under three years old.	Value of oxen and steers.	Milch Cows.	Heifers.	Value of cows and heifers.
Barnstable, .	2,235	$174,398 00	554	546	$37,890 00	3,764	1,357	$111,177 00
Berkshire, .	6,795	543,462 00	3,755	3,436	284,098 00	18,096	5,580	549,526 00
Bristol, .	5,490	502,898 00	3,118	992	191,142 00	9,306	1,455	277,803 00
Dukes, .	367	28,295 00	347	301	25,919 00	764	278	28,249 00
Essex, .	7,099	651,472 00	5,136	2,793	305,040 00	11,799	1,345	363,035 00
Franklin, .	4,467	342,419 00	4,812	4,531	346,668 00	9,501	3,828	415,077 00
Hampden, .	4,890	404,481 00	5,602	2,687	305,168 00	9,731	3,084	301,057 00
Hampshire, .	5,029	387,438 00	3,504	3,399	267,687 00	10,062	3,974	349,247 00
Middlesex, .	12,712	1,152,953 00	5,897	1,098	341,073 00	22,563	2,388	674,079 00
Nantucket, .	346	34,665 00	62	59	4,512 00	548	205	17,928 00
Norfolk, .	7,390	769,416 00	2,079	292	131,469 00	9,995	985	327,715 00
Plymouth, .	4,896	392,110 00	2,775	1,124	174,039 00	8,004	1,513	267,798 00
Suffolk, .	5,121	780,615 00	50	1	2,860 00	519	6	15,455 00
Worcester, .	13,484	1,120,267 00	12,534	6,027	828,776 00	33,917	9,443	1,194,145 00
Totals, .	80,321	$7,284,889 00	50,225	27,286	$3,246,341 00	148,569	35,441	$4,892,291 00

* See Note (47.)

BUTTER, CHEESE AND HONEY.

COUNTIES.	Pounds of Butter.	Val. of Butter.	Pounds of Cheese	Val. of Cheese.	Pounds of Honey	Val. of Honey.
Barnstable,	194,327	$61,836 00	1,325	$87 50	- -	- -
Berkshire,	1,262,845	243,748 76	2,658,192	168,167 16	23,083	$3,242 86
Bristol,	333,853	75,550 85	79,633	8,493 34	5,477	1,168 39
Dukes,	28,382	7,112 20	3,987	493 00	- -	- -
Essex,	533,853	121,434 00	80,063	7,915 00	3,223	664 00
Franklin,	884,307	171,722 40	233,337	20,505 25	4,039	661 45
Hampden,	729,637	145,813 36	381,721	34,707 05	7,900	7,910 33
Hampshire,	931,295	184,422 01	336,015	31,757 94	5,937	970 33
Middlesex,	838,748	192,735 20	72,695	6,322 16	5,889	983 44
Nantucket,	24,152	7,155 60	- -	- -	- -	- -
Norfolk,	316,254	77,538 00	42,277	3,983 55	5,073	949,66
Plymouth,	399,878	101,725 85	82,501	9,131 53	5,046	942 04
Suffolk,	500	100 00	- -	- -	100	15 00
Worcester,	1,637,978	287,663 60	1,791,030	172,687 07	7,910	1,529 59
Totals,	8,116,009	$1,678,557 83	5,762,776	$464,250 55	73,677	$19,037 09

COUNTIES.	CORN, INDIAN AND BROOM.*								WHEAT.†		
	Acres of Indian Corn.	Bushels of Indian Corn, per acre.	Value of Indian Corn.	Acres of Broom Corn.	Pounds of Broom Brush, per acre.	Value of Broom Brush.	Bush'ls of Broom Seed, per acre.	Value of Broom Seed.	Acres of Wheat.	Bush. of Wheat, per acre.	Value of Wheat.
Barnstable,	3,524	20	$71,777 20	-	-	-	-	-	40½	13	$1,034 00
Berkshire,	9,158½	32	282,066 50	-	-	-	-	-	513½	17	14,873 00
Bristol,	7,786½	27	186,032 00	-	-	-	-	-	27	17	806 00
Dukes,	763	21	15,216 00	-	-	-	-	-	-	-	-
Essex,	5,471½	34	232,034 90	-	-	-	-	-	90	14	2,466 00
Franklin,	7,925½	32	265,739 52	1,084½	581	$48,269 50	44	$13,105 87	542	15	15,411 00
Hampden,	8,816½	25	232,158 45	44	799	2,953 30	60	610 87	115	13	2,752 69
Hampshire,	10,041	29	327,477 10	1,938½	620	136,335 20	50	40,268 00	370½	15	8,870 75
Middlesex,	11,446	29	370,086 30	-	-	-	-	-	201	13	6,225 75
Nantucket,	380	21	7,895 70	-	-	-	-	-	2½	10	37 50
Norfolk,	4,299	35	143,520 45	-	-	-	-	-	17	16	546 25
Plymouth,	5,171	27	136,649 18	-	-	-	-	-	30	17	854 00
Suffolk,	88	37	3,838 00	-	-	-	-	-	1	30	78 00
Worcester,	16,185½	30	545,617 67	2	400	80 00	-	-	650¼	15	19,973 55
Totals,	91,056	28½	$2,820,108 97	3,069	600	$187,638 00	51	$53,984 74	2,600¼	$15\frac{10}{13}$	$73,928 49

* See Note (48.)

† See Note (49.)

COUNTIES.	RYE.*			BARLEY.†			OATS.‡		
	Acres of Rye.	Bushels of Rye, per acre.	Value of same.	Acres of Barley.	Bushels of Barley, per acre.	Value of same.	Acres of Oats.	Bushels of Oats per acre.	Value of same.
Barnstable,	2,043	7	$20,049 50	138¼	14	$2,439 00	410	18	$4,744 00
Berkshire,	5,034½	14	80,424 47	442½	22	10,110 30	9,650½	30	157,221 45
Bristol,	1,612½	14	20,752 17	176	18	3,519 00	2,326	21	28,648 30
Dukes,	197	7	1,522 00	2	17	42 50	168	18	1,790 50
Essex,	1,012	16	20,258 25	824½	22	15,339 30	1,167½	24	18,489 90
Franklin,	4,427	13	52,706 27	353	19	6,181 75	3,059½	26	42,094 38
Hampden,	10,272	10	100,781 15	44	21	7,540 00	3,281	24	42,176 64
Hampshire,	7,635	11	97,755 93	137	24	4,720 53	2,866	26	42,716 55
Middlesex,	3,601¾	13	60,984 00	432½	19	8,497 00	3,194¾	24	51,700 95
Nantucket,	13	9	117 00	23	24	644 00	66	19	772 20
Norfolk,	992	16	18,522 75	365¼	19	8,058 75	581½	22	6,982 32
Plymouth,	1,227¾	11	16,438 00	120½	17	2,472 87	923	21	11,836 38
Suffolk,	108	20	2,175 00	23	23	212 00	- -	-	- -
Worcester,	3,967½	13	67,715 04	1,890	20	40,381 45	9,930	27	154,555 67
Totals,	42,143	$12\frac{6}{14}$	$560,201 53	4,971½	20	$110,158 45	37,623¼	$21\frac{1}{13}$	$563,729 24

* See Note (50.)

† See Note (51.)

‡ See Note (52.)

COUNTIES.	POTATOES.*			ONIONS.			TURNIPS.		
	Acres of Potatoes	Bushels of Potatoes, per acre.	Val. of Potatoes.	Acres of Onions.	Bushels of Onions, per acre.	Value of Onions.	Acres of Turnips.	Bushels of Turnips, per acre.	Value of Turnips
Barnstable,	915	72 1/2	$50,126 00	34 1/2	151 5/6	$4,000 00	81	149 1/2	$4,790 00
Berkshire,	3,958	110	213,182 20	18	289 4/9	1,351 60	96 1/4	276	4,005 50
Bristol,	2,955 2/3	72	156,236 95	21 5/8	352 1/5	4,170 50	228 3/4	234 1/4	13,938 32
Dukes,	102	113	10,162 00	1/4	632	106 00	28 1/2	228	2,153 00
Essex,	3,138 1/2	92 1/2	236,878 75	521 5/6	338 1/2	147,136 00	109 1/4	241 1/2	8,471 00
Franklin,	2,658 1/4	93	105,548 03	5 3/4	189 3/4	990 25	17 1/2	254 1/2	1,370 40
Hampden,	3,326	93 2/5	175,156 85	14 1/2	360 3/4	3,343 40	209 1/4	228 1/2	8,622 62
Hampshire,	3,156	101	181,717 49	8 5/6	420 5/7	2,454 50	534 1/4	200	3,298 50
Middlesex,	6,583 1/2	85 1/9	475,537 15	42 3/4	260 2/3	7,486 10	405 1/2	313 1/2	29,596 47
Nantucket,	72	108	7,776 00	5	187	516 00	51	152	3,100 40
Norfolk,	2,644	106 1/2	214,690 90	62 5/6	241 1/2	6,490 00	210 1/2	264 1/2	14,523 25
Plymouth,	2,935 1/2	79	143,038 88	9	313 7/10	2,066 30	102 1/2	243 2/3	8,736 60
Suffolk,	99	90	8,202 00	1/2	-	- -	21	200	1,120 00
Worcester,	9,439 1/2	96 1/2	543,653 22	24 1/2	332 1/5	7,336 40	172	246 1/2	12,625 00
Totals,	41,982 11/12	93 5/7	$2,521,906 42	769 7/8	313	$187,446 45	2,267 1/4	231	$116,351 06

* See Note (53.)

COUNTIES.	CARROTS.			BEETS AND OTHER ESCULENT VEGETABLES.				MILLET.	
	Acres of Carrots.	Bushels of Carrots, per acre.	Value of Carrots.	Acres of Beets and other Esculent Vegetables.	Value of same.	Acres cultivated in all other Grain or Root Crops.	Value of same.	Acres of Millet.	Value of Millet.
Barnstable,	36	220½	$2,110 50	62½	$2,840 00	21	$700 00	-	- -
Berkshire, . .	45½	515	5,179 53	18⅛	1,228 75	5,081	31,738 25	-	- -
Bristol, . .	14⅜	369	1,021 40	208¼	20,560 00	241	14,507 50	107¾	$1,699 00
Dukes, . .	2	350	210 00	- -	- -	- -	- -	-	- -
Essex, . .	448¼	451	18,861 55	375½	45,278 50	2,484	55,691 75	10	324 00
Franklin, . .	32	516	4,463 66	½	30 00	98	1,566 50	4¾	92 00
Hampden, . .	39¼	400	4,745 33	151¼	21,384 00	1,184¼	16,561 00	31¾	365 00*
Hampshire, .	21½	616	3,338 11	43	1,300 00	348	3,342 00	14	175 00
Middlesex, .	260½	438	37,077 36	1,913¾	275,829 00	807	103,656 00	72½	1,292 00
Nantucket, .	17	331½	1,690 65	95	9,535 00	- -	- -	-	- -
Norfolk, . .	246	427	23,793 87	402½	45,568 00	138	6,581 00	27	571 00
Plymouth, . .	58¾	373½	7,849 31	127¼	11,021 00	96½	7,569 00	2	28 00
Suffolk, . .	18	500	2,880 00	63	3,987 50	- -	- -	-	- -
Worcester, .	240¾	473	34,819 95	393	46,006 50	712¾	44,286 75	33½	963 00
Totals, .	1,479⅞	427⅐	$148,041 22	3,853⅝	$484,568 25	11,211½	$286,202 75	303¼	$5,509 00

* Value of three-fourths of an acre of Millet, in Southwick, omitted in the returns.

HAY.*

COUNTIES.	Acres of English Mowing.	Tons of English Hay.	Value of English Hay.	Tons of Wet Meadow or Swale Hay.	Value of Wet Meadow or Swale Hay.	Tons of Salt Hay.	Value of Salt Hay.
Barnstable,	4,391	5,526	$87,266 00	937	$11,865 00	7,370	$51,037 00
Berkshire,	76,962	75,948	752,960 00	5,242	30,838 00	-	-
Bristol,	34,597	28,234½	509,566 00	6,124¼	57,238 00	1,645½	12,040 00
Dukes,	1,539	1,810	26,957 00	612	5,051 00	399	3,459 00
Essex,	33,565	36,393¾	654,432 00	10,124½	83,904 00	11,422	107,683 00
Franklin,	43,049	41,392	475,303 00	7,957	53,413 00	-	-
Hampden,	29,720	35,947	425,416 00	9,977	63,380 00	-	-
Hampshire,	41,270	38,700½	489,403 00	9,496	66,441 00	-	-
Middlesex,	61,452¾	61,578¾	1,207,438 00	25,990½	251,220 00	2,356½	25,294 00
Nantucket,	1,425	2,463	39,328 00	179	1,790 00	209	1,463 00
Norfolk,	30,042	28,444	568,592 00	11,732	104,171 00	2,445	27,392 00
Plymouth,	22,610¾	19,948¼	355,985 00	8,391	68,379 00	5,088	40,480 00
Suffolk,	740	1,039	23,702 00	-	-	1,180	16,720 00
Worcester,	117,116¾	109,919¾	1,715,658 00	32,389	257,053 00	-	-
Totals,	498,480¼	487,344½	$7,362,006 00	129,151¼	$1,054,743 00	32,115	$285,568 00

* See Note (53.)

COUNTIES.	APPLE AND PEAR TREES, CHERRIES, NUTS, BERRIES, &c.*					HOPS.†			TOBACCO.	
	Apple Trees cultivated for their fruit.	Value of Apples.	Pear Trees cultivated for their fruit.	Value of Pears.	Value of Cherries, Nuts, Berries and all fruit not otherwise enumerated.	Number of acres of hops.	Pounds of hops, per acre.	Value of Hops.	Acres of Tobacco.	Value of Tobacco.
Barnstable,	25,939	$10,080 00	2,124	$803 00	-	-	-	-	-	-
Berkshire,	121,275	56,118 24	4,223	4,440 00	-	3	600	$324 00	2	$250 00
Bristol,	157,161	53,260 00	22,168	3,737 00	$500 00	-	-	-	-	-
Dukes,	7,733	1,521 00	118	100 00	-	-	-	-	-	-
Essex,	239,127	166,905 65	27,023	12,227 45	16,952 00	No ret'n.	No ret'n.	80	-	-
Franklin,	66,009	40,929 90	953	1,080 00	1,301 00	54	778½	10,302 50	93½	12,403 00
Hampden,	148,694	48,702 00	2,700	1,623 00	1,637 32	-	-	-	170½	21,220 74
Hampshire,	78,892	40,392 50	2,073	1,202 00	470 00	3	2,400	480 00	155	23,600 00
Middlesex,	351,586	297,395 24	42,684	24,352 00	38,502 00	112	604$\frac{3}{7}$	21,625 00	-	-
Nantucket,	-	-	6	40 00	489 00	-	-	-	-	-
Norfolk,	175,723	101,667 00	41,941	23,416 00	18,650 50	No ret'n.	No ret'n.	10 00	-	-
Plymouth,	194,521	62,069 35	15,572	3,471 76	3,744 00	-	-	-	-	-
Suffolk,	4,500	5,818 00	1,020	2,830 00	-	-	-	-	-	-
Worcester,	465,740	236,402 92	22,787	8,822 00	23,590 00	93¾	587	14,719 36	-	-
Totals,	2,236,900	$1,121,261 80	185,392	$88,144 21	$105,835 82	265¾	655½	$47,461 66	421	$57,473 74

* See Note (54.)

† See Note (55.)

COUNTIES.	CRANBERRIES.*		BEESWAX.		CASKS.				
	Acres of Cranberries.	Value of Cranberries.	Pounds of Beeswax.	Value of Beeswax.	Establishments for the manufacture of Casks	Capital invested.	Casks manufactured.	Value of Casks.	Hands employed.
Barnstable,	197	$16,916 00	-	-	3	$5,300 00	5,600	$7,158 00	7
Berkshire,	-	-	509½	$153 12	21	8,825 00	111,690	25,958 00	52
Bristol,	380	12,282 00	165	60 22	33	83,297 00	454,025	234,385 00	208
Dukes,	14	1,297 00	-	-	2	1,750 00	2,000	2,450 00	3
Essex,	370	8,488 00	39	14 63	43	42,300 00	164,657	76,267 00	105
Franklin,	9⅛	505 00	99½	35 49	1	800 00	400	500 00	1
Hampden,	13½	439 00	169	61 67	7	260 00	3,700	1,200 00	7
Hampshire,	5	40 00	209	78 00	2	300 00	Not returned.	800 00	3
Middlesex,	2,554⅝	29,274 00	87	34 74	25	25,750 00	401,560	114,358 00	161
Nantucket,	19¾	1,140 00	-	-	9	11,500 00	20,250	25,312 00	26
Norfolk,	897	30,000 00	543	269 00	3	6,000 00	166,000	77,000 00	33
Plymouth,	361½	12,098 85	350	168 80	13	14,210 00	317,150	65,086 00	54
Suffolk,	-	-	-	-	17	50,200 00	158,000	168,000 00	148
Worcester,	641¼	22,720 00	153½	67 10	14	7,455 00	41,400	3,900 00	20
Totals,	5,462¾	$135,199 85	2,324½	$942 77	193	$257,947 00	1,846,432	$802,374 00	828

* (See Note (56.)

COUNTIES.	FRINGE AND TASSELS.					STONE AND EARTHENWARE.			
	Establishments for the manufacture of Fringe and Tassels.	Capital invested.	Value of Fringe and Tassels manufactured.	Males employed.	Females empl'y'd	Establishments for the manufacture of stone and earthenware.	Capital invested.	Value of Stone and Earthenware manufactured.	Hands employed.
Barnstable,	-	-	-	-	-	-	-	-	-
Berkshire,	-	-	-	-	-	-	-	-	-
Bristol,	-	-	-	-	-	5	$17,000 00	$28,200 00	21
Dukes,	-	-	-	-	-	-	-	-	-
Essex,	-	-	-	-	-	3	250 00	3,300 00	4
Franklin,	-	-	-	-	-	2	4,500 00	12,950 00	11
Hampden,	-	-	-	-	-	-	-	-	-
Hampshire,	-	-	-	-	-	-	-	-	-
Middlesex,	1	$4,000 00	$6,000 00	8	6	4	14,500 00	40,000 00	33
Nantucket,	-	-	-	-	-	-	-	-	-
Norfolk,	2	53,000 00	362,000 00	66	56	-	-	-	-
Plymouth,	2	9,500 00	65,000 00	41	114	-	-	-	-
Suffolk,	-	-	-	-	-	1	15,000 00	20,000 00	29
Worcester,	-	-	-	-	-	2	10,000 00	21,000 00	20
Totals,	5	$66,500 00	$433,000 00	115	176	17	$61,250 00	$125,450 00	118

COUNTIES.	SASHES, DOORS AND BLINDS.				GAS.				PICKLES AND PRESERVES.			
	Establishments for the manufacture of Sashes Doors & Blinds.	Capital invested.	Value manufactured.	Hands employed.	Establishments for the manufacture of Gas.	Capital invested.	Value of Gas manufactured.	Hands employed.	Establishments for the manufacture of Preserves and Pickles.	Capital invested.	Value when manufactured.	Hands employed.
Barnstable, . .	3	$2,500 00	$5,652 00	8	1	$800	-	-	-	-	-	-
Berkshire, . .	6	10,100 00	20,000 00	19	2	35,000	$15,350 00	4	-	-	-	-
Bristol. . .	6	17,000 00	40,450 00	41	3	200,000	141,059 95	21	-	-	-	-
Dukes, . .	-	-	-	-	-	-	-	-	-	-	-	-
Essex, . .	14	40,600 00	98,919 46	87	9	455,100	92,718 26	34	-	-	-	-
Franklin, . .	7	12,100 00	28,650 00	32	-	-	-	-	-	-	-	-
Hampden, . .	4	30,500 00	107,500 00	107	2	87,000	†30,074 26	8	-	-	-	-
Hampshire, .	3	18,800 00	49,500 00	20	1	28,000	1,200 00	1	-	-	-	-
Middlesex, .	21	111,500 00	358,913 00	235	4	430,000	115,000 00	37	3	$80,000	$201,000	60
Nantucket. .	-	-	-	-	1	40,000	14,600 00	4	-	-	-	-
Norfolk, . .	5	12,200 00	39,700 00	31	4	206,000	33,000 00	12	1	800	2,000	2
Plymouth, . .	2	5,000 00	5,000 00	13	1	40,000	Just commenced.	4	-	-	-	-
Suffolk, . .	7	12,800 00	44,500 00	33	4	1,041,000	445,000 00	176	3	65,000	130,000	87
Worcester, .	31	55,880 00	138,175 00	148	5	171,000	44,330 00	17	4	5,500	13,858	36
Totals, .	109	$328,980 00*	$936,959 46	774	37	$2,733,900	$932,332 47	318	11	$151,300	$346,858	185

* Amount of capital in S. Danvers, Shirley and Westborough, is not returned.

† Value of Coke, $107.88.

COUNTIES.	DISTILLERIES.						BREWERIES.				
	Distilleries.	Capital invested.	Barrels of Alcohol Distilled.	Barrels of all other Liquors Distilled.	Value of all Liquors Distilled.	Hands employed.	Breweries.	Capital invested.	Barrels of Beer manufactured.	Value of Beer manufactured.	Hands employed.
Barnstable,	-	-	-	-	-	-	-	-	-	-	-
Berkshire,	2	$2,100	900	102	$13,600	5	-	-	-	-	-
Bristol,	-	-	-	-	-	-	1	-	1,000	$3,500 00	3
Dukes,	-	-	-	-	-	-	-	-	-	-	-
Essex,	3	23,000	-	4,837	57,204	9	4	$3,400	305	7,469 60	9
Franklin,	1	500	-	40	1,024	1	-	-	-	-	-
Hampden,	8*	1,350	-	76½	2,000	5	1	250	170	841 50	2
Hampshire,	2	-	-	-	-	-	-	-	-	-	-
Middlesex,	2	28,000	-	1,200	135,000	6	6	16,100	9,400	47,300 00	23
Nantucket,	-	-	-	-	-	-	-	-	-	-	-
Norfolk,	1	60,000	20,000	-	450,000	14	3	25,000	7,800	50,000 00	18
Plymouth,	-	-	-	-	-	-	1	225	100	520 00	2
Suffolk,	9	850,000	55,612	79,397	2,495,000	107	7	67,600	47,800	238,408 00	56
Worcester,	-	-	-	-	-	-	4	8,400	2,950	7,800 00	20
Totals,	28	$964,950	76,512	85,652½	$3,153,828	147	27	$120,975	69,525	$355,839 10	133

* Two in Blandford are unemployed.

COUNTIES.	FRICTION MATCHES.					INDIA RUBBER GOODS.				
	Establishments for the manufacture of Friction Matches.	Capital invested.	Gross of Matches manufactured.	Value of Matches manufactured.	Hands employed.	Establishments for the manufacture of India Rubber Goods.	Capital invested.	Value of Goods manufactured.	Males employed.	Females employ'd.
Barnstable,	-	-	-	-	-	-	-	-	-	-
Berkshire,	-	-	-	-	-	-	-	-	-	-
Bristol,	-	-	-	-	-	-	-	-	-	-
Dukes,	-	-	-	-	-	-	-	-	-	-
Essex,	-	-	-	-	-	1	$60,000 00	$125,000 00	16	33
Franklin,	2	$2,900 00	56,000	$6,200 00	8	-	-	-	-	-
Hampden,	-	-	-	-	-	1	8,000 00	18,000 00	5	18
Hampshire,	1	400 00	25,000	1,250 00	2	1	110,000 00	150,000 00	60	70
Middlesex,	-	-	-	-	-	1	100,000 00	225,000 00	65	75
Nantucket,	-	-	-	-	-	-	-	-	-	-
Norfolk,	-	-	-	-	-	1	160,000 00	450,000 00	110	10
Plymouth,	-	-	-	-	-	-	-	-	-	-
Suffolk,	1	10,000 00	110,000	50,000 00	60	-	-	-	-	-
Worcester,	3	19,500 00	109,000	38,300 00	80	-	-	-	-	-
Totals,	7	$32,800 00	300,000	$95,750 00	150	5	$438,000 00	$968,000 00	256	206

COUNTIES.	BAKERIES.					TYPE AND STEREOTYPE FOUNDERIES.				
	Bakeries.	Capital Invested.	Barrels of Flour consumed.	Value of Bread manufactured.	Hands employed.	Type and Stereotype Founderies.	Capital invested.	Value of Type, &c., manufactured.	Males employed.	Females employ'd.
Barnstable,	2	$2,700 00	800	$11,100 00	5	-	-	-	-	-
Berkshire,	4	9,750 00	3,175	33,522 50	20	-	-	-	-	-
Bristol,	19	63,500 00	22,687	319,507 00	102	-	-	-	-	-
Dukes,	1	600 00	300	6,000 00	3	-	-	-	-	-
Essex,	47	162,100 00	41,666	622,000 00	215	1	$2,000 00	$4,500 00	3	-
Franklin,	1	2,000 00	500	6,000 00	5	-	-	-	-	-
Hampden,	1	3,100 00	1,000	20,000 00	12	1	300 00	1,200 00	1	-
Hampshire,	1	3,000 00	1,200	18,000 00	8	1	1,000 00	1,200 00	2	1
Middlesex,	38	120,900 00	53,745	921,770 00	262	2	17,000 00	71,000 00	95	-
Nantucket,	2	1,100 00	1,200	14,600 00	6	-	-	-	-	-
Norfolk,	23	84,400 00	24,550	390,600 00	146	-	-	-	-	-
Plymouth,	5	16,550 00	2,676	47,400 00	31	-	-	-	-	-
Suffolk,	53	131,700 00	64,519	965,810 00	230	6	96,000 00	230,000 00	160	54
Worcester,	16	38,600 00	15,972	222,300 00	92	1	500 00	1,200 00	2	-
Totals,	213	$640,000 00	233,990	$3,592,609 50	1,137	12	$116,800 00	$309,100 00	263	55

COUNTIES.	BOXES.				CONFECTIONERY.				MAPLE SUGAR.†	
	Establishments for the manufacture of Boxes	Capital invested.	Value of Boxes manufactured.	Hands employed.	Number of Establishments for the manufacture of Confectionery.	Value of Confectionery manufactured.	Capital invested.	Hands employed.	Pounds of Maple Sugar manufactured.	Value of the same
Barnstable,	-	-	-	-	-	-	-	-	-	-
Berkshire,	10	$14,000 00	$11,791 00	21	-	-	-	-	102,465	$8,481 30
Bristol,	13	30,825 00	80,300 00	54	-	-	-	-	-	-
Dukes,	-	-	-	-	-	-	-	-	-	-
Essex,	12	48,900 00	117,290 00	67	4	$46,076 00	$6,000 00	20	-	-
Franklin,	10	5,200 00	13,180 00	22	2	7,000 00	2,800 00	5	123,056	11,477 12
Hampden,	3	10,600 00	26,000 00	13	1	75,000 00	8,000 00	40	233,000	26,700 00
Hampshire,	8	2,850 00	8,775 00	15	-	-	-	-	61,920	5,635 00
Middlesex,	24	109,200 00	237,616 00	118	2	110,000 00	30,000 00	-	-	-
Nantucket,	2	640 00	1,170 00	3	-	-	-	-	-	-
Norfolk,	21	42,550 00	114,991 83	98	2	36,000 00	5,500 00	-	-	-
Plymouth,	33	88,350 00	116,248 00	127	1*	4,500 00	-	-	-	-
Suffolk,	9	17,400 00	72,000 00	71	-	-	-	-	-	-
Worcester,	54	68,610 00	198,422 00	183	-	-	-	-	-	-
Totals,	199	$439,125 00	$997,783 83	792	12	$278,576 00	$52,300 00	65	520,441	$52,293 42

* Manufacture fifteen tons.

† See Note, (57.)

COUNTIES.	PORT MONNAIES, POCKET BOOKS & WALLETS.*				CLOTHING & TAILORING ESTAB'MTS.			SWINE.	
	Number of dozens manufactured.	Value.	Capital invested.	Hands employed.	Value.	Capital invested.	Hands employed.	Number of Swine	Value of Swine.
Barnstable,	-	-	-	-	-	-	-	1,378	$16,386 00
Berkshire,	-	-	-	-	-	-	-	3,324	29,763 10
Bristol,	-	-	-	-	$37,000 00	$8,000 00	18	6,153	60,425 00
Dukes,	-	-	-	-	-	-	-	146	1,460 00
Essex,	-	-	-	-	16,600 00	-	-	3,369	54,209 50
Franklin,	81,400	$207,300 00	$23,000 00	226	4,000 00	-	38	4,100	41,133 00
Hampden,	-	-	-	-	183,600 00	58,250 00	380	3,138	25,525 00
Hampshire,	-	-	-	-	37,750 00	6,000 00	75	2,051	14,035 00
Middlesex,	-	-	-	-	91,900 00	175,850 00	989	4,874	62,134 00
Nantucket,	-	-	-	-	-	-	-	541	10,112 00
Norfolk,	-	-	-	-	$30,000 00	$5,000 00	13	6,763	89,230 11
Plymouth,	-	3,000 00	1,500 00	5	107,046 00	-	245	4,253	57,113 00
Suffolk,	-	6,000 00	2,000 00	4	8,500,000 00	2,500,000 00	No ret'n.	-	-
Worcester,	2,250	46,400 00	10,500 00	64	54,000 00	17,500 00	-	11,023	120,011 00
Totals,	83,650	$262,700 00	$37,000 00	299	$9,061,896 00	$2,770,600 00	1,758	51,113	$581,536 71

* See Note (58.)

COUNTIES.	MILK.		POULTRY AND EGGS.	ICE BUSINESS.			
	Number of quarts of Milk.	Value of Milk.	Value of Poultry and Eggs.	Tons prepared for market.	Value of Ice.	Capital invested.	Hands employed.
Barnstable,	- -	- -	$22,106 00	- -	- -	- -	-
Berkshire,	- -	$1,215 00	2,611 00	- -	- -	- -	-
Bristol,	619,034	24,356 36	3,575 50	16,200	$10,000 00	$16,000 00	10
Dukes,	- -	- -	- -	- -	- -	- -	-
Essex,	1,811,936	94,591 93	- -	13,900	76,200 00	25,000 00	65
Franklin,	- -	- -	2,576 70	- -	- -	- -	-
Hampden,	393,283	17,735 00	2,154 33	- -	- -	- -	-
Hampshire,	- -	- -	5,615 00	- -	- -	- -	-
Middlesex,	4,309,084	348,938 80	1,200 00	366,200	550,400 00	660,700 00	362
Nantucket,	- -	- -	- -	- -	- -	- -	-
Norfolk,	2,584,404	94,225 70	- -	- -	- -	- -	-
Plymouth,	121,240	9,486 00	6,912 00	800	2,500 00	- -	-
Suffolk,	476,220	32,263 75	- -	- -	- -	- -	-
Worcester,	2,888,464	133,075 36	5,938 00	- -	- -	- -	-
Totals,	13,203,665	$755,887 90	$52,688 53*	387,100	$639,100 00	$701,700 00	437

* No value returned from Adams and Hanover.

PRINTING.

COUNTIES.	Value of all Printing done during the year.	The various kinds of Printing done.	Number of Daily Newspapers published.	Number of Weekly Papers published.	Number of Tri-weekly, Semi-weekly, Bi-weekly, Monthly, Bi-monthly, Quarterly and Yearly Publications.	Capital invested.	Males employed.	Females employ'd.
Barnstable,	$4,625 00	Book, Job and Newspaper.	–	3	– –	$3,650 00	11	1
Berkshire,	10,788 00	Newspaper, Job, &c.	–	6	– –	6,800 00	16	2
Bristol,	14,000 00	Books, Pamphlets, Newspapers, &c.	3	7	– –	16,500 00	28	–
Dukes,	2,585 00	Job and Newspaper.	–	1	– –	1,200 00	3	–
Essex,	70,970 00	Book, Job and Newspaper.	2	15	5	59,050 00	113	16
Franklin,	10,700 00	Book, Job, and Newspaper.	–	3	– –	9,000 00	13	4
Hampden,	54,100 00	Book, Card, Newspaper, &c.	3	8	– –	26,500 00	57	6
Hampshire,	9,000 00	Book, Job and Newspaper.	–	3	– –	9,700 00	15	–
Middlesex,	271,026 00	Book, Pamphlet, Newspaper, Plain and Ornamental Job.	4	10	4	100,600 00	96	34
Nantucket,	4,500 00	Newspaper and Job.	–	2	1	2,500 00	7	–
Norfolk,	5,000 00	Book, Job and Newspaper.	–	3	–	3,000 00	6	–
Plymouth,	17,700 00	Book, Pamphlet, Newspaper and Job, of all kinds.	–	8	– –	11,400 00	30	1
Suffolk,	807,280 00	Book, Card, Magazine, Wood-cut, Copper-Plate, Lithograph, Fancy Job, Newsp'r &c.	13	59	60	442,450 00	484	74
Worcester,	69,044 00	Book, Card, Job, Newspaper, &c.	2	11	8	57,200 00	92	25
Totals,	$1,351,318		27	139	78	$749,550 00	971	163

COUNTIES.	BOOKBINDING.					MISCELLANEOUS ARTICLES NOT ELSEWHERE ENUMERATED IN TABULAR FORM.		
	Number of Books bound during the year.	Value of Book-binding done.	Capital Invested.	Males employed.	Females employ'd	Value of Grave-stones Wheel-wright Stock, Baskets, Carpenters' Tools, Umbrellas, & a variety of other articles not elsewhere enumerated.	Capital Invested.	Hands employed.
Barnstable, . .	- -	- -	- -	-	-	$26,660 00	$227,832 00	32
Berkshire, .	5,000	$3,000 00	$1,300 00	4	2	198,237 00	56,625 00	149
Bristol, . .	3,000	13,250 00	1,450 00	6	-	798,216 00	232,550 00	518
Dukes, . .	- -	- -	- -	-	-	7,090 00	- -	9
Essex, . .	36,500	10,000 00	2,150 00	11	8	1,505,119 00	688,400 00	967
Franklin, . .	Not returned.	6,000 00	2,500 00	5	3	179,469 90	71,000 00	286
Hampden, .	8,000	5,500 00	2,000 00	5	4	364,763 00	63,675 00	231
Hampshire, .	10,000	6,000 00	3,000 00	5	3	194,579 00	59,700 00	191
Middlesex, .	142,706	23,734 00	5,850 00	17	22	1,614,770 92	562,675 00	1,155
Nantucket, .	- -	- -	- -	-	-	12,582 00	- -	-
Norfolk, . .	- -	- -	- -	-	-	1,777,037 00	334,600 00	716
Plymouth, . .	- -	- -	- -	-	-	198,991 63	73,290 00	234
Suffolk, . .	496,888	78,500 00	29,200 00	73	130	3,315,100 00	993,300 00	1,426
Worcester, .	158,147	1,306 00	4,750 00	12	14	1,564,141 50	438,700 00	2,187
Totals, . .	860,241	$147,290 00	$52,200 00	138	186	$11,756,756 95	$3,802,347 00	8,101

SUMMARY

Of the preceding Tables, showing the value of the articles manufactured or produced in the Commonwealth, the amount of capital invested, and the number of hands employed, with a comparative summary of the returns of 1845.

ARTICLES.	1855. Value.	1855. Capital invested.	1855. Hands employed.	1845. Value.	1845. Capital invested.	1845. Hands employed.
Cotton Goods of all kinds,	$26,140,538 32	$31,961,000	34,787	$12,193,449	$17,739,000	20,710
Calico,	5,213,000 00	1,980,000	1,157	4,779,817	1,401,500	2,053
Goods Bleached and Colored,	5,111,200 00	659,000	644	2,264,700	200,500	325
Woollen Goods of all kinds,	12,105,514 34	7,305,500	10,090	8,877,478	5,604,002	7,372
Carpeting,	1,362,819 00	2,264,172	1,614	834,322	488,000	1,034
Worsted,	1,448,740 00	1,236,000	1,062	654,566	514,000	846
Hosiery and Yarn,	207,160 00	69,980	256	94,892	42,500	238
Linen,	1,440,000 00	550,000	910	145,000	79,000	192
Silk,	300,000 00	55,000	138	150,477	38,000	156
Rolled and Slit Iron and Nails,	5,512,816 00	2,342,825	3,025	2,738,300	1,906,400	1,729
Anchors, Chain Cables, &c.,	915,980 00	739,600	547	538,966	377,685	422
Pig Iron,	641,540 00	567,400	323	148,761	155,000	235

Hollow Ware and Castings other than Pig Iron,	3,256,538 00	1,613,600	2,276	1,280,141	713,270	1,267
Machinery, ...	4,089,590 00	2,484,000	3,740	2,022,648	1,103,850	2,421
Steam Engines and Boilers, ...	3,255,000 00	2,099,500	2,638	208,546	127,000	221
Fire Engines, ...	50,000 00	- -	45	37,800	- -	42
Scythes, ...	120,532 00	66,000	144	113,935	69,590	171
Axes, Hatchets and other Edge Tools, . .	626,654 00	409,860	484	94,441	48,225	94
Cutlery, ...	573,625 00	398,200	705	148,175	68,725	197
Screws, ...	180,000 00	120,000	230	- -	- -	-
Butts or Hinges, ...	22,000 00	15,000	38	25,390	3,500	49
Door Handles and Latches, ...	39,100 00	12,000	29	3,200	750	10
Locks, ...	66,700 00	24,500	84	60,070	23,600	75
Tacks and Brads, ...	621,212 00	278,950	370	253,687	123,225	269
Shovels, Spades, Forks and Hoes, . .	894,515 00	408,075	681	275,212	123,950	259
Ploughs and other Agricultural Implements, .	763,980 86	189,300	433	121,691	58,575	158
Iron Railing, Fences and Safes, ...	656,400 00	239,600	371	129,300	53,000	87
Copper, ...	1,685,500 00	626,300	320	610,950	329,000	197
Brass Articles, ...	1,504,050 00	515,300	540	331,890	167,600	145

SUMMARY—Continued.

ARTICLES.	1855. Value.	1855. Capital invested.	1855. Hands employed.	1845. Value.	1845. Capital invested.	1845. Hands employed.
Britannia Ware,	$302,000 00	$158,000	332	$102,550	$49,350	93
Buttons,	267,120 00	172,500	229	56,080	51,500	60
Glass,	2,648,125 00	1,805,500	1,887	758,300	700,200	630
Starch,	195,800 00	161,000	48	119,950	37,500	39
Chemical Preparations,	1,124,765 00	1,095,600	340	331,965	251,700	113
Paper,	4,141,847 00	2,564,500	2,630	1,750,273	1,144,537	1,369
Musical Instruments,	2,295,680 00	1,280,700	1,765	548,625	293,100	427
Clocks,	100,000 00*	17,000	26	54,975	10,350	40
Sewing Machines,	300,000 00*	97,000	184	– –	– –	–
Daguerreotypes,	605,439 00*	139,875	260	– –	– –	–
Chronometers, Watches, Gold and Silver Ware and Jewelry,	2,105,200 00	720,500	1,263	305,623	126,225	293
Brushes,	484,500 00	267,600	429	153,900	68,875	220
Saddles, Harnesses and Trunks,	1,220,049 00	327,807	966	422,794	144,540	648

Upholstery,	1,876,800 00	554,250	600	354,261	124,700	275
Hats and Caps,	1,926,105 00*	350,373	1,042	734,942	213,793	1,003
Cordage,	2,478,410 00*	636,400	1,000	906,321	543,930	647
Boats,	130,161 00*	58,550	212	82,943	- -	164
Vessels,	4,643,450 00*	1,940,700	3,592	1,172,147	- -	1,017
Masts and Spars,	247,638 12*	199,900	167	- -	- -	-
Sails,	921,299 79	168,050	519	- -	- -	-
Cards,	440,240 00	196,600	154	323,845	171,500	147
Salt,	350,971 00	187,324	261	79,980	399,285	584
Railroad Cars, Coaches and other Vehicles,	2,352,955 00	949,770	2,491	1,343,576	553,434	1,881
Lead,	340,000 00	165,000	68	90,880	72,700	50
Sugar Refined,	2,056,430 00	- -	315	940,000	410,000	106
Sperm Candles and Oil,	6,813,291 38	3,282,013	412	3,613,796	2,451,917	306
Soap and Tallow Candles,	7,720,533 58	1,582,500	445	836,156	405,872	343
Powder,	228,125 00	54,000	54	165,500	120,000	49
Fire-Arms,	391,475 00	132,500	282	260,819	62,848	357

* Estimate.

SUMMARY—Continued.

ARTICLES.	1855. Value.	1855. Capital invested.	1855. Hands employed.	1845. Value.	1845. Capital invested.	1845. Hands employed.
Cannon,	$54,151 00	$50,000	40	$82,000	$120,000	48
Chocolate,	197,013 00*	103,000	57	81,672	47,500	27
Chairs and Cabinet Ware,	3,969,982 00	1,913,615	4,243	1,476,679	477,374	2,594
Tin Ware,	1,451,240 00	570,975	1,131	793,624	343,710	719
White Lead and other Paints,	910,190 00	171,000	71	356,200	253,500	106
Combs,	557,422 00	271,060	611	198,965	73,100	340
Linseed Oil,	890,000 00	600,000	93	181,100	77,000	34
Camphene and Burning Fluid,	462,600 00*	135,500	33	- -	- -	-
Glue and Gum,	532,650 00	124,450	138	387,575	283,675	93
Cotton Gins,	99,000 00	114,000	100	45,444	75,000	48
Flour,	2,040,040 00	607,450	173	174,805	44,550	30
Leather, tanned and curried,	10,934,416 00	4,152,426	3,143	3,836,657	1,900,545	2,043
Patent and Enamelled Leather,	1,271,942 00	227,700	400	- -	- -	-

Boots and Shoes,	37,489,923 00	No return.	74,326	14,799,140	– –	45,877
Straw Bonnets, Hats, and Braid,	4,905,553 00*	– –	14,511	1,649,496	– –	13,311
Bricks,	2,627,165 00	– –	1,109	612,832	– –	1,407
Mathematical Instruments,	204,850 00	– –	76	54,050	– –	68
Snuff, Tobacco and Cigars,	988,790 00	– –	775	324,639	– –	572
Building Stone,	1,585,213 00	– –	2,205	1,065,599	– –	1,849
Marble,	561,650 00	– –	455	220,004	– –	312
Lime,	94,907 00	– –	110	43,629	– –	80
Mineral Coal and Iron Ore,	111,475 00	– –	225	21,669	– –	78
Charcoal,	237,469 08	– –	689	– –	– –	–
Whips,	505,500 00	– –	367	111,947	– –	526
Blacking,	75,800 00	– –	60	10,422	– –	35
Blocks and Pumps,	314,510 00	– –	296	127,249	– –	204
Mechanics' Tools,	1,142,614 00	– –	1,048	161,899	– –	256
Wooden Ware,	745,711 00	– –	610	416,366	– –	806
Corn and other Brooms,	323,135 00	– –	260	200,814	– –	313

* Estimate.

SUMMARY—Continued.

ARTICLES.	1855. Value.	1855. Capital invested.	1855. Hands employed.	1845. Value.	1845. Capital invested.	1845. Hands employed.
Gold Pens,	$64,885 00*	$28,500	31	- -	- -	-
Lasts and Shoe Pegs,	192,350 00	- -	-	$98,351	- -	84
Lumber,	3,664,462 56	- -	3,413	921,106	- -	2,506
Firewood,	2,960,915 00	- -	5,325	1,088,656	- -	2,925
Whale Oil and Bone,	7,766,996 00	14,546,548	11,364	10,371,167	$11,805,910	11,378
Mackerel and Cod,	2,829,640 00	3,696,436	10,551	1,484,137	1,238,640	7,866
Alewives, Shad and Salmon,	73,156 00	- -	485	- -	- -	-
Sheep and Wool,	464,889 00	- -	-	923,420	- -	-
Horses, Oxen, Cows and Calves,	15,423,521 00	- -	-	8,778,317	- -	-
Butter, Cheese and Honey,	2,161,845 47	- -	-	1,528,089	- -	-
Corn, Indian and Broom,	3,061,731 71	- -	-	1,438,788	- -	-
Wheat,	73,928 49	- -	-	54,502	- -	-
Rye,	560,201 53	- -	-	328,033	- -	-

Barley,	110,158 45	– –	–	72,261	– –	–
Oats,	563,729 24	– –	–	405,657	– –	–
Potatoes,	2,521,906 42	– –	–	1,309,030	– –	–
Onions,	187,446 45					
Turnips,	116,351 06					
Carrots,	148,041 22	– –	–	530,181	– –	–
Beets,	484,568 25					
Other Grain and Root Crops,	286,202 75					
Millet,	5,509 00	– –	–	8,476	– –	–
Hay,	8,702,317 00	– –	–	5,214,357	– –	–
Apples, Pears, &c.,	1,315,241 83	– –	–	755,382	– –	–
Hops,	47,461 66	– –	–	32,251	– –	–
Tobacco,	57,473 74	– –	–	16,686	– –	–
Cranberries,	135,199 85	– –	–	– –	– –	–
Beeswax,	942 77	– –	–	981	– –	–
Casks,	802,374 00	257,947	828	269,935	– –	487

* Estimate.

SUMMARY—Continued.

ARTICLES.	1855.			1845.		
	Value.	Capital invested.	Hands employed.	Value.	Capital invested.	Hands employed.
Fringe and Tassels,	$433,000 00	$66,500	291	$54,300	$11,700	106
Stone and Earthen Ware,	125,450 00	61,250	118	52,025	15,500	72
Sashes, Doors and Blinds,	936,959 46	328,980	774	180,181	– –	215
Gas,	932,332 47	2,733,900	318	– –	– –	–
Pickles and Preserves,	346,858 00	151,300	185	– –	– –	–
Alcohol and other Distilled Liquors,	3,153,828 00	964,950	147	– –	– –	–
Beer,	355,839 10	120,975	133	Included in	gen'al summary	in 1845.
Friction Matches,	95,750 00	32,800	150	– –	– –	–
India Rubber Goods,	968,000 00	438,000	462	– –	– –	
Bread,	3,592,609 50	640,000	1,137	Included in	gen'al summary,	in 1845.
Types and Stereotype Plates,	309,100 00	116,800	318	" "	" "	"
Boxes of all kinds,	997,783 83	439,125	792	215,105	– –	235
Confectionery,	278,576 00	52,300	65	– –	– –	–

Maple Sugar,	52,293 42	-	-	41,443	-	-
Porte-monnaies, Pocket-books, &c.,	262,700 00	37,000	299	-	-	-
Clothing,	9,061,896 00	2,770,600	1,758	-	-	-
Swine,	581,536 71	-	-	917,435	-	-
Milk,	755,887 90	-	-	304,917	-	-
Poultry and Eggs,	52,688 53	-	-	25,891	-	-
Ice,	639,100 00	701,700	-	-	-	-
Printing,	1,351,318 00	749,550	1,134	-	-	-
Bookbinding,	147,290 00	52,200	324	-	-	-
Gravestones, Wheelwright Stock, Baskets, Umbrellas and a variety of other articles not elsewhere enumerated,	11,756,756 95	3,802,347	8,101	5,231,723	2,410,760	3,281
Various articles embraced in the Notes, and not in the Tables,	1,051,657 00	366,200	396	-	-	-
Totals,	$295,820,681 79	$120,693,258	245,908	$124,735,264	$59,145,767	152,766

NOTES.

(1.) Cotton.—Lancaster Quilts, in the manufacture of which, at Clinton, $125,000 is invested, 249,493 pounds of cotton consumed, 1,600 spindles used, and 40 males and 60 females employed, are not embraced in the table; shoe-strings, manufactured by an establishment in Carver, to the amount of $20,000, are likewise omitted. In the returns from Amherst, Boylston, Brookfield, Coleraine, Lancaster, Northbridge, Northampton, Sunderland and Westfield, the amount of capital invested is omitted; those from Boxford give neither capital, value of manufactured goods, nor the number of hands employed; Concord returns embrace neither capital nor the number of hands, while, in numberless instances, either the quantity of raw material used, the class of goods manufactured, their value, or some other material statement is omitted.

(2.) Bleaching and Coloring.—The value of goods bleached is omitted in the returns from South Danvers and Foxborough; no capital is returned from Medway, the mill, the operations of which, for six months, are embraced in the table, having been burned down.

(3.) Woollen.—Not included in the table are 15,094 embossed table covers, value, $25,000, manufactured in Salisbury; 143 yards roller cloth, value, $350, and 97 yards of woollen shawls, value, $390, manufactured in Southbridge; and 275,000 pounds of wool and cotton, consumed in the manufacture of satinets in Stockbridge. Eleven towns fail to return the amount of capital invested; five, the number of sets of machinery; four, the quantity of wool consumed; four, the value of the fabrics manufactured; six, the number of hands employed, and from one or two the returns are deficient in all of these respects.

(4.) Carpeting.—Not included in the table are four mills for the manufacture of painted carpeting, (two in Essex, one in Middlesex and one in Norfolk,) having an aggregate capital of $12,500, producing 88,000 yards, and employing 28 hands. From two mills in Middlesex there are no returns of the quantity manufactured, and from one no return of capital. One mill in Norfolk and two in Nantucket make rag carpets only.

(5.) Worsted.—The number of establishments in Chelmsford and Framingham is omitted in the returns, and the owner of a mill in Sudbury refuses to give any information as to the value of his manufactures, or the amount of his capital. The establishment in Essex County manufactures mousseline de laines; that in Norfolk County manufactures fancy worsteds; one of those in Worcester County manufactures mousseline de laines, and the other, coach lace, 689 lbs. of silk being used in the manufacture of the last-named fabric. There is also an establishment for printing mousseline de laines at Southbridge, in Worcester County, which prints 4,500,000 yards, valued at $675,000, has a capital of $150,000, and employs 140 males and 20 females.

(6.) Hosiery.—From the establishments for the manufacture of shirts and drawers in Woburn and Worcester, the quantity manufactured is not returned; the description of goods manufactured in the establishment at Oxford is omitted, and the returns from Norfolk County are exceedingly defective throughout.

(7.) Silk.—There is an establishment in Newton for the manufacture of ribbons, fringes and trimmings. Value of goods manufactured, $38,000; capital, $20,000; males employed, 16; females employed, 35.

(8.) Rolling, Slitting and Nail Machines.—There are, in addition, 15 machines in operation in Shirley, for the manufacture of horse nails, and there is a new mill in process of erection in Somerset, with a capital of $60,000. There is also in Plymouth an establishment for the manufacture of zinc, nails and brads, where there are eight machines in operation, zinc manufactured to the value of $8,500, nails and brads to the value of $10,000, and where $10,000 capital and fifteen hands are employed. The value of iron manufactured at one mill in Danvers, the quantity and value of nails made, and the amount of capital invested, are not given in the returns; neither is the number of machines in Roxbury.

(9.) Forges.—No particulars are returned of the business of three forges in Wellfleet and three in Nahant. The number of hands employed in seven at Beverly, and the number of hands and amount of capital employed in four at Newbury, are not returned. From seven forges in South Hadley nothing but the amount of capital and the number of hands is returned. One forge in Norfolk County is connected with nail works.

(10.) Hollow Ware and Castings.—Two furnaces in Berkshire, included in the table, are not in operation, and of one in Hampden no particulars are given.

(11.) Axes, Hatchets and Edge Tools.—There is no return of the value of the article manufactured in Lawrence, Essex County; none of the number of axes made or the amount of capital invested in Sharon, Norfolk County, and none of the number of tools made in Millbury, Worcester County.

(12.) Tacks and Brads.—The number of mills in Duxbury is omitted in the returns. A mill in Plympton returns 170,100,000 as the whole number of tacks and brads made; one in South Scituate, 375,000,000, and one in Abington, 1,405,-300,000.

(13.) Ploughs and other Agricultural Implements.—The number of manufactories in Sandisfield; the amount of capital invested in Tyringham, Coleraine, Leverett and Hardwick; and the number of articles manufactured in Shirley and Fitchburg, are all omitted in the returns.

(14.) Copper.—Not included in the table, is an establishment at Taunton for the manufacture of copper and brass kettles, where 300,000 kettles, valued at $109,000, are manufactured, $25,000 invested, and ten men employed. At a manufactory in North Brookfield, copper and sheet iron are produced to the value of $2,000, and one man is employed. The weight of copper manufactured in Boston is not returned.

(15.) Brass Founderies.—The returns from one, a cannon foundery at Chicopee, are embraced in another department.

(16.) Paper.—From New Marlborough, Berkshire County, and Middleton, Essex County, the value, instead of the quantity, of the stock used is returned, the amount being stated in the first case at $41,000, and in the last at $10,000. The quantity of paper manufactured in Huntington, Hampden County, is not returned, nor the quantity of stock used or the amount of capital invested in the business in Shirley, Middlesex County. At Natick, Middlesex County, is a mill for the manufacture of paper pulp, which is not embraced in the table. It uses 490 tons of stock, manufactures pulp to the value of $70,475, has $16,500 capital, and employs twelve hands. Not included, likewise, is an establishment for the manufacture of sand paper, at Winchendon, Worcester County, which makes 400 reams of sand paper, valued at $1,200, employs $200 capital, and one hand.

(17.) Piano-Fortes, and other Musical Instruments.—The towns of Pittsfield, Berkshire County; New Bedford, Bristol County; Beverly, Haverhill and Lawrence, in Essex County; Springfield, West Springfield and Westfield, in Hampden County; Cambridge, Marlborough, Reading, Townsend and Waltham, in Middlesex County; Canton, in Norfolk County; Chelsea, in Suffolk County; and Worcester city, make no return of the *number* of musical instruments manufactured. Montague, in Franklin County, specifies 300 piano-forte cases, but makes no return of their *value*. North Bridgewater, in Plymouth County, returns all the particulars, except the number of establishments.

(18.) Daguerreotypes.—The number of Daguerreotypes taken in Great Barrington, Berkshire County, and the amount of capital invested, are not returned.

(19.) Chronometers, Watches, &c.—From an establishment in New Bedford, no returns have been given.

(20.) Saddles, Harnesses, &c.—Hancock, Berkshire County, returns no capital; Quincy, Norfolk County, no particulars; West Brookfield, Worcester County, no value of manufactures; and Westminster, in the same county, the number of manufactories only.

(21.) Hats and Caps.—The number of hands employed in the manufactory at West Brookfield is not returned.

(22.) Cordage.—Eight establishments in Essex County manufacture lines; three of them return 4,230 dozens lines manufactured, and five the value—$24,000—instead of the number. There is no return of capital from the manufactory in Marblehead; the manufactory in Hampden County is not in operation, and from that in Southborough, Worcester County, $3,000 is returned as the value of the cordage made, while the number of pounds is omitted.

(23.) Boats.—The number of establishments for boat building in Swampscott, Essex County, and Franklin, Norfolk County, as well as the amount of capital and number of hands employed in South Hadley, Hampshire County, is not given in the returns.

(24.) VESSELS LAUNCHED.—There is no return of the amount of capital invested in ship building in New Bedford, or of the amount of capital and number of hands employed in Amesbury.

(25.) MASTS AND SPARS.—The proprietor of one mast and spar shed in Fairhaven, Bristol County, refused to give the assessors any information touching his business. Twenty thousand dollars is returned as the value of the masts and spars manufactured in Salem, Essex County, the number being omitted; and $2,000 is returned as the value of those manufactured in Hingham, Plymouth County, where the number is likewise omitted.

(26.) RAILROAD CARS, &c.—Ipswich, in Essex County, and Deerfield, in Franklin County, make no return of capital; Attleborough, in Bristol County, and Ware, in Hampshire, return neither the amount of capital invested nor the number of hands employed; Gill, in Franklin County, returns neither the amount of capital nor the number of establishments, and Shrewsbury, neither the number of establishments nor of employees; Abington, in Plymouth County, returns the capital of only one out of four establishments, and Rutland, in Worcester County, makes no return of the value of the vehicles manufactured.

(27.) LEAD.—At the manufactory in Salem, Essex County, both sheet and white lead are manufactured.

(28.) FIRE ARMS.—$137,000 comprises the amount of the manufacture at the United States Armory, in Springfield, which is included in the aggregate of Hampden County, in the column of the "value of fire arms."

(29.) WHITE LEAD AND OTHER PAINTS.—Returns from Needham, Norfolk County, do not specify the number of establishments, but give $18,000 (which sum is included in the table) as the "value of white lead, chrome green and vermillion." Essex County makes no return of the number of hands employed.

(30.) FLOUR MILLS.—From the town of New Marlborough, in Berkshire County, no return is made of the value of flour, or the amount of capital invested, but the sum of $8,000 is returned as the value of the mills in that place. Holyoke, Hampden County, returns neither value, capital, nor the number of hands employed. East-hampton makes no return of the number of barrels, and Hatfield returns one "custom mill," but omits all other particulars.

(31.) CURRYING ESTABLISHMENTS.—The towns of Deerfield, in Franklin County, West Roxbury, in Norfolk County, and North Brookfield in Worcester County, make no returns of the amount of capital invested. Melrose, in Middlesex County, returns neither value, capital, nor the number of hands employed.

(32.) PATENT AND ENAMELLED LEATHER.—Wilmington, in Middlesex County, returns "one manufactory just commenced," but omits all other particulars. Worcester city returns one establishment for the manufacture of "enamelled leather *cloth*," but specifies no further particulars. This establishment is not included in the table.

(33.) Boots and Shoes.—Hardwick, in Worcester County, makes no return of the number of pairs of boots or shoes, but returns the aggregate value, and the number of persons employed, which are included in the table. The town of Mansfield, in Bristol County, besides its regular returns, gives the following statistics: "Boots and shoes bottomed for manufacturers out of town, 12,000 pairs; value, $3,000." Wenham, Essex County, in addition to its regular statistics gives the following statement: "There are 205,000 pairs of shoes made in this town for dealers in Danvers and Lynn; value, $36,560; men employed, 160." The foregoing particulars are presumed to be included in the table in the county aggregates of the several towns, wherein are located the establishments for which the articles were made.

(34.) Straw Bonnets and Hats.—Berkley, in Bristol County, returns, 7,595 straw bonnets and hats (which are included in the table) and omits all other statistics, but adds that the articles enumerated were "made in private families." Greenwich, in Hampshire County, after giving the pecuniary value of the palm leaf hats made in that town, submits the following information in the appropriate place for the number of employees: "Females employed, almost all in the town, when occupied with nothing of more importance." Petersham, in Worcester County, adds to its enumeration of palm-leaf hats, that they are "made in families."

(35.) Charcoal.—The number of hands employed in the manufacture of charcoal is omitted in the returns from Adams and Otis in Berkshire County; Norton and Raynham, in Bristol County; Warwick, in Franklin County; Monson and Wilbraham, in Hampden County; Huntington, in Hampshire County; Dunstable and Tewksbury, in Middlesex; Foxborough, in Norfolk; Rochester, in Plymouth; and Ashburnham, Leominster, Northbridge, Phillipston, Princeton and West Brookfield, in Worcester County.

(36.) Blacking.—The number of hands employed in the manufacture of blacking, in Gloucester, Essex County, is not returned.

(37.) Mechanics' Tools.—The number of hands employed on mechanics' tools in Weymouth, Norfolk County, is not returned.

(38.) Wooden Ware.—The number of hands employed in the manufacture of wooden ware, in Westport, Bristol County; in Northfield and Whately, Franklin County, and in Goshen, Hampshire County, is not returned.

(39.) Corn and other Brooms.—The number of hands engaged in the manufacture of brooms in Shirley, Middlesex County, is not returned.

(40.) Gold Pens.—The following statistics, in the returns from Williamsburg, Hampshire County, are not embraced in the table: "Gold and silver pencil cases manufactured, 40,000; capital, $12,000; men employed, 24; females employed, 2."

(41.) Lumber.—The following towns fail to return the number of hands engaged in the preparation of lumber for market: Stockbridge, Fall River, Norton, Middleton, Gill, Warwick, Whately, Blandford, Chicopee, Huntington, Chelmsford, Dunstable, Framingham, Groton, Littleton, Pepperell, Tyngsborough, Wilmington, Dedham,

Foxborough, Marshfield, N. Bridgewater, Hardwick, Leominster, Paxton, Princeton, Shrewsbury, Southborough, West Boylston. The quantity of lumber is omitted in the returns from Framingham, and the value in those from Pembroke.

(42.) FIREWOOD.—The following towns make no return of the number of persons employed in preparing firewood for market, viz.: Great Barrington, Lanesborough, New Marlborough and Tyringham, in Berkshire County; Fairhaven, New Bedford, Norton and Westport, in Bristol County; Tisbury, in Dukes County; Gloucester, Hamilton and Ipswich, in Essex County; Gill, Warwick and Whately, in Franklin County; Blandford, Chicopee, Monson and Palmer, in Hampden County; Chesterfield and Northampton, in Hampshire County; Burlington, Dunstable, Framingham, Lexington, Lincoln, Littleton, Melrose, Pepperell, Stoneham and Wilmington, in Middlesex County; Brookline, Dedham, Foxborough, Quincy and Wrentham, in Norfolk County; Marshfield and South Scituate, in Plymouth County; Hardwick, Lancaster, Leominster, New Braintree, Northborough, North Brookfield, Paxton, Phillipston, Princeton, Shrewsbury, West Boylston and West Brookfield, in Worcester County.

(43.) WHALE FISHERY.—Besides the deficiencies indicated in the table, the cities of Fall River and Lynn return neither the quantity of sperm nor whale oil, nor the value of either.

(44.) MACKEREL AND COD FISHERIES.—Truro, in Barnstable County, returns the number of vessels employed in the cod and mackerel fishery, their aggregate tonnage, the number of bushels of salt consumed, the capital invested, and the number of hands employed, but omits all other particulars. Beverly, Essex County, adds to its full returns the following item: "Codfish Oil, 425 barrels; value, $8,925." Marblehead, same county, adds the following: "Value of cod liver oil *for currying purposes*, $7,217." Nahant, same county, omits the number of bushels of salt consumed. The return from Nantucket states that the fish are taken "in boats." Marshfield, in Plymouth County, returns only the value of codfish taken, and the number of hands employed, and Plympton, in the same county, only the quantity of fish, the value, and the number of employees.

(45.) ALEWIVES, SHAD AND SALMON.—The towns of Falmouth, in Barnstable County, Westport, in Bristol County, and Holyoke, in Hampden County, and the city of Lynn, in Essex County, make no return of the number of hands employed in the alewive, shad and salmon fishery. Appended to the return from Watertown, Middlesex County, is the following item: "Value of other fish taken, $1,200." Too late to be inserted in the proper place, came the following return from Edgartown: "Barrels of herrings or alewives caught, 1,130; value, $3,390; hands employed, 9."

(46.) SHEEP AND WOOL.—The town of Salisbury, Essex County, makes no return of the value of sheep. From the following places no return is made of the number of pounds of wool produced: New Bedford, Bristol County; Wendell, Franklin County; Chesterfield, Hampshire County; Chelmsford, Concord, Hopkinton, Newton and Wilmington, in Middlesex County; Dedham and Dorchester, in Norfolk County; Abington, Plymouth County; and Bolton, Gardner, Phillipston and West Boylston, in Worcester County.

(47.) Horses, Oxen, Cows and Calves.—From three of the four districts into which Haverhill seems to have been divided, the assessors return the whole number of "neat cattle," without regard to the classifications contemplated in the official inquiries. The number thus returned is included in the table under the head of "oxen over three years old." "Neat cattle," only, are likewise returned from Shutesbury and Monson. Hatfield makes the following supplementary return, which is not included in the table: "Beef cows, 242; gross value, $7,640."

(48.) Corn, Indian and Broom.—From Haverhill and Swampscott, in Essex County, from Monson, in Hampden, and Sudbury, in Middlesex, the number of acres appropriated to the cultivation of corn is not returned.

(49.) Wheat.—The value of the wheat raised in Abington is not returned.

(50.) Rye.—The number of acres is not returned from Haverhill, Swampscott, Monson or Sudbury.

(51.) Barley.—The number of acres is not returned from Haverhill, Swampscott, Sudbury or Wilmington, nor the value from Winthrop.

(52.) Oats.—The number of acres is not returned from Monson or Sudbury.

(53.) Potatoes, Onions, Turnips, &c.—The statistics from Haverhill, Monson and Sudbury, with regard to the crops of potatoes, onions, turnips, carrots, beets and other vegetables, and hay, are in conformity with the instructions to assessors in no particular. In the returns from many other towns the number of acres cultivated, and the average yield per acre, are omitted.

(54.) Apples, Pears, &c.—In twenty-one towns, the number of trees, or the value of fruit, is omitted.

(55.) Hops.—Pepperell and Wilmington return only the gross quantity and value.

(56.) Cranberries.—Either the number of acres, or the value of cranberries, is omitted in the returns from fifteen towns.

(57.) Maple Sugar.—The value of maple sugar made in Otis is included in the "gross value of all other articles," returned from that town, and 1,700 pounds made in Savoy, is included with "sugar refined."

(58.) Porte Monnaies.—The quantity manufactured in Plymouth and Suffolk Counties, as well as in Lancaster and Millbury, in Worcester County, is not returned; nor is there any return at all from one establishment in the city of Worcester.

ERRATA.

[Most of the following errors are corrected in the Tables.]

Page 11. Value of Corn: For $69,157, *read* $6,915.

Page 30. Value of Charcoal: For $36,400, *read* $3,640.

Page 54. Value of Oats: For $47,520, *read* $5,940.

Page 119. Value of Boots and Shoes: For $1,000, *read* $11,225.

Page 217. Number of Hides tanned: The " $ " is altogether superfluous.

Page 228. Indian Corn: For 125 bushels, *read* 125 acres; and for 2,500 bushels per acre, *read* 25.

Page 338. Shovels &c.: For $300, *read* $3,000.

Page 350. Keg Staves and Headings, should *read* as follows: Establishments, 13; Keg Staves m'd, 3,600,000; val., $10,000; Keg Heads, 1,250,000; val., $12,000.

Page 374. Copper Manufactories: For $10,000,000, *read* $500,000.

Page 410. Carpeting: For $2,000, *read* $10,000.

Page 421. Boots and Shoes: For 15,000 pairs of Shoes made, *read* 52,500 pairs; and for 20 men employed, *read* 63.

Page 505. Lumber: For 1,700 ft., *read* 1,700,000 ft.

Page 551. Scythes: For 7,200 doz., *read* 7,200 Scythes.

Page 570. Pounds of Cotton Yarn m'd and not made into Cloth: For 3.321,146, *read* 3,321,646. Value of Cotton Yarn manufactured in Essex County: For 38,131,22, *read* 38,131,77.

Page 574. Yards of Flannel or Blanketing m'd in Dukes: Omit the two right hand ciphers.

INDEX

TO COUNTIES AND TOWNS.

INDEX

TO THE TABLES.

www.ingramcontent.com/pod-product-compliance
Lightning Source LLC
LaVergne TN
LVHW021050110826
845150LV00001B/30

9781425567781